1001 ACTIVITIES

Making a Density Column (page 45)

Do you know why some objects float while others sink? Understanding density will help you explain this. Make a density column, and move to the head of your class!

A Nutty Idea (page 604)

Why not give someone the gift of nature for Christmas this year? This nutty wreath is unique and easy to make!

Thar She Blows! (page 251)

There's no need to run for cover from this model of a real erupting volcano! Use household items to create your volcano. You can even decorate it to look like the real thing. Then add vinegar, and watch it erupt. It's lava time!

Each activity has been rated with a difficulty level: simple, medium, or challenging. The number of symbols will guide you:

 Activity is simple.

 Activity is of medium difficulty.

 Activity is challenging.

Before you begin a project, ask an adult to review it. Decide together whether or not you will need help. You should be able to do the simple projects and most of the medium projects by yourself, but you may need help with the harder ones.

1001
WAYS TO EXPLORE
SCIENCE & NATURE

Peter Rillero, Ph.D.

 Publications International, Ltd.

Peter Rillero, Ph.D., is an associate professor of science education at Arizona State University West in Phoenix. He is the author of *Totally Gross Chemistry, Totally Creepy Bugs,* and *Super Science Fair Projects.* In addition, Rillero coauthored the best-selling high-school biology textbook in the United States and is consulting editor for the journal *Science Activities.* Rillero has taught high-school science in New York City and Kenya, as well as college science in Costa Rica. As a Fulbright Scholar, he lectured in science education at the University of Akureyri in Iceland.

Contributors: Maria Birmingham; Karen E. Bledsoe; Marilee Robin Burton; Jamie Gabriel; Nancy Goodman; Kelly Milner Halls; Lise Hoffman; Suzanne Lieurance; Susan A. Miller, Ed.D.; Candyce Norvell; Phyllis J. Perry; Joseph Peters, Ph.D.

Interior illustrations: Kate Flanagan

Additional illustrations: Terri and Joe Chicko, Anne Kennedy, Ellen Joy Sasaki, George Ulrich

Covers: Photography by Brian Warling; Illustrations by Rémy Simard

CONTENTS

◆◆◆◆◆◆◆

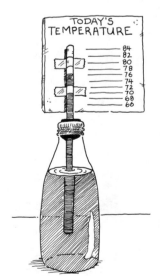

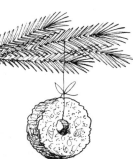

WHAT A WONDERFUL WORLD!

◆▶◆▶◆▶◆▶◆

Dear Parents and Teachers—

The activities in this book are designed to challenge your child to explore the world around them. Each project includes one, two, or three test tubes to indicate the difficulty level. Your child may need help with activites that are rated three test tubes. You know your child's abilities best—review each project before they begin to judge whether your help will be necessary. Some activites include a CAUTION. Such projects may require the use of a sharp blade, flames, or hazardous chemicals. An adult should always supervise use of these materials to prevent injuries.

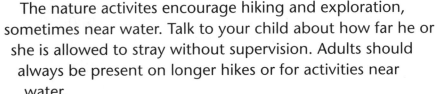

As you review the experiments in this book, you may decide that safety goggles and a smock or apron are necessary for some activities, especially those that use ammonia, vinegar, bleach, or spray paint. Have these items on hand, and encourage your child to use them where appropriate. Noxious chemicals such as bleach, ammonia, and spray paint should only be used under adult supervision in a well-ventilated area.

The nature activites encourage hiking and exploration, sometimes near water. Talk to your child about how far he or she is allowed to stray without supervision. Adults should always be present on longer hikes or for activities near water.

This should be an enjoyable, creative learning experience for children. Encourage their creativity and interests as they discover the wonders of the world!

Hey Kids—

The natural world is everywhere for you to see, but it does charge for admission. Its secrets are revealed only to those who are willing to open their eyes and ears, to touch and smell—and sometime even taste! When some people think of science, they think of boring textbooks and complicated formulas. Actually, science is just a way of looking at the world around us and at the things we find in it every day.

When we open our senses and mind to the world around us, we walk on paths of science, discovery, and adventure. In any new place, a guide facilitates learning. A guide keeps us from making dangerous and costly mistakes. A guide sets up experiences to promote learning. A guide poses questions to provoke thought. Let this book be your guide on the path to understanding the world.

To learn about the world and about science, it is not enough to read this book; you must *do* this book. The hands-on activities provide concrete experiences that will last a lifetime. Don't feel that you need to do all the activities in the book. Start with the ones that are most interesting to you. You'll find that once you open your senses and mind to the world, you will want to keep them open. You will want to keep making new discoveries.

Before you begin any of the projects in this book, you should know a couple of things. Each project has one or more test tubes. These show how difficult the activity is.

 Simple projects get one test tube,

 medium projects get two, and

 challenging projects get three.

If you'd like to do one of the challenging projects but think it might be too hard, get help from an adult or an older brother or sister.

Remember: Part of being a scientist is being responsible in what you do. Always think about how you can do a project safely. Don't leave an experiment unattended unless you're sure it is safe to do so. If you have pets or younger

brothers or sisters, be sure that the project poses no danger to them. Make sure you always clean up after an experiment and dispose of materials properly.

When you head outdoors, use common sense and be alert for all hazards. Always take an adult with you when you explore—especially when you are going near water. Hike only on established trails. Going off-trail increases your chances of getting lost. Know and obey the rules and regulations of public lands. When you gather materials from nature, take only what you need. Never take so much of any one thing that you leave a "scar." Watch animals from a safe distance—animals may bite, claw, kick, or peck if they feel threatened.

Always get adult permission to do a project. Show the adult the activity, and get approval before you start. Some projects contain a CAUTION. These projects involve things such as flames, sharp objects, or hazardous chemicals. You should only do these with adult help.

Once you choose a project to try, read the instructions carefully. Most of the activities in this book use items that you can find around the house, but a few may require a trip to the store. Before you begin, make sure you have enough time. Some experiments can be done in ten minutes, but others have to sit for hours or days. You'll need to take care of them during that time.

Some experiments may turn out differently than you expect. That happens to all scientists. If it happens to you, try to figure out why. Do the project again and see if that makes a difference. For projects that work as you expect, try to explain what happened. Observe what happens, think about it, and learn about the world.

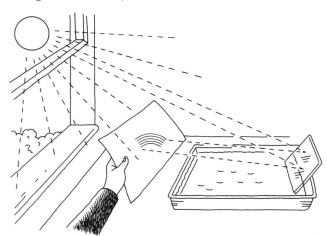

You will find that discovery leads to appreciation, and appreciation leads to discovery. May your explorations be filled with adventure, discovery, and appreciation as you realize what a wonderful world we have!

CHEMISTRY CONNECTIONS

◆▷◆▷◆▷◆▷

In chemistry, we study matter, its properties, its structure, and the way it acts. In this chapter, you'll learn some of the ways that materials interact with one another. You'll explore the differences between physical changes and chemical reactions, and you'll also learn how to study the characteristics of different materials.

Liquid Density

◆▷◆▷◆▷◆▷

Density has to do with how tightly packed an object is. If two substances have the same weight, but one takes up more space, the larger one is less tightly packed, or less *dense.* A less dense object will float on, or be supported by, a more dense object.

Try some (or all!) of the projects that follow, and you'll become an expert on what will float—and what won't.

Heavy Water, Heavier Salt Water

◆◆◆◆◆◆◆

Different liquids have different densities.

What You'll Need
- measuring cup
- water
- scale
- pen and paper
- large container
- salt

Fill a measuring cup with 1 cup of water. Use a scale to measure how much the water weighs, and write down the weight. Pour the water into a large container, and add a little bit more water to it. Mix as much salt into the water as it will hold. Pour the salt water into the measuring cup so that you have 1 cup of very salty water. Use the scale to measure how much the salt water weighs. Did the salt change the water's density?

The salt water and freshwater you weighed each took up the same amount of space. This means that they had the same volume. However, one of them weighed more than the other, or was more dense. When 2 substances have the same volume but different weights, we say that their density is different; the heavier substance has a greater density. In this case, the salt water was more dense than the freshwater. If you had difficulty proving that with this activity, try Layered Look on page 12.

Bottled Sea: Catch a Wave

◆◆◆◆◆◆◆

Catch waves without leaving home when you make a sea-in-a-bottle.

What You'll Need
- clear plastic bottle with top
- water
- blue food coloring
- mineral oil

Fill a plastic bottle ⅔ of the way with water. Add blue food coloring and swirl. Fill the rest of the bottle with clear mineral oil so there's no room for air. Then put the top on the bottle and close tightly.

Lay the bottle on its side, and you'll get a layer of oil on top with a layer of blue water underneath it. That's because the water is heavier (more dense) than the oil. Tilt the bottle from side to side slowly, and watch the wave flow.

Egg-citing Levitation

◄►◄►◄►◄►

Why did the chicken make the egg float? To get to the other salt.

What You'll Need
- bowl
- water
- egg
- salt
- spoon
- measuring cup and spoon

Fill a bowl with enough water to cover an egg. Place the egg in the water. Does the egg float or sink? The egg sinks because it is more dense than the water. Now add salt to the water, and stir gently, being careful not to break the egg. Keep adding salt until the egg floats. You will need about 4 tablespoons of salt for every 1½ cups of water.

Did the salt change the water's density? The liquids inside an egg are more dense than water, so the egg usually sinks in water. Adding salt to water makes the water more dense. When enough salt is added, the egg will be less dense than the water. The egg will rise. You have produced the levitation of an egg!

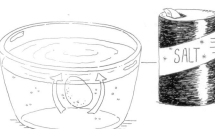

Viva South America!

◄►◄►◄►◄►

Vegetable oil, corn syrup, and water have different densities.

In one container, mix ½ cup of corn syrup with red food coloring. In the other container, mix ½ cup of water with blue food coloring. Two or three drops of food coloring will be enough. Pour enough of the red syrup mixture into a tall, thin glass to fill it about ⅓ of the way. Next, gently pour the same amount of the blue colored water into the glass. Then pour the same amount of natural yellow vegetable oil into the glass.

What You'll Need
- 2 containers
- measuring cup
- corn syrup
- red and blue food coloring
- water
- tall, thin glass
- vegetable oil

The syrup is more dense than the other solutions, so it stays at the bottom of the glass. The oil is less dense, so it floats on top of the other layers. You'll have 3 distinct layers that form the color pattern used in the flags of several South American countries, including Venezuela, Colombia, and Ecuador. Find flags from other countries, and duplicate their patterns using different food coloring.

Layered Look

▶▶▶▶▶▶▶

Freshwater floats on top of salt water because it is less dense.

What You'll Need
- 4 clear glasses
- water
- salt
- measuring cup and spoon
- food coloring
- eyedropper or spoon

In a clear glass, combine 1 cup of water and 3 or 4 tablespoons of salt to make salt water. Pour half of your salt water into another glass, and add food coloring. Fill a third glass with freshwater from the tap (this should be the same temperature as the salt water). Using an eyedropper, put a small amount of colored salt water on top of the clear freshwater. The salt water sinks to the bottom. Get another glass of freshwater, and add some food coloring to it. Using the eyedropper, add a small amount of the colored freshwater to the top of the clear salt water. The freshwater stays at the top.

A substance with less density will float on top of a substance with more density. The freshwater floats on top of the saltwater because it is less dense. Likewise, the salt water sinks in freshwater because it is more dense.

Layered Look: Hot and Cold

▶▶▶▶▶▶▶

Hot water floats on top of cold water because it is less dense.

Fill one cup halfway with hot water and another cup halfway with cold water. In a third cup, add red food coloring to some hot water. In a fourth cup, add blue food coloring to some cold water. Using an eyedropper, put a little red hot water into the cup of clear cold water. The red hot water stays at the top. Using the eyedropper, put a little blue cold water into the cup of clear hot water. The blue cold water sinks to the bottom.

What You'll Need
- 4 clear cups
- water
- red and blue food coloring
- eyedropper or spoon

What happened? Hot water floats on top of cold water because it is less dense. Likewise, cold water sinks in hot water because it is more dense. Heated molecules have more energy than cool molecules. The energy of warm molecules causes them to move farther apart from each other. This makes them less dense.

Pop Up and Pop Down

◆▶◆▶◆▶◆▶

Objects that look the same can have different densities.

Fill a bathtub, basin, aquarium, or other large container with water. Place several unopened cans of different kinds of soda into the water. Some of the cans will be heavier, or more dense, than water, and some will be less dense than water. The less dense cans will float, and the more dense cans will sink. Watch the cans, and note which ones float and which ones sink. What's the difference between the floaters and the sinkers? Do you think the cans are different or the soda is different? Can you form a hypothesis about which types of soda tend to sink and which types float? Use some other brands of soda to test your hypothesis.

If you add salt to the water, the water will become more dense. Can you predict how this might affect the cans of soda? Add salt to the water to see if your prediction was correct.

Drop It—Slowly!

◆▶◆▶◆▶◆▶

Water has different densities when it takes on other forms.

What You'll Need
- clear bowl
- corn oil
- ice cube

In Layered Look: Hot and Cold (see page 12), you saw that hot water was less dense than cold water, but what about ice? The density of a substance changes depending on temperature because the volume of the substance changes with temperature. *Volume* is a measure of how much space a substance takes up, and as volume increases, density decreases. Most often, things have a greater volume when they are warmer and a lesser volume when they are colder. Water is sometimes an exception to this rule, though; it actually has greater volume and less density when it's frozen than when it's liquid. You can use this fact to perform a very simple, but very cool, demonstration.

Fill a clear bowl halfway with corn oil, drop an ice cube in it, and sit back and watch. You'll notice right away that the ice cube floats on top of the oil. This is because the ice weighs less than the amount of oil needed to fill up the same volume. Eventually, the ice will melt and form drops of water. The liquid water has a lesser volume than the frozen water—the same amount takes up less space. This means that the liquid water is more dense than the frozen water; it is also more dense than the oil. The drops of water will form almost perfect spheres and sink slowly to the bottom of the oil.

Shake Down

◆▸◆▸◆▸◆▸

See some cool effects that involve density, sinking, and floating.

What You'll Need
- jar with lid
- water
- vegetable oil
- green food coloring
- salt
- measuring spoon

Fill a jar halfway with water. Add vegetable oil to the jar until it is ⅔ full. Add a drop of green food coloring to the jar, and observe the result. Then sprinkle ½ teaspoon salt on top of the oil and watch what happens to the salt.

The drop of food coloring gently fell through the oil to the water and turned the water green. Food coloring has a water base, so it is heavier than the oil. The salt fell down through the oil and through the water to the bottom of the jar because it is more dense than the oil and the water. As some of the salt fell, it carried some oil with it in drops. This is because, as a unit, the salt–oil drops are heavier than water. The oil stayed at the bottom of the jar. When the salt dissolved in the water, the oil rose up. You can make the oil rise more quickly by gently shaking the jar.

Acids and Bases

◆▸◆▸◆▸◆▸

In chemistry, materials can be grouped by their properties, or characteristics. One property is pH, which tells you whether a substance is an acid, a base, or a neutral. The pH values of materials are extremely important in chemistry but also in areas such as gardening, fish keeping, cooking, and construction. We measure pH on a scale of 1 to 14, where 7 is neutral, 1 is the most acidic, and 14 is the most basic. When doing these projects, be careful handling the materials; some of them can stain or damage clothing.

Cabbage Patch Chemist

◆◆◆◆◆◆

Is it an acid or a base?
Would you believe that cabbage can tell you the answer?

What You'll Need
- purple cabbage
- knife
- pot
- water
- measuring cup
- stove
- strainer
- jar
- 2 clear cups
- vinegar
- clear ammonia

Caution: This project requires adult supervision.

Chop some purple cabbage into small pieces, and put it into a pot with 2 cups of water. With adult help, bring the water to a boil on the stove. Reduce the heat, and let it simmer for 10 minutes. The water will turn purplish. Remove the pot from the heat. Allow the purplish liquid to cool. Strain the cabbage, and pour the liquid into a jar.

Divide the purple liquid into 2 clear cups. Pour a bit of vinegar into the first cup, and note the color change. Pour a bit of ammonia into the other cup, and note the color change.

What happened? Vinegar is an acid. It caused the color of the cabbage juice to change from purplish to a more reddish color. Ammonia is a weak base. It caused the color to change to green. Cabbage juice can be used to tell if chemicals are acids or bases.

Neutralize Me

◆◆◆◆◆◆

Produce neutral solutions by combining acids and bases.

Put a small amount of vinegar in one cup and a small amount of ammonia in another. Use the purple cabbage juice or other pH indicator (such as litmus paper) to test the vinegar and ammonia to see if they are acid, base, or neutral. Then mix some vinegar and ammonia together in a third cup, and use your pH indicator to see if the new mixture is an acid, a base, or a neutral. Can you mix the vinegar and ammonia together in the correct amount to make a completely neutral mixture?

What You'll Need
- 3 clear cups
- vinegar
- ammonia
- purple cabbage juice (see Cabbage Patch Chemist, above) or other pH indicator

Working on Eggshells

◆◆◆◆◆◆◆

How do you make an eggshell disappear? It's not magic, it's chemistry!

Carefully place a hard-boiled egg in a jar; pour in enough vinegar to completely cover the egg. Close the jar securely, and leave it for 24 to 48 hours. When the time has passed, examine the egg. Carefully pick it up. How has the egg changed? The vinegar reacts with the calcium in the shell and leaves the egg with no shell. Bet you never thought you could use chemistry to make an eggshell disappear!

What You'll Need
- hard-boiled egg
- jar with lid
- vinegar

Invent Your Own
Acid-Base Indicator

◆◆◆◆◆◆◆

Did you know colors in some fruits, vegetables, and flowers may change in response to acids or bases? Try this experiment to see for yourself!

Gather some fruits, vegetables, and colored flower petals (lilies, asters, irises, daisies, or petunias). Soak each item in a small jar with rubbing alcohol for 30 to 60 minutes. Then, separate each of the resulting colored solutions into 2 containers. Add some vinegar (an acid) to one container and some ammonia (a base) to the other. Repeat this process for each colored solution. If the color of the substance changes, the substance is an acid-base indicator. Compare your results for different flowers, fruits, and vegetables to determine which one is the best acid-base indicator.

What You'll Need
- different-colored fruits, vegetables, and flower petals
- small jars
- rubbing alcohol
- several small containers
- vinegar
- clear ammonia

Acid Rain Is a Pain

◆◆◆◆◆◆◆

Sometimes chemicals get in the air and mix with water to form "acid rain." It can cause damage to a lot of things on Earth, including plants.

Find a place where you can grow 3 potted plants for several weeks; make sure the plants all experience the same growing conditions—sunlight, temperature, and so on. Label the plants and 3 spray bottles "REGULAR RAIN," "ACID RAIN," and "EXTREME ACID RAIN." Fill the regular rain bottle with tap water. Fill the acid rain bottle ⅔ of the way with tap water and ⅓ of the way with vinegar. Fill the extreme acid rain bottle ⅓ of the way with tap water and ⅔ of the way with vinegar. Measure and record the heights of the plants.

Water each plant with the type of rain indicated on its label. Every week, measure the growth of the plants. After a few weeks, compare the effects that the different types of rain had on the plants.

What You'll Need
- 3 potted plants of equal size
- 3 spray bottles
- paper and pen
- tape
- water
- vinegar
- ruler

What Am I, Acid or Base?

◆◆◆◆◆◆◆

Some household materials are acids and others are bases. Can you predict which?

What You'll Need
- miscellaneous household items
- purple cabbage juice (see Cabbage Patch Chemist on page 15) or other pH indicator

Gather up common household items such as aspirin, milk, clear vinegar, orange juice, soda pop, antacids, milk of magnesia, coffee, and baking soda. Use the purple cabbage juice or another pH indicator (such as litmus paper) to test the materials to see if they are acid, base, or neutral. After you've tested a few materials, see if you can predict which category the next one falls into. Think about what the substance is used for and how it smells before you make your prediction.

Dissolving Figures

◆◆◆◆◆◆◆

Why are marble statues dissolving outdoors? Blame it on the rain!

Caution: Do not spray vinegar at any person or animal. Keep vinegar off clothing.

Use a plastic knife to carve a face or other simple design into a piece of chalk. A stick of jumbo sidewalk chalk (available at craft stores) will be easiest to carve, but any kind of chalk will work. Once you've carved your design, stand the chalk up in a pie pan using the clay as a base. You have your "marble" sculpture!

Set the pie pan in a deep sink. Add vinegar to a spray bottle, and use it to mist your chalk sculpture. Observe what happens as you spray the vinegar. Repeat every day for a week. What has happened to your sculpture?

Vinegar is an acid. It breaks down the calcium carbonate in the chalk and produces carbon dioxide gas, which you might have seen bubbling away. In a similar way, acid rain attacks the calcium carbonate in marble sculptures. Of course, your sculpture dissolved much faster than marble would, because vinegar contains more acid than acid rain, and chalk is softer than marble.

> **What You'll Need**
> - dull knife
> - chalk
> - clay
> - pie pan
> - sink
> - vinegar
> - spray bottle

Chemical Reactions

◆◆◆◆◆◆◆

Matter is made of molecules. Molecules are the smallest particles of a substance, but they still have the same properties as the original substance. How small is a molecule? It is way too small to be seen. Chemists study how molecules interact. Sometimes molecules interact with each other, but they remain the same. This is a physical change. Other times they interact, and the molecules change to form new molecules. This is a chemical change.

Rust Steals Steel Wool

Steel is acted upon by water and oxygen to form rust.

Take two 1-inch balls of steel wool, and put each one into a glass. Add water to one glass so it covers half of the ball. Do not add water to the other glass. Observe both pieces of steel wool after a few days. Rust has formed on the wet steel wool but not on the dry steel wool. This is a chemical reaction called *oxidation*, in which oxygen combines with other

What You'll Need
- steel wool
- ruler
- 2 glasses
- water

molecules. The iron molecules in the steel wool combine with oxygen molecules to form rust molecules (ferric oxide). This is a chemical change because it creates new molecules. The presence of water made it easier for the oxygen from the air to attach to the iron. This is why the moist steel wool rusted but the dry steel wool did not.

Woolly Heat

Rusting is a chemical reaction. Does this chemical reaction produce heat?

What You'll Need
- steel wool
- ruler
- bowl
- vinegar
- clock or watch
- thermometer
- napkin
- pen and paper

Place a small wad of steel wool (about 2 inches across) into a bowl. Pour enough vinegar in the bowl to cover the steel wool. After 10 minutes, take the rusted steel wool out of the vinegar, and mold it gently around the bottom of a thermometer. Wrap a napkin over the steel wool so you can hold the thermometer comfortably. Read the temperature on the thermometer and write it down. Record the temperature every 5 minutes until it no longer changes.

The temperature rises, showing that heat is produced by this reaction. In chemical terms, this is an *exothermic,* or heat-producing, reaction. Rusting is an oxidation reaction; oxygen is added, and heat is given off. This is similar to when things burn because oxygen is added and heat is given off. Of course, burning occurs more rapidly than rusting.

Match Made in Heaven

◆◆◆◆◆◆◆

Burning matches make a product that will cause them to stick together.

Caution: This project requires adult supervision.

Ask an adult to put the heads and bodies of 2 wooden matches together, and then strike one match against a lighting surface. Both matches will start blazing. Blow out both matches, and observe that the sticks have united to become one.

What happened? The head of a match burns, or oxidizes, when oxygen combines with the material at the head of the match. The combustion produces a new substance—a cinder type of material with holes and pockets. When the matches are burned together, the cinder material of the matches combines and holds them together.

Potato Versus Liver

◆◆◆◆◆◆◆

Can you guess which will cause the most bubbles?

Your mom or dad can purchase the liver needed for this project at the grocery store. (If they can't find liver, chicken or beef meat will also work.) Cut a cube of potato and a cube of liver; make sure the cubes are equal in size. Place the potato cube in one glass and the liver cube in the other. Pour equal amounts of hydrogen peroxide to cover each cube. Which reaction seemed to occur the fastest?

What You'll Need
- dull knife
- potato
- beef or chicken liver
- ruler
- 2 glasses
- hydrogen peroxide
- pen and paper

You probably noticed more bubbles in the glass containing the liver. These bubbles are caused by an enzyme (called *cata-lase*) that breaks hydrogen peroxide into water and

oxygen (the bubbles are caused by the oxygen coming up out of the water). Both the potato and the liver have this enzyme, but the liver has far more of it than the potato. That's because one of the functions of the liver is to clean the blood; it encounters more hydrogen peroxide than a potato would.

Foam Home

◆◆◆◆◆◆◆

Vinegar and baking soda produce a chemical reaction and release carbon dioxide. The carbon dioxide gas can produce a physical change in soap.

What You'll Need
- bowl
- baking soda
- measuring cup and spoon
- dishwashing liquid
- vinegar

Place ¼ cup baking soda in a bowl. Put 1 squirt of dishwashing liquid on the baking soda. Pour in ¼ cup of vinegar. The baking soda and vinegar chemically react to produce carbon dioxide gas. This gas causes the dishwashing liquid to produce millions of bubbles. This physical change produces foam.

Apple Science

◆◆◆◆◆◆◆

The inside of an apple will undergo a chemical change when exposed to oxygen. You can prevent this reaction, but you can't reverse it.

Cut an apple in half. Then cut each half into 3 sections, so you have 6 wedges of apple. Use a cotton swab to paint lemon juice on the white fleshy parts of 3 wedges. Paint water on the white fleshy parts of the other 3 wedges. Place the apple wedges on a paper towel, and observe every 15 minutes for a few hours. Record your observations.

What happened? The apples that were soaked in water turned brown when exposed to air. This is a chemical reaction called *oxidation,* in which oxygen combines with other molecules. The apples soaked in lemon juice did not change color.

What You'll Need
- apple
- dull knife
- cotton swabs
- lemon juice
- water
- paper towel
- clock or kitchen timer

The juice prevented oxidation. Put some lemon juice on apples that have become oxidized. Does the lemon juice reverse the reaction? The lemon juice prevented the reaction, but it cannot reverse it once it has occurred. It is usually not very easy to reverse a chemical reaction.

Brown and Blue

◆◆◆◆◆◆◆

Do your favorite foods contain starch?
Make an indicator solution to find out.

Caution: This project requires adult supervision. Iodine is a poison. Keep it away from your mouth, and wash your hands after using it.

Make an iodine solution by adding 10 drops of tincture of iodine to ½ cup of water. Using an eyedropper, place a drop of the iodine solution on a pile of cornstarch. Note the change in color—iodine turns blue in the presence

of starch. Now use this test to see what foods contain starch. Place the iodine on bread and other foods (such as potatoes and cooked rice) to see if they contain starch. The iodine is called an *indicator solution,* because it indicates the presence of starch.

It's a Gas, Gas, Gas

◆◆◆◆◆◆◆

You can't see carbon dioxide, but you'll know it's there when you perform this balloon experiment.

Blow up a balloon a few times to stretch the rubber. Put 3 tablespoons of baking soda into a small bottle. Pour enough vinegar into the bottle to cover the baking soda. Stretch the open end of the balloon over the mouth of the bottle. The baking soda and vinegar produce

carbon dioxide gas when they combine, and the gas will rise and fill the balloon partway.

Raising Raisins

◀◆▶◆▶◆▶

Raisins rise and fall in this chemical reaction.

What You'll Need
- tall glass
- raisins
- vinegar
- baking soda

Put a few raisins in the bottom of a tall glass. Add vinegar until it fills ¾ of the glass. Observe the raisins. They just rest at the bottom of the glass. Now, add a pinch of baking soda so that some bubbles form (but not too much or it will foam wildly).

What happened? The vinegar and baking soda produce a chemical reaction that creates carbon dioxide bubbles. The bubbles attach to the raisins causing them to rise. The bubbles act like water wings on the raisins. When the bubbles pop at the surface, the raisins fall back down.

Fire Extinguisher

◀◆▶◆▶◆▶

Create a gas to extinguish a flame using a common chemical reaction.

What You'll Need
- 2 candles
- glass mixing bowl
- clay
- baking soda
- matches
- vinegar

Caution: This project requires adult supervision.

Find 2 candles, such as a short votive candle and a longer birthday candle, and place them in a glass mixing bowl. You'll need to stick the birthday candle in clay to keep it upright. Cover the bottom of the bowl with a layer of baking soda. Then have an adult light both candles. Slowly pour the vinegar down one edge of the bowl. When most of the baking soda is moistened, stop pouring. Observe what happens.

Fire is a chemical reaction that requires oxygen. Carbon dioxide gas smothers flames. When you mixed the baking soda and vinegar, you produced bubbling. This was due to the production of carbon dioxide gas from a chemical reaction. You might have expected the carbon dioxide to just float up and away, but it is denser than air so it fills the bowl starting from the bottom. The small candle goes out first because it is closest to the bottom of the bowl. As the bowl fills, the taller candle is extinguished as well.

Hot Reactions

◆▶◆▶◆▶◆

How does temperature affect the rate of this reaction?

What You'll Need
- 3 glasses
- paper and pen
- tape
- pitcher
- water
- ice
- 3 antacid tablets

Find 3 glasses of the same shape and size. Use slips of paper and tape to label your glasses A, B, and C. Pour tap water into Glass B so that it is ¾ full. Allow it to sit for a while so its temperature becomes room temperature. Fill a pitcher with water and ice. Pour the ice water (not the cubes) from this pitcher into Glass A. Then run the hot water faucet to produce warm water. Add this to Glass C. Do not use scalding hot water—warm water will be sufficient. Be sure the water levels in Glasses A and C match that of Glass B.

Drop an antacid tablet into each glass. Compare the amount of bubbling in the glasses. How does temperature affect the rate of this reaction?

Antacid tablets contain sodium bicarbonate and citric acid. When they combine in water, a chemical reaction occurs producing sodium citrate and carbon dioxide gas. The sodium citrate is a base that helps neutralize acids in stomachs. The carbon dioxide gas bubbles through the water. The higher the temperature, the faster this reaction occurs.

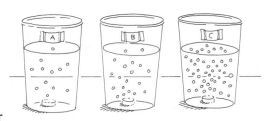

Enough to Make Your Milk Curdle

◆▶◆▶◆▶◆

Acid makes milk curdle. This process is a chemical reaction.

Add 2 teaspoons vinegar or lemon juice to ½ cup of skim milk. Stir the milk, and observe the clumps that form. You have just witnessed milk curdling. The proteins in the milk have reacted with the acid and undergone a chemical change.

What You'll Need
- vinegar or lemon juice
- skim milk
- measuring cup and spoon

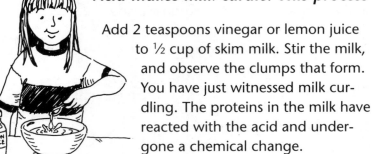

Cool Flashes

◆▶◆▶◆▶◆

Produce a chemical reaction that causes light to flash from your mouth.

What You'll Need
● Wint-O-Green Life Savers®

Many chemical reactions give off heat; some also give off light. When you chew Wint-O-Green Life Savers you cause chemical bonds to break. This results in green flashes of light.

Go into a very dark place with a partner. Have your partner chew a Life Saver candy with his mouth open. What do you see? You should see green flashes of light, almost as if your partner has a mouth full of fireflies! Now it's your turn to chew the candy and let your partner observe.

Experiment with other flavors of Life Savers and also with other wintergreen candies. You'll discover that only the Wint-O-Green Life Saver candies produce the green flashes. Why do you think that is?

Energy and Chemical Reactions

◆▶◆▶◆▶◆

Some chemical reactions take place whenever the materials involved come in contact with each other. Others need additional sources of energy to start the reaction. This energy can come from many sources and be supplied in many forms, including light and heat. In this section, you will use energy from lightbulbs, stoves, warm water, toasters, and eggbeaters to energize chemical reactions.

Caramel Chemistry

◆▸◆▸◆▸◆

Heat can cause a chemical change to sugar.

Caution: This project requires adult supervision.

Measure about ½ cup sugar into a deep nonstick pan. Place the pan on the stove over low heat. Continuously stir the sugar as you gradually increase the heat. Eventually, the sugar will melt and break down to form carbon. Caramel is a combination of sugar and carbon. Remove the pan from the heat when the sugar is straw colored. The sugar has been converted to caramel through a chemical reaction. If you heat the sugar too long, it will turn the dark brown color of carbon and lose all of its sweetness—an interesting chemical change but not very tasty!

> **What You'll Need**
> ● sugar
> ● measuring cup
> ● nonstick pan
> ● stove
> ● large wooden spoon
> ● water

Now dissolve the caramel in water to make it taste better. This is a physical change. Slowly add ½ cup of water to the caramel. Don't add this too quickly, as the caramel is hot and might splatter the water and burn you. Place the pan back on the stove over low heat, and stir the mixture until the caramel dissolves in the water. When it has cooled, taste the mixture. The caramel tastes different from the original white sugar because it is a different substance.

You're Toast!

◆▸◆▸◆▸◆

*The production of charcoal is a chemical reaction
that is dependent upon heat.*

> **What You'll Need**
> ● bread
> ● toaster

Place bread into a toaster, and toast it a little longer than usual. Observe the charcoal that is produced on the bread. In this chemical reaction, the carbohydrates of the bread combine with oxygen. Heat is necessary to produce the oxidation of the bread.

Whip It Good

◆◆◆◆◆◆

Beating egg whites causes the protein in them to denature.

Separate the yolk from the white of an egg, and put the egg white in a bowl. Egg whites consist of long protein molecules wound up like balls of yarn. Beat the egg white with a whisk or electric beater. In time, you will produce a meringue. The energy you supplied with the whisk unraveled the balls of protein and changed the properties of the egg white. Changing proteins this way is called *denaturing*.

What You'll Need
- egg
- bowl
- whisk or electric beater

 # Top Secret Invisible Ink

◆◆◆◆◆◆

*Write an invisible message, then amaze your friends
by making it appear.*

What You'll Need
- toothpick
- lemon juice
- paper
- heat source
- vinegar or milk (optional)

Caution: This project requires adult supervision.

Dip the tip of a toothpick into lemon juice, then use it to write a secret message on a piece of paper. Use lots of lemon juice for each letter you write. Allow the paper to dry until you can't see the writing anymore. Now move the paper back and forth over a heat source, such as a lightbulb or iron.

As the ink gets warm, your message is revealed.

What happened? The acid in the lemon juice breaks down the cellulose of the paper into sugars. The heat supplied tends to caramelize the sugars, making them brown and revealing the secret writing. Repeat this with vinegar or milk to find out which makes the best invisible ink.

Chill Out

◇◆◇◆◇◆◇

Heat is a necessary part of the chemical reaction that occurs when a candle burns.

Caution: This project requires adult supervision.

Cut a square of aluminum foil about 4 inches by 4 inches. In the middle of one side, cut a thin slit going to the middle of the square. Light a candle. Notice the burning of the flame. You are watching a chemical reaction. The heat causes the wax to be converted into simpler products, and this produces more heat, which causes the reaction to continue. Now cool things off a bit. Using tongs to hold the aluminum foil, carefully position the foil so the candle flame is inside the slit. Watch as the candle goes out.

The aluminum foil absorbs and reflects the heat of the flame. This pulls heat from the flame and from the candle. The heat needed to continue the chemical reaction was taken away, so the reaction stopped.

What You'll Need
- aluminum foil
- ruler
- scissors
- candle
- matches
- tongs

Eat, Yeast, and Be Merry

◇◆◇◆◇◆◇

This experiment is sure to get a rise out of you.

What You'll Need
- dry yeast
- sugar
- measuring cup and spoon
- 2 glasses
- water

Place ¼ teaspoon dry yeast and 4 teaspoons sugar in each glass. Add ¾ cup cold water to one glass and ¾ cup warm (not above 130°F) water to the other glass. Compare what happens to the yeast in the 2 glasses.

With the aid of heat, the yeast in the warm glass was able to break down the sugar, giving off alcohol and carbon dioxide. The carbon dioxide bubbled up in the solution. Without the added heat, the yeast in the cold glass could not break down the sugar. When people bake bread, they add yeast to flour and put it in a warm place. The yeast breaks down sugar and releases carbon dioxide, and the gas causes the bread to rise.

Presto Change-o!

◆◆◆◆◆◆◆

Seawater contains salt, which makes it unfit to drink. Here's how you can change salt water to freshwater.

What You'll Need

- pot
- water
- salt
- aluminum foil
- bowl
- stove

Caution: This project requires adult supervision.

Fill a pot with water. Now put in some salt. This is your "seawater." Use aluminum foil to make a "tent" that covers the pot and slopes over a wide, shallow bowl. With adult help, bring the water to a boil.

As the water boils and turns to steam, the steam will condense on the foil and drip into

the bowl. Let most of the water move from the pot to the bowl. Then let the water cool.

Look at the water in the bowl and taste it. How is it different from the water in the pot? What happened to the salt? This method of making freshwater is called *distillation* and is used to help provide water to areas where only seawater is available.

Physical Changes

◆◆◆◆◆◆◆

Just as in a chemical change, a physical change occurs when two substances interact or when energy is applied to one or more substances. Unlike a chemical change, though, the molecules of a substance stay the same after a physical change—no new substance is formed. Physical changes can make a substance look different in size, shape, or color.

Dried Fruit: Apple Chips

Removing water (dehydration) from fruit is a physical change.

What You'll Need
- 2 apples (or similar fruit)
- scale
- pen and paper
- knife
- plate

Caution: This project requires adult supervision.

Weigh 2 apples on a scale, and record their weight. Cut the apples into thin slices. Spread them on a plate, and leave them out for 3 days.

On the third day, observe the apple slices. How have they changed? Weigh all the slices. How does the weight of the dried slices compare with the original weight of the apples? They weigh less because the apples have lost water through evaporation. This is an example of a physical change.

Salt Solution

Physical changes can be reversed.

Put 2 teaspoons salt in a container. Add about ¼ cup warm water, and observe as the salt dissolves in the water and becomes invisible. This is a physical change. Place the container in a warm

What You'll Need
- measuring cup and spoon
- salt
- container
- water

spot where evaporation will occur quickly. Allow the solution to stand for 3 days so the water will evaporate. Notice that the salt is left behind. This is also a physical change. The physical change of dissolving the salt in water was reversed by the second physical change of the water evaporating.

Shrunken Heads

◆◆◆◆◆◆◆

Have fun with fruit when you use science to "shrink" an apple.

What You'll Need
- apple
- vegetable peeler
- knife
- string

Caution: This project requires adult supervision.

In Dried Fruit: Apple Chips (see page 30), you learned that the inside of an apple can lose water due to evaporation. Now you are going to have some more fun with this idea. Peel the skin from an apple with a vegetable peeler. Using a knife, carve a face into the apple. Hang the apple with a string tied to the stem, and let it dry for 3 days. Observe the appearance of the apple. It has lost water through evaporation. This is a physical change. Observe the face you carved into the apple. It looks shriveled up like a shrunken head or a witch's face that you could use as a Halloween decoration.

Gunk

◆◆◆◆◆◆◆

Cornstarch mixed with water has properties of both a liquid and a solid.

Pour 1 cup water into a bowl. Add cornstarch a little at a time, stirring as you go. You will need about 1½ cups cornstarch. Keep adding until it gets difficult to stir. When it is perfect, you can hit the solution with your hand and it will not splatter. Have fun with the gunk. Scoop some up, and let it dribble back into the bowl. Try to form some into a ball. Have a friend take a look. Slap your hand into the bowl, and watch as your friend jumps back expecting a splash, but no splash happens. When you've had enough fun with the gunk, throw it in the trash. Don't pour it down the drain, as it may clog the pipes.

What You'll Need
- water
- measuring cup
- bowl
- cornstarch
- spoon

Snowflake Science

◆◆◆◆◆◆

It is almost impossible to find 2 snowflakes exactly alike. Chemically they are identical, but they have physical differences.

What You'll Need
- fresh snowflakes
- black paper
- magnifying glass

Next time it is snowing, catch some snowflakes on a piece of black paper. Look at them carefully with a magnifying glass. Observe that all the snowflakes look different. They have different shapes and sizes, yet each is made of water. To be sure, allow the snow to melt and observe it as liquid.

# Balloon B-r-r-r-r and Balloon Sweat

◆◆◆◆◆◆

The size of a filled balloon depends upon its temperature.

Caution: This project requires adult supervision.

Fill a pot about halfway with water, and heat it over a medium heat on the stove. Fill a bowl about halfway with a mixture of ice and water. Blow up and knot a balloon. To measure the balloon's *circumference,* the distance around it, start by marking an X at the widest part of the balloon. Wrap a string around the balloon so that it begins and ends at the X, then measure the length of the string with a ruler. Write down this length. This is the balloon's circumference at room temperature. Put the balloon into the ice water for 3 minutes. Remove the balloon, and measure and record its circumference. Using tongs, hold the balloon in the warm water for 3 minutes; make sure the water is not too hot or the balloon will pop. Remove the balloon, and measure and record its circumference. Compare the 3 measurements you took of the balloon. How does temperature affect the size of the balloon?

What You'll Need
- pot
- water
- stove
- bowl
- ice
- balloon
- marker
- string
- ruler
- paper and pen
- clock or watch
- tongs

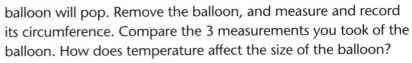

Coffee Filter Chemistry

◆◆◆◆◆◆

Is blue true blue? Perform chromatography with a coffee filter, and separate colors from colors.

Cut a strip of coffee-filter paper that is about an inch wide and 4 inches long. Use a blue or black marker to make a dot on the filter paper about 2 inches from the bottom. Make sure the dot is really dark. Fill the cup with about 1½ inches of water. Hang the filter paper strip from the pencil so that the filter paper rests in the water, but the marker dot is above the water. Observe the paper every 15 minutes for 2 hours.

What You'll Need
- scissors
- paper coffee filters
- ruler
- washable (water-soluble) color markers
- cup
- water
- pencil
- tape
- clock or watch

What happened? The water moves up the filter paper. As it travels, it dissolves the marker ink. You see different colors because dark markers are made of different color inks. The inks separate because they differ in how easily they are dissolved in water and how tightly they hold onto the paper.

Milk It

◆◆◆◆◆◆

Think that it's impossible? Now you can make water and oil mix.

Fill a glass jar about ¼ of the way with vegetable oil. Pour in water until the jar is ¾ full. Repeat with a second jar. Put lids on the jars securely and shake them. The oil and water mix, but in time, the liquids separate again, leaving the oil on top and water on the bottom. The oil floats because it is less dense than the water. Now add a squirt of dishwashing liquid to one of the jars. Shake both jars again.

What You'll Need
- 2 glass jars with lids
- vegetable oil
- water
- dishwashing liquid

Can you see a change? The detergent *emulsifies* the oil droplets, or breaks them into much smaller droplets. These small droplets remain suspended in the water and give the water a milky appearance. This kind of mixture is called an *emulsion*.

Candy-ography

Can candy be used in chromatography? Find out with this activity!

Chromatography is a technique for separating different substances. In this activity you will see if you can separate the colors found in different types of candy.

Put a small, round, colored candy in the center of a coffee filter. Use an eyedropper to place one drop of water on the candy. Observe what happens. Most candies are made to dissolve slowly in water. Add more drops of water, waiting about 30 seconds between each drop. Repeat this process using different colors of candy. Be sure to use a new coffee filter for each test.

The water dissolves the candy. As you add more drops, the water moves across the filter paper. As it moves, it brings the different colors in the candy with it. The colors separate because they differ in how easily they are dissolved in water and how tightly they hold on to the paper.

Glob to Globules

Find out if oil and alcohol mix.

Fill a glass jar halfway with rubbing alcohol. Add about 3 tablespoons of oil. What happens to the oil? Put the lid on tightly, and shake the jar.

You might have thought the oil would float on top of the alcohol. However, oil is denser than alcohol, so it sank to the bottom of the glass. When you shook the oil it broke up into smaller and smaller drops. Eventually the drops became suspended in the alcohol, forming a suspension. The oil does not dissolve in the alcohol; it just becomes smaller in size. This is a physical change. After about 20 minutes, the oil drops form back together, and you have 2 separate layers again.

Butter Me Up

Make butter magically appear with this tasty trick!

What You'll Need
- whipping cream
- bowl
- electric mixer or whisk

Pour a pint of whipping cream into a bowl, and whip it. With an electric mixer on high speed, this will take 7 to 9 minutes; with a whisk, it will take longer. Eventually, you will see butter forming into a ball. Pour off the liquid, and taste the butter.

Milk contains fat, and whipping cream contains even more fat. This fat is broken into small droplets and dissolved in the water of milk to form an emulsion. The energy you added to the cream by beating it made the small droplets of fat crash into each other and form bigger drops. The larger drops crashed into each other and formed even larger drops, and so on, until you had made one big drop of fat—butter. The process where small drops combine to form big drops is called *coalescing.*

Chemis-Tee

Perform chromatography with a T-shirt to make a cool design!

Caution: This project requires adult supervision.

After trying Coffee Filter Chemistry (see page 33), you're ready for a more challenging chromatography experiment! Find some old T-shirts to experiment with, but be sure to ask an adult for permission first. Using permanent markers draw different size circles with diameters of 1 inch to 3 inches.

What You'll Need
- T-shirt
- permanent markers
- coffee can
- rubbing alcohol
- eyedropper

Draw them with different colors. It will be easier to draw the circles if you keep the shirt taut over a coffee can.

Hold the center of one circle over the coffee can, and use an eyedropper to drop rubbing alcohol in the center of the circle. The alcohol will spread slowly outward and carry the pigments in the marker away from the circle. Slowly add new drops to the center of the circle, so the spot keeps spreading. Any extra alcohol will fall into the can. For larger circles, try putting several drops closer to the marker circle to create interesting flower-petal effects. Be sure to wash your new T-shirt before wearing it!

Ballooning Temperature

◆◆◆◆◆◆

Give new meaning to the "big bang" theory.

Caution: This project requires adult supervision.

What You'll Need
● helium balloons

Certain gases expand when exposed to heat. This experiment with helium balloons and hot summer days will show you how—and how much. Fill 4 balloons with helium at your local party or craft store. Ask the clerk to fill one half-full, one ¾-full, one just right, and one a little too full. Be sure to turn the air conditioning on in the car for the ride home. Once you get home, rush the balloons inside the cool house. One by one, take the balloons outside, starting with the half-full balloon, and watch what happens. You'll see just how helium expands with heat and what that expansion does to the latex in balloons.

Leonardo Da Salty

◆◆◆◆◆◆

Use science and salt to make amazing pictures!

What You'll Need
● newspaper
● water
● salt
● several containers
● food coloring
● paper
● paintbrushes or cotton swabs

Salt and food coloring both dissolve in water, which is a physical change. If the water evaporates, the salt and the food coloring are left behind, which is also a physical change. Use these physical changes to make great art!

Cover your work surface with newspaper. Mix warm water and salt together in several containers; add as much salt to each solution as it will hold—until no more salt will dissolve. Add a few drops of different food coloring to each container, and mix well.

Paint a picture on paper using the colored salt solutions. Put it on thick so that when it dries a lot of salt will be left behind. Let the painted paper sit for several hours until the water evaporates, and then observe. Notice how the color and salt remain on the paper. The interesting patterns of color around the salt crystals create a beautiful picture.

Bath Jelly

Here's a fascinating concoction to create in your own scientific laboratory (also known as your kitchen)! Use the bath jelly yourself, or give it as a gift to someone special.

What You'll Need
- water
- measuring cup
- saucepan
- pot holder
- hot pad
- 1 envelope unflavored gelatin
- mixing spoon
- bubble bath or liquid soap
- food coloring
- jar with lid
- small toy or seashells

Caution: This project requires adult supervision.

Measure ½ cup water into a saucepan. Have an adult heat the water until it boils and then move it to the table with the pot holder, using a hot pad to protect the table. Dissolve the gelatin in the boiling water.

When the gelatin is completely dissolved, add ½ cup bubble bath or soap and a few drops of food coloring slowly. Do not beat the mixture because it may become foamy. Stir gently to blend. Pour the mixture in a jar with a lid. Drop in a small toy or some pretty seashells. Put the jar in the refrigerator to set.

To use, place a small amount of jelly under tap water for a bubble bath, or use it as a shower gel.

Curious Combinations

When materials combine, the resulting substance may have different characteristics because of the way the molecules interact. In this section, you will mix different materials and observe the physical changes when these molecules meet.

Beads on the Beach

◆◆◆◆◆◆◆

When big particles mix with smaller particles, they may take up less space than when they were separate.

What You'll Need
- marbles or large beads
- 2-cup measuring cup
- large container
- sand or dirt

Carefully measure 1 cup marbles, and pour them into a large container. Carefully measure 1 cup sand, and combine it with the marbles in the container. Mix them around with your hand. You probably expect that you have 2 cups of the marble-sand mixture. If you pour the mixture into the measuring cup, you will see that's not correct. Do you know why?

The marbles have empty space around them, and the smaller sand particles can fill up that space. This makes the volume of the combined marble-sand mixture less than the combined volumes of the separate marbles and sand. This is a model for how some molecules combine when mixed.

Ocean Conductor

◆◆◆◆◆◆◆

Does water conduct electricity well? How about salt? Try for yourself and see!

Using the conductivity tester, touch the probes to a pile of salt. Notice that the bulb does not light. Put the probes in a cup of distilled water (or water that does not have a lot of dissolved materials in it); the bulb still doesn't light. Now add a few tablespoons of salt to the cup of water. Put the probes into the salt water; the bulb lights. Unlike the salt and the water sepa-

What You'll Need
- conductivity tester (see Conductors page 161)
- salt
- distilled water
- cup
- measuring spoon

rately, the saltwater solution is an electrical conductor because it has ions (charged particles) that conduct electricity.

So Sweet!

◆▷◆▷◆▷◆

When sugar and water are mixed, they may take up less space than when they were separate.

What You'll Need
- sugar
- 2-cup measuring cup
- container
- water
- wooden spoon

Carefully measure 1 cup sugar, and pour it into a container. Carefully measure 1 cup water, and add it to the sugar in the container. Mix them around with a spoon; you won't be able to dissolve all the sugar since there is not enough water. You probably expect that you have 2 cups of the sugar-water mixture. If you pour the mixture into the measuring cup, you will see that's not correct. Do you know why?

Water molecules are small, and sugar molecules are large. The smaller water molecules can fill in some of the empty space around the larger sugar molecules. This makes the volume of the combined substances less than the volume of the separate substances.

Deep Freeze?

◆▷◆▷◆▷◆

Why doesn't the ocean freeze in winter? Discover how salt can affect the properties of water.

What You'll Need
- 2 plastic cups
- water
- salt
- spoon
- freezer

Fill 2 cups halfway with water. Add some salt to one of the cups and stir it up. Now place both cups in the freezer or outside if temperatures are below freezing. Which one freezes first? You'll find that the salt in the water makes it harder to freeze. Depending on the amount of salt in it, salt water may need to be 25 degrees colder than freshwater to freeze! This is one of the reasons why salt is used to melt ice on sidewalks and streets. It's also one of the reasons why the ocean doesn't completely freeze when the weather gets cold.

Salt Water, Freshwater

◆▶◆▶◆▶◆

Try these fun experiments to learn what a pinch of salt can do!

Next time you're at the seaside, try this experiment to compare salt water to freshwater. First, to look at suds, pour 2 cups seawater in one bowl and 2 cups tap water in another bowl. Use a vegetable peeler to shave soap flakes from a bar of pure soap.

Put a teaspoon of flakes in each bowl. Beat with an eggbeater. Which makes better soapsuds, freshwater or salt water? Clean the bowls and do the same experiment with dishwashing liquid. Is there a difference?

What You'll Need
- seawater
- tap water
- 2 mixing bowls
- bar of pure soap
- vegetable peeler
- measuring cup and spoon
- eggbeater
- dishwashing liquid

Less Than the Sum

◆▶◆▶◆▶◆

50+50=100, right? Not in this activity!

What You'll Need
- graduated cylinder
- rubbing alcohol (the closer to 100% alcohol, the more dramatic the result)
- 2 large containers
- water
- tall jar
- measuring cup
- tape

If you have a graduated cylinder, measure 50 milliliters of rubbing alcohol, and pour it into a container. Then measure 50 milliliters of water, and add it to the container. Pour the combined liquids back into the graduated cylinder, and, like magic, you have less than 100 milliliters of solution.

Alternative Method: If you don't have a graduated cylinder, get a tall jar, such as an olive jar. Carefully measure ½ cup water, and pour it into the olive jar. Put a piece of tape on the outside of the jar to mark the water level. Pour the water into a container. Pour alcohol into the olive jar exactly up to the tape mark. Then pour the alcohol into the container with the water, and mix them together. Now pour some of the water-alcohol mixture from the container back into the jar, filling it exactly to the tape line. Pour this out into another container. You might expect the remaining mixture in the first container to fill the jar up to the tape line. But when you pour it in, you find it falls short of the line. You have less than 1 cup of the mixture, even though you started with ½ cup of water and ½ cup of alcohol.

The water molecules are smaller than the alcohol molecules. The water fills in the spaces around the alcohol, and the combined liquids take up less space.

What's the Matter?

◆▷◆▷◆▷◆▷

All physical objects are made up of matter. By studying different objects, you'll learn that all matter has mass, and all matter takes up space. You'll also learn how temperature and pressure affect matter. You'll find that matter can be solid, liquid, or gas and that these different kinds of matter are alike in some ways and different in others.

Matter

◆▷◆▷◆▷◆▷

Every object you can think of—your shoes, flowers, rocks, your fingernails, a balloon, the sun, orange juice—is made up of matter. One of the smallest units of matter is the atom, and atoms join together to form molecules. All of the everyday objects around us are made up of matter that has joined to form molecules.

Salt to Salt

◆◆◆◆◆◆◆

Molecules of one kind of matter can be mixed with molecules of another kind of matter.

What You'll Need
- salt
- measuring spoon
- dark paper
- magnifying glass
- hammer
- glass
- water
- spoon

Sprinkle a teaspoon of salt onto a piece of dark paper. Study the grains of salt with a magnifying glass. What shape do they have? Put another piece of paper on top of the salt. Use a hammer to lightly crush the salt into smaller pieces. Now what sizes and shapes are the grains of salt? Pour the tiny grains of salt into a glass of water, and stir. Can you see the salt? Taste the water. Is it salty? Put the cup of water in a sunny window for a couple of days. When the water has evaporated, some salt will be left in the cup. Scrape this salt back onto the dark paper. Use your magnifying glass to study the grains again. Do they look like the grains you started with?

Shape Shifter

◆◆◆◆◆◆◆

Liquids do not keep their own shape, but solids do.

Take 2 ice cubes from the freezer. Set one on a plate, and set the other in a cup. Notice that the ice cubes have a definite shape and that they stay in that shape. They are solids. We can't see the molecules that are in the ice, but a force is holding each molecule to the ones around it.

What You'll Need
- 2 ice cubes
- plate
- cup

Watch the ice cubes as they begin to warm up. As ice warms, the molecules begin to move faster. They slide over and around each other. When the molecules are moving fast enough, the force can't hold them in the cube shape. The ice melts and changes from a solid to a liquid.

Look at the melting ice on the plate. The liquid doesn't have a definite shape. It's just a puddle. The ice in the cup melts, and the liquid flows into the same shape as the cup.

Moving Molecules

◆◆◆◆◆◆◆

The molecules in an object are constantly in motion.

Fill a glass with water, and let it sit for a few minutes so the water appears still. Add a couple of drops of food coloring. Watch as the drops settle to the bottom of the water. Let the glass sit undisturbed for several hours. When you come back, you'll find that the food coloring has been spread throughout the whole glass of water. Try the project again. This time, use a glass of cold water and a glass of hot water. Check on the glasses every few minutes. Compare how long it takes the food coloring to spread throughout the hot water and the cold water.

What You'll Need
- 2 glasses
- water
- food coloring

Water molecules are constantly in motion, even if it looks like the water is still. The first time you did the experiment, the moving water molecules collided with the food coloring molecules and started them moving. After a time, the food coloring molecules were spread through the glass of water. The second time you did the experiment, you found that the food coloring spread through the hot water faster than through the cold water. This is because the molecules in hot water move faster than the molecules in cold water. This is true for every substance.

Sweet Racers

◆◆◆◆◆◆◆

Solids can be dissolved into liquids. Try it yourself with this tasty test.

What You'll Need
- 2 glasses
- water
- sugar cubes
- napkin
- hammer

Fill 2 glasses halfway with warm water. Wrap a cube of sugar in a napkin. Use a hammer to gently break the sugar cube into tiny pieces. Drop a whole sugar cube into one glass of water and the crushed sugar cube into the other glass of water at the same time. In which glass does the sugar dissolve faster?

Sugar dissolves in water when the sugar molecules are surrounded by water molecules. In the glass with the crushed sugar cube, the water molecules were able to surround the sugar molecules faster because the sugar molecules were spread out.

Sweet Success

❖❖❖❖❖❖

It's a race to disappear!

Use a marker to label 3 clear, plastic cups A, B, and C. Add tap water to Cup B so that it is ¾ full. Allow this cup to sit for a while so its temperature becomes room temperature. Set up a pitcher with ice water in it. Pour the water from this pitcher into Cup A. Then, run the hot water faucet to produce warm water. Add this to Cup C. Do not use water that is hot enough to burn you. Warm water will be sufficient. All 3 cups should have the same amount of water in them. Let the cups sit for a moment so that their contents are still.

What You'll Need
- 3 plastic cups
- marker
- water
- ice cubes
- pitcher
- sugar
- measuring spoon
- clock
- pen and paper

Add 1 teaspoon sugar to each cup and record the time. How long does it take for the sugar in each cup to disappear completely? Which type of water dissolved the sugar the fastest? Which dissolved sugar the slowest?

You probably found that the sugar dissolved fastest in warm water. The molecules in warm water move faster than the molecules in colder water. The faster moving molecules dissolve sugar quicker.

Density and Volume

❖❖❖❖❖❖

The density of an object is a measurement of its heaviness. Density includes an object's mass, or weight, and its volume, or the amount of space it takes up. If two objects weigh the same, but one takes up less space, the smaller one has a greater density. Understanding density will help explain other things, such as why some objects float while other objects sink.

Making a Density Column

◆◆◆◆◆◆◆

See density illustrated before your very eyes.

Fill a cup with water, add some red food coloring, and stir. Set a tall, narrow jar on a table. Using a turkey baster, slowly add the following to the jar in this order: corn syrup, glycerin, dishwashing liquid, colored water, vegetable oil, and rubbing alcohol. Add enough of each to fill about ⅙ of the jar. When you add each substance, put the tip of the baster on the side of the jar, and squeeze the bulb gently so the liquid slides down the side of the jar. Don't squirt it in. The liquids you've added will stay separate from one another; the less dense liquids will float on top of the more dense liquids. Take a cork, a marble, a paper clip, and several other small objects, and add them one at a time to the jar. The objects will float at different levels. Can you guess why?

What You'll Need
- cup
- water
- red food coloring
- spoon
- tall, narrow jar
- turkey baster
- corn syrup
- glycerin
- dishwashing liquid
- vegetable oil
- rubbing alcohol
- various small objects

Rock Space

◆◆◆◆◆◆◆

Rock your way to learning how to measure volume.

What You'll Need
- shoe box
- metric ruler
- paper and pen
- measuring cup that indicates milliliters
- water
- small rock

Measure the length, width, and height of a shoe box in centimeters. Write the measurements down, and then multiply the numbers (l × w × h). This is the volume of the box in cubic centimeters.

But how can you find the volume of something that doesn't have flat sides? Fill a measuring cup with 50 milliliters of water. Gently drop a rock into the water. Now how high is the water level in the measuring cup? Subtract 50 (the volume of the water) from the new measurement. This is the volume of the rock in milliliters.

When you put the rock into the water, it takes up space. That space used to have water in it, and the water has to go somewhere. The water level rises in the measuring cup by exactly the amount of space that the rock occupies.

Making a Hydrometer

Discover different densities with this homemade device.

What You'll Need

- 2 glasses
- water
- salt
- measuring cup
- spoon
- plastic drinking straw
- scissors
- plasticine clay
- string
- various liquids

Fill 2 glasses with water. Add ⅓ cup salt to one of the glasses, and stir it with a spoon. Set both glasses on a counter while you make your hydrometer.

Cut a plastic drinking straw so that it's a little longer than your glass. Put a small ball of plasticine clay (about the size of a marble) at the end of the straw. Be sure the clay makes a tight fit on the straw so that water won't leak into the straw.

Put the clay end of the straw into the glass of plain water; it should float just off the bottom. If it doesn't float, remove a little of the clay. When your straw and clay float, take the straw out of the water, and tie a piece of string around the middle of the straw. Put the straw back in the water. Slide the string to mark the water level on the straw. The straw is now a hydrometer. The higher the straw floats in a glass of liquid, the denser the liquid is.

Put your hydrometer into the glass of salt water. Where is the string? Is salt water more dense or less dense than freshwater? Use your hydrometer to check the density of other liquids, such as cooking oil or milk.

Marbles in Water

Pump up the volume without worrying about being too loud.

Pour 1 cup water into a 2-cup measuring cup. Drop 4 marbles into the water. What is the water level in the measuring cup now? Write this down. Drop 4 more marbles into the water. What is the level of the water in the measuring cup now? Can you predict, using the information that you have written down, what the level of water will be when you add 8 more marbles? Write down your prediction. Add 8 more marbles to the cup of water. Was your prediction correct?

What You'll Need

- water
- 2-cup measuring cup
- 16 marbles of the same size
- paper and pen

Density vs. Volume

◆▶◆▶◆▶◆▶

Liquids of the same volume may not have the same density.

What You'll Need
- identical jars with lids
- honey
- vegetable oil
- balance scale

Take 2 identical jars. Fill one with honey and the other with vegetable oil; put the lids on both jars. The honey and the vegetable oil have the same volume; they take up the same amount of space in the jars. Now compare their mass, or weight. Put the jar with honey on one side of a balance scale and the jar with vegetable oil on the other side. You'll see that one jar weighs more than the other. Substances with the same volume but different weights have different densities.

Bottle Diving

◆▶◆▶◆▶◆▶

Make a magical diver that rises and falls on your command.

Add water to an eyedropper so that it floats dropper-side down in a cup of water. Depending on the eyedropper, it will need to be about ½ to ⅔ full. Fill a clear 2-liter bottle with water, and replace the cap. If air remains at the top, remove the cap and completely fill the bottle. Put the eyedropper into the bottle. Put the cap back on. Now you are ready for some magic.

What You'll Need
- eyedropper
- water
- cup
- clear 2-liter bottle

Hold the bottle in your hand. Say "down diver" and squeeze the bottle. The diver falls. Then say "up diver" and stop squeezing the bottle. The diver rises.

Air is more highly compressible than water. When you squeeze the bottle, the water brings the compression to the air in the eyedropper. This air is compressed, and it takes up less space allowing water to enter the eyedropper. The eyedropper becomes denser, and it sinks. When you stop squeezing the bottle, the air expands in the eyedropper and pushes out some water making the eyedropper less dense so it rises.

If you squeeze the bottle and the eyedropper does not sink, take the eyedropper out and add more water to it. It might need to be a little denser to sink when you squeeze the bottle.

States of Matter

◆◆◆◆◆◆◆

Matter comes in 3 different states: solid, liquid, and gas. Solids can melt into liquids. When a solid is stirred into a liquid, it sometimes disappears. When it does, we say that the solid has dissolved to form a solution. Gases can dissolve in liquids and so can other liquids. In the same way, liquids can evaporate into gases, and gases can mix into other gases.

 # Less and Less and Less

◆◆◆◆◆◆◆

Water evaporates into the air.

Pour 1 cup of water into a clean jar. Immediately screw the lid onto the jar. Pour 1 cup of water into a second jar, but do not put a lid on this jar. Place both jars next to each other in a sunny window. With a marker, mark the level of the water in both jars on the outside. At the end of each day, mark the level of the water. After a week, what is the difference you see between the water level in the 2 jars?

   Heat from the sun made the water in both jars evaporate. In the jar with the lid, the water could not escape, and it condensed back into a liquid. In the jar with no lid, the water escaped into the air when it evaporated, so there was less and less water in the jar as the week went on.

Smelly Science

◆◆◆◆◆◆

Perfume molecules will move through the air.

What You'll Need
- 2 bottles of perfume
- shoe box

Ask a friend to sit across the room from you. Set a bottle of perfume on a table or counter, and open it. Put a second bottle of perfume inside a shoe box. Open this perfume bottle, and quickly put the lid on the shoe box. Set the shoe box next to the first perfume bottle. Ask your friend to tell you when he or she can smell the perfume from across the room.

It will take a little time for the molecules of perfume to move through the air. When your friend smells perfume, take the bottle of perfume out of the shoe box, and quickly close the shoe box again. Put the tops on both perfume bottles. Ask your friend to lift the shoe box lid and smell inside the box. The scent will be strong because the perfume molecules could not escape into the room.

Pop in a Balloon

◆◆◆◆◆◆

Gases can dissolve in a liquid.

What You'll Need
- bottle of soda pop
- balloon
- watch

Open up a bottle of soda pop, and set it on a table. Immediately slip the end of a balloon over the neck of the bottle. Pull the balloon's end well down over the bottle so that it fits tightly. Check on the balloon about every 10 minutes for any changes.

Soda pop is carbonated. This means that carbon dioxide gas has been dissolved in the liquid under high pressure. Opening the bottle releases the pressure, and the carbon dioxide gas begins to escape from the liquid. The balloon traps the carbon dioxide gas as it leaves the bottle, and then the gas inflates the balloon.

Growing Frozen

❖❖❖❖❖❖❖

What happens to the volume of water as it turns into ice?

What You'll Need
- plastic water bottle
- water
- marker
- freezer

Fill a clear, plastic water bottle half-full with water. Draw a line at the water level with the marker. When you freeze the water where do you think the new level will be? Draw a dotted line to show your prediction. Stand the bottle upright in the freezer, and leave it overnight. Take the bottle out of the freezer, and draw a line at the top of the ice line. How close was your prediction?

Most things get smaller as they get colder. This is because the molecules slow down and move closer together. Water generally behaves this way, with one exception. As water goes from 4°C to 0°C it expands and becomes less dense. Thus, ice (frozen water) takes up more space than liquid water.

Disappearing Act

❖❖❖❖❖❖❖

Solids can be dissolved in water, but different solids will dissolve in different amounts.

Pour ½ cup water into each of 3 small jars. Add ¼ teaspoon salt to the first jar, ¼ teaspoon sugar to the second jar, and ¼ teaspoon flour to the third jar. Put lids on the jars, and label each jar "SALT," "SUGAR," and "FLOUR." Shake each jar well. Which of the solids dissolved in water? Continue to add ¼ teaspoon of each solid to each labeled jar until the solutions are saturated, or until no more solids will dissolve. Keep track of how much of each solid you added.

What You'll Need
- water
- measuring cup and spoon
- 3 small jars with lids
- marker
- salt
- sugar
- flour
- pen and paper

Friction

◆◆◆◆◆◆◆►

Using energy creates heat. One way that energy can produce heat is through friction. When objects rub against each other, some energy is converted to heat through friction. Applying heat to matter can cause a change in the matter.

Swing Resistance

◆◆◆◆◆◆◆►

Pendulums swing back and forth.
Can you create a pendulum that more quickly swings less?

Tie a washer to the bottom of the string, then tape the top of the string to the side of a table. Make sure the pendulum can swing freely without hitting anything.

Cut one 30 cm strip of paper and one 15 cm strip. The point at which the pendulum hangs when it is not swinging is its resting point. Put the strips on the ground next to each other starting from the resting point. Use the 30 cm strip to help you pull the pendulum bob back 30 cm. Look at the clock and release the pendulum. Its first swings go almost all the way to the 30 cm mark, but over time the swings become shorter. Time how long it takes until the swings are reduced to 15 cm. Use the 15 cm strip to help you determine this.

Now, use tape to attach a wooden craft stick to the washer. Bring the bob to the 30 cm mark and release it again. Time how long until the swings are reduced to 15 cm.

What You'll Need
- string
- metal washer
- tape
- metric ruler
- scissors
- paper
- clock
- pencil
- wooden craft stick

You probably found that the swing of your pendulum shortened more quickly once you added the craft stick. This is because you increased the wind friction, or wind resistance, of the bob. Can you think of other materials you might add to the bob to slow it down? Which shapes do you think would add the most wind resistance?

Curly Fish

◆▷◆▷◆▷◆

Warm surfaces expand more quickly than cool surfaces.

What You'll Need
- celluloid
- scissors
- ruler
- bowl
- water

Cut a simple fish shape from a sheet of celluloid. Your fish should be about 4 inches long and 1 inch wide at the widest part of its body and 1 inch wide from tip to tip of its V-shaped tail. Drop the fish into a bowl of water.

Tell a friend that your fish is so lifelike it will curl up if taken out of water. Ask your friend to pick up the fish and lay it in his or her hand. Nothing will happen.

But if you rub your hands together vigorously and then ask your friend to put the fish flat on your open hand, the fish will curl its head and tail together within a few seconds.

The friction from rubbing your hands together created heat, and the heat was passed on to the fish. However, the plastic fish did not warm evenly. The bottom part touching your warm hand warmed faster and caused the plastic to expand, but the top, colder surface remained the same. This difference in the temperature of the top and bottom sides of the fish caused it to curl.

Pump It Up

◆▷◆▷◆▷◆

When we use energy, some of it can become heat.

What You'll Need
- bicycle
- bicycle pump
- air-pressure gauge

Take a bicycle and a bicycle pump that have been stored some-place cool. Feel the tires of the bicycle with your hands. They should feel cool to the touch. Feel the bicycle pump. It should also feel cool to the touch. Measure the pressure in the back tire. Then let half the air out of the back tire. Feel both tires again. They should still feel cool to your touch.

Now pump up the back tire. When it is full, feel both tires again. The back tire will feel much warmer than the front tire. The bicycle pump will feel warm, too.

You used energy to make air move from outside the tire to inside the tire. As the air moved, its mol-ecules bumped into the sides of the pump and the sides of the tire, causing friction. Some of your energy was used to overcome this friction. As the mole-cules moved against each other, they generated heat.

Hot Buttered Popcorn

◆▶▶▶▶◀◀◀◀

Heat causes popcorn kernels to explode.

What You'll Need
- popcorn
- air popper
- bowl

Caution: This project requires adult supervision.

There is a small amount of water inside a popcorn kernel. When enough heat is applied, the water turns to steam and expands, making the kernel burst. Put some popcorn into an air popper. Turn on the popper, and position a bowl to catch the popcorn. Soon you will start to hear the popping sound of the bursting hulls, and the popcorn will start filling your bowl.

As you enjoy your popcorn treat, you may find some "duds" left behind. These kernels were too dry—they didn't have enough steam to pop!

Ramp-age!

◆▶▶▶▶◀◀◀◀

When a block slides down a ramp, friction can slow it down.

Place one end of a wooden board on a stack of books to create a ramp. The ramp should be steep enough that the block will slide down it. If your ramp is not steep enough, add more books to your stack. Draw a starting line and a finish line on your ramp. Place the block at the starting line and time how long it takes to travel to the finish line. Record the time.

What You'll Need
- wooden board
- books
- wooden block
- pencil
- ruler
- stopwatch
- miscellaneous household materials

Now, try to find ways to make the block slide down the ramp faster. For example, you might try covering the ramp with waxed paper or spraying it with silicon spray. (Have an adult approve your materials before you use them.) Once you have explored ways to make the ramp faster, try to change the ramp so that the block doesn't slide at all. For example, you might try covering the surface with sandpaper. (Again, have an adult approve your choice of materials.)

You probably found that to make the block slide faster, you did something to decrease the friction of the ramp. To make it slide slower or to prevent it from sliding, you increased the friction.

The Real McCoy

◆▷◆▷◆▷◆

Ever heard the phrase "the real McCoy"?
Find out where the saying comes from.

What You'll Need
- pen and paper
- Internet access

Engineers work hard to reduce friction in machines with moving parts. Less friction means the parts last longer and the machine uses less energy. Elijah McCoy was a leader in this technology. He was born in Ontario, Canada, in 1843, the son of African American slaves who fled from Kentucky. As a child, he was very interested in mechanical things, so his parents sent him to Scotland to be educated as a mechanical engineer. Afterward, Elijah went to live in Detroit, Michigan. Because of his race he was not able to find work as an engineer and had to work instead as a laborer. One of his duties was oiling the train parts. This experience and his creativity led him to create and patent a self-oiling mechanism in trains.

Visit the U.S. Patent and Trademark Office on the Internet (http://www.uspto.gov/) to see a drawing and description from his actual patent application. Search for the patent using patent number 129,843. Engineers at the time were so impressed with this invention that they asked for "the real McCoy" when buying it. This expression is still used today to describe "the real thing." Elijah McCoy patented more than 60 inventions in his lifetime.

Hot Touch

◆▷◆▷◆▷◆

Friction creates heat.

On a camping trip or in a film, you may have seen someone start a fire by rapidly rubbing 2 sticks together near some tinder. The friction of the sticks caused enough heat to spark a fire. You can do a similar experiment without starting a fire.

What You'll Need
- 2 plastic pens
- hand towel

   Take 2 plastic pens, and feel them. They will probably feel cool to the touch. Set one of the pens aside. Take the other pen, and vigorously rub it with a hand towel for about a minute. Stop rubbing. Pick up the other pen and compare it to the pen you rubbed. Which of the pens feels warmer? The rubbed pen feels hot to the touch because the friction caused by rubbing it in a towel generated heat.

Tread on Me

◆◆◆◆◆◆◆

Which shoe bottoms give us the most friction?

Raid the closets in your house, and gather as many different kinds of shoes as you can find (high-heeled shoes, hiking boots, tennis shoes, etc.). Examine the shoes, and try to predict the relative amount of friction they would have on a wooden gym floor.

Now test your predictions. Create a steep hill by balancing a board on a tall stack of books. One by one, put shoes on the ramp and see how well they slide. The shoes that slide the most probably have the least amount of friction.

Think about this: In many cases we try to fight friction. But with shoes we need friction. It helps us stop and make turns. In fact, without friction, we couldn't even walk—our feet would simply slide backward.

What You'll Need
• shoes
• board
• books

Balloon Rocket Drag

◆◆◆◆◆◆◆

Which type of string is best for balloon rocket distance?

What You'll Need
• cylinder-shaped balloons
• ruler
• straw
• scissors
• tape
• waxed dental floss
• unwaxed dental floss
• cloth twine
• fishing line

To make the rocket, blow up the balloon and pinch the end to keep the air in. Have a partner use 2 pieces of tape to secure a 4-inch segment of straw to the balloon.

Decide which type of line you want to test first. Ask your partner to tie one end of the line to a chair, then thread the line through the straw attached to your balloon. Hold the other end of the line taut, and release the balloon. Measure how far the rocket travels.

Repeat with your other lines to see which is best. To make it a fair test, you'll need to have the same starting point for all the lines, and you'll want each balloon to have the same amount of air. Decide whether you should use the same balloon or if you should use a fresh balloon each time.

If you control all the variables, the difference in the distances will be due to the different lines. The longer the rocket travels, the less friction it experiences from the line.

Evaporation and Condensation

◆▶◆▶◆▶◆▶

During a rainstorm, water falls from the sky. It soaks into the ground and collects in puddles. After the rain stops and the sun begins to shine again, puddles dry up and the water disappears. The sun's heat makes the water turn into a gas, which rises up in the air. This process of a liquid turning into a gas is called *evaporation*. When the temperature of water vapor is lowered enough, it becomes liquid again—water. This process is called *condensation*.

 ## Disappearing Paintings

◆▶◆▶◆▶◆▶

Liquid evaporates if its temperature rises.

What You'll Need
● container
● water
● paintbrush

On a hot afternoon when the sun has been shining for several hours and the side-walk is warm, take a con-tainer of water and a clean paintbrush outside. Dip your brush into the water, and "paint" a picture on the side-walk. You might paint a cat, a tree, a rocket ship, or anything else you like to draw. Don't be too detailed; just make the outline, and add only a few details. Then stand back, and look at your picture. Admire it quickly because your "painting" will soon disappear. The water will evaporate into the warm air.

The Dew Point

It's easy to study water in all of its forms. Here we will take a look at the relationship between temperatures and water vapor.

What You'll Need
- metal can
- water
- food coloring
- ice cubes
- spoon

Fill a clean metal can with no label about ⅔ of the way with warm water, and add a few drops of food coloring. Let the can sit on a table for an hour until it reaches room temperature. Add ice cubes to the water one at a time, and stir with a spoon. Watch the outside of the can. After you add enough ice cubes, the outside of the can will become wet with small droplets of clear water.

Notice that the drops on the outside are clear and that the water inside the can is colored; the drops did not come from the water inside the can.

The air outside the can contains water vapor. When the vapor in the air came in contact with the cold can, the vapor's temperature lowered, and it condensed into water on the outside of the can.

Solar Still

Warmth from the sun causes moisture to evaporate from the soil.

What You'll Need
- shovel
- ruler
- bowl
- heavy clear plastic
- rocks

Find a spot in your yard that gets sun in the morning, and then get permission to dig a small hole there. Use a shovel to dig a hole 1 foot deep and 18 inches wide. Place a small bowl in the bottom of the hole. Cover the hole with a piece of heavy clear plastic. Drop a small rock into the middle of the plastic cover so that it sags down and is about 2 inches above the bowl. Fasten the plastic in place all around the hole using rocks for weights. Check the hole in the late afternoon. What did you find in your bowl?

Heat from the sun caused moisture in the soil to evaporate, or turn into a gas. The gas was trapped by the plastic cover. As the gas cooled, it turned back to liquid water and dripped into the bowl.

Quick Dry

◆◆◆◆◆◆◆

Water evaporates fastest in warm, dry places.

What You'll Need
- large rag
- scissors
- bowl
- water
- pen and paper

Cut a large rag into 6 strips of cloth that are about the same width and length. Soak all of the strips of cloth in a bowl of water until they are completely wet.

Find 6 different places to put your strips of cloth, such as on a sunny window ledge, on a shelf in the refrigerator, on a tree branch in the shade, on a tree branch in the sun, in a garage wadded up on the floor, or flat on a cement surface in a sunny spot. Write the places down on a piece of paper.

Think about each place, and predict where the cloth will dry the fastest. Number each place 1 through 6 on the paper, with 1 being where the cloth will dry fastest and 6 being where the cloth will dry slowest. Check the strips of cloth often. How did you do on your predictions? Why did the cloth dry fast in some places and slow in others?

Solid to Liquid to Solid

◆◆◆◆◆◆◆

Solids can change into liquids, and liquids can change into solids.

What You'll Need
- can of frozen orange juice
- pitcher
- large spoon
- water
- 2 paper cups
- 2 wooden craft sticks
- freezer

Open a can of frozen orange juice, and spoon it into a large pitcher. Touch the frozen juice to feel that it is both solid and cold. Add water according to the package directions to make orange juice. Fill 2 paper cups about ⅔ of the way with orange juice. Put a craft stick into the liquid in each paper cup. Being careful not to spill, put the cups of juice into the freezer. Check them after 2 hours. Can you gently pull out the craft stick, or has the

liquid orange juice frozen solid around the stick? If it has frozen, peel off the paper cups. Now you and a friend can enjoy a frozen treat!

Water, Water Everywhere

◆▶◆▶◆▶◆

Cold air cannot hold as much water vapor as warm air.

What You'll Need
● hand mirror
● freezer

By using your powers of observation, you'll be able to see several examples of condensation. Put a hand mirror in the freezer until the mirror is cold. Take the mirror out, and hold it close to your face. Blow your warm breath onto the mirror. You will see a misty spot on the mirror made from drops of water.

The next time you get out of your bath or shower, look at the mirror in your bathroom. The bathroom mirror may be covered with drops of water. In both cases, where did the drops of water come from? What did temperature have to do with forming them?

The Great Summer Melt-Off

◆▶◆▶◆▶◆

How long does it take for ice to melt?

In this fun race, you and a friend team up to see how quickly you can cause ice to melt using only your fingers and hands.

Stuff the cups with ice, then fill them to the top with water. Mark each paper cup at the halfway point with a waterproof marker. That's how much water MUST remain in the cup to avoid being disqualified in the end.

What You'll Need
● paper cups
● ice cubes
● water
● waterproof marker

It's your job to melt the ice faster than your opponent can, using only the swirling action of your fingers and the heat of your hands to make it happen. And remember, the cup must remain at least half-full or you're out of the competition.

Condensation Pie

◆◆◆◆◆◆

Learn about evaporation and condensation as you make a condensation pie.

Fill the bottom of a pie tin with water. Stretch a layer of plastic wrap over the pie tin so that the top of the pie tin is completely covered. Put a rubber band around the plastic to hold it in place. Place the "pie" in the sunshine, and observe it every 15 minutes. If your friends ask what you're doing, tell them you are making a condensation pie.

What You'll Need
- pie tin
- water
- plastic wrap
- rubber band
- clock or watch

The temperature influences the rate of evaporation. The hotter the water in the pie tin, the faster the evaporation occurs. This is similar to evaporation from lakes and oceans. The warmer the water, the faster the evaporation. Evaporation happens when the liquid water becomes water vapor in the air.

As the amount of water vapor increases, some of it condenses onto the plastic covering the pie tin. As the water drops get bigger in size, you see this condensation as a fog on the bottom of the plastic.

Bubble Bottle

◆◆◆◆◆◆

How can you make your beautiful bubbles last longer?

What You'll Need
- clear plastic container with lid
- bubble solution and wand
- watch

Find a clear plastic container with a lid. Add a little bubble solution to the container. Blow some bubbles, then catch them in the container. Time how long these bubbles take to pop. Now catch some new bubbles, but this time put the lid on the container. How much time passes before these bubbles pop?

You probably found the covered bubbles last a lot longer. As the bubble solution evaporates, the bubble weakens until it pops. When you put the lid on the container, evaporation slowed down. As a result, the bubble didn't lose water as fast, and it lasted longer.

Air Pressure

◆▷◆▷◆▷◆▷

We live in a sea of air that we call the *atmosphere*. The atmosphere contains gases, including nitrogen and oxygen. Like all other types of matter, this air has mass and volume, and its weight can exert pressure. Its volume also changes depending on its temperature.

 # Guess the Weight

◇▷◇▷◇▷◇▷

How can you estimate the weight of a car by using air pressure?

What You'll Need
- car
- chalk
- ruler
- tire-pressure gauge
- paper
- pencil
- calculator

Caution: This project requires adult supervision.

Before beginning this project, ask an adult to park their car in a safe place with no traffic, such as your driveway. Have the adult make sure the car is in park, the parking brake is on, and the engine is off.

Only part of a car's tire touches the ground at one time; the shape of this contact area is a rectangle. The adult can use a piece of chalk to draw 3 lines on the ground around one of the tires. The first line should be along the side of the tire. The second line should be in front of the tire. The third line should be in back of the tire. These 3 lines almost form a rectangle.

Now, have everybody stand far away from the car while the adult carefully moves it. Then connect the 3 chalk lines so that you have a rectangle. The area of the rectangle is equal to its length multiplied by its width. Find the area of the rectangle, and record the number.

Have the adult use a tire-pressure gauge to find the pressure in the tire. Record the pressure. The force down, or weight of the car on one tire, is equal to the area multiplied by the pressure. Multiply the area by the pressure to find the force acting on one tire. Now multiply this force by 4 (because a car has 4 tires) to find the approximate weight of the car.

Burn Out

◆◆◆◆◆◆

A candle needs oxygen to burn.

Caution: This project requires adult supervision.

Take a candle that is about 4 inches long, and carefully light it with a match. Tilt the candle over a saucer so that some wax drips into the saucer. Be careful! This wax is hot! After you have a small puddle of wax in the saucer, blow out the candle. Then place the bottom of the candle into the puddle of melted wax. This wax puddle will dry and hold your candle.

What You'll Need
- candle
- matches
- saucer
- tall glass

Carefully light the candle again. Observe it. The candle should burn brightly. Now put a tall glass over the candle. The lip of the glass should rest on the saucer. Watch what happens. The flame will burn for a while, and then it will go out. The candle has used up all the oxygen in the glass. Without oxygen, the candle cannot burn.

Flame Out

◆◆◆◆◆◆

Investigate the densities of gases in this hot experiment.

What You'll Need
- cardboard tube
- scissors
- ruler
- candle
- candleholder
- matches
- glass
- baking soda
- measuring spoon
- vinegar

Caution: This project requires adult supervision.

Cut a 10-inch section of cardboard tube. Put a candle in a candleholder in a safe place on a table. Light the candle. Put 1 teaspoon baking soda into an empty glass. Add 1 inch of vinegar to the glass. You will see bubbles forming. These bubbles contain carbon dioxide gas, which is formed as the vinegar and baking soda mix together. Hold up the cardboard tube, and tip it down toward the candle flame (but don't get it too close or it will burn). Carefully pour the bubbles from the glass into the tube and toward the flame without getting liquid into the flame. What happens to the flame?

As you poured the bubbles into the tube, the carbon dioxide gas traveled down the tube and came out the other end, covering the flame and keeping oxygen from it. The flame went out.

Spinning Snake

◆◆◆◆◆◆◆

Use warm air to breathe "life" into a paper snake.

What You'll Need
- paper plate
- markers
- scissors
- thread

Draw an oval shape in the center of a lightweight paper plate. Starting at the oval, draw a spiral line around and around 4 or 5 times until it reaches the edge of the plate. Use scissors to cut along the spiral line from the outside edge to the center oval. Draw eyes to make the center oval of the plate into a snake's head. Poke a small hole into the center of the head. Put a thread through the hole from the top, and tie a big knot in it so the thread will not pull through. Color the snake's body with stripes. Hang the snake by the thread above a heat source, such as a radiator or heating vent. Watch to see what your snake does.

What happened? Heat from the heat source caused air to rise up toward your snake. As the air molecules bumped into you spiral-shaped snake, they caused it to spin.

A Tight Squeeze

◆◆◆◆◆◆◆

Fire uses oxygen and lowers air pressure in a sealed container.

Caution: This project requires adult supervision.

Find a bottle, such as a carafe, with a neck slightly smaller than a peeled egg. Peel the shell from a hard-boiled egg, and check to be sure that the egg just fits into the neck of the bottle and will not fall through.

What You'll Need
- carafe
- hard-boiled egg
- paper
- taper or long candle
- matches
- pitcher of water

Crumple a piece of paper, and drop it inside the carafe. Use a taper or a long candle to light the paper at the bottom of the carafe. Quickly pop the egg into the neck of the bottle. Watch the egg get pulled into the bottle as the paper burns. Pour water into the bottle to extinguish the fire if necessary.

Can you guess what happened? As the paper burns, it uses oxygen. Because the egg is sealing the neck of the bottle, no more air can get in to replace the oxygen. This reduces the air pressure in the carafe until the outer air pressure is strong enough to push the egg into the carafe.

Up and Down

A gas will have a greater volume as its temperature increases and a lesser volume as its temperature decreases.

What You'll Need
- balloon
- soda pop bottle
- 2 buckets
- water
- ice cubes
- clock

Fasten a balloon onto the neck of an empty soda pop bottle that has been sitting overnight and is at room temperature. Feel the bottle. It will be neither hot nor cold. Then put the bottle into a bucket of ice water, and leave it there for 15 minutes. Feel the bottle. It is cold. Now put the bottle into a bucket of hot water. The balloon inflates. If you put the bottle back into the ice water, the balloon will deflate.

When you put the bottle in the hot water, you added heat energy to the air in the bottle. This made the air molecules move around more and spread out, so they took up more space. Some of the air went into the balloon and inflated it. When you put the bottle back into the ice water, you took heat energy away from the air in the bottle. This made the air molecules move less and take up less space, so the balloon deflated.

Balloon in a Glass

Air presses in all directions.

What You'll Need
- balloon
- clear plastic glass

Hold a balloon so that it dangles down into an empty glass. Hold the glass in one hand and the balloon in the other as you blow into the balloon. As you inflate the balloon, the part of the balloon trapped in the glass will swell out and touch the sides of the glass. Continue to blow. In a few more puffs, you can remove the hand holding the glass. You can lift the glass by holding the end of the balloon. The air pressure inside the balloon exerts force outward in all directions.

Unspillable Water

◄►◄►◄►◄►

Air pressure can be stronger than gravity.

Fill a juice glass with water. Let the water run over so the rim of the glass gets wet. Be sure you fill the glass right up to the top. Place a 4×6-inch index card on top of the full glass of water. Press the card down securely with your hand so it makes a good seal all around the wet lip of the glass. Working over a sink, hold the card in place with one hand as you turn the glass over. Carefully let go of the index card. The card will stay in place, and the water will stay in the glass.

What You'll Need
- juice glass
- water
- 4×6-inch index card
- sink

What happened? The force of air pressure against the card was stronger than the force of gravity on the water. The air pressure held the card in place.

Water Fountain

◄►◄►◄►◄►

Moving air has less pushing power than still air.

What You'll Need
- tall glass
- water
- 2 drinking straws
- scissors
- plant

Fill a tall glass with water. Stand a straw in the water so the straw is about an inch above the top of the glass. If the straw is too long for your glass, cut it to the proper length with scissors. Place the glass on a table in front of a plant that you want to spray with water. Hold another straw at a right angle to the straw in the glass of water. The tip of the horizontal straw should just touch the tip of the upright straw. Blow hard through the horizontal straw, and you will create a spray.

Normally, the air presses down on all the water in the glass with equal force, both inside and outside the straw. However, when you blow air over the straw, the moving air doesn't press down as hard as the still air over the rest of the water. That means that the air presses down harder on the water outside the straw and forces the water inside the straw up until it sprays out the top.

Book Blast

◆▷◆▷◆▷◆

Can you huff and puff books off a table?

Stack 3 books on top of one another on a table. Challenge a friend to move the books by blowing at them. Your friend won't be able to move the books.

Now place a large plastic bag on the table, and put the 3 books on top of the bag. Leave the open end of the bag sticking out over the edge of the table. Hold the opening together, leaving as small a hole as possible. Blow into the bag. Stop to rest if you need to (but be sure to close off the bag opening so the air stays trapped inside). If you blow long and hard enough, the books will rise off the table. They will be supported by the compressed air in the plastic bag.

What You'll Need
- books
- large airtight plastic bag

Rocket Power

◆▷◆▷◆▷◆

Have a blast when you use compressed air to launch a rocket.

What You'll Need
- construction paper
- scissors
- tape
- 2 drinking straws
- ruler
- modeling clay
- empty bottle of dishwashing liquid

Caution: Never launch your rocket at anyone.

Cut a 3-inch square of construction paper diagonally so that you have 2 triangles. Fold each triangle in half, and tape the folded triangles to the end of a drinking straw so that they look like fins on a rocket. Cut 4 inches off the other end of the straw. With modeling clay, make a small pointed nose, and put it on the tip of the straw.

Push a second straw through the hole in the cap of an empty bottle of dishwashing liquid. (If the existing hole isn't big enough, ask an adult to use a scissors or knife to widen the hole.) Put modeling clay around the straw to help seal up any gaps in the cap. Slip the rocket straw onto the straw that sticks out of the bottle cap. Point the nose of your rocket up in the air. Squeeze the plastic bottle to launch your rocket.

Pinwheel

◆◆◆◆◆◆◆

Moving air molecules create a force that can cause a paper wheel to spin.

What You'll Need
- ruler
- paper
- scissors
- pencil with an eraser
- straight pin

Measure and cut a piece of paper to make an 8-inch square. Use a ruler to draw a diagonal line from one corner of the square to the opposite corner through the middle of the paper, and then do the same for the other corners. You have divided your square into 4 equal triangles. Put an X in the bottom-left corner of each of the triangles. Cut from each corner along the lines you drew halfway to the center of the square of paper. Bend each corner that has an X in it to the center of the paper so they all overlap, and then carefully put a straight pin through all 4 corners to hold them in place at the center of the paper. Put the point of the pin into the eraser on your pencil. You now have a simple pinwheel. You can swing the pinwheel, run with it, blow on it, or hold it in the wind. The moving air molecules will strike the paper and make it spin.

A Lasting Step

Did you know that the footprints of the astronauts who walked on the moon in the 1960s are still there? There are no winds on the moon to blow the prints away, so Neil Armstrong's "one small step for man" is still imprinted on the moon's surface.

Caved-In Can

Air pressure is strong enough to bend a can.

Caution: This project requires adult supervision.

Fill a large container with water and ice cubes. Set it aside to use later. Pour ½ cup water into an empty pop can. With adult supervision, put the can on a burner on the stove. When the water in the can starts to boil, you will see steam coming from the hole in the top of the can. Turn off the stove, and use tongs or pot holders to remove the can from the heat. Quickly put the can in the container of ice water, turning it upside down to rest on its top. Watch as the can cools.

What happened? When you heated the water in the can, it produced steam that forced the air out of the can. When you put the can in the ice water, its temperature lowered, and the steam condensed back into water. The pressure of the air outside the can was greater than the air pressure inside the can. The weight of the outside air crushed the can.

<aside>
What You'll Need
- large container
- water
- ice cubes
- measuring cup
- empty pop can
- stove
- tongs or pot holders
</aside>

Flight and Air Pressure

Air has volume and mass, and just like any other thing with volume and mass, it can cause friction. The force created by this friction is called air resistance. Like all friction, air resistance pushes against an object in motion and slows it down. People can harness the power of air pressure in many different ways.

Clinging Card

◆◆◆◆◆◆◆

Would you believe you can lift a card without touching it?
Try this experiment to find out how.

What You'll Need
- index card
- scissors
- ruler
- pencil
- pin
- empty spool of thread

Cut an index card into a 4-inch square. Mark the middle of the card. Put a pin into the middle of the card. Put an empty spool of thread over the pin so the pin stands in the center of the spool.

Pick up the spool and card, holding the card against the bottom of the spool with your finger. Blow into the spool. Continue blowing, and slowly remove your finger from the card. If you are blowing hard enough, the card will continue to stick to the empty spool.

The moving air from your blowing created a low-pressure area between the card and the spool. Normal air pressure beneath it held the card in place.

Out of the Wind

◆◆◆◆◆◆◆

A stream of air will follow a curved surface.

Caution: This project requires adult supervision.

Place a large plastic bottle at the edge of a table. Put a candle in a candleholder, and place it on the table a couple of inches behind the bottle. Ask an adult to light the candle. Blow hard on the side of the bottle that is nearest the edge of the table. The moving air will follow the curve of the bottle around to the back and put out the burning candle.

What You'll Need
- large plastic bottle
- candle
- candleholder
- matches

Spinners

◆◆◆◆◆◆◆

Air pressure can cause objects to move.

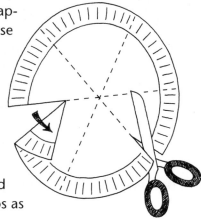

Hold an 8-inch paper plate in the palm of your hand so the plate is parallel to the floor. Drop the plate, and observe what happens. Retrieve the plate, and use a ruler to draw 3 lines that divide it into 6 equal pieces. Cut a slit 2½ inches long on each line from the outside edge of the plate toward the middle. Make a triangular flap along the left side of each section by folding the plate upward at each slit. Drop the plate again, and observe it as it falls.

The flaps caused your plate to spin as it fell the second time. Air molecules pushed against the surface of the flaps as the plate fell and made it spin.

Parachute Power

◆◆◆◆◆◆◆

The more air trapped beneath a canopy, the slower a parachute will fall.

Cut two 12-inch squares and two 8-inch squares of paper. Securely tape 10-inch pieces of string to all 4 corners of all 4 pieces of paper. Gather the 4 strings from one square of paper, and tie them to a paper clip. Repeat for the other 3 squares.

Drop an 8-inch square and a 12-inch square of paper at the same time from a staircase, porch, or deck. Which reaches the ground last, the big or the small parachute? Add 3 more paper clips to one of the 8-inch parachutes. Drop both 8-inch parachutes. Which one reaches the ground first? Put a small hole in the middle of one 12-inch parachute. Drop both 12-inch parachutes. Which one reaches the ground first?

You will find that the more surface area your parachute has, the slower it will fall. The larger surface encounters more air molecules as it falls, so it falls more slowly. A parachute with a heavier load falls faster because the force of gravity working against the air resistance is greater.

Paper Airplanes

◆◆◆◆◆◆

Shape is a factor in how well things fly through the air.

What You'll Need
- paper
- tape measure
- pen

Throw a flat sheet of notebook paper as far as you can, and then measure the distance it traveled. Try several times, and write down the greatest distance it traveled. Now wad the sheet of paper into a ball. Throw it several times, and measure the distance it traveled each time. Write down the greatest distance it traveled.

Take another sheet of notebook paper. Fold it into an airplane, such as the one shown. Throw the airplane several times. Does it travel farther than the other sheets you threw? Experiment with different designs for your plane. Which works best?

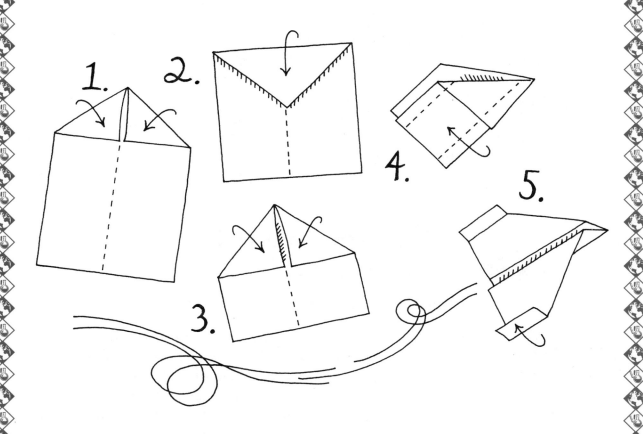

Fast and Slow Landing

◆◆◆◆◆◆◆

Take a look at how parachutes work with this airborne activity.

Cut an 8-inch square of paper. Tape a small rock to the middle of the paper. Wad the paper into a ball around the rock, and drop it from waist height off a staircase, porch, or deck. Ask a friend to use a watch with a second hand to time how long it takes the paper and rock to fall to the ground. Take the paper off the rock (don't be a litterbug!).

Tape a 10-inch piece of thread to each of the 4 corners of another 8-inch square of paper. Tape all 4 threads to the small

rock. When you lift the paper up, it will look something like a parachute, and the rock will hang underneath the center. Drop the rock from the same place, and time the fall.

What happened? When the paper was flat, it had a larger area than when it was crumpled into a ball. The paper ran into more air molecules on the way down, and the force of these additional air molecules slowed the paper and the rock as they fell.

Boomerang

◆◆◆◆◆◆◆

A boomerang is an example of active flight.

A paper airplane glides across the room making use of a condition we call *passive flight*. One of the earliest forms of active flight was the boomerang used by the Aborigines of Australia. You can make a simple boomerang that will work.

Draw your boomerang on an index card in a V-shape with the legs of the V open wide and each 2-inch leg looking like a long balloon. Cut out your boomerang, and balance it flat on 2 fingers of your left hand. Flick one of the legs with the forefinger of your right hand. It should take off like a little propeller and then return toward you.

Gyrocopter

This paper gyrocopter is just the thing to enjoy outside on a warm spring day—or anytime it's not too windy or cold.

What You'll Need
- paper
- ruler
- scissors or pinking shears
- paper clips

A *gyre* is a circular motion; a gyrocopter spins around when it flys. To explore gyre motion, make your own gyrocopter.

Cut out a 6½ × 1½-inch strip of paper. (Note: Using pinking shears will make the gyrocopter fly better, but ordinary scissors will work well too.) Starting at the top, cut a 3-inch slit down the middle of the strip to create a pair of wings. Fold the wings in opposite directions (see diagram). Attach a paper clip to the bottom of the strip for weight.

Drop the finished gyrocopter from an elevated spot, and watch it spin to the ground.

Now try experimenting. Make larger and smaller gyrocopters to see if size makes a difference when they fly. Think up other experiments you can try—make the wings longer, add 2 paper clips to the bottom.

Have gyrocopter races with friends who have made their own 'copters!

Wing It

This activity reveals one of the secrets of how planes fly.

In 1738, Daniel Bernoulli, a Swiss scientist, discovered that moving air has less pushing power than still air. This idea, called *Bernoulli's principle,* is used in the design of airplanes.

What You'll Need
- paper
- scissors
- ruler

To demonstrate the principle, cut a strip of paper 2 inches wide and 8 inches long. Take one corner of a 2-inch side of the strip in each hand, and hold it just below your lower lip. Gently blow across the strip of paper. You will see that the paper rises. The air you blow over the top of the paper is moving air, so it has less pushing power. The air pressure underneath the strip remains normal. The strong air pressure underneath pushes up and causes the strip of paper to lift. Wings of airplanes are shaped with curved tops to make the air move fast, and the fast-moving air along the top of the wing reduces air pressure and causes lift, an upward force that opposes gravity.

Water

◆◆◆◆◆◆◆

Water is an important substance for life on Earth. Pure, ordinary water is made of hydrogen and oxygen. When heated, water evaporates as gas. When cooled sufficiently, it freezes into a solid.

Strainers and Filters

◆◆◆◆◆◆◆

Strainers and filters separate bits of solid from a liquid.

What You'll Need
- knife
- orange
- hand juicer
- mesh strainer
- 2 bowls
- coffee filter

Caution: This project requires adult supervision.

Cut an orange in half with a knife. Use a hand juicer to squeeze out as much juice and pulp as you can from both halves of the orange. Hold a large mesh strainer over a bowl, and pour the juice and pulp into the strainer. Notice how quickly the liquid flows through the strainer. Check the strainer. It will probably contain seeds and large pieces of pulp. Rinse the strainer, and put a coffee filter in it. Now pour the juice through the filter into a second bowl. Notice that the juice flows more slowly through the filter. Look at the filter in the strainer. Did it catch more pieces of pulp?

The coffee filter trapped material that the metal strainer did not. If you look at the strainer, you can see that it has small holes in it that allow liquids and small particles to pass through but not larger particles. The coffee filter works in the same way, but its holes are so small you can't see them. Smaller holes mean that it will trap smaller particles.

A Filter at Work

◆◆◆◆◆◆◆

A filter can remove suspended substances from liquids.

What You'll Need
- water
- measuring cup and spoon
- 4 glasses
- sand
- sugar
- milk
- cocoa
- spoons
- coffee filters

Pour 1 cup water into each of 2 clean glasses. Add 1 tablespoon sand to the first glass. Add 1 tablespoon sugar to the second glass. Pour ¼ cup milk into a third glass, and add 1 teaspoon cocoa. Using a clean spoon each time, thoroughly stir the liquids. Place a coffee filter into the top of a clean glass. Hold the edges of the filter over the rim of the glass so that the filter does not slip inside. Slowly pour the sand mixture into the filter. Does the filter catch the sand? Rinse out the glass. Pour the sugar mixture into the glass through a clean filter. Does the filter catch the sugar? Dip your finger into the filtered water, and taste it. Is it sweet? Rinse out the glass. Pour the milk and cocoa mixture into the glass through a clean filter. Does the filter catch the cocoa? Your filters will catch some of the suspended substances but won't filter out substances that have been fully dissolved.

Water Magnifier

◆◆◆◆◆◆◆

One well-known quality of water is that it makes things wet! But did you know that water also makes things look larger than they really are?

What You'll Need
- piece of glass or plastic
- newspaper
- crayon
- eyedropper
- water

Get a small piece of clear glass or plastic. (A microscope slide is ideal.) Put the slide on top of a piece of newspaper that has small print on it. Now use a crayon to draw a small circle on the slide. Look closely at the print that is within the circle.

With an eyedropper, carefully put a drop of water in the circle. Now look at the print again. It looks larger because the water drop bends rays of light, magnifying the image.

Filtering Out Dirt

◆◆◆◆◆◆

You can filter suspended matter from water by using a wick.

What You'll Need
- 8-inch cardboard box
- 2 bowls
- water
- dirt
- wool yarn

Set an 8-inch-tall cardboard box on a table. Set a bowl of clean water on top of the box. Gently drop a small handful of dirt into the water. Much of the dirt will remain suspended in the water, and the water in the bowl will be discolored.

Set an empty bowl on the table right next to the cardboard box. Twist together several 1-foot strands of wool yarn to make a rope. Put one end of this rope, or wick, into the

bottom of the bowl of dirty water. Put the other end of the wick down into the empty bowl. After a while, drops of clear water will drip off of the free end of the wick into the empty bowl.

The material in your rope absorbs water and draws it from the bowl. It leaves the dirt behind, however, so the water that drips into the second bowl is clean.

All Kinds of Water

◆◆◆◆◆◆

Water doesn't just come in one shape.
It has 3 different states, depending on its temperature.

Caution: This project requires adult supervision.

To see all 3 states, put some ice cubes in a pan. With adult help, put the pan on the stove and turn on the heat. First the ice will begin turning to liquid, then the liquid will begin turning to steam. Ice and snow melt at 32°F (0°C), and water turns into steam at 212°F (100°C).

What You'll Need
- ice cubes
- pan
- stove

Over the Top

◆◆◆◆◆◆◆

Water expands when it freezes.

Fill a clean, plastic margarine tub with water. Make sure that the water level comes right up to the brim of the tub. Carefully place the tub of water in the freezer. Be very careful not to spill the water as you move the tub. The next day, remove the tub of water. Look at it carefully. The ice in the tub will be above the brim because water expands when it freezes.

What You'll Need
- plastic margarine tub
- water
- freezer

Sinking and Floating

◆◆◆◆◆◆◆

Objects that are more dense than water will sink in water. Objects that are less dense will float. Whether or not an object floats depends on the material it is made of and on how much space it occupies.

Sinking Sailors

◆◆◆◆◆◆◆

Paper sinks faster in soapy water than in plain water.

What You'll Need
- scissors
- newspaper
- ruler
- dishwashing liquid
- 2 large glasses
- water

Fold a piece of newspaper in half, and cut 2 identical human figures from it. The 2 "sailors" that you cut from the paper should be about 2 inches at their widest point and about 4 inches tall. Fill 2 glasses with water, and put some dishwashing liquid into one of the glasses. Hold each of the sailors above a glass of water. Drop them at the same time. Both will sink, but which will sink faster?

The sailor in the soapy water gets wet first and sinks faster because soap weakens the attraction between the water molecules.

Water Lines

◆◆◆◆◆◆◆

Does a block float higher in freshwater or salt water?

Have you ever wondered what happens to a boat as it sails from freshwater to salt water? Would the ship sink a little deeper into the freshwater, or would it float higher up? You can find out for yourself with this simple experiment.

What You'll Need
- wooden block
- large pot
- water
- 2 different colored pencils
- salt
- spoon

Float a wooden block in a pot filled with tap water. Draw a line at the watermark, then remove the block. Predict whether this water line would be higher, lower, or the same if the block floated in salt water.

Add some salt to the water in the pot and stir until it disappears. Add some more salt and stir. Keep doing this until the salt no longer disappears. Now test your prediction. Float the wooden block on the salt water. Draw a different color line to show where the salt water line is located. Was your prediction correct? Why did the block float higher in one type of water than in the other?

Up Submarine

◆◆◆◆◆◆◆

Air weighs less than water and can be used to make an object float.

What You'll Need

- plastic bottle with a narrow neck
- scissors
- 4 quarters
- tape
- plastic tubing
- modeling clay
- bathtub
- water

Cut 2 small holes, one above the other, in the side of a plastic bottle, such as an empty shampoo bottle. With adhesive tape, firmly attach 2 quarters on either side of both holes. Put a piece of plastic tubing (like the kind that is used in aquariums) into the neck of the bottle. Securely seal the opening of the bottle around the tubing with modeling clay.

Lower your submarine into a bathtub of water, keeping one end of the tubing above water. Hold your sub under the water until it fills up with water and sinks. Now blow through the end of the plastic tubing. As you blow, you will force air into the submarine and force water out the holes. As the submarine fills with air, it will rise to the surface. By blowing in or releasing air through the tubing, you can cause your submarine to rise or sink.

Air weighs less than water. When your submarine is filled with water, it is more dense and it sinks. When it is filled with air, it is less dense and it floats. Real submarines move up and down in the water in the same way.

Slow Down!

◆◆◆◆◆◆◆

Who can create the slowest diver?

In our hurried world, it seems that we are always trying to find ways to do things faster. Here is a good switch. Try to make the slowest underwater diver. Think of it as a submarine with tourists who want to enjoy the view.

Using film canisters with lids and

What You'll Need

- film canisters with lids
- various coins
- large basin
- water

coins, try to put the right combination of coins in the container so that it slowly sinks when placed into water. If the density of the canister and coins is less than the water, it will float. If the density is greater than the water, it will sink; the denser it is, the faster it will sink. Compete against your family members and friends to see who can make the slowest diver.

Testing PFDs

A PFD is a Personal Flotation Device.
Test one out in a pool and see how it works!

What You'll Need
- use of a pool
- any life jackets or other PFDs in your household

Caution: This project requires adult supervision.

Life jackets and other personal flotation devices (PFDs) are meant to keep you afloat if you accidentally fall into the water. However, they only work if you actually wear them properly. Don't think you can grab one quickly and put it on if your boat capsizes. You never know what will happen in an accident! If you've never tried out a PFD before, do so before you go boating. Get permission to try a life vest in a swimming pool. First, put the life vest on over a swim suit. Have an adult help you adjust the straps so it fits snugly. Then, with an adult in the pool to help you in case something goes wrong, jump in the pool and see what happens!

If the vest feels uncomfortable, or if it makes you float awkwardly, adjust the straps or try a different size or style. Once you find a vest that fits, test it out. Then put on clothes you would wear if you were boating or playing or fishing near open water. Put the life vest on over your clothes, adjust the straps, and jump in the pool. How does it feel? Will the vest keep you afloat with your clothes on? Knowing what it's like to float in a life vest will make things easier in an emergency.

A Floating Rock

Most rocks sink in water, but do you know which rock can actually float on water? The answer is pumice, a stone that was once volcanic lava. Pumice has lots of little holes in it that were formed by bubbles in the lava. The holes contain air, which keeps the rock afloat!

Gutter Gators

◆◆◆◆◆◆

Float these paper gators downstream.

The next time it looks like rain, block off a 15- to 20-foot section of your neighborhood gutter with plastic grocery bags filled with sand, dirt, or gravel. All you need is a shallow reservoir of water to give this gator race teeth.

As you wait for the storm to end (and your temporary dam to work), make five to ten 3-inch-long paper alligators out of bright green, thick biodegradable paper. Decorate them however you like—use your imagination. Make each one easy to tell from the next. Numbers (in waterproof marker) might be a good idea if your imagination runs a little dry.

Once the rain stops, stand on the sidewalk side of the uphill end of your temporary gutter-lake. STAY OUT OF THE STREET. Have a friend stand on the sidewalk side of the other end. Drop your paper gators in the water, then signal your friend to pull away the dirt-filled bags. Race alongside your waterlogged friends until the stream of water is completely gone. Which gator won the race? Were any held up along the way? Did any mysteriously vanish? You never know where those gutter gators will wind up. But it's always fun to find out.

Float or Sink

◆◆◆◆◆◆

Why do some objects float in water while others sink?

Fill a bathtub with water. Gather various objects from around the house to test, such as a paper clip, a lemon, a small sheet of aluminum foil, a plastic fork, a key, a wooden block, a cork, a strip of cloth, and a pencil. Make a list of all the objects on a piece of paper. Next to the name of each object, write "FLOAT" or "SINK" depending on what you think it will do. One by one, put the objects in the tub of water. Does the object float or sink? Were any of your predictions wrong? Did some objects, like the piece of foil, float or sink depending on how they were shaped?

Foiled Boats

◆━━◆━◆━◆━◆━━◆

Ahoy mate! Who can create a boat that holds the most stuff?

What You'll Need
- aluminum foil
- ruler
- pencil
- scissors
- large basin
- water
- paper clips

Cut out foil squares that are 2 inches wide and 2 inches long. Give one square to each person who will compete in the boat competition. Each person should manipulate their foil to create a shape that they think will float and hold the most weight. Allow 5 minutes to build the boats. As people build their boats, fill the basin with water.

After 5 minutes, ask everyone to gather around the basin and put their boat into the water. Give each person a handful of paper clips, and designate someone to act as judge. When the judge says 1, everybody puts 1 paper clip into their boats. When the judge says 2, everyone adds another paper clip. Keep adding paper clips as the judge counts. Eventually some boats will sink—foiled again! The boat that holds the most paper clips is the winner!

Examine the best boats. Is there something about their design that makes them hold more paper clips?

LIGHT AND SOUND SHOW

◆-◆-◆-◆-◆-◆-◆

Light and sound travel in waves. Light is a wave of energy; different colors of light have different levels of energy. Sound waves travel as vibrations through the air; different levels of vibration produce different sounds. Light waves travel in a straight line, but sound waves spread out in all directions. Both light and sound can be either reflected or absorbed by materials they run into. Light waves can also be *refracted,* or bent, when they run into certain substances.

Spectrum of Colors

◆-◆-◆-◆-◆-◆-◆

Sunlight contains all the colors of the rainbow blended together to make white light. These colors are red, orange, yellow, green, blue, indigo, and violet. But when sunlight shines on different things, not all colors are reflected equally. Some things, like grass, appear green to us because only the green light is reflected to our eyes; the rest of the colors are absorbed by the grass. Colors are only visible when light shines on objects.

Blue Skies

◇◆◇◆◇◆◇

How waves of light color your world.

Why is the sky blue? When the white light of the sun filters through our atmosphere, it scatters into every color of the rainbow and every possible wavelength. Our atmosphere makes it blue. This simple experiment will give you an idea of how that scattering works and why weather patterns can cause such a colorful shift.

Turn a flashlight on outside at night. Set the flashlight on a table so its beam shines in midair in front of you. Now sprinkle flour in front of the beam. You should see dozens of white flashes as each piece of flour or dust reflects light waves and sends the color signal straight to your eyes. That's how our atmosphere sends flashes of color to your eyes to make the sky seem so blue.

Changing Colors

◇◆◇◆◇◆◇

Experiment with color filters—you'll find that they let through light the same color as themselves.

Take 5 pieces of 9×12-inch cardboard, and cut out the centers, leaving a frame that is 1½ inches wide all around. Using tape, securely fasten a sheet of colored cellophane to each cardboard frame. These frames now hold 5 color filters.

Look through one of the filters. What does it do to the colors of objects in the room? Try another. Look through 2 filters at a time. What do you see? Draw simple pictures or shapes on several pieces of white paper, using only one color of marker for each

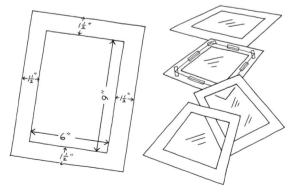

piece of paper. View each picture through a filter that is the same color as the picture. What do you see? Look at the pictures through filters of different colors. Continue to experiment with your filters.

Make Your Own Rainbow

Light may look white, but it is actually made up of a rainbow of colors.

What You'll Need
- shallow pan
- water
- mirror
- white paper

With a little patience, you will be able to make your own rainbow. Fill a shallow pan with water, and place it on a table right in front of a sunny window. Now put a small mirror in the water at the end of the pan. Slant the mirror so that it is facing the window.

Next, hold a sheet of white paper between the window and the pan of water. Slowly tilt the mirror back and forth to catch the light at different angles as it passes through the water and hits the mirror. The light will reflect from the mirror and pass through the water. As it passes through the water, it will bend. If you angle the mirror in just the right way, the light will bend enough to make a rainbow that will show up on the paper. Be patient and keep trying; sometimes it can take a while.

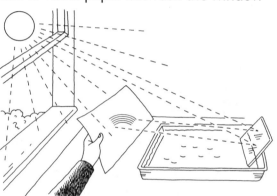

Rainbows Everywhere

Water drops can bend white light and break it into different colors.

Be on the watch for rainbows. The fine spray made by lawn sprinklers, mist from waterfalls, and the sun shining on a layer of rain can all cause rainbows. How many colors can you see in a rainbow? If you are lucky enough to see the sun reflect on 2 layers of rain, you may see a double rainbow!

Prisms

◆◆◆◆◆◆

Here's another way to sneak a peek at the rainbow that lives in light.

What You'll Need
- cardboard
- scissors
- prism
- white paper

Cut a slit in a large piece of cardboard. Place the cardboard in a sunny window so that a shaft of sunlight shines through the slit. In one hand, hold a prism in front of the cardboard so that the sunlight passes through it. With your other hand, hold a sheet of white paper so that the light passing through the prism shines on it. You will see a rainbow of colors on the paper.

Mixing Lights

◆◆◆◆◆◆

You can mix colored light to produce new colors.

Cut a few holes in the top of a 12-inch square box to let out heat. Cut a square 5 inches wide and 3 inches high in one side of the box; the bottom of the square should be an inch above the bottom of the box. Cut a hole in the other end of the box big enough for a lightbulb to fit through. Put the socket through the hole and into the box, and screw the lightbulb into the socket.

Cut out a 4×6-inch piece of black paper; then cut 3 vertical rectangles that are each 2 inches tall and ¾ of an inch wide in the black paper. Tape a strip of red cellophane over the leftmost hole, tape a strip of blue cellophane over the center hole, and tape a strip of green cellophane over the rightmost hole. Tape the black paper with the color filters over the square you cut in the side of the box. Lay a sheet of white paper in front of the filters.

What You'll Need
- 12-inch square box
- scissors
- ruler
- lightbulb
- a cord with a plug at one end and a socket at the other
- black paper
- red, blue, and green cellophane
- tape
- white paper
- mirror

Plug in the light cord, and then turn out the lights in the room. The light from your box will shine through the filters onto the white paper, showing red, blue, and green light. Use a mirror to reflect the red light onto the green light. What color do you create? What other colors can you create?

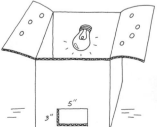

Color Mix-Up

◆◆◆◆◆◆

Instead of separating colors from white light, this activity combines colors to make white. It's like a reverse rainbow!

Cover the lens of a flashlight with red cellophane, and hold the cellophane in place with a rubber band. Cover the lens of a second flashlight with blue cellophane, and hold it in place with a rubber band. Cover the lens of a third flashlight with yellow cellophane, and secure it with a rubber band.

Set a sheet of white paper on the floor. Darken the room. Shine the red flashlight on the paper, and you will see a red spot. Shine the blue flashlight on the paper, and you'll see a blue spot. The yellow flashlight will produce a yellow spot.

Now overlap the spots of light from the yellow and blue flashlights; you will see a green spot. Ask a friend to shine the red light on your green spot, and the light will be almost white.

What You'll Need
- 3 flashlights
- cellophane in red, blue, and yellow
- rubber bands
- white paper

A Colorful Spinner

◆◆◆◆◆◆

Spin a color wheel to see how primary colors mix to form other colors.

What You'll Need
- cardboard
- ruler
- scissors
- pencil
- markers
- string

Cut a 4-inch circle from a piece of cardboard. Mark the middle with a pencil, and then divide the circle into 3 equal sections. Color the first section red, the second blue, and the third yellow. Using the pencil, poke a hole on either side of the center point ½ inch from the center. One hole should be in the red section; the other should be in the blue section.

Thread a 3-foot piece of string through one hole and back through the other. Tie the 2 ends of the string together. Slip 2 fingers of each hand through the loops in the ends of the string. Twirl the spinner around about a dozen times until the string is twisted.

Pull your hands apart firmly, and the string will start to unwind, making the spinner twist rapidly. When your hands are apart and the string is unwound, the momentum will cause the string to twist the other way. Move your hands toward each other to let the string twist. Repeat these motions over and over. If you time them right, you can get the spinner moving quickly. Look at the colored side of the spinner. What color do you see? The primary colors mix to form other colors.

Not Just Black and White

◆▶◆▶◆▶◆▶

Different colors will be seen when you view spinning black-and-white circles.

Draw and cut out 3 circles of white paper that are each 5½ inches in diameter. Put a small hole in the center of each circle. Draw and cut out a circle of black paper that is 5½ inches in diameter. Cut the black circle in half. Cut one of the halves in half.

Use these materials to make several different disks. Glue a black half-circle onto a white circle so that the disk is half black and half white. Glue a black ¼-circle onto a white circle so that the disk is ¼ black and ¾ white. Using a black marker, divide one white disk into 8 pie-wedge shapes. Color some of the pie wedges black, leaving others white.

Wrap some tape around the middle of a knitting needle. Put the knitting needle through the middle of a 6-inch paper plate, and push the plate down to rest on the tape. Spin the plate. Be sure it spins smoothly and doesn't wobble. Use this as your spinner. Poke the knitting needle through the hole in the center of one disk, and let the disk rest on the paper plate. Spin the plate, and look at the disk as it spins. What colors do you see? Do you see different colors when the disk is spinning quickly or slowly? Spin the other disks to see what colors they produce.

What You'll Need
- white paper
- pencil
- ruler
- scissors
- black paper
- glue
- black marker
- tape
- knitting needle
- paper plate

Mixing Pigments

◆▶◆▶◆▶◆▶

By mixing primary colors, you can produce new colors.

What You'll Need
- watercolors
- paintbrush
- jar of water
- white saucer
- paper

Dip a paintbrush into a jar of water and then into blue watercolor paint. Drop some of this blue paint onto a white saucer. Rinse your brush in the water. Pick up some yellow watercolor paint on the brush, and drop some of this onto the blue paint on your saucer. Use your brush to mix these 2 colors. You will have a shade of green. Rinse the paintbrush. In the same way, combine red and yellow to make orange on another spot on the saucer. Rinse the paintbrush again, and combine red and blue to create violet. Now, use your primary colors and the new colors you created to paint a picture.

Black to Colors

Black isn't just black but a whole bunch of colors rolled into one!

What You'll Need
- paper towels
- ruler
- scissors
- pencil
- tape
- glass
- black felt-tip marker
- rubbing alcohol

Take a white paper towel, and cut a strip 2 inches wide. Tape the strip to a pencil, and lay the pencil across the rim of a glass so the paper towel hangs into the glass. Cut the paper towel so that the bottom of it just touches the bottom of the glass as it hangs from the pencil. Draw a ¼-inch stripe on the paper towel about 1½ inches from the loose end with a black marker.

Pour 1 inch of rubbing alcohol into the glass. Set the pencil on top of the glass so that the towel is in the rubbing alcohol and the black marker line is above the alcohol. Let the materials sit for an hour; check on them now and then. Has the black stripe on the paper towel changed?

The color in the marker's ink was created by combining several other colors. As the alcohol was absorbed by the paper towel and traveled upward, it took some of the ink with it. It carried the different colors different distances, so they appeared in layers on the paper towel above the black line.

Colors at a Distance

Lighting and distance make certain colors easier to see than others.

What You'll Need
- hanger
- strips of cloth
- paper and pen

Ask a friend to tie narrow strips of different-color cloth to the bottom of a coat hanger so that the strips hang down neatly. Have your friend hang the coat hanger on a tree limb some distance from you.

Divide a sheet of paper into 2 columns. Write your name at the top of one column and your friend's name at the top of the other column. Down the left side, list the colors of your strips of cloth: yellow, orange, red, green, blue, black, and so on. Carry the sheet of paper and your pen, and walk toward the strips of cloth. As soon as you can see a color, write the number "1" on the paper under your name and next to the color you see to indicate that you saw that color first. Continue numbering all the colors as you see them. Now let your friend have a turn. Do you both agree on which color you were able to see first?

Plant Dyes

◆◆◆◆◆◆

You can makes dyes of primary and secondary colors from plants.

What You'll Need

- cloth
- laundry-marking pen
- pen and paper
- knife
- beet
- cutting board
- saucepan
- water
- stove
- strainer
- container
- tongs
- hanger
- clothespins
- carrot
- onion skins
- tea
- coffee
- blueberries

Caution: This project requires adult supervision. These dyes can stain your clothes or other materials.

Number several squares of cloth with a laundry-marking pen. Write the numbers in a column on a sheet of paper. Carefully chop a beet into tiny pieces. Put a small amount of water in a saucepan, and drop the chopped beets into the water. Boil for an hour, adding a little water to replace any that boils away. Strain the liquid into a container. Pour the strained liquid back into the saucepan, and drop the cloth labeled "1" into it. Boil for 15 minutes. Carefully remove the cloth with tongs. Hang it with a clothespin on a coat hanger outdoors to dry. Write "BEETS" next to the "1" on your paper. Repeat this process with a carrot, onion skins, tea, coffee, and blueberries. When you're finished, compare the colors of the cloth pieces.

Light and Heat

◆◆◆◆◆◆

Light is a form of energy. Heat is also a form of energy. Sometimes an energy source will produce light and heat at the same time. Sometimes the energy in light can be used to produce heat.

Burning Sun

◆◆◆◆◆◆◆

By focusing the sun's light, you can create a spot of great heat.

Caution: This project requires adult supervision.

On a clear, sunny day, place a sheet of white paper on a concrete or asphalt surface. Hold a magnifying glass a few inches above the paper, and you will see a spot of light on the paper.

Move the magnifying glass around to get the smallest spot of light possible on the paper. Hold it in this position, and watch the paper. In a short time, the focused light will burn a hole in the paper. When you're done, pour some water on the paper to make sure it's no longer burning. Be careful! Don't focus light on your skin or clothing or anything else that might burn.

Bulb in a Box

◆◆◆◆◆◆◆

A lighted bulb gives off heat.

Cut a hole in the end of a shoe box, and put the lightbulb socket into the box through the hole. Screw a 60-watt lightbulb into the socket, but don't turn it on yet. Place a thermometer inside the shoe box, and put the lid on the box. After 15 minutes,

read the temperature inside the shoe box, and write it down.

Put the thermometer back in the box. Turn on the lightbulb. Be sure that the bulb is lit and is not touching the thermometer. Put the lid on the box. After 15 minutes, turn off the lightbulb. Being careful not to touch the hot lightbulb, read the temperature inside the box, and write it down. Compare the 2 temperatures.

The lightbulb generates both light and heat. The heat from the bulb raised the temperature of the air in the shoe box, so the thermometer had a higher reading the second time.

Sun-Dried Fruit

◆◆◆◆◆◆◆

Use the power of the sun to make tasty fruit snacks.

What You'll Need
- fruit (apples, plums, peaches, apricots, pears)
- dull knife
- 1-inch-deep baking dishes
- cheesecloth
- tape
- peeler (optional)
- lemon juice (optional)

Watch the weather reports and make sure that sun is predicted for several days, because it may take that long to dry your fruit. Wash the fruit and peel it if you like. Remove seeds or cores and slice the fruit ¼ of an inch thick. If you want, dip the fruit in lemon juice to keep it from turning quite so brown. Spread the fruit slices in baking dishes. Cover the dishes with a layer of cheesecloth to keep the insects off. Tape the edges of the cheesecloth into place. Check the fruit each night.

Measuring Heat from Sunlight

◆◆◆◆◆◆◆

An object exposed to sunlight will become hotter than a similar object in the shade.

Put cardboard in front of a window to block the light from part of the windowsill. Set 2 thermometers that are indicating the same temperature on the windowsill. Be sure that one thermometer is in direct sunlight and the other is in the shade you created by putting cardboard in the window.

What You'll Need
- cardboard
- 2 thermometers
- clock

Wait 15 minutes, and then check the thermometers. Did both temperatures stay the same? Why not?

Some of the energy in the sunlight was converted to heat when it struck the thermometer. That heat raised the temperature reading on the thermometer. The other thermometer registered a lower temperature because it was not exposed to sunlight.

Brew Some Sun Tea

Use solar energy to make easy and delicious iced tea.

What You'll Need
- one-quart glass jar with lid
- 3 teabags
- measuring cup
- water
- ice cubes
- glass
- sugar and lemon (optional)

On a hot, sunny day, wash a jar in soapy water and rinse it clean. Drop in 3 bags of your favorite tea. (Citrus-flavored herb teas are particularly good for this.) Pour in 3 cups of cold water. Seal the jar and put it outside for 2 or 3 hours, keeping it in the hot sun.

Bring the jar indoors and remove the teabags. Put a few ice cubes in a glass and pour in the tea. Add sugar and lemon, if desired, and enjoy your tea! Leftover tea should be stored in the refrigerator. Try this with different teas. Which kind do you like best?

Opaque, Transparent, Translucent

We can say that an object is opaque, transparent, or translucent. If it is opaque, it will not let any light pass through. Transparent objects transmit light; we can see through them. Translucent objects pass light, but they diffuse it so that objects cannot be clearly distinguished.

Shadow Clock

◆◆◆◆◆◆

Explore the case of the moving shadow.

What You'll Need
- chalk
- watch or clock

On a sunny morning, draw an arrow with chalk on your patio or driveway. Ask a friend to stand facing in the direction of the arrow with one foot on either side of the arrow. Now trace around your friend's shadow with chalk. Is it a long or short shadow? Is it

in front of your friend or behind your friend? Inside the shadow, write down the time.

Every 2 hours, ask your friend to come back and stand in the same spot. Each time, trace around your friend's shadow, and write the time inside this shadow.

At the end of the day, look at the shadow tracings. Why are some shadows in front of where your friend stood and some behind? Why are some shadows small and some long?

Projecting Images

◆◆◆◆◆◆

Let the light in to see a projected image more clearly.

What You'll Need
- 5-gallon aquarium
- water
- stiff white paper
- tape measure
- slide and slide projector
- milk
- measuring cup
- eyedropper
- large spoon

Fill a 5-gallon aquarium ⅔ of the way with water. Prop up a sheet of stiff white paper about 65 inches behind the aquarium. Put a slide in a slide projector, set the projector on the table in front of the aquarium, and project the slide through the water and onto the sheet of white paper. You will need to focus the projector, and you may need to move the sheet of paper to get a good, sharp image.

Measure out 1 cup of milk. Using an eyedropper, put three drops of milk into the aquarium, and stir. Now look at the image on the paper. It will be blurred because the milk and water mixture doesn't permit as much light to pass through. Now mix in the remainder of the milk. Does any light pass through?

See-Through Shirt

◆◆◆◆◆◆◆

Learn the difference between opaque and translucent with this activity.

What You'll Need
● T-shirt

If you hold a T-shirt out at arm's length in front of you and try to look through the T-shirt to see a wall behind it, you will be unable to see the wall. The T-shirt blocks the light, so it appears to be opaque.

Now pull the T-shirt down over your head, and try to look through it. You will be able to see the wall. When your eyes are close enough to the T-shirt, the shirt is translucent. Although the view is less clear, you can still see through the shirt. Try this with other materials, such as a towel, a handkerchief, a scarf, a tablecloth, or a sweater.

Shadow Puppets

◆◆◆◆◆◆◆

When rays of light are blocked by an object, a shadow is formed. The nearer the object is to the light, the bigger the shadow is.

With a couple of friends, plan a shadow puppet show to share with family or other friends. Cut puppet shapes out of construction paper. For Halloween, for example, you might cut out the shape of a witch, a cat, a ghost, and so on. To do a woodland story, you might cut out simple shapes of a deer, rabbit, bird, and squirrel. Tape each of your puppet shapes

What You'll Need
● construction paper
● scissors
● pencil
● wooden sticks
● tape
● cassette and cassette recorder
● sheet
● 2 flashlights

onto a thin stick of wood so that they will be easy to hold.

Plan the story you are going to tell, and record it into a tape recorder. You can include background music if you want. Drape a sheet over a doorway. When it is show time, the audience will sit on one side of the door while the puppeteers sit on the other side. Turn on the tape. While 2 friends shine flashlights at the sheet, operate the stick puppets in front of the flashlights. The audience will see the shadows of the puppets on the sheet in the doorway.

Through the Drinking Glass

◆◆◆◆◆◆◆

Water can be changed from transparent to translucent to opaque.

Cut a small, interesting picture from a page of a magazine. Fill a clear glass halfway with water. Place the glass on top of the picture that you have cut from the magazine. Look down into the glass through the water. You will be able to see the picture clearly because the water is transparent. In a bowl, mix a little cornstarch with water. Put a little of the cornstarch mixture into the glass of water above the picture. The water is no longer clear and transparent. This solution is translucent; you will still be able to see the magazine picture, but the picture will be partially obscured. Add the rest of the cornstarch mixture. The water in the glass will become opaque; you will no longer be able to see the picture through the water.

What You'll Need
- old magazine
- scissors
- glass
- water
- bowl
- cornstarch
- spoon

No Oil Shortage

◆◆◆◆◆◆◆

Do you know which of your favorite foods contains the most oil? Test their translucency to find out!

What You'll Need
- brown paper shopping bag
- scissors
- oil
- eyedropper
- rolling pin
- assorted foods

Cut up a paper shopping bag so that you end up with several squares of brown paper. Using an eyedropper, place a few drops of oil on a square of paper. You'll see that the paper becomes translucent, or almost see-through, where you applied the oil. Now, use a rolling pin to crush walnuts or french fries on a square of brown paper. Does the paper turn translucent? If so, oil is present. The larger the translucent spot, the more oil the food contains.

Use this as a fat test on other foods around your kitchen, such as butter, cereal, bread, and potato chips. Put each food item on a clean square of brown paper and crush with a rolling pin. Which food contains the most oil?

Oil and fat are very similar. They both contain lots of calories. Oil is a liquid at room temperature; fat is a solid at room temperature.

Reflection and Refraction

Most objects are visible because they reflect light, or cause light to bounce off of them. Reflections can fool you; if you look in a mirror and wink your left eye, it appears that the right eye of the image in the mirror is winking. Light can also be refracted. This means that its path bends as it passes through a substance because the substance makes it travel at a different speed.

Arctic Light

Watch how the reflective properties of ice cause this arctic light to give off a warm, welcoming glow on a winter night.

What You'll Need
- water
- large metal mixing bowl
- plastic yogurt container
- small stones or coins
- votive candle
- large tray with sides
- matches

Caution: This project requires adult supervision.

Pour a few inches of water into the mixing bowl. Fill the yogurt container with stones or coins, then center it in the bowl. Slowly pour more water into the bowl so that it nearly reaches the rim of the yogurt container. Place the bowl in the freezer until the water is frozen.

When frozen, remove the ice from the mold. If the ice doesn't come out easily, run warm water on the outside of the bowl and the ice should slip out. Then dump out the stones or coins from the yogurt container, and pour in warm water to loosen it. Remove the container, and place the ice candle-holder on the tray.

Now it's time for sparkling fun. Place a votive candle in the opening, and have an adult light it. If you're fascinated by the way the light looks through the ice, go to your local library for some further study on light.

Hot, Hotter, Hottest

❖❖❖❖❖❖❖

Some colors and materials are better at reflecting the heat of the sun than others.

Fill 4 resealable plastic storage bags with water, and seal them tightly. Place the bags outside in a sunny spot on the sidewalk, driveway, or patio where they will not be disturbed. Wrap one bag in a sheet of white construction paper, one in a sheet of orange construction paper, one in a sheet of black construction paper, and one in a sheet of aluminum foil. Predict what effect the different wrappings will have on how the sun's energy heats the water in each bag. Which will be the warmest? Which will be the coolest? Using a thermometer, measure the temperature of the water in each bag after an hour. Were your predictions correct?

What You'll Need
- 4 resealable plastic storage bags
- water
- white, orange, and black construction paper
- tape
- aluminum foil
- thermometer
- pen and paper

A Kaleidoscope

❖❖❖❖❖❖❖

Everything looks topsy-turvy in this test of reflection.

What You'll Need
- 3 small mirrors of the same size
- tape
- waxed paper
- pencil
- scissors
- construction paper

To make a kaleidoscope, tape 3 small mirrors together, with the reflective sides facing in, to create a triangle. Stand the mirrors up on a piece of waxed paper, and trace around the bottom of the mirrors. Cut out this triangle shape, and then tape the piece of waxed paper in place at the bottom of the 3 mirrors. Cut out many small pieces and shapes from colored sheets of construction paper, and drop them inside the mirrors. Give your kaleidoscope a shake, then look inside. You will see some interesting patterns. The mirrors will reflect interesting shapes and colors.

Split Personality

◆◆◆◆◆◆

A mirror reverses images from left to right.

Cut a picture of a person's face from a magazine. Cut the picture in half vertically, and glue the right half of the face onto a sheet of white paper. Now place the paper flat on a table. Hold a mirror in the middle of the paper so that the mirror touches the line where you cut the picture in half. Look at the picture and the image in the mirror. You will see what appears to be a complete face again.

Pinhole Camera

◆◆◆◆◆◆

The image in a pinhole camera is upside down.

Cut a 1-inch square in the bottom of an empty oatmeal box. Tape a piece of aluminum foil over the 1-inch square. Prick a hole in the middle of the aluminum foil using a fine needle. Tape a piece of tissue paper over the open end of the oatmeal box. On a bright, sunny day, point the box at a house or tree across the street. Look through your pinhole camera. You will be able to see an image of the house or tree on the piece of tissue paper, but the image will be upside down.

On and On and On

◆◆◆◆◆◆

Mirrors can be placed to create multiple reflections.

Stand with your back to a large wall mirror in good light. Hold a large hand mirror up in front of you, just below eye level, in front of your nose. Look at the reflection in the hand mirror. You may need to adjust the position of the hand mirror, but you will soon see a reflection in the mirror that is multiplied many times. How many reflections can you count?

Mirror Writing

◆◆◆◆◆◆◆

Use a mirror to write a backward message to a friend.

What You'll Need
- mirror
- paper and pen

Prop a mirror upright on a table, and set a piece of paper on the table so it can be clearly seen in the mirror. Try to write a short message to a friend, but don't look at the sheet of paper on the table. Instead, look at the paper's reflection in the mirror. This may take several practice tries. After you've written your message, your friend can hold it up in front of a mirror and easily read what you wrote.

Up with Periscopes

◆◆◆◆◆◆◆

How do people in submarines see the surface? With a periscope!

Tape the spout of a clean cardboard milk carton closed. Imagine the top part of the milk carton is a tent supported by a long column. Face the opening of the milk carton (and tent) toward you. The following directions are given from this perspective.

Cut a 1-inch square hole on the right side of the tent. On the bottom left of the milk-carton column cut a viewing hole that is a 1½-inch square.

What You'll Need
- quart milk carton
- tape
- scissors
- ruler
- cardboard
- aluminum foil
- glue
- soft cloth

Cut out two 1½-inch squares of cardboard and two 2-inch squares of aluminum foil. Try not to fold or crinkle the middle part of the aluminum foil. Glue the dull side of each foil square onto each of the cardboard squares. Smooth with a soft cloth to form a flat surface. Allow to dry, and you have your 2 mirrors.

Now, cut out a periscope maintenance door. The door should start 1 inch above the bottom left viewing hole and end about 2 inches from the tentlike part of the milk carton. Tape one mirror onto the inside left surface of the tent. Place the bottom mirror into the bottom of the column on the right side. Adjust the angle of the mirror until you can look through the viewing hole and see the reflection in the upper mirror. Then tape it into place. Close your periscope maintenance door with tape. You're ready to test out your periscope!

Peekaboo

◆◆◆◆◆◆◆

The path followed by light rays is reversible.

What You'll Need

- clay
- 2 small mirrors
- white paper
- pencil
- black construction paper
- ruler
- scissors
- lamp
- protractor

Using a lump of clay to help hold it in place, center a small mirror on the edge of a sheet of white paper. Draw a line on the paper to show the front edge of the mirror.

Take a sheet of 9×12-inch black paper. Mark the middle of the paper. Fold back a flap at each end that is 3×9 inches. Cut a 1/16-inch slit from the middle of the 12-inch side of the paper to within 1 inch of the top of the paper. Stand this black paper shield, using the flaps to help hold it up, on the end of the white paper opposite the mirror, a little to the right of center. Set a lamp about 3 yards behind the black shield so that the light will shine through the slit.

Turn on the lamp, and turn off the other lights in the room. The light shining through the slit in the shield will make a narrow beam on the sheet of white paper. Draw lines on the white paper that trace the path of the light beam both before and after it strikes the mirror. With a protractor, measure the angle between the mirror and the incoming beam of light, and then measure the angle between the mirror and the beam of reflected light. How do they compare?

Now set a second mirror on the white paper so it is in the path of the reflected beam of light. What does it do to the reflected light? Turn the mirror slightly from side to side to make the light reflect back along the same path it was following.

The light traveled toward the first mirror at a fixed angle, and the mirror reflected the light at exactly that same angle but in a different direction. The second mirror did the same thing. However, when you changed the position of the second mirror by moving it from side to side, you caused the light to strike it at a different angle. This changed the path of the light reflected by the second mirror.

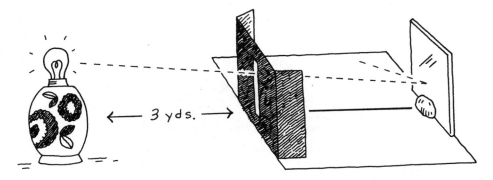

← 3 yds. →

Producing Sounds

The sounds we hear are caused by vibrations. When the vibrations reach your ear, they cause your eardrums to vibrate, and your brain perceives the vibrations as sound. Things sound different to us when they vibrate at different rates.

Frying-Pan Chimes

◄►◄►◄►◄►

Sound waves can be passed from one object to another and can even be amplified!

What You'll Need
- string
- scissors
- tape
- frying pan
- silverware

Cut 5 pieces of string, each about 15 inches long. Tie one end of a piece of string just beneath the tines of a dinner fork. Tape the other end of the string inside a frying pan, on the side directly opposite the handle. Repeat this process with other pieces of silverware. When you hold the frying pan by its handle, the silverware will dangle down on strings and bang into one another. Shake the pan, and listen to the sound it produces.

When the silverware pieces struck each other, they vibrated. The vibrations from each piece traveled up the strings at the same time and caused the pan to vibrate. The large pan amplified the combined vibrations and produced the sounds.

Sound in the Sea
Sound travels well through water. How fast it travels depends mostly on the water's temperature.

Bouncing Cereal

◆◆◆◆◆◆◆

Make objects jump at your thunderous command!

Stretch a piece of plastic wrap tightly over the top of a metal bowl. Secure it in place with a tight rubber band. Put a small handful of cereal flakes on top of the plastic wrap. Stand near the bowl, and loudly bang a cookie sheet with a spoon. Watch the cereal flakes.

What happened to the cereal? Striking the cookie sheet produced sound waves—vibrations—that traveled through the air. When the vibrations struck the plastic wrap, it vibrated, too, and that caused the cereal to move.

What You'll Need
- plastic wrap
- metal bowl
- rubber band
- cereal flakes
- cookie sheet
- spoon

Sympathetic Vibrations

◆◆◆◆◆◆◆

We can't see sound waves, but we can see their effect.

What You'll Need
- 2 identical wine glasses
- water
- pencil
- short piece of fine wire

Pour water into a wine glass until it is ⅓ full. Tap the side with a pencil. It will make a musical sound. By adding more or less water, you can change the sound. The tapping causes the side of the glass to vibrate.

Pour exactly the same amount of water into a second wine glass. When you tap both glasses with a pencil, they will give the same sound. If there is a difference in the sound, add a little water to one glass until they make the same sound. Stand the wine glasses on a table about 4 inches apart. Place a piece of fine wire across the top of the glass that is farthest from you. Strike the closest glass, and watch the wire on the other glass. It will move slightly. The wire responds to your tapping on the other glass because the glasses vibrate in sympathy. If you continue to tap, the wire on the far glass will gradually move enough to fall.

Bottle Music

Did you know you could make music with bottles filled with water?

Stand 8 empty bottles side by side on a table in front of you. Fill the bottle on the left about ¼ of the way with water. Add water to the next bottle so that the water level is a bit higher than in the first bottle. Continue adding water to the bottles so that each one has a little bit more water in it than the bottle on its left. Blow across the opening of the bottle on the left, and you'll hear a low note. Blow across the bottle on the right, and you'll hear a high note. By adjusting the amount of water in each bottle, you can produce a whole musical scale.

What You'll Need
- 8 empty glass bottles
- water

When you blow across the bottle's opening, you cause the air inside to vibrate, which produces a sound. The amount of air in the bottle affects the sound it makes. The bottles with more air produce low sounds, and the bottles with less air produce high sounds.

Rubber Bands

Make a cardboard-box guitar to see how different vibrations create different sounds.

What You'll Need
- cardboard box
- 3 long rubber bands
- ruler

Stretch 3 rubber bands around a small, sturdy cardboard box that is about 8 inches square and 2 inches deep. Space the rubber bands about 2 inches apart.

Pluck each of the rubber bands. Do they make a sound? Do they sound alike? Pull the middle rubber band tighter, and tie a knot to shorten it a little. Pull one of the other rubber bands very tight, and tie a knot to shorten it. Pluck the rubber bands again. Which one produces the highest sound? Which one produces the lowest sound?

By pulling the rubber bands tighter, you changed the rate at which they vibrate. The change in vibration rate caused a change in the sound they made.

Animal Sounds

◆►◆►◆►◆►

You can create animal sounds just by varying the vibrations on this simple instrument!

What You'll Need
- 1-quart milk carton
- scissors
- strong string
- paper towel
- water

Cut off the top of a 1-quart milk carton 4 inches from the bottom. Using scissors, punch a small hole in the center of the bottom of the carton, and thread the end of a 24-inch piece of strong string through the hole. Tie several knots to make a large knot that will not pull through the hole.

Wet a paper towel, squeezing out the excess water. Hold the milk carton in one hand, and put the wet paper towel around the string about 10 inches from the carton. Give the wet towel a quick pull while pressing it with your fingers. It will make a squawking noise that is amplified by the milk carton.

By varying how much string you leave between the wet towel and the box, you will be able to produce sounds resembling a rooster's crow and a lion's roar.

Teakettle Sounds

◆►◆►◆►◆►

Whistle while you work on this sound experiment.

What You'll Need
- teakettle
- water
- stove

Caution: This project requires adult supervision.

Bring water to a boil in a teakettle. Listen to the whistling sound the kettle makes. Whistle a note of the same pitch, imitating the sound of the kettle as closely as you can. You will hear only one sound. Now whistle a note that is higher than the sound of the teakettle. Listen closely as you whistle. Instead of hearing 2 sounds, you will hear 3!

If the kettle's note has 500 vibrations a second, and you whistle higher at a note of 600 vibrations a second, the third low note you hear is the difference between the first two, or a note that is 100 vibrations a second. The source of the extra note is the motion of the air particles in the waves of sound.

Fish Line Music

◆◆◆◆◆◆◆

The rate that something vibrates determines the sound that it makes.

What You'll Need
- smooth board
- pencil
- ruler
- hammer
- ten 1-inch nails
- scissors
- nylon fishing line

Lay a 16×6×1-inch board flat on the table in front of you so that one of the 6-inch sides is nearest you. Draw 5 straight pencil lines down the length of the board about 1 inch apart, beginning an inch down from the top and 1 inch in from the left side. Pound a nail about ½ inch deep at the top of each line.

Cut 5 pieces of nylon fishing line in the following lengths: 14, 12, 10, 8, and 6 inches. Tie a loose slipknot in both ends of each piece of fishing line. Put the slipknot of the 14-inch piece of fishing line over the top left nail on your board, and pull it tight. Put the slipknot at the other end of the fishing line over a loose nail, and stretch the line as tightly as you can toward the bottom of the leftmost

pencil line that you drew. Hammer the nail into the board about ½ inch deep. Nail the other pieces of fishing line onto the board in the same way. Work from left to right on the board, each time using the longest piece of fishing line that you have left.

You now have a musical instrument. Pluck each string with your index finger. Which string has the highest sound? Which has the lowest?

A Kazoo

◆◆◆◆◆◆◆

Vibrating air against paper will make a musical sound.

Stretch a 4-inch square of waxed paper over the end of a cardboard tube from a roll of paper towels. Put a rubber band around the tube to hold the waxed paper in place. Use a pen point to poke a hole in the tube about 1½ inches from the covered end of the tube. Now hold the open end of the tube to your mouth, and hum a tune into it. The waxed paper will vibrate and hum your tune along with you.

What You'll Need
- paper-towel tube
- waxed paper
- rubber band
- pen

Bull Roarer

◆▶◆▶◆▶◆▶

An object in motion can cause sound waves.

What You'll Need
- wooden paint stirrer
- drill
- string

Caution: This project requires adult supervision.

Ask an adult to drill a hole in a wooden paint stirrer, about ½ inch from the end of the handle. (If you do not have a paint stirrer, any thin strip of wood about a foot long will work.) Securely tie a piece of sturdy string through the hole in the stick. Find a place where you can safely twirl the stick; be sure that no people or objects are in your way. Rapidly twirl the stick around in front of you in a circle. It will make a big roar of sound. As the stick moves through the air, it begins to spin, then it catches the air and causes air molecules to vibrate. The vibrating air molecules produce the sound you hear.

Nature's Noisemaker

◆▶◆▶◆▶◆▶

It's easy to make grass whistle.
All you need is a blade of green grass, and 2 thumbs.

Put your thumbs together, and hold the blade of grass between them. Blow into the crack between your thumbs, so the air flows over the grass. You should hear a whistling sound. If you don't hear anything, move the blade of grass a little, and try again. You'll soon get the hang of it.

Sound Waves

When sound travels through the air, it causes the air molecules to vibrate back and forth at a regular rate. Sound waves can also travel through other mediums including liquids, such as water, and solids, such as metal, by making the molecules of water or metal vibrate back and forth. Sound waves travel different distances and at different speeds through different mediums. Sound waves are reflected if the vibrations bounce off of an object, and they are absorbed if the vibrations are stopped by an object.

Be a Sound Detective

Does sound travel better through some materials than others? Find out for yourself!

If you've ever watched old westerns, you may have seen a character put one ear to the ground and announce that the cavalry was coming or listen to the rail of a train track and know that a train was on its way. Does this really work? To find out, go to a playground with a partner on a warm day. Have your partner go to the other side of the playground, then run back. Raise your hand as soon as you can hear the sound of your partner's running feet. Now have your partner run across the playground again, but this time put your ear to the ground. See if you can hear your partner's feet sooner.

When it's not too hot or too cold, find a long, metal object such as a chain-link fence post (watch out for loose metal). Stand at one end and have your partner tap the post. Then put your ear to the rail and have your partner tap again. Does it sound different? Does it seem louder? Try the same experiment with the materials around you. Does sound travel better through some materials than others? Do some materials muffle sound?

Sound waves are waves of energy that move the molecules of the substance they travel through. Air molecules are much farther apart than the molecules of solid metal. Consider the density of the material (that is, how close together the molecules are) as you try to figure out why sound would move through metal better than through air.

Locating Echoes

◆▸▸▸▸▸◀◀◀◀

Can you find good echoes in your community?

Echoes are sound waves that begin in one place, bounce off an object, and can be heard in another place. How far away must you be from an object to hear an echo? What kinds of objects produce echoes? Find a large building or a huge wall near your home. (Make sure the loud noises won't disturb anyone.) Shout "Echo!" at the wall and listen for an echo. Back away from the wall a few steps at a time and see how far away you must be before you hear an echo. Try the same activity near a large tree and see what happens. Do you hear an echo, or does the shape of the tree muffle the sound? Try making echoes in different areas around your neighborhood and record the best places to hear them.

Sound Barriers

◆▸▸▸▸▸◀◀◀◀

Find out how sound can be stopped.

Go into your backyard and stand about as far from your partner as your house is wide. (That should be about 30 feet or so.) Try to talk to one another. As long as there is nothing between you and your partner, you should be able to hear one another fairly well, though you may have to raise your voice a little. Now stand on one side of a house while your partner stands on the other side. Try to shout something to your partner and see if you can be heard clearly. Have your partner shout something at you. What happened? You may have heard something, but perhaps you could not make out what your partner was saying. Was the sound weak and distorted? Try the same experiment with a wall between you and your partner. Try it with a fence, a window, a blanket, and other types of barriers. Does the thickness of the barrier matter?

Sound Wave Model

◆◆◆◆◆◆◆

Use this model to find out how sounds move through the air.

Cut 6 pieces of thread, each 10 inches long, and attach one end of each thread to a glass marble using tape. Now tie the other end of each thread to the horizontal piece of a coat hanger, leaving about 1 inch between each thread that you tie.

What You'll Need
- thread
- scissors
- 6 glass marbles
- tape
- coat hanger

Hang the hook of the coat hanger from a shower-curtain rod. Pull back one of the end marbles. Let the marble go so that it strikes the next marble. Watch what happens. It hits the second marble, which swings to the side and hits the third marble, and so on.

Sound travels through the air in the same way. A vibration causes one molecule of air to move from side to side and bump into another molecule, which then moves from side to side at the same rate and bumps into a third molecule.

Tick Tick Tick

◆◆◆◆◆◆◆

A balloon containing carbon dioxide will amplify sound waves.

What You'll Need
- baking soda
- measuring spoon
- narrow-necked bottle
- vinegar
- balloon
- ticking clock

Put 2 tablespoons baking soda into a narrow-necked bottle. Add 3 tablespoons vinegar. Pull the opening of a balloon down over the neck of the bottle so that it fits tightly. The balloon will become filled with carbon dioxide gas produced by the baking soda and vinegar.

Hold up a ticking clock about a foot from your ear. You will be able to hear the ticking sound. Now, hold the inflated balloon up to your ear with one hand while you hold the ticking clock on the other side of the balloon about a foot away. The ticking of the clock will be much more distinct. The balloon filled with carbon dioxide acts as a kind of lens that focuses the sound wave.

Solids and Sound

◆▸◆▸◆▸◆▸◆

Solid objects can carry sound vibrations and make them louder.

Fill a metal bowl with water. Take a pair of scissors, and cut the air. Listen to the sound. Now submerge the scissors in the bowl of water, and open and close the scissors while you hold your ear to the metal bowl. Does it sound different?

Hit the tines of a fork against the edge of a table, and listen to the sound. Then hit the tines of a fork against the edge of a table, and quickly touch the end of the fork handle to the table. Is the sound louder?

Do sound waves sound the same to you when they travel through the air as they do when they travel through other mediums?

What You'll Need
- metal bowl
- water
- scissors
- fork
- table

Reflecting Sound

◆▸◆▸◆▸◆▸◆

You can use umbrellas to help sound travel long distances.

What You'll Need
- 2 umbrellas
- yardstick
- 2 pieces of sturdy, bendable wire
- a watch that ticks loudly
- tape

Lay 2 open umbrellas on the ground so that the handles face each other about 2 yards apart. Twist the middle of a piece of sturdy bendable wire around the handle of one umbrella. Push both ends of the wire into the ground to support the umbrella so that it is horizontal with the ground. Repeat with the other umbrella.

Move a ticking watch along the handle of one umbrella to find the spot where the ticking sounds loudest. Tape the watch in place at that spot. Now move to the other umbrella, and hold your ear to the corresponding spot on the umbrella handle. You should be able to hear the watch.

The sound of the watch strikes the inside of the umbrella it's attached to and bounces off of it. The sound waves then strike the inside of the other umbrella and bounce off at the same angle. The shape of the umbrella focuses the sound waves at a single point along the handle.

Sound Path

◆◆◆◆◆◆◆

Sound waves can travel through a piece of thread.

What You'll Need
- thread
- 2 forks
- 3 spoons

Tie a fork to the middle of a 30-inch piece of thread. Hold the free ends of the thread to your ears. Lean forward from the waist so that the fork hangs freely and does not touch you or your clothing. Have a friend hold a fork and a spoon and strike them together while you listen. You will hear a soft sound. Now ask your friend

to strike the fork hanging from your neck with a spoon. The noise will travel along the thread, and you will hear it quite loudly. Now tie a spoon to the thread on either side of the fork. Again hold the free ends of the thread to your ears. Ask a friend to strike the spoons and the fork with another spoon. You will hear a series of bell-like tones.

A Simple Telephone

◆◆◆◆◆◆◆

Sound travels through string better than it travels through the air.

Use a pen to punch a small hole in the middle of the bottom of each of 2 plastic containers, such as cottage cheese containers. Thread one end of a 12-foot piece of string through the hole in each container so that the end is inside the container. Tie knots in each end so that the string will not pull out through the hole.

What You'll Need
- pen, nail, or other pointed object
- 2 plastic containers
- 12 feet string

Hold one container, and give the other to a friend. Walk far enough apart so that the string between the containers is pulled tight. The string should

not be touching anything in the middle. Ask your friend to hold the container up over one ear while you whisper into the other container. Your voice will make the string vibrate. The vibration will travel along the string to the other container, and your friend will clearly hear what you whispered. Now listen while your friend whispers. Build other phones that use different lengths of string and different kinds of containers, and compare how well they work.

May the Force Be with You

✦✦✦✦✦✦

Any kind of push or pull on an object is a force. We see examples of this every day in moving cars, falling leaves, spinning tops, and in other familiar sights. The same forces that cause the movements we see every day also govern how planets move and how galaxies form. They play a big part in everything that happens everywhere in the universe, from a pin dropping to a star exploding. When we study force, we look at where different forces come from, how they are applied, and how they affect the movement of objects.

Gravity

✦✦✦✦✦✦

Gravity is the attraction between physical objects. You see gravity at work any time you see an object fall to the ground. All objects exert gravity; the sun, the earth, you, and a single strand of your hair all draw other objects toward them to some degree. However, gravity is only noticeable when it's very strong.

Tides Come and Go

❖❖❖❖❖❖❖

The moon's gravity causes a regular movement of the oceans.

Caution: This project requires adult supervision.

If you've ever spent the day at the ocean, you may have noticed that the water level at the shore changed throughout the day. The water creeped up the beach steadily and then gradually slipped out again. This rise and fall of ocean waters is called the *tide*. The moon causes the tide by the gravitational pull it exerts as it travels around the earth every day.

    If you ever spend the day by the ocean, pay attention to the changes in the tide as they occur. Or check weather reports in a local newspaper or other source to see what that day's tides were like. Check for several days in a row, or check one day each week for several weeks. Track the tides over time to see how they change.

Journey to the Center of Gravity

❖❖❖❖❖❖❖

Get centered to get a grip on reality.

What You'll Need
- paper clip
- notebook paper
- pencil
- tape

Bend a paper clip open to make an L-shape. Put the tip of the short side of the paper clip on the tip of your index finger, and try to balance it. The paper clip will fall off. Take a half sheet of notebook paper, and roll it into a small tube around a pencil. Use tape at both ends of the paper to keep the tube from unrolling. Remove the pencil. Tape the end of the long side of the paper clip to the end of the tube of paper. Now try to balance the paper clip on your index finger.

    What caused the change here? By adding more weight to the bottom of the paper clip, you changed the paper clip's center of gravity—the point where the force of gravity is equal on either side. That allowed you to balance the clip on your finger.

Lift an Adult

◆◆◆◆◆◆◆

You'll feel strong when you lift an adult, but it's really gravity at work!

The earth's gravity exerts a force on you that keeps you planted on the ground. An adult may be able to overcome that force by exerting an upward force to lift you in the air. But chances are very good that you cannot exert enough upward force to lift your mother or father off the ground—unless you use a lever.

Take a plank about 6 feet long, 1 inch or more thick, and 6 to 12 inches wide. Put a block of wood about 1 foot tall and at least as wide as the plank under the plank about 1 foot from the end. Lift up the long end of the plank until the shorter end touches the

floor. Ask your mother or father to stand on the short end. When you step on the long end of the lever, your body weight will exert a downward force on one end of the plank, which will exert enough upward force on the other end to overcome gravity and lift your parent off the ground. If it doesn't work at first, move the block closer to the end of the plank where your parent is standing.

Gravity on Pins

◆◆◆◆◆◆◆

Can you rest a water balloon on pins without popping it? Find out!

Cut a 4×4-inch square from a polystyrene plate. Put 3 straight pins through the square. Now go outside to a place that is okay to get wet. Stand the square on the ground so that the points of the pins are in the air. Place a water balloon on the pins. The balloon will burst. Add 3 more pins and try again. The balloon will probably burst this time, too. Add 3 more pins and try again. Eventually, you will add enough pins to support the weight of the balloon so that it doesn't burst.

The force of gravity acts downward. This causes the balloon to have weight. When it acts on one pin the weight causes the balloon to be punctured. However, when the weight is spread out over enough pins, the pins can support the balloon without puncturing through the rubber.

Dilute Gravity

◆◆◆◆◆◆◆

Studying gravity is easier when we slow it down.

Galileo wanted to experiment with gravity and acceleration by timing how long it took for objects to fall. Unfortunately, when he was alive, the clocks were rather primitive, and they could not accurately measure the time for a falling object. Galileo decided he would slow down gravity through the use of inclined planes so he could better time their fall.

You can also study the effects of gravity through the use of an inclined plane. Use a wooden board as your plane. Put one end on a couple of books so it slopes downward. Put a toy car on the plane and make sure it rolls down. If it doesn't, add more books. For this activity, the slower the car rolls, the better.

Draw a starting line on the board. Place the front of the car on this line; release the car, and start the stopwatch. When 1 second is up, yell "one," and have your partner mark where the car is on the board. You might have to practice this a few times to get it right. Then, go back to the start. Release your car and start the watch. After 2 seconds, yell "two." Have your partner mark where the car is after 2 seconds. Continue in this way until the car has no more room. Then measure the distances between the starting line and the first mark, and then the next mark, and the next. These distances equal how far the car went in a single second.

You will notice that the distance traveled each second is greater and greater. That is because the car is accelerating due to gravity. Each second it goes faster, and each second it goes a greater distance.

Laws of Gravity

Gravity may be a very powerful force, but it does have to obey some rules. For instance, the more mass an object has (the heavier it is), the greater that object's gravitational pull. Gravitational pull is also affected by distance; as 2 objects get closer to each other, the pull between them increases.

Gravity and Mass

◆◆◆◆◆◆◆

The strength of gravity depends on the mass of the objects that are attracting each other.

One of Isaac Newton's discoveries was that the strength of gravity depends on the mass of the objects attracting one another. Therefore, the same object would weigh less on the moon than on Earth, because the moon, being smaller than Earth, would attract that object less strongly. You cannot change the size of the earth or easily travel to the moon, but you can illustrate Newton's principle by changing the mass of a handy object here on Earth.

What You'll Need
- 5-pound bag of sugar
- scale
- bowl

Weigh a 5-pound sack of sugar. Pour about half of it out into a bowl. Weigh the sack again. The sack now weighs about half of what it did originally, right? That's because you cut the mass of the sugar sack in half. You've proved that half the mass is attracted by the earth with half the force.

Falling Marbles

◆◆◆◆◆◆◆

Heavy and light objects fall at the same speed.

What You'll Need
- 15 marbles
- 2 resealable plastic bags

Put 5 marbles in a plastic bag, and seal it. Put 10 marbles in another plastic bag, and seal it. Raise both bags of marbles above your head as high as you can. Release the bags at exactly the same time, and drop them onto a carpet. Listen for the moment that they strike the floor, and you'll know that they landed at the same time.

One bag obviously weighed more than the other, so you might have expected it to fall faster. The force that makes objects fall on Earth, though, is the gravitational attraction of the earth itself. As with any object, the strength of the earth's gravitational pull is determined by the earth's mass. Since the earth's mass is always the same, it exerts the same pull on any 2 objects that are the same distance from it.

High Bounce

You'll have a ball with gravity when you try this experiment.

What You'll Need
- assorted balls
- pen and paper
- cardboard
- tape measure

Collect some different balls (tennis ball, beach ball, softball, rubber ball, football, basketball, golf ball, etc.). Make a graph that has the names of the different balls across the bottom and height in feet along the side.

Test the different balls to see which bounces best on a concrete floor, porch, or driveway. Drop them one at a time from the same height in front of a tall sheet of cardboard, and mark on the cardboard how high each one bounced. Measure each bounce, and indicate it on your graph.

All the balls gained the same amount of energy when they fell. When they struck the ground, the downward force from gravity was converted into upward force that worked against gravity to send the ball up in the air. The different materials and sizes of the balls affected how well each could convert the energy into upward force.

Two Thuds or One?

Gravity exerts the same force on a moving object and a stationary object.

Caution: This project requires adult supervision.

What You'll Need
- grooved ruler
- wooden board
- roofing tacks
- hammer
- block of wood
- 2 marbles

Lay a grooved ruler on a wooden board about 1 inch thick, 6 inches wide, and 1 foot long. Hammer roofing tacks close to one end of the ruler, on either side, so that the broad heads hold the ruler firmly to the board at one end. Wedge a 3-inch wooden block under the other end of the ruler. Have a friend stand by ready to help. Let a marble roll down the groove of the ruler. This will launch the marble horizontally. At the exact

moment the marble leaves the end of the ruler, have your friend drop a second marble from exactly the same height. What happens?

Both marbles hit the ground at the same time, even though one was traveling horizontally and the other was not. Gravity exerted the same force over the marbles, even though one of them was in motion.

Target Practice

◆▸▸▸▸▸◆

Beanbag tossing takes a tricky turn when motion and gravity are part of the game.

What You'll Need
- black paper
- ruler
- scissors
- bicycle
- beanbag

Challenge a friend to target practice. From a sheet of black paper, cut out 2 black circles. Make a 1-inch-diameter circle and a 6-inch-diameter circle.

In a safe place, you and your friend can take turns riding past the target on your bike and trying to drop a beanbag on the target as you go by without stopping. After several tries, you'll learn when to drop the beanbag. Do you drop it when you are directly over the target? When you and your friend can hit the 6-inch target, try the 1-inch target.

Simple Siphon

◆▸▸▸▸▸◆

Gravity affects the flow of water.

What You'll Need
- 2 large jars
- water
- 3-foot length of clean plastic tubing

Fill a jar halfway with water, and set it on a table. Set a second jar next to the first. Now put one end of a 3-foot piece of plastic tubing into the jar containing the water and the other end in the empty jar. Lift the jar with water up so it is level with your head. Does anything happen?

Now set the jar down, and take the tubing out of the empty jar. Put the tubing in your mouth, and suck up water until the tubing is filled with water. Hold your thumb over the end of the tubing to keep the water from running out, and carefully lift the jar containing the water up so it is level with your head. Put the tubing into the empty jar, and remove your thumb. Watch what the water does this time.

The part of the tubing that ran between the 2 jars was much longer than the part that was in the jar containing the water; the longer section of tubing had more water in it than the other section, so the downward water pressure in the longer section of tubing was much greater. This greater water pressure was enough force to overcome the pull of gravity on the water in the jar, so the water was drawn up through the tubing.

Milk Carton Waterwheel

◆◀◀◀◀◀◆◆

Issac Newton's third law states, "Every action has an equal and opposite reaction." Have fun proving that law by making a waterwheel—but do this project outside because it is quite wet!

What You'll Need
- ½-gallon paper milk carton
- pencil
- scissors
- string
- water

Caution: This project requires adult supervision.

This is a fun way to play with water on a hot, sunny day. Put on your thinking cap and your bathing suit! Use a pencil to poke a hole in the bottom left-hand corner of each of the 4 sides of a ½-gallon paper milk carton. With scissors, poke a hole in the top flap of the milk carton (you may need adult help with this). Tie a string through this hole, and tie the carton to a branch or something from which it can suspend. While covering the holes in the milk carton with your fingers, have a helper pour water into the carton.

When the carton is filled, take your fingers off the holes and see what happens to the milk carton as the water flows out. You've created a waterwheel!

Water-Pressure Gauge

◆◆◆◆◆◆◆

Gravity works its force on everything on Earth. In this project, gravity puts the pressure on water.

What You'll Need
- pencil
- ½-gallon paper milk carton
- ruler
- tape
- water
- sink

Use a pencil point to poke 3 holes, one directly above the other, on one side of an empty ½-gallon milk carton. One hole should be about 1 inch from the bottom of the container; the middle hole should be 3 inches above the first; and the third hole should be 3 inches above the middle hole.

Put a piece of tape down the side of the container to cover up the 3 holes. Fill the carton with water, and set it down in the sink. Pull off the piece of tape, and watch the water flow from the holes. You'll see that the water shoots out the greatest distance from the bottom hole and the least distance from the top hole. You'll also see that the water from each hole squirts less and less far as time passes.

As gravity pulls down on the water, the water exerts a downward force that we call water pressure. The more water you have, the greater the amount of downward force it will produce. The force of water pressure that made the water squirt out of the holes was stronger at the bottom of the carton than at the top because the bottom had more water above it pressing down. That's why the water squirted farther from the bottom hole. As the water drained from the carton, the amount of water pressure decreased, and the water didn't squirt as far.

Paths of Objects

The movement of objects can occur in a straight, curved, or irregular path. The way that force is applied makes a difference in the path that an object will follow.

Pendulum Patterns

◆▶◆▶◆▶◆▶

Catch a glimpse of the pattern of a swinging pendulum.

Place 2 chairs about 3 feet apart, and cover the floor between the chairs with a large piece of dark paper. Lay a broom handle across the backs of the chairs. Poke a small hole in the bottom of a paper cup. Tape a 6-inch string to the paper cup on either side to form a handle. Tie the handle of the paper cup to a 3-foot piece of string, and then tie the string to the middle of the broom handle between the 2 chairs.

Hold your finger over the hole in the bottom of the paper cup, and fill the cup with salt. Then pull the cup toward one of the corners of the sheet of dark paper. Release both your finger and the

cup. The cup will swing like a pendulum in a pattern, and you will be able to see that pattern by looking at the salt that drops onto the paper.

What You'll Need
- 2 chairs
- ruler
- dark paper
- broom
- paper cup
- scissors
- string
- tape
- salt

Swinging Together

◆▶◆▶◆▶◆▶

Motion can transfer from one moving object to another.

What You'll Need
- 2 chairs
- rope
- ruler
- scissors
- 2 paper cups
- string
- 4 marbles

Place 2 chairs about 4 feet apart. Tie a rope between the backs of the chairs. Punch 2 holes opposite one another in the lip of a paper cup. Thread a 4-inch string through the holes, and tie a knot to make a handle for the cup. Repeat this process with a second cup. Tie a 2-foot-long piece of string to the handle of each cup. Tie the free ends of the strings to the rope stretched between the 2 chairs; tie the strings so they are about a foot apart. Put 2 marbles in each cup. Hold one cup to the side, and then release it. Watch as it begins to swing. What happens to the other cup?

Ghost Walk

◆◆◆◆◆◆◆

*Energy from a wound-up rubber band can
make an object move along a path.*

What You'll Need
- rubber band
- empty spool of thread
- toothpick
- tape
- candle
- knife
- unsharpened pencil
- white handkerchief

Caution: This project requires adult supervision.

Thread a rubber band through an empty spool of thread. Slip half a toothpick through the rubber band at one end, and use a piece of tape to stick the toothpick to the bottom of the spool. Slice a 1-inch-thick piece of wax from a candle, and poke a small hole through the center of it. Thread the other end of the rubber band through the candle ring, and then put a pencil through the end of the rubber band. Set the spool on the table so the toothpick side is touching the table surface. Wind the pencil around several times, and hold it in place. Cover the spool with a white handkerchief, and then let it go. Watch your little ghost creep across the table.

Whirligig

◆◆◆◆◆◆◆

*Centrifugal force causes spinning objects to
move toward the outside of a circle.*

Take a half sheet of notebook paper, and wad it up into a small ball. Stick the end of a 2-foot piece of string into the ball of paper, and tape it to the paper. Cut a cardboard tube from a roll of paper towels in half, and thread the string through one half of the cardboard tube. Wad a full sheet of paper into a tight ball. Stick the other end of the piece of string into the large ball of paper, and tape it to the paper.

What You'll Need
- paper
- string
- scissors
- tape
- paper-towel tube

Let the small ball stick out of the tube about 5 inches at the top, while the large ball hangs down from the bottom. Grasp the tube in one hand, and move your hand in a small circular motion so that the small ball spins around the tube. Spin it faster and faster, and watch the large ball begin to rise. Continue moving your hand, and pull down on the large ball. Watch what happens to the speed of the small ball.

Watch an Ounce Lift a Pound

◆▷◆▷◆▷◆

Centrifugal force increases when speed increases.

What You'll Need
- fishing line
- empty wooden cotton spool
- a 1-ounce object
- a 1-pound rock

Thread a 5-foot piece of fishing line through an empty wooden cotton spool. At one end, securely fasten a 1-ounce object that can be whirled about without danger. Fasten a 1-pound rock to the other end of the fishing line.

Grip the spool so that you are also holding the string beneath it. Let the heavy rock dangle down about 10 inches. Rotate the light object in a horizontal circle above your head. When the light object is spinning around fast, you can release your grip on the string below the spool. As you continue to spin the light object, you will see the heavy object begin to rise on the string that goes through the spool. (Be sure to use a strong line and fasten objects securely so that the objects don't fly off!)

Some of the energy you used to spin the light object around generated a centrifugal force that caused the object to move in a circle. As you applied more energy, the centrifugal force became strong enough to lift the heavy object.

Path of a Ball

◆▷◆▷◆▷◆

Bouncing a ball is a fun way to learn how force affects the path of objects!

Take a small ball with a good bounce, and throw it straight at a smooth wall. Watch the ball carefully. If it hits the wall straight on, it will bounce straight back to you. Now move to

What You'll Need
- small ball

the side and throw the ball so that it hits the wall at an angle. Watch the ball carefully. It will not bounce back to you; instead it will bounce off the wall at an angle equal to the angle at which it struck the wall. Move to another spot where you can throw the ball so that it hits the wall at an even sharper angle. Again watch the path of the ball bounce. It will be equal to the sharp angle at which the ball struck the wall.

Catapult

◆◆◆◆◆◆◆

How far can you make an eraser fly?

What You'll Need
- wooden block
- ruler
- eraser
- pen and paper

Find a place to do this project where you're sure the eraser won't hit anything or anyone. Place a small wooden block on a table. Rest the center of a ruler on the block. Put a small eraser on one end of the ruler, and quickly push the opposite end down to the table. Notice that both ends of the ruler travel the same distance. Measure how far the eraser was thrown, and write it down.

This time, rest the ruler on the block so that the block is about 2 inches from one end of the ruler; that end will be up in the air, and the other end will rest on the table. Put the eraser on the end of the ruler that is resting on the table. Give a sharp blow to the other end of the ruler. Notice that the one end of the ruler moves several times farther than the other end. Measure the distance that the eraser was thrown, and compare it to the previous measurement.

The block of wood was acting as a *fulcrum,* which transferred the force from one end of the ruler to the other. The ruler was acting as a *lever.* The closer the fulcrum is to one end of the lever, the more force it will transfer to the other end.

Curve Balls

◆◆◆◆◆◆◆

Does a curve ball really curve in flight?

What You'll Need
- table-tennis ball
- waterproof marker
- playing field marked with straight lines (like a baseball diamond)
- paper-towel tube

This activity requires either a windless day or a large indoor space (like your school gym). To prepare, color half of the table-tennis ball with the marker. This will help you see what happens to it in flight. Stand on a marked line on the playing field or gym and try to throw the ball straight down the line. What path does the ball take?

Now, put the ball in one end of the paper-towel tube. Holding the other end, fling the ball out of the tube, trying to throw it straight. What path does it take now? Try this several times. You should see the ball spin. The axis of the spin is perpendicular to the flight path of the ball. The spin actually changes the path of the ball and makes it fly in a curve!

Laws of Motion

Three basic rules govern how things move, or how they react when force is applied to them. First, a stationary object will stay in place, and a moving object will keep moving until a force acts on it; this is called *inertia.* Second, the effect that force has on an object depends on the amount of force and the mass of the object. Third, applying force to an object results in an equal force being applied in the opposite direction.

Balloon Wheels

◇━━━━━━◇

Use Issac Newton's laws to move your toy cars without gravity!

What You'll Need
- old toy cars
- double-sided tape
- balloon

Newton's third law states that for every action there is an equal and opposite reaction. It explains how jet and rocket engines work. In this activity, you'll unleash the power of Newton's third law on toy cars.

Place double-sided tape on the top of a toy car. (Note: The tape may be hard to remove from the top of your car; you may damage the car's paint when you remove it.) Blow up a balloon and stick it to the top of the car with the balloon valve pointing toward the back of the car. Point the car in a direction with a lot of smooth floor space. Release the balloon valve.

As the air moves backward out of the balloon, it pushes the balloon and the attached car forward, demonstrating Newton's third law. If the balloon flies off the car without moving it, try a little less air in the balloon, a lighter car or one with smoother wheels, or give the car a little push as you release the balloon.

Seesaw Balance

◆◆◆◆◆◆

Turn a seesaw into a balance and find out how scales work.

What You'll Need
- seesaw
- two or more partners

Have you ever wondered how the scale at the doctor's office works? How can small weights balance your own larger weight? Use a seesaw to find out. Before you begin, however, agree that no one will jump off the seesaw while another person is sitting on it. The sudden jolt can cause serious injury. First, sit on one end of the seesaw and have a partner

sit on the other end. Is the seesaw balanced? Have the heavier person move toward the middle of the seesaw until it balances. Notice that neither of you changed your weight; only your position changed.

Now have 2 people sit on one side of the seesaw and one person on the other. Decide together how to move people so that the seesaw becomes level. Should the 2 people move to the middle, or should the single person move?

Spinning Swings

◆◆◆◆◆◆

How do ice-skaters spin so fast? Find out on a playground swing.

What You'll Need
- swing set
- partner
- stopwatch

Only do this activity if your parents say it's okay to get a little dizzy! Sit on the swing and have your partner turn you slowly around and around until the swing is wound up tightly. Have a stopwatch ready, and when your partner lets go, time how long it takes for the swing to unwind. Next, try the same thing with your arms and

legs stretched out as far as they will go. This puts some of your weight away from the center of mass. Time how long it takes for the swing to unwind.

Now, do the same thing but pull your arms and legs in close to your body. This brings all your weight close to your center. Did you go faster? Next time you see skaters on television or in a show, watch how they hold their arms when they spin. The closer their arms are to their bodies, the faster they can whirl.

Swing on a Pendulum

◆◆◆◆◆◆◆

Discover the physics of a pendulum on the playground swing.

You probably know that the harder you pump on a swing, the higher you go. You probably feel like you're going faster, too. But how does this affect the swing's *periodicity*—that is, does the swing actually go back and forth more times per minute? Sit in a swing and have your partner push you gently. Time how many times you go back and forth in one minute. Don't pump the swing. Just let it go on its own. Your partner can use a stopwatch to time precisely one minute while you count. Next, have your partner push you as hard as possible. Again, don't pump the swing. Count how many times you go back and forth in one minute. Is it any different? Now try the same experiment, but pump the swing yourself. Does adding a force affect the periodicity of the swing?

Breaking the String

◆◆◆◆◆◆◆

An object at rest will remain at rest until a force makes it move.

Cut a 2-foot piece of thread, and tie one end securely around a 6×4×2-inch block of wood. Tie the other end to a secure horizontal pole (such as a porch railing) so the block of wood hangs from it. Cut another 2-foot piece of thread, and tie one end of it securely around the block of wood also. Let the other end hang down freely. Now gently pull down on the lower piece of thread. Continue to pull slowly and steadily, increasing pressure until the upper thread breaks.

What You'll Need
- scissors
- ruler
- thread
- block of wood

Set up your experiment again. This time, instead of pulling slowly and steadily, give a sharp, powerful tug to the bottom thread. This time the bottom thread will snap.

The block of wood was at rest. When you pulled down steadily with increasing force, you overcame the block's inertia, pulling it downward and causing it to pull on the top thread and break it. When you pulled down quickly, you did not generate enough force to overcome the block's inertia; all of the energy was applied to the lower thread, causing it to break.

Pulley Power

◆◆◆◆◆◆

Avoid too much lifting grief; let a pulley give you some relief!

Caution: This project requires adult supervision.

Open the flaps of an empty 1-quart milk carton, and put 24 marbles inside. Close up the carton, and punch a hole through the top with a scissors. Push a 3-inch piece of strong string through the hole, and tie the string in a knot to form a loop. Take a coat hanger, and use wire cutters to carefully cut off the long straight piece on the bottom. (Save this for Using a Roller on page 130.) Bend the 2 short arms of the coat hanger through the hole in the center of an empty spool of thread until the ends of the arms touch each other. Put the hook of the coat hanger through the loop of string you tied to the milk carton.

Set a dowel on a table so it extends 6 inches over the side of the table; set some heavy books on top of the dowel to hold it in place. Place the milk carton on the floor beneath the dowel.

First lift the milk carton 6 inches off the floor by holding the carton by the flaps and pulling it up in your hands. Now tie one end of a 5-foot piece of string to the dowel.

(Save this for Using a Roller on page 130.)

What You'll Need
- empty 1-quart milk carton
- 24 marbles
- scissors
- string
- ruler
- metal coat hanger
- wire cutters
- empty spool of thread
- dowel
- books

Pass the other end of the string under the spool of thread. Lift the carton of marbles about 6 inches off the floor by pulling the string 12 inches. You have created a *pulley*. The milk carton will feel only half as heavy as it did before. Pulling the string twice the distance that you raise the carton means you need to exert only half the force to lift it.

Using a Roller

◆◆◆◆◆◆

Using a ramp can really help get a job rolling!

What You'll Need
- books
- ruler
- thin metal rod (such as the bottom piece cut from a coat hanger with wire cutters)
- empty spool of thread
- string
- scissors
- toy car
- empty margarine tub
- marbles
- paper and pen
- cardboard

Put 2 stacks of books, 9 inches apart, at the edge of a table. Each stack should be 9 inches tall and placed so that part of each stack of books sticks out over the edge of the table. Place a thin metal rod through an empty spool of thread, and rest the rod across the stack of books. Add a few more books to each stack to hold the rod in place. Tie a 2-foot piece of string to the front of a toy car. Put the car on the table beneath the rod, and put the other end of the piece of string up over the spool of thread.

Punch 2 holes opposite each other in the rim of an empty margarine tub. Tie an 8-inch piece of string through the holes to form a handle for the tub. Tie the other end of the string that is attached to the toy car to the handle of your tub.

Add marbles to the margarine tub, one at a time, until there is enough weight to lift the toy car 5 inches into the air. Empty the tub, and count the marbles. Write the number down.

Add a third stack of books, 5 inches high, between the other 2 stacks. Use a sturdy piece of cardboard to make a ramp (which is an *inclined plane*) between the top of the middle stack of books and the table. Put the toy car at the bottom of the ramp.

Put marbles, one by one, into the tub until there's enough weight to pull the toy car to the top of the ramp. Empty the tub, and count the marbles. Write the number down.

By using a ramp to help, did it take more or less weight to lift the toy car?

Blast Off

◆◆◆◆◆◆

*According to one of Isaac Newton's laws of motion,
for every action there is an equal and opposite reaction.*

What You'll Need
- two 3-foot dowels
- hammer
- fishing line
- measuring tape
- drinking straw
- scissors
- empty, plastic screw-top bottle
- vinegar
- tape
- baking soda
- measuring spoon
- tissue paper

Caution: This project requires adult supervision.

Carefully pound two 3-foot dowels into the ground about 6 feet apart. Tie a 7-foot piece of fishing line to one dowel, thread the loose end through a drinking straw, and then tie the other end to the second dowel, stretching the string tightly between the dowels.

Ask an adult to use scissors to poke a hole through the cap of an empty, plastic screw-top bottle, such as a shampoo bottle. Remove the cap from the bottle. Pour an inch of vinegar in the bottle. Recap the bottle. Tape the bottle to the straw on the fishing line so the bottle is horizontal. Slide the bottle along the fishing line all the way to one end so that the cap is next to the dowel.

Put 3 teaspoons of baking soda into a small piece of tissue paper. Roll the paper up, slip it into the bottle, and quickly screw the cap back on the bottle.

Carefully shake the bottle back and forth for a few seconds, and then let go of the bottle. The bottle will travel the length of the fishing line, propelled like a rocket.

The baking soda and vinegar produced carbon dioxide gas when they were mixed together. The gas was forced out of the hole in the bottle cap. As the gas pushed backward out of the bottle, it exerted an equal force in the opposite direction, which propelled the bottle forward.

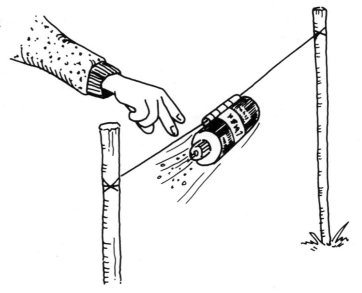

Water-Powered Boat

◆◆◆◆◆◆◆

This homemade boat doesn't need a motor or sails to make it go.

What You'll Need
- dull knife
- empty 1-quart milk carton
- pencil
- paper cup
- bendable drinking straw
- water
- sink or bathtub

Carefully cut an empty 1-quart milk carton in half lengthwise. You only need one half, so set the other half aside. Set your half down on the table so you can see the inside of the carton. The top of the milk carton will be the prow, or front, of your boat; the bottom will be the stern, or the back. Using a pencil, make a hole just big enough for a drinking straw to fit, near the bottom and in the center of the boat's stern.

Poke a hole of the same size in the side of a paper cup ½-inch up from the bottom. Bend a bendable drinking straw into an L-shape. Put the long end of the straw through the hole in the boat's stern. Now put the short end of the straw through the hole in the cup, and set the cup inside the boat.

Fill your sink or bathtub with water, and put the boat in it. Be sure that the straw poking out from the boat is below the water's surface. Hold a finger over the end of the straw in the paper cup while you fill the cup with water. Take your finger off the straw, and watch your boat sail.

Gravity made the water flow out of the cup, through the straw, and into the sink. As it was forced out of the straw, the water exerted an equal force in the opposite direction, which propelled the boat forward.

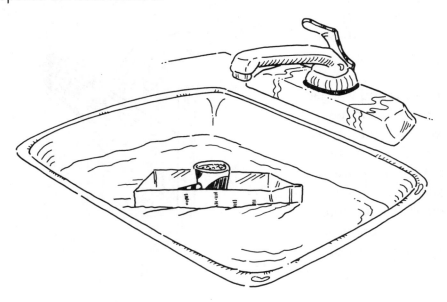

Rolling Oats Race

❖❖❖❖❖❖❖

Force is needed to overcome inertia.

Tape a heavy metal washer to the inside of an empty oatmeal box halfway between the top and bottom. Tape a second washer directly across from the first one, and put the lid back on the box. Take the lid off of a second oatmeal box. Tape a heavy metal washer to the underside of the lid, directly in the center. Put a washer inside the box, and tape it to the bottom, directly in the center. Put the lid back on the box. Put a mark on the lid of this box so you can tell the 2 boxes apart.

Arrange a large sheet of sturdy cardboard so one end rests on the seat of a chair and the opposite end rests on the floor. Use this ramp as a raceway for your 2 oatmeal boxes. Hold them at the top of the ramp, one in each hand, and release them at exactly the same time. Which one reaches the bottom first? Race them down the ramp several times. Does the same one always win?

What You'll Need
● 4 identical metal washers
● 2 empty oatmeal boxes with lids
● tape
● marker
● cardboard
● chair

The box with the washers taped to the sides was always slower than the other one. As the slow box rolled, the washers on the side moved in a circular path. As the fast box rolled, the washers on the top and bottom stayed in one place. Gravity exerted an equal force on the 2 boxes, but some of that force had to be used to overcome the inertia of the washers in the slow box. More of the force was available to make the fast box roll, so it rolled faster.

Starting and Stopping

◆◆◆◆◆◆◆

An object in motion will keep moving until a force stops it.

Put 3 rocks in the back of a toy truck as cargo. Push the truck forward quickly so that it picks up momentum, and then stop it suddenly. Watch to see what the rocks do when the truck is stopped.

What You'll Need
● 3 rocks
● toy truck

The rocks in the back of the truck were in motion. When you applied force to the truck to stop it, the rocks continued moving until they were stopped by hitting the side of the truck.

Skateboard Load

◆◆◆◆◆◆◆

When a skateboard rolls down a hill, does a heavier or lighter rider roll faster?

Galileo dropped 2 objects with different weights from the Leaning Tower of Pisa. Both hit the ground at the same time. Galileo determined that objects with different weights have the same acceleration due to gravity. But in a soapbox or pinewood derby, rules limit how heavy your car can be. Is it because a heavier car is faster than a light car? Grab your skateboard, and see for yourself.

What You'll Need
- skateboard
- chalk
- stopwatch
- pen and paper
- old telephone books

Find a straight sloping pathway. Draw a starting line and a finish line. Release your empty skateboard (don't push it!) and time how long it takes to get from start to finish. Record your data. Add a few heavy telephone books to the skateboard. Time how long it takes to get from start to finish, and record your data. Repeat this a few more times with increasing amounts of books on the skateboard. Analyze your data; does more weight make the skateboard go faster?

You probably found that more weight *did* make the skateboard roll faster. Was Galileo wrong? Not exactly. Galileo was excluding *friction* from his analysis. If the amount of friction slowing the skateboard is the same, then more *momentum* helps overcome the friction. Adding books to the skateboard increased its mass and gave it greater momentum to battle friction.

Simple Machines

◆◆◆◆◆◆◆

Simple machines, such as the lever, inclined plane, and pulley, have been used for thousands of years. These machines enable us to do work with less effort. Have you ever ridden your bike up a huge hill? You might have started zigzagging up the hill to make it a bit easier or you might have shifted into a lower gear. This helped you decrease the effort. But you still had to work to get up the hill.

Inclined to Rise

◆◆◆◆◆◆◆

See how an inclined plane helps reduce the effort to lift a load.

Cut a piece of string 3 inches long and tape one end to a wooden block. Tie the other end to a rubber band. Let the block hang from the rubber band. Slowly lift the block; have a partner measure the length of the rubber band as you lift. Record this data. Now create an inclined plane using a board and a stack of books. Start out by making the inclined plane very steep; add more books if you need to. As you steadily pull the block up the inclined plane have your partner move the ruler along and measure the length of the rubber band. Make the measurement as the block is moving slowly up the plane. Record your data. Now remove a book or two to make the inclined plane less steep. Pull the block up the plane again, measuring the length of the rubber band, and record your data. Remove some more books and repeat.

> **What You'll Need**
> - tape
> - string
> - wooden block
> - rubber band
> - ruler
> - pen and paper
> - wooden board
> - books

The rubber band stretched the most when you held the block without the inclined plane because you were using the most force. The inclined plane enabled you to lift the block with less force. The more gradual the inclined plane, the less force you used.

Screwy Inclined Plane

◆◆◆◆◆◆◆

Is a screw really just an inclined plane?

> **What You'll Need**
> - paper
> - scissors
> - pencil
> - tape
> - screw

Cut a triangle out of paper. Hold this triangle up, and you can easily see how it could be an inclined plane. Move a piece of paper up the inclined plane to see how it could make lifting a load easier.

Now, roll the triangle onto the pencil. Start rolling with the wide side of the triangle. Tape the end point of the triangle down, and remove the pencil.

Compare a screw to your rolled-up inclined plane. Can you see that they are similar? A screw is a kind of simple machine; it is a modified inclined plane.

Magic Brooms

◆◆◆◆◆◆

Use brooms to demonstrate how pulleys can help a small force exert a larger force.

What You'll Need
- 2 volunteers
- 2 brooms
- nylon rope

Give 2 volunteers each a broom. Ask them to hold the brooms in front of themselves and face each other. Now you will connect the brooms with a rope to make a pulley. Tie one end of the rope to one of the brooms. Then weave the rope over and under the second broom, back over and under the first broom, back over and under the second broom, and, finally, back over and under the first broom. Make sure your rope is long enough to wrap around both brooms twice and still leave some rope at the end. Now you have a pulleylike arrangement. Ask your volunteers to use all their strength to keep the brooms apart. At the same time, grab the end of the rope and try to pull the brooms together. Because of the pulley action, you can easily overcome the strength of your 2 volunteers, forcing the brooms together.

Muscle Lever

◆◆◆◆◆◆

How can you make it easier to lift a weight in a curl?

Search your kitchen for canned goods to use as dumbbells. Hold a can in your hand with your arm down by your side. Keeping your upper arm still, slowly move the dumbbell up to your shoulder. Now, ask a partner to hold

What You'll Need
- canned goods
- partner

the can closer to your elbow to see if it is easier to lift. Your partner should just hold the can in place without making it harder or easier to lift. Do a curl in this position. Repeat a third time, with the partner holding the can just below your elbow.

You probably found that the can was easier to lift as it got closer to your elbow. Your arm acts like a third-class lever. If you curl a dumbbell that is one pound, your bicep has to exert a force of several pounds to lift it. Moving the weight closer to the fulcrum (your elbow) decreases the force needed.

Inclined Calculations

◆◆◆◆◆◆◆

How do simple machines allow us to use less force to do the same amount of work?

Machines often enable us to use less force to do work—in other words, machines can make work easier. But how can you measure the amount of work a task requires? Work is equal to the force applied multiplied by the distance moved. The formula is: Work=Force×Distance.

To use less force, you must move that force over a longer distance. In this activity, you will measure the distance traveled by a load on an inclined plane. From this information, you can calculate the amount of force used.

Suppose you want to lift a one-kilogram weight to a height of one meter. If you just bend down and lift it, the distance the load travels is one meter. The work is equal to 10 joules.

Now imagine that you are going to lift the one-kilogram weight using inclined planes of various slopes. Measure a spot on the wall that is one meter high, and mark it with your chalk. This is your destination height. Now make a steeply inclined plane from the floor to the chalk mark with the tape measure. (This is much easier if you have a partner to help you.) Record the distance the weight would travel on this plane. Then repeat for a slightly less steep plane. Repeat for a very gentle slope.

work = force × distance

Calculate the effort needed in each case using the formula: Work=Force×Distance. Assume there is no friction and the work is 10 joules in each case. You solve the equation for force, so Force=Work÷Distance. For example, if the length of the inclined plane is 1.5 meters, then the force, or effort, needed is found with the following formula: F=10 Joules÷2 meters. So, Force=5 Newtons (the units used to measure energy).

Once you complete your calculations, compare the answers. Did you discover that the gentle slope required less force than the steep one?

Leaping Lincolns

◆◆◆◆◆◆

How can you get the highest bounce from a penny?

What You'll Need
- 12-inch ruler
- pencil
- penny
- quarter
- yardstick

Put the pencil under the ruler at the 4-inch mark. The pencil acts as a fulcrum. Place a penny on the 1-inch mark of the ruler. Use your yardstick to measure a height of 30 inches, then drop the quarter down onto the ruler. Where on the ruler should you drop the quarter to make the penny jump the highest?

The penny jumps the highest when the quarter hits farther away from the fulcrum. This idea is important in levers: The greater the distance from the fulcrum, the greater the turning force.

Washer Lever

◆◆◆◆◆◆

Can you get everything to balance out when you experiment with a lever?

What You'll Need
- meter stick
- triangular block
- 3 large washers of equal size

Balance a meter stick on a triangular block so all the metric numbers are facing up; the meter stick should balance on the 50 cm mark. The triangle acts as a fulcrum. Use your materials to solve the following problems:

(A) Place one washer 20 cm away from the fulcrum. Now, place a second washer on the other side so that the ruler is balanced. (B) Place one washer 30 cm from the fulcrum. Can you position a washer on the other side to balance the ruler? (C) Place one washer 20 cm away from the fulcrum. Where can you put a 2-washer stack on the other side to balance? (D) Place 2 washers 20 cm from the fulcrum. Where can you put one washer on the other side to balance the ruler?

You probably found the following: (A) With one washer 20 cm away from the fulcrum, the ruler balances with a washer 20 cm away on the other side. (B) With one washer 30 cm away from the fulcrum, the ruler balances with a washer 30 cm away on the other side. (C) With one washer 20 cm away from the fulcrum, the ruler balances with a 2-washer stack 10 cm away on the other side. (D) With 2 washers 20 cm away from the fulcrum, the ruler balances with one washer 40 cm away on the other side.

Movable Pulley

◆◇◆◇◆◇◆

A movable pulley decreases the amount of effort required to lift a load.

What You'll Need

- string
- scissors
- ruler
- tape
- wooden block
- rubber band
- pen and paper
- empty thread spool
- wire

Start by cutting 2 pieces of string. One should be short, about 2 or 3 inches. The other should be much longer, approximately 1 yard. Tape one end of the short string to a wooden block; tie the other end to a rubber band. Let the block hang from the rubber band. Slowly lift the block; have a partner measure the length of the rubber band as you lift. Record this data. This indicates the relative amount of force you need to lift the block without the pulley.

To make the pulley, start with an empty thread spool. Push a 4-inch length of wire through the spool hole. Join the ends of the wire up to make a triangle and twist them together. Untie the end of the string from your rubber band, and use it to tie the block to the wire where it is twisted together.

Tie one end of the long piece of string to a doorknob. Tie the other end to your rubber band. Rest the pulley on this string so the string wraps under the spool and the block hangs from the metal triangle (as shown in the illustration). Pull the rubber band and string up. Have your partner measure the stretch in the rubber band.

Did you notice that the rubber band stretched the most when you just held the block without the pulley? That is because you were using more force. The moving pulley allows you to lift the block with about half the force.

Dramatic Lever

◆◆◆◆◆◆◆◆

Use a little math to understand how a lever works.

What You'll Need
- 9 large washers
- tape
- meter stick
- triangular wood block

If you tried the activity Washer Lever (see page 138) you gained experience with levers. In this activity, the fulcrum will be at the 50 cm mark of the meter stick. The ruler should balance. Your load will always be 5 cm away from the fulcrum. Your effort will start close to the fulcrum and then move away. You will see how big of a load you can support for each effort. Use your materials to solve the following problems: (A) If one washer is 10 cm away from the fulcrum, how many washers will be needed for balance 5 cm from the fulcrum on the other side? (B) If one washer is 20 cm away from the fulcrum, how many washers will be needed 5 cm from the fulcrum on the other side? (C) If one washer is 40 cm away from the fulcrum, how many washers will be needed on the other side 5 cm from the fulcrum?

You probably found the following answers (A) 2, (B) 4, and (C) 8. Some simple math can help you understand how your lever worked. When you have balance, the force distance on one side of the fulcrum equals the force distance on the other side. You could weigh your washer to find its force, but for now let's just call it a Washer Weight (WW). In situation A, the formula is expressed as $10 \text{ cm} \times 1 \text{ WW} = 5 \text{ cm} \times 2 \text{ WW}$. Both sides equal 10, so it is in balance. In situation C, the formula is expressed as $40 \text{ cm} \times 1 \text{ WW} = 5 \text{ cm} \times 8 \text{ WW}$. Can you come up with a formula for situation B?

Magnets and Metal

◆◆◆◆◆◆◆◆

Magnetism is a property of the molecules of certain substances, such as iron, that will attract or repel other magnetized objects. In a magnet, the molecules line up in a way that creates a force. When a magnet is free to turn, it can be used to indicate the direction of the earth's magnetism. The end of a magnet that points to Earth's North Pole is called the north pole of the magnet.

Magnetic Minerals

Is there iron in your cereal? With a little help from science, you can perform some breakfast-table magic.

The iron that your body needs to make healthy blood is the same iron that is found in the earth. If the cereal you eat for breakfast is high in iron, it should be attracted to a magnet.

What You'll Need
- cereal
- plastic bag
- rolling pin
- strong magnet

Put some cereal in a plastic bag and use a rolling pin to crush it into powder. Then, touch the magnet to the powder. Does the cereal cling to the magnet?

Magnets and Rust

Magnets can lose some of their magnetism.

What You'll Need
- horseshoe magnet
- a can of small nails
- paper and pen
- jar
- water

Many things can weaken a magnet. For instance, they can be spoiled by being repeatedly banged so that molecules are jarred and disarranged. In this experiment, you'll find out if rust weakens a magnet.

Dip a shiny horseshoe magnet into a can of small nails. Count how many nails it attracts. Repeat this 3 times, counting the number of nails attracted each time and taking the average. Then put the magnet in a jar of water, and leave it there until its surface is rusted. Repeat your test of the magnet with the can of nails. Does the rust have any effect on the magnet's strength?

An Electromagnet

Electricity can produce magnetism.

Caution: Wires can become hot during this activity.

Wind a 3-foot piece of electrical wire around a long iron bolt about 20 times; make the loops close together, and leave about 10 inches of wire loose on each end of the coil. Connect the 2 loose ends of the wire to a 6-volt battery. The bolt is now an electromagnet and will attract metal containing iron. Test the electromagnet using paper clips, spoons, and other household items to see how strong it is. Disconnect the wire from the battery, and see if the magnet still works.

As electricity from the battery flowed through the wire, it caused the molecules in the bolt to align themselves in a way that created a magnetic force, and the bolt became a magnet.

Magnet Merry-Go-Round

A turning magnet will pull steel objects in a circle.

Tape 2 small magnets to the turntable of an old record player. Turn on the record player. Place several thumbtacks on a sheet of thin cardboard. Hold the cardboard above the turntable. Slowly lower the sheet of cardboard over the turntable until you almost touch it. The magnetism will be exerted through the

cardboard and will pull the thumbtacks around and around as the magnets spin on the turntable.

Keep Your Distance

❖❖❖❖❖❖❖❖

Depending on which poles are brought together, magnets will either attract or repel each other.

What You'll Need
- pencil
- 6 doughnut-shape magnets

Hold a pencil upright like a flagpole with your hand at the bottom. Put 6 doughnut-shape magnets on the pencil, being sure to reverse every other one so that they will repel (push away from) each other. Now move the pencil into a horizontal position. What happens to the magnets?

Strong Attraction

❖❖❖❖❖❖❖❖

Only objects containing iron are attracted to magnets.

Gather small objects from around the house (such as a paper clip, nail, hairpin, thumbtack, plastic spoon, wooden block, table-tennis ball, toy car, penny, aluminum foil, pop can, tin can, cup, fork, belt buckle, etc.)

What You'll Need
- various household items
- horseshoe magnet

and make a guess as to whether or not they contain iron. Then test them to find out. Hold an object to the ends of a horseshoe magnet. If the object contains iron, it will be attracted to the magnet. If it does not contain iron, it will not be attracted. How often did you guess correctly?

Lines of Force

The force of magnetism extends out from a magnet in all directions to form an area we call the *field* of the magnet. Objects affected by magnetism will feel the force of a magnet if they pass into its field. The field takes the shape of lines extending from the magnet, which we call *lines of force.*

Dispersing Magnetism

◆◆◆◆◆◆

The force of magnetism cannot be exerted through steel.

What You'll Need
- magnet
- paper clip
- aluminum cake pan
- plastic
- cardboard
- steel cookie sheet

A magnet will attract a steel paper clip through many different objects. Hold the magnet under an *aluminum* cake pan. Put a paper clip in the pan; there is a strong attraction. By moving the magnet, you can move the paper clip all around the pan. Do the same test, putting a piece of plastic and then a piece of cardboard between the magnet and the paper clip. Again, there is a strong attraction, and you can move the clip.

Now put the paper clip on a *steel* cookie sheet. Put the magnet underneath. Instead of passing right through the sheet, the magnetism is dispersed. Depending on the strength of the magnet, either there will be no attraction or the attraction will be much weaker than it was through the other objects.

Magnet Maze

◆◆◆◆◆◆

The force of magnetism can be exerted through paper.

What You'll Need
- paper plate
- pencil
- paper clip
- bar magnet
- timer

Draw an interesting maze with lots of twists and turns and some dead-ends on the surface of a large, white paper plate. Make the path of your maze slightly wider than the width of a paper clip. When the maze is finished, ask a friend to hold the plate. Place a paper clip at the start of the maze. Holding a bar magnet beneath the paper plate, try to guide the paper clip through the maze without touching any of the lines. If the paper clip crosses a line, change places, and let your friend try to guide the clip through the maze. You might want to time yourselves to see how long it takes to move through the maze.

Right Through the Glass

◆▸◆▸◆▸◆▸

The force of magnetism can be exerted through glass.

Set several small metal objects, such as thumbtacks, nails, and paper clips, on a table. Move a bar magnet across the table toward one of the metal objects. When the magnet is close enough to the object, it will cause the object to move toward it. Try this with several of the objects.

Now take all of the metal objects that were attracted to the bar magnet, and drop them into a glass jar. Hold the bar magnet to the outside bottom of the jar. Put your hand across the mouth of the jar, and turn it upside down while holding the magnet in place at the jar's bottom. Remove your hand from the jar opening. The metal objects don't fall. The magnetism passes through the glass and attracts the objects, holding them in place. If you remove the magnet, the objects will fall.

Magnet Outlines

◆▸◆▸◆▸◆▸

Magnets exert their force on objects that move into their field.

Place 2 bar magnets on a table. Put them with unlike poles facing each other, about an inch apart; unlike poles attract each other. Cover the magnets with a sheet of thin paper. Sprinkle some iron filings onto the paper. Observe the pattern that the iron filings make. The filings show you a 2-dimensional version of the field generated by each magnet. Looking at the shape of the fields, you can see how the 2 magnets affect each other at the points where their fields meet.

Repeat this experiment, but this time set the magnets on the table with like poles facing each other, about an inch apart. Like poles repel each other. The lines of force from each magnet will appear to be different at the point where they intersect.

Horseshoe Field

◆◆◆◆◆◆◆

Magnets create lines of force that form a magnetic field.

Place a horseshoe magnet on a table, and cover it with a sheet of thin paper. Sprinkle iron filings on the paper. Observe the pattern that the iron filings make as they are attracted to the magnet. This pattern gives you an idea of the shape of the field generated by the magnet. The filings show you a 2-dimensional version of the field; the real field extends out from the magnet in all directions.

Experiment with other magnets around your house to see what patterns they make.

Transferring Magnetism

It is possible to transfer magnetism from a magnet to another iron or steel object. When this is done, the object to which the magnetism has been transferred will behave like a magnet for a period of time.

Paper Clip Chain

◆◆◆◆◆◆◆

Magnetism can be passed by induction.

Take a strong magnet, and hold a paper clip to it. Touch a second paper clip to the first one that is hanging from the magnet. The second paper clip will be attracted to the first one because the first clip has become a magnet. Continue adding paper clips in this way to see how long of a chain you can create. Take the first paper clip off the magnet. Do the other paper clips stay joined together, or do the other paper clips immediately fall?

Magnetic Screwdriver

◆▶◆▶◆▶◆▶

You can use an electromagnet to magnetize a screwdriver.

What You'll Need
- screwdriver
- screws
- electrical wire
- ruler
- 6-volt battery with screw-down terminals

Put a screwdriver next to several screws. If the screwdriver is not magnetized, nothing will happen. Coil a 3-foot piece of electrical wire around the metal shaft of the screwdriver about 20 times; make the loops close together, and leave about 10 inches of wire loose on each side of the coil. Connect the 2 loose ends of the wire to a 6-volt battery. The electric current flowing through the wire makes the screwdriver into a magnet. In a short time, the screwdriver will have become magnetized. Remove the screwdriver from the coil, and touch it to the screws. Do the screws cling to the screwdriver now?

Checking Magnetic Poles

◆▶◆▶◆▶◆▶

Opposite poles of a magnet attract.

What You'll Need
- fine thread
- tape
- strong bar magnet
- marker
- large sewing needle
- iron nail

Tape a fine piece of thread to a doorway that is not near metal objects. Tie the loose end of the thread around the middle of a bar magnet. Let the magnet hang freely. The magnet will slowly align itself with the earth's magnetic field, and one end will point north. Mark that end of your magnet with an N.

Now hold a large sewing needle by the eye, and stroke it repeatedly with the bar magnet toward the point. Always stroke it in the same direction, and hold the magnet away from the needle when you are moving it back to the eye of the needle. After 2 dozen strokes, test your needle. If the magnetism has been successfully transferred to the needle, the needle will now attract an iron nail. Now tie a thread to the center of the needle, and suspend it from the doorway. Notice whether the eye or the point of the needle points north. Now approach the north end of the needle with the north end of the bar magnet. What happens?

By rubbing the needle with the magnet, you transferred the magnet's magnetic properties to the needle. Once magnetized, the needle behaved the same way any other magnet would.

Hot Needles

◆▸▸▸▸▸◆

A magnetized needle will quickly lose its magnetism if the needle is heated.

Caution: This project requires adult supervision.

Magnetize a needle by stroking it in the same direction along a bar magnet about 2 dozen times. Hold the magnet away from the needle when you are moving it back to the eye of the needle. Test the needle with a paper clip to make sure it is magnetized. Put a candle securely in a candle-holder, and light it. Using tongs, hold the needle in the flame of the candle for a few seconds. Take the needle out of the flame. Still holding the needle with the tongs, use the paper clip to test the needle to see if it's still magnetized. If the needle is still magnetic, put it back into the flame for a few more seconds, and test it again.

What happened? The heat energy from the candle caused the molecules in the needle to move around in a way that disrupted the needle's magnetic field.

Timely Magnetism

◆▸▸▸▸▸◆

You can magnetize a needle, but the magnetism will eventually leave the needle.

Take a steel needle, and stroke it 2 dozen times, in the same direction each time, along a bar magnet. Each time, hold the needle away from the magnet as you move it in position to the top of the needle to stroke it again. Determine whether or not the needle is magnetized by seeing if it attracts a paper clip. If it is not magnetized, stroke it against the bar magnet until it is.

Once you've shown that your needle is magnetized, write down the time and date. Check the needle several times throughout the day to see if it is still magnetized. Each time, write down the time and whether or not the needle is still magnetized. Continue to check your needle a couple of times a day until it is no longer magnetized; write down the time and results each time you check your magnet. How long did it take for the needle to lose its magnetism?

Mighty Magnet

Some magnets are stronger than others.

What You'll Need
- thread
- ruler
- scissors
- 2 needles
- 2 bar magnets
- tape
- 2 paper clips

With a friend, thread each of 2 needles with a 3-foot piece of thread. Tie a knot in the end of each thread so the knot will stay in the needle's eye. Magnetize both needles at the same time by stroking each one against a strong bar magnet repeatedly in the same direction. Tape the thread from both needles to a doorway so that the needles dangle down about a foot apart. Touch a paper clip to each needle so that it is suspended in the doorway.

Now wait to see which magnet lasts longer. How long does each needle remain magnetized? Which paper clip fell first, and which remained hanging from its magnet? How much longer did the remaining paper clip stay attached to its magnet?

Surface Tension

Surface tension is a property of liquids that causes the surface to behave something like an elastic skin. The molecules in the surface layer are strongly attracted by the molecules of liquid in the layer underneath, but they are not attracted by the molecules of air above them. This makes the molecules of the liquid stick together to some degree.

Break the Tension

The force of surface tension can be overcome.

What You'll Need
- bowl
- water
- paper clip
- fork
- bar of soap

Fill a small bowl halfway with water. Using a fork, gently lower a paper clip on top of the water. Pull the fork away carefully, and the paper clip will float. Look closely at the water around the paper clip. You may be able to see that the top of the water looks stretched. Very gently touch the top of the water with a bar of soap. The paper clip will sink.

The soap interferes with the attraction that the water molecules have for each other. By disrupting the attraction, the soap breaks the surface tension that was supporting the paper clip.

Wet Needle

Water has surface tension that can support objects.

Fill a bowl halfway with water. Drop a needle point-end first into the water, and watch as the needle sinks. Try setting the needle gently on the water lengthwise, and watch what happens. The needle will still sink.

Now take a piece of tissue paper about 3 inches square. Lay the needle on the piece of tissue paper, and gently set the tissue on the surface of the water in the bowl. The tissue with the needle on it will float and support the needle. When the tissue gets soaked with water, it will sink. But the needle will remain floating. Look at the needle through a magnifying glass. Can you see little dents around the needle in the water? It almost looks as if the surface of the water has a "skin."

What You'll Need
- bowl
- water
- needle
- ruler
- tissue paper
- magnifying glass

The molecules of water at the surface were attracted to each other by surface tension. The force of the surface tension was greater than the force of gravity on the needle, so the water held the needle.

It's a Tense Situation

◆◆◆◆◆◆◆

How high can you fill a glass with water? This experiment will demonstrate the power of surface tension.

Fill a glass to the very top with water. Then use an eyedropper to add water, very gently, one drop at a time. You'll see that

you can add drops until the water level is actually above the rim of the glass! How is this possible?

What You'll Need
- glass
- water
- eyedropper

Here's the explanation: The water molecules are attracted to one another but not to air molecules. So, as long as they possibly can, the water molecules will stick together in the glass rather than fall over the edge of the glass. This tendency of water molecules to stick together is called "surface tension." Surface tension gives water the appearance of having a "skin" across the top of the glass. This is also why small droplets of water stay in a round shape rather than spreading out in all directions.

Absorb or Repel?

◆◆◆◆◆◆◆

Some materials absorb and some materials repel water.

What You'll Need
- paper and pen
- various household items
- water
- eyedropper
- magnifying glass

Label a sheet of paper "ABSORBS WATER." Label a second sheet of paper "REPELS WATER." Then find various objects around your house, such as pieces of cloth, a cotton ball, waxed paper, aluminum foil, newspaper, a magazine page, or a coffee filter. Predict whether the objects will absorb or repel water, and write your predictions down on the appropriate sheet of paper.

Set the objects on a table. Use an eyedropper to drop a few drops of water on each object. Use a magnifying glass to look closely at the water on each object to study how it interacts with the object's surface. Were you right or wrong on most of your predictions?

The looseness or firmness of an object's surface is called its *porousness,* and it plays an important role in how water acts on the object's surface. The ability of a substance to attract or repel water molecules also plays a role. Things that soak up water are said to absorb water. If water beads on a surface, that object is said to repel water.

Power Boat

Create a powerboat that cuts through surface tension.

What You'll Need
- foil
- scissors
- tub
- water
- toothpick
- dishwashing liquid

Following the shape of the diagram below, cut a small, flat boat out of foil. Place the boat carefully in a tub of water so that it floats gently. Use a toothpick to drop one drop of dishwashing liquid on the small nick at the back of the boat. This soap acts like a motor. Observe what happens.

The soap breaks the surface tension of the water in the back of the boat, and the boat is pulled forward. The boat stops when the soap has spread throughout the surface of the water.

Come and Go Magic Toothpicks

Use science to create a magic trick. Toothpicks come to your magic wand and then move away.

Moisten one end of a "magic" wand (a wooden dowel or chopstick), and dip it into sugar to coat it. Rub the other end of the wand across a bar of soap.

Float 2 toothpicks in a tub of water. Say "come to me toothpicks," and stick the sugared end of the wand in the water very close to the toothpicks. The toothpicks move toward the wand. Say, "go away now" and stick the soapy end of the wand between the toothpicks. The toothpicks now move away.

What You'll Need
- wooden dowel or chopstick
- sugar
- bar of soap
- toothpicks
- tub
- water

When you stick the sugar end of the wand into the water, the sugar dissolves in the water and pulls the water toward it, making the toothpicks come closer. When you stick the soapy end into the water, the soap spreads through the top of the water, breaking the surface tension of the water. The tension on the other side of the toothpicks pulls them away from the wand.

Bubbles, Bubbles Everywhere

◆─◆─◆─◆─◆─◆

Bubbles get their shape from surface tension.

Add ½ cup dishwashing liquid and 2 teaspoons glycerin to ½ gallon water in a large container. Mix the materials together, and let them sit overnight. The next day, pour the mixture into a plastic dishpan out in your backyard. Shape chenille stems into circles of different sizes. Cut a circle of

plastic from a soda pop ring, and staple it to a craft stick. Dip these devices into the bubble solution, and gently blow through the circles to make bubbles. Circles of different sizes will make bubbles of different sizes.

What You'll Need
- dishwashing liquid
- measuring cup and spoon
- glycerin
- water
- large container
- dishpan
- chenille stems
- plastic soda pop ring
- scissors
- stapler
- wooden craft sticks

How to Skip a Rock

◆─◆─◆─◆─◆─◆

Once you get the hang of it, learn the physics of rock-skipping.

What You'll Need
- flat rocks

If you've ever wondered how to skip rocks across a surface, here's your chance to learn. First, find a calm body of water. Then, find some flat rocks. The perfect stone for skipping has rounded edges, is flat on both sides, and fits in the palm of your hand. It can be bigger if it's not too heavy or smaller if it's not too light.

For best results, throw sidearm so that the flat side skips across the water as it spins. If you throw just right, the rock should bounce across the surface of the water. To understand how rock-skipping works, picture yourself at a swimming pool ready to dive into the water. If you dive just right, your arms and head cut into the water and your body slips through the surface. Now drop a stone edge-first into the water. Like a diver, the rock cuts through the surface instead of bouncing.

Cutting Water

You can split a water drop into smaller drops, and you can put small water drops together.

What You'll Need

- glass
- water
- food coloring
- spoon
- eyedropper
- waxed paper
- toothpick
- drinking straw

Put a drop of food coloring into a glass of water; stir until all of the water is evenly colored. Using an eyedropper, gently put several drops of the colored water onto a sheet of waxed paper. Look at the circular shape of the drops.

With a toothpick, try to cut a water drop in half. Can you do it? With a drinking straw, blow gently to try to put 2 water drops together. Can you do it?

The surface tension of water pulls the water molecules in a drop toward each other; the

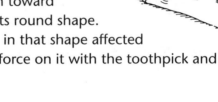

molecules in the outer layer are drawn in toward the center of the drop, giving the drop its round shape. The surface tension that holds the water in that shape affected how the water acted when you exerted force on it with the toothpick and the straw.

Flat Drops

Overpower surface tension to change a water drop's shape.

What You'll Need

- glass
- water
- straw
- vinyl tablecloth
- magnifying glass
- toothpick
- dishwashing liquid

Fill a glass with water. Suck some of the water up in a straw, and quickly put your finger over the end of the straw to hold in the water. Gently release some water from the straw onto a vinyl tablecloth so that it forms several drops. Using a magnifying glass, look at the circular shape of the water drops. Now dip the end of a toothpick into some dishwashing liquid. Gently touch the tip of the toothpick to some of the water drops, and observe how the shape of the water drops changes.

The surface tension of water pulls water molecules in a drop toward each other; the molecules in the outer layer are drawn in toward the center of the drop, giving the drop its round shape. The dishwashing liquid interfered with the attraction that the water molecules had for each other and changed the shape of the drops.

ENERGIZE ME

◆━◆━◆━◆

Anytime anything changes in the physical world, energy is involved. A moving car, a glowing lightbulb, and boiling water all depend on energy. Energy is the ability to do work or to make something change. Heat, electricity, and chemical energy are different forms of energy. Even though we use energy, we can never make or destroy any of it. We can only convert it from one form to another. In this chapter, you will explore types of energy around you and see how energy is converted from one form into another.

Forms of Energy

◆━◆━◆━◆

Scientists think of energy in 2 basic ways. Potential energy is energy that is stored, or not being used. Kinetic energy is energy that causes motion. Potential energy can change into kinetic energy, and kinetic energy can change into potential energy. For example, a ball held above the ground has potential energy. If the ball is dropped, the potential energy is converted into kinetic energy.

In the Swing of Things

In a pendulum, energy is repeatedly changed back and forth
from kinetic energy to potential energy.

Caution: Be certain the swinging pendulum will not strike a
person or a fragile object.

Tie a weight, such as a bolt, a key, or a rock, to the end of a
string. Tie the other end of the string to a railing or tape it to a
table so that the string and weight can freely swing. Keeping
the string taut, pull back the weight. While you are holding
the weight, it has no kinetic energy because it is not moving. All of its energy is potential
energy. Release the weight, and watch it swing. As it swings downward, the potential

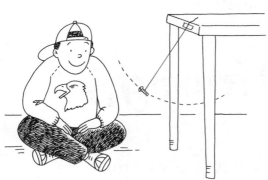

energy is converted into kinetic energy. When it
reaches the bottom of its swing, all the energy is
kinetic energy. As the weight starts rising up, the
kinetic energy is converted into potential energy.
When it reaches the high point of its swing, all
of the kinetic energy is converted to potential
energy. As the weight starts to fall downward,
the process starts again. This conversion of
potential energy to kinetic energy and back will
continue as long as the pendulum swings.

The Twist

A rubber band can hold potential energy and convert it to kinetic energy.

Loop a rubber band around the U-shaped part of a padlock,
and lock the padlock. Hold the end of the rubber band in one
hand so the lock hangs from it, and turn the lock around
5 times with your other hand. As the rubber band twists, it
stores some of the energy you used to turn the lock as poten-
tial energy. Now release the lock. The spinning lock has energy of motion, or kinetic
energy. As it spins, it winds the rubber band in the other direction, and the rubber band
again stores potential energy, which will be released when the lock spins the other way.
Eventually the lock will stop twisting because it loses energy to friction.

The Come-Back Can

Put the principles of potential and kinetic energy to work.

Caution: This project requires adult supervision.

Use a hammer and nail to poke a hole in the center of the bottom of a coffee can. Use the nail to poke a hole in the center of the coffee-can lid. Tie a weight, such as a washer, nut, or bolt, to the middle of a rubber band. Put the rubber band through the hole in the bottom of the can, so that one loop of the rubber band sticks outside the can and the rest of the rubber band (and the weight) is inside the can. Put a dowel through the loop to hold it in place on the outside of the can. Put the other end of

<table>
<tr><td>What You'll Need</td></tr>
<tr><td>

- hammer
- nail
- coffee can with plastic lid
- rubber band
- weight
- 2 dowels
</td></tr>
</table>

the rubber band through the lid from the inside, so that a small loop of rubber band sticks out of the lid. Put the other dowel through this loop to hold it in place on top of the lid. Put the lid on the coffee can. Roll the can away from you on the floor. When it starts slowing down, yell, "Come back!" When the can stops rolling, it should reverse direction and roll back toward you. If it doesn't work, try using a different size of rubber band.

Tennis Cannon

Transferring energy from one object to another can be a blast.

<table>
<tr><td>What You'll Need</td></tr>
<tr><td>

- basketball
- tennis ball
</td></tr>
</table>

Hold a basketball in one hand and a tennis ball in the other, and drop them to the ground from the same height. Watch carefully to see how high they bounce. Did one bounce higher than the other? Now hold the basketball in one hand, and place the tennis ball on top of the basketball with your other hand. Drop them to the ground together. Watch to see how high they bounce.

The tennis ball and basketball have energy from falling. The amount of energy depends on the weight of the object. The basketball is much heavier, so it contains much more energy. When the tennis ball and basketball hit the ground, all of the energy of the falling basketball is transferred to the tennis ball, and it launches the tennis ball like a cannon.

Slingshot Science

A slingshot converts potential energy into kinetic energy.

Caution: This project requires adult supervision. Never use your slingshot to shoot at anyone or anything.

Hammer 2 nails about 3 inches apart into a piece of wood. Loop a thick rubber band from one nail to the other. Find a place where you can safely fling plastic caps without hitting anyone or anything. Place a plastic cap in the center of the rubber band, and pull back on the rubber band. Release the rubber band, and watch as the rubber band flings the cap. The energy you used to pull the rubber band back was stored as potential energy while you held the rubber band in place. When you released it, the potential energy was converted into the kinetic energy of the moving plastic cap.

What You'll Need
- hammer
- nails
- ruler
- block of wood
- thick rubber band
- small plastic caps

Wheel Fun

Raised water has potential energy and releases it as kinetic energy when it falls.

What You'll Need
- 2 thin wires
- cork
- 14 paper clips
- running water

Place one thin wire in each end of a cork. Straighten the first curve in each of the paper clips. Insert the ends of 12 paper clips into the middle of the cork at even intervals around its diameter. Arrange the paper clips so all of the loops are in line with one another. You now have a waterwheel. Pick up the waterwheel with the 2 remaining paper clips by slipping the loop of one paper clip over the wire in each end of the cork. Turn on a faucet, and hold the waterwheel under the running water so that the water strikes the paper clips.

The water in the faucet has potential energy. When it falls, that energy is converted to kinetic energy. Your waterwheel captured some of that energy and used it to spin around. Large waterwheels have been used for centuries to grind wheat and corn. Today, water turbines use the same principle to generate electricity.

Waterwheel Challenge

◆▸◆▸◆▸◆

You can design your own waterwheel to convert the potential energy of water into kinetic energy.

This is the Waterwheel Challenge! After reading and doing the activity Wheel Fun (see page 158), you are ready for this challenge. Design and construct your own waterwheel that will spin when placed under water. Build several waterwheels, using different materials or altering your design slightly to see which one works best.

Car Talk

◆▸◆▸◆▸◆

Moving cars get their kinetic energy from the stored chemical energy in gasoline. The design of the car influences how far it can go with the same amount of energy.

A moving car has kinetic energy—the energy of motion. This energy comes from the stored energy in gasoline. Have an adult take you to a new-car dealership. Each car has a sticker in the window that tells the number of miles the car can go with one gallon of gas; this is called *gas mileage*. Each car has a different number for driving on highways and for driving in cities. Compare cars that can go a long distance on one gallon of gasoline with cars that can go shorter distances. What differences can you see between the cars? Talk with the adult who brought you about why certain cars have higher or lower mileage numbers.

Energy Conductors

Conductors allow energy to flow through them easily. Insulators make it difficult for energy to flow through them. We use conductors to transfer energy from one place to another. We use insulators to keep food hot and to make electrical wires safe to handle.

I'm Melting

Different materials conduct heat at different rates.

Gather several flat surfaces made from different materials, such as a ceramic plate, plastic plate, steel pot, or wooden bowl. Take several ice cubes that are about the same size, and put one on each surface. Let them sit undisturbed, and watch as the ice melts. Write down the surfaces in the order that their ice cubes melted.

Ice needs heat to melt. Some heat will come from the surface it is on. Ice will melt faster on a surface that is a good conductor of heat and slower on a surface that is not a good conductor.

What You'll Need
- different flat materials
- ice cubes
- pen and paper

Heat Sheet

Different materials conduct heat at different rates.

What You'll Need
- paper
- scissors
- ruler
- aluminum foil
- 2 thermometers
- pen and paper

Cut a strip of paper about 8 inches long and 2 inches wide. Cut a strip of aluminum foil the same size. Wrap about 1 inch of the paper around the bulb of a thermometer. Wrap about 1 inch of the aluminum foil around the bulb of another thermometer. Find a windowsill that has an area in the shade and an area in the sun. Put the 2 thermometers on the windowsill so that the thermometers are completely in the shade but the ends of the paper and aluminum foil are in the sun. Record the starting temperatures for both thermometers. Then record the temperatures every few minutes.

The thermometer with the foil heated to a higher temperature because the aluminum is a better conductor of heat. Energy from the sunlight heated the aluminum foil and paper. Aluminum is a good conductor of heat, so it transferred much of the heat to the thermometer. Paper is a poor conductor of heat, so it transferred little of the heat to the thermometer.

Hot Mugs

◆▶◆▶◆▶◆

Insulators can be used to keep things warm or to keep things cool.

What You'll Need
- mugs made of different materials
- water
- measuring cup
- thermometer
- paper and pen
- clock

Gather a variety of mugs made from different materials, such as ceramic, glass, or plastic. It is best if the mugs are all about the same size. Using a measuring cup, carefully fill each mug with the same amount of hot water. Take the temperature of each mug every 3 minutes with a thermometer. Make a chart to record all the temperatures. Take a total of 7 readings on each mug. Which material makes the best insulator?

Conductors

◆▶◆▶◆▶◆

Some materials allow electricity to flow through them and some do not.

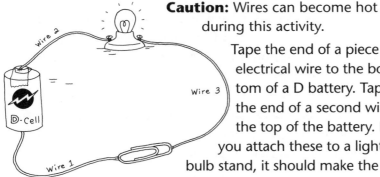

Caution: Wires can become hot during this activity.

Tape the end of a piece of electrical wire to the bottom of a D battery. Tape the end of a second wire to the top of the battery. If you attach these to a lightbulb stand, it should make the lightbulb light. (If you have a lightbulb with no stand, hold one wire at the bottom of the bulb, and hold the other wire on the side to light the bulb.)

What You'll Need
- electrical wire
- D battery
- tape
- 1.5-volt lightbulb and stand
- pencil
- household objects

Disconnect the first wire from the lightbulb, and connect a third wire to the bulb in its place. Wire 1 will have one end connected to the battery and the other end free. Wire 2 will have one end connected to the battery and the other end connected to the bulb. Wire 3 will have one end connected to the bulb and the other end free.

Touch the end of wire 1 to the end of wire 3; the lightbulb should light. These 2 wires are the probes. Touch the ends of the probes to a pencil, making sure the probes don't touch each other. If the pencil is an electrical conductor, the electricity from the battery will flow through it and light the bulb. If the pencil is an electrical insulator, the bulb will not light. Test other household objects (such as a paper clip, fabric, key, spoon, etc.) to see if they are insulators or conductors.

Baked Ice Cream

◆◆◆◆◆◆

Have you ever seen a restaurant serve baked ice cream? In this activity, you'll find out how to cook and enjoy baked ice cream.

Caution: This project requires adult supervision.

How can you *bake* ice cream? Well, if you insulate the ice cream well enough, it can withstand the heat of the oven. An insulator is a weak conductor of heat energy. In this activity, you'll see an insulator in action. You'll end up with a tasty treat, too!

A mixture of egg whites will form our insulating top. Beat 2 egg whites in a bowl with an electric mixer. Add 1 tablespoon of sugar for each egg white. Beat the mixture until it forms peaks like a mountain. Don't overbeat, or it will become too runny. You'll need to repeat this process for each cookie you want to make.

What You'll Need
- egg whites
- bowl
- electric mixer
- measuring spoon
- sugar
- oven
- cookie sheet
- ice cream
- cookies
- spoon

Preheat oven to 450°F. Put your cookies on a cookie sheet. Place one firm scoop of ice cream onto each cookie. Top the ice cream and the cookie with the whipped egg whites. Bake the ice cream for 3 to 5 minutes. Remove the cookie sheet from the oven when the egg whites get brown.

You'll notice that the cookie got warm, but most of the ice cream remained frozen. That's because the egg whites and cookie form a layer of insulation that prevents the heat from penetrating to the ice cream. Be sure to let the "insulation" cool before enjoying your delicious creation!

Friction

When surfaces rub against each other, they create friction. The molecules from the 2 surfaces catch on each other as they pass back and forth. Getting the molecules to move past each other uses up energy, so friction slows things down. It also makes the molecules vibrate, which generates heat.

Shaken, Not Stirred

◆◆◆◆◆◆

Friction is what heats up this experiment.

Fill a coffee can halfway with sand. Measure the temperature of the sand, and write it down. Remove the thermometer, place the lid securely on the can, and shake the can rapidly for a few minutes. Measure the temperature of the sand, and write it down again. Repeat the test one more time.

The energy you used to shake the can made the sand particles rub against each other and against the side of the can. This created friction, and the friction produced heat.

Rough Stuff

◆◆◆◆◆◆

Sandpaper rubbed on wood produces friction and heat.

Feel a piece of wood to roughly determine its temperature. Now rub it with some sandpaper. Do this vigorously for about a minute. Now feel the wood. It is very warm. Sandpaper creates a great deal of friction when it is rubbed on wood. In addition to sanding the wood to make it smoother, the friction creates heat.

Hot Hands

◆◆◆◆◆◆

Friction produces heat.

Rub your hands together. Do this quickly, and feel the heat produced. When your hands rub against each other, they produce friction. This friction produces heat.

Give Me a Break

◆▷◆▷◆▷◆

Friction uses up the energy of a moving object.

When you squeeze the hand brake of a bike, you cause 2 pieces of rubber to pinch the rim of the tire. When the tire is moving, the contact between the rubber and the moving rim produces friction. This friction uses some of the kinetic energy

What You'll Need
● bicycle with hand brakes

of the tires to make the molecules in the 2 surfaces move past each other, and it uses the rest of the kinetic energy in the tires to produce heat. Before you get on your bike, feel the rubber of the rear brake pads to roughly determine their temperature. Get on your bicycle, and pedal to build speed. Now put the rear brakes on so the bicycle comes to a slow stop. Get off your bike, and feel the rear brake pads. They will be warm, or even hot, from the heat produced by the friction. Disc brakes on a car stop the car using the same principle.

Balloon Hovercraft

◆▷◆▷◆▷◆

Air can be used as a lubricant to reduce friction between objects.

What You'll Need
● plastic soda bottle
● knife
● nail or other sturdy pointed object
● balloon

Caution: This project requires adult supervision.

Carefully cut off the top of a large plastic soda bottle about 2 inches from the top of the bottle (you may need an adult's help with this). Cut evenly so the bottle top will sit flat. Poke a small hole in the bottle cap with a nail. Screw the cap back on the bottle top, and set the bottle top on a flat surface. Gently push the bottle top to see how far it will slide over the table top. Blow up a balloon. Pinch the neck of the balloon to keep the air from escaping, and stretch the opening of the balloon securely over the bottle cap. Let go of the balloon, and watch as the bottle top rises above the table. Gently push the bottle top, and it will glide easily over the surface of the table.

As the air escaped from the balloon through the opening in the cap, it pushed down against the table and lifted the bottle top. The bottle was no longer touching the table, so there was less friction for the bottle top to overcome and it could move farther.

Hot Wired

◆▸▸▸▸▸◆

Friction can be produced by moving a single substance.

What You'll Need
- thick wire

Take a piece of thick wire, such as a coat hanger, and feel it to roughly determine its temperature. Bend the wire back and forth in the same spot 8 or 10 times. (Don't bend it too many times, or it may break and have sharp points on the ends.) Now feel the spot you were bending. The wire has become warm in this area.

The bending caused friction between the molecules in that area of the wire. The friction produced heat energy, which you felt when you touched the wire.

Slide Friction

◆▸▸▸▸▸◆

Learn about the force of friction and how it is reduced.

What You'll Need
- playground slide
- items to be tested (toys with wheels, wooden blocks, rocks)
- stopwatch
- partner
- waxed paper
- water

Friction is a force that stops motion. If there were no friction in the world, anything that starts moving in one direction would never stop. If you slide a wooden block across a floor, friction between the block and the floor makes the block stop. In this activity, you'll find out how friction affects an object and how friction can be reduced. Lay out your items to be tested and decide which ones will go down the slide the fastest. Test each item one at a time. With your stopwatch ready, have your partner hold one item at the top of the slide and release it on your signal. See how long it takes for the item to reach the bottom. Which objects go the fastest? What qualities made them move faster than others?

Now, take one of the objects and rub the bottom of it with waxed paper. See how long it takes for it to reach the bottom of the slide. Try setting it on a square of waxed paper and see if that reduces friction. Wet the slide and see what effect water has. Will the items move faster or slower? Does the amount of water matter?

Static Electricity

Static electricity occurs when a charge builds up in an object. Objects become charged by either losing or gaining electrons. Electrons have a negative charge, so an object becomes negatively charged if it gains electrons. If an object loses electrons, it becomes positively charged. Remember: Static electricity activities don't work well if it's too humid. If the activities don't work, try them on a drier day.

Electro-Detecto

◆▶◆▶◆▶◆▶

Make a device that detects electrical charges.

Find a bottle and a cork that will seal it. With a nail, make a small hole through the center of the cork from top to bottom. Push a 6-inch piece of heavy electrical wire through the hole. Leave about 1 inch of wire above the top of the cork.

Bend the wire coming from the bottom of the cork into a flat hook, shaped like the bottom of a coat hanger. Cut a piece of thin aluminum foil into a strip 1 inch long and ¼ inch wide.

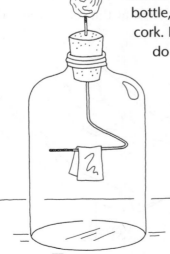

What You'll Need
- bottle
- cork
- nail
- heavy electrical wire
- ruler
- scissors
- thin foil

Fold the strip in half, and hang it on the flat hook. Put the hook and foil into the bottle, and seal the opening with the cork. Make sure the foil and the hook do not touch the sides or bottom of the bottle. Roll up another piece of aluminum foil into a tight ball about 1 inch in diameter around the wire sticking out of the cork. Make sure that the ball is smooth and tightly packed.

You have just built a functional electroscope that will tell you if any object carries a charge. If you hold an object with a charge near the foil ball, the object will draw the opposite charge through the wire from the foil strip. The 2 sides of the strip will then have the same charge and repel each other.

You Repulse Me

Once you change the charge of these balloons they won't want to be anywhere near each other.

Blow up 2 balloons. Tie each to a string about 15 inches long. Tape the strings to the edge of a table so the balloons hang

down about an inch apart from each other. Charge one balloon by rubbing it with a cloth. Then charge the other balloon in the same way. Let both balloons hang near each other, and watch what they do.

Rubbing balloons with the cloth transferred electrons to the balloons. This made both balloons negatively charged. When the balloons were brought near each other, the charge acted to push the balloons away from each other. Objects with the same charge repel each other.

What You'll Need
- 2 balloons
- string
- scissors
- ruler
- tape
- cloth (wool, polyester, or nylon)

You Shock Me

When you charge an object, it will lose its charge through another conductor.

You have probably gotten shocks from static electricity many times. Rub your feet on carpet as you walk in a room. Touch a metal doorknob. Do this again, and touch a friend. As you rubbed your feet along the carpet, your body picked up an electrical charge. When you touched something that conducted electricity, such as a metal object or another person, the charge passed from you to the other conductor. One or both of you felt a shock, and you may have even seen a spark.

Sticky Balloons

◆◆◆◆◆◆◆

*A charged object can stick to a neutral object
by inducing an opposite charge.*

What You'll Need
- balloon
- cloth (wool, polyester, or nylon)
- clock or stopwatch
- pen and paper

Rub a cloth on a balloon, or rub a balloon on your hair. Put the balloon up against a wall, and let go. Time how long it stays on the wall. Try different cloths and different wall surfaces to see which makes the balloon stick the longest. Make sure you rub it the same number of times for each test to make the comparisons fair.

The balloon rubbed with the cloth became

negatively charged. When brought near the wall, the negatively charged balloon repelled electrons in the surface of the wall, and created a positive charge on the surface of the wall. Opposite charges attract, so the negative balloon stuck to the positive wall surface. But as the balloon lost charge to the air and wall, the attraction decreased, and eventually the balloon fell.

Trickle Down Activity

◆◆◆◆◆◆◆

A charged object can curve the path of water trickling from a faucet.

What You'll Need
- balloon or comb
- cloth (wool, polyester, or nylon)
- faucet

Charge a balloon or comb by rubbing it with a cloth. Turn a faucet on so the water falls in a slow, gentle stream. Place the balloon or comb near the falling water, and watch how the water acts.

By rubbing the balloon or comb, you caused it to have a charge of static electricity. The negative charge of the object acted to repel the negative charge that the moving water had, causing the water to change its path.

Detecting Charged Objects

◆◆◆◆◆◆◆

An electroscope can detect the amount of charge an object contains.

What You'll Need
- balloon or comb
- cloth (wool, polyester, or nylon)
- electroscope (see Electro-Detecto on page 166)

Turn a balloon or comb into a charged object by rubbing it with a cloth. Bring the charged object near (but don't touch) the foil ball at the top of the electroscope. Watch the foil leaves swing apart. Rub the balloon or comb with the cloth again for a longer time to increase the charge. Hold the charged object near the foil ball of the electroscope again, and observe the leaves of the foil strip. Do they move even farther this time?

Charging by Conduction

◆◆◆◆◆◆◆

Place a charge on an electoscope by touching it with a charged object.

Turn a balloon or plastic comb into a charged object by rubbing it with a cloth. Then rub the charged object on top of the electroscope. Repeat this several times until the electroscope's foil leaves swing apart. Placing a charge on the electroscope by touching it with a charged object is called charging by conduction. As you add more charge, the leaves swing farther apart. The leaves of the electroscope stay apart as long as they have a charge. Touch the top of the electroscope with your finger. Instantly, the leaves of the electroscope fall together.

What You'll Need
- balloon or comb
- cloth (wool, polyester, or nylon)
- electroscope (see Electro-Detecto on page 166)

When you rub the charged object on the electroscope, the negative charge on the object is transferred to the ball of the electroscope. These negative charges are conducted to the leaves of the electroscope. When the charge buildup is sufficient, the leaves will push away from each other. The more charge you add, the more they push away. When you touch the electroscope with your finger, you give a path for the electrons to leave the electroscope. When the leaves of the electroscope lose their charge, they will stop repelling each other.

Charging by Induction

◆◇◆◇◆◇◆

You'll get a charge out of this one!

Turn a balloon or plastic comb into a charged object by rubbing it with a cloth. Bring the charged object near (but do not touch) the ball of the electroscope. When the foil leaves push apart, keep the balloon or comb near, and touch the ball of the electroscope with your finger. The leaves collapse. Remove your finger, and remove the balloon or comb. Notice the leaves now repel each other. They have been charged by induction. Now bring a charged balloon or comb near the electroscope. The leaves repel each other with less force; they move closer together.

Holding the negatively charged object near the top of the electroscope pushed electrons from the top of the electroscope, and some went to the bottom. When you touched the top, some of the electrons left the electroscope and entered your body. When you removed your finger and the charged object, the electroscope became positively charged. Bringing a negatively charged object near the top of the electroscope then caused the leaves to fall. This is because electrons are pushed into the leaves, reducing the positive charge. If you touch the electroscope with a wire or your finger, it will lose its charge.

Charge Me Up!

Electrons have a negative charge and form layers (or shells) around the nucleus of an atom. Objects become charged because they gain or lose electrons. A positively charged object lost electrons, and a negatively charged object gained electrons.

Snake Charmer

◆◆◆◆◆◆

A charged object can stick to a neutral object by inducing an opposite charge.

Tape one end of a 5-inch piece of string to a table top. Charge a balloon by rubbing it with a cloth. Bring the balloon near the untaped end of string to make the string rise off the table. Move the balloon back and forth to make the string sway.
The balloon rubbed with the cloth became negatively charged. When brought near the string, it repelled the electrons at the surface of the string. The surface of the string became positively charged and was attracted to the balloon. You can see that the energy of static electricity can be used to do work, such as lifting up the string. Do you think you could charge the balloon enough so that it would lift up the table? Why not?

What You'll Need
- string
- scissors
- ruler
- tape
- balloon
- cloth (wool, polyester, or nylon)

Static Cling Jacks

◆◆◆◆◆◆

Have fun with static electricity in this "charged" game.

What You'll Need
- paper
- plastic comb
- cloth (wool, polyester, or nylon)

Tear a sheet of thin paper into small pieces. Rub a comb with a cloth to give it a charge. Hold the comb near the pieces of paper, and watch as they cling to the comb. Play a version of the game jacks called Static Cling Jacks with a friend or by yourself. Put the pieces of paper in a pile. Rub the comb a little so that it picks up a single piece of paper. Rub the comb a little more so it picks up exactly 2 pieces of paper. Then try for 3. Keep going until you pick up more or less than the correct number. At this point, you lose your turn and the next player goes. When it is your turn, you start with 1 piece of paper again. Can you work your way up to 8 pieces of paper?

No Shock

◆▷◆▷◆▷◆▷

Can you take the shock out of a shock?

Rub your feet on carpet to build up a static charge, then touch a metal doorknob. You will get a shock as a spark jumps from your finger to the doorknob.

Now try the same activity again, but this time hold a paper clip in your hand. Don't let your fingers touch the doorknob; let the paper clip approach it instead. Were you shocked?

The paper clip conducted electricity, so even though a spark was produced you did not feel a shock. The electricity still flowed through your body, but your fingers were away from the spark and it did not affect you.

Current Electricity

◆▷◆▷◆▷◆▷

Current electricity is the flow of electrons. To make a current of electricity, the electrons need to flow in a complete, unbroken circle. The path for electricity is called a circuit. If the circuit is not complete, the electrons will not be able to flow. Moving electrons contain energy, and this energy can be used in many ways. Remember that electricity is a powerful force, and it can be dangerous. The projects in this section use small amounts of electricity generated by batteries. Never experiment with the electricity that flows through the outlets in your house; it is much more powerful and can cause serious injury.

Power Meters

◆▸◆▸◆▸◆▸◆

*Learn to read the electrical power meter for your home,
then help your family save electricity!*

What You'll Need
● paper and pen

With an adult, find the electrical power meter for your home. It contains 4 dials in a row. Read the number each dial is pointing to, and write them all down in order from left to right; if the pointer is between 2 numbers, choose the lower number. This gives you a 4-digit number of kilowatt hours of electricity. Read your home's meter at the start of the week. Then read it at the end of the week. Subtract the first number from the second number. The difference is the amount of electricity used in your home between the 2 meter readings.

Think of ways to save electricity, such as turning off lights and appliances when you're not using them. Use these approaches during the next week, and then check the meter again to see if you and your family used less electricity the second week than you did the first week.

Light On

◆▸◆▸◆▸◆▸◆

Electricity doesn't do much good unless it has a complete circuit.

Caution: Wires can become hot during this activity.

Do you think you can create a complete electrical circuit using just a lightbulb, a wire, and a D battery? To make a complete circuit, you have to create a path that allows electrons to flow from the battery to the lightbulb and back

What You'll Need
● 1.5-volt flashlight bulb
● electrical wire
● D battery
● tape

to the battery. If you do that, electrical current will flow through your circuit and cause the lightbulb to light. The solution to this problem is to tape a wire to the bottom of the battery, hold the lightbulb on top of the battery, and then attach the wire to the side of the lightbulb. This combination gives a complete circuit for the electricity to flow.

Light On Brighter

◆━◆━◆━◆━◆▶

You can make a complete circuit with 2 batteries.

What You'll Need
- 1.5-volt flashlight bulb
- electrical wire
- two D batteries
- tape

Caution: Wires can become hot during this activity.

This is a new challenge. Do you think you can create a complete electrical circuit using just a lightbulb, a wire, and two D batteries? Remember, you still have to make a complete path for the electrons to flow from the batteries to the lightbulb and back to the batteries. The solution to this problem is to stack the batteries on top of each other, with the bottom of one battery on the top of the other. Then tape a wire to the bottom of the bottom battery, hold the lightbulb on top of the top battery, and attach the wire to the side of the lightbulb. How does the brightness of this bulb compare to when only one battery was used?

Battery Tester

◆━◆━◆━◆━◆▶

A battery tester can be made with wire and a flashlight bulb.

Caution: Wires can become hot during this activity. Do not test large batteries such as those used for cars.

Twist a small loop in the center of a 5-inch piece of stiff electrical wire; this loop will be used as a handle for your tester. If you are using very thick wire, you can use pliers to help twist the loop. Wrap the top end of the wire around the metal bottom of a 1.5-volt lightbulb. Curl the other end up and around so it points toward the bottom of the lightbulb. Leave a little less space between the wire end and the bulb than a battery would occupy.

What You'll Need
- electrical wire
- ruler
- pliers
- 1.5-volt flashlight bulb
- batteries

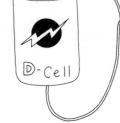

D-Cell

To use your battery tester, slide a battery into the tester so the top of the battery makes contact with the bottom of the bulb and the bottom of the battery makes contact with the free end of the wire. Use a new battery to make sure your tester is working. If it doesn't work, check the connections. When it does work, start testing the D batteries around your home. If batteries do not light the bulb, they have lost their power. Some batteries may be weak and will only dimly light the bulb.

Light Is Right!

◆▶◆▶◆▶◆▶

Complete electrical circuits are the key to succeeding at this game.

What You'll Need
- cardboard
- brads
- marker
- electrical wire
- 1.5-volt flashlight bulb
- 9-volt battery
- tape

Caution: Wires can become hot during this activity.

In this project, you'll create a quiz card. Think of pairs of items that can be matched. They can be states and their capitals, sports teams and their cities, chemical names and their formulas, or anything else you can think of. Push 6 brads into a piece of cardboard in 2 vertical rows of 3 each. If you chose states and capitals, make the left row represent the states and the right row represent the capitals. Write the names of the states and capitals on the cardboard next to the brads.

On the back of the cardboard, connect an electrical wire to each brad that represents a state; connect the other end of each wire to the brad that represents that state's capital. Tape a 1.5-volt lightbulb to the back of the cardboard so it sticks above the top, and tape a 9-volt battery to the cardboard just below the bulb. Connect a wire from one terminal of the battery to the bottom of the bulb, and tape it in place. Connect another wire to the side of the base of the bulb. This wire should be long enough so that the other end can reach the front of the cardboard and touch any of the brads on the left; it will be one probe. Connect a wire to the other terminal of the battery. This wire should be long enough so that the other end can reach the front of the cardboard and touch any of the brads on the right; it will be the other probe. Cover the back of the quiz board with another sheet of cardboard.

Now touch the probe for the left side to any of the brads on the left. Choose the matching answer, and touch that brad with the other probe. The light should light. Positive reinforcement for a correct answer!

Design your own more complex quiz cards. Have more than 3 questions. Have some answers match with more than one correct item. For a real challenge, try to make a board that has a buzzer that goes off if you select the wrong answer, as well as a light that goes on for the correct answer.

Switch It

◆◆◆◆◆◆◆

A switch can be used to open and close a circuit.

What You'll Need

- 1.5-volt flashlight lightbulb
- socket for bulb
- electrical wire
- D battery
- tape
- aluminum foil
- scissors
- ruler

Caution: Wires can become hot during this activity.

Screw a 1.5-volt lightbulb into a socket, and connect a wire to each of the screws of the socket. Tape one wire to the bottom of a D battery. Tape the other wire to the top of the battery. The bulb should light. Remove the wire from the bottom of the battery.

Now make a switch. Cut a strip of aluminum foil about 2 inches long and 1 inch wide. Fold it in half lengthwise, and then fold it over about ⅓ of the way from the end. Tape the shorter end of the strip to the tabletop. Cut another strip of aluminum foil about 1 inch long and 1 inch wide, and fold it in half lengthwise. Tape this strip to the tabletop so that when the longer strip is held flat on the table, they make contact with each other. Take the wire that had been on the bottom of the battery, and slide the free end under one of the pieces of aluminum foil; tape it in place. Slide the end of a third wire under the other piece of aluminum foil, tape it in place, and tape the other end to the bottom of the battery. You have just made a complete circuit with a switch.

Push down the folded piece of aluminum foil so it touches the other piece of aluminum foil. The bulb will light up. When the foil pieces are touching, the electrons have a complete path to flow from the battery to the bulb and back. When the foil pieces are not touching, the electrons do not have a complete path, and the bulb will not light.

Magnetism

When electrons flow through a wire, they create magnetic fields. The discovery that moving electrons create magnetic fields was the first step in developing electric motors. It also led to the creation of the generator, which we use to produce electrical power.

Electromagnetic Moments

◆▸◆▸◆▸◆▸◆

A solenoid can be made more powerful by putting a metal object in its center.

What You'll Need
- electrical wire
- D battery
- paper clips
- iron nail

Caution: Wires can become hot during this activity.

Coil a length of electrical wire so that it looks like a spring. This is called a *solenoid.* Connect one end of the wire to the top of a battery, and connect the other end to the bottom of the D battery. The current flowing through the solenoid creates a magnetic field. See how many paper clips you can pick up with the solenoid. It might not work well because the magnetic field is not concentrated. Now wrap the same wire around an iron nail; make the same number of coils in the wire as you did the first time. Connect the wire to the battery. See how many paper clips the solenoid can pick up.

You were able to pick up more paper clips the second time because the nail concentrated the magnetic field.

Coiled Magnetism

◆▸◆▸◆▸◆▸◆

A coiled wire produces a stronger magnetic field than an uncoiled wire.

Caution: Wires can become hot during this activity.

Cut the cardboard tube from a roll of paper towels in half. Coil electrical wire around one half of the cardboard tube so that it looks like a spring. This is called a *solenoid.* Connect one end of the wire to the top of a D battery. Connect the other end to the bottom of the battery. Move a compass to different locations around the solenoid, and note which direction the compass needle points. On one end

What You'll Need
- paper-towel tube
- scissors
- electrical wire
- D battery
- compass

of the solenoid, the compass needle points toward the center of the tube. On the other end, it points away from the center of the tube. Take another piece of wire, and attach one end to the top of the battery and the other end to the bottom of the battery. Compare the strength of the solenoid with the strength of a single stretched-out wire. The solenoid produces a bigger magnetic field.

D-Cell

Nail Puller

❖❖❖❖❖❖

Create an electromagnet that pulls nails toward it.

Caution: This project requires adult supervision.

Create an electric solenoid by wrapping wire around the larger nail. Leave at least 6 inches of wire sticking out at the start of your coil. Try to have at least 50 coils around the nail. The more coils you have, the greater the strength of the magnetic field. Leave at least 7 inches of wire at the end of your coil. With an adult's help, strip about ½ inch of the insulation from both ends of the wire.

Tape two D cell batteries so that they are stacked up with the positive end of the bottom battery connected to the negative part of the top battery. Tape the 6-inch end of the wire to the bottom of the battery. Pull the larger nail out of the solenoid. Place the smaller nail at the opening of the solenoid with the sharp part of the nail pointing into the solenoid tube. Now briefly touch the 7-inch end of the wire to the top of the battery. What happens?

When the wires are connected to the batteries, the nail gets pulled in. When the solenoid has an electric current flow, a magnetic field is created. An opposite pole is induced into the nail, and the nail is attracted into the electromagnet.

What You'll Need
- large nail
- wire with insulation
- ruler
- wire stripper
- two D cell batteries
- tape
- slightly smaller nail

Compass Turbulence

❖❖❖❖❖❖

Electricity flowing through a wire creates a magnetic field.

What You'll Need
- compass
- electrical wire
- D battery

Caution: Wires can become hot during this activity.

Hold a compass next to a piece of electrical wire. Note that the compass points to the north. Connect one end of the wire to the top of a D battery and the other to the bottom. Hold the compass near the wire now. Does the compass still point to the north? Move the compass to different locations around the wire to see how it is affected.

The electricity flowing through the wire created a magnetic field around the wire. The magnetic field attracted the needle of the compass and caused it to change directions.

Energy from the Sun

The sun is an enormous nuclear furnace. Every second, tons of matter in the sun are converted to energy through nuclear fusion. Much of this energy is projected out into space as light and heat, and some of it reaches the earth in the form of sunlight and heat. The energy in sunlight is the source of most of the energy available to us on Earth, regardless of what form the energy takes.

Sun Patches

◆◆◆◆◆◆◆

Plants use the sun to make food.

What You'll Need
- geranium plant
- aluminum foil
- tape
- water
- pot
- stove
- tongs
- rubbing alcohol
- coffee mug
- spoon
- iodine
- measuring cup
- eyedropper

Caution: This project requires adult supervision.

Put a geranium plant in a dark area for 3 days. Then cover a couple of leaves with aluminum foil (tape the foil in place if necessary), and leave the other leaves uncovered. Put the plant in the sun for 3 days.

On the fourth day, remove 2 leaves that were not covered with foil. Heat a pot of water until it boils, and place the leaves in the pot for 2 minutes. Turn off the heat, and remove the pot from the stove. Remove the leaves from the pot with tongs.

Pour about 1 inch of rubbing alcohol into a large coffee mug. Put the mug into the pot of hot water. (NOTE: Alcohol should not be directly heated on the stove because it can burn.)

Place the leaves into the alcohol in the mug. The warm alcohol helps to remove the green chlorophyll from the leaves. Stir the solution to help the process. Remove the white leaves, and allow them to dry. Put about 10 drops of iodine into ½ cup of water to make an iodine solution. Place a drop of iodine solution on the leaves. The iodine should turn a blue-black color, indicating there is starch in the leaves.

Repeat this process with leaves that were covered with aluminum foil and did not get light. This time, the iodine will not change color because there is no starch in the leaves.

The plant's leaves use the sun's energy to create sugars, which the plant then converts into starch. When the leaves don't receive sunlight, there is no energy available to them to make food.

Sun-Baked

◆◆◆◆◆◆◆

What can the sun do to your skin?

What You'll Need
- soft leather scraps
- block of wood
- stapler
- marker
- sunscreen
- baby oil
- water

Ever wondered what too much sun can do to your skin? To get an idea, try this weird and wacky experiment using soft leather scraps. Take 4 scraps of leather and staple them to a block of wood. Use a marker to label the strips "SUNSCREEN," "BABY OIL," "WATER," and "NATURAL." Then rub a thick layer of sunscreen across the top of the sunscreen strip, baby oil over the baby oil strip, and water on the water strip. Don't put anything on the natural strip.

On a very hot summer day, take the strips of leather outside and let them bake in the sun. The next hot, sunny day, reapply the sunscreen, baby oil, and water and repeat the process. Keep doing this every hot, sunny day. At the end of the summer, closely examine how the strips of leather held up. Now imagine that the leather is your own skin.

Sun Power

◆◆◆◆◆◆◆

The sun is a source of energy.

Think about the different sources of energy you see or use everyday. Electrical energy in your home is generated by power plants that may use water, wind, or coal to generate electricity. Your family car uses gasoline, which is a fossil fuel that contains chemical energy. Your body takes the chemical energy from the foods you eat and uses it throughout the day in many ways.

Do some research into each of these types of energy. Find out where it comes from. Where does the energy in the food you eat come from? What are fossil fuels made from, and where do they get the chemical energy they contain? How do power plants use moving wind and water to make electricity, and where does the energy that makes the wind and water move come from? You may be surprised to learn that the sun is involved in every one of these processes.

Warm Planet, Cold Planet

◆◆◆◆◆◆

A covering that allows light to enter but slows the loss of heat causes an object to become warm.

What You'll Need
- 2 thermometers
- 2 identical jars
- clear plastic wrap
- clock or watch
- paper and pen

Put a thermometer into each of 2 identical jars. Cover one jar with clear plastic wrap, and leave the other one uncovered. Record the temperatures in both jars. Place both jars next to each other on a sunny windowsill for about 20 minutes. Check and record the temperatures of the jars every few minutes. Compare how quickly the temperatures of the jars rise. Take the jars off the windowsill, and put them somewhere out of the sun for about 20 minutes. Read and record the temperatures of the jars again every few minutes. Compare how quickly the temperatures of the jars fall.

The jar with the plastic wrap warmed faster and to a higher temperature than the jar without the plastic wrap. The plastic wrap let in the light, and it helped keep the heat inside. The other jar had no covering to hold in the heat. When you took the jars out of the sun, the one with the plastic wrap stayed warmer longer, again because the plastic wrap helped to keep in some of the heat. The gases in the earth's atmosphere act in a similar way. They let sunlight in and help the earth keep some of the heat. A planet without an atmosphere is usually cold because it loses heat quickly, just like the jar without the plastic wrap.

Humans: Bodies and History

◆▶▶▶▶◀◀◀◀◆

Human beings share many characteristics with animals, but we are also unique. Our bodies work in ways similar to other animals, and we have the same needs of food, air, shelter, and community. However, we are able to think in ways that no other creatures can, and we can create and use tools to shape much of our environment. In this chapter, you will learn about the way your body is built and about the ways we study our unique place in the world.

Muscles and Bones

◆▶▶▶▶◀◀◀◀◆

Your body contains more than 200 bones that are connected by strong tissues called *ligaments*. This skeletal system gives your body its shape. Working together with muscles, it also allows your body to move in different ways. The design of your skeleton and muscles influences how you are able to survive.

Need Knees

◆▸◆▸◆▸◆▸◆

What do you need knees for? Find out when you try this activity!

Joints are places where 2 or more bones meet, and you have them all over your body—neck, elbows, fingers, hips, knees, and ankles—just to name a few. Having joints makes your body more flexible and allows you to move. You use them every time you walk, jump, raise your arm, sit down, grab an object with your hand, or open your mouth. To get an idea of how important your joints are, try walking up stairs without bending your knees. You'll find that it is difficult or maybe even impossible. The shape of your knee and the way the bones move together allow you to bend your leg.

Skeletons in the Closet

◆▸◆▸◆▸◆▸◆

Different animals have different skeletal structures.

Look through a variety of reference books to find pictures of animal skeletons. Find as many different kinds of animals as you can. Look at the structure of the different skeletons. How are the bones arranged to give support in different animals?

What You'll Need
● reference books

How are the bones arranged to allow movement in different animals? Try to make predictions about the different animals' diets and habitats and about how they live in general based on clues in their skeletons. If you can't be sure where an animal lives or what it eats, can you at least predict where it does not live and what it does not eat? Look in the reference books for information that will tell you whether or not your predictions were correct.

Hollow Strength

◆◆◆◆◆◆◆

Long bones are hollow or filled with soft tissue, which helps them to be strong but light.

What You'll Need
- paper
- tape
- paper plate
- wooden blocks or other weights

Roll a sheet of notebook paper into a tube about an inch wide. Tape the tube closed so it doesn't unravel. Repeat twice more so you have 3 paper bones. Stand the bones up on their ends. Put a paper plate on top of the 3 rolls. The hollow rolls support the plate! Now start adding wooden blocks to the plate. Count how many blocks the plate can hold before it collapses the bones. These bones are strong, so they might be able to hold quite a few blocks.

Roll 3 more sheets of paper as tightly as you can, so there is no hollow section. These bones use the same amount of paper, but they are much thinner. Stand them on end, and put the plate on top of them. Put blocks on the plate until these bones collapse.

The hollow bones were able to support more weight. Having a hollow center gave them a better design and made them stronger. The large bones in your body are also hollow. This makes them strong, so they can support more weight, but light, so it takes less energy to move them.

Wing Ding

◆◆◆◆◆◆◆

The 4 bones of a chicken wing are designed to allow the chicken to flap its wings.

What You'll Need
- chicken wing
- pot
- water
- stove
- fork

Caution: This project requires adult supervision.

Boil a chicken wing in water for about 20 minutes. Carefully remove the meat from the bones without pulling the bones apart from each other. Examine how the bones are held together. The connective tissues holding bones together are called *ligaments*. Observe the 4 bones in the wing. How are they different? How do you think a chicken's leg bones would be different from its wing bones?

Breaking Bones

◆◀◆◀◆▶◆▶◆

What does the inside of a bone look like?

Get part of the leg bone of a cow or sheep from a butcher. Ask the butcher to cut the bone in half near the middle of the leg so you can see what the inside looks like. Observe the characteristics of the bone. You will see that the bone is composed of a tough outer layer called the *periosteum.* Underneath this is the compact bone, which gives the bone strength. The center is either hollow or contains a soft area called the *marrow.* The insides are not solid because this would make the bone too heavy. Make sure you wash your hands after this activity.

Proportional Dimensions

◆◀◆◀◆▶◆▶◆

Many parts of your body are designed in proportion to each other.

Measure the distance from your elbow to your wrist. Measure the distance from your elbow to your shoulder. These distances will be approximately the same.

Sway your hips back and forth, and find the top of your thigh bone. Measure from there to the top of your head. Now measure the distance from the top of your thigh bone to the bottom of your foot. These distances will be approximately the same.

Our skeletons play an important role in determining our size. Our body is arranged in proportions. Find other examples of things in proportion on your body.

What You'll Need
- measuring tape or ruler
- paper and pen

Get a Backbone

◄►◄►◄►◄►

Make a model of a backbone and see how your vertebrae work together.

The backbone is made of many bones called *vertebrae*. These are arranged in a line or column. To create a model of the human backbone, thread string through the center of several spools of thread, and tape the ends so they stay in place. Connect 5 larger spools to represent the lumbar vertebrae at the bottom; connect 12 medium spools to represent the thoracic vertebrae in the middle; and connect 7 small spools to represent the cervical vertebrae at the top. Place a balloon (or ball) on the spools to represent a head. Notice how your model backbone can move in a variety of directions. In your model, string holds the vertebrae together. In a real backbone, ligaments hold the vertebrae together.

What You'll Need
- 7 small, 12 medium, and 5 large spools of thread
- string
- tape
- balloon or ball

Flex Those Muscles

◄►◄►◄►◄►

Muscular contraction causes bones to move.

What You'll Need
- cardboard
- scissors
- ruler
- brad
- hole punch
- 2 rubber bands

Cut 2 cardboard rectangles about 7 inches long and 3 inches wide. Join the end of one piece of cardboard to the end of the other with a brad. Punch holes in the cardboard as indicated in the drawing. Cut 2 rubber bands, put them through the holes as indicated in the drawing, and retie them.

Make the arm move by pulling on the rubber bands. You'll see that pulling on one rubber band makes the arm bend and pulling on the other rubber band makes the arm straighten. Many of your muscles work in pairs like this, with one muscle pulling a bone in one direction and the other muscle pulling the bone in the other direction.

Upper arm

Triceps ←

→ Biceps

Forearm

Deboning

◆▸▸▸▸◆◆

Bones without calcium have less strength.

What You'll Need
- chicken leg bone
- vinegar
- container with lid

Remove the meat from a chicken leg bone. Place the bone in a container, and pour in vinegar until the bone is covered. Put a lid on the container, and leave it undisturbed. After 4 days, remove the bone. Rinse it with water. How is the bone different than when you started?

Senses

Human beings have 5 senses: sight, taste, touch, smell, and hearing. We rely on our senses to provide us with information about the world around us, and they are some of the most important traits we have for survival. Our senses also allow us to study the world and to enjoy it.

The Dominant Eye

◆▸▸▸▸◆◆

One of your eyes is stronger than the other.

Normally when you look at something, each of your eyes captures an image of the object and sends it to your brain. Your brain then combines the two signals into one image, and that's what you see. This system makes you better at judging distances. However, your brain does favor one eye over the other. Stretch your arm out in front of you with one finger raised. Look at an object a few feet away, and line your finger up with it. Now close your left eye so that you're looking at the object and your finger only with the right eye. Now switch, closing your right eye and looking with your left. Closing one of your eyes will make it seem like your finger jumps over to the side so it is no longer lined up with the object. The eye that you close when this happens is your dominant eye. Your brain pays more attention to the image from that eye than it does to the image from the other eye. Have some of your family or friends do this test to see which of their eyes is dominant.

Jiggly Gelatin Lenses

◆━━◆━━◆━━◆

Make these "Jiggly Gelatin Lenses" and find out how eyeglass lenses work.

What You'll Need

- water
- small pan
- stove
- pot holder
- package of lemon, pineapple, or other light-colored gelatin
- small mixing bowl
- measuring cup
- mixing spoon
- variety of rounded containers
- tray
- clear plastic wrap
- water
- newspaper
- dull knife (optional)

Caution: This project requires adult supervision.

Have an adult help you with boiling the water on the stove. Pour the gelatin into a mixing bowl, and add 1 cup of boiling water. Stir until all the gelatin dissolves. Choose a variety of rounded containers (ladles, ice-cream scoops, wine glasses, round bowls, round-bowl measuring spoons) to pour the gelatin into; use containers with round, smooth bottoms to give the lenses smooth, curved surfaces. Set the containers on a tray, and fill them with the gelatin mixture. Put the tray into the refrigerator, and chill the gelatin for at least 4 hours or until fully set.

When the gelatin is set, wet a piece of clear plastic wrap to prevent sticking. Wet your fingers, too. Run hot tap water over the outside of the containers, and, if necessary, coax the gelatin out with the tip of a warm, wet knife. Place the lenses on the plastic wrap, flat side down.

Place the plastic wrap over a sheet of newspaper. Slide the plastic wrap slowly over the paper while looking through a lens. Try all the lenses on the same word, then look at some pictures. Which lenses make the words look bigger? Which make them look wiggly? Why do different lenses make the same thing look different?

If you'd like to do some more exploring about lenses, check out some books from your school or local library.

No Taste

◆◆◆◆◆◆

The sense of smell is important for tasting food.

Next time you eat a meal, pinch your nose closed, and then taste the food. It does not taste as flavorful. Without the sense of smell, our tongues still detect sweet, sour, bitter, and salty tastes, but we don't detect the fragrance of the food. Fragrance plays a big part in how the food tastes. So next time you have to eat something with a taste you don't like, simply pinch your nose.

Good Taste

◆◆◆◆◆◆

We have taste thresholds for certain types of taste.

What You'll Need
- water
- sugar
- measuring cup
- 10 plastic cups
- marker
- salt
- paper towel
- cotton swabs
- paper and pen

Mix 1⅔ cups water and ¼ cup sugar to make a 12.5% sugar solution. Pour this in a plastic cup labeled "12.5% SUGAR." Add ½ cup of this sugar-and-water solution to 1½ cups water to make a 3.1% sugar solution, and label it "3.1% SUGAR." Add ½ cup of this to 1½ cups water to make a 0.78% sugar solution, and label it "0.78% SUGAR." Add ½ cup of this to 1½ cups water to make a 0.19% sugar solution, and label it "0.19% SUGAR." Make a series of salt solutions, following the above directions but using salt instead of sugar.

Rinse your mouth with water, and dry your tongue with a paper towel. Keeping the solutions out of your sight, have a friend place a clean cotton swab in one of the solutions and then put it on the middle of your tongue. Tell your partner if you can taste the solution and if it is sweet or salty. Your partner should write down whether or not you could taste the solution. Rinse your mouth and dry it, and have your partner try a different solution and record your response. Keep doing this until all the solutions are tested. Switch roles with your partner.

Which solutions could you taste, and which could you not taste? What was your threshold for sweet, and what was your threshold for salty? Was salt harder or easier to detect than sugar?

Sharp Hearing

◆◆◆◆◆◆◆

Hearing ability varies among individuals.

What You'll Need
● pen and paper
● tape recorder
● radio

Label a sheet of paper from 1 to 20. After every number, write a one-syllable word, such as beat, park, broom, etc. Speaking at the same volume level, read your list into a tape recorder. Pause long enough after each word so that some-one who heard the word would have time to write it down. Make a second list of different one-syllable words. Tape-record this second list at the same volume level on your tape recorder.

Prepare 2 sheets of paper for each of 4 participants, and number each sheet from 1 to 20. Test the participants one at a time. Seat each person the same distance from the tape recorder. Turn on some soft background music on a radio. Then play the first recorded list of words. Ask each participant to write down the list of words he or she hears. Check them against your master list to see how many errors were made.

Repeat this procedure with the second list of words, but this time play the back-ground music louder than before. After the participants write down the words, check to see if they made more or less mistakes when the background noise increased. Compare the results of the different individuals who took the test. Does someone in your group have the sharpest hearing?

Running Hot and Cold

◆◆◆◆◆◆◆

If your brain receives a signal from a sense organ long enough, it will start to get used to it.

Caution: This project requires adult supervision.

What You'll Need
● 3 jars
● water

Fill one jar with very hot water (but not too hot—you don't want to burn yourself!), one jar with warm water, and one jar with very cold water. Put one finger of your left hand in the hot water and one finger of your right hand in the cold water. Leave them in the water for a minute. Then put both fingers into the warm water at the same time. How does the water feel?

You made one finger warm and the other cold, and your brain got used to them being that way. When you put both fingers into water of the same temperature, your brain got a different feeling from each of them.

How Cold Is It?

◆◆◆◆◆◆◆

Take a dip to determine temperatures.

What You'll Need
- bowl
- water
- thermometer
- ice cubes
- pen and paper

We know the average healthy human body maintains a temperature of about 98.6 degrees. But can our bodies accurately read temperatures lower than that? Play this "dippy" game to find out. On a warm day, sit outside and dip a bare toe into a bowl of water and make a guess at what temperature the water actually is. Measure the real temperature with a thermometer and write it beside your guess. Now add some ice cubes to the bowl and guess again. Measure the correct temperature and write both figures down. Now carefully add warm water to the ice water (making sure it's not too hot to touch), stick your toe in, and repeat the process. See if your body even comes close to guessing the correct temperatures.

Toe-Tickle Challenge

◆◆◆◆◆◆◆

What can you see with your toes?

How much can you see with your toes? This fun game will help you find out. Have a friend blindfold you so that you can't see. Now, it's time to tickle your toes. And it's up to you to guess just what tickler your friend has decided to use. Is it a feather? Could it be a slice of juicy orange? Maybe it's the nose of a puppy. It's up to

What You'll Need
- blindfold
- 5 different soft, rough, or sticky substances

you to use your other senses to try and figure it out. Once your turn is complete, return the favor with your friend blindfolded.

Scent from Above

◆▶▶▶▶▶◀

Experience the sweet smell of success!

Some experts believe scent is the strongest of human senses. Test the theory with this nosey game. Blindfold each contestant when it is his or her turn. Give the contestant 30 seconds to identify as many objects as possible based on scent alone. Keep track on paper of what the players are smelling and what they guess the object might be. The person to successfully guess the most scents after everyone has had a turn wins the game. Be sure to have plenty of smelly items on hand so everyone has a distinctive new challenge.

Mystery Boxes

◆▶▶▶▶▶◀

Challenge your friends to discover—by touch only— what lies in your mystery boxes!

For each mystery box, tape the lid onto a shoe box and cut a hole in one end large enough to put your hand through. Cover the hole with paper. Cut 8 slits from one side of the paper to the other in a star shape, so that you can put your hand in but the hole will still be covered. Instead of cutting some paper, you could hang a small piece of fabric in front of the hole on the inside, forming a curtain.

Now put your mystery object inside the box. Remember that your friends trust you, so only use objects that won't harm them or make them feel bad in any way. Try shells, rocks, driftwood, leaves, twigs, or cones. Make up a riddle or a poem to go with each object. Write it on an index card and put it on the box. Then decorate the box.

Let your friends put a hand through the hole and try to guess what the object is. After everyone has made a guess, let someone take the object out for all to see.

A box without hinges, key or lid
Yet golden treasure inside is hid...

Sounds of Nature

◆◆◆◆◆◆◆

Understand how different parts of nature work together by learning to recognize the components.

What You'll Need
● paper and pens

This is the perfect outdoor activity to do with a friend on a lazy summer day.

Go outside, find a comfortable place to sit down, and close your eyes. (Try not to fall asleep.) Pay close attention to the sounds you hear. Do you hear birds? The wind? Crackling leaves? After about 5 minutes, write down all the sounds you've heard. Then compare lists. See if you or your friend heard something the other one missed.

Wade and Wonder

◆◆◆◆◆◆◆

Let your fingers guess the watery secrets.

Splashing around in a wading pool is fun, but you can only splash so long. If your energy runs out before the heat fades, try this with a partner. Drop 10 to 20 floating toys in the pool. Blindfold one player while the other acts as a guide. One by one, the guide should hand the toys to the blindfolded player. Can he or she guess which toy is which? Keep track of how many he or she gets right. Now switch places, and see how well you do.

What You'll Need
● wading pool
● floating toys
● blindfold

Singin' Sand

The next time you head to the beach, see if you can hear the sand sing. Some sand grains are covered with a gel. When the wind blows the grains around, they slide against each other. The gel causes the sand to make noises that sound like singing. La, la, la!

Are Two Ears Better than One?

◆◆◆◆◆◆

How do we know the direction of a sound?

What You'll Need
- blindfold
- pillow
- 2 spoons
- pen and paper

Blindfold a partner. Have your partner hold a pillow over one of his or her ears so that ear cannot hear. Then hit the bottom of 2 spoons together and ask your partner to point to the spoons. Repeat in different places around your partner, including some above their heads. Record how many times they were successful and how many times they failed.

Repeat the same procedure without having your partner cover his or her ears. Record how many times they were successful and how many times they failed. Compare the results of the 2 trials.

You probably found that your partner was more successful in telling direction when he or she used both ears. The brain interprets information from both ears to better know the direction of the sound.

Inheritance

All living things inherit their characteristics from their parents. Baby birds have feathers and hollow bones because their parents passed those features on to them. Baby fish have scales and gills because their parents passed those features on to them. Baby humans are able to think complex thoughts because their parents passed that feature on to them.

We Are Family

◆◆◆◆◆◆

Do brown eyes run in your family?
Make a list to see what you have in common.

What You'll Need
● paper and pen

We all have different physical features (unless we are identical twins); we have different eyes, hair, lips, hands, teeth, and fingers. Make a list of physical features, such as eye shape, skin tone, height (tall, medium, short), and so on. Compare yourself to a friend and then to your brother or sister. You probably have more physical characteristics in common with your brother or sister than you do with your friend. This is because we inherit our characteristics from our parents. We are similar to, but not exactly like, our parents. Each of our parents contributes the genetic materials that design our bodies. We have some characteristics of our mother, some of our father, and some that are unique to ourselves.

Like Mom, Like Dad, Like Me

◆◆◆◆◆◆

We have some characteristics of our mother and some of our father,
but we are not exactly like either.

Compare yourself to your mother and father. Compare your hair, eye, and skin characteristics. Look at other traits, including how you act or speak. What are some characteristics you have from your mother? What are some characteristics you have from your father? Do you have any characteristics that are a blend of characteristics of your mother and father? Compare yourself to your grandparents in the same way, and compare your mother and father to their parents. Can you see traits that your parents received from your grandparents? Can you see any that you received from your grandparents?

Guppy Genetics

◆◆◆◆◆◆

*Guppy babies are usually different from each other
and different from their parents.*

In this project, you will observe the babies produced by a
female fancy guppy. Consult with an expert at your local pet
shop about what you'll need to set up a balanced 10-gallon
freshwater aquarium. This will require time, effort, and money,
so get permission from your parents first. Put real or plastic
plants in the tank so the babies will have places to hide.

Buy 2 pregnant female fancy guppies for your aquarium.
Observe the females as they eat and their bellies get bigger.
Keep watching them every day. One day you will notice that
they are thinner and there are baby guppies hiding in many places in the tank.

As the babies grow older, compare them to each other. The more colorful fish are
males and the less colorful are females. Males also have longer fins. Compare the males
with other males and the females with other females and with their mother. They may
act differently. Their body color may be different. The fins or the tails may be different.
Give different names to the fish, and make a chart that identifies some of the characteristics or behaviors of each fish, such as color, tail shape, aggressiveness, and so on. The
young fish are different from each other and different from their mother, but they also
share similarities. Allow the young fish to grow into adults, and observe their offspring.

The Geep

◆◆◆◆◆◆

What do you get when you cross a goat and a sheep?

Scientists have successfully mated a species of goat with a species
of sheep to produce what they call a geep. For a long time, people have bred donkeys with horses to produce mules. Mules have
the intelligence of horses and the surefootedness of donkeys.

Find pictures of various animals in magazines or newspapers.
Cut out the pictures of 2 species, and glue them together so they
share body parts. Put your new animal on poster board. Give a
name to your new organism. Make several new animals, and for
each one, explain where it would live and how it would survive. Describe any advantages it
would have over its "parents" and over other animals living in the same area.

Taco Tongues

◆◆◆◆◆◆◆

Track tongue rolling through your family tree.

See if you can roll your tongue so that it resembles a taco. Then check with your relatives to see if they can do it. Can your parents do it? Can your sisters and brothers do it? Can your grandparents or great-grandparents do it? Can your aunts and uncles do it? Can your cousins do it?

What You'll Need
● markers
● paper

Now create a pedigree for this trait. A square will represent each male. A circle will represent each female. At the bottom of the page (in the same row) draw a circle or square for each of your siblings. On the next higher row put your parents. Connect your parents with a horizontal line as shown in the illustration. Draw a line down from this line to you and your brothers and sisters. Then label all the circles and squares with the names of the people. If a male can roll his tongue, then color his square black. Likewise, if a female can roll her tongue, color her circle black. If the person cannot roll his or her tongue, do not color the circle or square.

Do some of your relatives have the trait for taco tongues? If so, can you see any patterns in how the trait gets inherited?

Taco tongue is a dominant gene. We have 2 genes for every trait. If one gene is dominant, that means you will have the trait. If a person cannot roll their tongue, they do not have any taco tongue genes.

Individual Differences

Although organisms in a group may share many common traits, they will also be different in some ways. Kittens or puppies from the same litter often have different colors of fur or eyes, for instance. Animals in the same group can also differ in things like size. One may have better hearing than another or have quicker reflexes. Recognizing individual differences is an important part of studying living things.

A Sense of Balance

◆◆◆◆◆◆

Different things affect your sense of balance.

Use a piece of paper to make a chart with 5 columns. Label the top of the first column "NAME," the second column "EYES OPEN, LEFT FOOT," the third column "EYES OPEN, RIGHT FOOT," the fourth column "EYES CLOSED, LEFT FOOT," and the fifth column "EYES CLOSED, RIGHT FOOT."

Set a piece of 2×4-inch board in the middle of a carpet or lawn, making sure there is nothing nearby that might hurt a person who fell. Ask friends to stand on the board one at a time and balance on one foot, first the left foot and then the right foot. Use a stopwatch to time how long each person can keep their balance, and record the times on your paper. Then have your friends repeat this with their eyes closed. Do some people have a better sense of balance than others? Does having your eyes open or closed make a difference?

Pulse

◆◆◆◆◆◆

Different individuals have different pulse rates.

You may know that your pulse rate varies. After you exercise, for example, your heart beats faster. Pulse rates also vary from one individual to another. Do you think that younger or older people might have faster heart rates? Do you think that males or females will have faster heart rates? Is a person's pulse rate higher in the morning or evening? Write your predictions down.

Draw 5 columns on a sheet of paper, and label them "NAME," "AGE," "GENDER," "TIME," and "RATE." Ask friends and family members if you can test them. Put your first 2 fingers on the underside of the subject's wrist below the thumb. Count how many pulse beats you feel in 30 seconds, and multiply that number by 2. Record this on your chart, and fill in all the other information. Try to check each subject 4 times, twice in the morning and twice in evening. Does the information you gathered agree with your predictions?

Eye Spy

◆◆◆◆◆◆◆

The eyes have it.

Make the grid for a graph on a piece of paper. Up the left side, put the numbers 0 through 24, with 0 at the bottom left corner. Across the bottom of the sheet, list eye colors: "BROWN," "BLUE," "GREEN," and "HAZEL." On the school playground, at the swimming pool or park, or at some other place where you meet a lot of people you know, spend some time checking eye color. Write down each person's name and eye color. After you have checked 24 people, fill in your graph.

What You'll Need
- pen and paper
- crayons or markers

How many people had brown eyes? Draw a line to that number in the column above brown eyes. Color the column brown up to that number. Repeat this for the other 3 columns, coloring the blue-eyes column blue, the green-eyes column green, and the hazel-eyes column gold. Among this group of friends, what eye color was most common? What color was least common?

Blowhards

◆◆◆◆◆◆◆

Lung capacity varies among individuals.

What You'll Need
- pen and paper
- water
- large bowl
- empty 1-gallon jug with a cap
- plastic tubing
- marker
- antiseptic wipes

Make a chart with columns labeled "NAME," "AGE," "WEIGHT," "HEIGHT," and "CODE." For each person you test, fill in the information on the chart, and give a different code letter of the alphabet, starting with A.

Pour about 3 inches of water into a large bowl, and set it on a counter. Fill a 1-gallon jug with water, and screw on the cap. Place the jug upside down into the bowl of water. With the top of the jug below water, remove the cap, and slip a 3-foot length of clear plastic tubing into the jug.

Ask each subject to take a big breath and blow as much air as they can into the length of tubing. Mark the water level on the jug, and put the person's code letter by it. Wipe the tubing clean with an antiseptic wipe before another subject uses it. Compare the data you gathered from your test.

Fingerprint Fun

◆◆◆◆◆◆◆

Have fun uncovering fingerprints with this easy-to-make fingerprint kit!

Have your family gather in another room where you can't see them. Before they go, give them a jar of cold cream and a white envelope. Tell them that only one person should rub cold cream into his or her hands and then touch the envelope. They shouldn't tell you who does it, but you'll be able to tell by matching the fingerprints.

To Solve the Mystery: Before starting the game, create a fingerprint file for each family member. Write each person's name on a separate index card, and draw two 1-inch squares for the fingerprints. Rub the point of a pencil on a separate piece of paper until you have a solid 1-inch square. Roll each person's left thumb on the square to coat it with graphite, then press it on the sticky side of a piece of tape. Gently lift the tape, and press it onto one of the squares on the file card. Repeat for the right-hand thumb. (Be sure everyone washes their hands after being fingerprinted.)

To Dust for Prints: In a small dish, make some graphite powder by rubbing a pencil point against an emery board. Dip your paintbrush into the powder, and gently brush the entire surface of the envelope to expose the hidden prints. They will appear like magic.

To Match the Prints: Examine the prints on the envelope for arches, loops, whorls, and any broken lines in the ridges. Compare the dusted prints (which are backward) with the fingerprint file cards. Use a magnifying glass if you need to. Who touched the envelope?

What You'll Need
- cold cream
- white envelope
- pencils
- index cards
- ruler
- paper
- clear tape
- emery board
- small dish
- soft-bristle paintbrush
- magnifying glass (optional)

Nutrition and Health

Eating and exercising are 2 important ways to give our bodies what they need. Learning more about food and exercise and how they affect us can help us do a better job of caring for our bodies.

Spinning a Food Web

◆►◆►◆►◆

You belong to a food web that includes many organisms.

As a human being, you are part of a food web. One night after dinner, write down the major components of each food item that you ate. Make a list of all the components, and write down where each one came from. Draw a picture of yourself at the top of a large piece of poster board. From left to right across the middle of the poster board, draw pictures of the plants and animals that provided your dinner, and draw a line from them to you. Think about where these organisms got their energy—from the sun, from certain plants, from other animals? From left to right at the bottom of the poster board, draw pictures of the energy source used by each plant and animal you ate for dinner. Look at all the different organisms you have on your chart. For each organism, think of 2 more organisms that have a food relationship with it—an animal that eats it or is eaten by it or decomposers that break down the organism or its waste products. Draw these new organisms on your poster, and add lines to show the food relationships. Look at all the different creatures that you were connected to just by eating your dinner!

> **What You'll Need**
> - paper and pen
> - poster board
> - markers

Drive for Five

◆►◆►◆►◆

Fruits and vegetables are important parts of your diet.

Fruits and vegetables have a great deal of vitamins and nutrients that help people live healthier, longer, and more energetically. Experts on nutrition recommend that people eat at least 5 servings of fruits or vegetables each day.

> **What You'll Need**
> - paper and pen

Starting in the morning, write down the name of each fruit or vegetable that you eat during the day. A serving is roughly the size of an orange, ½ cup of cooked vegetables, ½ cup of canned fruit, or ¼ cup of 100 percent juice. Determine how close you came to eating 5 servings of fruits or vegetables during the day.

Read the Label

⬥⬥⬥⬥⬥⬥⬥

Different cereals may contain different amounts of nutrients.

What You'll Need
- various kinds of cereal
- pen and paper

Read the nutritional labels on cereal boxes. Make a chart that lists different vitamins, minerals, and nutrients down one side and lists the names of the cereals across the top. Put information from several types of cereals into your chart. Determine which has the most vitamin C for one serving. Which has the second most? Which has the least? Compare the cereals for the amount of iron they have and for other nutrients. Looking at all the nutrients, which cereals seem to be better for you? Make similar charts for other types of food.

What's the Skinny?

⬥⬥⬥⬥⬥⬥⬥

The amount of calories from fat varies in different foods.

Calories are units of food energy. Look at the nutritional information on food product labels from regular and reduced-fat foods (cheeses, salad dressings, soup, potato chips, crackers, etc.). Many of them will indicate what percentage of the food's total calories comes from fat. You can also calculate the percentage if you know the food's number of total calories

What You'll Need
- food labels
- calculator
- paper and pen

and the number of calories from fat, which are usually listed on the label; divide the calories of fat by the total calories and multiply by 100%.

Using the food labels you've collected, compare the percentage of calories from fat for the regular food products and their reduced-fat versions. Calculate the decrease in fat by dividing the original percentage by the reduced-fat percentage and multiplying by 100%. For example, suppose Paco's Tortilla Chips have 40% of their calories from fat, and Paco's Reduced-Fat Tortilla Chips have 20% of their calories from fat. Divide 20% by 40% and multiply by 100%; the result is 50%, which means the reduced-fat version of the tortilla chips has 50% less fat than the regular version.

Chain Game

❖❖❖❖❖❖❖

Each link in a food chain supports another link.

What You'll Need
- markers
- poster board
- 3×5-inch index cards
- dice

Design a game board based on a food chain. The path that you follow from Start to Finish might be along a river or a lake, through woods, or through a jungle. Draw a twisted path on the playing board, and design appropriate spaces on the board and pawns for the habitat you choose. If you choose a lake, for example, you might include a mosquito, a minnow, a large-mouth bass, and a human as spaces and as pawns. Some spaces will be colored and open. Mark several index cards "10 FOOD POINTS."

Players choose their markers, roll dice, and move the appropriate number of spaces. For example, if a player with the mosquito pawn lands on a human square, the player with the mosquito pawn gets a card and the player with the human pawn goes back to Start because mosquitoes bite humans. If a mosquito lands on a minnow square, the player with a minnow pawn gets a card, and the player with the mosquito pawn goes back to Start because minnows eat mosquitoes.

Continue the game until someone reaches the Finish space. Then have all the players add up the number of food points they have collected to see who has won.

Pyramid Power

❖❖❖❖❖❖❖

Following the food-guide pyramid can improve your diet.

What You'll Need
- paper
- marker
- old magazines
- scissors
- glue

The food-guide pyramid shows the different food groups and how many servings of each we should eat in a day. Draw the pyramid on a large sheet of paper. Find photos in magazines of foods you like to eat. Paste the pictures where they belong in the pyramid. Let each picture represent one serving, and show the recommended number of servings for each group. For example, you should paste 3–5 pictures for the vegetable group. Compare the foods you eat in one day with your food pyramid. Should you make any changes in your diet?

Thank Moo

◆◆◆◆◆◆◆

People rely on cows for many food products.

Visit a local grocery store, and look carefully through all the aisles. Try to find as many products that come from cows as you can. Look in the meat department and dairy department, of course, but check other places, too. Write down each type of food that you find. How many things are on your list?

Nut-rageous!

◆◆◆◆◆◆◆

Food contains energy for our bodies.

Caution: This project requires adult supervision.

Find different kinds of nuts (walnuts, pecans, cashews) that are about the same size. Stick one of the nuts on a needle, and stick the other end of the needle in a cork so it will stand by itself on a table. Put about ¼ inch of water in a metal cup. Measure the starting temperature of the water in the cup with a thermometer. Light the nut with a match. Using tongs, hold the cup over the flame. When the nut stops burning, record the temperature of the water. Compare that to the starting temperature to see how much the water's temperature increased. When the water cools to near its starting temperature, repeat with a different kind of nut. Which has the most energy?

Nuts contain a great deal of food energy in the form of oils. When we eat nuts, our bodies take this energy and either use it or store it as fat. When you burned the nuts, their food energy was released as light and heat, which raised the temperature of the water.

Sugar Buzz

◆◇◆◇◆◇◆

Carbohydrates are absorbed into the blood at different rates.

What You'll Need
- 2 glasses
- corn syrup
- red food coloring
- measuring spoon
- sugar
- flour

Sometimes if you eat too much sugar, your head feels a bit odd and may start to hurt. Some people call this a sugar buzz. This also causes your body to work to remove the sugar from the blood. When all of the sugar is removed, your body is hungry again. Starches do not rush into the blood as quickly as sugar does.

Fill 2 glasses halfway with corn syrup. Add 2 drops of red food coloring to each glass to make artificial blood. Place 1 teaspoon sugar on top of the "blood" in one glass and 1 teaspoon flour on top of the "blood" in the other glass. Watch how long it takes for the blood to absorb the sugar and flour.

The sugar is absorbed faster than the flour. The sugar is made of small molecules that dissolve faster than the large starch molecules in the flour. When we eat sugar, these small molecules quickly pass into our blood. When we eat starches, the molecules take longer to pass into our blood.

Large Lungs

◆◇◆◇◆◇◆

Blowing capacity varies from person to person.

What You'll Need
- balloons
- cloth tape measure
- paper and pen

Caution: Do not do this activity if you have asthma or any other breathing condition.

Give identical balloons to several friends. Instruct each one to blow up a balloon as much as possible with only one breath. Measure everyone's balloon, and write the numbers next to their names. Let the air out of the balloons, and repeat 2 more times. Take the average of the 3 tests. Who was able to blow the most air into their balloon? What enables him or her to do this? You may find that people who play musical instruments that require blowing, who do cardiovascular exercise, or who are large in size are able to blow harder.

Heart Power

◆◆◆◆◆◆◆◆

Can you work as hard as your heart does?

What You'll Need
- clock
- paper and pen

Our hearts beat constantly, 24 hours a day, without a rest. Close your hand into a tight fist. Your heart is about this size. See how long your hand muscles can work as hard as your heart. Look at a clock, and write down the exact time. Quickly open your hand, and stretch your fingers. Then quickly close your fingers into a tight fist. Open them and close them, open them and close them. Keep doing this until your hand is too tired. When you stop, look at the clock to see how long you were able to pump your hand. Your heart has to pump like that without stopping every second of every day. In one day, it beats 100,000 times and pumps 11,000 quarts of blood through your body.

Step Right Up!

◆◆◆◆◆◆◆◆

Exercise increases your breathing rate and your heart rate.

What You'll Need
- watch
- paper and pen
- stairs

Caution: Do not do this activity if you have heart or breathing problems.

Have a friend count the number of times you breathe in 30 seconds. Multiply this by 2 to get the number of times you breathe per minute. Record this number. Have your friend find your pulse and count the number of times your heart beats in 30 seconds. Multiply this by 2 to get the beats per minute. Record this number.

Stand at the bottom of a flight of stairs. Step up onto the first stair with your right foot and then with your left foot. Step down with your right foot and then with your left foot. Now step up with your left foot first and then your right foot. Step down with your left foot and then with your right foot. Continue stepping in this way for 30 seconds. Have your friend measure your breathing rate and pulse rate again. Compare these readings with the initial readings. How long does it take for these readings to return to normal?

As you exercised, your muscles were working, so they needed more oxygen. Your breathing rate increased to get more oxygen in your body, and your heart rate increased to get that oxygen to your muscles.

Neighborhood Theme Walks

◆ ▷ ◆ ▷ ◆ ▷ ◆

Take a walk with your family and keep your eyes open for something special!

Family theme walks are fun. They're a good way to provide the exercise everyone needs and a great way to get to know your neighborhood. However, when you walk, there are safety rules to remember. Make sure to stay on the sidewalk or shoulder—don't walk in the street. Be sure you walk on the left-hand side of the road whenever you can, so that you face traffic. Finally, cross the street only at street corners. Always look both ways and make sure it is safe to cross. Before you go, decide what theme to use. Here are some ideas:

Firsts: Look for the first daffodil of spring, the first rose of summer, the first barbecue cookout on the block.

Tally It Up: Tally the houses on your block and see what color is most popular. Do the same with cars. What else can you tally?

Alphabet Walks: Look for and name anything you see beginning with a certain letter.

Color Walks: Look for (and name) anything you see of a particular color. Or give each person a card cut from colored paper and have them try to find something that matches it exactly.

Coin-Flip Walk: At every street corner, flip a coin. If it's heads, turn right. If it's tails, turn left. See where you end up after a certain length of time, then reverse your direction and head home.

Bike Hike

◆◆◆◆◆◆◆

Take bike hikes with your family and watch your miles add up!

What You'll Need
- bicycles
- helmet for each rider
- water bottle
- snacks
- notebook
- pen or pencil
- national or world map
- pushpins
- marker

If your family is into biking, try planning some bike hikes with them. One great incentive to keep everyone biking is to plan an imaginary trip. Find out how far your "destination" is, then see how long it takes you to bike that many miles. When biking, be sure to observe these safety tips:

1) Inspect your bicycle before each ride. Inflate the tires, check the brakes, and lubricate the chain properly.

2) All riders, both adults and children, should wear helmets. Make sure your helmet protects your forehead. Always buckle the straps and make sure they fit snugly.

3) Remember, your bike is a moving vehicle. You must follow the rules of the road. Ride on the right-hand side. Obey all traffic signs and signals, using hand signals to indicate when you turn.

4) Be alert for cars at all times. Always assume that the driver doesn't see you. Watch for cars turning at corners or backing out of driveways.

If you're going to be out more than an hour, bring water and snacks. Use a map to plan your route and figure out how many miles you will travel. After a while you'll get pretty good at estimating how far you've biked. After each hike, record your mileage in a notebook. On a wall map, mark your town (and your "destination") with pushpins, then use a colored marker to note on a highway the number of miles you've biked.

See how long it takes you to bike around the country—or the world!

Workout Stations

◆◆◆◆◆◆◆

Have fun exercising at your own workout stations—
add posters that have directions for what to do at each one.

What You'll Need

- sticks or pieces of rope
- bath mat or nonslip rug
- jump rope
- canned goods (or paper-towel tubes, rocks, and tape)
- poster board
- markers
- blank cards
- transparent tape

Make 4 workout stations, each with a poster explaining what to do there. Mark off each station with sticks or pieces of rope. At the first station, place a bath mat or nonslip rug for sit-ups. The poster here should explain what a sit-up is. It should also say, "Do 10 sit-ups before moving to the next workout station."

At the second station, make a poster that explains what a push-up is. The poster should say, "Do 10 push-ups before moving to the next workout station." The third workout station should include a jump rope. The poster at this station should say, "Jump rope 10 times before moving to the next workout station."

At the fourth station, place some canned goods to use as lightweight dumbbells (or make your own by filling paper-towel tubes with rocks and taping the ends). Make a poster that says, "Do 10 curls for each arm with the dumbbells to complete your workout."

Before you begin working out, make sure you stretch out all your muscles—do some side bends, toe touches (no bouncing), and arm stretches. When you are done stretching, start your workout routine.

After you have mastered your circuit of exercises, add 2 more reps (repetitions of the exercise) to each workstation. Tape a blank card over the number on each poster, and write in the new number. After mastering each new number, add another 2 reps. You will be the fittest kid on your block—keep those muscles active and healthy!

Artifacts

Archaeology is the study of ancient people and civilizations. One of the ways we study ancient cultures is by examining artifacts that they left behind. Artifacts are any objects made by people for a specific purpose. By carefully examining artifacts, we can learn much about the people who used them.

 # Time Capsule

Time capsules help people in the future understand past cultures.

What You'll Need
- various objects
- resealable plastic container
- plastic bag
- shovel
- paper and pen

Gather objects that represent the current year. These can be baseball cards, newspapers, magazines, fashion items, or anything else you can imagine. You might write a letter that tells about yourself, your family, or your community. Put these items into a plastic container, and seal it securely. Put the plastic container into a plastic bag, and tie the bag closed.

Find someplace to bury the time capsule; make sure you have permission to do so. Dig a 3-foot hole in the ground, put your time capsule in, and cover it with dirt. Make a sign, and put it on the ground above the capsule, or make a map to the capsule. On your map or sign, indicate what year the time capsule should be opened. When it is opened, people will find artifacts that will give them some information about how you lived.

Sand Search

◆▸◆▸◆▸◆▸◆

Archaeologists can use sound waves and rods to find materials buried underground.

What You'll Need
- household objects
- sand
- 30 skewers or long sticks
- shovel

Archaeologists sometimes use equipment to send sound waves into the ground, and then they study the reflections of the waves to find artifacts below the surface. They can also insert long rods into the ground to help them determine what is below the surface. Gather up a few items from around the house, such as cups, plates, and small garden tools. Have a friend or family member bury an object in sand. Have them show you where it is buried, but don't let them tell you what the object is. Now sink a skewer into the sand so it just touches the object. Leave the skewer in the sand. Do this with about 30 skewers. Try and guess the shape of the object. Then guess what the object is. After you guess, carefully dig up the object to see if you are right. Then bury an object for your friend or family member to identify.

Find the Arrowhead

◆▸◆▸◆▸◆▸◆

Artifacts can be found in different ways.

It can be difficult for archaeologists to find artifacts from other cultures. Often, the items are buried below the ground and require careful digging by many people. Sometimes they are buried by natural forces and then exposed by wind and rain centuries later. Other times, artifacts can be found in exactly the same spot they were left by the person who used them. Next time you are out in the woods or in another uncultivated area, look for rocks that have been shaped into arrowheads. These artifacts were made by Native Americans to use in their arrows for hunting and warfare.

Moving Archaeology

◆◆◆◆◆◆

The things people own give clues about how they live.

Visit a moving sale or an estate sale with an adult, and look over the items being sold. Try to determine as much as you can about the people who own the sale items. For example, if they have lots of pet-care products, you might conclude that they are pet lovers. If they have lots of sports equipment, you might conclude that they are athletic. You can't be sure about your conclusions, but this is how archaeologists work. They draw conclusions based on what they find and then seek more facts to see if their conclusions were correct.

Old Age Home

◆◆◆◆◆◆

Objects in your home can tell a story if you know what questions to ask.

Working with an adult, identify the oldest object in your home that was made by people. This could be furniture, tools, letters, jewelry, photographs, or paintings. Once you have found the oldest item, try to answer some questions about it. What is the purpose of the object? Is it still used for the same purpose? When do you think it was made? Who originally owned the item? What can the object tell you about the original owner?

Kite Fishing

Kites have been used for centuries in Asia for fishing. A hook and bait are attached to a kite, which is then lowered into the water. Can you think of other objects we use today that might have had a different purpose in the past?

Nickel for Your Thoughts

◆◆◆◆◆◆

Artifacts can reveal things about the people who use them.

Things people left behind are artifacts; these can be tools, clothing, food, or furniture. Suppose you were an archaeologist and you were researching an ancient culture. If you found only some coins, what things could you learn about the culture? Examine some nickels with a friend or relative. Think of questions you can ask and answer about the objects. How were the objects made? How were they used? What do the words on them mean? Write down as many ideas as possible. For example, the coins tell you that this culture could melt and shape metals. They also tell you that the culture had a written language.

What You'll Need
- nickels
- paper and pen

Trash Talk

◆◆◆◆◆◆

People's garbage can provide clues about how they live.

What You'll Need
- rubber gloves

Caution: This project requires adult supervision; be careful of any sharp or otherwise dangerous objects you might find.

With an adult, go through your family's garbage. (Be sure to put rubber gloves on first.) If you were an archaeologist who didn't know your family, what conclusions would you make? You might guess the kinds of food your family eats or the appliances your family uses to cook. You might make conclusions about family members' hobbies or about work projects done around the home. Archaeologists often analyze the trash of ancient civilizations to learn more about their culture. Be sure to wash your hands with soap and water when you are finished.

Anthill Horde

◆◆◆◆◆◆

Ancient finds, tiny heroes.

Paleontologists know ants can be the masters of any prehistoric dig. They spend hours and hours of each day tunneling through the earth, improving their habitats. As they dig, they often find chunks of material that we might miss digging on our own.

What You'll Need
- gardening gloves
- insect repellent
- tiny jar with lid or cloth bag

As a result, paleontologists know to search the dirt piles of ants carefully for tiny prehistoric bits. For instance, tiny teeth are common in certain fossil-rich areas like Wyoming and Montana.

So the next time you see an anthill, don't stomp it! Study it! Put on your best gardening gloves, use insect repellent to keep you safe, and start looking. You just might find some fossil teeth of your own. Remember to ask the owner of the land permission to search for fossils first. And if you are on public land, give your discovery to a scientist. Keeping fossils found on public land is almost always against the law.

Sandstone Carving

◆◆◆◆◆◆

Will writing your initials in stone leave a lasting impression?

What You'll Need
- sandstone
- screwdriver or hammer and nail

Ancient peoples often carved their favorite stories into the faces of giant rocks. They left their history behind for us to study and explore. You can express yourself in stone, too, if you select the rock carefully. Be sure to ask before you carve and have an adult help you choose the right tools. Once you have permission, take a screwdriver or a hammer and nail. Carefully chisel your first initial into the side of the stone. Check back in a week, a month, and even a year to see if your carving has withstood the test of time. Wind and blowing dirt can blast your mark from the stone in a process called *erosion.*

Scientific Sifter

◆◆◆◆◆◆◆

Archaeologists and other scientists often sift through sand, dirt, and other materials to find small artifacts and treasures. Make your own scientific sifter to find treasures.

Cut the metal clips off an onion bag, then cut the bag so you have a flat piece of mesh. Cut 2 rectangles out of cardboard that are the size of the mesh. Cut a matching hole in each piece of cardboard that is at least 2 inches smaller than the size of the mesh. Using one piece of cardboard, stretch the mesh over the hole and staple it in place. Take the second piece of cardboard and lay it on top (over the staples). (If you'd like to make an extra-fine sifter, use 2 or 3 pieces of mesh.) Tape the cardboard pieces together at the outside edges with packing tape.

What You'll Need
- mesh onion or potato bag
- scissors
- cardboard
- ruler
- stapler
- packing tape
- magnifying glass
- notebook
- pencil
- reference books

   Now it's time to go outside to explore! Sift through some dirt in your backyard, some sand at the beach, or some soil in the garden. (Of course, you need to ask permission before digging or sifting!) How many treasures can you come up with? Did you find living creatures (be sure to put them back after examining them), interesting rocks, or shells?

Examine your findings with the magnifying glass, and then draw them in your notebook. You can sort, classify, and identify your treasures by comparing your drawings with pictures from reference books.

   Mom and Dad will appreciate that you only bring pictures of your treasures into the house!

Human Tools

Tools are one of the most common artifacts found by archaeologists. Tools are a part of technology; they make work easier or more precise. While a few other animals are known to use simple tools, humans create and use tools in a much more sophisticated way than any other creatures do.

Tooling Around

◆▸◆▸◆▸◆▸

Could you survive life on a desert island?

What You'll Need
● paper and pen

Imagine you are stranded on a deserted island. All you have with you are the clothes you are wearing, a small hunting knife, a book of matches, and a compass. It could be days, weeks, even months before you are rescued. Make a list of all the items you need to survive and of tools that will help you. For example, you need to eat and drink. Will you hunt, grow, or gather your food—or a combination of all three? What tools do you need to hunt, grow, or gather? Where will you find water, and how will you carry it and store it? Remember, you only have the items you were stranded with—all other tools you have to make from objects already on the island. (If you are unsure what objects would be on an island, ask an adult.) Since you have no idea when you will be rescued, you need to prepare yourself for a long stay. For example, what will you do when you run out of matches? You can turn this experiment into a game to play with your friends. Pretend the group of you are stranded and need to set up your own community. Will you have a government or laws? Will you trade with each other or have a system of money? How will you divide up the work?

Stick Raft

◆▸◆▸◆▸◆▸◆▸◆

A raft can be made by tying sticks together.

Gather some small sticks, and lay them side by side. Tie the sticks together securely so they make a raft. Put the raft in a container of water to see if it floats. Add some small objects, such as toy soldiers, washers, marbles, or paper clips, to see if your raft is able to support them. How many objects can the raft support before it sinks? Design a raft that will hold more objects. Rafts were one of the first types of boats people ever made.

What You'll Need
● sticks
● string
● scissors
● large container
● water
● various small objects

Building Bridges

◆◆◆◆◆◆

Bridges are used to cross over valleys, waterways, or roads.

What You'll Need
- magazines and reference books
- toothpicks
- glue

Find pictures of several different bridges, either in magazines or in reference books. Study the pictures carefully. What do they have in common? In what ways are they different? Do some of the designs seem stronger than others? Using toothpicks and glue, build a simple bridge that can cross a 5-inch span. Test your bridge to see how much weight it will support by resting different objects on top of it. Can you think of ways to change your bridge's design so it will be stronger?

Tool Tally

◆◆◆◆◆◆

People rely on a variety of tools every day.

You use a number of tools every day. Every time you use a tool, take a minute to write it down on a sheet of paper. You might easily recognize some items as tools, such as hammers or scissors or spoons. However, you may not realize that some things you use every day are tools, such as your toothbrush, your bicycle, your lunch box, and even the pen you're using to write. At the end of the day, count up the number of tools you have used. Think about what life would be like if you didn't have some of these tools available to you. Which of the tools on your list did people have 100 years ago? What about 1,000 years ago? For the tools they didn't have, what did they use instead?

What You'll Need
- paper and pen

Clay-Pot Refrigeration

◆◆◆◆◆◆

Porous ceramic pots can keep their contents cool.

This activity works best if done on a hot day. Seal the hole in the bottom of a clay flowerpot using either a cork or silicon sealant. Fill the pot with warm water, and add the same amount of warm water to a plastic container of about the same size as the pot. Measure the water temperature in each container, and write it down. Record the temperature every 20 minutes.

    You'll find that the water in the clay pot has a lower temperature than the water in the plastic container. You'll also find that the water level drops in the clay pot but not in the plastic container. The clay pot is porous; it allows water to slowly seep from the inside of the pot to the outside of the pot. When it reaches the outer part of the pot, the water evaporates, which cools the pot. People have used this method of refrigeration for thousands of years.

What You'll Need
- unglazed clay flowerpot
- cork or silicon sealant
- water
- plastic container
- measuring cup
- 2 thermometers
- pen and paper
- clock

Foil Fleet

◆◆◆◆◆◆

The design of a boat will affect how well it can perform.

What You'll Need
- aluminum foil
- scissors
- ruler
- large container
- water
- various small objects

Cut out four 6×6-inch squares of aluminum foil. Fold them into different shapes that will float on water. Put your boats in a container of water to see if they float. Add some small objects, such as toy soldiers, paper clips, or washers, to see if the boats support them. How many objects can each boat support before it sinks? Which boat holds the most? Design boats that will hold more objects.

How High is that Hill?

◆◆◆◆◆◆◆

Use a simple surveying tool to measure the height of any slope.

What You'll Need
- clear plastic jar
- waterproof marker
- tape measure
- paper and pen
- calculator

To measure the height of a slope, you'll need a tool called a *level*. Make a simple level by filling a jar about a ⅓ of the way with water. Put it on a flat table and, with a waterproof marker, make a ring around the jar at the water level. Then have your partner use a tape measure to measure the height from the floor to your eyes. Write this measurement down. Call this your "eye-level distance."

Stand at the bottom of the slope and hold the jar so that the water level is even with the ring on the jar. Look through the jar, across the surface of the water, and have your partner stand at the point on the hill that you can see across the water. Your partner is standing eye-level distance above you.

Now go up the hill and stand by your partner. Look across the level water again and have your partner move to the next point you can see on the hill. Your partner is now 2 eye-level distances up the hill. Continue doing this until your partner is on the top of the hill. Then multiply the number of eye-level distances you measured out by the number of inches from the floor to your eyes. This will tell you how many inches high the hill is. Divide by 12 to find out how many *feet* high it is.

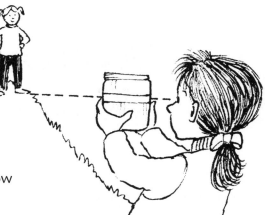

Clay Kitchen

◆◆◆◆◆◆◆

Clay can be used to make a variety of tools for eating.

What You'll Need
- clay
- paper and pen

Using clay, try to make as many eating tools as possible. Make a list of all the tools you made. If you can't make a specific tool (for example, a fork), try to make a substitute tool that will have the same function. You will find out that clay is a very useful material for making many kitchen tools. Before people were able to work with metal, they often used clay to make tools and household items.

Our Precious Planet

◆◆◆◆◆◆◆◆▶

You might have seen astronaut photographs of our Earth—half-lit and surrounded by nothing but the black of outer space. This view has helped many people realize that Earth is our home; we must all do our part so that it remains a beautiful place to live. As the earth rotates, the lit part experiences day, and the dark part experiences night. Earth science explores these aspects of Earth and how it has changed over time. These changes have produced fascinating geological features from tiny, delicate crystals to the vastness of the Grand Canyon.

Water, Water, Everywhere

◆◆◆◆◆◆◆◆▶

If life ever visited us from a distant planet, perhaps the thing they would find most amazing about the earth is all the water on it. Approximately ¾ of the earth is covered with water. That means this great blue ball is almost *entirely* covered with water!

Is that All There Is?

◆▷◆▷◆▷◆

Why is it so important to keep rivers and lakes clean? Make a chart showing how precious our freshwater supply really is.

What You'll Need
- poster board
- markers
- quarter or small cup

You can do this activity with a group of friends. Get a big piece of poster board and draw 100 circles, all the same size. (You can trace around a quarter or a very small cup. Just make sure there's room on your poster board for 100 circles, with some room left over.) Now color 97 of the circles all the same color. These circles will stand for all the salt water on Earth. Next, color 2 circles another color. These 2 circles will stand for all the frozen water on Earth.

How many circles are left? That's right, only one. That circle stands for all the fresh-water on Earth. Color it a third color. That circle has to provide all the water humans need for drinking, watering crops, and everything else.

Think of a title for your poster. Also, somewhere on the poster, make a key to explain what the chart means. See if you can put up your chart at a library or school.

"Read" a Creek

◁▷◆▷◆▷◆

You can learn a lot about a creek or stream—if you know where to look!

Caution: This project requires adult supervision.

If there is a creek or stream near where you live, spend some time walking along its banks. Be sure to have an adult go along with you. Pay close attention to the different kinds of plants and animals that live in the water and on the banks.

Look closely at the current. Is it the same everywhere, or is it faster in some places and slower in others? Can you think of reasons for the differences? (For one thing, the current is swifter where the water is shallow and slower where the water is deep.) What about the surface of the water? Is it smooth in some places and choppy in others? A small area of choppy water might mean there is a rock or large log under the surface.

Is the water level in the creek higher or lower than normal? You can tell by looking at the banks. If there is bare, damp soil along the banks, the creek is lower than normal. If you see green land plants or trees growing out of the water, the creek is higher than normal. Can you tell why the creek flows where it does? Does it go around obstacles, such as large rocks?

Just Passing Through

❖❖❖❖❖❖

It's amazing all the things that travel down the watery highway of a creek!

What You'll Need
- wire coat hanger
- screen or mesh
- gardening gloves
- duct tape

Caution: This project requires adult supervision.

Bend a wire coat hanger into a rough circle. Take a piece of old screen, and bend it around the coat hanger. (Be careful not to stick yourself with the screen. You may want to wear work gloves or gardening gloves while doing this.) Use duct tape to hold the screen in place.

Now go to a creek or stream with an adult. Put your screen into the current and hold it there for a few minutes. Take out the screen and see what the current has carried onto it. You might find seeds that will land on the creek's bank and grow into plants. Or, you might find water animals such as insects, minnows, or crayfish. (Put them back in the creek right away, so they stay alive.) You might even find something somebody lost a long way upstream.

Be an Explorer

❖❖❖❖❖❖

Discover uncharted territory! Visit a river, stream, lake, pond, or tide pool.

Caution: This project requires adult supervision.

In 1804–1806, Meriwether Lewis and William Clark were the first European-Americans to travel across what is now the western United States. They kept journals full of notes and drawings to tell the rest of the world about all the strange, new things they saw: plants, animals, mountains, and much more.

What You'll Need
- notebook
- pen

With an adult, visit a body of water near your home. Imagine that you are an explorer. Look closely at the plants, animals, rocks, and other natural elements. Tell about them in a journal. Finally, make a map of the area for explorers who will follow in your footsteps. Don't forget that explorers may find all kinds of surprises. Meriwether Lewis met a grizzly bear one day and had to jump into a river to escape!

Changing Shapes

◆─◆─◆─◆─◆─◆

Nothing in nature stays exactly the same. See how a body of water changes over time.

Caution: This project requires adult supervision.

What You'll Need
- yardstick
- paper and pen

Visit a body of water—a creek, river, pond, or lake—about once a week. Notice how it changes, and record your observations. Does the water level go up and down? (If you can get permission, stick a yardstick in the mud at the edge of the water. Then you'll be able to tell exactly how much the water rises and falls.) What happens when it rains? Or when it doesn't rain for a long time? When the water level goes up, what other changes occur? Does the water get muddier? Does it change color? How are plants and animals affected?

The Living Ocean

◆─◆─◆─◆─◆─◆

Oceans don't just contain salt water. They encompass many different living things. Make a diorama of this underwater world.

What You'll Need
- book about the ocean
- shoe box
- markers or paint
- paintbrush
- paper
- scissors
- clay (optional)
- decorations (optional)

When you think of the ocean, you probably think about swimming at the beach or going for a boat ride. Those are fun things, but they're not the only ways oceans are used. Oceans are home to many unusual and delicate forms of life, like starfish, algae, seahorses, coral, anemones, and of course lots of fish. Find a book about sea life, and learn about all the different things that are found in the world's oceans. Then choose a part of the ocean and make a diorama that shows what you learned. You may want to show a coral reef or a deep part of the ocean. What kind of animals or plants live there? On the inside bottom of a shoe box, draw or paint a blue background to represent water. You can cut and color paper fish and plants and glue them to the background. Then turn the shoe box on its side, and make the "floor" of your ocean. You might put in sand and shells, or make plants and animals (like lobster or crab) out of clay.

This Watery World

◆◆◆◆◆◆

About ¾ of the earth's surface is covered with water. Find out more when you read all about oceans or rivers.

Do you know the names of the world's 4 major oceans? (They are the Pacific, Atlantic, Indian, and Arctic.) How about the 2 longest rivers? (They're the Nile and the Amazon.) Before people even knew that the earth was round, great explorers sailed across oceans and down rivers to see what they could find. Some of the most fascinating creatures in the world live in oceans and rivers.

See if your library has some books on oceans and rivers. Then compare similarities and contrast the differences between them. You can do this by creating a chart or writing a report. Where can you find a whale or dolphin? A trout or catfish? How many ways can we protect these valuable bodies of water? You can even draw pictures to go with what you've learned.

Geology

◆◆◆◆◆◆

Rocks are constantly created, and rocks are constantly broken down. If you dig into the soil, you will quickly find small rocks. But what if you could dig deeper? Way down beneath the soil, there are much larger rocks. If you could drill past all the solid rock, you would eventually find melted rocks, or magma.

Rocky Rainbow

◆▶◆▶◆▶◆

How many colors can you find in your own backyard?

What You'll Need
- bag or plastic jar
- glue or duct tape
- poster board

Nature has created literally hundreds of differently colored rocks. Many of them can be found in your own yard. When you're feeling ready to explore, see how many different tones you can discover and collect in a single day's geological expedition. If you want, you can mount the stones on a piece of poster board. Just for fun, take your poster to a nearby natural history museum or geology professor. Ask why your rock specimens are the color they are. You might be fascinated to discover what chemicals work to give a rock its hue.

A Rockin' Recipe

◆▶◆▶◆▶◆

All rocks are made of minerals that have been combined by heat and pressure. You can make some edible "rocks" to show how this happens.

Caution: This project requires adult supervision.

With help from an adult, melt 40 marshmallows and 3 tablespoons butter or margarine in a pan, stirring them together. Measure out onto waxed paper 1 cup of any of the following: nuts (any kind you like), raisins, or chocolate chips.

What You'll Need
- 40 large marshmallows
- butter or margarine
- measuring cup and spoon
- pan
- stove
- waxed paper
- nuts, raisins, or chocolate chips
- puffed rice cereal
- large spoon
- rock-identifying book

Stir 6 cups of puffed rice cereal into the melted marshmallows and butter. Then use a large spoon to drop "hunks" of the mixture onto waxed paper. Let it cool just a little, until you can handle it without burning yourself. Be careful when handling this hot mixture! Coat your hands with butter. Then make rocks by combining the ingredients of your choice with the cereal/marshmallow mix. The melted marshmallows provide the heat. You provide the pressure. And you can make different kinds of "rocks" depending on which "minerals" you add. Look in a rock-identifying book to compare your rocks to real rocks. Did you make granite, marble, or perhaps something else?

Rock and Roll

<>-<>-<>-

Does shape affect how a rock rolls? You decide.

What You'll Need
- rocks
- watch with second hand
- pen and paper

Pick 6 differently shaped rocks of about the same size and weight. One might be rounded, one might be flat on one side, and one might be almost square or totally flat. One by one, release these rocks at the top of a steep hill and time how long each takes to roll to the bottom. Try to predict which rocks you think will move the fastest before letting them go. Compare your times and see how close your predictions came to being correct.

Mineral Testing Kit

<>-<>-<>-

Put together this simple kit for rock hounds.

Make a small, sturdy bag to carry your kit in: Cut two 6×8-inch pieces of canvas or denim and put them together, wrong side out. Sew 3 sides together. Fold over 1 inch of fabric on the top. Sew together to form a casing. Slit a seam open in the casing and slip a thick string through it.

    Into the bag, put a penny, a small piece of glass, a piece of unglazed tile, a file or pocket knife, a small bottle of vinegar, and an eyedropper. Now use your kit to test rocks and minerals to help you identify them.

    1. Use the tile to test the "streak" of the mineral. Do this by scratching the tile with your rock and seeing what color the scratches are.

    2. Vinegar is used to test for the presence of calcium carbonate. Put a drop of vinegar on the rock. If it fizzes, the rock contains calcium carbonate.

    3. The rest of the items test for hardness, on a hardness scale of 1 to 10: **1–2:** fingernail can scratch rock; **3:** penny can scratch rock; **4–5:** knife blade or file can scratch rock; **6:** glass can scratch rock; **7:** rock can scratch knife or file; rock can barely scratch glass; **8–10:** harder than common minerals.

    Use what you learn to identify the rocks in a reference book about rocks.

What You'll Need
- canvas or denim scraps
- scissors
- ruler
- needle and thread
- thick string
- penny
- small piece of glass
- piece of unglazed tile
- file or pocket knife
- small bottle of vinegar
- eyedropper
- rocks
- reference book about rocks

Mud Madness

◆◆◆◆◆◆◆

Here's mud in your eye! Getting dirty is the name of the game when it comes to building with mud.

Caution: This project requires adult supervision.

When you were younger, you probably loved to make mud pies. But now you can do more with mud than make a sloppy blob of goo. (This activity can get messy, so ask permission first and be sure to wear old clothes.) Using a stick, mix together some soil, flour, and water in a bucket until it's stiff and looks like dough. Now shape this mixture into a large rectangle (around 3 feet by 2 feet—about as big as a sofa cushion) and let it dry until it's firm. Once it's ready, have an adult cut the large brick into small bricks with a dull knife. You can use these bricks to build whatever you can imagine—a building, a city, a space station, or something else entirely. What muddy masterpiece can you create?

What You'll Need
- old clothes
- stick
- soil
- flour
- water
- bucket
- dull knife

Pebble Mosaic

◆◆◆◆◆◆◆

Make magnificent mosaic decorations from pebbles!

What You'll Need
- a variety of pebbles
- pencil
- plywood or particle board
- craft glue or tile grout

After you've collected lots of pretty pebbles in different colors and shapes, you can use them to make your mosaic. If you like, first use a pencil to draw a design on a piece of plywood. Then glue the pebbles on the design. Or, spread the plywood with grout, and push the pebbles into the grout.

A pebble mosaic makes a good trivet (used to hold hot pots). You can also make pebble mosaics to decorate flowerpots, vases, or lamps. What else could you decorate with pebbles?

Be a Rock Hound

❖❖❖❖❖❖❖

*Is it igneous or metamorphic? You'll find out
when you create your very own rock collection.*

What You'll Need

- rocks
- rock-identifying books
- box
- glue (optional)
- marker (optional)

No matter where you live, there are rocks around. But what kind of rocks depends on what part of the country you live in. In some regions, there are (literally) tons of granite lying around. In other regions, most of the rock is sandstone or limestone.

The kinds of rocks you find in a region depend on what kinds of minerals are found there. (Rocks are made out of minerals.) It also depends on what geologic "events" have happened in the area. For example, if a volcano ever dumped molten lava in your area, you'll find lots of igneous rocks. If your region was once under water, you'll find sedimentary rocks (rocks made when mud, sand, and minerals settle and harden). And if the earth has buckled, you'll find metamorphic rocks (rocks that have been changed by pressure and/or heat). These are the 3 basic kinds of rocks. All rocks fall into one of these 3 types.

Take a hike through your neighborhood and see how many different kinds of rocks you can find. Look along roads, streams, lakes, and excavations for rocks of different colors and different textures (smooth or rough, shiny or dull). But be careful!

Then see if you can identify your rocks. One way to identify rocks is to use a book that shows the different kinds. Check out a book from your library, and match your rock samples to pictures and descriptions in the book. The book will probably also tell you what minerals are in each kind of rock and how it was formed. Another way is to go to a rock shop. There you'll see samples of all different kinds of rocks, labeled with their names. Which ones look like rocks you found?

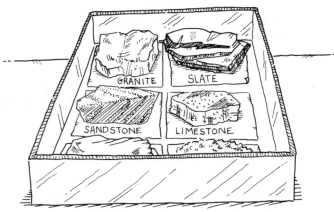

Keep expanding your rock collection as you find new and unusual rocks. Keep your rock collection in a box. You can glue each rock to the box and label it, or make a compartment for samples of each kind of rock.

Precious Jewels

◆▶◆▶◆▶◆

*Surprise someone you know with a special present—
jewelry made from natural gems.*

What You'll Need
- some interesting "found" stones
- jewelry fittings
- craft glue

How many times have you been walking along, looked down, and seen a really interesting rock? You pick it up, explore it, and put it in your pocket. It's easy and fun to make those special rocks into jewelry for yourself or your friends and family. After all, gemstones are just minerals that have been cut into shapes and then polished. (Sapphires, for instance, are made from a mineral called *corundum*.) Craft stores have all kinds of jewelry fittings. For example, they have pin backs—just glue one to the back of a special rock, and you have a beautiful pin. They also have glue-on fittings that you can use to make earrings, necklaces, bracelets, and rings.

Rock Hounder's Scavenger Hunt

◆▶◆▶◆▶◆

Rock steady with this geologic search.

Rock hounds are always on the prowl for new kinds of rocks. You can become a quick expert with this hunt. Ask your local librarian for books on rocks common to your hometown. Make a list of those rocks—including descriptions—and make photocopies while you're at the library. Once you get that list home, give it to your friends along with ordinary brown paper bags. Now team up in pairs and head out to find as many of those ordinary rocks as you can. The team with the most rocks gets to talk about their adventure first.

What You'll Need
- list of local rocks and descriptions
- paper bags
- markers

Ancient Messages

◆▸◆▸◆▸◆

Paint rocks to create petroglyphs, just like people did in ancient times.

"Petro" means rock and "glyph" means carving, so *petroglyphs* are rock carvings. Some ancient petroglyphs pointed the way to a stream or a shelter. Some might have told others, "Grog was here." These writings tell us about people who lived thousands of years ago. Here's how to make your own petroglyphs:

First, make your paint. Use crumbly rocks, dirt, or a mixture of both. Whatever you use, it should be colorful so it will show up when you paint it on a flat rock. Put the rocks in a paper bag, and pound them with a hammer to make a powder. Mix the powder with egg yolks, liquid soap, or liquid starch.

Now use your fingers to make petroglyphs on a large, flat rock. What do you have to say to people who will live thousands of years from now?

What You'll Need
- crumbly rocks or dirt
- paper bag
- hammer
- binding medium (such as egg yolks, liquid soap, or liquid starch)
- large flat rock

Go for the Gold

◆▸◆▸◆▸◆

You probably won't strike it rich gold panning, but it's fun to try!

What You'll Need
- old pie tin
- tweezers
- small bottle
- magnet

Caution: This project requires adult supervision.

Most areas of the country have at least a few streams that have yielded gold. Ask at the local Forest Service or Bureau of Land Management office to find out where to go near you.

Never go near the water without an adult nearby. Also, don't go in water that is deeper than your knees. Find a spot in the stream where the bottom is sandy and without too many rocks. Scoop up a handful of sand with plenty of water in your pie tin and swirl it around. Let the lighter sand spill out over the edge of the pan. Heavier materials, including iron and gold, will remain behind. The heavy sand is darker in color, too.

When the darker sand is all you have left in the pan, pour out the water and look closely. If you're lucky you'll see small specks of gold gleaming in it. Use tweezers to pick the gold from the sand and put it in your bottle. Later, let the gold and sand dry. Use a magnet to lift away the iron-rich dark sand, leaving the gold.

Be a Mineral Detective

◆◇◆◇◆◇◆

Calcium carbonate is one of the most common minerals in nature. See if you can discover some in your home.

Both eggshells and limestone contain calcium carbonate; some chalk is made from it as well. It's simple to find out whether or not a substance has calcium carbonate in it. Simply drop a sample into a jar of vinegar. If the vinegar dissolves (or partly dissolves) the substance, it contains calcium carbonate.

To try this, fill a wide-mouthed jar with vinegar. Gently place a whole egg in the jar. Watch the eggshell begin to fizz. Over a couple of days, it will completely dissolve! That's because an eggshell is almost all calcium carbonate.

What You'll Need
- wide-mouthed jar
- vinegar
- raw egg (in the shell)
- different kinds of chalk

Try the same thing with several different chalk samples. If the chalk is made from calcium carbonate, it will fizz and at least partly dissolve. Some chalk is made from another mineral called gypsum, which will not fizz and dissolve in vinegar.

Can Rocks Float?

◆◇◆◇◆◇◆

Even a rock can be full of surprises.

What You'll Need
- pumice
- bucket
- water

Most rocks drop with a "kerplop" to the bottom of a stream or a lake (or any body of water). But one volcanic rock won't sink like a stone when tossed into the drink. In fact, it will float and bob at the top. Don't believe it? Check out an air-filled rock called *pumice,* which is created by volcanic activity. It looks different from other rocks, and even feels light when you hold it in your hand, but it's a genuine rock and a must for any rock collector. Try to sink it in a bucket. It will float!

What Stone Are You?

◆▶◆▶◆▶

Were you born an amethyst, a peridot, or a zircon?
Learn all about your special birthstone.

What You'll Need
- encyclopedia or rock-identifying book
- paper clay
- tapestry needle
- paint
- paintbrush
- string

In ancient times, each month was said to have a special stone. Over time, people came up with at least 2 stones for most months. That stone—or stones—supposedly brought good luck to people who were born in that month. For example, the stone for January is garnet, a red gem. People born in January wore jewelry made with garnets.

These special stones became known as birthstones. Many people still wear their birthstones.

Find your birthstone on the following list. Learn as much about the stone as you can, including what it looks like and where it is found. Look up your stone in an encyclopedia or rock book. If you can, go to a rock shop so you can see your birthstone. Pay attention to the shape and color of your birthstone.

Using paper clay, create beads that resemble gemstones. Use a tapestry needle to make a hole in each bead. Let the beads dry overnight. Then paint the beads the same color as your birthstone. Since most stones have various shades, you may want to mix a few colors of paint together to get the right one. After the paint has dried, thread the beads on a short piece of string to make a bracelet or a long piece of string to make a necklace.

Month	Birthstone
January	garnet
February	amethyst
March	aquamarine or bloodstone
April	diamond
May	emerald or agate
June	pearl or moonstone
July	ruby or onyx
August	carnelian or peridot
September	sapphire or chrysolite
October	opal, beryl, or tourmaline
November	topaz
December	turquoise or zircon

Grow a Crystal "Garden"

◆▷◆▷◆▷◆

At one time, these were called "Depression gardens" because they were an inexpensive project for children during the Great Depression of the 1930s.

Caution: This project requires adult supervision.

Remember to be careful when working with any broken objects and when pouring ammonia.

Break coal, brick, clay flowerpots, or unglazed porcelain into chunks the size of walnuts. Place several in an old dish, clustering them near the center. (Don't overcrowd the dish.) In a mixing bowl, mix 4 tablespoons salt (not iodized), 4 tablespoons liquid bluing, 4 tablespoons water, and 1 tablespoon household ammonia. Pour the mixture very slowly over the broken pieces in your dish. Drip food coloring on the pieces sticking up out of the solution. Set the bowl aside in a place it won't be disturbed. (If you like, repeat the above directions using other colors of food coloring.) In a few hours you should see crystals "growing" in your garden.

To make crystal blossoms: Make a larger batch of the solution given above but leave out the ammonia. Make enough to completely cover the broken pieces in the dish (keep the pile low, under the rim of the dish). Add more solution every day or two to keep the same liquid level. After 2 weeks stop adding solution and allow the liquid to evaporate completely. Beautiful blossom shapes will form.

What You'll Need
- chunks of coal, brick, flowerpot pieces, or pieces of unglazed porcelain
- old shallow dishes about 6 inches wide
- measuring spoon
- mixing bowl
- salt (not iodized)
- liquid bluing
- water
- ammonia
- food coloring in several colors

Nature's Concrete

Make beautiful pottery and long-lasting sculptures with simple sand clay.

What You'll Need
- water
- clean sand
- measuring cup
- cornstarch
- pot or bowl
- spoon
- stove
- oven

Caution: This project requires adult supervision.

For thousands of years, people have mixed sand with other natural ingredients to make bricks, pots, and other things they need. You can do the same thing. With the help of a parent or adult, boil some water. For each cup of clean sand, mix ½ cup cornstarch and ½ cup boiling water in a sturdy pot or bowl. Stir the mixture several times as it cools.

Now, shape the mixture into pots and jars, or make sculptures of animals or other shapes. To harden the concrete, bake your creations in a 300°F oven for an hour. Let it cool completely before handling.

Candles in the Sand

Light up the darkness with these decorative candles created from sand.

Caution: This project requires adult supervision.

Sand, which is made of tiny grains of rock (usually quartz), has many uses. Bags full of sand keep rivers from jumping their banks and flooding the surrounding area. Sand sprinkled on icy sidewalks and roads can keep people and cars from slipping. Sand can even be used as a mold for making candles. Here's how:

What You'll Need
- wax or old candles
- old pan or coffee can
- stove
- cardboard box
- sand
- small candles
- oven mitts

With help from an adult, melt some wax on the stove (this is a good way to reuse old candles) in an old pan or an empty coffee can. Fill a cardboard box with damp sand. Use your fist to hollow out some holes in the sand. Put a small candle in the center of each hole. The candles' wicks should reach the tops of the holes. Finally, fill each hole around the small candle with melted wax. Be careful not to burn yourself with the hot wax! Let your candles sit overnight, then dig them out of the sand.

Art the Navajo Way

◆▸◆▸◆▸◆

The Navajo people have made sand paintings for centuries.

Navajo sand paintings almost always show nature: trees, plants, animals, lightning, and other wonders. You can make your own nature sand painting. You'll need several colors of sand. You can collect sand from nature, or buy it at a craft store. Cover your work surface with newspaper. Then take a piece of cardboard or poster board, and use a pencil to draw a nature picture.

Now mix white glue half-and-half with water. Use a paintbrush to paint a thin, even layer of the glue-and-water mixture every place where you want one color of sand. Sprinkle sand over the painted areas. Let dry for a few minutes, then turn your picture over and tap off the extra sand. (Do this over a trash can!) Repeat the process with the next color: Paint glue on all the areas that will be the same color. Sprinkle on the sand, let dry, and tap off. Repeat this until you've finished your sand painting.

What You'll Need
- newspaper
- colored sand
- cardboard or poster board
- pencil
- glue
- water
- cup or bowl
- paintbrush

Play with Clay

◆▸◆▸◆▸◆

There is natural clay all over the earth. See if you can find clay near you.

What You'll Need
- small shovel

Clay is soil that's made of very tiny bits of minerals and other elements. These tiny bits stick together, packing so close that they keep out water. That's what makes clay squishy and stretchy.

See if you can locate some natural clay where you live. Start by asking people who garden what they know about natural clay. They can tell you if there's a lot of it around. You'll have to dig for it—clay is usually under the topsoil. When you find something that you think might be clay, try rolling a piece of it into a ball. (You may need to add some water.) If it holds its shape, like modeling clay, it's clay. Clean all the rocks, leaves, twigs, and other debris out of the clay. Then use it to make a small pot. Pots made from natural clay aren't completely waterproof, but they can last a long time if you're careful with them.

'Tites or 'Mites?

◆▸◆▸◆▸◆◂◆

If you sat in a cave for thousands of years, you could watch stalactites and stalagmites form. Or you could make your own in a matter of days.

What You'll Need

- 2 jars
- water
- Epsom salts
- string
- small weights
- plate

Fill 2 jars with warm water. Mix in Epsom salts until no more will dissolve. Wet the string and tie a weight to each end. Drop one end of the string into each jar. Put a plate between the 2 jars, with the string hanging over the plate.

Check your "cave" at least once a day to see if stalactites and stalagmites have formed. By the way, if you're wondering which are 'tites and which are 'mites: Stalactites have to hold on tight to stay on the ceiling of the cave. Stalagmites have to be mighty to stand up on the floor of the cave.

Sand Museum

◆▸◆▸◆▸◆◂◆

Sand is composed of tiny particles. These particles, or grains, are different sizes, colors, and shapes.

Lift some sand in your hand. Pour it out, and you'll see that it behaves almost like a liquid. Look at the sand using a magnifying glass. What does one sand grain look like? Compare it to others. Do they have different sizes, shapes, and colors?

Now make a sand museum. Find grains of as many different colors and sizes as you can. Draw squares on a piece of dark paper, and glue

What You'll Need

- sand
- magnifying glass
- dark construction paper
- marker
- glue

similar sand grains in the center of each square. Pretend they are rare jewels, and give them descriptive but fun names, such as the "Ruby Crystal" or the "Black Star."

Soft and Hard

◆▶◆▶◆▶◆

Different minerals have different levels of hardness.

What You'll Need
- talcum powder
- gypsum (from drywall)
- penny
- sandpaper

Different minerals have different levels of hardness. To measure hardness, geologists determine a mineral's resistance to scratching. Friedrich Mohs created a scale of hardness for classifying different minerals, which we call the Mohs' scale.

You can see that talc is the softest mineral on the scale and diamond is the hardest.

Touch some talcum powder, and notice its softness. Then feel gypsum for its texture and hardness. Your fingernail can scratch minerals with a softness of about 2.5. A penny has a hardness of about 3. See if you can find minerals that can be scratched by a penny. Sandpaper is made with minerals such as corundum. These are very hard minerals. Gently touch your finger against some sandpaper to feel the hardness of these minerals.

Hardness	Mineral
1	talc
2	gypsum
3	calcite
4	fluorite
5	apatite
6	feldspar
7	quartz
8	topaz
9	corundum
10	diamond

Acid Test

◆▶◆▶◆▶◆

Some rocks and minerals contain calcium carbonate.

What You'll Need
- rocks
- small cups
- vinegar

Gather several small pieces of different kinds of rock. Place each piece into a different cup. Pour enough vinegar in each container to almost cover the rock. See if the rock starts fizzing. If it does, you'll know that the rock contains calcium carbonate; the acid in the vinegar reacts with the calcium carbonate to cause the fizzing. Rocks such as limestone, marble, calcite, and chalk react with the acid in this way. Acid rain can also break down rocks, just as vinegar can. Many ancient buildings and statues are made of marble, and acid rain is causing some of them to slowly dissolve.

Way Cool: Volcanic Rock

◄►◄►◄►◄►

The speed of cooling influences the size of particles in rocks.

Examine different types of volcanic rocks closely. Use a magnifying glass to determine if each one is coarse or fine grained. The fine textures occur when the lava cools quickly, and the rough textures occur when the lava cools slowly.

What You'll Need
- volcanic rocks
- magnifying glass

Fast Cool, Slow Cool

◄►◄►◄►◄►

Try this tasty experiment to see how rocks are formed.

What You'll Need
- metal container
- bowl of ice
- water
- measuring cup and spoon
- saucepan
- stove
- sugar
- spoon
- vanilla extract
- salt

Caution: This project requires adult supervision.

Making candy is a sweet way to learn about rocks. The way you cool the candy influences the size of the candy particles. This is similar to how some rocks are formed.

Put a metal container into a large bowl filled with ice; you will use this cool container later. Bring ½ cup water to a boil in a saucepan. Slowly add 2½ cups sugar, mixing it gently with a spoon. Add 2 teaspoons vanilla extract and ¼ teaspoon salt. Keep stirring the candy mixture as you heat it. Heat the mixture to a slow boil until the sugar dissolves. Be careful that the solution does not foam up and out of the pan. When the sugar is dissolved, turn off the stove.

Now it's time to let the mixture cool. Take the container that you cooled with ice, and carefully pour half of the candy mixture into it. The cool container will make the candy solution cool quickly. Leave the remaining candy mixture in the pot, and put it in a safe spot to cool. It will cool more slowly than the other mixture. As the mixtures cool, they will form into crystals. Observe the size of the crystals in the different containers.

The candy that cooled quickly produced small crystals. It looked sandy or sugary. The candy that cooled slowly produced larger crystals. It produced lumpy candy. Rocks that are formed through heating and cooling behave the same way. Granite is an igneous rock with large grains, and basalt is an igneous rock with small grains. Do you think granite and basalt cooled at different rates? Which one cooled faster?

Toast to Regolith!

◆━◆━◆━◆━◆

Regolith is a layer of loose rocks and soil that sits over solid rock. It is usually formed on Earth through erosion.

What You'll Need
- toast
- sandpaper

Make a piece of toast. Imagine that your toast is the hard, rocky surface of the earth. Rub your hand on one side of the toast. Note the crumbs and fine particles that fall off. The friction from your hand caused the erosion of the toast. Rub the other side of the toast with sandpaper. The rough surface rubs off more particles. Friction from wind and water, from sand blown by the wind, and from rocks carried by glaciers can cause erosion in rocks and create pebbles, sand, and dirt. Some of this is washed away by water to lakes and oceans, and some of it remains on land. We call the layer of sediment that covers the ground *regolith*.

What Is Sand?

◆━◆━◆━◆━◆━◆

Sand is more than something to use to make castles. Discover the mysteries in a handful of sand.

Where does sand come from? The sand itself will give you clues. The next time you hit the beach, sprinkle some sand on a sheet of white paper and look at it closely with a magnifying glass. What kinds of particles do you see? How many different colors do you see? Sprinkle some on black or dark-colored paper. Do particles stand out now that were hard to see on white paper? You'll also notice dark particles in the sand. Pass a magnet over your sand sample. Many of the dark particles will stick to the magnet. These are iron-rich minerals, such as magnetite. If you are patient, you can try sorting the sand particles into separate piles.

What You'll Need
- beach sand
- white paper
- magnifying glass
- black or dark-colored paper
- magnet
- small containers
- labels
- pencil or pen

Sand is made of tiny rock fragments eroded by water. Some of your sand grains are the same color as nearby rocks. You may find a lot of light-colored or even clear particles. Many of these are quartz, a mineral high in silica. Because most sand has a lot of quartz, it is used to manufacture glass.

If you visit beaches in different areas, start a sand collection. Find small, clear bottles or plastic containers. (Some film-developing shops will give you clear film canisters for free.) Scoop a sample of sand from the beach into a container, and label and date it.

Rockin' Paint

◆◆◆◆◆◆

Now you can make paint just as people did years ago...with rocks!

What You'll Need
- crumbly rocks
- charcoal
- soil
- clay
- paper bag
- rock
- old bowl
- cornstarch or corn syrup
- water
- paintbrush
- paper

Forget rock 'n' roll. It's time to rock 'n' paint! Make your own paint with materials like rocks, charcoal, soil, and clay. Gather crumbly rocks, charcoal, heavy pieces of soil, and clay in a paper bag and use a rock to crush them into a fine powder. (Watch your fingers!) Believe it or not, this powder will be the base for your paint. Mix the powder in a bowl with a little cornstarch and water (or just some corn syrup) to make a pastelike mixture. Now you're ready to create a masterpiece with your own homemade paint! Just dip a brush into the mixture and get to work painting on your paper. Have a look around your backyard and see what other things can be crushed to make paint and what materials don't work all that well. Try things like grass, flowers, leaves, or sticks. Hard rocks won't work too well. See if you can mix different colors that will add some flair to your works of art!

Sweet Crystals

◆◆◆◆◆◆

See how crystals form in nature, and make candy at the same time!

Caution: This project requires adult supervision.

With the help of an adult, boil half a cup of water in a saucepan. Add a cup of sugar a spoonful at a time until all the sugar is dissolved. Keep adding sugar until the solution turns into a clear syrup. Let it cool for about 10 minutes, then pour the syrup into a glass jar.

Now get a piece of string about 6 inches long. Tie one end of the string around a pencil, then tie the other end to a craft stick. Put the pencil on top of the jar so the craft stick hangs in the syrup.

Set your "crystal maker" aside. Take a look at it every day to see what's happening. In about a week, the syrup should be crystallized and ready to eat.

What You'll Need
- saucepan
- stove
- water
- measuring cup
- spoon
- sugar
- glass jar
- string
- pencil
- craft stick

This Garden Rocks!

◆◆◆◆◆◆

*If you're a rock lover, it's fun to make a garden
that features rocks, as well as plants.*

What You'll Need
- pen and paper
- garden plot
- rocks of different shapes and sizes
- plants

If you have a yard or garden area that already has some large rocks in it, you're in luck. If not, gather some rocks when you go out hiking. (A wagon or wheelbarrow comes in very handy!)

Begin arranging the rocks in your garden space. You may want to draw a plan of your rock garden first. It's a lot easier to move rocks around on paper than in the garden! Arrange the rocks in a design you like. It's nice to have one place in a garden that is the main attraction. If you have a favorite rock, put it in a place where it will be the "star" of the garden. Use more rocks to make a border around the garden, if you like.

Of course, you'll want plants in your garden, too. For ideas, here is a list of flowering plants that are popular in rock gardens. But which plants you choose will depend on where you live and what kinds of plants you like. Your rock garden could also be an herb garden! Or, you could plant different kinds of plants that all have the same color flowers. If you live where it's warm and dry, your rock garden could be a cactus garden, with many kinds of cacti.

Popular Rock-Garden Plants
Alyssum
Anemone
Azalea
Crocus
Cyclamen
Geranium
Iris
Narcissus
Phlox
Rhododendron

Collect Meteorites

◆▶◆▶◆▶◆

It's easy to collect particles from outer space.

What You'll Need
- bed sheet
- rock or bricks
- magnet
- plastic bottle

The earth is constantly bombarded with rocks from space. Most of them burn up in the atmosphere long before they touch the earth. Of the few that do drop to Earth, the vast majority are as fine as dust. Tiny stone meteorites are hard to find without a microscope, but iron meteorites are easy to collect. All you need is a magnet and a bed sheet. On a still, clear night, lay a sheet on the ground. (Make sure it's in the open, away from trees.) Hold the edges of the sheet down with rocks or bricks and leave it there all night. In the morning, examine the sheet. You'll notice it's a little bit dirty. Most of this dirt is dust from the air, but some of it came from space! Take a magnet and pass it slowly over the sheet. If there are any iron particles from meteorites, they will stick to the magnet. Gently scrape the iron particles off and store them in a container, such as a plastic bottle or a film canister. Meteorite particles make a great addition to your rock collection!

Extinction

Many groups of plants and animals have become extinct during Earth's history. Sometimes when plants or animals die, they leave behind impressions of their bodies in rock formations. We have learned much about extinct life-forms from these kinds of fossil remains.

Making an Impression

Leave your mark on the world when you create "fossils."

Fossils are imprints of plants and animals found in rocks. Here is one way fossils are made in nature: A leaf falls into wet, sandy ground. A flood deposits more sandy soil on top of the leaf, so that it is trapped there. Over thousands of years, the leaf decays and disappears. But as the sandy soil hardens into rock, the impression made by the leaf is left in the rock.

What You'll Need
- small natural object
- petroleum jelly
- paintbrush
- plaster of paris
- spoon
- water
- small disposable dish

You can see how fossils are created by making your own. First, choose an object for your fossil. It could be a shell, a leaf, an animal bone, or another object from nature. Coat the object with petroleum jelly. Next, pour some plaster of paris and some water in a small disposable dish, such as a margaring tub. Mix them together well. Let the plaster of paris and water sit for a few minutes, without stirring. Press the object into the plaster of paris and let everything dry. This will take at least one day. When the plaster of paris is completely dry, remove the object. The impression left behind is like a fossil.

Fossil Finds

Nature makes a lasting impression.

What You'll Need
- paper
- crayons

We think of fossils as ancient reminders captured in stone. But modern fossils are everywhere and are as close as the sidewalks under your feet. The next time you take a walk, keep your eyes on the cement to make a few modern-day fossil finds. The "fossil" could be an imprint from a shoe, the pecking of a persistent bird, or a chip made by some unseen tool. For extra fun, bring along paper and a crayon to make rubbings of what you discover. Just lay the paper over the "fossil" and rub a crayon across the spot to make an exact "copy" of the image on your page.

Fossil Junior

◆◆◆◆◆◆◆

Study how fossils begin.

What You'll Need
- small garden shovel
- old toothbrush

Before fossils turn to stone, they rest in dirt. Search for fossils-in-the-making to understand how the process actually works. First, ask your parents' permission before you dig in any part of their landscaped yard. Once you have the green light, dig carefully with a small garden shovel.

If you find a leaf or dead bug embedded in the soil, use an old toothbrush to carefully remove excess dirt from the "fossil." See if you can gently remove the bug or plant. Is there an impression left where the bug once was? Now imagine—left undisturbed, that bug might have been transformed into a fossil millions of years into the future.

City Fossil Hunt

◆◆◆◆◆◆◆

Look carefully to find fossils right in the middle of the city!

What You'll Need
- magnifying glass
- notebook
- pen or pencil

Fossils are made when animals or plants are trapped in sediment (such as mud, wet sand, or river silt). If conditions are right, minerals from the sediments slowly replace the material in the bones of the animals. Plant and animal parts can leave imprints in mud that dry and can be preserved for thousands of years. Eventually the sediments may turn to rock, such as sandstone, shale, limestone, or slate. Under heat and pressure, sedimentary rocks may change into metamorphic rocks such as marble.

Sometimes, sedimentary and metamorphic rocks are used to make buildings. Take a walk around your city and hunt for buildings using rocks in their construction. The rocks used most often are granite and marble. Granite was formed from hardened lava, so you won't find fossils in it. It's rare to find fossils in metamorphic rock, but observe them closely anyway. You may find a few fossils of seashells stretched and deformed along with the rock! If you can find a building that uses sedimentary rocks, you may be in luck. Look carefully for the remains of ancient creatures. They may be small, so use your magnifying glass to hunt for tiny shells. Keep track of your findings.

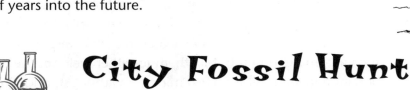

Long, Long Ago

◆▸▸▸▸▸◂

The earth is billions of years old.

Scientists divide all of the time that has occurred since the formation of the earth into eras. The 3 most recent eras are the Paleozoic era, which covers the time between 570 and 225 million years ago; the Mesozoic era, which lasted from 225 to 65 million years ago; and the Cenozoic era, which dates from 65 million years ago to the present. Use a reference book to find the dates of all the eras in Earth's history.

What You'll Need
- reference books
- roll of toilet paper
- calculator
- paper and pen

   Get a roll of toilet paper that has 1,000 sheets. You will use this to represent the passage of time over Earth's history. Since the earth is roughly 4.5 billion years old, each sheet of paper can represent 4.5 million years. To figure out how many sheets you need to represent each era in Earth's history, look in your reference books to find out how long each era lasted, and then divide that number by 4.5 million. Unwind the paper, carefully counting off each sheet, and mark each of the era boundaries. How much of the paper do you need to represent the amount of time humans have lived on Earth?

Shell Print

◆▸▸▸▸▸◂

Use clay to see how a fossil print might have been made.

What You'll Need
- newspaper
- air-drying modeling clay
- dull knife
- pencil
- small seashell
- leather strip

Real fossils are formed in several different ways. They can be actual hard remains of ancient organisms, parts of organisms that have been replaced by minerals, or impressions of the organisms that have been preserved in sediments. Using a shell and clay, you can imitate this process.

   Cover your work surface with newspaper. Start with a ⅜-inch-thick slab of air-drying modeling clay. Cut out a 2-inch diameter circle of clay. Use a pencil to poke a hole through the top of the clay circle. Press an interesting small seashell firmly into the circle of clay. Carefully remove the shell. It should leave a clear impression behind. The impression will resemble a fossil imprint. Allow the clay to air-dry, then thread a leather strip through the hole, and tie the ends in a knot. You can wear your shell imprint around your neck.

Life Chart

Geologic time periods have been given names, and different creatures lived during each period.

Find a geologic time chart in a reference book; check in encyclopedias or in books about dinosaurs or Earth's history. Use the information in the reference books to make a large chart on poster board. Give your chart 5 columns: "ERA," "PERIOD," "EPOCH," "MILLIONS OF YEARS AGO," and "CREATURES."

What You'll Need
- reference books
- poster board
- markers
- ruler

Down the first column, from top to bottom, print the names of 3 eras: "CENOZOIC," "MESOZOIC," and "PALEOZOIC." Using reference materials, complete the columns of your geologic time chart. For example, in the Period column for the Cenozoic, you will divide it into 2 periods: "QUATERNARY" and "TERTIARY." Under the Epoch column for Tertiary, you will print the names of 5 epochs: "PLIOCENE," "MIOCENE," "OLIGOCENE," "EOCENE," and "PALEOCENE." In the Millions of Years Ago column after Pliocene, you will print "5." Find one or two plants or animals that lived during each period, and draw them in the final column. A saber-toothed tiger, for example, might appear as a creature in the Quaternary Period.

Changes in the Earth

The surface of the earth is always changing. Plates below the earth's crust may push other plates up, forming mountain ranges and valleys. Volcanoes may erupt, forming mountains and islands. At the same time, forces also break down structures on Earth. Water seeps into rocks, freezes, and breaks the rocks. Wind, rain, and glaciers wear away rocky surfaces.

River Rock Mystery

◆◆◆◆◆◆

Well-rounded stones—imagine how they got that way.

Scoop up a bucket of river rocks and sand and what will you find? Smooth, rounded stones, more often than not. Examine a few of the stones, then imagine the journeys they've made downstream and figure out WHY they're more rounded than their mountainside friends. See if you can follow their trail to find out how they got to the river and where they came from.

What You'll Need
- bucket
- stream or riverbed

Washed Away

◆◆◆◆◆◆

Learn how erosion—when soil is washed away by wind or water—occurs.

What You'll Need
- 3 aluminum-foil cooking pans
- scissors
- 3 lengths of rubber or plastic tubing (½-inch in diameter)
- tape
- a mixture of soil, sand, and clay
- potting soil
- books
- 3 bowls
- cereal grains
- plant mister
- watering can

Poke a small hole in one end of each aluminum pan, near the upper rim. Put one end of a length of tubing into each hole, using tape to hold it there. Into each pan put a layer of the soil, sand, and clay mixture. Then add a layer of potting soil on top of that. Put all 3 pans indoors on a table where they will get sunlight. Rest all 3 pans on books to elevate the pans at about a 30-degree angle. The tubing should be on the bottom end of each pan. Put the free end of each tube into a bowl.

In one pan, make rows across the width of the pan and plant cereal grains in the rows. In another pan, make the rows lengthwise and plant the grain. Don't plant anything in the third pan. Use a plant mister to keep the grain moist until it sprouts. Continue to water the grain until the seedlings are about 2 inches tall. Don't do anything to the empty pan. Once the seedlings in the 2 pans are about 2 inches tall, begin using a watering can to sprinkle all 3 pans.

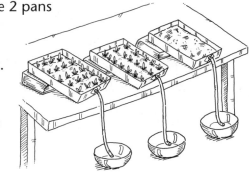

The watering can should have a spout that imitates rain. Each time you water the pans, watch the water that runs into the bowls. Which bowl collects more potting soil? Why? What could you do to prevent potting soil from eroding into the bowls?

What a Relief!

Every area of the earth has high places and low places. A relief map is a special kind of map that shows these highs and lows.

What You'll Need

- plywood
- marker
- plaster of paris or modeling clay
- paints
- paintbrushes

Whether it's your backyard or the whole United States, you'll find high and low points. A relief map is like a small model showing mountains, hills, and valleys. You can make a relief map on a piece of plywood. First, draw an outline of the area you're going to map. Then use plaster of paris or modeling clay to fill in the outline. Pile up the clay to show the high places! If you're mapping a large area, such as the state you live in, you'll need to look at a map that shows mountains and valleys. If you're mapping a small area such as your backyard, just map what you see.

After your map dries, paint it. Use different colors to highlight the highs and lows. For example, you could paint the highest mountaintops white like snow and the valleys green like plants.

The Flat Earth

About 2,300 years ago, a Greek scientist named Aristotle decided that the earth was round, not flat like other people believed. Most people laughed at Aristotle, and it wasn't until Columbus traveled to America in the late 1490s that others started to take Aristotle's theory seriously. There is still an organization called the Flat Earth Society, and its members believe that Aristotle made a mistake.

Powerful Plants

◆◇◆◇◆◇◆

You might think that rocks would be stronger than plants. But plants are strong enough to break through rock when they have to.

What You'll Need
- beans
- water
- bowl
- plaster of paris
- aluminum-foil baking pan

Soak a handful of beans in a bowl of water overnight. Pour plaster of paris into an aluminum-foil baking pan. The plaster of paris should be a couple of inches deep. Sprinkle the soaked beans on top. Cover the beans with another layer of plaster of paris that is about an inch thick. Watch what happens. When the beans sprout, they will break right through the rocklike plaster of paris.

You can see examples of this in nature. When you go for a walk, look for plants and trees growing up through rock. Or you might see tree roots breaking up a concrete sidewalk.

Layers of Time

◆◇◆◇◆◇◆

Stripes of mystery revealed.

Have you ever noticed the ribbons of colors that run throughout some roadside cliffs? Next time you pass one of these colorful rock formations, stop and make a sketch. Be as careful and accurate with colors as you can. Once you've finished

What You'll Need
- paper
- colored pencils or crayons
- self-addressed stamped envelope

your sketch, send a color copy of the drawing, along with its exact location, to the U.S. Geological Survey office and a local university geology department or local natural history museum asking what the colors mean. Be sure to enclose a self-addressed stamped envelope with your letter so that the scientists can write back about what they see between your colorful lines. You'll learn a lot about geology and ancient history.

That Settles It!

◆◆◆◆◆◆◆

When soil, sand, and other materials settle at the bottom of a lake or pond it is called sediment. Over time, layers of sediment can form rock.

Put a handful each of soil, sand, and gravel into a jar. Fill the jar with water. Put the lid on tightly. Shake the jar well until everything is mixed together. Now let the jar sit overnight. In the morning, see how the different things in the jar have settled. How would you describe what you see? What can you say about the layers? Compare your layers to what happens in a lake or pond.

What You'll Need
- jar with lid
- soil
- sand
- gravel
- water
- small plastic animals (optional)

If you want to see how fossilized critters are made, put small, plastic animals in with your soil, sand, and gravel mixture.

It's Your Fault

◆◆◆◆◆◆◆

A fault is a place where there is a break in the earth's crust. You can use clay to make your own model of a fault.

What You'll Need
- 3 different colors of clay
- a dull knife

Earthquakes often begin at a fault in the earth. If rock near a fault suddenly begins to move, it creates pressure, which causes an earthquake. Here's a simple way to show how it works:

Get 3 pieces of clay, each in a different color, and pound each piece into a flat rectangle. Stack them on top of one another and press them together. The 3 pieces of clay stand for layers of the earth's crust.

Use a dull knife to cut all the way through the layers, in the middle. Put the 2 sections of clay together, but don't match them up exactly as they were before you cut them apart. The cut is like a fault in the earth's crust.

Push in on the outside edges of both sections of clay. The clay along the "fault" will buckle and slide. Earthquake!

Thar She Blows!

◆◆◆◆◆◆◆

**There's no need to run for cover from this safe model
of a real erupting volcano.**

What You'll Need

- tall jar with lid
- measuring cup and spoon
- water
- baking soda
- dishwashing liquid
- red or orange food coloring
- large plastic container or wash basin
- dirt or sand
- vinegar
- plaster of paris (optional)
- paints (optional)
- paintbrushes (optional)
- pinecones (optional)

When a real volcano erupts, you don't want to be there. After all, the lava that spews out of a volcano is rock that is so hot it has become liquid. But you can get an idea what it's like by making your own volcano.

First, get a tall, thin jar. The kind of jar that pickles or olives come in works well. In the jar, mix together ¼ cup water, ¼ cup baking soda, 3 tablespoons dishwashing liquid, and a few drops of red or orange food coloring. Put the lid on the jar. Set the jar in the center of a big container. Next, build a "mountain" of dirt or sand around the jar. (It will work better if the dirt or sand is slightly wet.) If you'd like, you can cover the mountain with plaster of paris, and paint it to look like a real volcano. You can even decorate it with pinecones to look like trees.

Now... it's lava time! Take the lid off the jar, quickly pour in ¼ cup vinegar, and stand back. Watch your volcano erupt.

Sleeping Giants

Just because a volcano has been asleep for a long time does not mean that it is no longer a threat. One volcano that was asleep, called Mount St. Helens in the state of Washington, hadn't erupted since 1857. But, in 1980, it erupted violently, causing it to become more than 1,000 feet shorter than it had been.

There Goes the Beach!

◆◇◆◇◆◇◆

Water has the power to wear down rocks and soil—even beaches. You can make a beach-in-a-pan to see how erosion happens in nature.

What You'll Need
- large rectangular pan
- brick
- sand
- gravel
- water
- thick sponge

Set one end of your pan on a brick so the end of the pan is raised a few inches. Next, use sand and gravel to make a "beach" at the high end of the pan. (You may need to dampen the sand to make it stay in place.) Pour water into the low end of the pan until the water reaches the beach.

Now put a thick sponge in the water at the low end of the pan. Push down on the sponge to make "waves" in your ocean. Watch what the waves do to the beach. That's erosion!

Deep Sea Life

If you traveled downward in the ocean, below 330 feet, it would get darker and darker. Soon it would be as black as night. There are fish that live there, but they look quite strange. Some, like the lantern fish and the stomiatoids, have tiny glowing lights. Other fish have silvery sides that act like mirrors—and the angler fish has a projection that dangles from its head. It acts like bait, attracting other fish, which the angler fish can gobble up.

Pangaea Puzzle

◆◆◆◆◆◆

The continents of today may have been joined together in the past in one huge continent.

Find a map of the world that you can cut into pieces. Cut out all of the continents on the map. Think of them as pieces in a jigsaw puzzle. Try to fit the pieces together to form one big continent. Some scientists believe that

the continents were once joined together in one huge land-mass called Pangaea and that forces in the earth caused them to drift apart over many millions of years. When you created the Pangaea Puzzle, the continents fit together pretty well, but not perfectly. If they had been joined together before, why wouldn't the pieces of your map fit together perfectly now?

A Rocky Road

◆◆◆◆◆◆

Weathering of rocks breaks them into smaller pieces.

Rinse all the dirt or debris from a handful of pebbles. Look at the pebbles, noting their size and shape. Place them in the jar, and add water until they are covered. Screw on the lid of the jar. Shake the jar, and swirl the rocks for a total of 20 minutes or more.

Observe the contents of the jar. Can you see small pieces of rock, sand, and clay that have broken off the pebbles? Place 2 coffee filters over the mouth of the jar. Pour off the water. Examine the pebbles and particles.

The movement of the water broke the rock into smaller pieces. This kind of weathering happens in nature as water, wind, glaciers, and the earth's shifting crust break down rocks into smaller pieces.

Grazing Glaciers

❖❖❖❖❖❖❖

Glaciers erode land.

What You'll Need
- gravel
- paper cup
- water
- freezer
- scissors

Caution: This project requires adult supervision.

You are going to make a glacier. Put enough gravel in a paper cup to cover the bottom. Fill the cup ¾ of the way with water, and put it in the freezer. When the water is frozen, carefully cut away the bottom inch of paper from the cup. This exposes the ice and gravel but leaves a place for you to hold the ice.

Find a patch of soil. Rub the ice and gravel part of your "glacier" over the soil. What effects did this have on the soil? During the last ice age, many places in the north were overrun with glaciers. The movement of these glaciers removed soil and rock and left deep gouges in the earth.

This Will Crack You Up

❖❖❖❖❖❖❖

It's true, winter can be hard on everybody—even on rocks. See how the cold affects more than just your toes.

Put an egg in a sealed plastic bag and put the bag in the freezer overnight. In the morning, see what the freezing temperature did to the egg. When the egg freezes, it expands and breaks its shell. Winter freezes do the same thing to rocks that have moisture in them. The moisture expands as it freezes, causing the rocks to break. When you're out walking in the winter, see if you can find rocks that have been in

What You'll Need
- egg
- small resealable plastic bag
- freezer

nature's deep freeze. A rock that is broken into pieces but still lying in its original shape is probably a victim of winter's icy strength.

Clues of the Past

◆◆◆◆◆◆

Look for signs of Earth-shaping events.

What You'll Need
- A map of your community or a place of special interest

The surface of the earth is constantly moving as water and weather erode the rocks and move the soil. You can find evidence of recent geological events—and perhaps ancient events as well! Use a map to explore your community or some other special place. Mark what you find on your map. Floods, for example, leave watermarks on buildings. Also look for scouring of stream banks and for debris in tree branches.

Huge glaciers, which once scoured a large part of the North American continent, left distinctive marks behind. Large, exposed rock faces may have had long scratches cut into them as rocky undersides of glaciers passed over them. If you live in the northern United States, look for areas around your community that are flat and have many small lakes. These areas were scoured out by glaciers. Glaciers also "rafted" large rocks from one area of the country to another. Look for boulders of a kind of rock not normally found in your area.

Around the mountains, look for the same kind of scratches on rock faces that continental glaciers left behind. Also seek what geologists call U-shaped valleys. These are broad valleys cut by glaciers. Valleys cut by streams tend to be V-shaped. Also search for areas where soil has been exposed and eroded by running water. Too much erosion causes stream banks to collapse and can lead to landslides. If you see a very muddy stream, follow it upstream to see if the mud comes from erosion along the banks. Look also for signs of erosion control in your community, such as trees planted on bare slopes.

Core Knowledge

How do geologists take core samples of the layers of the earth?

Take one color of clay and roll it into 2 flat pancakes. Repeat with the other colors of clay. Then, mix up all the pancakes, and place them in a multicolored stack.

Now it is time to take a core sample. Use a plastic straw, and push it from the top of the stack down to the bottom of the stack. When you pull the straw back out, it will have clay inside. Use cuticle

scissors to cut the plastic straw away from the clay inside. Remove the clay core sample.

Examine the core sample. It reveals exactly how you stacked your color pancakes. In a similar way, geologists take core samples from the soil to study the layers of the earth. The deeper layers are the layers that were deposited first.

Earth's Rotation

The earth's rotation on its axis is responsible for producing night and day. When one side of the earth receives sunlight and experiences daytime, the other side gets no light and experiences nighttime. During the day, the sun's position in the sky can be used to tell time.

Sun Time

◆◆◆◆◆◆◆

What time is it? Check the sun!

Mold a piece of clay so that it will make a firm base. Put a stick into the clay so that it will stand upright. Put the stick on a blacktop or concrete surface where it can get light all day. Starting in the morning, draw a chalk line over the shadow of the stick at the start of each hour. Label the time near the line. Do this throughout the day. When you're done, you'll have a sundial that can be used to tell time. At any time during the next day, you can go look at where the stick's shadow falls, and tell what time it is by comparing it to the chalk marks you made. The sun's position in the sky changes gradually as the year goes on, so you'll need to reset your sundial each month by redrawing the chalk markings.

What You'll Need
- clay
- stick
- watch or clock
- chalk

Light/Night

◆◆◆◆◆◆◆

The earth's rotation produces day and night.

What You'll Need
- globe
- flashlight

Turn on a flashlight, and place it on a table in a darkened room. Hold a globe of the earth a few feet from the flashlight in its beam. Notice that half of the globe is lit up and half is dark. The dark side is night, and the light side is day. Rotate the globe clockwise, and watch how different parts of the world receive light and then fall into darkness. Can you see why the sun seems to rise in the east and set in the west?

Globe Trotters

◆◆◆◆◆◆◆

The amount of light reaching a hemisphere makes summer warm and winter cold.

What You'll Need
- lamp
- globe

Put a lamp in the middle of the room. Hold a globe about 5 or 6 feet from the lamp. Notice that the globe is tilted along its poles. This shows how the earth is tilted. Hold the globe upright, and position it so the North Pole tilts away from the light source. Observe how the light falls on the Northern Hemisphere (above the equator) and on the Southern Hemisphere (below the equator). You can see that the Southern Hemisphere gets more light. If the earth was in this position in its orbit, it would be summer in the Southern Hemisphere and winter in the Northern Hemisphere. Walk around the lamp in a circle, but move the globe as you walk so that the North Pole continues to point in the same direction. Notice that the way the light falls on the hemispheres changes as you walk around the lamp. When you're standing on the opposite side of the lamp, the Northern Hemisphere gets more light than the Southern Hemisphere. If the earth was in this position in its orbit, it would be summer in the Northern Hemisphere and winter in the Southern Hemisphere.

Flash Sun

◆◆◆◆◆◆◆

The earth's tilt helps create the differences in the seasons.

What You'll Need
- 2 similar flashlights

Many people think it is cold in the winter because the earth is farther from the sun during the winter season. This is not true. In fact, in the Northern Hemisphere, the sun is slightly closer to the earth during the winter. It is colder in the winter because the earth tilts away from the sun and the sun's intensity on the Northern Hemisphere decreases.

To picture this, take 2 flashlights. Stand close to a wall. Shine one light straight at the wall. Notice the round circle of light it makes. Point the other flashlight slightly upward, and shine it against the wall. Notice the larger oval area of light it makes. Both flashlights put off the same light and heat, but the first one concentrates it in a smaller area, and the other one spreads the light and heat over a greater area.

Hours in a Day

◆◆◆◆◆◆◆

A day is 24 hours long, but the amount of daylight in each day changes throughout the year.

What You'll Need
- notebook
- pen
- newspaper or radio (optional)

Keep a journal that records the hours of daylight in each day. Each morning if you are awake, record the time the sun rises. At the end of the day, record the time the sun sets. If you cannot observe the sunrise or sunset, check the times each day in the newspaper or on the radio. You will find that the days are shorter in winter than in summer. The longest day of the year is the summer solstice (around June 21), and the shortest day of the year is the winter solstice (around December 21).

Wheel of Time

◆▶◆▶◆▶◆

What time is it in Sydney, Australia, right now? With this activity, you'll be able to tell the time all over the world.

What You'll Need

- poster board
- scissors
- yardstick
- markers
- thumbtack
- large piece of cardboard
- watch

The world is divided into 24 time zones. When it's midnight in one time zone, on the side of the earth opposite from that spot, it's noon.

Cut a piece of poster board into a large circle. Draw lines that divide the circle into 24 equal wedge-shape pieces.

Write one hour of the day in each time zone. Start with 12 A.M. and go from there. Write the hours near the center of the circle. Write them in order, of course, and be sure to write whether each time is A.M. or P.M.

Put a thumbtack in the center of the circle, and attach the circle to a big piece of cardboard.

Now, use the table included here to write the name of each place next to its correct time zone outside the circle's edge on the cardboard.

Check your watch. What time is it where you are? Turn the circle until that time lines up with the name of a city in your time zone.

Now you can read your time-zone chart to tell what time it is right now in other cities all over the world.

1 A.M.	central Pacific Ocean
2 A.M.	Honolulu, Hawaii
3 A.M.	Anchorage, Alaska
4 A.M.	Los Angeles, California
5 A.M.	Denver, Colorado
6 A.M.	Chicago, Illinois
7 A.M.	New York, New York
8 A.M.	Caracas, Venezuela
9 A.M.	Rio de Janeiro, Brazil
10 A.M.	mid-Atlantic Ocean
11 A.M.	Reykjavik, Iceland
12 P.M.	London, England
1 P.M.	Paris, France
2 P.M.	Cairo, Egypt
3 P.M.	Moscow, Russia
4 P.M.	Dubai, United Arab Emirates
5 P.M.	Karachi, Pakistan
6 P.M.	Indian Ocean
7 P.M.	Bangkok, Thailand
8 P.M.	Beijing, China
9 P.M.	Tokyo, Japan
10 P.M.	Sydney, Australia
11 P.M.	western Pacific Ocean
12 A.M.	Auckland, New Zealand

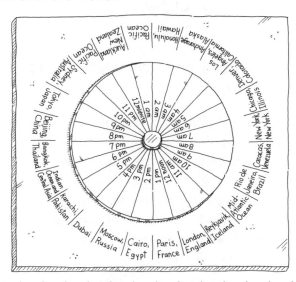

Sunrise, Sunset

▸▸▸▸▸▸▸

Find out how the sun wanders with the seasons.

What You'll Need
- sketch pad
- colored pencils

Find a place to sit where you can clearly see the eastern horizon. Sketch the horizon itself. Include any landmarks you see, such as buildings, hills, or trees. Next, find a place where you can see the western horizon and sketch that. On the first clear day of the month, go out at dawn to the spot where you sketched the eastern horizon. Watch where the sun rises and draw that in a different colored pencil on one of your eastern horizon drawings. At sunset, mark the position of the sun on a drawing of the western horizon.

Try this again on the first clear day of the next month. Mark the position of the sun on the same drawings. Has its position changed? You'll probably notice that it has. If you do this once in the winter and once in the summer, you'll see a big difference! If you're patient, try marking the position of the sun once a month for a year. Why does the sun seem to move? The direction of the tilt of the earth changes in relation to the sun as the earth moves around the sun. The changing angle makes the sun appear at dawn in changing positions on the horizon.

Sundials: Old and New

▸▸▸▸▸▸▸

There are a variety of structures for sundials.

Check out World Wide Web sites devoted to sundials. Do a search on the words "sundial" and "time," and then check out the sites. Sites can change from time to time, but here are some interesting sundial Web sites you might be able to find.

What You'll Need
- Internet access

The Richard Swenson Sundial is not only a functional sundial, but a modern work of art. To see this creation and to read the history of sundials, go to: **Select Sundial Links** at http://www.infraroth.de Of course, sundials have been around for a long time. To see ancient sundials, select **Orologi Solari** in the Astro Gallery at: http//www.mclink.it/mclink/astro

Make a Sundial

◆◆◆◆◆◆◆◆

Before there were clocks, ancient people used sundials to tell time.

What You'll Need

- thin cardboard
- ruler
- scissors
- tape
- wooden board
- pen or marker
- clock

Cut a piece of thin cardboard to the dimensions shown in the illustration. Tape the cardboard upright on a board. Put the sundial outdoors in a sunny place with the highest point of the triangle facing south. Starting as soon as it gets light, go to your sundial every hour on the hour, and mark where the shadow of the cardboard falls. For example, at 7 A.M., write "7 A.M." at the place where the shadow falls. Once all the hours are marked you can use your sundial to tell time. Make sure you place your sundial in exactly the same spot each time you use it.

Can you think of ways that clocks are an improvement over sundials? The most obvious is that clocks tell time at night, too, while sundials don't.

Preserving Nature's Resources

Do you recycle? Do you know what causes acid rain? Do you know why some animals and plants are endangered? In this section, you'll learn about some great craft projects that will show how much you care about the earth. You can help others learn what they can do to protect the earth's precious resources. What you help preserve today will be around for others to enjoy tomorrow.

Our Favorite Planet

◆◆◆◆◆◆

Considering that the earth is where you live,
you probably don't give it much thought.
You'll be surprised when you read about our amazing home.

What You'll Need

- one or more books about the earth
- pen and paper

Our planet is a pretty interesting place. Scientists think the earth is about 4,600,000,000 years old. (That's more than 4½ billion years.) It's 93,000,000 miles from the sun. (That's 93 million miles.) And at the center of the earth, the temperature is about 9,000 degrees. (That's very hot!)

Check out some books about the earth from your library, and see what else you can learn about your home. Write a report telling the most interesting things you learned from the books you read. Or try to find 10 fun facts to share with your friends. You can also invent an "Earth quiz" to test their knowledge of this amazing planet.

Life on Earth

While there may be life on other planets, none has yet been discovered. Certain conditions must be met before there can be life, and the earth has met them. The earth travels around the sun in almost a perfect circle, causing temperatures to remain fairly stable. Also, we are just the correct distance from the sun to allow water to remain liquid. If we were closer to the sun, the water would evaporate, and if the earth were farther away, the water would freeze.

Your Own World

◆◆◆◆◆◆◆

A diorama is a 3-D model of an area. Making a diorama is a good way to learn about a part of nature—and show what you've learned.

What You'll Need
- reference books
- shoe box
- markers
- craft glue
- nature decorations
- clay
- cotton balls

The world is made up of many different types of habitats or environments. To create your diorama, you'll first need to learn about one kind of habitat. You might pick the desert, woods, or someplace else. Learn about the plants and animals that live there, the different kinds of rocks and water sources, and anything else that makes that habitat unique.

Once you have a picture in your mind of what the area is like, you can create your diorama. Turn the shoe box on its side. On the sides and "roof" of the box, draw the background of your habitat. Use what is the "floor" of the shoe box to make the fore-

ground of your diorama. You might glue down sand and rocks for a desert or toy trees and a "lake" (shallow cup of water) for woods. Make plants and animals out of clay to populate your habitat. Glue cotton balls to the top of the box to put clouds in the sky.

Undoing Pollution

◆◆◆◆◆◆◆

We all know some things that cause water pollution. In this experiment, you'll learn just how hard it is to undo pollution.

Fill a 5-gallon bucket with clean water. Now, do your best to pollute the water. Throw in dirt, gravel, vegetable oil (to stand for toxic oil spills), trash (plastic packaging and any other kind of trash you've seen polluting water in nature), and other kinds of pollution. Yuck!

Now, here's the hard part: What can you do to decontaminate the water? You can use tongs, strainers, and anything else you can think of. Can you get the water really clean again?

What You'll Need
- bucket
- water
- pollutants (dirt, oil, trash)
- tongs
- strainer

Mini-Ecosystems

◂◆◂◆◂◆▸

For a science project—or just for fun—make a display of the world's forests, deserts, and grasslands.

What You'll Need

- aquarium or gallon glass jar
- charcoal for house plants
- potting soil
- sand
- ruler
- purchased or collected plants

"Biomes" are large areas of the earth that are determined by the plant communities that grow there. You can re-create the 6 major biomes of the earth in miniature using terrariums. Clean and dry an aquarium or gallon jar. Pour a ½-inch layer of charcoal in the bottom, then add about 4 inches of potting soil. (For a desert, use a mixture of ½ potting soil and ½ sand.) Buy your plants, or ask someone for permission to collect plants from their property or garden. Never collect plants from nature, because they could be endangered. Here is a list of biomes and some suggestions of plants you can use:

Tundra (such as northern Canada and Alaska): Try lichens, mosses, and any of the small alpine plants sold for rock gardens. These will need a sunny window.

Northern coniferous forest (such as southern Canada, northern United States): Try piggyback plants and small ferns.

Deciduous forest (such as eastern United States): Use violets, wintergreens, strawberries, and small ferns.

Grassland (such as the midwestern United States): Plant a prairie wildflower seed mix that includes several grasses.

Desert (such as the American southwest): Purchase cacti or aloe vera plants. Don't overwater or overfertilize. Leave the lid off.

Tropical rain forest (such as the Amazon Basin): Most common houseplants come from the tropics. Try African violets, creeping charlies, or aluminum plants.

What is Smog?

The word "smog" was created in 1905 and is a combination of the words "smoke" and "fog," the two main ingredients in smog. (Chemicals from pollution are also in smog.) Smog darkens the skies and pollutes the air. It is common in large cities and can be a serious threat to plants and animals.

Rain, Rain—Go Away

◆◆◆◆◆◆◆

Sometimes chemicals get in the air and mix with water to form "acid rain."

What You'll Need
- measuring cup
- water
- 2 jars
- vinegar
- sod

Put ¼ cup water in one of the jars. Ask an adult to cut 2 small squares of sod from your lawn or buy some sod at a nurs-ery. Push one square of sod down into the jar so that the sod's soil is in the water. Then put ¼ cup

vinegar in the other jar. Push the second square of sod down into the jar, so the soil is in the vinegar. Now place both jars in a warm, sunny place, and watch what happens over the next several days. Vinegar is an acid, like the acid in acid rain.

Acid rain is a worldwide problem. It can be caused by smoke from factories, burning coal, and even car exhaust. In addition to harming plants, acid rain pollutes bodies of water, kills fish, and destroys rocks and buildings!

Be an Eco-Scientist

◆◆◆◆◆◆◆

An "eco-strip" is a small strip of land that is part of an ecosystem. Create your own eco-strip.

What You'll Need
- sticks or large rocks
- field guides to rocks, plants, and animals
- notebook
- pen
- markers

You can make an eco-strip by marking off a section of land with sticks or large rocks. Choose a place such as a park, forest, beach, or other natural area. Then, study every detail of your eco-strip. This is a fun activity to do with a friend, because each of you will notice different things.

Use field guides to help you identify rocks, plants, and animals; record your findings in a notebook. Identify as many of the eco-strip's plants, animals, and rocks as you can. Look for signs of animals, such as tracks. Also look for ways in which humans have affected the eco-strip in good or bad ways. Maybe hikers have left trash, or maybe people have put out a basin of water that animals need in hot weather. Take notes about everything you observe. Finally, make a detailed map of the eco-strip.

What's It Good For?

◆▷◆▷◆▷◆

Everybody knows that recycling is one good way to help nature.
But there's another way, too: Reuse.

Recycling means saving things so they can be turned into new products. *Reusing* means using products in new ways, instead of throwing them away. For instance, a plastic milk jug is a product that can be reused in many ways. Here are some ideas:

- Make a watering can for flowers. All you need to do is have an adult cut off the top of the jug, above the handle.

- Plastic milk jugs with the tops cut off make great organizers for craft supplies. Use them to store your nature finds until you're ready to use them.
- Milk jugs are also good containers for sprouting seeds. Have an adult cut the top off to make a flowerpot. Then poke holes in the bottom for drainage. You can get your summer vegetables or flowers started inside and transplant them outdoors when the weather gets warmer.
- Make a "drinking fountain" for small wild animals by cutting the jug to make a shallow tray.

Can you think of other products that you could reuse instead of throwing them away? Each time you go to throw away a package or other product, ask yourself, "How could I use this again?"

Water Conservation

How much water do you think you use each day? A gallon? Twenty gallons? Believe it or not, the average person uses 100 gallons of water a day! We use 5–10 gallons a minute just to take a shower, and another gallon each time we brush our teeth. Since nature only has a limited amount of water, we all need to be careful that we don't waste our precious water supply—even if that means taking shorter showers.

Paper Making

◆▶◆▶◆▶◆▶◆

Recycle your old paper and make new, unique paper that you can't buy in any store!

What You'll Need
- stiff wire screen
- old paper
- bowl
- water
- blender
- dishpan or roasting pan
- rags or tea towels (use smooth cloth, not terry cloth)
- iron

Caution: This project requires adult supervision.

Recycling paper at home is fun and easy but a little messy! Do this in the kitchen and have a lot of towels ready for clean-up.

1. With the help of an adult, bend the sharp edges of the wire screen over and flatten them. You can also make a wooden frame and staple the screen onto it.

2. Tear white scrap paper into small pieces and soak them in a bowl of warm water.

3. Put the soaked paper in the blender with equal amounts of water and blend until mushy. Do not fill the blender more than half-full. If you have a lot of pulp, blend it in batches.

4. Pour the pulp into the dishpan or roasting pan. Add a gallon of warm tap water. You should have a thin slurry of paper pulp.

5. Tilt the screen away from you and dip it into the pan with a smooth motion. Hold it level under the water, then lift slowly and smoothly. There should be an even layer of pulp on the screen. Tilt the screen to let excess water run off.

6. Let the pulp dry a bit. Then lay a soft, absorbent towel or rag out on a table and quickly flip the screen over onto it. Blot the back of the screen with another rag to absorb excess water. Gently peel the screen from the sheet. This process of blotting and removing the fresh sheet is called *couching* (pronounced "cooching").

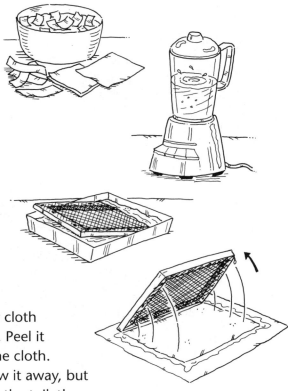

7. Let the paper air-dry, or place another cloth over it and have an adult iron it dry and flat. Peel it away while still damp so it doesn't fuse to the cloth. Save the leftover pulp by freezing it, or throw it away, but never pour it down the sink or flush it down the toilet!

Nature's Recycler

▶▶▶▶▶▶

Mother Nature recycles everything. Nature will even help you recycle your garbage, turning it into fertilizer called "compost."

What You'll Need
- plastic garbage can
- heavy-duty scissors or shears
- dry leaves, grass clippings, or straw
- vegetable matter
- small rake
- plant mister

To make your own composter, cut some holes in a garbage can. Put the garbage can outdoors in a place where animals won't get into it. Put in a layer of dry leaves, grass clippings, and/or straw. On top of that dry layer, you can start adding food scraps. Vegetable and fruit scraps make great compost. (Just don't put in any meat scraps or coffee grounds!)

Every few days, use a small rake to mix up your compost, then moisten it with a plant mister. Doing these things will help nature recycle your garbage faster. You can also keep adding more grass clippings and leaves. It will take 1 to 4 months to turn your garbage into fertilizer, depending on things like the temperature and humidity. Then you can use the fertilizer to help plants grow in a garden.

Vanishing Fish

At one time, there was more than enough food in the oceans for everybody to eat. But, as anglers have caught more and more fish, they have had to find new places to catch them. About 110 million tons of fish are caught each year, and many prized fish are disappearing. As the fish are vanishing, so are many other forms of water life, such as certain types of turtles and whales that survive on fish as their food source.

Speak Your Mind

▶▶▶▶▶▶

Voice your opinion about something in nature that you really care about.

What You'll Need
- stationery
- pen
- envelope
- stamp

Are you concerned about stray animals? Air pollution? The destruction of the rain forest? No matter where you live, you have people who represent you in government. Each area of the United States has two senators and at least one congressional representative. The job of these people is to listen to the people in their area and try to do something about their problems and concerns. So, why not write them a letter and tell them what's on your mind!

Be as specific as you can about what's bothering you. Tell them what you're doing to help and what you'd like them to do. Maybe they could try to get new laws passed to take better care of nature. You can even write to the President of the United States! After all, he's your leader, too.

Another way to make your voice heard is to write a letter to the editor of your local newspaper. Every newspaper has a page where it prints letters from readers. Many people read these letters, so it's a chance to tell a lot of people how you feel. Here are the addresses of your government officials:

(Your U.S. Senator's Name)
U.S. Senate
Washington, DC 20510

(Your U.S. Representative's Name)
U.S. House of Representatives
Washington, DC 20515

(President's Name)
The White House
1600 Pennsylvania Avenue
Washington, DC 20500

Taking Care of Nature

▶▶▶▶▶▶

It's important to learn how all the parts of the environment fit together.

All the parts of nature together are often called the *environment*. It's important to know how you fit in with the environment and what you can do to help keep the environment healthy and beautiful. Read a book to learn about the environment. After you learn more about the environment, come up with an activity that will help it. What can you do?

What You'll Need
- books about the environment

Count Me In

◆◆◆◆◆◆

There are many organizations that exist to help take care of nature.
Start a nature group of your own.

Some nature organizations focus on animals, while others turn their attention to saving the rain forests or mountains. Get a group of friends together to start your own organization. Ask a librarian about the different nature organizations. You may want to write to several groups and ask them to send you information about what they do. The organization will also tell you about things you can do to help nature. Then you can choose a focus for your nature group.

What You'll Need
- stationery
- pen
- envelopes
- stamps

Once your organization is formed, get together once a week or once a month to do things that will help you learn about and assist nature. You can even design a nature newsletter (see below) to keep everyone in your neighborhood informed.

Nature News

◆◆◆◆◆◆

After trying out a lot nature activities, share your discoveries with others.

If you have a typewriter or computer at home, you can use word processing and page layout programs to arrange your newsletter just like a real newspaper and add pictures. If you don't have either, you can still make your newsletter by hand on paper, using your neatest handwriting. Draw pictures or take photographs to paste onto the newsletter. You can "publish" your newsletter once a week and post it on your refrigerator, or make photocopies for your friends.

What You'll Need
- paper and pen
- typewriter or word processor
- notebook
- markers

How do you get stories to write about? Go out each day to observe what's going on outdoors. Take a notebook with you and write down what you see. As a reporter, remember to record "who," "what," "where," "when," "how," and "why" for any event. Here are some sample headlines to give you ideas:
- Bird's Nest Found in Neighborhood Tree
- First Rose Sighting of the Spring
- The Jones Family puts up Bird Feeder

What's Your Game?

◆◆◆◆◆◆◆◆

*It's fun to create your very own nature board game
and play it with your friends.*

What You'll Need
- poster board
- index cards
- markers
- small stones or coins
- dice

It may seem hard at first to make up a board game about nature. To get started, choose a theme such as "save the forest," "clean up that oil spill," or "recycle for life."

Then get out a board game that you like to play. You can use this game as a model for yours. Draw squares around the edges of your poster board as shown and think of things to write or draw in the squares. Remember, everything in the game should be about nature. For example, you could have a player lose a turn for throwing trash in a river or move ahead for picking up trash. Use your imagination!

Be sure to write down rules for your game. Again, use the rules from one of your games as a guide. Finally, try playing your game. You may find there are things you need to change. Keep working on it until your game goes smoothly!

Rainwater Blues

◆◆◆◆◆◆◆◆

*How clean is the air you breathe? The water you drink?
Rain can help you find out.*

If you've ever wondered what particles slip inside your body from the air you breathe or the water you drink, this is an interesting way to find out. Place a clean jar or cup in an open area just as it starts to rain. Collect as much rain as you can for the first hour of the storm. Now gather the rainwater and carefully pour it through a clean coffee filter, catching the

What You'll Need
- 2 clean jars or cups
- coffee filter

water in a second jar or cup. Peel open the coffee filter and see what the rain washed out of your atmosphere. You might look at breathing in a new way after checking out this environmental strain.

Noise Pollution

◆▶◆▶◆▶◆

Noise is one pollution that is often overlooked.

What You'll Need
- tape recorder (optional)

Walk around your neighborhood and listen for as many sounds as possible: cars, trucks, birds, dogs, lawn mowers, and all other noises. How many of these sounds do you normally notice? How many do you usually ignore? You may be so used to the noises that you don't notice them anymore. If you like, take a tape recorder with you as you listen. Record as many sounds as you can.

Make recordings of any sounds that you consider noise pollution. Is your neighborhood too loud? Use your memory (or your tape recorder) to remember the types of noises that bothered you the most. Then decide what you can do about them. Start with the noises that your own household produces. Some communities have banned leaf blowers because they are too noisy and cause pollution. If you have a leaf blower, consider using a broom to clean your sidewalks and a rake to collect leaves from your yard. It takes about the same amount of time and doesn't require that much effort. Gas-powered lawn mowers are also very noisy. Some people use push mowers instead—and get their exercise while they mow! Talk to your neighbors about ways you are reducing noise pollution. Maybe they'll follow your example.

Crunch!

Talk about noise! Astronomers agree that the most common feature in the solar system is the impact crater (created by striking comets and meteors). Entire planets, moons, and asteroids are covered with them.

Testing the Air

◆▶◆▶◆▶◆

How clean is the air around your home?

What You'll Need
- stiff cardboard
- scissors
- ruler
- hole punch
- string
- petroleum jelly
- magnifying glass
- rubber bands

With 2 simple tests, you can check the air for common pollutants. In the first test, measure how much dust, dirt, soot, and other floating material is in the air. To do this, cut 2 pieces of stiff cardboard into a 4-inch square. Punch a hole on one corner of one piece and put a string through it for hanging. Coat both sides with petroleum jelly and hang the cardboard up under the eaves of your house. Coat one side of the second piece and lay it flat in the shade, also sheltered under the eaves of your house. Leave both pieces in place for a day. Examine both cardboard squares with a magnifying glass and see if you can count the number of small particles sticking to them. Which has more particles: the cardboard that was lying flat or the one hanging?

To test for invisible gaseous pollutants, stretch 3 or 4 rubber bands over a piece of cardboard. Lay them in a shady place. Check the rubber bands each day. The faster they become brittle, the more pollutants there are in the air. Try both of these tests in 2 very different places to compare pollutant levels. You might try them in the middle of a city, then in a forest or in the country.

Save Our Breath

Want to help keep the air clean? Ask your parents not to idle their cars for long periods of time at a drive-through bank, dry cleaner, or restaurant. Ask them to turn their motors off while they wait, even if it's only for a few minutes. Every minute is important.

Chalk It Up

◆◆◆◆◆◆◆

Add some temporary colorful art to your urban world.

If you ever get tired of your urban jungle, take the chalk challenge and brighten your world. Open your favorite nature magazine to a color photograph. Now try to duplicate the brightest, most wonder-filled pictures right in your own front (or back) yard using chalk. Do you love the jungle and the monkeys that call it home? Chalk them in swinging across your driveway. Do you dream of colorful tropical birds? Draw them on the sidewalk beyond your front door. It will remind you how lucky you are to be a citizen of this wonderful world.

Taking Notice

◆◆◆◆◆◆◆

More power in your kid corner.

Keep track of how your community is doing when it comes to pollution. The next time you and your family jump in the car and head downtown, bring along your enviro-journal and keep your watchful eyes peeled.

Is there garbage on your city streets? Where is the garbage (and what kind of trash did you see)? Do cars around you belch out too much smoke and exhaust? Make a note of that, too. Is it easy to breathe the city air? Easy to see down the street? Don't forget to write that down.

Keep track of the environmental details you can see for yourself every time you head for the downtown streets. Then mail copies of those notes to your favorite newspaper or the governor's office. Let them know kids are keeping score, and everyone will win.

Operation Neighborhood

◆◆◆◆◆◆◆◆

When you help, others catch the fever.

Sometimes all it takes is one hero to start a wave of participation. You can be that hero by organizing a group of young volunteers to do a little neighborhood cleanup. Ask your friends if they care about the neighborhood they call home. If, like most kids, they answer "yes," tell them it's time to turn their good thoughts into good deeds.

What You'll Need
- work gloves
- trash bags
- broom
- dustpan

Get permission from friends and neighbors before you begin, then grab some work gloves and a big trash bag and dig in. Is there a broken-down fence scattered across the alley? Take the time to gather it up and toss it in the trash. Did somebody break glass bottles all over the street? Grab a broom and a dustpan and sweep that mess into the trash. You'll feel like a hero, and your streets will reflect how much you care.

Leave It to Nature

◆◆◆◆◆◆◆◆

Fall into community composting.

What You'll Need
- rake
- garbage bags

After you rake and bag your leaves, it's time to pick up the telephone. Call your local city government office and ask if they have a community compost location. If they do, talk mom and dad into loading the leaves into your family car instead of the trash-collection barrel. Bring your compost over to the community location and leave it there—allowing nature to break down the organic material and keeping trash landfills free for other disposables.

Live Christmas Tree

◆◆◆◆◆◆

Make Christmas a year-round activity.

What You'll Need:
- rooted Christmas tree
- shovel

They may cost a little more—sometimes a LOT more—but live, rooted Christmas trees are a great way to help reforest Planet Earth AND keep your holiday memories alive. Each year, have your family buy a rooted tree. In the spring, plant this living tribute to your family holiday traditions. In doing so, you make the yard look more beautiful and help the planet process both oxygen and carbon dioxide.

Such a Sap

◆◆◆◆◆◆

Plant a seed of hope.

Hundreds of rain forest acres are depleted every year by greedy corporations or by hungry locals trying to make a decent living. Either way, trees are vanishing, and with those trees, the oxygen supply and animal habitat they used to provide are vanishing, too.

What You'll Need:
- tree seedlings
- small shovel

You can't always stop deforestation in other countries. But you can help rebuild the ecosystem, starting with your own backyard. Buy tiny tree starts or saplings at your local home and garden center, or write to the National Arbor Day Foundation (100 Arbor Ave, Nebraska City, NE, 68410) to buy saplings. The sooner you plant, the sooner we all breathe a little easier.

Sand-Sift Saturday

❖❖❖❖❖❖

Make being beached good "clean" fun.

What You'll Need:
- rake
- work gloves
- trash bags

Ever noticed how much junk winds up in a playground sandbox? For some reason that scientists and philosophers have never discovered, a lot of people think children's sand pits are giant ashtrays or garbage cans. Until we figure out why this happens and how to stop it, make a difference by cleaning up the mess other people leave behind.

Help sift out the icky stuff left behind using an ordinary rake. Once you have a good-size pile of junk, slip on your work gloves and bag it up. You'll be doing your neighborhood (and the younger kids that look up to you) a big favor. But be especially careful of broken glass and anything that even LOOKS like a needle. If you find that type of waste in a sandbox, ask an adult for advice on what to do.

Earth Day Parade

❖❖❖❖❖❖

Celebrate in style.

When Earth Day rolls around on April 22, why not gather your friends together and have a recyclers' parade? Decorate your bicycles, your wagons, your dogs, and yourself with newspaper streamers, recycled cloth strips, bottle-cap noisemakers—anything you can string together using recycled goods. Make sure you have your parents take plenty of pictures. Then write to your local newspaper about your private parade. Next year, you might wind up in the newspapers you recycle. Be sure to clean up afterward.

What You'll Need:
- bicycles
- newspaper streamers
- recycled cloth strips
- bottle caps
- twigs
- branches
- leaves
- pinecones

Paper or Plastic?

◆◆◆◆◆◆◆

Just DO IT!

What You'll Need:
● 3 recycling bins

In the past 10 years, Americans have recycled more aluminum, plastic, and paper than ever before. We've even pocketed thousands of dollars for some of our efforts. But we still have a ways to go before we can say we recycle most of our reusable trash.

Ask your folks if you can keep 3 recycling bins on the back porch near your kitchen. When a plastic bottle is headed for the trash, reroute it to your plastic's recycle bin (don't forget to remove the cap before you do). Do the same for aluminum cans and newspapers. Then call your local city government to find out how to get these goodies to recycling centers. Many towns now offer curbside pickup in the same way they pick up traditional trash.

Beautify the Neighborhood

◆◆◆◆◆◆◆

Plan an outdoor cleanup project with family and neighbors.

You've probably seen a spot or two in your area that needs sprucing up. Perhaps the parking strip in front of your own house is full of weeds. Maybe the nearby park looks blah. First, list what to do: get permission, pull weeds, dig up soil,

What You'll Need:
● gardening tools
● plenty of helpers

reseed grass, plant trees, plant flowers. Cross things off your list that are too difficult, expensive, or hard to maintain, and check with your local government before fixing public property. Tell everyone about your idea. See if any neighbors, friends, or local clubs would like to help. Set a date to meet. When everyone is together, dig in! Everyone can help pull weeds. Adults can dig up hard soil and trim shrubs. Children can help plant flowers and small trees.

Billboard Bonanza

❖❖❖❖❖❖

How much is too much? You decide.

What You'll Need:
- notebook
- pen
- envelope
- stamp

The next time you go for a walk or a drive in the town or city with your parents, keep track of how many advertising billboards or advertising benches you see (and how far your drive was). Were too many billboards blocking the natural view? Too many ugly advertising messages on pedestrian benches? Keep an accurate record of what you saw and how it made you feel. Send the statistics to the governor of your state (ask your parents to help you find his or her address).

Green Clean

❖❖❖❖❖❖

How good are simple cleaners?

Environmentalists advocate homemade cleaners, saying they work as well as commercial brands, are less harmful to the environment, and are less expensive. In this activity you will evaluate the first and third claim.

What You'll Need
- vinegar
- measuring cup
- water
- spray bottle
- commercial window cleaner
- paper towels

A solution of vinegar and water is said to be an effective window cleaner. Add ¼ cup vinegar to 1 cup water, and pour this mixture into a spray bottle.

Now test your solution against a commercial window cleaner. Find 2 equally dirty windows. Clean one with the vinegar solution and the other with the commercial cleaner. Do they seem to be equally effective?

Compare the prices of the cleansers. What size bottle did the vinegar come in? How much did the bottle cost? Calculate the cost for ¼ cup of vinegar, which produced 1¼ cups of vinegar solution. Compare this to the cost of the commercial window cleaner. How much did the bottle of window cleaner cost? How much would 1¼ cups of the commercial window cleaner cost?

Recycle Band

▸▸▸▸▸▸▸

Celebrate recycling by making musical instruments!

Gather your friends in the yard or the park and make rhythm instruments out of recyclable containers. After you've cleaned out empty plastic bottles and coffee cans with lids, put a handful of uncooked beans and rice inside each one and tape the lids shut. Now that you've found a way to give old things new life, give your new percussion instruments a shake. Add your favorite songs, and you've got a musical tribute to recycling!

What You'll Need:
- clean plastic bottles, coffee cans, and margarine tubs (all with lids)
- uncooked pinto beans
- uncooked rice
- masking tape
- CD player
- favorite CD

Rot Not?

◂◂◂◂◂◂◂

Which things break down and which remain?

What You'll Need
- apple wedge
- aluminum foil
- glass bowl
- clear plastic wrap

We don't like it when our food spoils before we eat it, but our rotting waste is good for the environment. Imagine if nothing ever decayed—we would have huge mountains of fruit, leaves, dead organisms, and animal waste everywhere! When things decay they don't take up as much space in trash piles, and their nutrients can be reused by plants. In this activity, you'll compare the rate of decay in an apple wedge and a piece of aluminum foil.

Place the apple wedge and foil into a glass bowl. Cover the bowl with clear plastic wrap, and place it in a sunny window. Check the bowl once a day for the next 2 weeks. Does the apple change? The foil?

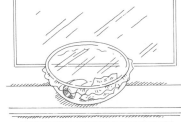

Some wastes that we produce remain in their current form for hundreds of years. This is often the case with synthetic materials, such as plastic jugs and aluminum cans. However, wastes that come from living things, such as food scraps and leaves, break down over time. We call this process *decay*. Although decay may seem gross, it is a good thing because it allows the nutrients in living things to return to the soil for plant use. Materials made from living things are said to be biodegradable. Biodegradable materials are good to use because when they decay they do not occupy as much space in landfills.

Compost Sculptures

◆▶◆▶◆▶◆

These decorative bags make interesting lawn sculptures, and you'll end up with some handy compost in the spring!

What You'll Need

- paper yard-waste bags
- crayons or permanent markers
- leaves
- string
- smaller brown paper bags
- twigs

You've probably seen those orange plastic bags that look like pumpkin faces and are filled with leaves. The ones you make will be even better for the environment. If you place them where they'll be protected during the winter, in a few months you'll have some compost in the bottom of the bags—just in time for your spring garden!

Before filling the yard-waste bags with leaves, decorate them with the crayons or markers. Animal faces, funny faces, or designs of any kind make interesting sculptures.

When finished, fill the bags with leaves. Tie the tops shut. You can add twigs for arms, use a smaller paper bag to make a hat—who knows where your imagination will take you!

Sorts of Packaging

◆▶◆▶◆▶◆

Which fast-food restaurant uses the most environmentally friendly packaging?

What You'll Need

- pen and paper

The next time you visit a fast-food restaurant, examine all the nonfood waste you throw away. Sort the trash by things that are biodegradable, such as paper products, and things that are not biodegradable, such as plastics. As you throw the stuff away, make a tally sheet. Write the name of the fast-food restaurant. Make 2 columns: "Not Biodegradable" and "Biodegradable." If the trash is not biodegradable, make a mark in the Not Biodegradable column. If it is biodegradable, put the mark in the Biodegradable column. Compare different fast-food restaurants. Which ones are the best at using biodegradable packaging? If you were to make suggestions to a restaurant, what would you suggest to help them increase the amount of biodegradable items they use?

Packing Powerful Peanuts

◆▷◆▷◆▷◆

Which peanuts are biodegradable?

If you've ever opened a box that came from a mail ship-
ment, you are probably familiar with packing peanuts.
They prevent the contents of the box from damage. Older
peanuts were made of a polystyrene material that did not
break down easily. Newer peanuts are made with starch.

What You'll Need
- polystyrene packing
  peanuts
- starch packing peanuts
- water
- 2 jars with lids

Compare new ecological packing peanuts with traditional polystyrene peanuts to see how long they take to
break down in water. Compare them under 2 conditions:
shaken and not shaken. For the shaken group, put some new peanuts and some old
peanuts into a jar filled with water. Fasten the lid securely, then shake them
to see how they respond. For the nonshaken group, put the
peanuts into a jar filled with water and replace the lid. Don't
shake them. Observe these once a day for one week.

You probably found that the starch peanuts broke
down faster than the polystyrene peanuts. These peanuts are
better for the environment because they take up less space in
landfills.

A Gallon a Day

◆▷◆▷◆▷◆

How much water do you use each day?

What You'll Need
- plastic gallon container
- water

To understand how vital water is to your daily existence,
see if you can get by using only a gallon of water for a
whole day. To prepare, fill a gallon jug with water. Try to
get through a whole day using only water from this
gallon. That means you will be using water from the jug
for hand washing, teeth brushing, face washing, dish rinsing, and drinking! Use the
water sparingly, and see if you can make it last the whole day! Hint: Some of the water
you can recycle, some you can't. Don't drink water you've used for washing your hands
(or anything else, for that matter) or brushing your teeth. But you could use water
you've washed your face in to wash your hands.

Costly Leaks

◆◆◆◆◆◆

It may be a drop in the bucket, but it certainly adds up.

What You'll Need
- faucet
- dishpan
- clock or watch
- measuring cup
- pencil and paper
- calculator

If you have a leaking faucet, use it to perform this experiment. If not, you'll need to simulate a leaky faucet by turning on a faucet so it produces a very slow drip. Place a dishpan in the sink, and collect the water from the dripping faucet for a 30-minute period. Then, pour the water into a measuring cup to see how much water was collected. Write this number down; this is the amount of water wasted in 30 minutes.

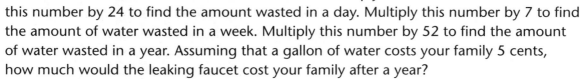

Multiply the amount of water wasted in 30 minutes by 2 to find the amount of water wasted in an hour. Multiply this number by 24 to find the amount wasted in a day. Multiply this number by 7 to find the amount of water wasted in a week. Multiply this number by 52 to find the amount of water wasted in a year. Assuming that a gallon of water costs your family 5 cents, how much would the leaking faucet cost your family after a year?

Fishmas Trees

◆◆◆◆◆◆

Ho, ho, ho—under the ice.

The next time you buy a live, cut Christmas tree, don't just throw it in the landfill when the ho-ho-hos are over. Rather than waste it, toss the whole tree—branches, needles, and all—on a frozen lake. (Be sure to get permission from your local parks department first!)

What You'll Need:
- discarded natural-cut Christmas tree

Now why would you do that? Well, you may be warm and toasty inside your house, but the wildlife in your town might not be. The discarded tree provides a nice windbreak and warm resting place for migrating birds who stop along the way. It even warms the water beneath the ice by several degrees, providing relief for winter-bound fish.

Weather Wonders

◆▸◆▸◆▸◆▸

It's an age-old question: What kind of weather will we have and how can we know? Some may laugh at the weather forecasters, but weather is tough to predict. So many things may change it! In this chapter you'll learn about wind, rain, snow, and many other things you see every day. As you learn, you'll notice sunlight, wind, and water all affect the weather.

Precipitation

◆▸◆▸◆▸◆▸◆▸

Have you ever asked yourself where rain and snow come from? Water evaporates from lakes, oceans, and rivers. In the sky, it condenses to form clouds. Under the right conditions, this moisture falls back to Earth as precipitation in the form of rain, snow, sleet, or hail.

Snow People Cookies

◆◆◆◆◆◆◆

These treats are great for a cold, snowy day.

What You'll Need
- 1 package (20 ounces) refrigerated chocolate-chip cookie dough
- cookie sheet
- oven
- cooling rack
- measuring cup and spoon
- powered sugar
- milk
- bowl
- spoon
- assorted small candies

Caution: This project requires adult supervision.

Preheat your oven to 375°F. Remove dough from wrapper according to package directions. Cut dough into 12 equal sections. Divide each section into 3 balls: small, medium, and large. For each snowman, place the 3 balls in a row, ¼-inch apart, on an ungreased cookie sheet. Repeat with remaining dough. Allow space between each snowman, so they have room to spread while baking.

Bake 10 to 12 minutes or until edges are very lightly browned. Cool 4 minutes on cookie sheets. Remove whole snowmen to wire racks; cool completely.

Mix 1½ cups powdered sugar and 2 tablespoons milk in medium bowl until smooth. This mixture is your snow! Pour over cookies. Let cookies stand for 20 minutes or until set.

Use assorted candies (such as candy corn, gumdrops, chocolate chips, and licorice) to create faces, hats, arms, and anything else you can think of to decorate your snow people. Makes 12 cookies.

Indoor Rainstorm

◆◆◆◆◆◆◆

No need to wait for a rainy day—just make some rain yourself!

Caution: This project requires adult supervision.

Ask an adult to bring a pot of water to a boil; let it cool slightly. Pour the water into a jar, and put on the lid. Place the jar on a towel. Then put ice cubes on the jar's lid. Watch a rainstorm begin in the jar as hot water condenses on the lid and rains down into the water.

Watching your "rainstorm" makes it easy to imagine what happens when a cold front (a mass of cold air) comes into contact with warm air: Moisture from the warm air is pushed up, clouds are formed, and soon it's raining.

What You'll Need
- pot
- water
- stove
- glass jar with lid
- towel
- ice cubes

Rain Gauge

◆◆◆◆◆◆

Next time it rains, keep track of just how wet it is out there with your own working rain gauge.

What You'll Need

- piece of thin wood (about 8 inches long and 4 inches wide)
- sandpaper
- old test tube or olive jar
- drill
- wire
- 6-inch plastic ruler
- acrylic paint
- paintbrush
- stake
- paper and pen
- spray paint (optional)
- modeling clay (optional)

Caution: This project requires adult supervision.

Sand the piece of wood smooth. If you wish, you can paint it with spray paint. If you are using an old test tube, press a small amount of modeling clay in the bottom to make it level.

Next, lay your test tube or olive jar on the board and mark the board so that the top of the jar or tube extends about an inch beyond the top edge of the board. Mark the board on both sides of the tube near the top and near the bottom. Have an adult drill small holes where you made marks. Wire the tube or olive jar to the board by running wire through the small holes and around the tube. Twist tightly in the back.

Use a ruler to help you paint marks on the side of the tube. Start from the bottom and paint heavy lines every inch. Then paint thin lines to mark ¼ inches. Fasten your rain gauge to a stake. Be sure to put it someplace where overhanging trees or large buildings won't block the rain. After a rain, check the tube to see how much rain fell. Then empty the gauge, and return it to the stake. Keep track of your readings on a chart.

Save It for a Sunny Day

It's hard to sit indoors all day, watching the rain fall from your seat at the window. Maybe you'd planned to play baseball that day, or maybe your family was going to have a picnic, but the festivities got rained out. But look on the bright side. There are places on Earth where it rains almost every single day! Those places are called tropical rain forests, and they get between 100 and 400 inches of rain every single year.

Who (or What) Can Resist?

◆◆◆◆◆◆

How can you stay dry when it rains?

What You'll Need
- cotton balls
- scraps of 5 different fabrics
- old newspapers
- piece of scrap wood
- stapler
- staple remover

Which clothes serve you best when you're caught in a sudden storm? Let a cotton ball be your guide. Take 5 ordinary cotton balls and 5 scraps of different fabrics and set them out on a table covered with old newspapers the next time it's ready to rain. Put the cotton balls on a scrap of wood and cover them with squares of cloth. Be sure to staple the cloth to the wood so the wind doesn't disrupt your experiment.

Leave the wood in the rain for about 5 minutes. Then bring it inside and use a staple remover to peel back the cloth, one cotton ball at a time. Which cotton ball stayed the driest? Which balls are completely soaked? What you find will help you decide what kind of coat to use when it rains.

Be a Cut-Up

◆◆◆◆◆◆

Nature's snowflakes are beautiful, but they don't last long. You can make long-lasting snowflakes out of construction paper.

What You'll Need
- paper
- marker
- plate
- scissors

Trace around a plate to make a circle on a piece of paper. (All nature's snowflakes are white, of course, but yours can be any color you like.) Cut out the circle.

Fold the circle in half. Then fold it in thirds. Fold it in half one more time.

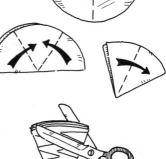

Use a scissors to cut small pieces out of the paper. Then unfold the circle to see what your snowflake looks like. Because of the way snow crystals form, every snowflake has 6 rays—just like your paper snowflakes.

Warm, Fuzzy Snow

◆◆◆◆◆◆

You can use cotton balls to create a 3-D winter scene that won't melt in the spring.

What You'll Need
- paint
- paintbrush
- shoe box
- cotton balls
- glue
- crayons
- glitter (optional)

Paint the inside of a shoe box. Use a good sky-colored paint like blue or gray. When the paint is dry, tilt the shoe box on its side, so the narrow part is faced down. Then make a snow scene using cotton balls for the snow. Use your imagination to make snow-covered hills and trees, snow people, snow animals, and more. (If you want, you can make your drawing in crayon first, then glue on the cotton.) Add glitter to make your snow sparkle like the real thing!

Snow Ice Cream

◆◆◆◆◆◆

Long ago, people figured out the easiest way to make ice cream is to use snow.

Scoop some freshly fallen snow into a big, chilled bowl. (Make sure the snow you take is clean and white. If the snow is brown or yellow, it will taste yucky.) Nestle the bowl in the snow to keep it cold while you make snow ice cream. Add a little sugar, a few drops of vanilla extract, and some very cold milk or cream. Stir together and eat. You might like to take your tasty treat inside to enjoy by a warm fire. Experiment with different flavors of snow ice cream. Try adding some cinnamon or cocoa powder.

What You'll Need
- clean snow
- bowl
- sugar
- vanilla extract
- milk or cream
- spoon
- cinnamon or cocoa powder (optional)

Stormy Weather

◆◆◆◆◆◆◆

You'll see nature in a whole new way when you take a walk outside in "bad" weather.

Most people make it a point to stay inside when the weather is "bad." And, most of the time, that's probably the best thing to do. But it can be interesting to go outdoors when it's rainy, snowy, or foggy. (Never go outside in a thunderstorm, snowstorm, or hailstorm. Severe weather can be dangerous.) Look for the birds and animals you usually see. How do they adapt to rain and snow? How are plants affected? Also, pay attention to what happens in nature after the rainy or snowy weather passes. What do animals do then? How do plants react? How does the sky look?

My, What Big Feet You Have

◆◆◆◆◆◆◆

Snowshoes allow people to walk on top of deep snow, instead of sinking into it. Make your own shoe-box snowshoes.

What You'll Need
- 2 shoe boxes or a few fallen evergreen boughs
- large rubber bands or old shoelaces

Snowshoes work by spreading a person's weight over a larger area of snow, so the snow can support the weight. Here are a couple of quick and easy ways to make snowshoes:

Use big rubber bands or shoelaces to strap shoe boxes or evergreen boughs to the bottoms of your boots. Now try walking in the snow. You'll find that walking in snowshoes is like walking in swim fins: It's important to lift the front of your foot high with each step.

Examine Snowflakes

You've heard that no 2 snowflakes are alike, right?
Take a look and see if it's true.

What You'll Need
- black construction paper
- magnifying glass

Do this activity on a snowy day. Put a piece of black construction paper outside where it's cold but not where it will get snowed on. Let the paper chill for several minutes.

Then catch snowflakes on the paper and look at them under a magnifying glass. Are they really all different from one another? In what ways are they all alike? Scientists have found that snowflakes come in 7 basic geometric shapes. However, snowflakes have infinite different—and beautiful—varieties within those categories.

When you go inside, you might want to draw snowflakes as they looked under the magnifying glass.

Snowflake Fact

Snowflakes are actually 6-sided ice crystals, ones that are created in clouds when the temperature is below freezing. For you to have good snow for snow people and snowball fights, the air has to stay cold as the snowflakes fall. Otherwise the ice crystals will melt. But, if the air is too cold throughout the snowflake's descent, the snow will not stick together well enough for snowballs.

Rainy-Day Pictures

Create your own masterpiece—with a little help from the rain!

What You'll Need
- paper
- water-soluble paint or markers

You've probably used lots of things to create pieces of art, like paint, markers, tissue paper, string, and even rocks. But have you ever used the rain to make a piece of artwork? This idea may sound all wet, but give it a try!

Use your paint or markers to draw shapes and lines on a piece of paper. Then bring on the rain! Place your piece of paper in the rain for about 20 seconds. When you take your "canvas" out of the rain, dry it out, and then check out your creation. Thanks to the rain, your shapes and lines will have turned into something else entirely!

When It Rains, It Pours

How much water does the average storm let loose?

They always say, "When it rains, it pours." But is that really true? Does it really pour, or is the average rainfall in your hometown more like a spurt or a trickle? Find out with this fun experiment.

The next time it looks like rain, place a measuring cup in a clear spot in your yard. Be sure to secure it by anchoring it in the ground or surrounding it with gravel so it doesn't tip over before you gather your information.

What You'll Need
- plastic measuring cup
- notebook
- pen or pencil
- clock or watch

Watch the clock and make a note of how many ounces of rain you collect every 2 hours. Do the same during the next storm—and the next. Now compare your figures to calculate whether it rains when it pours, or just gets things a little damp.

Get Wet

◆◆◆◆◆◆

Forget about those umbrellas! What's wrong with getting a little wet when the rain starts coming down?

What You'll Need
- raincoat
- rain hat
- waterproof boots

Don't stay cooped up in the house when there's a downpour. Toss on a raincoat and hat and a pair of waterproof boots and head outside! You'll be surprised how different the world is while the rain is coming down.

Once you're outside splashing through the rain, take a big whiff of the air. Do you notice a difference in the smell of rainy-day air? Look around and see if you can spot any animals or insects that you don't normally see when the sun's out. Watch your step. Chances are you'll see plenty of earthworms wiggling about in the rain.

Some trees have leaves that are made so that the rain glides off them. What other things do you see around your house that look different in the rain than they do when the sun is out?

The Sky Is Falling!

Raindrops aren't all that fall from the sky during a storm. In 1997, live toads rained down on the Mexican town of Villa Angel Flores. Experts think the toads may have been swept up into a tornado and tossed to Earth when the winds died down.

Let It Rain

Here's your chance to be a rainy-day detective. Find out what crawls around in your backyard when it rains.

Here's your mission...should you choose to accept it! Before it begins to rain, dig a hole in a garden bed and bury a glass jar up to its neck. Make sure the opening of the jar is not covered with dirt. Now place your "bait" (the cheese) in it. Find 4 small rocks and place them on the dirt around the jar.

Then put a small piece of wood on top of the rocks to keep the rain out of the jar. But be sure there's enough room between the wood and the jar so that the insects and other small creatures can crawl between them. Now your "trap" is set.

Once the rain has stopped, look in the jar to see what creatures went for the cheese. If you "caught" a slug, place it on a piece of glass or a chunk of clear plastic. That way, you can see its underside and watch how it moves. After you've taken a look at all the creatures, let them go on their way. Mission accomplished!

What You'll Need
- shovel
- glass jar
- piece of cheese
- 4 small rocks
- piece of wood
- piece of glass or clear plastic

Wet Scent

Have you ever noticed how great the air smells after a rainfall? Well, that's because the rain has cleaned it up! When it rains, raindrops wash away all the dust and dirt that are in the air.

Avalanche!

◆◆◆◆◆◆◆

Simulated disasters help you understand the real thing.

What You'll Need
- cardboard box (cut in half, corner to corner)
- scissors
- mittens
- cold water
- snow

Ever wondered how an avalanche works? Try this activity on for size. On a cold day, cut a cardboard box in half, corner to corner, creating a cardboard peak that will sit flat on the ground. Wet the box and let it freeze, peak to the sky. Once it's frozen, wet it again to create a second, smoother layer of ice. Now let snow blanket the icy peak. Will the snow slide off that steep sheet of ice? A soft bump will help you find out—and simulate a real avalanche.

Hail! Hail!
The Gang's All Here!

◆◆◆◆◆◆◆

Sometimes the sky rains solid.

How powerful is your average hailstorm? Try this experiment to find out if the hail in your area even makes a dent. The next time you anticipate a hailstorm, fill 3 large, plastic bowls halfway with sand or gravel. Then cover the top of the bowls, one with foil, one with plastic wrap, one with waxed paper. Use rubber bands to hold the paper in place. Set the bowls in an open space where the hail will strike often. Once the storm is over, examine the different bowls. What happened to the foil? The plastic wrap? The waxed paper? Explore the impact of hail firsthand.

What You'll Need
- 3 large plastic bowls
- sand or gravel
- aluminum foil
- plastic wrap
- waxed paper
- large rubber bands

Winter's Diamonds

◆◆◆◆◆◆◆

If you want to make icicles, don't forget the most important ingredient: a cold winter night.

What You'll Need
- sharp pencil
- plastic cup
- string
- needle or pin
- water

Using a sharp pencil, poke 3 or 4 holes around the lip of a plastic cup. Tie several inches of string through each hole, then tie the ends of the strings together to make a hanger for the cup. Use a needle or pin to poke a very small hole in the bottom of the cup. Be careful not to poke yourself. Fill the cup with water. The water should drip very slowly out of the hole in the bottom. On a cold night, before you go to bed, hang the cup outside on a branch or nail. Overnight, an icicle will form at the bottom of the cup.

Snow Painting

◆◆◆◆◆◆◆

Art on a snowy canvas.

What You'll Need
- food coloring
- measuring spoon
- water
- old bowls
- paintbrushes
- old, warm clothing

The next time your world turns into a winter wonderland of white, add a little color of your own. Add about 10 drops of food coloring in any shade you like to 3 teaspoons water in a bowl that you have permission to get dirty. (Use a different bowl for each color you want to make.) Carry your colorful "paint" outside.

Pack a 4×4-foot section of snow hard and firm to make your canvas. Now, splash that bright color onto the snow using your paintbrushes for an abstract splash. Or paint your favorite characters right on the snow. Be sure to wear older clothes that you can get dirty, because food coloring doesn't wash out of most fabrics.

Arctic Snow Goggles

◆◇◆◇◆◇◆

Make your own Arctic Snow Goggles with some everyday cardboard.

Caution: This project requires adult supervision.

Snow-covered areas are very bright places, even though they are very cold. That's because the sun's rays reflect off the snow. Those reflections can damage a person's eyesight. To protect their eyes from these harmful rays, the Inuit (native people of Canada, Alaska, and Greenland) wore goggles that they carved from wood or whalebone.

To make your own pair of snow goggles, draw an hourglass shape on the piece of cardboard. Be sure the shape is large enough to fit on the front of your face. Cut out the shape. Have an adult mark slits on the cardboard where your eyes are. (You hold the cardboard on your face, and the adult can mark the cardboard.) Have the adult use a craft or utility knife to cut out narrow eye slits. Punch holes in the upper corners of the goggles. Cut two 18-inch pieces of string. Feed an end of a piece of string through the hole on the side of the goggles, and tie a knot. Repeat for the other piece of string and the other hole.

Add a decorative border along the edges of your goggles with markers or colored pencils. Try out your goggles!

(Warning: These glasses reduce the glare of the sunlight reflecting off the snow—they are not protection from the sun! Never look directly at the sun, even with these goggles on! You could damage your eyes.)

> ### What You'll Need
> - cardboard
> - pencil
> - heavy-duty scissors
> - craft or utility knife
> - hole punch
> - string
> - ruler
> - markers or colored pencils

Can Frost

◆▶◆▶◆▶◆

Frost forms because of a change in temperature.

Remove the label from a small metal can and fill it ¼ of the way with water. Stir 4 tablespoons of salt into the water. Add enough crushed ice to fill the cup, and stir the solution. Observe what happens on the outside of the can.

The cold solution in the can lowered the temperature of the can. When the air outside the can came in contact with the cold can, the air's temperature also dropped. The amount of water vapor the air can hold depends on the air's temperature; it cannot hold as much water when it is cold. The water vapor condensed on the cold can, and the low temperature made the water freeze and form frost on the outside of the can.

What You'll Need
• small metal can
• water
• salt
• measuring spoon
• crushed ice
• spoon

Air

◆▶◆▶◆▶◆▶◆

A refreshing breeze cools your skin. Leaves dance in the autumn wind. The fierce winds of a tornado send people running for cover. Whether small or large, winds are created when air flows from regions of high pressure to regions of low pressure.

Clock the Wind

◆◆◆◆◆◆◆

How fast is the wind blowing today?
Make a wind-speed gauge that will tell you.

What You'll Need

- 2 hollow balls
- knife
- nails
- hammer
- 2 sticks of the same length
- paint and paintbrush
- 1 foot wooden 2×4
- drill
- wooden board for a base
- wax or oil
- clock or watch
- paper and pen

Caution: This project requires adult supervision.

First, take 2 small, hollow balls (rubber balls, tennis balls, or table-tennis balls will work well) and cut them in half. Nail the ball halves to the ends of 2 sticks with the cut sides facing outward as shown in the illustration. Paint one half ball, so it's a different color than the others. Next, nail the 2 sticks together at right angles so they form an X. Make sure you join the 2 sticks at their exact centers, so the joined sticks will balance on the nail. Use a long nail so that the end of the nail comes through both sticks.

Now make the base. Have an adult drill a hole in the end of a 1-foot length of a wooden 2×4. The hole should be a bit larger than the nail that holds the 2 sticks together. Attach the 2×4 to a wooden base, and set the nail in the drilled hole. (Put a little wax or oil in the hole so the gauge will turn easily.)

Now, put your wind-speed gauge in the wind. Count the number of times it turns around in 30 seconds. (Count by the painted half ball.) Write that number down and divide it by 5. The answer is the wind speed in miles per hour.

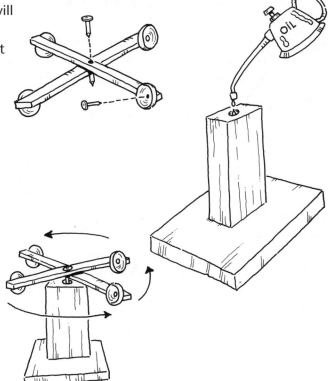

What Kind of Wind?

◆◆◆◆◆◆◆

*Be a wind detective! There are clues all around you
that help tell how fast the wind is blowing.*

In the early 1800s, a British admiral named Francis Beaufort came up with a system so that sailors had a way to describe the wind's strength that meant the same thing to everybody. The table below shows the Beaufort Scale, which describes how each level of wind looks both at sea and on land. Each day, look for clues to how strong the wind is. Is it a 0 day or a 7 day? Is it a light breeze or a fresh breeze?

The Beaufort Scale:

Type of wind		Clues at sea	Clues on land
0	Calm	Smooth water	Smoke rises straight up
1	Light air	Small ripples	Smoke drifts sideways
2	Light breeze	Small wavelets	Leaves and weather vanes move
3	Gentle breeze	Larger wavelets; foam	Twigs move
4	Moderate breeze	Small waves	Branches move; flags flap
5	Fresh breeze	Medium waves; spray	Small trees sway
6	Strong breeze	Large waves, up to 10 feet	Large branches sway
7	Strong wind	Waves 18–24 feet	Larger trees sway; flags stand straight out
8	Fresh gale	Waves up to 23–30 feet	Twigs break; hard to walk
9	Strong gale	Waves 25–33 feet	Signs blow down
10	Storm	Waves 29–40 feet	Trees fall over
11	Violent storm	Waves 37–50 feet, foam covers surface	Widespread damage
12	Hurricane	Waves 45–60 feet, heavy spray and foam	Widespread destruction

Blowing in the Wind

The wind is sometimes like a bus or train. It picks up passengers from one place and transports them to another.

What You'll Need
- cardboard
- hole punch
- string
- vegetable oil or petroleum jelly

Get a piece of cardboard that is the size of a piece of notebook paper or larger. Make a small hole on one end of the cardboard, and tie a piece of string through the hole. Smear one side of the cardboard with vegetable oil or petroleum jelly. On a windy day, hang the cardboard from a tree using the string. Make sure the oily side of the cardboard is facing the wind. Leave the cardboard in the wind for an hour or more. Then go back and see what the wind has carried onto the cardboard. You may find seeds, insects, pollen, dust, or other tidbits of nature.

Some plants (like the dandelion) use wind to help scatter their seeds far away. Sometimes the seeds can be carried for several miles or more! Small spiders can hang by their thread and let the wind blow them from spot to spot. What other ways can you think of to use wind?

Trade Winds

Have you ever heard the expression "trade winds"? If so, have you wondered where it came from? Well, wonder no more. Long ago, people delivered things that were for sale by ship. Buying and selling items was also known as "trade." Sailors knew about the steady bands of wind that blow all around the world, just above and below the equator. They called these winds the trade winds and used them to travel the world.

Wind Sock

◆◆◆◆◆◆◆

Socks do more than keep your toes warm. A wind sock can tell you which way the wind is blowing—and how fast, too!

What You'll Need
- yardstick
- light cloth such as muslin (one yard will make a large sock)
- scissors
- needle and thread
- wire
- fishing line
- thin wood
- paint
- paintbrush
- glue
- stake or old broom handle
- large nail
- hammer
- paper and pen

Use the yardstick to help you cut one square yard of light fabric. Fold it in half diagonally. Mark the center of one of the narrow edges. Cut from the mark to the corner at the other end. You will have 2 long triangles of fabric. Cut 2 inches off of the pointed end. Sew the long edges together to make a cone. (An adult may be able to help you sew with a sewing machine.) Shape light stiff wire into a hoop large enough to keep the large end of the cone open. Fold the edges of the fabric around the wire and sew in place. Cut 4 pieces of heavy fishing line, about 2 feet long. Poke 4 small holes through the fabric around the hoop at even distances. Tie a piece of fishing line through each. Cut a square of wood and paint letters for each of the 4 directions.

Glue the square to the top of the stake or old broom handle. Drive a nail through the center of the square. Tie the lines of your wind sock to the nail.

Hang your wind sock outside your home, making sure the letters are facing the correct direction, and observe the angles of the wind sock on different days. Note which angles go with what weather conditions. Make a chart of your information, and use the chart to help you estimate wind speed.

Make a Hygrometer

◆▶◆▶◆▶◆▶◆

*Sometimes people say, "It's not the heat, it's the humidity,"
to explain why hot weather bothers them. Use this instrument
to find out just how humid it is outside.*

What You'll Need

- 1 hair at least
  9 inches long
- ½ gallon
  cardboard milk
  carton
- scissors
- darning needle
- broom straw
- glue
- paper clip
- tape
- penny
- plain index card
- pen

Wash the hair clean with soap and water. Cut a small "H" in the side of the carton as shown, about ½ the length of the darning needle. Bend back the tabs, and push the needle through. Poke a broom straw into the eye of the needle and glue in place. At the end of the carton, cut a small slit and push the paper clip through it. Glue in place. Tape one end of the hair to the paper clip. Lay the hair over the needle, loop it around the needle once, then let it hang over the end of the box opposite the paper clip.

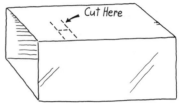

Tape the penny to the free end of the hair. Draw a half-circle on the index card and divide the half-circle with 10 marks. Label them 1 through 10 beginning on the left side. Glue the index card to the box under the broom straw. Take your completed hygrometer into the bathroom and run hot water in the shower until the mirror fogs up. The air is 100 percent humid and will cause the hair to stretch. Adjust the straw so it points to 10. Put the hygrometer outdoors in a sheltered place, such as under a porch. Tap it gently a few times before taking a reading, to make sure the straw isn't stuck in place.

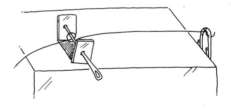

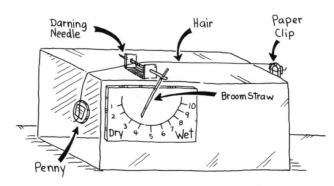

Fan of the Weather

❖❖❖❖❖❖❖❖

Wind can have an effect on temperature.

What You'll Need

- 2 thermometers
- paper and pen
- fan
- glass
- water
- paper towel

Read and record the temperatures shown on 2 thermometers. Place one in the breeze of a fan and the other away from the fan. What do you think will happen to the temperature of the thermometer in the breeze? Many people might suspect that this thermometer will cool off and show a lower temperature. But as you will find, this does not occur. The breeze on the thermometer does not lower its temperature.

Allow a small glass of water to warm to room temperature. Wet a paper towel with this water. Place a small wad of the wet paper towel on the bulb of one thermometer. Do nothing to the second thermometer. Place both thermometers in the breeze of the fan. Record the temperatures every couple of minutes.

The temperature of the thermometer with the wet towel on it dropped steadily. The breeze from the fan caused the water to evaporate, and as it evaporated, it used energy in the form of heat. This cooled the thermometer in the same way that your body cools itself when you perspire.

Foggy Notions

❖❖❖❖❖❖❖❖

Did you ever wonder what exactly fog is?
This project will help clear up the mystery.

What You'll Need

- bottle
- water
- rubbing alcohol
- ice cube

You've probably seen fog. That's because when fog is around, it's about all you can see. Well, fog is a cloud that forms very close to the ground. In nature, when a mass of cold air bumps into a mass of warm humid air, millions of tiny droplets of water are formed. That's fog. Here's a way to get some cold air and some warm air together and make fog:

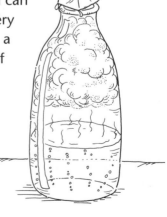

Fill a bottle ⅓ full with very hot water. Add a few drops of rubbing alcohol. Put a piece of ice over the top of the bottle and watch fog develop.

So Much Pressure!

◆▶◆▶◆▶◆

You can make a water barometer that will show you the changes in the air pressure.

What You'll Need
- 2 rulers
- modeling clay
- bowl
- water
- clear plastic bottle
- string
- scissors
- paper
- pen or pencil

First, stick a ruler into a lump of modeling clay. Then put the clay and ruler in the bottom of a bowl. (The ruler should be standing up straight.) Put 3 inches of water into the bowl.

Next get a narrow, clear plastic bottle. Fill it about ¾ full of water. Cover the top of the bottle with your hand, turn it upside down, and put it into the bowl next to the ruler. Once the bottle top is underwater, you can take your hand away. With the bottle still standing upside down, tie the ruler to the bottle with string.

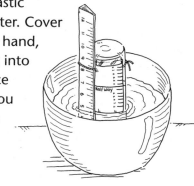

Cut a strip of paper about 4 inches long. Make a scale on it by making a mark every ¼ inch. Halfway down the strip, make a longer line to show the halfway mark. Tape this strip of paper to the bottle with the halfway mark at the same level as the water in the bottle.

Now you have a water barometer. The water in the bottle will move up and down as the air pressure changes. As the air pressure in the room increases, it will push down on the water in the bowl, forcing water up into the bottle. Then you can see yourself that the air pressure is high. If the air pressure is low, the bowl's water will rise, the bottle's water will sink, and you'll get a lower pressure reading.

Hot, Hot, Hot!

A Chinook is a hot and dry wind. In 1943, people in Rapid City, South Dakota, felt a Chinook raise their temperature from 10 to 55 degrees in just 15 minutes!

Tornado, Hold the Mayo

◆◆◆◆◆◆◆

Twirling currents trapped inside a jar.

What You'll Need
- clear mayonnaise jar with lid
- water
- food coloring
- measuring spoon
- dishwashing liquid
- vinegar

Do tornadoes make you dizzy? Do their spinning, twirling winds make you wonder how they work? Well, shake up a tornado of your own with this wild activity and study its spiraling vortex of currents without fear. Fill an ordinary clear mayonnaise jar about ⅔ of the way with water. Add a few drops of food coloring (any color) to the water. Then, add a teaspoon of dishwashing liquid and a teaspoon of vinegar. Screw the lid on good and tight to prevent leaks and extreme messes. Give the jar a good, hard shake, then give it a twist to set the liquid inside spinning. What you'll see is a tiny bottled cortex that looks just like a miniature tornado. You'll soon understand how the real thing works.

Bottled Cloud

◆◆◆◆◆◆◆

Make a little weather of your own.

Caution: This project requires adult supervision.

What You'll Need
- candle
- match
- clear glass 2-liter bottle

Clouds form when warm, particle-rich air meets cool, moist air. This fun activity can help you understand just how it works. On a cool day with little or no wind, head for your backyard and find a table. Ask your parents to help you light a candle. With help, turn your 2-liter glass bottle upside down and hold the candle inside the mouth of the bottle for about 10 seconds. (Don't use a plastic bottle. It could melt.) Once the bottle's mouth has cooled a little, form a seal around the bottle with your mouth and blow. Once you pull your mouth away, you should see a cloud form inside the bottle—just like in the skies above your home.

What a Blowhard!

◄◆◄◆◄◆►

From a breeze to a brawl, you'll know it all.

What You'll Need
- string
- hole punch
- scissors
- crepe paper
- newspaper
- light cloth
- heavy cloth

How hard is the wind blowing? Find out by making your own simple gauge. Using string, attach 4 strips cut to equal sizes—one each of crepe paper, newspaper, light cloth, and heavy cloth—to a branch or rain gutter. When the wind blows softly, the crepe paper will react. When it blows a little harder, the newspaper will flutter. As the wind increases in strength, the light cloth will wave. When the heavy cloth flaps, you will know the wind is blowing hard.

Wind Wondering

◄◆◄◆◄◆►

Any way the wind blows.

Which way does the wind blow? And how does that affect your environment? This colorful experiment will help you find out. Carefully staple or tape 6 crepe-paper streamers, each about 2 feet long, to a tree branch or clothesline. Anytime you see the paper flutter in the wind, take a few notes. Which way is the wind coming from? How long do the papers stay in motion? Write your notes on a piece of paper for at least a week. At the end of the

What You'll Need
- crepe-paper streamers
- stapler or tape
- notebook
- pen or pencil

week, check to see if there are any regular patterns. Does the wind seem to blow mostly from the east? Check the trees and plants growing in your yard. Do they tilt ever so slightly to the east? Could the wind have something to do with the leaning? Who knows for sure? That's what science is all about—asking good questions and doing your best to find answers.

Weather Vane

◆◆◆◆◆◆◆

How does a weather vane work? Find out by making your own.

What You'll Need
- heavy cardboard
- ruler
- scissors
- 2 pencils
- aluminum foil
- string
- nut, bolt, or other weight

Draw a wind vane, in the shape of an arrow, on a sheet of heavy cardboard. Your vane should be about 14 inches long and 5 inches wide, and the tail should be wider than the point. Cut the wind vane from the cardboard with scissors. Cover the arrow with aluminum foil so it can withstand the weather outside.

Balance the cardboard wind vane on the eraser end of a pencil, and mark the spot on the wind vane where it balances. Punch 2 holes side by side in the wind vane at this balance spot; each hole should be ½ inch from the edge of the vane. Tie an 18-inch piece of string through the top hole and a 12-inch piece of string through the bottom hole. Tie a nut or bolt to the bottom piece of string for a weight. Tie the top piece of string to a tree branch where the vane can swing easily without hitting anything.

When the wind blows, your wind vane will point directly into the wind. The larger surface of the tail provides more resistance to the wind and causes the point to face into the wind.

Can't Hide in a Cloud

Ever think you'd like to hide in a fluffy white cloud? Don't be fooled. Clouds can't hold your weight. Clouds are actually made of millions of tiny, cold water droplets, as well as some crystals of ice. So they'd be a pretty icky place to hide!

Turntable Winds

▶▶▶▶▶▶▶

*The earth's rotation causes winds to shift direction,
which affects weather patterns.*

Cut a circle from a sheet of paper about the same size as the turntable. Tape the paper circle to the surface of the turntable. Hold a ruler down on the paper, and draw a straight line as you have a friend slowly turn the turntable. Don't let the ruler turn. Look at the line. You'll see that the

line is curved, even though you followed the edge of the ruler. Now rotate the turntable slowly, and roll a marble across it. Notice how the marble's straight-line motion is curved by the rotation of the turntable. The turning of the table caused the marker line and marble to be deflected from their path across the paper. In a similar fashion, winds are deflected as the earth rotates.

What You'll Need
- paper
- scissors
- turntable, such as a lazy Susan, old record player, or microwave turntable
- tape
- ruler
- marker
- marble

Feeling Pressured?

▶▶▶▶▶▶▶

*You may not feel it, but the air around you has pressure. This simple
experiment will help demonstrate its invisible force.*

Fill a cup all the way to the top with water. Place an index card over the top of the cup. Hold the card in place, and turn the cup upside down. Slowly, carefully, let go of the index card. It should stay in place, held by the pressure of the air beneath it. Be sure to work over a sink in case your cup slips and the water spills.

What You'll Need
- cup
- water
- index card

Go Fly a Kite

◆◆◆◆◆◆◆

When you watch a kite sailing on the wind, you can almost imagine sailing up there yourself.

What You'll Need

- ruler
- 2 thin, lightweight wooden sticks
- string
- scissors
- tape
- colorful wrapping paper
- cloth strips

There's no better way to "see" the wind than to make and fly a kite. Here's how:

Make a cross out of 2 wooden sticks (one 36 inches long and the other 18 inches long), placing the shorter stick a foot from the top of the longer stick. Use string to fasten the sticks together where they cross. Put string around the outside of the crossed sticks to make a diamond shape, and connect the string to the ends of the sticks with tape. This will make the outline of the kite. Cut wrapping paper 1½ inches larger than the outline of the kite. Put the paper over the outline. Fold the extra 1½ inch over the string and tape it down.

Tie a ball of string to the place where the sticks are joined. Tie cloth strips to another piece of string, and attach the string to the pointy end of the kite for a tail. Now you're ready to sail on the wind.

Temperature

◇◇◇◇◇◇◇

Temperature is measured with thermometers. It is a measure of the average amount of moving energy in an object's particles. Many thermometers work because the liquid in the glass tube expands as it warms. The higher the column of liquid, the greater the temperature.

 ## As Warm as . . . Snow?

◇◇◇◇◇◇◇

We all know snow is cold, but can it help keep you warm?
Take a snowbank's temperature.

What You'll Need
- shovel
- 2 thermometers
- snow
- stick or branch
- warm clothing

For this activity, you'll need to wait for a day when it's very cold (at least 10°F or lower). Be sure to dress warmly! Find a large snowbank and dig a small hole deep into its base. Put a thermometer in the hole. Now put a second thermometer outside the snowbank (but also outside the rays of the sun). Put a stick or branch nearby to mark the spot. Leave both thermometers overnight.

The next day, compare the thermometers. Is there a difference in the temperatures outside and inside the snowbank? The colder it gets outside, the bigger the difference you'll find between the temperatures. This is because snow has the ability to insulate and protect things from even colder weather. And that's why when it gets really cold, small animals will tunnel into the snow to shelter themselves from the deep chill.

The Wind-Chill Factor

◆◆◆◆◆◆◆

Cold weather feels even colder when it's windy. Professional weather forecasters call this the "wind-chill factor."

Your body is normally surrounded by a thin layer of warm air, and it protects you. The wind, however, actually blows away that layer of warm air. So, you feel much colder on windy days. Using a thermometer, measure the temperature. Then calculate the speed of the wind with the wind-speed gauge. Combine the numbers on the chart below to determine the wind-chill factor. Use the wind-chill factor to help you dress for the weather. Bundle up for how cold it feels, not how cold it is!

Find the place on the chart where the wind speed and temperature meet. That's the wind-chill factor. Example: If the wind speed is 10 mph and the temperature is 25 degrees, the wind-chill factor is 10 degrees.

What You'll Need
- thermometer
- wind-speed gauge (see page 299)

Wind Speed, miles per hour	Temperature, Fahrenheit						
	30	25	20	15	10	5	0
0	30	25	20	15	10	5	0
5	27	22	16	11	6	0	-5
10	16	10	3	-3	-9	-15	-22
15	9	2	-5	-11	-18	-25	-31
20	4	-3	-10	-17	-24	-31	-39
25	1	-7	-15	-22	-29	-36	-44
30	-2	-11	-18	-27	-33	-43	-49

Ups and Downs

*Here's how you can keep track of temperature changes,
just like weather forecasters do.*

What You'll Need
- thermometer
- paper
- pen

Put a thermometer out-doors—out of the sun—and check it at the same time each day. Record the daily temperatures. Make a graph of your tempera-ture readings like the one in the picture. Every week or so, connect the dots on the graph to make a line showing the temperature ups and downs. Which day was coldest? Which was warmest? What trend do you see over time? Is it getting colder or warmer?

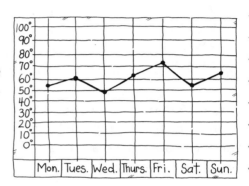

Cricket Degrees

*Did you know that crickets are nature's thermometers? Find out how to tell
the temperature by cricket chirps.*

Go out in the evening to a place where you know there are crickets. Single out the chirp of one cricket, and count its chirps for 14 seconds. Write down the number, and add 40 to it. The sum will tell you the temperature in degrees Fahrenheit.

What You'll Need
- stopwatch
- pencil
- paper

Don't Sweat It

◆━━◆━━◆━━◆

Cool down while you heat up.

What You'll Need
- towel
- watch
- water

Perspiration is the human body's natural cooling system. But does it really make a difference? There's one way to find out. The next time a hot day settles on your hometown, take a towel outside and sit in the sun for 30 minutes. For the first 15 minutes, wipe away every drop of sweat you can find as soon as you feel it sneak out. Don't wait an instant. Once those 15 minutes are complete, sit as you normally would, just letting the perspiration pour. Which 15 minutes felt cooler? The answer will give you a whole new perspective on the beauty of a really good sweat. As soon as you're done, go inside and drink some water to rehydrate!

Just How Hot Is It?

◆━━◆━━◆━━◆

Most thermometers are made with mercury, a poisonous liquid metal. But you can make a safe thermometer using water.

Fill a small soft-drink bottle almost full of water (about ⅘ full). Color the water with food coloring. Put a clear drinking straw in the bottle so that the straw goes halfway down into the

What You'll Need
- soft-drink bottle
- water
- food coloring
- clear drinking straw
- modeling clay
- index card
- tape
- pen or pencil

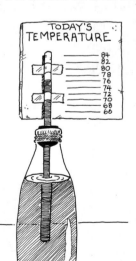

bottle. Use modeling clay to seal the top of the bottle and hold the straw in place. Tape an index card to the straw. You will use the card as a scale. Make a mark on the card to show where the water level is.

Now move your thermometer to a sunny place. Does the water rise? Mark the index card to show the new water level. (You may want to mark it with an "S" so you'll know which mark is which.) Check your thermometer at different times of the day to see how the temperature varies. You can also compare it with the weather section of your local newspaper to see if your readings match the "official" temperature.

Stay Cool, Stay Warm

◆▶◆▶◆▶◆▶

The way you dress can affect your personal environment.

Whether the weather is hot or cold, the colors you wear can affect your body temperature. Want to test the theory? Take 2 identical drinking glasses. Wrap one in black paper, and tape it securely. Wrap the other in white paper, and tape it in place. Now fill both glasses with lukewarm water, and put them on a porch or picnic table. Allow the glasses to stand undisturbed in direct

sunlight for about an hour. Now use a thermometer to measure the temperature of the water inside each glass. Then decide which color clothes will help you stay warm or cool. Odds are that your choice will be crystal clear.

What You'll Need
- 2 identical drinking glasses
- one sheet of black paper
- one sheet of white paper
- tape
- water
- thermometer

Hot Spots

◆▶◆▶◆▶◆▶

Where are the hottest spots on a hot day?

What You'll Need
- outdoor thermometer or soil thermometer
- notebook
- pencil or pen
- miscellaneous materials

If you're like most kids, you've tried to walk barefoot on asphalt on a hot day—and regretted it! What you got was a lesson on how some materials capture heat better than others. In this activity, you'll find out how well other materials absorb heat. On a warm, sunny day, go outdoors with a thermometer. Any outdoor thermometer will do, but a soil thermometer (available at a garden center) is useful because it has a strong metal probe that you can stick into the dirt.

Check the air temperature, and write it down. Then find different kinds of materials that are in the sun: soil, grass, bark dust, asphalt, metal, water. Hold the bulb end of the thermometer against each material, wait a few minutes, and write down the temperature. Which materials absorbed heat the most? How many were warmer than air? How many were cooler?

Gum Wrapper Thermometer

◆◆◆◆◆◆◆

Make a simple thermometer and find out how hot it really is!

What You'll Need

- foil gum wrapper (foil on one side and paper on the other)
- scissors
- spool (or similar item)
- tape
- glue
- index cards
- pencil or pen
- store-bought thermometer

Foil gum wrappers are made of 2 different materials: metal foil and paper. Both react a little differently to heat. The metal foil actually expands a little bit more than the paper as it gets hot. Because the different layers of the wrapper expand and contract at different rates, the wrapper will actually bend as the temperature changes.

Cut a long pointer from a gum wrapper. Tape one end of the pointer to the side of a spool. Glue the spool on its end atop an index card. That's all there is to it! But wait—how do you know how hot or cold it is? If you want actual numbers, you'll have to check a regular thermometer. Once you do that, mark the current temperature on the index card wherever the pointer is pointing. When the temperature changes, mark the new temperature on your homemade thermometer. You'll find that the gum wrapper thermometer isn't terribly precise; humidity can affect its accuracy. Still, it can tell you whether it is hotter today than yesterday, and maybe that's all the precision you want!

Watch Your Skin!

Did you know that if you're not careful, you can get a sunburn even on a cloudy day? Ultraviolet radiation that comes from the sun can go right through clouds, especially if the cloud layer is thin.

The Heat Is On

◆▶◆▶◆▶

Land warms up faster than water.

What You'll Need
- 2 containers
- soil
- water
- 2 thermometers
- tape
- lamp
- pen and paper
- watch or clock

Fill a container halfway with soil. Fill another container ¼ of the way with water. Place a thermometer in each container just underneath the surface of the soil and water, and tape them into position on the sides of the containers. Check the temperature of the soil and of the water. Add more water to the container to make it half full and to make the water temperature the same as the soil temperature. If the water is cooler than the soil, add warm water; if the water is warmer than the soil, add cool water. Put a lamp over the con-

tainers so they both get the same amount of light and heat. Record the temperature every 2 minutes. Do this for about 20 minutes.

What happened? The soil warmed at a faster rate than the water did. More energy is needed to raise the temperature of water than of land.

Hot Air

◆▶◆▶◆▶

Warm air rises.

Caution: This project requires adult supervision.

Use a thermometer to measure the air temperature near the floor in a room with poor air circulation, such as a garage. Write this down. With an adult's help, stand on a stepladder, and measure the temperature of the room at the highest point you can safely reach. Write this down. How are the temperatures different?

What You'll Need
- thermometer
- pen and paper
- stepladder

The temperature near the ceiling was higher than the temperature near the floor because warm air is less dense than cold air, so it rises. This is an important principle in weather. When hot air rises, air from someplace else blows in. This movement creates wind and storms, which help to move moisture all across the earth.

It's the Humidity

Humidity affects how hot we feel.

What You'll Need
● paper and pen
● weather reports

During the summer, make a chart with 3 columns; make the third column much wider than the first and second. Label the first column "TEMPERATURE." Label the second column "HUMIDITY." Label the third column "HOW I FEEL." Each day for 2 weeks during the summer, find out the day's humidity and high temperature from the newspaper or television, and record these numbers in your chart. Also record how hot or uncomfortable the weather made you feel that day. Compare the information from the different days.

If the temperature of 2 days is the same but the humidity is different, we would usually feel hotter on the day with the higher humidity. This happens because it is more difficult for the sweat of our bodies to evaporate on humid days. Normally sweat evaporates, cooling our bodies. But on humid days, the sweat evaporates slower.

Forecasts

How's the weather today? What will it be like tomorrow? Ever since ancient times people have asked these same questions. While modern weather instruments can give us better and better long-range forecasts, the weather wisdom of our ancestors is still useful today. Learn to watch for weather signs, as people did long ago, and make some modern weather instruments of your own. Try making your own weather predictions based on what you've learned, and see how often your predictions come true. Maybe you'll develop sympathy for the weather forecasters on television!

Natural Math

◆▷◆▷◆▷◆

*You don't have to be a weather forecaster to calculate
how far away lightning is. Just take a look.*

What You'll Need

- stopwatch or watch with a second hand
- paper and pen

Caution: This project requires adult supervision.

Where there is lightning, there is thunder. Since light travels faster than sound, you see the flash before you hear the sound. You can use the thunder to figure out how far away the lightning is. Watch for a flash of lightning. When you see it, use a stopwatch or second hand to count the seconds between the flash and the thunder that follows it. Write down the number of seconds, and divide that number by 5. The answer tells you how far away from you the lightning was in miles.

Did you know that not all lightning bolts touch the earth? In fact, ⅔ of all lightning occurs between clouds or within the same cloud. But that doesn't mean it's safe to go out in a thunderstorm! During a storm, avoid tall objects (like trees) and don't touch anything metal. You should also stay away from electrical appliances, telephones, and water until the storm is over.

"What Was That?"

◆▷◆▷◆▷◆

*Make up your own legend to explain thunder and lightning—
or any other weather phenomenon.*

What You'll Need

- paper
- markers

In ancient times, people had no way to know what thunder and lightning were or what caused them. So they made up stories to "explain" these mysteries. One American Indian tribe believed that thunder and lightning were the signs of gods attacking evil men on Earth. In fact, most ancient people thought thunder was the sound of gods either talking or fighting, and lightning flashes were their spears.

Imagine that you lived long before modern science. Make up a legend of your own to explain thunder and lightning. Write your legend, and draw pictures to illustrate it.

Weather Station

◆▶◆▶◆▶◆

Use your readings to track the weather. Then try to make predictions.

Caution: This project requires adult supervision.

In a ventilated area, paint the stake and peg board white using outdoor spray paint. Be sure to wear safety goggles and have an adult supervise. Nail the pegboard to the stake so the top of the board is a foot below the top of the stake. Use wire to fasten a thermometer and rain gauge to the pegboard. Fasten a weather vane or wind sock to the top of the stake. The north side of the wind vane's direction indicator should be on the same side as the thermometer. Find an open area with no over-hanging trees or large buildings in the way. Have an adult help you dig a hole about 18 inches deep. Sink your stake into the bottom of it so that the side of the station with the thermome-ter is facing north. Then fill the hole back in, and stomp the soil down firmly. Keep a weather notebook. Take readings of temperature, wind direction (and speed, if you made the wind sock), and rainfall daily. If you have a hygrome-ter and a barometer, you can add readings of humidity and air pressure to your notebook. Compare your readings to those you see in the newspaper. See if you can predict the weather.

What You'll Need
- stake
- small piece of peg board (about 8 inches wide and 1 foot long)
- white spray paint
- safety goggles
- wire
- thermometer
- rain gauge (see page 287)
- wind sock or weather vane (see pages 302 and 308)
- shovel
- notebook
- hygrometer (see page 303), optional
- barometer (see page 305), optional

Forecast: More Weather

◆▶◆▶◆▶◆

Weather maps show more than just temperatures. Learn how to read one.

What You'll Need
- newspaper
- weather map

Take time to learn how to read the weather map in your local newspaper. Check the key to learn what all the different sym-bols and colors mean. You might see numbers that stand for high and low temperatures, lines that show warm and cold fronts, and symbols that point out where it may rain or snow. These symbols are used by meteorologists (weather experts) all over the world. Read the weather map every day for at least a week. What weather patterns do you see?

Weather Folktales

◆◆◆◆◆◆

See which old beliefs are based on fact and which are pure fancy!

Our ancestors didn't have television weather forecasters, satellite weather photos, or fancy instruments to predict the weather. They had to rely on signs from nature. Some old folklore predictions are highly accurate, while others are mere superstition.

Here are some folk sayings about the weather. Which ones do you think give accurate predictions? Make your own observations of these signs to find out, then record them in your notebook. Which do you think are more reliable: signs that rely on animals or signs that relate to the sky and clouds?

1. Red sky in the morning, sailors take warning. Red sky at night, sailor's delight.
2. Crows on the fence mean rain; crows on the ground mean fine weather.
3. If a cow moos 3 times in a row, rain will come soon.
4. A ring around the sun or moon means rain is coming soon.
5. Roosters crowing at night predict rain.
6. High clouds mean fine weather; low clouds mean rain is coming.
7. Wide brown bands on a woolly bear caterpillar mean a mild winter.

All Kinds of Weather

◆◆◆◆◆◆

The answers to all your weather questions are as close as your library.

Have you ever wondered what are the coldest, hottest, rainiest, and snowiest places on Earth? Antarctica is the coldest at -128.6°F and Al Aziziyah, Libya, is the hottest at 136°F. The rainiest place in the world, Kukui, Hawaii, gets 460 inches every year, and Washington's Mount Rainier Paradise Ranger Station, the snowiest place, gets 1,122 inches in the winter season.

Or, have you wondered what causes tornadoes, thunder, or lightning? If so, check out some books about weather and find out. Discover your own fun weather facts, write them down, and share them with others.

What's the Weather Like?

◆▷◆▷◆▷◆

You don't need a crystal ball to predict when it's going to rain.
All it takes is a little practice!

Predicting the weather isn't a cinch, but you can look for hints about whether it's about to rain. First, listen to the weather report on the radio. If rain is on the way, grab a notepad and head out. There are plenty of signs in nature to alert you if umbrella weather is coming. For instance, some flowers—like tulips and dandelions—close up when rain is heading in. Clover folds its leaves. Some trees know it's going to rain, so they turn their leaves over to keep their tops dry.

Many spiders take down their webs before a heavy rainstorm. Cows gather together and lie down in a field before the rain hits, and dogs often smell the air before a rainfall.

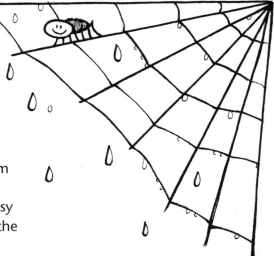

You'll also notice that noises are a lot clearer and smells are much stronger just before it rains. When you're outside, keep an eye, ear, or nose out to see if any of these things happen around your home. Write them on your notepad. If you do the same thing before a few more rainfalls, you'll see how easy it is to predict rain without even listening to the weather report!

Weather Journal

◆▶◆▶◆▶◆▶

Document weather trends.

Keeping a weather journal can teach you about weather patterns and help you forecast the weather conditions to come. Just get an ordinary spiral notebook at your grocery or department store. Check the weather outside, watch the forecast on television, and make a few

notes each day. Now go outside, watch the weather, and add your own personal notes to those mentioned on TV. See if you can guess what the weather will be like the next day, and write down your prediction. (Be sure to mention in the next day's entry if your prediction was right!) Before you know it, you'll begin to recognize weather trends. You'll be a junior weather forecaster, even if you never get to make your predictions on TV.

Newspaper Weather

◆▶◆▶◆▶◆▶

The weather of places is influenced by where the places are located.

In the weather section of your newspaper, look at the big map of the United States. Choose some cities, and keep track of their temperature highs. Choose one city far north, such as Albany, NY, and one far south, such as El Paso, TX. Choose one city by the ocean, such as San Diego, CA, and one city more inland, such as Phoenix, AZ. Choose one city high in the

mountains, such as Denver, CO, and one city on low land, such as Kansas City, MO. Make a chart with the names of the cities down the side and the days of the week across the top. Use the chart to record the temperature of each city for one week.

The temperature of each city changed during the week but probably by only a few degrees. The northern city was probably colder than the southern city. The city near the ocean probably had less severe weather than the more inland city; if it was summer, it was not as hot, and if it was winter, it was not as cold. The city in the mountains was probably colder than the city on low land.

Animal Instincts

◆◇◆◇◆◇◆◇

Can the mood of your pet help you predict weather shifts?

What You'll Need
- pet
- weather forecasts
- notebook
- pencil

Do you have a pet cat, dog, or rabbit? Does the weather affect your animal's moods? Keep track of how pets act on sunny and stormy days. Do they get restless when a rain storm is about to hit? Do they get sleepy when the day is bound to get hot? Do they pace when a hurricane is approaching? Watch closely and keep good notes of how they act before and after the weather changes. Soon, you'll know if your pet suffers from any weather-related moods—and if they can foretell weather patterns or trends.

Can Animals Fly? Yes!

Animals play a large part in the history of air travel. In 1782, 2 French brothers began test flights with hot-air balloons. They even sent a sheep, a duck, and a rooster up on a flight! The animals went on an 8-minute, 2-mile trip before the balloon touched down safely.

Skywatching

Since the beginning of humankind, people have gazed up at the sky and wondered: "What are the stars? What are the clouds? What is a rainbow?" Even today, with modern telescopes and satellites, there is still much we don't know about what's "up there." In this chapter you will find lots of activities to help you learn about the sky, the planets, the stars, and more. Take some time to explore, for astronomy is a field where amateurs are still making important contributions. Maybe the next big discovery will be yours!

Our Sun

There are millions of stars in our galaxy, and the sun is just one of them. The sun, however, is the center of our solar system; all of the planets in our solar system revolve around the sun. The diameter of the sun is about 865,000 miles, which is more than 100 times that of the earth. More than one million planets the size of the earth would fit into the sun.

Sunshine Cookies

◆◆◆◆◆◆◆

Bring rays of sunshine to a gloomy, cloudy day
with a batch of smiling sun cookies.

What You'll Need

- measuring cup and spoon
- butter, softened
- sugar
- 3 mixing bowls
- electric mixer
- 1 egg
- flour
- salt
- ½ lemon
- frozen lemonade concentrate, thawed
- powdered sugar
- meringue powder
- cookie sheets
- rolling pin
- 3-inch round cookie cutter
- 1 egg, beaten
- thin pretzel sticks
- oven
- cooling racks
- yellow paste food coloring
- water
- gummy fruit candy
- black licorice strings

Caution: This project requires adult supervision.

Beat ¾ cup butter and ¾ cup sugar in large bowl at high speed of electric mixer until fluffy. Add egg; beat well. Combine 2¼ cups all-purpose flour, ¼ teaspoon salt, and grated peel of ½ lemon in medium bowl. Add to butter mixture. Stir in 1 teaspoon lemonade concentrate. Refrigerate for 2 hours.

Prepare the icing: Combine 6 tablespoons of frozen lemonade concentrate with 3¼ cups sifted powdered sugar and 3 tablespoons meringue powder in large bowl. Beat at high speed of electric mixer until smooth. Cover; let stand at room temperature.

Preheat oven to 350°F. Grease cookie sheets.

Roll dough on floured surface to ⅛-inch thickness. Using cookie cutter, cut out cookies and place on cookie sheets. Brush cookies with beaten egg. Arrange pretzel sticks around the edge of the cookies to represent sunshine rays; press gently into cookies. Bake 10 minutes or until lightly browned. Remove to wire racks; cool completely.

Add food coloring to icing. Add water, 1 tablespoon at a time, to icing, until thick but pourable consistency. Turn cookies over; spoon icing in centers and spread it out over cookies.

Decorate cookies with gummy fruit candy and licorice to make a face like the one in the illustration. Let stand one hour or until dry. Makes about 3 dozen cookies.

See It Safely

◆▶▶▶▶◀

Use this eclipse viewer to watch a solar eclipse safely.

A solar eclipse happens when the moon comes between the earth and the sun. The moon blocks out the sun, and the earth gets dark in the daytime. Caution: looking at an eclipse—or looking at the sun on any day—can cause blindness, because the sun's light is so strong. You can make a viewer that will allow you to see an eclipse safely.

What You'll Need
- 2 pieces of cardboard
- pin or nail

Get 2 pieces of cardboard, each about the size of a piece of notebook paper. Poke a small hole in the middle of one piece of cardboard with a pin or nail. At the time of an eclipse, hold the piece with the hole up to the sun, with the other piece of cardboard beneath it, as shown. Look at the second piece of cardboard. You should see a circle with a "bite" taken out of it; the bite is the shadow of the moon in front of the sun.

Catch the Sun

◆▶▶▶▶▶◀

Create shimmery stationery or hang your creations as sun-catchers.

What You'll Need
- colored writing paper
- scissors
- newspaper
- waxed paper
- pressed plants (see page 626)
- ironing board and iron
- hole punch (optional)

Caution: This project requires adult supervision.

Fold a piece of colored writing paper in half and cut it to the size you want. Unfold it and lay it out on a sheet of newspaper. Tear off a piece of waxed paper and lay it over your cut paper. Arrange the pressed plants on the half of the paper that will be the front of your card until you have a design you like. Tear off another sheet of waxed paper and lay it on the first. Now carefully slide the waxed paper stack off of the paper and onto the newspaper. Cover with another sheet of newspaper and carry the whole thing to an ironing board. Have an adult use a warm iron to fuse the waxed paper together. Then, trim the waxed paper to fit the colored paper and fold in half with the colored paper inside. The plants will form the front of the card.

For a sun-catcher: Take the fused waxed paper and cut around the flowers. Punch a hole in the top and hang your creation in a window.

Solar-Powered Pictures

◆◆◆◆◆◆

Here is a way to make shadow pictures from sunlight.

What You'll Need
- flat objects
- scissors
- stiff cardboard
- flat pan
- water
- light-sensitive paper (such as Sunprint brand paper)
- glass baking dish or sheet of clear acrylic

First, assemble the materials you want to make prints from. Grass, leaves, and flowers make good prints. You can also look around the house for small objects such as keys, paper clips, and shaped erasers. Cut a sheet of stiff cardboard a little larger than the printing paper. In a dim place, lay your objects on the cardboard and decide how to arrange them. Then set the objects aside and make a print.

Pour water in a flat pan and have it ready to develop your prints. Open the package of light-sensitive paper and remove one sheet. Lay the sheet on the cardboard, then arrange your objects on the paper. Set the glass baking dish or clear acrylic on the paper. Lift the whole stack and set in bright sun for 3 to 5 minutes. Remove the paper and soak in the water for about 1 minute. Set your print in a shady place to dry. You will see white shadows on a blue background.

Frame your finished prints and decorate your bedroom wall with them, or use them to make cards, bookmarks, party invitations, or anything else you can think of.

Hot As Sun
Humans may have landed on the moon already but you can bet they'll never land on the sun. The sun, which is 43 million miles away from the earth, has a temperature of about 15 million degrees Celsius. Ouch!

Sun Portraits

◆▸◆▸◆▸◆

Calling all Picassos! Use the sun to draw a self-portrait.

What You'll Need
- large piece of paper
- rocks
- markers
- paint
- paintbrush
- leaves, sticks, or seeds
- glue

On a sunny morning, place a large piece of paper on the ground and put some rocks on the corners of it to keep it from blowing away. Stand next to the paper so your shadow falls on it. Then have your friend trace the outline of your shadow onto the page. You can do the same for your friend.

Now you're ready to get a little creative with your shadowy self. Using paint or markers, color your shadow or make

crazy designs inside of it. If you like, make a collage inside your shadow by gluing leaves, sticks, or seeds to the paper. Come back to your creation later in the day and trace another shadow next to the one you traced earlier. Since the sun is in a different place in the sky, your shadow will have a whole new look.

Big Sun

◆▸◆▸◆▸◆

If the earth were the size of a penny, how big would the sun be?

What You'll Need
- penny
- ruler
- chalk

The sun is about 862,000 miles in diameter. The earth is about 8,000 miles in diameter. To picture how much larger the sun is, pretend the earth is the size of a penny.

Place a penny on a sidewalk. This is now the size of the earth. Measure from the center of the penny to a distance of 40 inches. Put a dot on the sidewalk with your chalk. Measure this distance 6 different places around the penny, and place a dot in each spot. Then connect all these dots into a big circle around the penny. The penny represents the size of the earth; the chalk circle represents the size of the sun.

It might surprise you that the sun is so much bigger than the earth. After all, the sun looks small when we see it. The sun looks small because it is very, very far away.

Test Suntan Lotion

◆◀◆◀◆◀◆

How well does your favorite lotion protect against sun rays?

What You'll Need
- stiff cardboard
- scissors
- light-sensitive paper (such as Sunprint brand paper)
- plastic wrap
- tape
- various suncreens and tanning lotions
- keys or other flat objects
- paper clips
- flat pan
- water
- watch or timer

Sunscreen and tanning lotions screen out radiation. It's the ultraviolet (UV) waves in sunlight—not the sun's heat—that browns skin and can cause sunburn or skin cancer. Many people use sunscreen to prevent UV damage. To test sunscreen and tanning lotions, make testing frames from cardboard and plastic wrap. Cut a square of cardboard 4 inches wider and longer than the light-sensitive paper sheets. Cut a hole in the center of the cardboard the same size as the light-sensitive paper. Cover the hole with plastic wrap and tape in place. Cut a second square of cardboard the same size as the first to go under the frame. Make as many testing frames as you need to test the various brands of lotion you have.

Put a dab of sunscreen on the plastic wrap of one frame. Spread it thinly and evenly over the entire surface. Lay a sheet of light-sensitive paper in the middle of the solid cardboard square. Set a key or similar flat object in the middle of the paper, and cover with the testing frame. Paper clip the frame to the cardboard to hold everything together.

Set the stack in bright sunlight for exactly 3 minutes. Bring indoors. Remove the paper and soak it in a flat pan filled with water for exactly 1 minute. Let the paper dry completely. Repeat the process with a clean frame for each lotion. Do one test using just the frame and no lotion at all for comparison. Which lotion worked best? Remember, the darker the paper, the more sunlight came through.

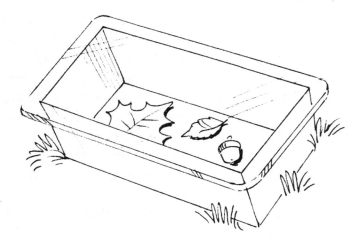

Night Colors

◆◆◆◆◆◆

See the light show that nature puts on every evening.

You've probably seen a few spectacular sunrises and sunsets, but have you ever watched the whole sky to see how the colors change as the sun goes down?

On a clear evening, find a place to sit where you can watch the eastern and western horizons. Use watercolors or colored pencils to record the night sky an hour before sunset. What you should see in the east is white light near the horizon, pale blue just above it, and blue in the bowl of the sky. The western sky will look warmer than the eastern sky.

What You'll Need
- notepad and pencil
- watercolors or colored pencils
- watch

Twenty minutes before sunset, you may see pale orange at the eastern horizon, white above that, and shades of blue above that. The western sky will be full of yellows, oranges, and pinks. As the sun sets, look east to see dark blue at the horizon, brilliant shades of red, orange, or purple at the level of the setting sun's rays, and pale yellow and deep blue high above. The western sky should glow orange. If you look carefully, you might see a rare flash of green light just as the sun disappears below the horizon.

Just after sunset, the western horizon will be bright and warm with pink bands fading into purple. In the east, you'll see dark blue at the horizon, purple above that, and red in the bowl of the sky.

Twenty minutes after sunset, the western horizon may still be yellow or orange, but above is a band of rosy pink fading into purple. The eastern horizon is turning dark purple, with blue above that and purple or red in the bowl of the sky.

If there is a lot of smoke or dust in the air, the colors may be different. Heavy pollution can produce spectacular orange and red sunsets.

The Moon

The moon is the closest astronomical object to our planet. Because it is so close, we know a great deal about it. People have studied it carefully for centuries, even when the technology for space observation was limited. The moon is also the only object in space that people have ever visited.

Time Flies

Learn about the parts of the moon's cycle with a lunar phases flip book.

What You'll Need
- 16 plain white index cards
- black marker
- heavy-duty stapler

The moon is a great example of nature's cycles. Every 29½ days, the moon goes through a complete cycle. At the beginning of the cycle, the moon is invisible. This happens when the moon comes between the sun and the earth, so that sunlight only shines on the backside of the moon where we can't see it. As the moon moves around the earth, we see more of the sunlit part of the moon. Halfway through the cycle we see a full moon. At that time, the whole face of the moon is lit up by the sun. Then we see less and less of the moon until finally it is invisible again.

On 16 index cards, draw the phases as shown on this page. Draw each "moon" on the right half of the card. Stack the cards in order, with the first one on top of the stack. Staple all the cards together on the left side, or just hold the cards together firmly. With your other hand, flip through the stack to see the moon's phases.

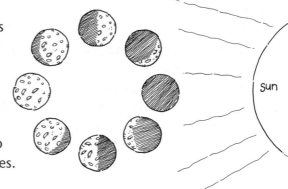

The Toad in the Moon?

◆◆◆◆◆◆◆

There are lots of stories that try to explain the shadows on the moon. Now it's your turn to make up a legend.

What You'll Need
● paper and pen

People in different parts of the world have had different ideas about just who, or what, is "in the moon." In the United States, we look at the shadows on the full moon and say it is "the man in the moon." In Germany, people say that man was sent there for something he did wrong. In Africa, the Masai people say it's "the woman in the moon." And in China, they say it's a rabbit or a toad.

Take a good look at the full moon. What do you see there? Write a story telling who, or what, is in the moon, and how it got there. Then see what stories your friends can tell.

Going Through a Phase

◆◆◆◆◆◆◆

Make a model of the sun, Earth, and moon to show the phases of the moon.

Stick a pencil into a plastic foam ball. The ball stands for the moon. Use the pencil as a handle.

Darken the room, and turn on a lamp that doesn't have a shade. Put the lamp at eye level in the middle of the room. Now face the lamp. The lamp is the sun and you are the earth! Hold the plastic foam ball directly between you and the light. The side of the ball that is facing you will be dark. This is called the new moon.

What You'll Need
● pencil
● plastic foam ball
● lamp without a shade

Now, hold the ball at arm's length while you turn in place. You might want to hold the ball above your head so the light can always reach it as you turn. Watch the ball. It will go through the phases of the moon as different sides of the ball are hit. When you are between the lamp and the ball, with the light shining completely on the ball, the ball will look like a full moon.

Moon Models

◆◆◆◆◆◆

Learn what causes moon phases.

Many people think that the moon's phases are caused by the shadow of the earth moving across the face of the moon, but that isn't true. When the earth's shadow blots out the moon, we call this a lunar eclipse. To find out what really causes moon phases, do this simple demonstration with 2 friends. One person, holding a flashlight and standing near a garage in the dark is the sun. A second person, standing a few feet away, is the earth. The third person, the moon, carries a softball "in orbit" around the earth.

Have the "moon" stand directly between the "earth" and the "sun." The "earth" should see the unlit side of the moon. This is what happens when we see a new moon. We're seeing the "night side" of the moon.

Now ask the "moon" to move left of the "earth." Now the earth should see the sun side of the softball lit up and the other side in shadow. This represents a "first quarter" moon, which is really a half-moon.

Next, the "moon" stands in back of the "earth." There should be enough light reaching the softball to light up the whole side that faces the "earth." This represents a full moon.

Finally, the "moon" moves to the right of the "earth." Again, the "earth" should see half the ball lit up and half in shadow. This represents the last quarter moon. Like the first quarter moon, this is really a half-moon.

Now track the moon for a month. This is easy to do when the moon is full, because it rises just after sundown, but after that, the moon rises and sets later. Do you ever see the moon in the day? Can you figure out why?

Space Dust

Did you know that gravity on the moon is only 1/6 as powerful as on Earth? The first moonwalkers, astronauts Neil Armstrong and Buzz Aldrin, reported that when they kicked dust with their boots, every grain landed exactly the same distance away!

Explore the Moon

◆◆◆◆◆◆◆

"Travel" to the moon with binoculars and "explore" its features.

What You'll Need
- binoculars
- paper and pencil
- reference books (optional)

Choose a clear night with a full or nearly full moon. (The moon will rise shortly after sunset.) Sit comfortably outdoors in a place where you can see the moon. Use binoculars to look closely. What features to do you see? How many large craters do you see? Can you count the small craters? You should be able to spot Tycho crater near the southern pole and Copernicus crater near the equator and slightly west of center. Both of these craters have long, radiating, extending lines that you should be able to see through your binoculars.

These rays were caused by material flung out when the crater was created by a meteor impact. Look for the flat plains called "seas" (which don't hold water). These may have been created years and years ago when huge meteorites struck the moon and blew away huge basins that soon filled with liquid lava. The 3 most visible seas (or *maria,* as they are often called) are the Sea of Showers near the northern pole, the Sea of Serenity near the equator and to the east, and the Sea of Tranquility, just south of the Sea of Serenity.

Now draw your own moon map. Start with a large circle, then fill in all the craters and seas that you observe. Label the larger features. You can use other reference books to find names for the smaller features. If you prefer, pretend that you are the first person to explore the moon and name the features yourself!

Head, Ball, Moon

◆◆◆◆◆◆◆

Sometimes we only see a slice of the moon lit up because of our angle of view when we look at the moon.

Next time you are outside and you can see the moon during the day, get a big ball, like a basketball or a soccer ball. Stand in a sunny spot, face the moon, and hold the ball in front of you as if you were giving it to the moon. Your head, the ball, and the moon should all be lined up. Look at how the sunlight is shining on the ball. Although half of the ball is lit up, you can only see a portion of the lit ball. Now look at the moon. The portion of the ball you see lit up is the same as the portion of the moon that is lit up.

What You'll Need
● large ball

Moon Map

◆◆◆◆◆◆◆

The moon appears to change shape as it orbits around the earth and is lit by the sun.

What You'll Need
● pen and paper
● calendar

Find a place outside where you can see the sky from the southeast to the southwest and where you can also see several landmarks on the horizon, such as buildings or trees. Draw the view of the horizon with the landmarks on a sheet of paper. Mark the exact spot you are standing in so you can find it again.

You are going to plot the moon's position and its image every day for a month. You may wish to start on a night with a full moon or a new moon. At the same time every night, observe the moon from the spot where you drew your map. Draw the moon's position on the map, and write the date inside it. On a calendar, draw what the moon looks like in the square for that day. As the month goes on, you will see how the moon changes position in the sky and how the part of the moon that is lit by the sun changes.

I'll Be Back

◆▶◆▶◆▶◆

The terminator is the point on the moon (or on any planet) where day and night meet.

Focus binoculars or a telescope on the moon. Find the terminator, which is the line where day meets night on the moon. The lighting near the terminator makes it a great area for observing structures on the moon. Can you see any mountains or valleys?

Boxed Moon

◆▶◆▶◆▶◆

Simulate the phases of the moon with this exercise in perception.

Cut a hole in one end of a shoe box big enough for a flashlight to fit through. Then cut 8 peepholes around the box as indicated in the drawing. Glue a spool of thread to the center of the bottom of the box. Glue a tennis ball on top of the spool. Prop the flashlight on a stack of books, and shine its light through the hole. Look at the image of the moon from the eight different peepholes around the box. What does the moon look like from each peephole?

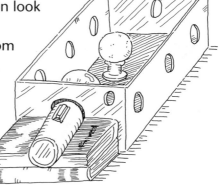

As you look at the ball from different angles, different parts of it will appear to be lit up. Our view of the moon changes in the same way. The amount of sunlight hitting the moon does not change throughout the month (unless there is a lunar eclipse, which is rare). Our view of the moon changes because we see it from different angles as it orbits around the earth.

Looking at a Lunar Eclipse

❖❖❖❖❖❖

A lunar eclipse occurs when the earth blocks light to the moon.

Lunar eclipses don't happen very often, but when they do, they are exciting. Newspapers and television stations will inform you when one will occur in your area. You should not look directly at a solar eclipse, but it is safe to look at a lunar eclipse. When the next lunar eclipse occurs in your area, arrange to be in a place that offers a clear view, and watch as the eclipse takes place. You will be able to see the shadow of the earth slowly cross over the moon.

Understanding Totality

❖❖❖❖❖❖

A total eclipse occurs when a shadow, called an umbra,
falls on a region of the earth.

In a dark room, put a large ball, such as a soccer ball, on a table. Then put a flashlight on a stack of books so that the light beam shines on the middle of the ball. Tape a string to a smaller ball, such as a tennis ball, and hold the smaller ball in the path of the light to make a shadow on the larger ball. This will be a model of a solar eclipse, where the large ball is the earth, the small ball is the moon, and the flashlight is the sun.

What You'll Need
- large ball
- flashlight
- books
- small ball
- string
- tape

If you hold the ball at the right distance, you will see a very dark shadow on the large ball surrounded by a lighter shadow. The dark shadow is called the *umbra,* and the lighter shadow is called the *penumbra*. If you were in the spot on Earth where the umbra falls, you would experience a total eclipse. If you were in the spot on Earth where the penumbra falls, you would experience a partial eclipse.

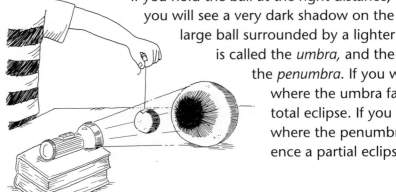

Hula-Hoop Eclipse

Solar eclipses are caused by the moon blocking light to the earth. Lunar eclipses are caused by the earth blocking light to the moon.

What You'll Need
- table-tennis ball
- glue
- string
- hula hoop or cardboard ring
- lamp

Glue a table-tennis ball to a piece of string. Tie the string to a hula hoop or cardboard ring. Turn off all the lights in the room except one lamp. Face the lamp, and stand in the middle of the hula hoop so the ball is between you and the lamp. The lamp represents the sun, the ball represents the moon, and you are the earth. Watch how the light falls on the ball. Turn your body and the hula hoop, and watch how the light on the ball changes. When you are facing the lamp, notice how the ball puts a shadow on your body. This is what happens during a solar eclipse. If you were standing on the earth where the moon's shadow fell, you would be in the moon's shadow, and it would seem as if the sun had been covered. Continue rotating around until you have your back to the sun. Now your body blocks light to the ball. During a lunar eclipse, the shadow of the earth makes it seem as if the moon has been covered.

Clouds

Clouds create endless fascination. At times, they are so immense it looks like we could walk on them. This would be a miracle greater than walking on water. Clouds form when water vapor condenses into tiny drops of water on particles of dust. You cannot walk on floating dust, and you cannot walk on clouds.

Identifying Clouds

◆◆◆◆◆◆

All clouds are made of tiny droplets of water. Yet clouds come in all shapes and sizes and bring different kinds of weather.

What You'll Need
● pen and paper

The main kinds of clouds are listed below. They're listed from the lowest to the highest in the sky. What type of clouds are in the sky right now? Keep a record of the clouds you see each day. You can draw the clouds and keep a count of how many days you see each type of cloud. Maybe you'll be able to see them all!

Low clouds (up to 6,500 feet)

Fog: Clouds in contact with the ground.

Stratus: Low sheets of clouds that form less than a mile above the earth. Like a thick blanket over the earth, they bring dark, gray days—and, sometimes, drizzle.

Nimbostratus: A very thick, dark layer of clouds that bring rain. (Nimbus is Latin for rain.)

Cumulus: These are the big, white fluffy clouds that float by on sunny days. They usually mean good weather.

Stratocumulus: Cumulus clouds pressed together in layers.

Cumulonimbus: These clouds pile up into towering mountains called "thunderheads." They may bring thunderstorms. At their worst, they create tornadoes.

Middle clouds (6,500 to 20,000 feet)

Altocumulus: These are rows of clouds shaped like long rolls.

Altostratus: Thin, gray, layered clouds that look like a veil in front of the sun.

High clouds (20,000 to 40,000 feet)

Cirrus: These long, wispy clouds are often called "mare's tails." Can you guess why?

Cirrocumulus: These rows of long, thin clouds are sometimes called "mackerel sky" because they resemble fish scales or ripples in water.

Cirrostratus: These form thin layers of high clouds that often cause a halo around the sun or moon.

Clouds Overhead

❖❖❖❖❖❖

A good way to remember the different clouds is to make a mobile.

What You'll Need:
- poster board
- scissors
- cotton balls
- glue
- string
- dowel
- paint and paintbrush (optional)

For each kind of cloud, cut its shape out of poster board. Glue cotton balls to both sides of the shape to make it look like a cloud. Make each cloud look like the real thing as much as you can. For a cumulus cloud, bunch up lots of cotton balls to make it fluffy. For a cirrus cloud, stretch out the cotton balls to make them thin and wispy. You could use a little gray paint (just mix a little black into white) to make some of the clouds gray.

When all your clouds are assembled and the glue is dry, make a small hole in each one. Then tie a piece of string through each hole. Nimbostratus clouds should have the longest string, since they're closest to Earth. Cirrus clouds should have the shortest string, since they're the highest clouds.

Now tie all the clouds to a dowel. Finally, tie a piece of string around the middle of the dowel, and use it to hang your mobile.

As Clouds Roll By

❖❖❖❖❖❖

Build this cloud chaser and see the wind blow!

What You'll Need
- cardboard
- marker
- tape
- small mirror
- compass

Swooooosh! There goes the wind . . . and now you can see it! First, mark out north, south, east, and west on the outside edge of a piece of cardboard. Include other directions, like northeast, if you like. Then tape a small mirror to the cardboard so that the compass directions form a circle around the mirror. Now you're ready to chase the wind!

Place your cloud chaser on the ground so it faces north. You can do this by matching north on your cloud chaser with north on your compass. Lie next to your cloud chaser and watch the reflection of the clouds in the mirror. Once you see which way the clouds are moving, you'll know that's the same direction that the wind is blowing.

Cloudy Caper

◆◆◆◆◆◆◆

Look to the sky for imaginary fun.

Lots of kids have never taken the time to sit and stare at the clouds in the sky. If you're one of those kids, it's time you settled back for a fluffy white look. Lay on your back in an open field and look up at the sky. What do you see? Ordinary clouds? Or clouds shaped like your favorite cartoon or mythical beast? Do you see a cloud shaped like a fire truck or a circus tent? You never know what's going to shape up until you try.

Planets

◆◆◆◆◆◆◆

Large objects that circle stars are called planets. Nine planets, including our Earth, orbit our Sun. Jupiter is the largest planet in our solar system, and Pluto is the smallest. Recently, astronomers have detected signs that there are planets orbiting other stars.

Peas in Space!

◆▸◆▸◆▸◆

Or would you rather have the walnuts?
Make a true scale model of the solar system.

What You'll Need
- a ball that is about 27 inches in diameter (such as a beach ball)
- 5 peas
- 1 orange
- 1 tangerine
- 2 walnuts
- tape measure

You've probably seen lots of drawings and diagrams of the solar system. But, to make the drawings fit on a piece of paper, the artists have to draw the planets closer together than they really are. In this activity, you'll make a scale model of the solar system. You'll be surprised to see how much bigger some planets are than others and how far apart some of them are.

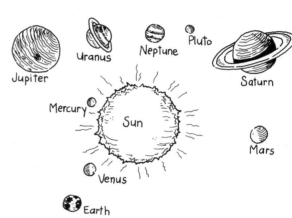

Make your model in a large open space that will represent, uh, space! Put a beach ball or other large ball at one end of the space. The ball is the sun. Place the other objects as follows. (Remember to measure each planet from the sun.)

Planet	Object	Distance from the Sun
Mercury	Pea	1¾ inches
Venus	Pea	3¼ inches
Earth	Pea	4½ inches
Mars	Pea	7 inches
Jupiter	Orange	2 feet
Saturn	Tangerine	3 feet, 7 inches
Uranus	Walnut	7 feet, 3 inches
Neptune	Walnut	11 feet, 4 inches
Pluto	Pea	14 feet, 10 inches

Travel to Outer Space

◆◆◆◆◆◆

Imagine what it would be like to float among the planets, stars, and comets!

What You'll Need
- scissors
- cardboard or heavy paper
- decorations (paint, aluminum foil, or glitter)
- pin
- thread or nylon line
- 2 dowel rods or sticks

If you hang a space mobile in your room, you can look up and imagine you're there. Cut out and color shapes to make planets, stars, spaceships, and other objects found in outer space. Use interesting materials such as glow-in-the-dark paint, aluminum foil, and glitter. Also use your imagination, and include anything you think might be found in space: alien monsters? giant dough-nuts? It's your universe!

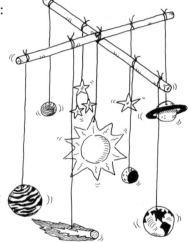

Next use a pin to make a small hole through each shape you made. Tie a piece of thread or nylon line through each hole. Next, cross one dowel rod over the other at a right angle. Tie the dowels together, then tie your shapes to the dowels. Tie different shapes at different heights. Finally, tie a strong thread or piece of nylon line around the dowels to hang your mobile. You've got your head in the stars!

Lost in Space?

◆◆◆◆◆◆

There is so much to learn about space and the solar system! Explore the galaxy without even leaving your home.

What are comets made of? Why do the planets in our solar system orbit around the Sun? What is a galaxy? How long would it take to travel to Pluto? You can learn the answers to these questions and a lot more about space by reading about it. Find some books at your library. After you've learned all about space, write a story in which you pretend you are a space traveler. Put some of the things you learned in your story, to make it seem more real.

What You'll Need
- books about space
- paper
- pen

Planetary Walk

◆▸◆▸◆▸◆

Take a stroll through the solar system in 1,000 paces!

Have you ever wondered how far apart the planets really are? This planetary walk will show you just how much space there is in outer space! An 8-inch ball will be the Sun. Now, glue or tape the "planets" to individual index cards, and use bright markers to label them as follows: the pinheads are Mercury, Mars, and Pluto (Pluto is actually smaller than Mercury and Mars, so if you can find a very small-headed pin, use it), the peppercorns are Venus and Earth, the walnut is Jupiter, the acorn is Saturn, and the peanuts are Neptune and Uranus.

Use your own stride as a unit of measurement. With a yardstick, practice taking steps one yard long. Each step will represent 3,600,000 miles! Now set your "Sun" on the edge of a large park or on the sidewalk of a long, straight street. Take 10 one-yard steps from the sun and put down your Mercury card. Does this seem a long way away? Proportionally it's in the right place. Mercury is about 36,000,000 miles from the Sun.

Take 9 more steps and set down Venus. Take 7 steps and put down Earth. Now take 14 steps and put down Mars. You've taken 40 steps from the Sun. Earth and Mars look lonely so far from the Sun and the other planets. Yet this is how they are in space. From Mars, take 95 paces and set down Jupiter. From Jupiter, it's 112 steps to Saturn. Take 249 more paces and put down Uranus. You're halfway across the solar system!

Next is Neptune, which is 281 paces from Uranus. From Neptune, take 242 paces, and put down your last card, Pluto. You've gone 1,019 paces, or just over a half a mile. The Sun probably looks like a speck, if you can see it at all. If you were standing on Pluto's surface, the sun would look about as bright as the other stars around it. Pluto is, on the average, 3,660,000,000 miles from the Sun!

Watching for Planets

◆◆◆◆◆◆◆

Can you find the planets in the night sky?

What You'll Need
- star chart
- binoculars or telescope (optional)

Of the 9 planets in our solar system, 5 (besides Earth) can be seen with the naked eye. People in ancient times called the planets "wandering stars" because these bright objects appeared to change position while other stars seemed to stay in place. Try to spot the wandering stars yourself. You need only your eyes, but a pair of binoculars or a telescope offers a better look. Venus is the easiest planet to find. Look in the western sky just after the sun goes down. You can also spot it in the early morning sky just before sunrise.

The rest of the planets are harder to find. Consult an almanac or planetary table to track their movements. Watch your local newspaper or an astronomy magazine for information on which planets are visible. Use a star chart to locate the constellation where the planet will be. The planets appear to move through the constellations associated with the zodiac, so become familiar with these constellations. Once you spot a bright object that doesn't seem to belong to the constellation, try observing it through binoculars or a telescope. With most home telescopes, you can see the red spot on Jupiter and the rings of Saturn.

Constellations

◆▷◆▷◆▷◆

In big cities, people have difficulty seeing the beauty of the night sky because of all the artificial light shining into the atmosphere. When city people visit the country, they often gasp when they see the view of the night sky on a clear night. Ancient people had a wonderful view of the night sky, and they spent a great deal of time studying the stars. They remembered stars by thinking of the groups of stars as representing gods or things on Earth. These groups of stars are called *constellations*.

 ## It's Raining Stars

◆▷◆▷◆▷◆

Turn your umbrella into your own private planetarium.

What You'll Need
- black umbrella
- white chalk
- star chart

Do this activity on a crystal-clear night when the moon is either invisible or very small. If you can, go to a place where there are few or no human-made lights.

Ask an adult if you can mark up an old, black umbrella with chalk. Open the umbrella and hold it over your head. Point the tip of the umbrella at the North Star. (Use a star chart to find the North Star, or ask an adult to help you.) Look up at the underside of the umbrella. You may see the stars shining through. Use white chalk to mark on the umbrella each place where you see a star. (This will be easier if someone else holds the umbrella for you.) If you can't see the stars through the umbrella, just look in the sky and mark the stars in the same positions as you see them in the sky. When you've marked all the stars you can see, take the umbrella inside. Compare your marks to a star chart. What stars and constellations did you mark? Draw lines connecting the constellations, and label them with their names.

Star Theater

◆◆◆◆◆◆◆

You'll be the star when you learn the shapes
of some constellations and put on a show for your family!

Caution: This project requires adult supervision.

Clean the cans and use pliers to flatten any sharp points. Lay the end of the can on the tracing paper and draw circles with a pencil. Lay the marked tracing paper on a picture of a constellation in a book and trace a constellation inside of each circle, using dots to represent stars. If a constellation won't fit in the circle, you can try drawing it freehand. Cut out the circles, and use a pin to poke a hole where each star is marked. Then turn each circle over so the constellation is backward, and tape one to the closed end of the steel can. Use a hammer and a thin finishing nail to punch a hole through each pin hole. (Always be careful when using a hammer!) Remove the paper.

Write the name of each constellation on a piece of masking tape and attach each piece of masking tape to the can it represents. This is so you can remember which constellation is which. Shine a flashlight into the open end of the can to shine the constellation on the ceiling. You can shroud the open end of the can in black cloth to shut out excess light when you put on a star show for your family.

Star Light, Star Bright

On a clear night, you can probably see only 3,000 stars out of the millions of stars in the sky. Some stars appear much brighter than others. This is because they are either larger, have a stronger light, or are closer to the earth than other stars. The star nearest to the earth, other than our sun, is Proxima Centauri, which is about 25 trillion miles away!

The Sky Is Falling!

◆▷▷▷▷▷◆

There is nothing as breathtaking as a shooting star. Find out when and where you can scan the skies for meteor showers.

Space is chock-full of tiny planetlike spheres known as asteroids. That is, they're tiny by space standards; a very small asteroid might fit inside your house. Millions of fragments from asteroids can fall into the earth's atmosphere. When one of these fragments comes close to Earth and burns up, it makes a streak of light that can be seen in the night sky. This streak is called a *meteor,* or a shooting star.

Most of these fragments burn up completely in the atmosphere. But once in a while one lands on Earth. When that happens, it's called a *meteorite.*

Skywatchers have learned that there are certain times and places when lots of meteors can be seen. These events are called *meteor showers,* and they're worth staying up late for. (The best time to see meteors is after midnight, and the best place is away from city lights.) Here are the times and places of some of the biggest meteor showers. Use a star map to find the places listed.

When	Where
January 1–3	Eastern sky, between Boötes and Draco. This is called the Quadrantid meteor shower, and it's the flashiest one of the year!
April 20–22	Northeastern sky, between Vega and Hercules.
May 4–6	Eastern sky, to the southwest of the Square of Pegasus.
August 10–13	Northeastern sky, around Perseus. Called the Perseids, this is the most famous meteor shower and is second only to the Quadrantids in the number of meteors.
October 20–23	Eastern sky, between Orion and Gemini.
November 3–10	Northeastern sky, between Taurus, Auriga, and Perseus.
December 10–12	Eastern sky, in Gemini.

Twinkle, Twinkle

◆◇◆◇◆◇◆

Stars appear to twinkle when their light passes through Earth's atmosphere.

Look into the night sky, and focus your eyes on a star. Observe how the light seems to become slightly brighter and dimmer at times. The star appears to be moving, slightly left to right, slightly up and down. But the light the star gives off is fairly constant, and the star is not making any rapid movements. The twinkle effect occurs as light from the star strikes molecules in our atmosphere. These molecules cause the light to make small changes in its path.

Speck-tral Stars

◆◇◆◇◆◇◆

Constellations are groups of stars in the sky. They are often given names based on their shape.

Thousands of years ago, people noticed the groups of stars and gave them names based on the shapes they seemed to form. Pegasus the Horse, Orion the Hunter, and Ursa Minor the Little Bear all got their names this way. Often, different cultures gave the groups their own names. What we call the Big Dipper, the Vikings called the Wagon, the Chinese called the Emperor's Chariot, and the English called a Plow.

What You'll Need
- newspaper
- white paper
- paint
- paintbrush
- pencil

Spread some newspaper on the floor or over a table. Place a sheet of white paper in the middle of the newspaper. Dip a paintbrush into paint. Hold the brush over the paper, and tap your hand so small paint specks fall on the paper. Think of these as stars, and examine them for patterns or shapes you recognize that could be constellations. Connect the paint specks with a pencil to form shapes you can recognize. Then paint more detailed pictures of the image. Write names for your constellations.

Latitude, Altitude, Time

◆▸◆▸◆▸◆▸

Measure your latitude by the North Star.

Long before our modern navigation systems were developed, people in ancient times navigated by the stars. The ancient Greeks, in fact, knew that the world was round and invented a system we still use to map and measure the globe. They divided the globe into latitude lines based upon the apparent altitude of the North Star above the horizon.

To find your own latitude, go outdoors on a clear night and look for the North Star. Tie a key or other weight to one end of a piece of string; tie the other end to the cross bar of a protractor. Turn the protractor so that the curved edge faces downward. Tilt it so that the string hangs exactly at "zero." Slowly tilt the protractor and look along the straight edge until you can see the North Star. Notice which degree mark the string now crosses. This indicates how many degrees above the horizon the North Star is. This figure is also your degree of latitude.

You can measure the altitude above the horizon of any star using the same technique, but latitude lines are based only on the angle of the North Star. Try to estimate a star's altitude above the horizon with your fingers. If you hold your hand out at arm's length, the width of a finger is approximately 4 degrees. Your hand minus the thumb (4 finger widths) is usually 15 to 16 degrees. All hands and arms are not alike, however, so check this measurement with the protractor.

Starry, Starry Night

◆▸◆▸◆▸◆▸

Twinkle, twinkle, I take notes.

Are all stars the same color and brightness? Not at all. Each has dozens of distinctive qualities and characteristics based on age, distance, and light pollution. Take the time to study the starry night and make note of the different colors you see.

See if you can find out why some stars seem bigger, brighter, or more colorful than others. Then hit the library or your family encyclopedia to find out if all the lights in the sky are actually stars at all.

Astrolabe

◆◆◆◆◆◆◆

Learn how to measure the position of stars with this simple instrument.

When scientists describe the position of a star in the sky, they measure its position relative to the horizon. An instrument called an *astrolabe* measures how high above the horizon the star is in degrees. Here's how to make your own astrolabe.

Tie a 12-inch piece of string to the hole in the middle of the crossbar on the protractor. Tie a weight to the other end of the string. Hold the protractor so that the curved part is down and the 0 degree mark is closest to you. Sit on the ground, and look along the flat edge of the protractor with your eye at the zero mark.

Point the flat edge at the star whose position you want to measure. Once you have the star at the end of your sight, hold the string against the side of the protractor.

Note the degree mark the string touches. Write this down in your notebook. This number tells you how many degrees above the horizon your star is.

Take readings for several stars. Return every 30 minutes and take new readings. Notice the pattern of the stars as they appear to move across the sky as the earth turns.

What You'll Need
- string
- ruler
- plastic protractor
- weight (washer, rock, or fishing weight)
- pen
- notebook
- flashlight (to see what you're writing)

Stellar Stories

◆◆◆◆◆◆◆

This is your chance to wish upon a star.

What You'll Need
- paper
- pen
- markers

In ancient times, people all over the world made up stories to explain what the stars are or where they came from. Some people believed that when people died, they became stars. If you didn't know that stars were giant balls of flaming gas millions of miles away, what would you think? Be creative, and make up a story to explain the stars. What are they? Why are there so many of them? Why do they twinkle? Make an illustrated storybook that tells your "star story." And don't forget to give your story a title!

Star Light, Star Bright

◆◆◆◆◆◆◆

Some stars appear to be brighter than others.

Cut four 1×4-inch rectangles next to each other on a piece of cardboard. Tape a sheet of cellophane over all 4 rectangles. Then tape cellophane over the last 3 rectangles. Then tape cellophane over the last 2 rectangles and finally over the last rectangle only.

View the night sky with your brightness detector. Notice you can see more stars when you look through fewer cellophane sheets.

Only the light from the brightest stars is able to penetrate all 4 sheets. Try to find a star that you can see with 1 sheet but not with 2 sheets. Call this a 1 star. Find a star you can see with 2 sheets but not 3. Call this a 2 star. Find a star you can see with 3 sheets but not 4, and call this a 3 star. Any star you can see through all 4 sheets is a 4 star. Which type of star can you find most often? A star's brightness on Earth depends upon 2 things: the amount of light the star is putting out and how far it is from Earth.

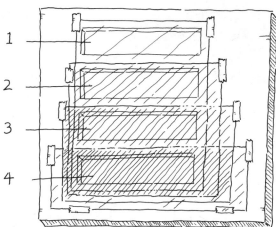

What's a Moonbow?

Most people have seen a rainbow, but how many have seen a moonbow? A moonbow occurs when 3 conditions are met: the moon will be full that night, it has just rained, and the moon has just risen. When all those conditions happen at the same time, a moonbow may appear.

Planetarium Presentations

❖❖❖❖❖❖

Turn your living room into a planetarium!

On one end of the shoe box, cut a hole just big enough for a flashlight to fit into. Cut a rectangle out of the other end of the shoe box. Draw dots on a piece of paper to represent the stars of a constellation, and poke holes through the dots with a pin; do this for several different constellations. Put one of the sheets over the rectangular hole in the box, and tape it in place. Support the flashlight with a stack of books, and put it into the hole in the other end of the box. In a darkened room, turn on the flashlight, and project your constellation onto a wall. Quiz your friends or family to see if they can identify the different constellations.

Happy Trails

❖❖❖❖❖❖

Circular star trails are produced on film when a camera shutter is left open and pointed at the night sky.

On a clear night, set up your camera on a tripod so that it points toward the North Star. Open the camera to its widest aperture, and set the shutter to be open for 2 hours. When you develop the film, you will see that the stars' positions in the sky have changed. Streaks of light show their path. This is a result of the earth's rotation. You'll see also that the star streaks on the film all circle around the North Star.

Map of the Stars

◆◆◆◆◆◆

Star light, star bright, the first star I see tonight . . .

What You'll Need
● star charts

The patterns of stars remain the same, but their positions in the sky change. Star charts help us find constellations in the sky. (Star charts are available at book stores or on the Internet.)

Bring a star chart outside on a clear night. Set the chart to the correct date and time. Hold the chart in front of you as you face north. Look at the chart and sky to see if you can find constellations. Find the Big Dipper and the Little Dipper. At the end of the handle of the Little Dipper is the North Star. Another way to find the North Star is from the Big Dipper. The part of the cup away from the handle is made of 2 stars. Start from the bottom star, and follow an imaginary line to the upper star. This will point you to the North Star. The North Star is important in navigation because it can always be used to identify which direction is north. All the other stars seem to rotate around this star.

Little Dipper   North Star

Big Dipper   To North Star

Star Map

◆◆◆◆◆◆◆◆◆◆

A constellation's position in the sky changes as Earth rotates.

What You'll Need
● paper and pen

Find a place outside where you can see the sky from the southeast to the southwest and where you can also see several landmarks on the horizon, such as buildings or trees. Draw the view of the horizon with the landmarks on a sheet of paper. Mark the exact spot you are standing in so you will be able to find it again. When night approaches, stand in that spot again, and look for a constellation or group of stars in the southern sky. Put a dot to represent the group on your landscape map, and write the time next to it. Every hour for the next 3 hours or more, return to the spot, and mark the time and the group's location on your map.

Dip into the Seasons

◆◆◆◆◆◆◆◆◆◆

The positions of stars change from month to month.

Every month the stars in the sky rotate by ¹⁄₁₂ of the way across the sky, sort of like every 60 minutes the hour hand on a clock moves ¹⁄₁₂ of the way around the clock. Go outside at 9:30 P.M. Find the Big Dipper, and note where it is in relation to the North Star. Record the season. Do this for the other 3 seasons of the year.

What You'll Need
● paper and pen

The Big Dipper's position around the North Star changed during the different seasons. The drawing shows the constellation's approximate positions for the different seasons at 9:30 P.M.

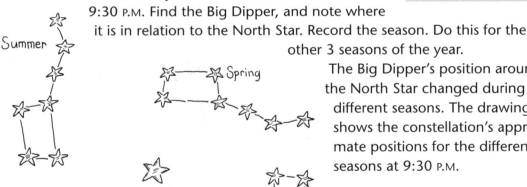

Plants All Around Us

◆▷◆▷◆▷◆▷

A tiny seed can become an enormous tree or a gorgeous flower. How does it happen? Discover the mysteries hidden in seeds, flowers, and plants with the activities in this chapter. Go outdoors to enjoy the wonders of trees. Try some of the gardening activities to grow flowers of your own and use them to make lovely art projects. Or turn your garden into a fun place to play by growing a bean teepee or a sunflower fort. Let's get growing!

Seeds

◁▷◆▷◆▷◆▷

It is fascinating to see a seed start to grow into a new plant. A seed contains genes from a male plant and from a female plant, just as you contain genes from your father and mother. With the right conditions, including warmth and moisture, seeds germinate, or sprout.

Seed Jewelry

◆◆◆◆◆◆

Create a fashion statement by making jewelry from nature's treasures.

First you will need to collect your seeds. Save seeds from watermelons, cantaloupes, apples, pumpkins, squash, and anything else you can find. Wash them in a sieve and let them dry thoroughly. If they're in season, you can also find some ears of "Indian" corn and remove the colorful corn seeds.

When you have enough seeds, lay them out on white paper and think about how you'd like to arrange them. Soak the seeds you plan to use for a few hours until soft. Use a plain sewing needle and strong thread or unwaxed dental floss to string your seeds. (Always be careful when handling a needle!) You can make necklaces from single, double, or even triple strands of seeds. Tie barrel-type jewelry fasteners (available at craft stores) to the ends of your string for shorter necklaces, chokers, or bracelets. For earrings, glue seeds into flower shapes on earring backs. If you like, you can add shine to your finished jewelry with clear acrylic spray. Ask an adult to help you, and be sure to work in a well-ventilated area.

What You'll Need
- large seeds
- sieve
- white paper
- water
- needle
- strong thread or unwaxed dental floss
- barrel-type jewelry fasteners
- earring backs
- strong craft glue
- spray acrylic (optional)

Save a Seed

◆◆◆◆◆◆

Recycle seeds nature's way.

What You'll Need
- summer plants as they begin to seed
- jar, coffee can, or seed pot with lid

Long before there were seed companies, farmers collected the seeds from one season's plants and put them away for the next year's planting. You can do the same thing. When your plants stop growing and go dormant, gather up the seeds for planting next spring. It's the best way to recycle—nature-style!

Speckled Plants

◆▸◆▸◆▸◆

Make a mosaic to show the many colors of plants.

What You'll Need
- variety of dried beans, seeds, and peas
- cardboard, poster board, or plywood
- marker or crayon
- craft glue

Start with a trip to a grocery store. (If possible, go to one that sells a wide variety of beans and peas in bulk, so you can buy just a handful of each.) Check out all the different kinds of dried (not canned) beans and peas. You should find beans in black, red, brown, white, and speckles. You'll find bright green peas and light green lima beans. Lentils come in many colors, including pink! Don't forget to check out seeds, too: tiny black poppy seeds, stripy sunflower seeds, green pumpkin seeds, and whatever else strikes your fancy.

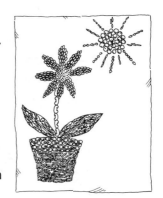

Collect as many different shapes, sizes, and colors of beans and seeds as you can. Then use them to make a mosaic. Make a drawing on a piece of cardboard, poster board, or plywood. Then glue on beans and seeds to fill in your drawing.

Seed Pot

◆▸◆▸◆▸◆

Protecting yesterday's seeds for tomorrow's harvest.

What You'll Need
- modeling clay
- oven
- cookie sheet
- aluminum foil
- tempera paint
- paintbrush
- seeds

Caution: This project requires adult supervision.

Ancient tribes kept their precious seeds in clay pots for safe-keeping between planting seasons. You can make a seed pot of your own. Buy some inexpensive modeling clay at your local craft store. (Be sure it's the kind of clay that bakes to a permanent finish in your oven.) Now mold a clay pot with a fairly broad opening, or "mouth." Roll a clay ball big enough to fit on that clay opening without slipping inside the pot.

With help, bake both pieces in your oven on a cookie sheet lined with aluminum foil at the temperature and time length mentioned on the clay packaging. Once the pot cools, paint the outside with tempera paint. Then keep your leftover and collected seeds safe and dry until it's time to plant again. You'll be following in some proud and ancient footsteps when you do.

Plant Your Socks?

◇◆◇◆◇◆◇

Imagine what would happen if your socks started to sprout.

What You'll Need
- pair of old tube socks
- shallow aluminum-foil pan
- water

Get a pair of old tube socks, and put them on over your shoes. Go for a walk through a field of tall grass and weeds. (The best time to do this is in the early fall, but you can try it in spring and summer, too.) Carefully take off the socks once they are covered with seeds. When you get home, put the socks in a shallow aluminum-foil pan with a little water in the bottom. There should be just enough water to make the socks wet—no more. Put the pan in a place indoors where it will get plenty of light, and keep those socks moist. In a few days, the seeds that stuck to your socks will begin to sprout. Let your sock garden grow for a while to see what kinds of plants you have.

Seed Collection

◇◆◇◆◇◆◇

Collect seeds and discover nature's tiny treasures!

What You'll Need:
- clear film canisters or envelopes
- seeds
- newspaper
- cardboard (optional)
- glue (optional)
- paper (optional)
- pen (optional)

Before you begin, decide how you want to organize your collection. Clear plastic film canisters are useful for storing seeds; they are waterproof and you can see the seeds. Ask for them at any store that develops film. You can also store seeds in paper envelopes, which can be kept in a shoebox.

Collect seeds in late summer and fall. Watch for wild fruits to ripen. Remove the seeds from the fruits and let them dry on newspaper before storing them. Watch for maple seeds to drop. Oaks will drop acorns in the fall. These are seeds, too. Let pinecones dry indoors, then pull out the scales and look for seeds. As flowers finish blooming, leave some on the plant so you can collect the seeds they make. To collect weed seeds, wear socks over your shoes and walk through weeds or a meadow. Look at the seeds stuck to your socks! Make sure the seeds are dry before you store them, or they will mold. Put each kind of seed in a different container. If you want to make a seed display, glue different kinds of seeds to cardboard and make a paper label for each.

Seed Bank

◆◆◆◆◆◆

Plants save for a rainy day by putting their seeds in seed banks!

Seeds that fall to the ground don't grow right away. They wait until conditions are right. To grow plants from a seed bank yourself, collect soil from any natural area (such as a dark forest or under a shrub) that hasn't had herbicides or pesticides applied to it. Scrape away any decaying plant material and dig enough soil to fill your pan ½ to 1 inch deep.

What You'll Need
- clean soil
- trowel
- aluminum baking pan
- water
- plastic wrap

Water the soil so that it is moist but not soggy. Cover the pan with plastic wrap to keep it moist. Set in a warm place and wait. After about a week, young plants will be growing. Where do they come from? They sprouted from seeds already in the soil. This is what we call a seed bank. Try this with soil from various places. How is the seed bank in a forest different from the seed bank in a meadow? Try garden soil, too.

Flying Seeds

◆◆◆◆◆◆

Discover how the wind can send some seeds flying.

What You'll Need
- wind-dispersed seeds (maple, elm, dandelion, thistle)
- sticks (optional)

In the fall, collect wind-blown seeds. Look for seeds with wings, such as maple and elm, or with downy parachutes, like the dandelion or thistle. These seeds are built so that the wind will scatter them far from their parent plant. Have a friend stand carefully near an open window on the second floor of a home and toss a handful of winged seeds toward the ground.

Watch them to see how far they sail. If possible, mark the farthest seed with a tall stick. Note also how the seeds land. Do they fall flat, or do they spin so fast that they drill themselves into the ground? Now have your partner drop dandelion or thistle seeds. (Make sure they are separated from one another first.) Do they drop to the ground, or do they float for miles? Can you mark the farthest one? Try this activity on both a breezy day and a still day to compare how far the seeds spread.

Chilly Veggies

◆━◆━◆━◆━◆

Seeds will still germinate after being frozen.

What You'll Need

- dried peas and lima beans
- envelopes
- freezer
- 4 pots
- rocks
- sand
- potting soil
- marker
- water

Put 6 dried peas and 6 dried beans in an envelope. Put the envelope in your freezer for 2 days. Put 6 dried peas and 6 dried beans in another envelope. Put that envelope in a drawer for 2 days.

Prepare 4 pots for planting. Put about 1 inch of small rocks in the bottom of each pot. Cover the rocks with 1 inch of sand, and cover the sand with 4 inches of potting soil. Label the pots as "FROZEN PEAS," "PLAIN PEAS," "FROZEN BEANS," and "PLAIN BEANS."

Plant your peas and beans in the appropriate pots. Water them to keep

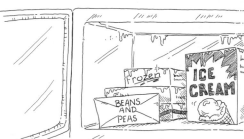

the soil moist but not wet. Put all 4 pots in a sunny window, and observe them for several weeks. Did the frozen seeds grow?

Temperature and Seeds

◆━◆━◆━◆━◆

Temperature can affect how fast seeds germinate.

Get 3 empty wide-mouthed jars, such as mayonnaise jars. Put 2 inches of small rocks at the bottom of each jar. Cover the rocks with 2 inches of sand. Then add 4 inches of potting soil.

Plant 4 of the same kind of flower seeds in each jar, following the directions on the package to find out how deep the seeds should be planted. Put the 3 jars in different places: in the refrigerator, on top of the refrigerator near the back, and near a cold garage wall. Water each of the jars occasionally so that the soil is moist but not wet. Observe the 3 jars each day, and write down what you see. Do the seeds in one of the jars germinate faster than in the others? What do you think caused any differences you observed?

What You'll Need

- 3 wide-mouthed jars
- ruler
- small rocks
- sand
- potting soil
- flower seeds
- water
- refrigerator
- pen and paper

Fresh Air

◆◆◆◆◆◆

Seeds need air to sprout.

What You'll Need
- 2 glass jars with lids
- dried peas
- water

Fill 2 glass jars with dried peas. Add a little water to both jars, and put on the lids. Shake the jars to be sure that every pea gets wet. Take the lid off one jar, and leave the lid on the other. Put the jars side by side in a sunny window for several days. Add water as it evaporates from the open jar. Observe the peas every day to look for any changes.

What happened? The pea seeds in the open jar sprouted, but the seeds in the sealed jar did not because they received no air. Seeds and plants need air to grow.

Seed Hunt

◆◆◆◆◆◆

Be on the lookout for seeds!

Visit a park, garden, or other planted area at the time of year when the plants growing there are producing seeds. Collect a few seeds from as many different plants as possible. Study each seed carefully. Does it have stickers or burrs that might

What You'll Need
- paper
- tape
- marker

get caught in animals' fur or in people's clothing? These stickers allow the seed to be carried from one spot to another. Is the seed inside a fruit that might be eaten by a bird or animal and eventually be eliminated by the animal in another spot? Does the seed have a parachute of some kind that enables it to fly? Classify your seeds by putting them into groups, perhaps based on how they are transported. Tape the seeds on sheets of paper labeled with the group names, and identify the plants they came from if you can.

Way Down Deep

◆◆◆◆◆◆

The depth at which seeds are planted can affect how well and how fast they grow.

Place 2 inches of small rocks in the bottom of an empty aquarium. Cover these with 2 inches of sand, and cover the sand with 8 inches of potting soil. Plant 16 corn seeds about an inch apart from each other in the aquarium; plant 4 of the seeds 1 inch deep in the soil, 4 seeds 2 inches deep, 4 seeds 4 inches deep, and 4 seeds 6 inches deep. Put the seeds near the glass wall of the aquarium so you can see them. Tape black paper over the outside of the glass to cover the seeds.

Water your seeds occasionally to keep the soil damp but not wet. Lift the paper to look at your seeds every day. Write down your observations and the date. Measure the length of roots and stems. Always tape the black paper back in place.

After 6 weeks, cut off the parts of each group of plants that are growing above the soil. Use a scale to weigh each group of plants. What do you think is the best depth for planting corn seeds?

What You'll Need
- empty aquarium
- small rocks
- sand
- potting soil
- ruler
- corn seeds
- ruler
- black paper
- tape
- pen and paper
- scissors
- scale

Seeds and Veins

◆◆◆◆◆◆

Can you tell the difference between a monocot and a dicot?

What You'll Need
- leaves
- magnifying glass (optional)

Scientists divide most seed-making plants into 2 groups: monocots and dicots. The seed of a dicot has 2 halves, which are food parts and become the 2 first leaves of the plant. The seed of a monocot has only one part. These plants also differ in their leaves. Dicots have leaves with veins that look like nets with strands that cross over each other. Monocots have leaves with veins that run parallel to one another.

Collect leaves from a variety of plants: flowering plants, such as daffodils and poppies; trees, such as oak, maple, aspen, and hickory; vegetables, such as beans and corn; and different grasses, palms, and shrubs. Spread the leaves out on a table, and look carefully at the veining in the leaves. You may want to use a magnifying glass. Separate the leaves into dicots and monocots by the way the veins in the leaves look.

Seed Keeping

◆ ▶ ◆ ▶ ◆ ▶ ◆

Many people save seeds from their gardens so they can be used to start next year's harvest. Make this drying frame so you can save seeds, too!

Caution: This project requires adult supervision.

To make 2 shallow boxes, measure and mark an inch up from the bottom of each box on all 4 corners. Connect the marks using the yardstick to help you make straight lines. Ask an adult to use the craft knife to cut the boxes along the sides. Then, on the bottom of the first box, measure and mark an inch in from all the sides. This will make a rectangular opening. Ask an adult to use the craft knife to cut the opening. This box is the frame.

Cut a rectangle of screen cloth an inch longer and an inch wider than the rectangular opening of the frame. Lay the screen over the opening on the inside of the frame. Tape the screen in place with plastic tape (stretch the screen tightly as you tape). Tape a piece of white paper to the inside bottom of the other box with clear tape. This is the seed box.

> **What You'll Need**
> - 2 small cardboard boxes with 10×10-inch bottoms
> - pencil
> - yardstick
> - craft knife
> - piece of nylon screen cloth
> - colored plastic tape
> - white paper
> - clear tape
> - clear vinyl adhesive paper

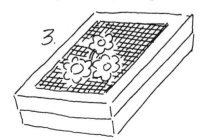

Cover both the frame and the seed box with clear adhesive vinyl paper, leaving only the screen and white paper uncovered. Cut 2 triangles out of scraps of cardboard. Place a triangle in each of 2 opposite corners of the seed box, and tape them into position with strips of the vinyl adhesive paper.

To use the frame: Set the frame section on top of the seed box with the screen side down. Place dead flower heads or seedpods on the screen. As the flowers and seedpods dry, the seeds will fall through the screen to the white paper in the seed box. Note: This sifter works only for small seeds—ones that can fit through the screen. But you can use the frame as a drying frame for plants with larger seeds.

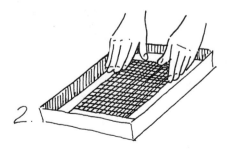

Sunlight, Water, Air, and Soil

Plants need sunlight, water, and air to thrive and be healthy. Plants use light from the sun to convert carbon dioxide and water into food and oxygen in a process called *photosynthesis*. Plants also take other important nutrients that they need from the soil.

 ## Root-View Box

Plants grow up out of the soil and down into the ground.
Use this special box to watch how roots grow.

What You'll Need

- ½-gallon paper milk carton
- scissors
- ruler
- sheet of glass, clear acrylic, or stiff clear plastic packaging
- craft glue or tape
- potting soil
- seeds of vegetables with large roots
- pan or tray
- water
- cardboard

Cut off the top of the milk carton and punch a few holes in the bottom for drainage. Cut a window in the side, leaving a ½ inch margin all the way around the window. Have an adult cut a sheet of glass or clear acrylic to fit the window inside the box. Another option is to check all the plastic packaging that is thrown away in your house for a piece of stiff, clear plastic that will fit the window. Glue or tape the plastic to the inside of box. Let it dry completely.

Now fill the box with potting soil. Plant seeds of carrots, radishes, or other root vegetables right up against the side of the box where the window is. Set the carton on a pan or tray to catch extra water, then water the seeds well. Put a bit of cardboard under the bottom of the box on the side opposite the window. This will tilt the box slightly, so the roots will grow right up against the window. Check the plant's growth to see how the roots are developing. Be sure to give your plants enough water and light.

"Look Mom, No Dirt!"

◆━◆━◆━◆━◆

*Believe it or not, while most plants in nature grow in soil,
it's possible to grow plants without it.*

Put a piece of wire mesh (like a piece of old screen) in the
bottom of an empty aquarium. Bend the ends of the mesh so
that it makes a shelf that is several inches above the bottom of
the aquarium. Mix plant food into some water, and pour the
water into the aquarium. The water level
should be just below
the mesh. Put some
sphagnum moss on
top of the mesh. Then
sprinkle some bean or corn seeds onto the moss,
and water them well. Keep the seeds watered.
Even though there's no soil, the seeds will sprout
and send roots down through the mesh into the
water that contains plant food.

> **What You'll Need**
> - wire mesh
> - aquarium
> - plant food
> - water
> - sphagnum moss
> - bean or corn
>   seeds

Cycle of Life

◆━◆━◆━◆━◆

A small plant can demonstrate nature's ability to recycle.

> **What You'll Need**
> - small potted plant
> - wide-mouthed jar
>   with lid

Water a small potted plant well. Then
put the plant—pot and all—in a big,
wide-mouthed jar and put the lid on
tightly. Put the jar where it will get sunlight, and leave it there for 30 days. (Be
careful that it doesn't get too hot or you
could hurt the plant.) Observe what happens in the jar. Droplets of
water will collect on the jar and drip down into the soil so the plant
can use the water again. Because this is a self-contained system,
the plant can live "on its own" inside the sealed jar.

The Need for Light

◆◆◆◆◆◆

What happens when plants don't get light?

This activity will harm the plants you observe, so please get permission beforehand. Try to find a weedy patch that hasn't been planted recently. In your notebook, sketch the plants you see in your weed patch. Note their shapes, sizes, and colors. Now cover the weed patch with a board or a brick. Weigh the board down with a rock or brick if you need to.

Leave the cover in place for a week. After a week is up, lift the board. What differences do you see? Write down and sketch the changes in your notebook. If you want, put the board back and wait another week. What happens to the plants if they don't get light? How long can they survive without light?

What You'll Need
- weedy patch of ground
- notebook
- pencil or pen
- board or brick
- large rock (optional)

I See the Light

◆◆◆◆◆◆

No matter what, plants always grow toward light!

What You'll Need
- plastic cup
- potting soil
- pinto beans
- scissors
- cardboard
- tape
- shoe box
- water

First, punch a few drainage holes in the bottom of a cup, add some potting soil, and plant a few pinto beans. Water the beans and put them in a warm place. Next tape 2 pieces of cardboard into a shoe box to make a maze, as shown. Cut a hole in one end of the shoe box. Keep the soil moist until the beans sprout, then put the cup in the shoe box. Put the lid on the shoe box.

Take the lid off the box every day to look at the bean plants and to water them as needed. Always make sure to put the lid back. Which way are the plants growing? See how long it takes them to grow out of the hole, into the light.

Surviving in the Desert

◆▶◆▶◆▶◆

Have you ever wondered how desert plants live on very little water?

Wet 3 paper towels until they are saturated with water but not dripping. Put the first paper towel flat on a cookie sheet. Roll up the second paper towel, paper clip it to keep it rolled up, and put it on the cookie sheet, too. Put the third paper towel on a piece of waxed paper that is the same size. Roll up the waxed paper and the paper towel together, and paper clip them so they stay rolled up.

Leave all 3 paper towels where they are for 24 hours. Then check them. The flat one will be dry. The rolled one will be dry or mostly dry. But the paper towel that is rolled up with the waxed paper will still be wet.

Now, you may be asking, "What does this have to do with plants in the desert?" Here's the answer: Cacti and other desert plants are like the paper towel that is rolled up with waxed paper. These plants have waxy coverings that keep moisture from evaporating into the dry desert air. That's part of the reason they can survive on the little water they get in the desert.

Respiring Plants

◆▶◆▶◆▶◆

How do plants take in oxygen?

Even though plants don't have nostrils or mouths like people do, they still need to take in air. There's a way to find out how plants breathe. Just take a small plant that has plenty of leaves and place it on an outdoor windowsill. Cover the tops (not the bottoms) of 5 of the plant's leaves with a thick coating of petroleum jelly. Then, cover the bottom sides only of 5 other leaves with another thick layer of jelly. Make a chart and keep track of how each leaf looks every day. Watch your plant for a week, and see if you can figure out which side of the leaf needs to be uncoated to bring in fresh air.

Colorful Carnation

◆▶◆▶◆▶◆

In this project, you can actually watch a flower "drink" water.

Caution: This project requires adult supervision.

Get a white carnation with a long stem. With help from an adult, very carefully cut the carnation's stem lengthwise, from the bottom to about halfway up to the flower. Now fill 2 glasses with water. Use food coloring to color the water in one of the glasses dark red. Color the water in the other glass dark blue. Put the glasses right next to each other. Put half of the carnation stem into each glass. Check the carnation a day later, and 2 days later. Can you tell that the carnation has been drinking the water? You'll notice that the water travels up the tubes into the stem to reach the other parts of the plant.

Water on the Move

◆▶◆▶◆▶◆

What happens to the water that plants take in through their roots?

The "plumbing system" of trees and other plants carries water on a one-way trip from roots to leaves. Evaporation of water on the surface of the leaves is one force that helps move the water. To see this, try a simple experiment. On a sunny morning, find a tree branch that you can reach easily. Cover a cluster of leaves with a plastic bag and tie the bag in place with string. Leave in place until evening.

When you return, notice how much water has collected in the bag. Remove the bag, being careful not to spill any water. Gently dip the water out by teaspoons. How much water did the leaves give off in one day? Divide this amount by the number of leaves in the bag to find out how much one single leaf gives off. Just for fun, estimate how many leaves are on the tree, then multiply by the amount of water one single leaf gave off. How much water did the tree give off in a day?

Beans in the Dark

◆◆◆◆◆◆◆

Cast some light on learning about plant growth.

Soak 6 lima beans overnight in a glass of water. Take 2 plastic foam cups, and put about an inch of small rocks in the bottom of each one. Add an inch of sand to each cup on top of the rocks, and then add about 4 inches of potting soil to each cup.

Plant the 6 bean seeds, 3 in each cup. Water each cup to keep the soil moist but not wet. Put one cup in a sunny windowsill and the other in a dark closet. Check on your beans every day to see how they're growing. Are you surprised by the results?

After several days, the plants growing on your windowsill will be healthy and green. The plants in the closet will be very pale, but they might be taller than the other plants. Plant cells have special light receptors. When they don't get enough light, they signal the plant to grow long and thin to seek out a light source. Since there's limited light, the plants in the closet don't produce the chlorophyll that makes the plants green and also absorbs sunlight to produce food. If you move the pale plants next to the green plants in the window, the pale plants will become green in time.

What You'll Need
- lima beans
- glass
- water
- 2 plastic foam cups
- ruler
- small rocks
- sand
- potting soil

Life on a Brick

◆◆◆◆◆◆◆

You can grow grass on a brick!

What You'll Need
- nonglazed porous brick
- bowl
- water
- pie tin
- grass seed

Many plants can adapt to very difficult growing conditions. Grass seeds, for example, can sprout in less than ideal locations. Soak a nonglazed brick overnight in a bowl of water. The next day, put the brick in a pie tin. Set the pie tin in a sunny spot. Pour water over the brick so that it runs down into the tin until the brick is sitting in about ½ inch of water.

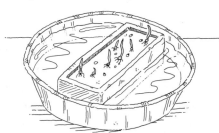

Sprinkle grass seed on the top of the brick. The grass seeds will sprout into plants.

Strong and Puny

◆▶◆▶◆▶◆▶

What kind of water makes plants grow strongest?

What You'll Need
- 6 plants
- 6 pots
- potting soil
- water
- vinegar
- plant fertilizer
- pen and paper

Take 6 plants of the same variety, and plant them in pots with the same mixture of soil. Put them side by side in a warm sunny spot where they'll be exposed to the same temperatures and amount of sunlight. Give each of the plants the same amount of water, but water 2 of them with ordinary tap water, water 2 with vinegar water (1 tablespoonful vinegar to 1 pint water), and water 2 with water that contains added plant fertilizer. Observe the plants

over several weeks, and make notes to describe their growth. Can you see differences between those that received vinegar water, those that received tap water, and those that received fertilizer?

Down and Dirty

◆▶◆▶◆▶◆▶

Soil contains microscopic animals that breathe.

Drop a large handful of garden soil into the bottom of a big empty jar. Pour some limewater into a small container. Note what the limewater looks like. Set the container of limewater, uncovered, inside the large jar so it rests on top of the soil. Tightly screw on the lid of the large jar, and leave it undis-

What You'll Need
- garden soil
- jar with a lid
- small container
- limewater (available at a drugstore)

turbed. In 2 or 3 days, look at the limewater to see if it has changed in any way.

The soil contains many microscopic animals. These animals take in oxygen and release carbon dioxide as a waste product, just as you do when you breathe. The limewater turned a milky color because the carbon dioxide produced by the organisms in the soil combined with the limewater to produce chalk. Your garden soil may contain bacteria, protozoans, and threadlike worms called *nematodes*.

Thirsty Spud

◇◇◇◇◇◇

Living cells are able to absorb and pass on water.

What You'll Need
- potato
- vegetable peeler
- knife
- spoon
- pan
- water
- sugar

Caution: This project requires adult supervision.

Cut the ends from a potato, and discard them. Peel a 1-inch strip of skin from the bottom of the potato. Using a knife and spoon, scoop out a cavity about an inch deep in the top of the potato. Stand the potato up in a pan filled with water so that the peeled bottom is in the water. Put a spoonful of sugar in the cavity in the top of the potato. Let the potato stand in the water for 24 hours, and then check to see if any changes have occurred.

What happened? The cells of the potato drew water up from the pan to the top of the potato. Individual cells took in water molecules from the water in the pan and passed them on to the cells above them in a process called *osmosis*.

See Cells

◇◇◇◇◇◇

Take a closer look at plants than you ever have before.

Set up your microscope on a table (if you do not have your own microscope, you may be able to borrow one from your school). Find a plant with thin leaves, such as elodea (a common freshwater aquarium plant), or use a piece of onion skin. Place a leaf on a glass slide. Add a drop of water, and place a cover slide over the leaf and water. Look at the slide under your microscope. You should see box-shaped structures. These are plant cells. If you look closely, you should be able to see tiny green parts in the cells. These contain chlorophyll, which gives the plant its color and helps the plant produce food.

What You'll Need
- microscope with about 50-power magnification
- a leaf with thin leaves or an onion skin
- glass slides
- water
- eyedropper

Yeast Feast

◆◆◆◆◆◆

A yeast plant can't make its own food.

What You'll Need
- yeast
- bowl
- water
- spoon
- 2 glasses
- measuring cup and spoon
- sugar

Pour 2 packages of yeast into a small bowl. Add 1 cup warm water, and stir to dissolve the yeast. Split this mixture between the glasses.

Mix 1 tablespoon sugar into one of the glasses. Set both glasses in a warm spot, and check on them frequently. The one with the sugar will soon be foaming with bubbles.

What happened? Yeast is a plant, but unlike green plants, it cannot make its own food.

When you supplied food in the form of sugar, the yeast began to consume the sugar and produce carbon dioxide gas and alcohol. The foam is made up of bubbles of gas.

Light at Night

◆◆◆◆◆◆

See how plants respond to increased light.

Soak 8 lima beans in water overnight. Prepare 4 flowerpots for planting. Put an inch of small rocks in the bottom of each pot. Put an inch of sand over the gravel and 4 inches of potting soil over the sand. Plant 2 lima beans in each pot. Water to keep the soil moist but not wet. Label 2 of the pots "NIGHT LIGHT." Put all 4 pots in a sunny window by day. Put the 2 "Night Light" pots under a fluorescent light each evening, and put them back in the window with the other 2 plants each morning. Observe the growth of the plants over several weeks. Do the plants getting light at night grow faster than the others?

What You'll Need
- lima beans
- water
- 4 flowerpots
- ruler
- small rocks
- sand
- potting soil
- marker
- fluorescent light

Bubble, Bubble

◆▶◆▶◆▶◆

Plants give off oxygen as they make food.

Fill a clean jar about ⅔ of the way with tap water. Put a shoot of Canadian pondweed in the water. Put the jar in a sunny window. On a sheet of paper, write down the time that you placed the jar in the window. Look at the jar every 30 minutes, and write down the time and what you see. Before long, you'll be able to observe bubbles of oxygen rising in the water. Put the jar in a dark closet in your house. Look at the jar every 30 minutes, and write down the time and what you see.

What You'll Need
- jar
- water
- Canadian pondweed
- paper and pen
- clock

Did you notice a difference in the jar when it was in the closet? While the plant was receiving sunlight, it was able to carry out photosynthesis. As a part of this process, the plant produced oxygen as a waste product, which made bubbles in the water. Without sunlight, the plant could not carry out photosynthesis.

Who Needs Dirt?

◆▶◆▶◆▶◆

You can grow a sweet potato plant without soil.

What You'll Need
- toothpicks
- sweet potato
- glass
- water

Insert 3 toothpicks around a sweet potato near the large end so they stick out to the sides in different directions. Fill a glass most of the way with water. Put the sweet potato into the glass small-end first, and rest the toothpicks on the rim so they hold up the sweet potato. There should be enough water in the glass so that about ¾ of the sweet potato is covered. Put the jar in a sunny spot for several days. Add water as needed. Soon you will have a beautiful vine growing from the top of the potato.

Usually you put a plant into the soil to make it grow, but you can grow some plants without soil. When the sweet potato plant was growing with its roots in the soil and its leaves in the sun, it produced food through photosynthesis and stored carbohydrates in the potato. This stored food in the sweet potato provided the energy needed to grow a new plant.

Trees: Nature's Giants

Trees, like all other plants, need sunlight and carbon dioxide to make their own food. In the process, trees take carbon dioxide from the air and put back oxygen. As you learn about trees with the activities in this section, remember how important trees are. Only use wood that has fallen from the tree. Use bark that has peeled from the tree itself or from fallen twigs. Gather only what leaves you need and leave the rest.

Pinecone Flowers

Turn ordinary pinecones into pretty flower decorations.

What You'll Need
- pinecones
- knife
- craft glue
- cardboard
- twigs or dry grass
- dried leaves
- large seeds or small alder cones
- spray paint or glitter (optional)

Caution: This project requires adult supervision.

Collect small pinecones outdoors. Brush off dirt or leaves. If the cones are closed, dry them in a warm oven for several hours until they open.

Have an adult cut the pinecones in half vertically. Use a large blob of strong glue to glue the bottom halves of the pinecones to the piece of cardboard. Glue on twigs or dry grass to represent flower stems. Glue dried leaves on the twigs. Allow to dry completely before moving.

Make smaller flowers by pulling the bracts from the cones and gluing them individually to the board in a flower shape. Use a large seed or a tiny alder cone for a center.

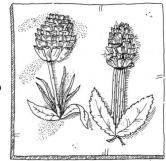

Pinecone flowers look nice plain, but you can dress them up by dipping the cones in glue, then roll in glitter before gluing to the board.

Knock on Wood

◆◆◆◆◆◆

Trees give us more than a shady spot on hot summer days.
Find the products that trees provide.

Do you have a baseball bat? How about a pencil? Does your home have a wooden table or chairs? There are so many things made from trees it's hard to count them all! Try to walk around your house and find as many things as you can that came from trees. Look for wooden items, as well as paper and cardboard. Don't forget to count fruit—such as apples—that grows on trees.

Colors in a Leaf

◆◆◆◆◆◆

Even green leaves have more colors than you may think!

What You'll Need
- coffee filter
- scissors
- leaves
- coin
- rubbing alcohol
- jar
- pencil
- tape
- foil

Leaves have a green pigment called *chlorophyll* that they use to capture sunlight. But did you know that leaves also have pigments of other colors to capture colors of light that chlorophyll misses? You can use chromatography to see the many colors in a leaf.

Cut a strip an inch wide from a coffee filter. Cut one end of the strip to a point. Place a leaf on the paper ¼ inch above the cut. Roll the edge of a coin over the leaf, pressing green leaf juice into the paper. Let the paper dry, and repeat the process with 3 different leaves.

Pour a ½-inch layer of rubbing alcohol into the bottom of a jar. Tape your paper strip to the middle of a pencil and hang it so that the very tip of the strip touches the alcohol. The colored strip of leaf "juices" should not touch the alcohol. You may have to adjust the length of the strip. Lay a piece of foil over the top of the jar to keep the alcohol from evaporating. Watch carefully as the alcohol moves up the filter paper, carrying the pigments along with it. In 10 to 20 minutes the colors should be separated. Do not allow them to run to the top of the paper. How many colors do you see? Could you see them in the leaf itself? The finished paper is called a *chromatograph*. Let it dry and use your chromatograph for a special bookmark.

Twig Collecting

◆▶◆▶◆▶◆

Make a collection of twigs gathered from trees in winter.

What You'll Need
- plant shears
- index cards
- tape
- pencil
- tree-identification book
- magnifying glass

The twigs of each kind of tree have unique shapes and characteristics. You can collect an assortment of tree twigs to compare. If you have a good tree-identification book, you can even identify the trees they came from. The best time for collecting twigs is in February or March, long after trees have lost their leaves but before they have begun to bud.

(Get permission before doing the following!) Carefully cut twigs from a variety of trees (one twig from each tree), and tape them to index cards. Note the color and texture of the twig. Also, write down the name of the tree if you know it.

Study the different characteristics of the twig parts using the magnifying glass. Twig parts include the *terminal bud* that will become new growth; *bud scales* to protect new leaves or flowers; *leaf scars* that show where stems of old leaves were attached; *bud scale scars* that show where last year's buds were and how much the twig grew over the year; *bundle scars* that show where sap flowed to leaves; *lenticels,* the tiny holes through which bark "breathes"; and *pith,* the twig center.

Leaf Scents

◆▶◆▶◆▶◆

Can you identify your trees by scent alone?

If you've ever smelled herbs, you know that leaves can have powerful scents. Some we like very much and use for cooking or perfumes. Others we don't like at all. All leaves have distinctive scents, though most aren't as strong as herbs. Find out for yourself what tree leaves smell like.

What You'll Need
- leaves

Start with trees or shrubs in your own yard. Pick a leaf from a tree and crush it in your hand. Hold it to your nose and sniff. What does it smell like? Some leaves smell musty. Conifers have a strong pine-oil odor. Other leaves may smell fresh or sharp. Try this with as many kinds of trees and shrubs as you can find. Then test yourself. Close your eyes and have someone crush a leaf for you to smell, or make a pile of different leaves and draw from it with your eyes closed. Can you identify trees and shrubs by their scents?

Tree Storybook

◆▷◆▷◆▷◆

Make your own books to help you learn about trees.

To make a tree book, fold 2 sheets of white paper in half. Fold the construction paper in half and insert the white paper. Staple together along the spine. Make one book for each kind of tree you're interested in. Take a photo of the tree (or draw it) and glue the picture to the cover of the book. Learn the tree's name from an adult or at the library.

Hold the first page of the book against the tree's bark. Rub a crayon over the page to make a pattern. Pick a leaf, flatten it, and glue it into your book. If your tree sheds flowers, pick and press one. If your tree loses branches, find a small winter twig. Glue it on the third page. Then use pages 4 and 5 to describe what is living in the tree.

Tree Tales

◆▷◆▷◆▷◆

You walk by trees in your neighborhood every day—learn all about them.

At the library, check out a field guide to trees that grow in your area. It will have pictures, descriptions, and information about each kind of tree. Then take the field guide out into your neighborhood, and see how many of the trees you can find. Learn the name of each tree. Pay attention to what kind of leaves, seeds, and bark each tree has. Which trees have flowers, fruits, or nuts? Which trees are home to animals?

As the seasons change, keep a record of which trees' leaves change color and fall off and which trees are the first to leaf out in the spring. You could even make your own field guide to trees in your neighborhood. Your guide could include the name of each tree, a drawing, a leaf from the tree (or tracing of a leaf), information about the tree, and details of where in the neighborhood each kind of tree can be found.

How to Plant a Tree

◆▶◆▶◆▶◆▶

Planting trees is good for the earth—but they will only live if you plant them correctly.

Caution: This project requires adult supervision.

A tree seedling needs 4 things to live: clean air, the right amount of water, good soil, and the right amount of sunlight. When you buy the tree be sure to ask where to plant it. Some seedlings like shade, whereas others need more sun.

With help from an adult, dig a hole deep enough to cover the roots of the tree seedling. Use your shovel to loosen the soil in the bottom of the hole. Pile a mound of loose soil in the middle of the hole. Put the seedling into the hole up to the "root collar," spreading the roots out over the mound of dirt. Fill in with loose dirt and stomp down well to prevent large air pockets. Add more dirt until the ground is level. Be certain that all the roots are in the hole. Don't let any of them turn up in a J shape, whether they stick out of the dirt or not. This is called *J-rooting* and can cause the seedling to die. Water the seedling immediately. Water will help settle the soil down and fill in any remaining air pockets.

After the tree is in the ground, it still may be unstable—especially if it has a thin trunk. If you think it needs support, place 2 or 3 wooden stakes in the ground just outside of where the roots are. Use elastic ties or nylon hose to hold the tree in place. Don't tie them too tight or let them dig into the trunk. The tree should be able to move slightly in the wind. Remove the stakes as soon as the tree can support itself (usually within a year).

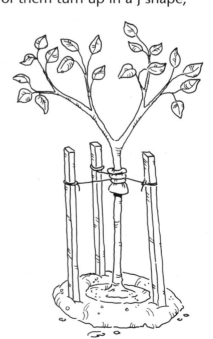

Adopt a Tree

◆▷▷▷▷◁◀

Just like people, each tree is different in its own way.

Pick a tree that you would like to study for one year. It should be a tree that you'll be able to visit at least once a month. Get a notebook that you can use to make a diary of the tree's life for the year.

To begin, identify what kind of tree it is. Look closely at the tree's bark, leaves, any fruits or nuts, etc. Use a camera to take a picture of the tree, or draw its picture.

For the next year, visit the tree at least once a month. Each time you visit, make notes in the diary about what is happening in the life of the tree. Can you see signs of growth? Does the tree lose its leaves in winter? Does it produce flowers, berries, seed pods, or nuts? Does the tree ever show signs of stress, such as wilting leaves from lack of rain or damage from frost? Do animals make homes in your tree? Add a new picture of the tree each time you visit, too. At the end of the year, you'll have a complete report of your tree's life and growth.

Count the Rings

◆▷▷▷▷◁◀

Here's an easy way to figure out a tree's age.

Find a tree that has been cut down. Use sandpaper to sand the surface of the stump until it is very smooth and you can see the rings. Start at the center of the stump, and count the rings. Each set of light and dark lines counts as one ring. Each ring stands for one year in the tree's life. How old was the tree? Notice that some of the rings are wider than others. Wide rings show years when the tree grew a lot. Narrow rings show years when the tree grew less. Can you think of reasons why the tree might have grown more in some years than in others?

How Tall Is It?

◆◆◆◆◆◆◆

How can you measure the height of a tree when it's really tall? Here's a neat trick to help you do it.

What You'll Need
- partner
- yardstick or tape measure

You'll need a partner to do this activity. Use a yardstick to measure a straight line 60 feet away from the tree you want to measure. Then have your partner stand there and hold the yardstick straight up with the bottom touching the ground. (A yardstick will work for trees that are up to 30 feet tall. For very tall trees, you can do this activity with a metal tape measure instead of a yardstick.)

Now walk 6 feet past your partner. (You'll be 66 feet away from the tree.) Lie down with your head very close to the ground at the 66-foot mark. Now look up at the tree and notice where the top of the tree comes to on the yardstick. Have your partner mark that spot. (You'll have to guide your partner to make the mark in the right place by saying, "A little lower...a little higher..." until he or she finds the right place.) The height of the tree is about 10 times the height marked on the yardstick. For example, if the mark on the yardstick is at 24 inches, the tree is about 240 inches (20 feet) tall. Calculate how tall your tree is by multiplying your yardstick measurement by 10.

Tree Growth

A tree will grow differently in a windy climate than in a calm climate. If a strong wind usually blows from one direction, for example, the tree's trunk and branches will grow the way the wind pushes them. If a tree grows in a thick forest, the trunk will grow more narrowly, and the branches will grow more heavily at the top of the tree, where the leaves can find light.

True Poetree

Write a poem in praise of our wooded friends.

What You'll Need
- paper
- pencil
- markers (optional)

Trees have always been a favorite subject of poets. Here is part of a poem that Robert Frost wrote about birch trees:

When I see birches bend to left and right
Across the lines of straighter darker trees,
I like to think some boy's been swinging them.
But swinging doesn't bend them down to stay

As ice-storms do. Often you must have seen them
Loaded with ice a sunny winter morning
After a rain. . . .
— from "Birches"

Try writing your own poem about a tree. It could be a tree you planted, a tree you like to swing in, or even a tree in your imagination. Your poem can rhyme, or not—it's up to you! If you like, draw a picture of the tree to go with your poem.

Meet a Tree

Here's a fun game that will test how well you know the trees in your neighborhood.

What You'll Need
- blindfold

In this game you will use all your senses but sight to explore a tree, then see if you can find that tree again once your sight is restored. Play the game in a wooded area or in a park where there are lots of trees.

Divide the players up into 2-person teams. One person on each team puts on a blindfold. The partner turns the blindfolded person around 2 or 3 times, then leads the person in a zigzag path to a tree. The partner must be very careful to lead the blindfolded person around dangers. The blindfolded person then has as much time as he or she wants to explore the tree, to feel the texture of the bark, find bumps or hollows, and find patches of moss or other features of the tree. When the blindfolded person is done, the partner leads him or her in a zigzag path away from the tree, turning the blindfolded person around 2 or 3 times in the middle. The blindfolded person takes the blindfold off and tries to find the same tree. Then the partners switch places. What did you discover about your tree that you never noticed before?

State Trees

Every state has an official tree. Find your state tree, and learn all about it.

What You'll Need
- encyclopedia or almanac
- field guide to trees
- paper and pen (optional)

Look up your state in the list to find out what your state tree is. Then, look up the tree in an encyclopedia or field guide to read about it. Why do you think the tree was chosen? If you want, you can even write a story about your state tree. See if you can find your state tree in nature.

Alabama	Southern pine	**Montana**	Ponderosa pine
Alaska	Sitka spruce	**Nebraska**	Cottonwood
Arizona	Paloverde	**Nevada**	Single-leaf piñon
Arkansas	Pine		and bristlecone
California	California redwood		pine
Colorado	Colorado blue spruce	**New Hampshire**	White birch
Connecticut	White oak	**New Jersey**	Red oak
Delaware	American holly	**New Mexico**	Piñon
District of	Scarlet oak	**New York**	Sugar maple
Columbia		**North Carolina**	Pine
Florida	Sabal palmetto palm	**North Dakota**	American elm
Georgia	Live oak	**Ohio**	Buckeye
Hawaii	Kukui (Candlenut)	**Oklahoma**	Redbud
Idaho	White pine	**Oregon**	Douglas fir
Illinois	White oak	**Pennsylvania**	Hemlock
Indiana	Tulip poplar	**Rhode Island**	Red maple
Iowa	Oak	**South Carolina**	Palmetto
Kansas	Cottonwood	**South Dakota**	Black hills spruce
Kentucky	Tulip poplar	**Tennessee**	Tulip poplar
Louisiana	Cypress	**Texas**	Pecan
Maine	Eastern white pine	**Utah**	Blue spruce
Maryland	White oak	**Vermont**	Sugar maple
Massachusetts	American elm	**Virginia**	Dogwood
Michigan	White pine	**Washington**	Western hemlock
Minnesota	Red pine	**West Virginia**	Sugar maple
Mississippi	Magnolia	**Wisconsin**	Sugar maple
Missouri	Dogwood	**Wyoming**	Cottonwood

Bark Rubbings

◆◆◆◆◆◆◆

*Tree bark and leaves have many interesting patterns
that can be "collected" by making rubbings.*

What You'll Need

- large crayon or colored chalk
- thin paper
- trees
- hair spray
- craft glue
- notebook
- pen

Do this project on a dry day, because wet tree bark will make your paper tear. Peel the paper from a large crayon, or use a thick piece of sidewalk chalk. Press a sheet of thin paper up against the bark of a tree. Gently rub the side of the crayon or chalk on the paper until the pattern of the bark shows. Compare rubbings from different trees. Which bark patterns make the nicest rubbings?

Can you tell which rubbing came from which kind of tree? For leaf rubbings, lay the leaves flat on a hard, smooth surface. Cover the leaves with paper and rub the side of the crayon or chalk on the paper.

Ask an adult to spray the pictures with hair spray to keep the chalk from smearing. Glue your rubbings in a scrapbook to make a "Bark Book." Include some interesting facts about the trees.

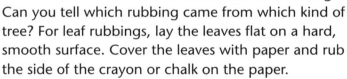

What Is Bark?

Bark is really the skin of the tree. It surrounds the trunk and branches, and it protects the tree. Trees grow wider each year, with the newest layer of wood growing right underneath the bark. Each tree has its own unique pattern of bark, and some trees have quite unusual bark. The blistered mahogany, for example, has bark that actually blisters.

Wood Collection

◆◆◆◆◆◆

Learn about the beauties of wood with this special collection.

Caution: This project requires adult supervision.

Begin by collecting wood in a nearby forest or woodlands. Use only fallen branches, choosing solid branches about 2 to 3 inches in diameter. Have an adult saw off a 6-inch length of branch. Check the leaves remaining on the branch to find out what kind of tree the branch came from. Allow the wood to dry for about 2 weeks. You can ask at the lumber store for small scraps of wood from trees that may not grow in your area. Try to get scraps about 2 inches square and 6 inches long.

What You'll Need
- branches or scraps of wood from lumber store
- saw
- sturdy vise
- sandpaper
- brush
- varnish

Put your branch or wood scrap upright in a sturdy vise and have an adult help you make a 2-inch deep lengthwise cut down the middle. Make a second cut crosswise until your saw meets the base of the first cut. Remove the piece of wood. Sand the cut surface until smooth, then ask an adult to help you varnish it. This will beautifully highlight both the lengthwise grain and the cross-grain.

Leafy Bleach Prints

◆◆◆◆◆◆

Use "reverse" bleach prints to make beautiful greeting cards.

What You'll Need
- newspaper
- smock or apron
- colored paper
- rubber gloves
- bleach
- small glass dish
- old paintbrush or cotton swab
- assortment of leaves
- markers (optional)

Caution: Bleach can irritate skin and eyes. Wear rubber gloves when doing this project, and have an adult help you.

Cover your work surface with newspaper. Put a smock or apron on to protect your clothes from the bleach. Lay a sheet of colored paper out on the newspaper. Have an adult help you pour a little bleach into a small glass dish. Use an old paintbrush or cotton swab to paint the back of a leaf with bleach, then press the leaf bleach-side down on the paper. Lift off the leaf. In a moment or two you will see a bleached-out print of the leaf. After you have made a nice arrangement of prints on the paper, you can hang it up for a picture, or fold it in half and make a greeting card.

Preserving Leaves

◆▶◆▶◆▶◆

Make beautiful bronzed leafy branches to decorate your home.

Caution: This project requires adult supervision.

With help from an adult, mix a solution of 1 part glycerine and 2 parts hot water. The amount you mix up depends on

how many branches you want to pre-serve, but you should make enough to cover the bottom of your jar or bucket several inches deep.

Ask an adult for permission to cut branches about 18 inches long, or use prunings from shrubs in your yard. Trees or shrubs with firm, waxy leaves work the best. Carefully crush the cut ends of the branches with a hammer, peel away

the bark, and stand them up in the glycerine mixture. Let them sit about 3 weeks. The branches will absorb the glycerine slowly through the miniature pipelines in their stems. The leaves will turn a bronze color and feel slightly greasy when preservation is complete. Wipe off the ends of the branches, and arrange in a pretty vase.

What You'll Need
- glycerine (available at drug, farm, and garden stores)
- water
- jar or bucket
- branch cut from a leafy shrub (from spring or fall prunings)
- hammer

Leaf Skeletons

◆▶◆▶◆▶◆

Leaf skeletons are fun to make for collections or for decoration. Here's one method you can try.

What You'll Need
- tree leaves
- newspaper
- old shoe brush
- brown paper
- craft glue

Collect fresh tree leaves. Place an entire newspaper on a table and put the leaf on top of it. Pound with an old shoe brush. Don't pound so hard that you tear the leaf, but just enough to wear away the soft green material between the leaf veins. Allow the skeleton to dry.

Mount the skeletons in a scrapbook for a collection, or use them to decorate. Cover a nature book or tree manual with brown paper and glue leaf skeletons to it.

Leaf Batik

◆◀◆◀◆◀◆▶

The shapes of leaves inspire batik designs in this project.
Make some wall hangings for your room!

Caution: This project requires adult supervision.

Gather several leaves with interesting shapes. Use a green crayon to trace the shape of the leaves onto a piece of fabric. With help from an adult, put some peeled, broken green crayons in a can. Then put the can in a pan of boiling water to melt the crayons. Never melt wax or crayons directly on a stove burner. They can catch fire.

Using an old paintbrush, spread melted crayon into the leaf shape on your fabric; coat it completely. Then give it time to dry.

Mix a light-colored, cold-water dye with water according to the instructions on the package. Crumple your fabric and dip it in the dye. Allow to dry.

Melt paraffin wax in a can in boiling water. Paint branch shapes or any other shapes you like with the paraffin. Crumple your fabric and dip it into a darker dye. Allow to dry.

What You'll Need
- leaves
- green crayons
- fabric
- cans
- pan
- stove
- water
- old paintbrushes
- cold-water dye (in 2 colors that can mix)
- paraffin wax
- newspaper
- iron

Roll your fabric hard in your hands to break up the wax and peel off as much as you can. Place the fabric between several sheets of newspaper and have an adult help you iron it. The iron will melt the wax, which will be absorbed by the newspaper. Replace the newspaper often, until most of the wax is gone.

Treasure Tree

◆◆◆◆◆◆◆

Here's one way to remember your next nature trip. Make a special "tree" to display the treasures you find along the way.

When you are on a walk in the woods you may come across lots of interesting treasures you want to take home: pinecones, pretty leaves, discarded eggshells from wild bird nests, old snail shells. Rather than take everything home that attracts your eye, pick out a few of the most interesting items and make a treasure tree to display them.

Find a dead tree branch with many side limbs. Clean it off and let it dry. Mix enough plaster of paris to nearly fill a coffee can, peanut can, or can of similar size. Stick the base of the branch into the plaster. Allow it to dry. Using markers, draw a nature setting or a decorative design on construction paper; then glue it to the can.

Use yarn to hang your treasures from the branches. You can change the decorations each time you take a walk. Remember to take only a few of the most interesting things and leave the rest for others to enjoy.

What You'll Need
- nature objects
- interesting branch with many side branches
- coffee or peanut can
- plaster of paris
- construction paper
- markers
- craft glue
- yarn
- scissors

Plant Buddies

◆◆◆◆◆◆◆

Some plants rely on others to help them grow.

What You'll Need
- mossy tree

When you're in a forest, look for plants that grow on trees. Scientists call these plants *epiphytes.* Their relationship is *symbiotic,* a scientific word that means "living together." Moss is an epiphyte. Look closely at moss growing on a tree. Moss, a simple plant, does not have true roots, but tiny rootlike structures help the plant cling to the side of the tree. Bits of dead bark collect and rot, providing nutrients for the moss. Look for other epiphytes. In some areas, licorice fern grows on oak tree limbs. Mistletoe, another epiphyte, is a parasite. Its roots bore into oaks and spruces and draw out moisture and sap.

Fill 'er Up

❖❖❖❖❖❖❖

Who doesn't love the fresh scent of pine? Pine needles make a good—and good-smelling—filling for a pin cushion.

Start with a small cloth bag that is sewn shut on 3 sides. Stuff the bag very full with crushed pine needles. With adult help, use a needle and thread to sew the bag closed. This makes a lovely gift for people who sew. Or you can use it yourself to keep track of any pins or needles you need for other projects.

What You'll Need
- small cloth bag
- pine needles
- needle
- thread

Fire Starters

❖❖❖❖❖❖❖

Surprise someone with a fireplace with a basket of useful fire starters.

What You'll Need
- small pinecones
- paraffin wax
- metal juice can
- pan
- water
- stove
- newspaper
- waxed paper
- scissors
- tongs
- salt
- basket or bucket
- ribbon

Caution: This project requires adult supervision.

Gather small pinecones outdoors. Clean off any dirt or leaves. If the cones are closed, put them in a warm oven for several hours until they dry out and open up.

Break a block of paraffin wax into pieces and put the pieces in a large metal juice can. Put the can in a pan of water, and have an adult help you heat it slowly until the wax is melted. Never put a container of wax directly on a stove burner. It can catch fire.

Spread newspapers on your work surface. Cut some squares of waxed paper and lay them on the newspaper. Set the pan with the wax on the newspaper (the hot water will help to keep it melted). Pick up a pinecone in the tongs and dip it in the wax. Set the cone upright on a square of waxed paper. Sprinkle the cone with salt. Continue with the rest of your cones. Allow the cones to cool completely, then pile them into a basket or bucket. Tie a ribbon into a big bow on the handle. One or two of these cones is enough to start a fire in the fireplace. The salt makes them burn with a bright yellow flame.

Hammered Leaf Prints

◆▸▸▸▸▸◆

Make a truly one-of-a-kind T-shirt, bandanna, or wall hanging!

What You'll Need

- small board (½ to 1 inch thick)
- newspaper
- 100% cotton garment or fabric
- leaves
- waxed paper
- masking tape
- hammer
- measuring cup and spoon
- alum
- water
- salt

Caution: This project requires adult supervision.

Cover a small board with 2 or 3 layers of newspaper. Lay your fabric on the board. If you are printing a T-shirt, open up the bottom and slip the board and newspaper inside. Arrange a variety of leaves on the fabric. Cover with a sheet of waxed paper, and tape the corners of the waxed paper to the fabric. With help from an adult, pound with the hammer until you have pounded every part of the leaf. When you are done, lift off the waxed paper. You'll see a leaf print.

To set the print: Soak for 2 minutes in a mixture of 3 tablespoons alum in a gallon of warm water. Wring, then soak in a mixture of ¼ cup salt in a gallon of warm water. Remove the fabric, rub off any clinging bits of leaf, wring, and let it dry. Wash by hand in cold water.

Nuts About Ink

◆▸▸▸▸▸◆

You can make your own special ink using walnut shells.

Caution: This project requires adult supervision.

Remove the walnuts from their shells. Wrap the shells in a towel and crush them with a hammer. Put the crushed shells in a saucepan with some water. With help from an adult, heat until the water boils, then simmer the walnut shells for 45 minutes.

Let cool for 15 minutes, then pour the mixture through a strainer into a jar. Add to the jar ½ teaspoon vinegar and ½ teaspoon salt. Stir until the salt dissolves. Use your "walnut" ink immediately, or put the lid on the jar to store it.

What You'll Need

- 8 walnuts
- nutcracker
- towel
- hammer
- saucepan
- water
- stove
- strainer
- jar with lid
- measuring spoon
- vinegar
- salt

An Early Spring

◆▶◆▶◆▶◆

"Forcing" is the technique used to make winter twigs bloom indoors.

Check shrubs in your yard for flower buds that are just beginning to swell. Forsythia, flowering plum, flowering cherry, or pussy willows work well for this. Be sure to get permission before cutting! With adult help, cut branches about 2 feet long or longer if you can. Put the branches in a bucket of water right away and bring them indoors. Find a large vase with a wide mouth and fill it with water. For longest-lasting branches, put the cut end of the branch in the vase, and, holding it under the water, cut an inch off the end. Leave your vase in a sunny window. In a week or so the buds will burst out into blossoms.

What You'll Need
- winter twigs in bud, cut from flowering shrubs or trees
- clippers
- bucket
- water
- vase

Sweet Sap

◁▶◁▶◁▶◁

Maple syrup is a delicious treat straight from nature.

What You'll Need
- maple tree
- drill with ½-inch bit
- small tube or pipe
- hammer and nail
- bucket
- aluminum foil
- large pot
- stove
- butter
- candy thermometer
- strainer

Caution: This project requires adult supervision.

On an early spring day, go out searching for maple trees. If the tree you find is on private property, ask for permission to tap one. Have an adult drill a hole 2 inches deep into the south-facing side of the tree. Drill the hole so that it slants upward into the tree slightly.

Push a piece of tubing or pipe into the hole. Hammer a nail into the tree just above the hole. Hang a bucket on the nail to catch the sap that will drip from the tubing. Cover the bucket with aluminum foil. It may take a few hours or longer to gather a gallon of sap.

When you have about a gallon of sap, remove the tubing and nail from the tree. Take the sap home and put it in a very large pot. Bring it to a boil. Much of the sap must be evaporated to make the syrup. Add a pat of butter to keep the sap from boiling over. Use a candy thermometer to check the sap's temperature. When it reaches 219°F, it's done. Strain the syrup, let it cool, and serve!

Grow a Tropical Tree

◄►◄►◄►◄►

Enjoy a mango, papaya, or pomegranate.
Then grow the tree it comes from!

What You'll Need

- tropical fruit pits (from mango) or seeds (from papaya or pomegranate)
- knife
- vegetable brush
- potting soil
- flowerpots
- water
- flat dish
- paper towels
- plastic wrap

Caution: This project requires adult supervision.

Tropical fruit plants are fun to grow, but it takes lots of patience. Getting them to sprout is the hardest part.

Mango: Begin with a very ripe mango. Have an adult help you cut the pit from the fruit and clean it with a vegetable brush under running water. Plant the flat pit in potting soil with one edge up. Cover it completely. Keep it watered, and wait a long time. Mangoes may take 3 months to sprout. About 1 out of 4 will not sprout at all. Keep the plants in a humid room and away from cold windows. Once every few months, allow the soil to go completely dry.

Papaya: Have an adult help you cut the fruit open and remove the small seeds from their fleshy coating (called an *aril*). Line the bottom of a flat dish with wet paper towels and lay the seeds on it. Cover with plastic wrap and set in a warm place. When the seeds just begin to sprout, rinse them in fresh water and plant in moist potting soil. Keep the seedlings out of direct sunlight until they are about 6 inches tall.

Pomegranate: Prepare and sprout the seeds as you did for papayas. Pomegranates are desert plants, so keep them in a dry room.

Leaf Stencils

◆◆◆◆◆◆

Leaves make lovely artwork—and unique greeting cards and stationery.

Make easy and safe spray paint by adding water to tempera paint to thin it. Then put the different colors of paint in different spray bottles.

Collect a variety of leaves with interesting shapes. Cover your work surface with newspaper. (The newspaper should be bigger than the paper you will be using so it will catch the "over spray" when you paint.) Put a few of the leaves you collected on a piece of paper on top of the newspaper.

What You'll Need
- tempera paints
- water
- spray bottles
- leaves
- newspaper
- white paper
- crayons (optional)

Spray paint the leaves. (Be sure to spray around the leaves, too.) Let the paint dry, then take away the leaves. The image is called a *stencil.* You can also rub crayons along the edges of the leaves instead of using spray paint to create your stencil.

Make your leaf stencils into greeting cards, or make stationery by painting with light-colored paints. Overlap several leaves for an intricate design.

Trees, Trees, Trees

◆◆◆◆◆◆

Trees have a variety of uses in our environment. Read books—created from trees and written about them—to find out all sorts of information.

What You'll Need
- books about trees
- pen
- paper

Trees can be used for fun, as well as shelter. Where do you think tree houses come from? Did you know the oldest living tree—a 4,700-year-old pine tree in California—is named "Methuselah"? Or that in Arizona there's a forest of "petrified" trees that are actually 200-million-year-old fossils? Find a book about trees that interests you. You might learn about acorns, leaves, or paper-making. Afterward, write a story about what you discovered.

Flower Fun

◆◆◆◆◆◆◆

A flower garden can be anything from a half-acre plot to a flowerpot. If you are fortunate, you might have a small plot of ground to call your own where you can plant anything you like. In this section, you'll learn how to have spring flowers in the winter, how to attract butterflies to your yard, and how to eat your roses! This section is full of activities to guide you in growing both indoor and outdoor flowers. And the flowers you grow can be used for some fun crafts and activities.

 ## Sunflower Fort

◆◆◆◆◆◆◆

Grow your own leafy playhouse!

Late in spring, when the weather is warm, mark a 7-foot square in the garden (get permission first). Dig the ground around the edges a foot deep. The soil should be loose and crumbly. Push a stake in the ground at each corner. Mark the "doorway" with stakes. To help you plant seeds in straight lines, tie string to a doorway stake and run the string around the stakes in a square around your fort. Plant seeds an inch deep and 6 inches apart. (Poke a hole in the dirt with your finger, put a seed in, and cover it up.) Plant seeds around the edges of your fort—but not the doorway. Water the seeds.

What You'll Need
- 7×7-foot garden patch
- shovel
- short stakes
- string
- tall-growing sunflower seeds (such as giant greystripe or Russian mammoth)
- cheesecloth (optional)

Cover the seeds with a layer of cheesecloth to protect them from squirrels. Leave the cloth loose so the plants can grow; weigh down the edges with dirt. When the plants are several inches tall, remove the cheesecloth. Thin out the plants; sunflowers get huge and need the room. Keep the plants watered—sunflowers need plenty of moisture.

Grass Flowers

◆◆◆◆◆◆◆

Do grasses have flowers? Use your observation skills to learn.

What is a flower? The reproductive part of a flowering plant. A flower may have anthers that make pollen, an ovary that makes seeds, or both. Plants pollinated by insects have bright petals, but plants pollinated by wind don't need to "advertise."

What You'll Need
● magnifying glass

Visit a grassy meadow in early spring, just when the grasses form their seed heads. Observe the heads with your magnifying glass. Green or papery structures called *bracts* hold the seed. Return to the meadow until you see small dangling structures sticking out between the bracts. Some are *anthers,* which make pollen. They hang outside of the bracts so that when they ripen and split open, pollen scatters to the wind.

My Family Flag

◆◆◆◆◆◆◆

Your family colors—or your country's—in bloom.

What You'll Need
● paper
● pencils or pens
● garden spot
● gardening tools
● colorful bedding plants (petunias work well)

Does your family have its own crest? If not, maybe it's time you made one! Design a family symbol or flag on paper. Make it simple but unique to your "clan." Then plant colorful bedding plants with that design in a big, easy-to-see flower bed. If you can't think of a family flag, plant a design like the good old Stars and Stripes of the American flag and watch your neighbors grin.

Night and Day Scent Tower

◆◆◆◆◆◆◆

Grow vines with scented flowers that you can enjoy day and night!

What You'll Need

- moonflower seeds
- sandpaper
- cup
- water
- sweet-pea seeds
- large pot (12 inches or wider) with saucer
- potting soil
- 3 bamboo poles about 6 feet long
- string
- scissors

Wait until spring warms up before planting these flowers. Notice that moonflower seeds are as hard as rocks. Take 6 seeds and place them between 2 sheets of sandpaper. Rub the sheets together for about a minute. Then put the seeds in warm water to soak overnight. The sandpaper roughs up the seed coat, which can then soak up water.

Now soak 6 sweet-pea seeds in warm water overnight (they don't need sanding). While the seeds soak, fill the pot with soil to within about an inch of the rim. Water the soil well. Take 3 bamboo poles and tie them together at one end. Spread the other ends and stick them in the pot to form a tripod for your plants to climb. You can also use a small trellis. After your seeds have soaked, plant them an inch or so apart around the edge of the pot. Set the pot in a warm, sunny place. Keep the soil moist.

When the vines are tall, they will flower. Sweet peas, which bloom in the day, have a sweet, spicy scent. Moonflowers bloom at night. Their rich perfume attracts big luna moths.

Nature's Perfume

◆◆◆◆◆◆◆

Give your nose a treat by planting lovely scented geraniums

Some plants have leaves that smell good. An example is the scented geranium. Its scent can range from peppermint to lemon to nutmeg—even coconut! You can grow them in pots indoors or outdoors in summer. Buy some small potted geraniums at a plant nursery. Be sure to tell the nursery worker that you want "scented" geraniums, because there are many varieties of geraniums that are not scented. Let your friends sniff them and guess the scents.

What You'll Need

- potted scented-leaf geranium plants

Hummingbird Honey

◆◆◆◆◆◆

Attract these little wonders to your garden.

What You'll Need
- plants or seeds
- water

Did you know that hummingbirds have no sense of smell? It's true. They depend on sight, not scent, to find the flowers from which they love to drink. Plant a garden alive with the plants they crave to make your yard a hummingbird haven.

Which plants you use depends on where you live. In the Southwest, you might plant red sages or honeysuckle; in the Pacific Northwest, currants or Indian paintbrushes; in the Southeast, trumpet creepers or mimosas; and in the Midwest and Northeast, bee balms and red buckeyes.

Ask your local nursery manager for other plant suggestions. And remember, red is a hummingbird favorite. Be sure your garden has shade as well as sunshine, and always water with a fine mist. Hummingbirds love to bathe in misty water clouds.

Sunny Flower Garden

◆◆◆◆◆◆

Plants from the nursery make a colorful splash in your yard.

Choose a garden spot that gets 6 or more hours of sun a day. Pull weeds, and dig up soil until it crumbles. Spread a 1-inch layer of bagged compost over the soil, and mix it in. Then buy plants at a garden center. Buy small, healthy annuals that aren't flowering.

Set your plants on the bed, and arrange them. Give the young plants plenty of room. With your trowel, dig a hole for each plant. Turn the pot over, and tap the plant into your hand. Loosen the root ball with your fingers, and set the roots into the soil. Water your plants with a sprinkler every few days. Pick your flowers often to keep the plants blooming.

What You'll Need
- 4×3-foot garden patch (get permission)
- shovel
- bagged compost
- plants
- trowel
- hose
- small sprinkler

Flower Scents

◆▶◆▶◆▶◆

All flowers have a scent, though it may be hard to notice.

Scent is one way to attract insects, which have keen senses of smell. Strongly scented flowers such as lavender, roses, and lilies need powerful smells to attract insects. Flowers pollinated by hummingbirds don't have scents—birds don't have a good sense of smell. But do these flowers have any odor?

Go through the yard and collect several types of open flowers. (Get permission first.) Do they have scents? Some will have a strong, obvious odor, but others will have little or no odor. Take the flowers that don't have much smell and crush them in your hand. All flowers have some sort of scent. Next, close your eyes and have a friend hold crushed flowers under your nose. Can you identify flowers by smell alone?

Living Bouquets

◆▶◆▶◆▶◆▶

If you have no room for flower beds, use a pot or window box!

Planting living bouquets outdoors in big pots is especially fun if you pick out your own plants! Go to a garden center, choose some annuals (plants that die at the end of the growing season), then see what kinds of plants look nice together. Go for leaf combinations, too, such as dark green, silvery, and fuzzy leaves.

When you get home, pour some soil into large pots, set the plants gently in them, and fill in soil around them. Water until the liquid runs out the pots and into the saucers. Set the pots in a sunny place. Water daily (twice a day in hot weather), and pick off dry or dying leaves. Feed the plants with a good plant fertilizer, following instructions on the label.

Herb/Flower Nosegays

◆▸◆▸◆▸◆

Can you crack the code? Discover how you and your friends can send secret messages—with flowers!

Nosegays were small, scented bouquets that ladies of old carried when they went out walking, because the streets in the Middle Ages were smelly! Nosegays could also be used to pass secret messages, for people have given many flowers symbolic meanings.

Select a large flower to form the center of your nosegay, such as a daisy or a partially opened rose. Wrap the stem in florist's tape. Next, surround the center flower with a ring of flowers or herbs and wrap tightly with florist's tape. Keep adding layers until the nosegay is as big as you want it to be. Use ferns or large green leaves for the outer layer.

If you'd like to send a friend a floral message in a nosegay, here are what some flowers and herbs symbolize.

Alyssum	noble character	**Holly**	good health
Apple blossom	beauty and goodness	**Juniper**	protection
		Lemon balm	sympathy
Bracken fern	enchantment	**Marjoram**	innocence, blushes
Buttercup	radiance	**Mint**	virtue, character, riches
Chamomile	courage		
Carnation, pink	encouragement	**Pansy**	kind thoughts
Carnation, red	I must see you	**Rose, pink**	purity
Carnation, white	devotion	**Rose, white**	love
Cherry blossom	increase of friendship	**Rosemary**	remembrance
		Strawberry leaves	perfection
Daisy	innocence	**Thyme**	virtue, honesty
Fennel	strength	**Zinnia**	thoughts of absent friends
Forget-me-not	remembrance		
Fuchsia	warning		

Flower-By-Numbers

◆◆◆◆◆◆◆

Plants can be classified by the types of flowers they produce.

Seed-making plants can be classified into dicots or monocots by counting the flower parts. Flowers that have their petals and stamens in groups of 4 or 5 are dicots. Flowers that have petals and stamens in groups of 3, 6, or 9 are monocots.

Label one sheet of paper "DICOTS" and another sheet "MONOCOTS." Look through magazines for pictures of flowers. If the picture is clear enough, count the petals and the stamens sticking up from the center of the flowers. Cut each flower out, and glue it to the appropriate sheet of paper based on the number of petals and stamens it has. Identify as many of the flowers as you can by name.

What You'll Need
- pen and paper
- old magazines
- scissors
- glue

Fruit-Peel Flowers

◆◆◆◆◆◆◆

Try making these unusual Victorian flower decorations.

What You'll Need
- peels from citrus fruits
- knife
- spoon
- scissors
- cookie sheet
- oven
- candy box
- black paper or cloth
- craft glue
- small seeds

Caution: This project requires adult supervision.

Back in Victorian days, artificial flowers were often made from paper or feathers but sometimes from the peels of oranges, lemons, and grapefruit. To make these flowers, first peel some oranges or other citrus fruits. Use the edge of a spoon to carefully scrape away the white part of the peel until you see fine lines close to the outer, colored part. Rinse and dry the peels; use scissors to cut into the shapes of flower petals and leaves. With help from an adult, spread them out on a cookie sheet and dry in a warm oven (no hotter than 150°F). Don't let them overdry or they will be brittle. When the shapes are dry they will curl into natural petal shapes.

Next, line an empty candy box with black paper or cloth. Use strong glue to glue the petals into flower shapes on the black background. You can use small seeds from oranges or lemons for flower centers.

Rose Beads

❖❖❖❖❖❖❖

These lovely beads, which were popular in Victorian times for making necklaces and rosaries, will keep their scent for decades.

Caution: This project requires adult supervision.

If someone in your family has some old rose beads, you know how long they stay sweet-smelling! These beads are easier than ever to make thanks to the modern food processor.

Pick the roses early in the morning before the sun drives off some of the scent. Choose roses with similar scents, or blend scents that go well together. Most colors will blend well, as the beads will all darken to a mahogany color.

Ask an adult to put one handful of petals in the food processor at a time and process them until you have a thick paste. You may add a few drops of water if needed or even a bit of rose oil if you have it. If necessary, you can spoon the paste into a jar and keep it refrigerated while you wait for more roses to bloom.

When you have enough paste, roll it into pea-size beads. Run a pin through each bead, and stick the pin into a piece of cardboard. Let the beads dry thoroughly. String on light fishing line or dental floss.

What You'll Need
- rose petals
- food processor or blender
- spoon
- jar with lid
- straight pins
- corrugated cardboard
- light fishing line or dental floss
- needle
- water or rose oil (optional)

Nature's Forecasters

Did you know that the petals of the scarlet pimpernel have been used to predict rain? In England, gardeners watch this flower closely. If the amount of water in the air climbs up to 80 percent, the petals of the scarlet pimpernel close up, probably to protect itself from the water. The gardeners then expect rain to fall.

Plant a Rainbow

◂▸▸▸▸▸▸◂

Here's how to make an earth-bound rainbow
that's as colorful as a rainbow in the sky.

What You'll Need
- garden plot
- seeds of annual plants and flowers (see below)

For your rainbow garden, use seeds of plants in all colors of the rainbow. You can plant different colors of the same plant or a different plant for each color. You could even plant them in the shape of a rainbow! These flowers are summer-blooming annuals that will bloom well in all climate zones:

Color	Plant
Red and pink	Dianthus, petunia, verbena, zinnia
Yellow and orange	Calendula, marigold, zinnia
Green	Any nonflowering, leafy green plant, such as mint
Blue and purple	Dianthus, petunia, verbena, zinnia

Late Bloomers

◂▸▸▸▸▸▸◂

Find flowers, berries, and leaves for a beautiful winter bouquet.

What You'll Need
- field guide to plants

Most people think flowers only grow in the spring and summer, but there are several hardy winter-blooming plants. For example, a flower called the Christmas rose blooms in December and stays colorful all the way to early spring. And as long as they get some sunlight, pansies and violas will bloom in cold climates. See if you can find some winter blooms in your neighborhood.

Also look for plants that make bright-colored berries in the winter. Depending on where you live, you might find the berry-bearing bushes listed here. All are evergreen, which means their leaves stay green in winter. The berries may be red, orange, yellow, purple, or white. (Never eat the berries. They may be poisonous.) Use a field guide to plants to help you identify more flowers and plants for your winter bouquet.

Winter Flowers	Winter Berries
Christmas rose (Helleborus)	Barberry (Berberis)
Erysimum	Euonymus
Pansy	Holly (Ilex)
Polyanthus	Nandina
Viola	Pyracantha

Tame the Wildflowers!

◆◆◆◆◆◆

They're called wildflowers because they grow wild.
But you can also grow wildflowers in your garden.

Wildflowers are hardy plants that are used to growing and blooming without a lot of pampering. You may be able to buy wildflower seeds, or you can collect them in nature. (First check to see if there are laws in your area about harvesting wildflower seeds.) Here's how to do it: Pay attention to what wildflowers grow in your area. You'll often see them in parks and meadows and along roadsides. Of course, they're most noticeable when they're blooming. Different wildflowers bloom at different times, from spring through summer and into fall.

What You'll Need
- wildflower seeds
- small garden clippers
- small paper bag or envelope
- a garden plot

When you see a type of wildflower that you like, watch it closely. The seed heads of most wildflowers are ready to pick 3 or 4 weeks after they bloom. Use small garden clippers to clip off the seed heads, including the stems. Put them in a small paper bag or envelope and store them at room temperature in a dry place. Only take a few seed heads in any area. That way, you'll leave plenty of seeds for nature to grow next year's wild crop. And if you're on private property, get permission first.

In most cases, you'll plant the seeds in late summer or early fall. Wildflowers like lots of sunlight. Plant them in broken-up soil, and be sure the seeds are covered with soil. Otherwise, they'll become birdseed! Water the seeds well when you first plant them. If it doesn't rain, keep the seeds watered. The following spring, you'll have "tame" wildflowers.

Wonderful Wildflowers

There are more than 15,000 different kinds of wildflowers found in the United States and Canada alone. Their unusual names include flower-of-an-hour, yellow false garlic, tufted loosestrife, and stinking Benjamin. Beyond those 15,000 wildflowers, there is a huge assortment of non-flowering wild plants, including interrupted ferns and silver moss.

Stately Flowers

◆◆◆◆◆◆◆

Each state has an official flower—a flower that grows in the state and is a symbol of the state. Grow your state's flower.

What You'll Need
- encyclopedia or almanac
- pot and potting soil
- seeds or seedlings

Find out from the list below what your state flower is. Why do you think that flower was picked as a symbol of your state? What about other states? Do any states share the same flower? Does your town or county have its own official flower? You can grow your state flower, either from seeds or from a seedling you buy at a nursery. Or pick another state. Maybe you want to try to grow all the states!

State	Flower
Alabama	Camellia
Alaska	Forget-me-not
Arizona	Saguaro cactus blossom
Arkansas	Apple blossom
California	Golden poppy
Colorado	Rocky mountain columbine
Connecticut	Mountain laurel
Delaware	Peach blossom
District of Columbia	American beauty rose
Florida	Orange blossom
Georgia	Cherokee rose
Hawaii	Yellow hibiscus
Idaho	Syringa
Illinois	Native violet
Indiana	Peony
Iowa	Wild rose
Kansas	Native sunflower
Kentucky	Goldenrod
Louisiana	Magnolia
Maine	White pinecone and tassel
Maryland	Black-eyed Susan
Massachusetts	Mayflower
Michigan	Apple blossom
Minnesota	Pink and white lady's-slipper
Mississippi	Magnolia
Missouri	Hawthorn
Montana	Bitterroot
Nebraska	Goldenrod
Nevada	Sagebrush
New Hampshire	Purple lilac
New Jersey	Purple violet
New Mexico	Yucca
New York	Rose
North Carolina	Dogwood
North Dakota	Wild prairie rose
Ohio	Scarlet carnation
Oklahoma	Mistletoe
Oregon	Oregon grape
Pennsylvania	Mountain laurel
Rhode Island	Violet
South Carolina	Yellow jessamine
South Dakota	Pasqueflower
Tennessee	Iris
Texas	Bluebonnet
Utah	Sego lily
Vermont	Red clover
Virginia	Dogwood
Washington	Western rhododendron
West Virginia	Big rhododendron
Wisconsin	Wood violet
Wyoming	Indian paintbrush

Moonlight Blooms

◆◆◆◆◆◆

Most flowers bloom in daylight, but a few special ones bloom only at night.

Night-blooming plants are pollinated by night-flying moths, and they smell great. In late spring, plant some night-blooming flowers such as the ones listed below. Or ask at a plant nursery for the names of other night bloomers that grow in your area. You can grow the flowers from seeds or from seedlings. Plant them in the ground or in pots. Either way, plant them in a place where you'll be able to enjoy their sweet scents.

Evening primrose *(Oenothera biennis)*

Evening-scented stock *(Matthiola longipetala)*

Flowering tobacco *(Nicotiana)*

Thorn apple *(Datura)*

Moonflower *(Ipomoea alba)*

Invent a Flower

◆◆◆◆◆◆

There are lots of interesting flowers in nature. Try to create your own.

Can you guess just how big the world's biggest flowers are? Well, they're called rafflesia, and they can be as much as 3 feet wide and weigh as much as 15 pounds. They have almost no leaves and no stems—they're all flower! You've probably never seen one, since they only grow in the rain forests of Indonesia. Other unusual flowers include the bee flower, which looks so much like a bee that real bees get confused. And there's actually a flower called the carrion flower (carrion means *dead flesh*) that looks and smells like dead meat.

What wild kinds of flowers can you come up with? Find out by inventing a flower. Gather parts of different flowers and plants: leaves, stems, flowers, seeds, etc. Or, cut out plant and flower parts from pictures in old magazines. Glue the parts together on a piece of cardboard or poster board to make a crazy new flower.

Flower Power

◆◆◆◆◆◆◆

Hydrangea flowers can be different colors, depending on where they grow.

What You'll Need

- red cabbage, shredded
- measuring cup and spoon
- heat-proof pitcher
- water
- pot
- stove
- strainer
- jar
- glass
- baking soda
- white vinegar

Caution: This project requires adult supervision.

Put 1 cup of shredded red cabbage in a heat-proof pitcher. With help from an adult, bring some water to a boil. Pour the boiling water over the cabbage and let it steep for at least 5 minutes. Then pour the liquid into a jar through a strainer to remove the cabbage. Throw the cabbage away.

Put a few teaspoons of the liquid in a glass; it should be reddish-purple. Stir some baking soda into the glass, ⅛ teaspoon to start. Keep adding baking soda until the liquid turns green. Next, stir white vinegar into the glass, ½ teaspoon at a time. Keep adding vinegar until the liquid turns back to red.

Why did the liquid turn different colors? The solution with the baking soda is alkaline, and the solution with the vinegar is acid. Plant pigments (colors) are affected by alkaline and acidic substances. The alkali made the cabbage broth turn green; the acid made it turn back to red. Soil can vary in how acid or alkaline it is—just like the 2 liquids varied. A hydrangea growing in very alkaline soil produces greenish flowers.

Calling All Butterflies

◆◆◆◆◆◆◆

Plant a special garden that will attract butterflies.

There are more than 10,000 known species of butterfly in the world. Of course, there aren't that many in your neighborhood, but chances are good you can find quite a few different varieties. First go to a plant nursery and look for the plants listed below. The best time to plant a butterfly garden is in late spring or early summer. Try to find other plants that help attract butterflies in your area.

What You'll Need

- garden plot
- seeds or seedlings of plants butterflies enjoy (see below)

Milkweed, a favorite of Monarch butterflies
Butterfly bush (also called Buddleia)
Butterfly weed (also called Asclepias tuberosa)

Veggie Flowers

◆◆◆◆◆◆

Did you know that some vegetables actually grow flowers?

Plants such as potatoes, carrots, turnips, radishes, sweet potatoes, and beets are very talented; they produce vegetables
one year and flowers the next. Here's how to prove it:

Cut the bottom half off some of the root vegetables just
mentioned. Push the top half of each vegetable into some
potting mix in a garden or pot. (A potato prefers to grow in
water. Put the potato in a jar of water. Half the potato should
be underwater, and the potato should not be touching the
bottom of the jar. Stick toothpicks in the potato to keep it
from touching the bottom.) Keep the veggies well watered.
Soon, they'll sprout stems and leaves. And after that, they'll
blossom. Notice the different kinds of flowers produced by the different vegetables.
What is your favorite kind of flowering vegetable?

What You'll Need
- root vegetables
- garden plot (or
  some pots and
  potting mix with
  plenty of sand or
  vermiculite)
- jar
- water
- toothpicks

Beautiful Bulbs

◆◆◆◆◆◆

Brighten your winter by growing fresh spring flowers—indoors!

What You'll Need
- narcissus or
  hyacinth bulbs
- shallow dish
- pebbles or
  aquarium gravel
- water

Narcissus and hyacinth bulbs can be grown indoors using the
technique called *forcing.* To force a bulb, you trick it into
thinking it's springtime.

Buy some Paperwhite narcissus bulbs or any type of
hyacinth bulb at a garden store. Find a dish about 3 or
4 inches deep and pour in about 1 or 1½
inches of pebbles. Set 3 or 4 bulbs upright
in the dish and fill in around them with
more pebbles. Leave the tops of the
bulbs sticking out. Add water up to the top of the pebbles. Set the
dish in a cool, dark place for 2 weeks, adding water as needed, to allow
roots to form. After 2 weeks, bring the dish out into a well-lit room but
out of direct light. When the leaves are well developed and flower
buds are forming, set the dish in a sunny window. Start your bulbs
in October for Christmas blossoms or in January for Easter. You
can try other spring flowers such as daffodils, crocus, or tulips.

Flower Story

◆▶▶▶▶▶◀

Flowers are a wonderful source of material for story writing. They're fun, they're colorful, and the possibilities are endless.

Go exploring and observe all the different types of flowers you see in your neighborhood. The field guide can help you identify the different plants you find in nature. Remember to only go exploring during daylight and stay in a familiar area. Bring a notebook along, a pencil, and maybe some crayons so you can get the colors right. After you've done this "research" you're ready to start writing. Write a story, creating a world where only flowers exist. Make up flower people, flower buildings, anything you want. You can even draw pictures to go along with the story. Just have fun and be creative!

What You'll Need
- field guide to plants
- notebook
- pencil
- crayons (optional)

What's Your Name?

◆▶▶▶▶▶◀

Personalize your flower garden by planting seeds that will flower in the shape of your name.

What You'll Need
- flower box
- soil
- sharp stick or pencil
- flower seeds (such as alyssum)

Prepare the soil in a large, rectangular flower box or in a garden. Use a sharp stick or pencil to write your name in the dirt. Then sprinkle flower seeds in the marks you made. Sprinkle loose soil over the seeds, and keep them watered. Soon, you'll see your name sprouting from the ground in bright green! Keep watering your name, and watch it bloom.

Drying Flowers

❖❖❖❖❖❖❖

Preserve the beauty of flowers. Even fragile flowers can be dried to enjoy for years.

What You'll Need
- scissors
- fresh-cut flowers
- sand
- leak-proof box (such as a shoe box)
- spoon

Cut the flowers early in the day, after the dew has dried. Pour a layer of sand into a box. Lay your flowers on the sand with at least an inch of space between them. Gently spoon more sand over the flowers, making sure it gets between petals, until the flowers are covered. If the box is deep enough, you can add another layer of flowers.

If the flowers are delicate, find a box deep enough for them to stand upright. Pour a layer of sand on the bottom and stick the flower stems into it. Carefully pour more sand around the flowers until they are covered.

Leave the boxes alone for at least 2 weeks (larger flowers will take more time to dry than smaller ones). At the end of that time, carefully pour out some of the sand and check your flowers for dryness. If they have not dried completely, start the process over and check again in a few days.

Garden Variety

❖❖❖❖❖❖❖

People have grown plants in gardens for thousands of years. Plants add beauty to our homes and buildings. They give us useful and fun things, such as pumpkins for Halloween. Not only do plants give us oxygen, but some plants can also give us cleaner air.

Two-Headed Transplant

◆◆◆◆◆◆◆

Graft similar plants together to make your own unique garden creation.

What You'll Need
- knife
- rubbing alcohol
- 2 small, columnlike cactus plants of the same diameter
- yarn
- thick gardening gloves

Caution: This project requires adult supervision.

Dip a sharp knife into rubbing alcohol to sterilize it. Get 2 small, columnlike cactus plants in pots. Put a piece of yarn underneath each of the cactus-plant pots; the yarn should be long enough so that the ends can be tied together at the top of the plant. Put on thick gardening gloves to protect your hands while you handle the plants. Slice off the top of each cactus plant. Do not touch the cut surfaces of the plants.

Switch the tops of the 2 plants. Carefully press the new top onto the base of each

cactus plant. Take the yarn under each pot, and securely tie the ends at the top of each plant to hold the new top in place. Put the pots in a sunny window. After a month, the grafts should heal, and you can remove the yarn from your plants.

Carve It Out

◆◆◆◆◆◆◆

Make your mark with a pumpkin.

Plant dwarf pumpkin seeds or starts in a sunny spot in your garden. Watch them grow from seeds, to flowers, to melons. When they are yellow and just about to turn orange, carve your name in the skin of the pumpkin with a clean, sharp nail. (Be careful!) As the pumpkin grows, the skin will scar over your marks, leaving a very personal signature.

What You'll Need
- sunny garden spot
- dwarf pumpkin seeds or starts
- clean nail

Perfect Planter

◄►◄►◄►◄►

You'll want to make several of these perfect planters from empty milk or juice cartons. Give them as gifts, or start your own nursery.

What You'll Need

- empty paper milk or juice cartons (washed and clean)
- scissors
- construction paper
- glue or tape
- old magazines
- crayons or colored pencils
- craft sticks
- potting soil
- flower seeds or seedlings

Open the top of an empty paper milk or juice carton. Cut the top off to make a 4- to 6-inch planter. Use construction paper to cover all 4 sides of the planter, then tape or glue the paper in place. Decorate the construction paper with magazine pictures and drawings. You could draw the flowers you will grow in your planter, or you could draw anything you want. That's where your imagination comes in handy!

Cut a small square of construction paper to make a marker. Write the name and draw a picture of the flower you will grow in the planter. Attach the marker to a craft stick with glue or tape.

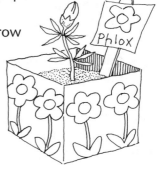

Fill the planter ¾ full with potting soil. Plant the seeds in the soil, or transplant a seedling to the decorated container. Add your plant marker.

Now watch your garden grow!

Good Old Days

◄►◄►◄►◄►

Gardeners are lucky to live in modern times.

If we need gardening tools, we just pull out our cash and head for the lawn and garden supply store. But it wasn't always so. Not so long ago, our ancestors had to make their own tools, often relying on sharp sticks and stones to help break up the soil. So the next time you plant a garden, step back in time a few hundred years. Plant one section the old-fashioned way—with rocks and sticks for gardening tools and seeds your ancient ancestors might have had. Take it a step further and carry water in clay pots to give your growing plants a drink. You'll get a whole new appreciation for how easy this tough job has become.

What You'll Need

- sharp rock
- digging stick
- seeds
- clay pots

Hothouse

◆◆◆◆◆◆

A greenhouse collects and stores heat.

What You'll Need

- cardboard box
- scissors
- ruler
- pencil
- newspaper
- tape
- aluminum foil
- empty soup cans
- water
- plastic wrap
- rubber bands
- seedlings in pots
- heavy plastic

Find a cardboard box about 14 inches deep, 10 inches high, and 12 inches wide, and cut off the top. Cut off one of the 10×14-inch sides of the box; this will be the front of your greenhouse. On both of the 10×12-inch sides, draw a line from the front bottom corner to the back top corner; cut along the lines so that you remove a triangular piece from each of the 2 sides. Cut a flap in both sides; each flap should be 4 inches across and 1 inch high. By bending these flaps open or closed, you will be able to control airflow in your greenhouse.

Tape several layers of newspaper to the outside of the back wall for insulation. Tape aluminum foil to the inside of the back wall for a reflector.

Place the greenhouse in a sunny spot outdoors. Fill several empty soup cans with water, and cover the tops of the cans with plastic wrap held in place with rubber bands. Place the cans in a row against the back wall; they will help to store heat in your greenhouse. Put several seedlings in pots inside the greenhouse.

Tape a large piece of heavy clear plastic to the top of the back wall, and pull it over the top and front of the greenhouse; the plastic should be wide enough to cover the greenhouse and long enough to tuck at least 1 foot under the greenhouse. Lift this cover when you want to water your seedlings.

PLASTIC DROP-CLOTH

NEWSPAPER

FOIL

Grow a Garden

◆►◆►◆►◆►

Put your green thumb to work and grow plants from scratch!

Ready to grow your own plants? A few days before you start, ask your family to save the seeds they find in any fruit they eat. That way, when you're ready to plant, you'll have plenty of seeds to use.

Once you have 8 to 10 fruit seeds, fill a small dish with water and soak the seeds for a day or so. Then fill a flowerpot with soil. Bury the seeds about a ¼ of an inch deep in the soil and water them. Over the next few weeks, watch your seeds carefully. Keep the pot in a sunny place and water the seeds every couple of days. Soon you'll see plants pop through the soil.

What You'll Need
- seeds from fruit (like apples, oranges, grapefruit, lemons, or limes)
- small dish
- water
- flowerpot
- soil

Bottle Terrarium

◆►◆►◆►◆►

Recycle old pop bottles by turning them into habitats for houseplants.

What You'll Need
- clean 2-liter soda bottle with black plastic base (and label removed)
- scissors
- potting soil
- charcoal
- plants
- water

First remove the black plastic base from the bottom of your soda bottle and set it aside. This will be the bottom of your terrarium. Use scissors to cut off the top of the bottle just below the "shoulder" of the bottle. When turned over, the bottle forms a clear dome over your terrarium.

Now sprinkle about ½ inch of crushed charcoal (you can buy it at your gardening store) in the bottom of the black-plastic base. Fill the base with potting soil up to about ½ inch from the top. Plant some small houseplants, woodland plants, seeds, or cuttings in the base. Water them until the soil is moist but not soggy. Cover the plants with the clear plastic dome you made from the rest of the bottle. Place your bottle terrarium in a sunny spot and water it regularly.

If you collect wild plants or seeds for your terrarium, be sure to collect on private property with permission only. Never collect plants from parks, state lands, or federal lands.

The Lowdown on Dirt

When it comes to supporting plant life, not all dirt is equal.

Look in your yard for areas where plants grow poorly. Is the soil trampled and hard? Is the soil soft and loose where plants grow well? Look for sandy or heavy, claylike soil. Gather samples of different soils and fill a flowerpot with each kind.

Label your flowerpots: "Hard, baked soil near the sidewalk," "Loose, fluffy soil from the flower bed," etc. Water the pots, then plant 2 or 3 bean seeds in each. Put a stake in each pot for the beans to climb. Keep the pots moist (but not soggy) while the beans sprout. Notice which beans sprout first. Measure the height of the plants every few days until the beans flower. Keep a chart. Which soil was the best?

Garden Nite-Nite

Eating isn't the last step when it comes to your garden.

Even if your garden has been a huge success—you've grown and eaten strawberries, green beans, corn, or watermelons—your work as a farmer isn't finished. If you love the land, the onset of winter means payback time. Before the snow and chill officially arrive, put your garden to bed. Gently clip down what's left of your plants and rake them back into your garden plot. That will feed the soil during the long winter months and help make it full of nutrients come next year. If you take care of your garden in the winter, it will take care of you next spring.

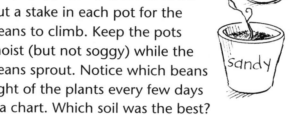

Jack (or Joan or Jim or Judy) & the Beanstalk

◆◆◆◆◆◆◆

Magic (even without those magic beans).

What You'll Need
- garden spot
- 3 equal-length dowel rods or branches
- pole bean seeds
- water
- plastic villagers

Fiction becomes fact—almost—thanks to this fantasy garden plot complete with little plastic figures. The next time you plant pole beans (the "reach for the stars" vines that crawl way up stakes and fences), set up a tiny village, too. Arrange plastic people at the base of the plant and the pole you stake down for it to climb. Before you know it, your fantasy folk will be settled around a gigantic adventure. You'll grow your imagination along with those beans.

Dig It Up

◆◆◆◆◆◆◆

Use these tips before you plant to pick the perfect piece of soil.

Choose a place that gets 6 or more hours of direct sunshine each day. Your garden needs that life-giving light. Make sure your plot of ground is near a water source, a hose, or an irrigation spout. Be sure your land is level so

What You'll Need
- soil checklist (below)

water won't run off (taking your seeds and topsoil with it). Make sure the soil is alive—search for organisms such as worms and organic matter such as sticks and leaf bits to help feed your crops. With these tips in mind, you're sure to be a real green thumb.

1. Make sure your garden plot is weed-free.
2. Remove large rocks from your soil before you plant.
3. Add compost or manure to your soil for extra nutrients.
4. Are earthworms a part of your garden? If not, add some.

A Garden of Good Scents

◆◆◆◆◆◆◆

Grow sweet-smelling plants that delight the nose and the eyes.

Choose a garden spot and prepare the soil as noted in Sunny Flower Garden (see page 398). Then, make 2 paths by pressing a foot wide strip of soil down the middle of the garden and a second one going across. Cover the paths with bark mulch about 2 inches deep. Buy your plants or seeds at a garden center.

Set the plants out and arrange them the way you wish. Use the labels in the pots to help you decide where to place them. Sow seeds according to the directions on the package. When everything is planted, run a sprinkler about a half an hour. Water deeply twice a week during dry weather and pull out weeds often.

When your garden is ready, make a sign that says "Please Touch the Plants!" Then invite friends inside. Some plants that release scents when touched are sweet alyssum, heliotrope, nasturtium, scented geraniums, basil, English violets, lavender, pinks, thyme, sage, and oregano.

What You'll Need
- patch of sunny ground about 5 feet wide and 6 feet long (get permission first)
- shovel
- trowel
- bagged compost
- bagged bark mulch
- plants or seeds
- hose
- small sprinkler
- cardboard
- scissors
- marker

Wagon Wonders

◆◆◆◆◆◆◆

Planting smaller gardens in creative places can be fun!

What You'll Need
- wagon
- soil
- bedding plants

Plant a red, white, and blue garden in your favorite wagon. You'll not only have a fun flowerbed, but you will also have a Fourth of July float for a neighborhood parade. Use simple

bedding plants like petunias in bedding soil. Keep them watered but not too wet. Before you know it, you'll have a beautiful garden on wheels.

Free Plants!

Get new plants for free by taking cuttings of old ones.

What You'll Need
- houseplants (such as African violet, begonia, or geranium)
- scissors
- small bottle
- flowerpots
- potting soil
- vermiculite or perlite (optional)

With the help of an adult, cut a section of a houseplant stem with 5 or 6 leaves on it. Trim away any flowers and cut off the bottom 3 leaves. Then fill a small bottle with water and place the stem of the cutting into the water. The remaining leaves will hold the cutting in place. Put the bottle near a sunny window but not in direct sunlight. Add water to the bottle as needed to keep the stem in water.

After a few weeks the cutting should have long roots and be ready for planting. Fill a small flowerpot with potting soil up to about ½ inch from the top. Dig a hole large enough for the roots. Lower the cutting in, and carefully cover the roots.

You can also start cuttings in vermiculite or perlite, which are heat-expanded rocks. You can buy them at a garden store. Fill a small jar with vermiculite or perlite, and add water. Take a cutting as described above. Poke a hole in the vermiculite or perlite, and lower the cutting into it. Allow roots to grow for 3 weeks, adding water as needed. After the roots have grown, replant the plant in potting soil.

Mini-Garden

Victorian kids made "fairy gardens." Create your own version!

What You'll Need
- shady 3×3-foot garden spot (get permission)
- rocks, sticks, and moss
- shade-loving plants
- trowel
- toy animals or dolls

In the shelter of a large, shady shrub, you can design a miniature world. Use dolls and toy animals as inhabitants, if you like, or pretend (as Victorian children did) that the "little people" visit your garden when you're not looking. First, decide where the edges of your garden will be. Mark the edges with a tiny wall made of rocks or sticks. Use stones to make paths. Build miniature houses by stacking sticks or stones log-cabin style. Cover the houses with moss. Fill the

rest of the space with shade-loving plants. Try such annuals as impatiens, coleus, polka-dot plants, and violas, or such perennials as dwarf ferns, dwarf hostas, and violets.

Bean Teepee

◆▷◆▷◆▷◆▷

Make a cool, leafy hiding place in the summer!

In late spring, when the weather warms up, pick a spot in the garden about 4 feet on each side. Make sure the ground is ready to plant. (See Sunny Flower Garden on page 398 if you're starting with uncultivated soil.) Tie your stakes together at the top and set them upright in the middle of the patch. Spread the bottom ends out to make a circle. Leave an opening between 2 stakes wide enough for a "door."

Soak your bean seeds overnight, then plant 4 or 5 an inch deep at the bottom of each pole. Keep the seeds watered while they sprout. They should find the stakes themselves and climb upward. By mid-summer, your bean teepee should be ready. Spread a tarp on the ground inside, and call your friends!

Spoon It Up!

◆▷◆▷◆▷◆▷

How long does it take to fill a bowl the old-fashioned way?

There was a time when farmers had to carry buckets of water from rivers or ponds to water their crops. Bucket by bucket, they carried the load. Want a quick and crazy way to appreciate that kind of work? See how long it takes to move a bowl full of water into an empty bowl—carrying just one spoonful at a time.

Set 2 bowls on opposite sides of a yard or small playing field. As soon as the stopwatch starts, begin to transport water from a full bowl to an empty bowl one spoon at a time. Do your best not to spill as you go. Then throw your hands over your head when your mission is complete. The stopwatch can tell you just how long it took. Your powers of reason will tell you how much longer it might take to irrigate a plot of old farming acreage, one bucket at a time.

Water Sprayers

Cool off and keep your garden watered
with a yard full of homemade sprinklers.

What You'll Need

- strong stake or old broomstick
- hammer
- 18-inch length of rubber tubing
- hose
- old rubber glove
- scissors
- tin can
- nail
- string

Caution: This project requires adult supervision.

Watering your garden or yard may feel like a chore at times. But water is an important ingredient in your garden's success. Try these sprinkler ideas out on a hot day and have fun watering your garden—and yourself! Just be careful not to trample any of your plants as you enjoy this wet project.

Water Whip: Use a hammer to drive a stake or an old broomstick into the ground. Take a piece of rubber tubing at least ½ inch in diameter and stretch one end over the end of a garden hose. Tie the hose to the stake so that the rubber tubing can flap freely at the top. Turn on the water, and adjust the height of the hose and the water pressure until the tubing waves around on its own, spraying water as it goes.

Water Hand: Poke holes in the fingertips of an old rubber glove, such as a dishwashing glove. Tie the cuff of the glove tightly over the end of a hose. Fasten the water hand to a stake so it sprays upright, or drape the hose over a tree branch to make a "handy" shower!

Tin-Can Shower: Use a nail to punch holes around the bottom edge of a large tin can. Punch 2 more holes at the top and insert a string to hang the can from a branch. Fill the can with water. As water sprays out through the holes, the can will spin!

Mini-Greenhouses

◆◆◆◆◆◆◆

Winter is the perfect time to start seeds indoors for a spring garden.

What You'll Need
- small pots or containers
- scissors
- potting soil
- water
- flower or vegetable seeds
- clear plastic bags
- twist ties

Punch some holes in the bottom of your containers for drainage. Fill them with potting soil. Use sterile soil so the seedlings won't catch a fungal disease called "damping off." Wet the soil, and set the containers aside to drain.

Plant only 2 or 3 seeds in each container. As a rule, plant the seed no deeper than 4 times its diameter. (Plant lettuce seeds on top of the soil because they need light to sprout.) Put each container in a clear plastic bag, such as the kind that grocers use for fruits and vegetables. Gather up the mouth of the bag and blow into it, then tie off the top with a twist-tie

to make a miniature greenhouse. Set the greenhouse in a warm room. Once you see sprouts, put your greenhouses in a sunny window. It's also a good idea to take the green-houses outdoors on warm days where they can get more sun for a few hours each day.

The first green "leaves" on your seedlings are called "seed leaves." They are not true leaves but parts of the seed. Wait until the seedlings have at least 4 true leaves and are tall and strong before transplanting them outdoors.

It's Planting Time!

◆◆◆◆◆◆◆

Different vegetables have different growing seasons.

Find out what vegetables grow in your area and what time of year each vegetable should be planted. (Check the library for books and magazines on vegetable gardening, or ask a gar-dener or farmer you know.) Then make a chart that shows each vegetable, when to plant it, and when to harvest it. Your chart could also give other information, such as how much water to give the vegetable plant and what pests to watch out for. You can use the poster to grow your own vegetables, or give it to someone who likes to garden.

What You'll Need
- gardening book
- poster board
- markers

Natural Dyes

◆▶▶▶▶▶◀

Before there were chemical dyes, people had to make their own dyes from plant materials. Try your hand at dyeing a shirt or bandanna.

What You'll Need

- wool or cotton material to dye
- laundry detergent
- a variety of colorful plant material (see suggestions below)
- knife
- glass bowl
- water
- old stainless-steel pans
- stove
- sieve
- alum (available in the spice rack at grocery stores)
- measuring spoon

Caution: This project requires adult supervision.

1. Wash cotton or wool material in plain detergent with no fabric softener.

2. Cut up your plant materials. Chop up or crush hard materials such as roots. Soak them overnight in a glass bowl with just enough water to cover them.

3. Pour the contents of the bowl into a stainless-steel pan. Bring to a boil on the stove, and simmer gently for about an hour. Check it frequently, and add water when needed.

4. Strain the dye through a sieve to remove plant material. Allow the liquid to cool.

5. Measure the liquid. For every quart of dye, add ½ ounce alum (about a tablespoon). Alum is a *mordant*. That means it helps set the dye.

6. Wet your fabric and wring it out, then put it in the steel pan with your dye. Put the pan on the stove, and simmer slowly until the fabric is just a little darker than you want it. (The fabric will look lighter when it dries.) Remember that natural colors will be soft, not bright.

7. Move the pan to the sink, and pour everything through a sieve. Run a little cold water over your fabric to cool and rinse it, then wring it out, and hang it up to dry outdoors where the drips won't hurt anything.

Here are some of the colors you can make from common plants:

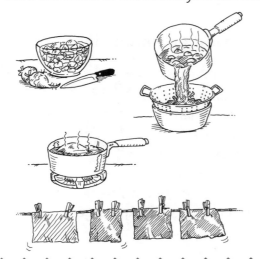

Plant	Color
Onion skins	yellow
Goldenrod flowers	yellow
Carrots	yellow
Red onions	pink
Raspberries	pink
Beets	rose
Coffee	brown
Nut hulls (not shells)	brown
Grass	green
Spinach	green

Pumpkin Tunnel

❖❖❖❖❖❖

Rediscover pumpkins: They aren't just for Halloween.

To build your tunnel, you'll need a sunny area of the garden about 5 feet wide. Have an adult cut a piece of mesh 5 feet wide and about 6 feet long. Shape it into an arch, pushing the ends of the wire on the 5-foot long sides into the soil. Plant pumpkin, gourd, or cucumber seeds along the sides, or use transplants. As the plants grow, they will cover the mesh and make a nice tunnel to play in.

If concrete mesh is hard to find, you can make your tunnel from poles. Stick 5 poles in the ground a foot apart, then make another line of poles 3 feet away. Tie the tops to a cross pole to form the shape of a tunnel. Plant your seeds at the base of each pole. As the plants grow, you may want to tie them to the poles with strips of rag to help them climb. Cover the floor of your tunnel with grass clippings or straw for comfort.

What You'll Need
- garden space
- heavy concrete reinforcement mesh or 11 poles about 5 feet long
- pumpkin, gourd, or cucumber seeds
- rag strips
- grass clippings or straw

The Cat's Meow

❖❖❖❖❖❖

Cats go crazy for catnip, whether it's still growing or made into a toy.

What You'll Need
- felt
- scissors
- pen
- needle
- thread
- catnip

Catnip is an herb that you can buy at a plant nursery and grow in a pot or garden. Cats love to play in it and eat it. Plant some catnip in a place where a cat can enjoy it.

Cut a piece of felt into an interesting shape, such as a mouse! Lay the shape on another piece of felt and trace around it. Cut out your tracing to make a second shape that's exactly the same as the first. With help from an adult, use a needle and thread to sew the 2 pieces of felt together, but leave a small opening. Stuff the toy with catnip, then sew it shut.

Plant Succession

◆◆◆◆◆◆◆

From weeds to trees, here's how Mother Nature takes back her land.

If you have a lawn, you know that somebody has to mow it all summer long. (Maybe it's you!) Did you ever wonder what would happen if the lawn didn't get mowed? Other plants might start growing in and around the grass. After that, small bushes and shrubs would begin to grow. If you live in an area where there are woods, trees would eventually grow.

This process is called *plant succession.* In some areas, you can see plant succession happening in nature. Look for land that was once farmland or pasture that has been abandoned. Once you've found a piece of land to study, check on it several times throughout the year. Keep a journal, and take notes on the land's progress. Nature will gradually reclaim this land, covering it with native plants, shrubs, and trees.

Garden Markers

◆◆◆◆◆◆◆

These attractive painted signs make nice gifts for gardeners.

What You'll Need
- seed packets
- markers
- thin scrap wood
- coping saw
- acrylic paint
- paintbrush
- spray varnish
- small nails
- hammer
- small stakes

Caution: This project requires adult supervision.

Some people like to mark their garden rows with stakes and stick the empty seed packet on top of the stake. Painted garden markers are a much prettier way to show what you've planted.

Use pictures from seed packets to help you draw 4- to 6-inch-wide pictures of the vegetables your family likes to plant in the garden. Trace the outline of each picture onto thin scrap wood, and have an adult cut the shapes out with a coping saw. Paint in the shapes with acrylic paints. Let the paint dry. Ask an adult to help you cover with 3 coats of spray varnish,

allowing the varnish to dry between coats. Be sure to work in a well-ventilated area and use a type of varnish that is suitable for the outdoors. Carefully nail the painted shapes to garden stakes about 2 feet long.

Venus's-flytraps

◄►◄►◄►

Carnivorous plants can be easy and fun to raise
if you give them the right environment.

What You'll Need

- fish bowl or 1 gallon glass jar (or Bottle Terrarium—see page 414)
- charcoal (use the kind prepared for house plants)
- potting soil
- sand
- peat moss
- old mixing bowl
- water
- Venus's-flytrap plant
- insects or tiny bits of raw meat

Pour a 1-inch layer of crushed charcoal into the bottom of the terrarium. Mix 3 parts potting soil with 1 part sand and 1 part peat moss in an old mixing bowl. Add water until the mix is moist but not soggy. Put about 3 inches of the mix into the terrarium. Now dig a small hole for your plant. Carefully remove the Venus's-flytrap from its pot, and plant it in the hole. Put a cover on the terrarium. You need to keep your plant moist. Most purchased Venus's-flytrap plants die because of improper care. The air in your living room is too dry for them. Venus's-flytraps are bog plants, so they need humid air and wet soil to survive.

The Venus's-flytrap eats insects because it needs nutrients; bog soils are low in nutrients. You can feed your plant small insects or tiny bits of raw meat. Put a bit of meat on a leaf and gently tap it to make the leaf close. Be aware that Venus's-flytraps are becoming rare because of overcollection. Many are collected illegally. When you buy yours, check the label to see if it is greenhouse-raised or collected from the wild. Be sure to only purchase greenhouse-raised plants.

Map Your Yard

◆◆◆◆◆◆◆

How well do you think you know your yard?
Find out when you draw a nature map.

What You'll Need
- large piece of paper
- markers
- field guide to plants and trees

First, try to draw a map of your yard from memory. No peeking outside! How much can you remember? When you're finished, take a look and compare, then make another yard map that shows how much you know about nature. Map all the trees, shrubs, flowers, and so on. Label them with their names. Also include any other interesting features of your yard, such as large rocks and animal homes.

Plantastic Plants

◆◆◆◆◆◆◆

The science and art of growing plants is called "horticulture."
Read about it, and maybe you'll grow a green thumb.

What You'll Need
- books about plants
- pen
- paper

There's a whole world of plants out there. At the library, find a book about plants, flowers, or gardening. See what you can learn. Then, do something with what you learned. You might plant your first garden or grow just one flower.

Afterward, write about the experience. Or, you might make a picture book showing the life cycle of a plant. Be sure to give the book a title and sign the author's name...yours!

Step on It

❖❖❖❖❖❖

Make walkways for your garden.

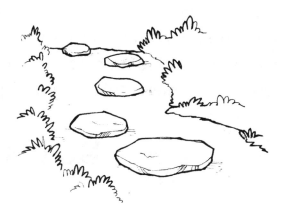

One way to use the larger stones you discover on your geologic journeys is to make them into stepping stones for your gardens, yard, or flowerbeds—especially to help you make a safe path to where you keep the garden hose. Just take your flat, heavy stones and put them about 6 inches apart on a trail, either between rows in your garden or in flowerbeds near the spigot for the hose.

Plant Comparisons

❖❖❖❖❖❖

Plants of the same species have individual differences.

Find 2 plants of the same species. You can use houseplants, plants from a vegetable garden, shrubs in your yard, or plants you find in the wild. Look at the 2 plants closely, and write down as many physical similarities as you can find between them. Look at things such as color, thickness of branches, shape of leaves, basic structure, and so on. Write "SIMILARI-

TIES" at the top of a piece of paper, and write down all the things the plants have in common. Now look at the plants to find ways that they are different. Look at the number of leaves, overall size, shape of branches, and anything else that occurs to you. Write "DIFFERENCES" at the top of another sheet of paper, and write down all the ways that the 2 plants are different from each other.

Edibles

◆▶◆▶◆▶◆▶

Of all the reasons to grow plants in a garden, one of the most important and fun reasons is to eat what plants provide. From the sugar in candy to the flour in bread, from the orange of a tree to the leaves of lettuce, our diet is full of yummy plant products.

 ## Box Garden

◆▶◆▶◆▶◆▶

Turn a wooden fruit crate into a miniature salad garden.

What You'll Need
- wooden fruit crate
- newspaper
- potting soil
- garden soil or compost
- water
- vegetable seeds (leaf lettuce, miniature carrots, radishes, and bush tomatoes)

In the winter, fruit shipped from places like South America often comes in wooden crates. Ask your grocer to save one for you. Line the crate with 4 or 5 layers of newspaper. Fill with a mixture of half potting soil and half garden soil or compost. Water the soil and allow the box to drain. Make 2 long furrows the length of the box, one near the front, the other right down the middle. Divide the front row in half. In one half sprinkle seeds for miniature carrots. In the other half sprinkle radish seeds. In the middle row, sprinkle leaf lettuce seeds. Plant the seeds thinly.

The back half of the box is for your bush tomatoes. Poke a hole about ½ inch deep and drop 2 or 3 tomato seeds in it. Cover the seeds. When they sprout wait until they are about 2 inches tall, then cut away the weaker plants, leaving one strong one.

Keep the box outside in a sunny place and water it every day. Thin the plants if they need it. Pull the carrots when they are about an inch across. Cut the lettuce when the leaves are about 6 to 8 inches tall.

Popcorn Plants

◆▸◆▸◆▸◆▸

No butter is required when you grow this popcorn garden!

We know that popcorn makes a great snack at the movies. It
can also be turned into a plant. When you're ready to get
popping, put a few paper towels in a plastic bag and soak
them with water. Now place a few popcorn kernels in the bag
so they sit on top of the paper towels. Zip the bag up and
tape it to an object (like a fence) where it can get plenty of
sunlight.

What You'll Need
- paper towels
- plastic bag that zips shut
- water
- unpopped kernels of popcorn
- tape
- planter pot
- soil

Keep an eye on the kernels over the next week or so. If the
towels dry up, pour some more water into the bag until the
towels soak it up.

Once you see small plants growing, place them in a pot
filled with soil. Keep the soil moist, and watch your popcorn plants reach for the sky!

Stop and Eat the Roses

◆▸◆▸◆▸◆▸

Some flowers look good, smell good, AND taste good!

What You'll Need
- rose blooms
- stove
- sugar syrup
- pot
- waxed paper

Caution: This project requires adult supervision.

Grow or buy some organically grown roses. (Since you're
going to eat them, you don't want the roses to have chemical
fertilizer or pesticides on them.) When the roses bloom, pick
some. Have an adult carefully dip them into boiling sugar
syrup. Put them on waxed paper to cool.
When they are cool enough to handle,
spread out the petals and let the flowers dry
in the sun or in a warm (not hot) oven. Then help yourself to rose
candy.

There's another part of the rose plant that tastes
good. In the late summer or early fall, roses form
"rose hips." When the rose hips turn red, they are
ripe and ready to eat. Just remove the seeds. Rose-
hips have a lot of vitamin C. They can also be used
to make tea.

Taste-Test Garden

◆▶◆▶◆▶◆

How long is a matter of taste!

When is the best time to harvest your garden crops? Read your seed envelope instructions, then try this experiment. Beginning about a week before your carrots or radishes are supposed to be ripe, pull a single sample and take a healthy bite (make sure you clean the dirt off and rinse the sample first). How does it taste 7 days early? Write it down. How about 6 days early? Five days early? And so on. When you plant your garden the next year, you'll know exactly how long it takes to grow the garden that you think tastes just right.

What You'll Need
- carrot or radish patch
- pad of paper
- pencil
- ruler

Carrot Basket

◆▶◆▶◆▶◆

Make a hanging carrot basket that would make any rabbit jealous.

What You'll Need
- large carrot (at least 2 inches across) or parsnip
- knife
- ruler
- apple corer
- toothpicks
- string
- scissors
- potting soil
- grass seed

If you use a carrot for this project, find one of the novelty types that is at least 2 inches in diameter and still has its top. If you can't find one, use a parsnip or other thick root vegetable with the top still on.

Cut off the bottom of your vegetable, leaving the top 3 inches with the leaves. Next cut off the foliage, leaving about 2 inches of leafy stem. Use an apple corer to hollow out the vegetable top. (Turned upside down, the vegetable top makes a basket.) With toothpicks, poke 4 evenly spaced holes around the cut edge of the basket. Cut 4 pieces of string about 2 feet long and tie one in each of the holes. Tie the strings together at the top. Fill the basket with potting soil and plant grass seed on top. Hang your basket up. If you keep the soil moist, it will sprout grass on top, while the vegetable tops will grow again, curling around the basket as they reach up for the sun. If you want, you can plant alfalfa seeds or the seeds of small flowers in your basket.

Pineapple Party

❖❖❖❖❖❖❖

Grow your own tangy beauties from just a leaf.

What You'll Need
- pineapple
- knife
- shallow pan
- water
- pot
- soil

Believe it or not, you can use the leafy end of a store-bought pineapple to grow a great plant. In fact, it may even triple its size by the time 12 months have passed. Just pick a pineapple with a good, leafy top. Cut that top off, leaving about an inch of fruit attached. Set the pineapple top in a shallow pan, like an old layer-cake pan, filled with water. Once it begins to root, plant it in rich soil and keep the dirt moist (but not too wet). To protect the tropical wonder from extreme cold, bring it inside when the weather drops below 45 degrees.

Fruit Leather

❖❖❖❖❖❖❖

Cook up some fruit rolls that are as much fun to make as they are to eat!

Caution: This project requires adult supervision.

What You'll Need
- fruit (such as plums, peaches, and apricots)
- peeler
- knife
- measuring cup
- sugar
- water
- stove
- saucepan
- blender
- plastic wrap
- cookie sheets
- oven
- jar

You can make your own fruit rolls! Peel fresh fruit, cut it up into small pieces, and put it in a measuring cup. For every quart of fruit, add ½ cup sugar and ½ cup water. Put the mixture into a saucepan and simmer on the stove until the fruit is soft and can be mashed up. Watch carefully to prevent scorching, and add more water as needed. Pour the cooked fruit into a blender and blend it into a thick puree.

Next, cut large squares of plastic wrap and lay them on cookie sheets. Pour ¼ to ½ cup fruit puree onto each square and spread it out into a thin layer. Put the cookie sheets in an oven heated to no more than 150°F, leaving the oven door slightly open. Allow the puree to dry until leathery. Don't overdry the leather or else it will turn crisp!

When the leather is done, roll it up in its plastic wrap and store in a jar. Peel it from the plastic wrap when you're ready to eat it. Yum! Plums, apricots, and peaches seem to make the best homemade leather, but you can experiment with other fruits as well.

A Spot of Tea

Many herbs and flowers can be used to make delicious tea.

Caution: This project requires adult supervision.

Try growing your own herbs for tea. Mint grows fast and can be grown indoors under a full-spectrum "grow light." Or you can harvest wild herbs and flowers for tea. Just be sure an adult goes with you to help you make sure that the herbs you're harvesting are okay to eat. Red clover is often found growing wild, and it makes a good tea.

Make tea from fresh herbs and flowers right after you gather them. Ask an adult to pour boiling water over them and let them steep for about 5 minutes. Then pour the tea through a strainer to remove the herbs. Add a little sugar or honey, if you like.

What You'll Need
- herbs or flowers that make good tea (chamomile, red clover, or mint)
- hot water
- strainer
- sugar or honey (optional)

Vegetable in a Bottle

This trick will mystify everyone—but it takes a lot of patience!

What You'll Need
- clear plastic bottle with a narrow mouth
- garden vegetable plant (such as cucumber or zucchini)
- wooden box (optional)

Find someone friendly who has a vegetable garden and who is willing to help you. Watch for a garden plant to blossom and set fruit. Cucumbers, zucchini, or gourds work well for this. Slip the tiny vegetable—still attached to the stem—into the neck of a plastic bottle. Be careful not to break the stem. Make sure the bottle is shaded under the leaves of the plant, or cover the bottle with a wooden box to keep the sun from heating the bottle too much. Now wait for the vegetable to grow. Once it's big enough to nearly fill the bottle, cut the stem and go show your friends. See if they can figure out how the vegetable got in the bottle. Then you can cut away the bottle to get the vegetable out.

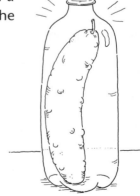

Sun Jam

◆◆◆◆◆◆◆

Make delicious strawberry preserves using the heat of the sun.

Caution: This project requires adult supervision.

Make this jam when the weather will be hot and sunny for several days. Cut your washed berries in half and put them in a saucepan. Add 4 cups sugar, stir, and let the pan sit 30 minutes. With adult help, heat the mixture on the stove medium-high until it boils. Turn the heat to low and simmer 15 minutes. Next, with adult help, pour the hot mix into a glass baking dish. Let it cool 15 minutes, then cover the pan in plastic wrap. Leave the pan in the sun all day. Stir the berries gently 2 or 3 times during the day. Bring the pan inside at night. It will take 2 or 3 days for the mixture to thicken. When the preserves are ready, store them in the refrigerator. Sometimes this recipe works, sometimes it doesn't—every batch is different. If your preserves don't jell, use them for strawberry syrup!

What You'll Need
- 1 quart of ripe strawberries (small berries rather than large ones)
- knife
- 10-inch saucepan
- measuring cup
- sugar
- stove
- large spoon
- large glass baking dish
- clear plastic wrap
- container

Kinda Corny

◆◆◆◆◆◆◆

Plant for a colorful harvest!

What You'll Need
- Indian corn seeds

Do you love the way that colorful brown, yellow, and orange Indian corn brightens up the autumn? You can plant your own series of stalks long before the summer turns to fall. Head for your favorite general or gardening store in March, April, or May. Gather up seed packets of colorful corn varieties. Plant them as instructed on the packages. By the time fall comes around, you'll have grown your own rainbow of maize to harvest and enjoy.

Onion/Garlic Braids

After harvesting onions or garlic, make them into braids.

What You'll Need
- onions or garlic with tops intact
- newspaper
- string

Begin with whole, undamaged onions or garlic. If you dig them from your garden be sure to clean off as much dirt as you can. Do not cut off the tops because you will need these to braid. Lay the onions or garlic out on newspapers in a cool, dry, sheltered place until the tops are dry.

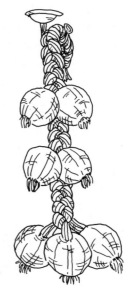

When they are ready, take 3 of your onions and braid the tops together for a few inches. Lay 2 more onions alongside right where the braid stops, separate their tops into the 3 strands you are braiding, and braid for another few inches. Add 2 more onions, and keep going. When you have about 2 feet of onions in your braid, stop adding onions. Braid the remainder of the tops together and tie the braid off with string. Loop the braid over onto itself and tie the loop with more string. Hang the braid in the kitchen, preferably from a hook on the ceiling, where air will circulate around the onions.

Make a garlic braid the same way, but leave only an inch or two between the bulbs. Garlic bulbs are much smaller than onions so they can be laid closer together.

Grow Carrots

Carrots are fun to grow—and even more fun to eat!

What You'll Need
- carrots
- knife
- flat dishes or deep saucers
- potting soil or pebbles
- water
- flowerpot

Start with carrots that have leafy tops. Cut off the tops, leaving about 2 inches of greens. Cut off the top inch of the carrot, and plant it in potting soil or fine pebbles in a dish. Leave the greens above the surface. Keep the soil barely moist. If using pebbles, add fresh water every other day. When the carrots begin to sprout new leaves, plant in soil in a flowerpot.

Sun-Dried Tomatoes

◆◆◆◆◆◆◆

These tomatoes are easy to make as a gift for gourmets.

Caution: This project requires adult supervision.

For this project, use only fresh, fully ripe tomatoes without any bruises. Cut the tomatoes in half and use a spoon to scoop out the seeds. Large tomatoes should be cut into quarters. Spread the tomatoes evenly on a cookie sheet. Put in an oven set to 150°F and dry until most of the moisture is gone but the tomatoes are still soft. Next, put the tomatoes in a bowl and sprinkle with red wine vinegar, then cover the bowl and allow to sit for at least 15 minutes. The vinegar helps preserve the tomatoes, and adds flavor. Pack the dried tomatoes loosely into a jar and pour in olive oil until completely covered. Cover the top of the jar with plastic wrap, then put on the lid. Store in the refrigerator.

What You'll Need
- tomatoes from garden or U-pick farm (plum tomatoes are best)
- knife
- spoon
- cookie sheets
- oven
- bowl
- red wine vinegar
- jar with lid
- olive oil
- plastic wrap

Something Nutty

◆◆◆◆◆◆◆

Go nuts! Grow nuts!

What You'll Need
- peanut seeds or starts

Why grow carrots when you can go completely nuts? Try your hand at growing delicious peanuts. You can buy seeds from a gardening store or even raw peanuts from the grocery store—the same nuts you like to munch on will grow into new plants! Remove the shells and plant the seeds about ¾ of an inch deep in sandy soil, about a foot apart, in the spring. Mound the soil around the plants after they flower to help with pollination. In about 4 months, your peanuts will mature—you'll know it's time when the leaves start to turn yellow. Remember, your harvest will be underground. Peanuts are actually roots!

Sugar, Sugar

◆◆◆◆◆◆◆

Sugar cane is the perfect remedy for a sweet tooth.

What You'll Need

- sugar cane
- knife
- potting soil
- large flowerpot (about 8 inches)
- matches
- candle

Caution: This project requires adult supervision.

Most people don't know that sugar cane is a type of grass. Like grass, it grows quickly and easily into an attractive plant. Find a fresh-cut section of sugar cane at least a foot long. (You may have to look in a specialty grocery store.) Look near the joints in the stem for a shield-shaped bud from which new stalks will grow. Below the buds are tiny holes where roots will grow. Ask an adult to cut the stalk off 2 inches below the bud and about an inch above the next joint.

Fill a flowerpot with potting soil up to about 2 inches from the rim. Stick the cane into the soil so that the bud is just barely covered. Have an adult help you light the candle and drip melted wax onto the other end of the cane to keep it from drying out. Keep the soil barely moist. In a week or so the bud will sprout. When the new sprout is about 6 inches high, add another 1½ inches of potting soil.

As more sprouts grow you can cut the sprouts, peel them, and cut them into sticks to stir hot drinks with.

Strawbarrel

◆◆◆◆◆◆◆

This project is berry much fun in a little bitty space.

Even if you don't have room for a garden, you probably have room for a strawbarrel. Fill a large half-barrel or outdoor planter with good, rich garden soil or potting soil. Then plant 6 strawberry starts (which you can buy at any garden store) in the soil. Make certain to water your berry plants every day, keeping the soil damp but not soaking wet. Also make sure your berries get at least 6 hours of sunlight a day. Before you know it, you'll be gobbling strawberries you grew yourself—even if you live downtown!

What You'll Need

- large planting pot
- potting soil
- strawberry starts
- water

A Kitchen Garden

◆◇◆◇◆◇◆

Look in your kitchen to find all sorts of fun things to grow!

Nearly any ripe seed will grow into a new plant. Collect seeds from fruits such as lemons and other citrus fruits or grapes. Then fill some flowerpots with potting soil up to ½ inch from the top. Plant your seeds, and watch them grow. Here are some special instructions for each:

Citrus fruits: Don't allow the seeds to dry out at all. Plant them right away in a mix of 3 parts potting soil and 1 part sand. Keep them well watered—but not soggy. These plants like a lot of light.

Grapes: Grape seeds usually sprout easily. Keep them in a sunny window, and give the plant something to climb on.

Kiwi: Collect these tiny seeds with a

toothpick and place them on a moist paper towel. Roll up the towel, put it in a plastic bag, and place it in the refrigerator for 2 weeks. Kiwi seeds need a cold period before they sprout. Plant on top of moist potting soil and cover with plastic wrap until the plants sprout. Be sure to give the young plants something to climb on.

> ### What You'll Need
> - fruit seeds (lemons, oranges, kiwis, grapes)
> - potting soil
> - sand
> - flowerpots
> - toothpick
> - paper towels
> - plastic bag
> - plastic wrap

Grow a Pizza

◆◇◆◇◆◇◆

When you're hungry for pizza, you can get one without ordering out.

> ### What You'll Need
> - plants that grow pizza ingredients (tomatoes, green peppers, onions, herbs)
> - a garden plot or large pots

Of course, growing your own pizza takes a little longer than having it delivered, but it can be worth the wait. What veggies do you like on your pizza? Grow them from seeds or seedlings starting in the spring, and plan a home-grown pizza party sometime in the summer. In addition to tomatoes, green peppers, and other pizza veggies, you can grow herbs for your pizza. Basil and oregano are the most commonly used. You might also try chives, rosemary, or other herbs. They're all easy to grow in small pots or in a garden.

When your pizza garden is ready all you'll need is a pizza crust, some cheese, and a few hungry friends.

Shout About Sprouts

◆◆◆◆◆◆

It's easy and fun to grow tasty sprouts for salads and sandwiches.

What You'll Need
- alfalfa seeds
- measuring spoon
- quart jar
- water
- cheesecloth
- rubber band

Wash and dry the jar. Measure 2 teaspoons of alfalfa seeds into the jar. Fill the jar half-full of water. Cover the top with 3 layers of cheesecloth, holding the layers in place with a rubber band. Swirl the jar around to rinse all the seeds, and pour the water out through the cheesecloth.

Place the jar in a warm, dry place, like a cupboard. The seeds should begin to sprout in a day or so. Each day, take the jar out, add more water, swirl to rinse the seeds, and pour the water out through the cheesecloth. When the sprouts are about 2 inches long, place the jar in a sunny window for a few days to green up. Keep rinsing the sprouts every day. After the sprouts have greened, put them in the refrigerator.

You Are What We Eat

◆◆◆◆◆◆

Classify plants according to the part of the plant that people use for food.

Label a sheet of paper "ROOTS." Look through magazines for pictures of plants with roots that people use for food, and write the plant name on your paper. You might include radishes, carrots, and beets. What others can you find? Label another sheet of paper "LEAVES." Look for magazine pictures of plants to include on this sheet.

What You'll Need
- pen and paper
- old magazines
- scissors
- tape

Among them might be lettuce, spinach, and cabbage. What others can you find? Label a sheet of paper "SEEDS." Look for magazine pictures of plants to include on this sheet. You might include peas, beans, and nuts.

What others can you find? Label a sheet of paper "FRUITS." Look for magazine pictures of plants to include on this sheet. You might include pears, peaches, apples, and grapefruit. What others can you find? What other sheets might you label and include in your classification system?

Dried Fruit Treats

▷▶▷▶▷▶▷▶

Turn this summer's harvest into tasty winter treats.

What You'll Need
- fruit
- peeler
- knife
- cookie sheets
- oven
- nuts
- measuring cup and spoon
- glass jar
- meat grinder
- lemon juice
- shredded coconut
- plastic wrap

Caution: This project requires adult supervision.

Begin with some fresh, ripe fruit without bruises. With adult supervision, peel and slice larger fruits, removing seeds or pits. Slices should be about ¼ inch thick. Small berries can be dried whole, but bigger berries (such as strawberries) should be sliced. You can also buy bananas when they are inexpensive, slice them, and dry them.

To dry fruit: Spread the slices in a single layer on a cookie sheet. Put in an oven set to 150°F, and dry until most of the moisture is gone but the fruit is still soft. Since you aren't using preservatives, the fruit will be brown. Pack into a jar, and allow to sit a week or so before using. Eat your fruit as it is, or make fruit treats.

To make fruit treats: Measure out about 2 cups of dried fruit and 1 cup of nuts. Use a meat grinder to chop up the nuts and fruits finely. Moisten with about a tablespoon of lemon juice. Shape into small balls or logs. Roll in shredded coconut. Wrap each treat in plastic wrap. Pack into a pretty jar for a gift.

A Berry Nice Ink

Write a secret note using special ink made from fresh berries.

Wear a smock to protect your clothes from stains. Put a cup of ripe raspberries, blackberries, or blueberries into a strainer. Put the strainer over a large jar. Use the back of a spoon to crush the berries so their juice falls into the jar. Squeeze as much juice out of the berries as you can.

Add to the jar a teaspoon vinegar and a teaspoon salt, and stir until the salt is dissolved. Use your berry ink right away, because it will spoil quickly.

What You'll Need
- smock
- berries
- measuring cup and spoon
- strainer
- jar
- spoon
- vinegar
- salt
- paper

Rose-Petal Jam

Make this sweet, fragrant treat from the flower garden.

What You'll Need
- rose petals
- scale
- measuring cup and spoon
- water
- pan
- sugar
- lemon juice
- stove
- spoon
- cold saucer
- pot holder
- jam jars

Caution: This project requires adult supervision.

Gather some roses in the morning after the dew has dried. Try to pick all of one kind, or find scents that will blend well together. Pick off the petals and cut off the white ends.

For every half pound of rose petals, add 1 cup of water. With help from an adult, simmer 5 minutes on the stove to soften the petals. Add 1¼ cups sugar and 3 tablespoons lemon juice. Bring to a boil, then simmer for about 30 minutes until the mixture is thick. To test the jam, pour a few drops from a spoon onto a cold saucer and allow the jam to cool. If it seems jellylike, the jam is ready. Take the pan off of the stove and allow it to cool for 10 minutes.

Sterilize clean jam jars by pouring a half inch of boiling water into them. Allow it to steam a few minutes, then turn the jar upside down on a dish rack. Be sure to use a pot holder when handling hot jars! Now fill the hot jars with jam. Each half pound of rose petals will make about a pint of jam. Close the jars, and keep the jam in the refrigerator.

Make Berry Jam

◆▷◆▷◆▷◆

Jazz up your peanut butter with this tasty jam.

What You'll Need

- small bowl or plate
- several jars with lids
- 2 pounds of fresh berries that are just slightly underripe
- fresh lemon juice
- measuring spoon
- large pot
- stove
- wooden spoon
- granulated sugar

If wild berries grow where you live, you can pick them and make them into jam. Or get your berries at a pick-them-yourself farm or roadside stand. Here's how to make jam from strawberries, blackberries, raspberries, or blueberries:

First, put a small bowl or plate in the refrigerator to chill. Next, put the jars that will hold the jam into the dishwasher, and run the dishwasher through a full cycle, including hot dry. The jars should still be warm when you're ready to pour in the jam.

Put 2 pounds clean berries and 4 teaspoons fresh-squeezed lemon juice in a very large pot or kettle. (Jam will froth and expand while it's cooking, so make sure there's plenty of extra room in the pot.) The berries should be just a little underripe, because ripe berries will make runny jam.

Use a big wooden spoon to squash the berries a little so that some of the juice is squeezed out. With adult supervision, cook the berries over low heat, stirring them all the time. Let the berries come to a boil. (Turn up the heat a little if you need to.) As soon as they are boiling, lower the heat and simmer the berries for 5 minutes. Don't forget to keep stirring!

Add 1½ pounds sugar gradually until it is all dissolved. Then turn the heat all the way up to high and boil the jam for at least 5 minutes. (How long it takes depends on what kind of berries you have and how ripe they are.) The mixture will be foamy. Remember to keep stirring and to watch the jam closely so it doesn't boil over.

After about 5 minutes, test the jam to see if it is done. To do this, use the wooden spoon to place a few drops of jam onto the bowl that you have chilled. Put the bowl back in the fridge so the jam will cool. If the jam forms a "skin" that holds together when you touch it, it's ready. If not, cook the jam for another 5 minutes, then test it again.

When the jam is ready, pour it into the clean, warm jars. Seal the jars. When they're cool, store in the refrigerator.

Growing Herbs

◆▷◆▷◆▷◆

Food tastes extra-special when prepared with fresh herbs!

Fill some medium-sized flowerpots (about 4 to 6 inches) with potting soil. Water the soil completely, and let the pots drain. Sprinkle a few herb seeds on top, and press them into the soil. Large seeds, such as parsley, may have to be soaked for a few hours before planting to help them sprout. Cover the pots with plastic wrap, and set them in a warm place to sprout. Herb seeds may take 2 weeks to sprout.

Once the seedlings are up, set the pots in a sunny window. Remove the plastic wrap, and lay it loosely on top of the pots to help keep moisture in but allow air to circulate. Remove it completely when the plants have several true leaves. Water the plants when the soil feels a little dry. Let it dry out completely once or twice in the fall. Use a plant mister or spray bottle to mist the plants weekly.

What You'll Need
- flowerpots
- potting soil
- water
- herb seeds (basil, sage, mint, parsley, thyme, and marjoram)
- plastic wrap
- plant mister

Drying Your Herbs

◆▷◆▷◆▷◆

Hang your favorite herbs out to dry.

What You'll Need
- plant shears
- string
- clothespins
- airtight spice containers
- labels

Once you grow your herbs, transplant them to an outside garden, and watch them thrive, it's time for the harvest. The best time to harvest most herbs is just as they begin to bloom. Once you pick them, run a string across a dry, dark place just outside your back door or a window. Add a dozen or more clothespins across that line of string. Now

hang your favorite herbs roots up, top-leaf-down on that string. As the herbs dry and crumble, take them down and store them in labeled, airtight containers until you're ready to use them for cooking!

Candied Violets

◆◆◆◆◆◆◆

What's purple and sweet and looks great on a cake?

Caution: This project requires adult supervision.

Candied violets make a very special decoration for cakes, cupcakes, or frosted cookies.

    Pick some violet flowers from violets you have grown yourself or violets growing wild. (If you pick wild violets, be sure they haven't been sprayed with pesticides or chemical fertilizers. Also, be very sure that the flowers you're picking are violets. Ask an experienced adult to look at them. Not all pretty flowers are edible!) Lay the violet blossoms on a cookie sheet, and carefully paint them with egg white. Then sprinkle them with plenty of sugar. Bake them in the oven at 300°F for about 45 minutes. When cool, use your candied violets to decorate pastries.

What You'll Need
- violet blossoms
- cookie sheet
- egg white
- small paintbrush
- granulated sugar
- oven

Sunflower Cookies

◆◆◆◆◆◆◆

These yummy sunflower treats are great for all kinds of flower nuts!

What You'll Need
- oven
- 1 package (20 ounces) refrigerated peanut-butter cookie dough
- measuring cup
- all-purpose flour
- large bowl
- rolling pin
- wooden spoon
- cookie sheet
- knife
- chocolate frosting
- unsalted sunflower seeds
- decorations: yellow and green icing

Caution: This project requires adult supervision.

Preheat your oven to 375°F. Remove dough from wrapper according to package directions; place in a large bowl; add ⅓ cup flour. Mix dough and flour well with a wooden spoon.

    Divide dough into 8 equal sections; then, divide each section in half. Roll half a section of dough into a ball; flatten on cookie sheet to 2½-inch thickness. Roll other half into 5-inch long rope. Cut 2 inches from rope for stem. Cut remaining 3 inches into 10 equal sections; roll into small balls for petals. Repeat with remaining dough.

    Assemble your cookies, then bake 10 to 11 minutes or until lightly browned. Cool 4 minutes on cookie sheets. Remove to wire racks; cool completely.

    Spread chocolate frosting in the center of each cookie; sprinkle with ½ cup sunflower seeds. Decorate petals with yellow icing and decorate stem with green icing. Makes 8 cookies.

Blanched Nuts

◆◇◆◇◆◇◆

Blanching is a different and delicious way to prepare nuts.

Caution: This project requires adult supervision.

While this activity works best with almonds, you can try it with other nuts such as hazelnuts.

Crack the nuts, and remove them from their shells. Place the shelled nuts in a large steel or glass mixing bowl. Pour enough boiling water over the nuts to cover them and let them sit until the brown skins loosen. This will take about 10 minutes. Have an adult help you check the nuts. When the brown skins are loose enough, remove the nuts from the water. Let them cool slightly, then slip the skins off with your fingers and place the nuts in another bowl. If the water your nuts are soaking in cools off too much and the skins become hard to slip off, add more boiling water and wait for it to cool just enough to handle. This process of skinning nuts is called *blanching.*

For every pound of nuts you have, melt a tablespoon of butter in a small pan. Pour the butter over the nuts and toss until they are coated. Spread the nuts out on a cookie sheet, sprinkle with salt, and roast in a 325°F oven until golden, about 10 minutes.

What You'll Need
- almonds or hazelnuts
- nutcracker
- 2 mixing bowls
- boiling water
- cookie sheet
- butter
- salt
- pan
- oven

Apple Rings

◆◇◆◇◆◇◆

This garland made from dried apples is a nice decoration that will make your house smell wonderful.

What You'll Need
- apples
- apple corer
- knife
- twine

Caution: This project requires adult supervision.

Have an adult help you core and slice several red-skinned apples. String the apple slices on a piece of twine. Make your garland as long as you like. When you're done, hang the garland up in your kitchen. In dry weather, the apples will slowly dry out and fill the kitchen with a fresh scent.

Inside Insects (and Other Little Lives)

◆◆◆◆◆◆◆

Do spiders give you the creeps? Do bugs gross you out? Do worms make you squirm? Let the activities in this chapter help you overcome your fears of these tiny beasts, some of which are among the most useful animals on Earth. Where would we be if bees stopped pollinating the flowers on fruit trees and other crops? What would happen to our soil if worms suddenly disappeared? Try these activities to learn why these small animals are so important.

Up Close and Personal

◆◆◆◆◆◆◆

The best way to get to know a bug is to take a good look at it. Making models can help us learn more. The best way to get up close is to catch some safe bugs and look closely at the structures of these unique animals.

Clothespin Butterfly

◆◆◆◆◆◆

Pin down a fluttering friend.

What You'll Need
- white paper
- pencil
- ruler
- scissors
- colored paper
- sequins
- craft glue
- clothespin
- wiggle eyes
- chenille stems
- magnetic strip (optional)

Butterflies are amazing. They flutter in the wind like real-life fairies, colorfully floating on air. You can make your own butterflies with paper, glue, and clothespins—and a little imagination.

Draw a 5×5-inch bow-tie shape on a piece of white paper, making sure the shape narrows to about 1 inch at the center. Cut out the shape; this is your butterfly. Decorate the wings with bits of paper, sequins—anything colorful. Glue the butterfly to the bottom of a clothespin. Add wiggle eyes and chenille-stem antennae to your butterfly.

Now you've got a magical butterfly you need never set free! Add a magnetic strip to the other side of the clothespin, and your butterfly becomes a refrigerator magnet. It can hold notes, your report card, and coupons for mom!

Moth Feeder

◆◆◆◆◆◆

Attract some beautiful nighttime moths with this easy feeder.

Did you know that there are more types of moths in the world than butterflies? Some moths even have brilliantly colored hind wings to scare off enemies. Here's how to attract them: Mix a ½ cup fruit juice with a tablespoon sugar. Dip cotton balls in the

mixture. Tie a string to each cotton ball, and hang them near a window or an outdoor light. Watch to see what kind of moths you attract. If you are lucky, you might see large Luna moths feeding at your cotton-ball "feeder."

What You'll Need
- fruit juice
- sugar
- measuring cup and spoon
- cotton balls
- string

Don't be afraid that moths coming into the house will ruin your wool clothes. Adult moths feed on nectar. Only the larvae (caterpillars) of one species of moth feed on wool. Much of the damage we blame on moths is actually caused by Dermestid beetles.

Gotcha!

Have you seen movies in which someone digs a pit as a trap for a lion or tiger? You can make the same kind of trap— only yours will be for much smaller game.

Make your safe insect trap in a place where there's likely to be a lot of bug traffic. Under a bush is good. First get a glass jar. Dig a hole that is the same size as the jar, so you can set the jar down in the hole. The lip of the jar should be about even with the ground.

Now put 4 small, flat rocks around the lip of the jar, and set a board on the rocks. The board will keep rain and bug-eating animals out of the jar. The rocks allow enough room for bugs to fall into the trap. Leave your trap overnight. In the morning, see what you've caught. Can you identify them? After you've studied your bug collection, be sure to let them go and fill up the hole you dug.

Spider "Sniffing"

With this simple trick, you can track down spiders at night with a flashlight. Really!

Your friends may think you're crazy when you say you're going spider sniffing, but give them each a flashlight and invite them to come with you and they'll be amazed.

Hunt for spiders in open fields where there are lots of shrubs. Go out at night, and walk slowly through the area. Turn on the flashlight, and hold it directly in front of your nose so that you can look down it. Look in the shrubs and in tall tufts of grass. You'll be able to spot spiders by the bright, jewellike glitter of their eyes. The colors are breathtaking.

Once you've spotted a spider, get as close to it as you can. Try to figure out what kind it is. If it sits still long enough, make a drawing. Then return to the area in the daytime and notice what spiders you see. Find out if the same spiders come out in the day and the night.

Insect "Collection"

◆◆◆◆◆◆◆

*Hunt for insects and other small creatures when the weather is warm.
You can collect them harmlessly by letting them crawl onto your pencil.*

You can find insects and other small creatures in shrubs, trees, in the layer of leaves on the ground, and around lights at night. Capture a few insects in a jar, then gently transfer them to smaller jars or bug boxes.

What You'll Need
- small jar
- magnifying glass (or a "bug box" with a magnifying lens)
- notebook
- pencil

Use a magnifying glass to take a closer look at your bugs. Count the number of legs first. Insects have 6 legs. Spiders (and a spiderlike animal called a *Harvestman*) have 8 legs. Isopods (often called *pill bugs*) have even more. Look at the shape of the body.

Does it have a "waist" (the narrow area between the thorax and abdomen) as ants and hornets do? Does it have a wide shell as beetles and many true bugs often have? What about wings? Not all insects have wings. If yours does, look at the pattern of veins, which are often used to tell one species from another.

Carefully draw each of the features in your notebook as you observe. You may want to make separate drawings of the top and bottom views and close-up studies of wings, legs, eyes, or mouth parts. Let your bugs go as soon as you can. Then find more to add to your "collection."

Invent an Insect

◆◆◆◆◆◆◆

*What does a doodlebug look like? It's all in your imagination
when you create your own crazy bug critters!*

What You'll Need
- cardboard or foam egg carton
- scissors
- craft glue
- decorations

Cut 3 linked sections out of the egg carton to make an insect body. Now, add the insect's other parts: head, antennae, legs (6, of course), and so on, using uncooked pasta, straws, packing peanuts, buttons—anything you find around the house. What is your bug's name? Does it have a story?

A Creepy Crawly Game

◆◇◆◇◆◇◆

**Here's a fun game you can play with your friends.
The object is to be the first to make your own "Beetle."**

This is a game for 2 or more players. Each player needs a sheet of drawing paper and some markers. You will roll the dice to draw a beetle. Here's what you must roll to draw each part:

1 beetle's head
2 beetle's body
3 leg
4 leg
5 leg
6 leg
7 leg
8 leg
9 eye
10 eye
11 antenna
12 antenna

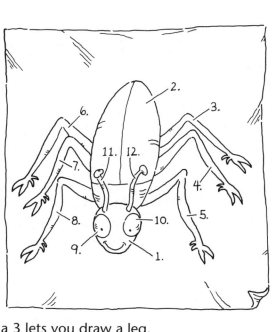

Roll both dice each time, but only draw one beetle part for each roll. Here are 2 examples to show you how it works:

1. Let's say you roll a 1 and a 2. You can draw either the beetle's head (1) or body (2), but not both. Or, you can draw a leg, because 1 plus 2 equals 3, and a 3 lets you draw a leg.

2. Let's say you roll a 5 and a 6. You can either draw one leg (because both 5 and 6 are for a leg), or you can add 5 plus 6 to make 11, and draw an antenna. If your beetle already has all 6 legs and 2 antennae, skip a turn.

Use different colors to make your beetle special. Whoever finishes his or her beetle first wins.

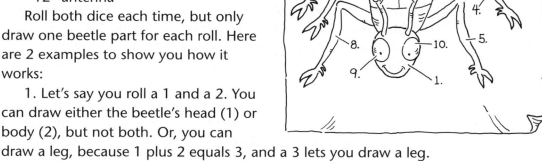

Creature Feature

⬥⬥⬥⬥⬥⬥

There are lots of interesting, creepy, crawly creatures!
Which is your favorite?

If you could be any kind of small creature, what would you be? An ant? A dragonfly? A spider? Check out some books from your library about your favorite small creatures. Then write your own story or poem about a day in the life of an insect, spider, or other small creature: Where does it live? How does it work? What does it eat? Be creative and have fun!

What You'll Need
- books or poems on small creatures
- paper
- pen

Patterned Butterflies

⬥⬥⬥⬥⬥⬥

These beautiful butterflies look like they're made
from stained glass! Study the patterns on real butterflies,
and see if you can re-create some of those patterns.

What You'll Need
- butterfly reference books
- large sheet of paper
- marker
- tissue paper in many colors
- waxed paper
- liquid starch
- paintbrushes
- scissors
- tape

Study some reference books about butterflies to decide which butterfly you want to create. Draw a butterfly outline on the large sheet of paper. Tear the colored tissue into 3-inch shapes. Place a sheet of waxed paper over the butterfly outline. Use the liquid starch to paint tissue pieces onto the waxed paper, filling in the outline of the butterfly with a mosaic of different colors. Add 1 or 2 more layers of tissue, and allow your butterfly to dry overnight. Cut out the butterfly, following the outline on the underlying paper. Slowly peel the tissue-paper butterfly off the waxed paper. Tape your butterfly to the window, and let the sun shine through!

Butterfly Net

▸▸▸▸▸▸▸

Make your own net to capture butterflies and other small creatures for examination and study.

What You'll Need

- plastic mesh bag (such as the bag onions come in)
- scissors
- chenille stems
- tape
- long cardboard tube
- drawing paper
- markers or crayons
- butterfly reference books from the library

Cut the clamp off the end of a mesh onion bag (leave the other end clamped). Next, make a rim for the net by fastening 2 chenille stems together by twisting the ends. Thread the stems in and out along the top edge of the mesh bag. When you're finished, secure the ends of the rim with tape.

For a handle, use a very stiff cardboard tube (like the kind found in a roll of wrapping paper). On one end of the tube, cut a slit on each side. Insert the rim of the net into the slits, and tape it in place.

Now it's time to go out and explore the natural world. When you find and capture a butterfly, examine it quickly and then draw it. After you let the butterfly free, you can look it up in a book to determine what type it is and learn more about it. Collect several pages of drawings, and make your own butterfly book.

You'll be a butterfly expert in no time!

Micro-Hike

◄◆◆◆◆◆►

Take a tiny hike into a tiny world and discover what lives there.

What You'll Need
- string
- scissors
- short stakes
- magnifying glasses
- pen and paper (optional)
- toothpicks (optional)

Measure out about 20 to 30 feet of string. Tie each end to a short stake, such as a tent stake. Take your string and stakes outdoors, and stretch the string across an area with some variation. You might run it across part of a lawn, under an arching shrub, and alongside a flower bed. The string doesn't have to be straight; it can run along the base of a fence or beside a pond or stream. Secure the line with more stakes if necessary. Make sure that you and every person who will be "hiking" with you has a magnifying glass.

Start at one end of the string on your hands and knees. Use your magnifying glass to examine everything under the string. Look for different kinds of plants, including moss between the grass blades or under a shrub. Look for fungi of different forms. Find animals such as insects, spiders, and worms.

Move slowly down the string, searching for every living thing you can find. You might end up taking a whole hour to hike! You never know what interesting things you'll find. When you're done, write down what you've seen or compare your observations with those of others who "hiked" with you. What interesting things did they see that you missed? When you're all done, use paper and toothpicks to make tiny signs to mark the most interesting discoveries. Then invite others to take your hike!

Hold on Tight!

If you were searching for a big nightcrawler to use as bait for fishing, you might have a hard time pulling it out of the ground. This creature's body has 150 rings, or segments, with 8 little bristles on each segment. So, it has 1,200 little feet to grab onto the dirt and to hold on tightly!

Behavior

◆▸◆▸◆▸◆▸◆

Wouldn't it be great if we could talk to bugs and have them tell us all about their lives? Unfortunately, bugs don't speak our language, so the best way to find out about their lives is to observe their behaviors. By piecing together behaviors, a bug's life is revealed.

Ant Farm

◆▸◆▸◆▸◆▸◆

Ants work together as a community to survive.

Many animals live in a type of community. In an ant colony, some ants gather food, some care for the young, and a queen ant lays the eggs. If you capture ants, you may find only worker ants and not have a complete colony. But whatever ants you find will be interesting to observe.

An ant farm may be a tall, narrow frame of plastic or wood and glass, with a very fine mesh opening that admits air but will not allow ants to escape. Many ant farms are about 12 inches wide, 10 inches tall, and 2 inches deep. Inside, they contain sand and dirt that fills about ⅔ of the space.

Once you have your ant farm and have purchased or captured ants, you can spend many hours in observation. The ants require little care. Put a piece of blotting paper or sponge in one side of the farm, and add water to this as needed. At the other side, add small amounts of different foods, and record the ants' reactions. You might try bread, syrup, sugar water, egg, cheese, lettuce, or a dead insect. Remove any food after 2 days if the ants are not eating it.

What You'll Need
- secure ant farm
- blotting paper or sponge
- ants
- water
- food scraps
- pen and paper

Moth Navigation

❖❖❖❖❖❖❖

Why do moths fly into candles and lamps?

What You'll Need
- street (with street lamp)

On a night when the moon is full, stand on a street where you can see the moon. Turn your head so that you see the moon over one shoulder. Now walk down the sidewalk and watch the moon over your shoulder. Note that you don't have to move your head as you go. The moon seems to follow you. (It doesn't really, of course.)

Now find a lit street lamp. Look over one shoulder at it. Walk and watch the lamp over the same shoulder. Feel like you're walking in circles? To keep the lamp over the same shoulder, you have to walk around it.

Moths use the moon to navigate. The moon doesn't move out of position if the moth flies in a straight line. But street lamps are confusing. If the moth flies in a straight line, it thinks the lamp's position has changed. As the moth continues, the lamp "moves" again. The moth flies in circles, moving closer and closer until it is trapped.

Warm Bugs, Cold Bugs

❖❖❖❖❖❖❖

How do insects react to changes in temperature outdoors?

If a sunny flower garden is in your yard or a nearby park, you can easily discover what effects temperature has on insects. Spring is a good time to do this, because the temperature can be warm one day and cold the next. On a warm day, check an outdoor thermometer to see the temperature. Take your notebook, and sit near a flower

What You'll Need
- outdoor thermometer
- notebook
- pencil

border where you can see insects. Choose a patch of flowers about a yard square. Every few minutes, count how many insects fly around in the flowers. On a cold day, repeat the experiment. Watch the same flowers and count the number of flying insects. On which day were the insects most active? How could this affect the plants if those insects pollinate some of the flowers?

Worm Observations

◆▷◆▷◆▷◆

Worms are interesting if you observe them up close.

Carefully dig up some worms in a garden, and put them in a plastic container filled with moist dirt. Prepare a worm-friendly surface for your observations. Lay 3 paper towels on top of each other on a waterproof surface, and moisten the paper until very wet. Set a worm on the wet paper towel.

On the outside: Look for a wide, thick band around the worm's middle. This is called a *clitellum*. It is closest to the head end. Look at the head with your magnifying glass. See if you can find the mouth, with its overhanging lip. Notice that the worm's body is made up of segments. Each segment has 2 pairs of special bristles (called *setae*). Wet your fingers and run them down the worm's body to feel the rough setae.

Getting around: Let the worm crawl on the paper towel. When it wants to move, it becomes long and thin. If you touch it, the worm contracts and becomes thicker. The worm has 2 layers of muscles; those running around the body squeeze the worm and make it thinner and longer. Those running end to end make the worm shorter and thicker.

Heartbeats: Find a light-colored worm. Wet its upper surface, and use your magnifying glass to observe the upper surface near the head. Look for the worm's 5 beating hearts.

Strong reactions: Dip a cotton swab in alcohol or nail-polish remover. Hold the swab close to the worm's head, but DON'T touch the worm with the strong chemical. What happens when the swab is near the head? Does the worm move? Hold the swab near the tail, then near the middle. Can the worm detect where the fumes are? How does it react?

Can Insects See Color?

◆▷◆▷◆▷◆▷

Set up an experiment to test the color vision of bees.

What You'll Need
- sugar
- water
- measuring cup
- pan
- stove
- colored paper
- scissors
- ruler
- clear plastic cups
- tape
- heavy washers
- notebook
- pen
- watch

Caution: This project requires adult supervision.

Make nectar to attract bees by mixing ¼ cup sugar with 1 cup water. With help, heat the mixture slowly in a pan on the stove until the sugar dissolves. Let the mix cool.

Then, cut squares of colored paper 4 inches on each side. Use red, orange, yellow, green, blue, deep blue, violet, white, black, and gray. Cut the bottoms off as many clear plastic cups as you have squares of paper to make shallow "dishes." Tape the squares to the top of an outdoor table. Set a cup bottom on each square. Add a washer to weigh it down, then pour in some of the sugar mixture you made.

Wait patiently for the bees. Which colors do they land on? To keep track, make a table in your notebook. Every 10 minutes, check the experiment. Count the number of bees on each color, and write that down next to each color. The next time you check, put your counts in another column of boxes.

At the end of the day, remove the dishes. The next day, do the experiment again. Do the bees visit their favorite square even if no food is on it?

Now confuse the bees. Next to the colored squares, set out gray squares similar in shade to the colored squares. If bees see color, they should land mostly on the colored squares. If they can't, they should visit the gray squares too.

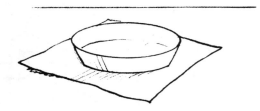

Be an Isopod Expert

Whether you call them pill bugs, sow bugs, or potato bugs, isopods are fun to observe.

What You'll Need
- jar
- garden gloves
- damp soil
- foil
- ruler
- scissors
- black paper
- small desk lamp
- sand
- water
- 2 teacups

Isopods go by many names. The round ones that roll up are pill bugs. Those with flat bodies that don't roll are sow bugs. Both may be called wood lice, roly-polies, or potato bugs. Isopods are not bugs or lice—they are crustaceans related to crabs, lobsters, and crayfish.

Take a jar and collect a dozen or so isopods. Wearing gloves, look under flowerpots, beneath big rocks, under logs or boards, and in compost heaps. Put some damp soil or rotted wood in the jar for the animals to hide in.

Now experiment to see what kind of environment isopods prefer. Test one factor at a time to decide which factors are most important to the animals. When you are done with the experiments, return the isopods to where you found them.

Make an isopod runway. Cut a large piece of foil, and fold it in half for strength. Fold it into a box shape measuring about 8 inches long, 2 inches wide, and 2 inches deep. Then try the following tests.

Light vs. dark: Cover ⅓ of the length of the runway with black paper. Shine a small desk lamp on the other end. Place the isopods in the middle, and see which end they settle down into.

Dry vs. wet: Put dry sand in one end of the runway. Put wet sand in the other end. Put the isopods in the middle and see which end they prefer.

Cold vs. warm: Fill one teacup with hot water and the other with cold. Set the runway on the teacups, one at each end. Put the isopods in the middle, and see which end they prefer.

Floral Advertising

◆▷◆▷◆▷◆

Flowers are like billboards. But what are they advertising for?

Look at the different flowers in a large garden. Can you guess what pollinates each kind? If you can't tell, here are some clues. Hummingbirds are attracted to bright red and orange flowers, especially tube-shape flowers that hang down. Hummingbird flowers offer lots of nectar but don't have much scent—birds don't have a keen sense of smell.

Bees are drawn toward blue and purple flowers that offer lots of nectar and pollen. They also are attracted to white and yellow flowers, even though they don't see yellow all that well. Why? Because these flowers may have ultraviolet markings that bees see but we can't! Bee flowers may be wide tubes or flat landing platforms.

Butterflies need nectar, and purple, yellow, or red butterfly-pollinated flowers offer plenty. Such flowers are either long tubes that a butterfly's tongue extends into or flat platforms where a butterfly can land and sip nectar. They are often scented; butterflies have an excellent sense of smell.

Moths fly at night, so moth-pollinated flowers are bright white (colors aren't visible at night). Moth-pollinated flowers are often tubular and usually richly scented. Many open only at night and all offer nectar.

Amazing But True!

◆▶◆▶◆▶◆

Create a quiz game using wacky facts about bugs!

What You'll Need
- books about insects
- index cards
- markers
- Internet access (optional)

Frogs and rabbits can jump, but have you ever heard of a "jumping bean"? This type of Mexican bean seed has a small caterpillar living inside of it. When the caterpillar moves, the bean has to move, too. This jumping can last for several months until the caterpillar finally emerges from the bean as a small moth!

Now, here's your challenge! Borrow some books on insects from the library or do some research on the Internet. What kind of amazing but true bug behavior can you uncover? Choose some of your favorite facts to use as clues in a buggy quiz game. Write each clue on a separate index card. Be sure to include the answers on the back. For example, a clue might be "This bug lives in a bean before it becomes a moth." The answer on the back of the card would read "Caterpillar in a Mexican bean seed." You can even draw a picture of the bug to go along with the answer. Quiz your friends and family members to see how much they know about insects. Then ask them to create some cards of their own, and quiz you.

Caution: Tunnel Ahead

◆▶◆▶◆▶◆

Turn beetle tunnels into works of art when you make these one-of-a-kind rubbings.

When you go for a walk in the woods, look for a fallen log. If the bark has fallen off or is loose, you may see tunnels made on the log by beetles. The tunnels make interesting designs. You can preserve the designs by making a rubbing of the tunnels. Put a sheet of paper over the tunnels, and rub over the paper lightly with a colored pencil or the side of a crayon. Can you trace the path the beetles made?

What You'll Need
- fallen log
- paper
- colored pencil or crayon

Snail Locomotion

◆◆◆◆◆◆◆

Slow-moving snails are great for studying animal motion.

If you find a snail in your garden and turn it over, you'll see that it uses a large, muscular foot to crawl along. But how does this boneless creature get around on one foot? To find out, get a pane of clear plastic or acrylic. Prop one end of the plastic on books or a brick. Position it so that you can look up through the glass from underneath. Now you have a transparent runway for watching snails.

Gather a few snails from the garden. Mark each snail with a small dot of acrylic paint on the shell. Use a different color for each snail to tell them apart. Wet the glass runway, and place a snail in the middle. Once it begins moving, watch from underneath. The foot can grip the glass while rippling muscles move it forward. The slime layer lubricates the surface so the foot doesn't get injured. Now put several marked snails in the middle of the glass. Line them up so they face the same direction. Draw their positions in your notebook at the start. Draw their new positions every 5 minutes. Do the snails move at random, or do you detect patterns in their motion?

If you don't have land snails in your area, try a similar experiment with aquarium snails. Mark some snails with paint, then put them back in the aquarium. Watch them crawl up the sides of the glass, and note whether they move in a pattern. If you let algae grow on the sides of the aquarium, snails will leave trails as they eat the algae.

What's the Buzz?

◆◆◆◆◆◆

What do bees and ballerinas have in common?
Learn about the amazing antics of the busy little bee.

You probably already know that each kind of animal has its own language. Birds have all different kinds of calls and songs. Dogs bark, cats meow, and dolphins "click." And what about bees? Well, they use their own kind of sign language.

What You'll Need
● field guide to insects or other reference book

They communicate with one another by dancing. For example, a honeybee that has found food tells other bees about it by flying in a circle if the food is nearby and in a figure eight if it's far away.

At the library, check out a field guide to insects or a book about bees. Learn more about how bees communicate. Spend some time watching bees. Finally, see if you can dance like a bee. Try imitating the different patterns you've read about.

Weather Bugs Bugs

◆◆◆◆◆◆

Does weather slow down your favorite pest?

What You'll Need
● clean, clear jar with a lid full of air holes
● pancake syrup
● fly
● refrigerator

Summer is definitely the season of the buzzing, bothersome fly. Hordes of them seem to invade your house and your yard as soon as the weather turns warm. But why do they vanish when the cool, short days return? Cold weather bugs some bugs. This activity will show you how much.

Capture an ordinary housefly in a clear plastic or glass jar (use a bit of pancake syrup to lure your fly into the jar). Be sure the jar has air holes so your experiment subject won't suffer as

you hold it captive. See how fast and active the fly is even while inside the jar? Now, place the jar inside your fridge for half an hour.

Retrieve the jar, and watch the fly now. Has the temporary chill slowed it down? Release the fly outside once your experiment is complete.

Let's Go Skating

If you're lucky, you've had the chance to go skating on a frozen pond in the winter. But you've never gone skating on a pond in summer—unless you're a water strider.

Caution: This project requires adult supervision.

Water striders are insects that live on the surface of a pond or river. They have long, skinny legs that allow them to spread their weight (which isn't much!) over the water's surface, so they don't sink. With an adult, go to a nearby pond or stream, and see if you can spot any water striders. Look in places where the water is calm. If you do, you'll understand why they're also called "pond skaters." Just don't try it yourself!

Making Tracks

You may not think that snails can do much. But with a little help from you, they can be artists!

What You'll Need
- garden snails
- black construction paper
- talcum powder

Have a snail hunt, and see if you can collect several snails. (Be gentle! Those shells may be fragile!) Snails are nocturnal, which means they like to sleep during the day and come out at night. You can usually find them sleeping in damp dark places, such as under a rock. One way to catch snails is to put a large clay flowerpot upside down, with one side propped up, overnight in a garden.

Once you've found some snails, put them on a sheet of black construction paper and let them do what they do—crawl around. You'll be able to see the slimy trail they leave. When the paper is crisscrossed with snail tracks, carefully put the snails back where you found them. Sprinkle talcum powder on their tracks. Tap off the excess talcum powder, and admire your snail art.

Light up the Night

◆▶◆▶◆▶◆

Fireflies have their own built-in flashlights.
Catch and observe some of these amazing creatures.

As you may know, fireflies are also called lightning bugs. Those tiny, blinking lights add beauty and mystery to a summer night. But, for fire-

What You'll Need
- fireflies
- glass jar

flies, they also serve a purpose. They're flashing a code to try to find a mate. In fact, different kinds of fireflies have different colors of lights and blink them at different speeds.

It's fun to catch and watch fireflies—as long as you're gentle and you let them go after a few minutes. You're likely to find fireflies hovering over tall grass on summer evenings. Hold up a big glass jar, and move toward the flashing lights. When you capture a firefly, put your hand over the top of the jar. Time the flashes to see how far apart they are. Then catch another firefly, and see if the flashes are timed the same—or different.

Worm Races

◆▶◆▶◆▶◆

Do worms prefer damp or dry places?
Find out in this race to the finish line!

What You'll Need
- books
- paper
- water
- worms

Put 2 books on a table, leaving a 1-inch gap between them. Lay a piece of paper over each book. Sprinkle water on one of the pieces of paper. Place a worm on the dry paper, and watch as it crosses the gap between the books to get to the moist paper. Put several worms onto the dry paper. Watch to see which one crosses over to the other side first.

Frozen Cocoons

◆▶◆▶◆▶◆

Cocoons from certain kinds of moths can survive freezing temperatures.

At the right time of year in your area, go out and gather 4 moth cocoons. Try to find cocoons that look the same and are from the same kind of moth.

Prepare 5 jars (1 small jar and 4 large jars) by putting a few holes in each lid for ventilation. In the 4 large jars, add a

branch with leaves from a plant that was growing near where you found the cocoons. Label 2 jars "FROZEN" and 2 jars "NOT FROZEN."

Put 2 cocoons in the small jar in your freezer. Put each of the other 2 cocoons in a large jar labeled "NOT FROZEN." After 6 hours, move the cocoons from the freezer into the 2 jars labeled "FROZEN." Store all 4 jars in a dark place.

Once in a while, sprinkle the cocoons with just a few drops of water. Check the jars regularly. How many moths hatch? Are these moths able to survive freezing temperatures? Be sure to release any moths that hatch.

Jumping Contest

◆▶◆▶◆▶◆

Some grasshoppers are better jumpers than others.

Catch several grasshoppers, and keep them in a large jar with holes poked in the lid. Place a large piece of paper on a flat surface outdoors. Put a grasshopper at the end of the paper. When it jumps, ask a friend to mark the landing spot. Measure the distance that it jumped. If possible, catch the grasshopper, and let it jump again.

Take the average of its jumps. Repeat this with all of your grasshoppers. Did you find one that was an exceptional jumper? Be sure to return the grasshoppers to where you found them.

Jumpin' Jiminy!

Most insects don't like cold weather, but snow fleas love it!

Have you ever been out on a winter day and seen what looked like pepper sprinkled on the snow? Have you seen that pepper start to jump up and down? If so, you've seen snow fleas.

The good news is, snow fleas aren't really fleas. But it's easy to see how they got their name, since they look like tiny fleas when they bounce around in the snow. Snow fleas are also called springtails, and that's an even better name for them. You see, they have a taillike feature that works like a pogo stick. You might say that springtails have a built-in ejection seat!

If you've never seen snow fleas, look for them under trees on sunny winter days. Just search for what looks like specks of pepper that are jumping up and down!

Why do you suppose snow fleas act that way? Make a list of other creatures that jump up and down. Although these creatures share the same behavior, they may jump up and down for different reasons.

Look up the creatures on your list in a reference book. Then make a chart of the information you find. Remember to include the type of creature, the origin, and the size, as well as the reasons behind the jumping behavior. You may even want to draw pictures to go along with your chart.

Food

All bugs eat. Some things they eat seem gross to humans. What do you think the dung beetle eats? Here is a hint: Other scientific terms for dung are scat and feces. Yech! Other things bugs eat seem pure and clean, such as a butterfly sipping the nectar from a flower.

Hungry Ants

❖❖❖❖❖❖❖

What kinds of food do our small friends like?

Find an anthill somewhere around your house, either on a sidewalk or a patch of dirt. Make sure it's in use by looking for signs of activity. Once you've found an active anthill, plan a test to find out what different types of foods the ants enjoy eating.

Spread some honey on a couple of leaves or blades of grass, lay out some small bread crumbs, spread out a little sugar, tear up lettuce into tiny pieces, and spoon out a bit of tuna fish. Make sure the different foods are at least an inch apart and that they're an equal distance from the ant colony. Come back a few minutes after you've put the food out to see what the ants are taking and what they're leaving. What do the foods the ants take have in common? What about the foods they don't want?

Worm Food

❖❖❖❖❖❖❖

Have you ever tried feeding worms?

Pick a spot on a lawn with thick, green grass and soft soil. Worms will be active in this area. When the lawn has been mowed and watered and the grass is short, lay out some fallen leaves. Cover the leaves with netting, and use tent stakes to hold the netting in place. (This will keep the leaves from blowing away.) In your notebook, sketch the pattern of leaves exactly as you see them. Label this picture "Start."

Check the netting the next day. Have any leaves disappeared? Draw what you see, and label the picture "Day 1." Continue checking the netting each day to see if more leaves disappear. Make a new drawing each day. Worms like to grab leaves and pull them down in their burrows to munch on later. You probably won't see all the leaves disappear, but worms active in the spot you choose will probably take away some of them.

Honeybee Cookies

◆◆◆◆◆◆◆

*Take a break from your insect exploring to bake these cookies—
the perfect treat for a buzzzy day!*

What You'll Need

- electric mixer
- 2 medium bowls
- measuring cup and spoon
- shortening
- sugar
- honey
- egg
- vanilla
- all-purpose flour
- cornmeal
- baking powder
- salt
- plastic wrap
- oven
- cookie sheets
- cooling racks
- decorations: yellow and black icing
- gummy fruit

Caution: This project requires adult supervision.

In a medium bowl, use an electric mixer to beat ¾ cup shortening, ½ cup sugar, and ¼ cup honey at medium speed until fluffy. Add 1 egg and ½ teaspoon vanilla; mix until well blended.

Combine 2 cups flour, ½ cup cornmeal, 1 teaspoon baking powder, and ½ teaspoon salt in medium bowl. Add to shortening mixture, mix at low speed until well blended.

Cover with plastic wrap; refrigerate several hours or overnight.

Preheat oven to 375°F. Divide dough into 24 equal sections. Shape each section into oval-shaped ball. Place 2 inches apart on ungreased cookie sheets.

Bake 10 to 12 minutes or until lightly browned. Cool 2 minutes on cookie sheets. Remove to cooling racks; cool completely. Decorate with icings and gummy fruit to create honeybees. Makes 2 dozen cookies.

Toadville

◆◆◆◆◆◆◆

*You know that toads don't REALLY give us warts.
Did you know they eat lots of insect pests, too?*

Why not invite those little croakers to move in by creating toad habitats? Use a broken pot or bowl turned with the curved side up as a toad shelter. Line the ground beneath the pot with moist mosses and leaves. Make sure you put the pots near an area sure to be watered. Then wait for the toads. They'll eat lots of bugs and give you plenty to look at.

What You'll Need

- broken ceramic flowerpot or bowl
- mosses and soft leaves

Beetle Trap

◆◆◆◆◆◆◆

Some creatures consume parts of dead animals.

What You'll Need
- shovel
- coffee can
- food for bait
- rocks

There are thousands and thousands of different kinds of beetles that live all over the world. Many of them are scavengers that move about at night looking for dead animals to consume. You might be able to trap one of these beetles, take a close look at it, and release it again.

With permission from your parent, dig a hole somewhere in your yard deep enough so that you can put a coffee can into the hole with its rim level with the ground. Put some food with a strong odor, such as cheese or tuna, in the can. Place the can in the hole. Put a small rock on the ground on either side of the hole, and then lay a large, flat rock over the hole, resting on the small rocks. This "lid" will prevent someone from stepping in the hole, and it will also keep out rain.

Leave your trap in place overnight. Check it the next morning to see if you have caught a beetle. You might need to wait several nights or try different spots in your yard. Be sure to fill in any holes you dig and to release any beetles that you catch!

Butterfly Puddles

◆◆◆◆◆◆◆

Give butterflies a helping hand by offering them a drink.

Butterflies cannot sip water from ponds or other bodies of water. The surface tension of the water is too strong for their delicate wings. These insects must drink water from nectar and other moist substances. Male butterflies often "puddle" in the summertime at muddy spots which provide butterflies with the water and minerals they need.

What You'll Need
- flat pan (such as a pie pan)
- garden soil
- water

You can provide a mud puddle for butterflies to gather in. Fill an old pie pan or other shallow pan nearly to the rim with plain dirt, which is rich in minerals. Add water to make soupy mud. Set your homemade mud puddle out where lots of flowers attract butterflies. Add enough water each day to keep the mud very wet. Watch the puddle over several days. You may see butterflies landing on the mud for a drink.

Habitats

◆▶◆▶◆▶◆

The place an animal lives is called its *habitat.* Organisms from different habitats often have different characteristics. For example, an organism that lives in the desert has more adaptations for conserving water than a rain forest dweller. Studying how an organism meets its needs in its habitat is an important part of ecology.

 # Lawn Census

◆▶◆▶◆▶◆

How do lawn plants and animals adapt to survive?

Before your lawn is about to be mowed, investigate what lives there. Find out what kind of grass should grow there. Look for grass of a different color or with larger or smaller blades. Find different kinds of weeds. You may not have names for all the plants, but you can describe and draw them in your notebook.

What You'll Need
- notebook
- pencil
- magnifying glass

Then get down on your hands and knees and look for animal life. Use your magnifying glass to discover beetles, spiders, worms, grubs, and other lawn animals. Write down what you see.

The morning after the lawn is mowed, do a second survey. Are the same weeds still alive? Is it the way they grow that helps them survive? Some weeds creep between grass blades, while some form flat, saucerlike rosettes of leaves that smother the grass and stay away from mower blades. Hunt for lawn animals again. How do they avoid the mower?

Mini-Sanctuary

◆◆◆◆◆◆

Create homes for the smallest wildlife in your yard!

Get permission to use a sheltered corner of the yard. Don't clear away old sticks and weeds, which give shelter and food to the creatures you want to protect. Place broken clay pots upside down in the shade for snails and toads. Make a small rock pile in the sun for flying insects and small reptiles. Prop up a brick with small flat rocks for insects to inhabit. Set out old wood as homes for beetles and ants.

   Many weeds serve as food for butterflies and rodents, but pull big vines like blackberries or large, aggressive shrubs that could take over the space. Once you're done, draw a sign reading, "Mini-wildlife refuge. Come and enjoy!" That way, visitors won't clean up the "mess"!

Snail Shelters

◆◆◆◆◆◆

Can snails find their way home?

If you have snails in your garden, try this experiment. Soak an unglazed clay flowerpot in water and put it upside down in the garden—preferably in thick foliage where snails may be present. Prop one side up with a small rock so that snails can get inside. Leave overnight. Check the pot the next day to see if snails are inside. They like cool, moist, dark hiding places.

   If the pot has 6 or more snails, mark each with a small dot of the acrylic paint on the shell. Look in the pot the next day. How many marked snails returned? Are there new ones?

A Sticky Situation

Are your spider senses tingling? Get close to a spider's web.

What You'll Need
- spiderweb
- bottle of hair spray
- black construction paper
- scissors

It's amazing how an itsy-bitsy spider builds its fancy web. It's even more incredible to see the finished product up close. Find a spiderweb outside that doesn't have a spider in it. Then spray the web lightly— and carefully—with hair spray. (And don't worry. Spiders build webs quickly, so it isn't a big deal to borrow this spider's home.) You want the web to be stiff, so you might have to spray 3 or 4 times.

Now get the construction paper ready behind the web. Carefully cut the strands holding the web to its supports. Catch the web with the construction paper as it comes loose. When the web is on the paper, give it another shot of hair spray so that it sticks to the page. Now, have a look at the way the web is made. It's quite a buggy creation!

Dirt Cups

If worms live in dirt, where do gummy worms live? Make a model of a worm's home in the soil—a model that's good enough to eat!

Put 2 or 3 gummy worms on the bottom of a plastic cup. Cover "worms" with a scoop of your favorite flavor of ice cream. Top with crushed cookies and chocolate syrup to make the cup look like a pot of soil. Then feel free to decorate with additional gummy worms or plastic flowers.

What You'll Need
- plastic cup
- gummy worms
- ice cream
- 4 chocolate sandwich cookies, crushed
- chocolate syrup
- plastic flowers (optional)

The Underside of Nature

◆◆◆◆◆◆

*There's a whole side of nature that no one ever sees—
the underside! See what lives under a rock.*

Take a walk in a wooded area. When you come across a big rock, turn it over. You'll be amazed at the busy world that's under there. Check out all the creatures that live under the rock.

Do you recognize any of them? You might find beetles, worms, or centipedes. You might even find an entire ant colony hidden from sight! Many types of creatures will make their home under a rock during the day and come out at night, when they are protected by darkness. After your visit, be sure to put the rock back exactly as it was, so life on the underside can get back to normal.

Find the Hiding Place

◆◆◆◆◆◆

*If you've ever looked closely at small plants and trees,
you may have noticed bumps on their leaves or stems. Those bumps—
called **galls**—are made by tiny insects.*

What You'll Need
- galls
- glass jar

If the gall contains holes, it tells you that the bugs "holed up" there have left. A gall that doesn't have holes is still hiding some insects. Go for a walk and look for galls on plants and trees. Oak trees are a favorite hiding place of gall-making insects. If you find some galls without holes, pick the part of the plant with the gall (be sure to get permission first). Put it in a glass jar and cover the jar loosely, so air can get in. Keep an eye on the gall. If you're lucky you might see tiny bugs coming out of hiding. After they do, take the jar outside and gently put its contents on the ground.

It's Not Just Dirt

There's more to dirt than just dirt. Discover what's in the soil.

What You'll Need
- pie pan
- garden soil
- water

Fill a pie pan with soil collected from an outdoor garden. Bring the pie pan indoors, and place it where it gets sunlight. Keep the pie pan away from open windows, so nothing gets into the pan from outside. Water the soil to keep it moist. Observe the soil each day. Do you see any earthworms or tiny insects? Is anything sprouting or growing? When you're finished, put the soil and all its creatures back in the garden.

Butterfly House

Give migrating and hibernating butterflies a place to live.

What You'll Need
- hand saw
- pine lumber (6″×½″×7′)
- scrap of pine (8″ wide)
- ruler
- hammer
- nails
- pieces of tree bark or floral moss

Caution: This project requires adult supervision.

When butterflies migrate they need to find shelter from bad weather. Usually they seek shelter in cracks of trees or buildings. Some butterflies hibernate in the winter and need shelter to protect them from winter cold. You can build a butterfly house to help migrating and hibernating butterflies. First, cut pine boards to the following dimensions:

Two sides: 6″×18″. Cut the top at an angle so that one side is 18 inches long and the other side is 17 inches long. **One back:** 4½″×18″. **One front:** 4½″×17″. **One bottom:** 4½″×6″. **One top:** 7″×7″.

Next, cut three 12-inch long slits in the front. Make the slits an inch wide, with one several inches higher than the others. (See illustration.) Nail the bark or moss to the back piece to give the butterflies something to cling to.

Lay the back down, bark-side up, and stand one of the side pieces up against it with the longer sides in back. Hold and nail in place. Do the same with the other side. Put the front in between the 2 side pieces and nail in place. Nail on the bottom and the top. Mount the house on a post in the shade.

Soil Wildlife

Discover a community of creatures living under the soil!

What You'll Need
- trowel
- shallow dish
- magnifying glass
- notebook
- pencil or pen

Go outside with a trowel, and dig around under large shrubs where leaves have fallen. Brush aside the top layer, and dig up some of the partially decayed leaves and the soil underneath them. Spread your sample out in a shallow dish, and observe it with a magnifying glass. Record and draw the organisms you see, such as:

Earthworms: Easy to recognize by their segmented bodies.

Beetles: These insects have 6 legs and a hard, shiny look. They may be black, metallic green, gold, or blue.

Grubs: These larvae of beetles and flies are wormlike but thick-bodied with many stumpy legs.

Springtails: These tiny, pale, wingless insects, usually white or pale gray, have a special structure on their abdomens that they use to spring high into the air.

Spiders: Unlike insects, spiders have 8 legs. Not all spiders weave webs. Some live and hunt near the ground.

Mites: These have 8 legs, like spiders, but are round-bodied.

Centipedes: Centipedes have one pair of legs per segment. They can bite, since they are predators.

Millipedes: They resemble centipedes, but their legs are shorter, and they have 2 pairs of legs per segment. Millipedes do not bite.

Beetles, earthworms, springtails, and millipedes feed on dead plant material. By breaking leaves into tiny pieces, they make it easy for bacteria and fungi to complete the decay process. Centipedes and spiders are predators.

Life Cycles

◆▷◆▷◆▷◆

Organisms grow. Some organisms reproduce or have offspring. All organisms die, and their atoms recycle back into the environment. The offspring grow, some reproduce, and they die. The torch of life flows through generations. The materials of life move through different living things.

 ## Explore a Rotting Log!

◆▷◆▷◆▷◆

Rotting logs are home to some fascinating creatures.

What You'll Need
- decaying log
- garden gloves
- magnifying glass
- clear plastic jar
- notebook
- pencil

Next time you are exploring a forest or woodland, look for a decaying log. When you find a soft one, spend time discovering the organisms that live there. Put on your garden gloves and get down on your hands and knees. Using your magnifying glass for a better look at the surface, look to see what lives there. You may find green plants, such as moss or small seedlings. You may find insects, such as beetles or termites. There may be other small creatures, such as wood lice and spiders.

If you want a closer look at a small creature, catch it in the jar and observe it. (Let it go when you are done.) Record your discoveries in your notebook. If you don't know the name of something you've found, draw its picture. If the wood is soft, break off a piece to see what kinds of creatures live inside. Termites, ants, and wood-boring beetles often live in logs. Replace the wood when you are done. Record what you find in your notebook.

Now turn the log over and see what lives underneath. The wood may be so rotten that it resembles soil. This is nature's way of recycling. The nutrients that made up the tree's tissue are being returned to the soil for other plants to use. Lots of organisms here are associated with decay, such as millipedes that eat dead plant material, insects that also feed on the dead wood, and earthworms.

Caddisfly Houses

❖❖❖❖❖❖

Watch caddisfly nymphs build their cases from material around them.

What You'll Need
- caddisfly nymphs
- plastic cups
- sand
- dead leaves
- dry grass
- stopwatch

Mothlike caddisflies lay their eggs in ponds, marshes, or streams. The nymphs that hatch are aquatic. To protect themselves, they build cases from the materials around them. The nymphs, camouflaged in their cases, can extend their bodies to feed. One kind of caddisfly builds a case resembling a miniature pinecone, bristling with bits of dead leaves. Another builds a long, narrow, cone-shaped case.

Find caddisfly nymphs in clear, shallow water at ponds and streams. You may be able to catch them with your hands. You can also catch them with a dip net (see Pond Dipping, page 554). When you've collected several nymphs, fill some plastic cups with pond water, one for each nymph. Gently remove the nymphs from their cases and put them in the plastic cups. In one cup, break apart the nymph's old case and see if the nymph will use it. In another, try broken-up dead leaves. In another, try sand, dry grass, or anything else "natural." Time the nymphs to see how long it takes them to build cases.

Before letting the nymphs go, offer them the same material their original cases were built from and let them make new protective cases.

Wiggly Workers

❖❖❖❖❖❖

Earthworms have been called "a gardener's best friend." Find out why.

What You'll Need
- wide-mouthed jar
- garden soil
- peat
- sand
- water
- earthworms
- dead leaves
- paper bag

Find a large wide-mouthed jar. Put in a layer of soil, a layer of peat, and a layer of sand. Water the soil well. Now dig some worms from a garden and put them in your wormery. Don't bury the worms! Just cover them with some dead leaves. Set a paper bag over the top of the jar. This will keep out light but let in oxygen. Put the jar in a cool place out of direct sunlight.

Check the jar frequently. Can you guess why gardeners like earthworms? They digest soil through their bodies, loosening it and mixing nutrients. Plants grow better in looser soil with lots of oxygen. Be sure to put the worms back once you've seen them work.

Butterfly Fun

❖❖❖❖❖❖❖

Why should you crawl when you can fly?

Make a caterpillar hatchery in a large glass jar or aquarium. Put a layer of potting soil in the bottom of the container. Put a stick in the soil, and lean the top of the stick against the side of the container. You're now ready to find a caterpillar. You'll find them feeding on leaves of plants like cabbages. When you find one, pay attention to what kind of leaves it is eating. (Different caterpillars eat different plants.) Gently pick up the caterpillar and plenty of the leaves, and put them in the hatchery. Put a lid or cover on the hatchery, but make sure air can get in.

Be sure to check on your caterpillar every day. Caterpillars have huge appetites! In its new home, the caterpillar will keep munching leaves (make sure it always has some) until it begins making a cocoon (also called a *chrysalis*). The caterpillar will come out of its cocoon as a butterfly. You won't recognize it! When that happens, take the hatchery outside and let the new creature fly away.

Decomposers

❖❖❖❖❖❖❖

Is it the end or just the beginning?

In nature, everything happens in cycles. Water moves in a cycle from rivers to oceans to clouds, back to Earth in the form of rain, which runs back into rivers, and so on. In this activity, you'll see part of the life cycle of plants. Decomposition is the last

stage of a plant's life cycle. But, in a way, it's also the first stage. That's how cycles work.

Take a few bites out of an apple. Put the apple outdoors in a damp area where animals won't bother it. Leave the apple outside overnight.

The next day, go see the apple. Do you see any decomposers at work? Decomposers are living things that break down the apple and turn it back into soil. Decomposers like flies and worms may be gross, but they're important!

The apple is made of elements such as carbon, hydrogen, and oxygen. It's no coincidence that soil is made of the same elements. Decomposers turn the apple back into soil, so new apples can grow. In fact, if no one disturbs your apple, and if the weather is right, the seeds in that apple just might sprout into new apple trees, putting down roots in soil that was once your apple. It's just one of nature's many cycles.

Break Down

❖❖❖❖❖❖❖

Microorganisms cause dead organic matter to decay.

Gather leaves and grass clippings, and pack them into a large clear jar. Add a few drops of water, and loosely screw the cap onto the jar. Be sure not to screw the cap tightly because gases will be given off that could break a tightly sealed jar.

Store the jar in a dark, warm place. Check on it every few days, and observe any changes. Write down your observations, along with the date.

What You'll Need
- glass jar with a lid
- fresh leaves and grass cuttings
- water
- pen and paper

What happened? Microorganisms that feed on dead matter were able to grow in your jar. In feeding on the grass and leaves, they broke it down into a dark brown mixture that would, in the wild, become a part of the soil.

Mealworms

❖❖❖❖❖❖❖

The complete life cycle of a mealworm takes 6 months.

What You'll Need
- mealworms
- large container
- small container
- ruler
- oatmeal or bran
- apple or potato
- mesh cloth
- rubber bands
- cardboard

Mealworms are the larval stage of the darkling beetle. They go through a complete life cycle in 6 months. To raise mealworms, you must meet their needs for food, water, shelter, air, and community.

Buy several dozen mealworms from a pet store or a biological supply house. Get a glass or plastic container about 10 inches across and at least 4 inches deep that they will use for shelter. Put 2 inches of oatmeal or wheat bran in the bottom of the container for food. Put an apple or potato in the container; the mealworms will use this as a source of water. Cover the container with a mesh cloth held in place by a rubber band. Lay a loose piece of cardboard on top to help keep in moisture.

The mealworms will develop into pupae. The pupae should be moved into another glass or plastic container with an inch of food in the bottom and covered with mesh cloth until they hatch into beetles. (If you leave the pupae in the large container, they may be eaten.) When the pupae hatch, return the beetles to the large container. The adult beetles will lay small eggs that will hatch into mealworms.

OUR FUN, FEATHERED FRIENDS

❖▷▷▷▷▷❖

Few animals are easier to watch than birds. Maybe that's why feeding backyard birds is so popular. Songbirds are protected by federal law, yet many birds still have problems surviving because people shoot them, cats hunt them, and construction and development destroy their nesting areas. The activities in this chapter will help you learn about birds and give you ideas about how you can help them survive.

Individual Differences

❖▷▷▷▷▷❖

Their feathers, beaks, wings, and feet make them obvious—they are birds. Yet, if you compare bird species you will find lots of differences. They may eat different foods, such as seeds, insects, or fish. They may move in different ways, such as walking, flying, or swimming.

Is Bigger Faster?

<><><><><>

How do birds take off for flight?

What You'll Need
- stopwatch
- notebook
- pencil or pen

Are bigger birds faster birds? Are smaller birds in more danger? Are the answers as obvious as they seem? Study your neighborhood birds to find out. Sit quietly somewhere that birds like to search for food, water, and shelter. Time exactly how long it takes each species to go from ground to treetop. Keep careful notes. You may find that while bigger birds have stronger wings, they also have more weight to launch into flight. You may find that smaller birds beat their wings faster but rise no faster than their bigger, more powerful friends. You may discover that it depends entirely on the individual bird. But whatever you observe, you're sure to find the study is a real "tweet."

Look at that Beak!

<><><><><>

And those feet, too! Learn how birds use their beaks and feet to help them survive in the wild.

One of the easiest ways to identify different birds is by looking at their beaks. Some have sharp beaks for pecking. Others have long, wide, flat, or curved beaks. How does each bird's beak help it get food? (A pelican's beak, for example, expands to hold the fish it catches.) Now think about birds' feet. Some have powerful feet with claws, called *talons.*

What You'll Need
- field guide to birds
- poster board
- markers

Other feet, like a duck's webbed feet, are designed to help birds swim. How does a bird's feet help it move around in its habitat?

Look through a field guide to birds and pay special attention to birds' beaks and feet. Then make a chart showing the beaks and feet of different birds and telling how they help the birds survive.

Sapsuckers and Woodpeckers

◆▸▸▸▸▸▸

Follow the clues to find out what's been in your trees!

Sapsuckers and woodpeckers have chisellike beaks that they use to drill holes in trees. Both feed along tree trunks but eat different kinds of foods. Woodpeckers eat insects and drill for them with their beaks. Sapsuckers punch holes in trees, then lick up the sweet sap with their long tongues. Look around your yard or a park for trees with small holes in them. Notice the pattern of the holes.

Woodpeckers eat insects wherever they find them, leaving holes randomly scattered around the tree. Sapsuckers feed more systematically. They will patiently drill a straight line of holes across the tree trunk. By the time the bird finishes drilling the last hole, the first is full of sap. The bird then drinks the sap from each hole, first to last, in turn. When the holes stop dripping sap, the sapsucker drills some more. If you see horizontal rows of holes along a tree trunk, you know the sapsuckers have been at work. If you like, hide behind a bush or a tree near the tree where woodpeckers or sapsuckers have been working. If you're patient enough, the birds might return and you can watch them feed.

What a Beak!

The South American swordbill is a bird whose bill is as long as its head and body put together! This bird lives in the South American rain forest, and it needs a long beak to gather food—the nectar from the long, tube-shape flowers of the passiflora plant. The bird's bill can be as long as 4 full inches.

Owl Eyes

◆◆◆◆◆◆◆

Can an owl really see better than you at night?
We'll shed some light on night vision.

When it's almost dark, go outside and try your best to see. (Go to an area where there are no outdoor lights.) Pay attention to how much you can see: The outline of a tree or house? A cat moving? Now, look through binoculars. Can you see more?

You can see better through binoculars because they take in more light than your eyes can. But even with binoculars, you're no match for an owl. Owls' eyes take in about 100 times more light than yours, so they can see quite well at night.

Did You Call Me?

◆◆◆◆◆◆◆

Learn to identify and imitate birdcalls.

Go to an area where there are lots of birds, and eavesdrop on their conversations. Listen and look at the same time, and begin to learn which sounds are made by which birds. If you know how, you can actually get birds to come close to you so

you can watch and listen to them. One way is to buy a birdcall at a nature store. Or, try this method: Open your lips but keep your teeth together. Put your tongue lightly against the back of your teeth, and blow out. Stand very still while you do this, so the birds notice the sound but don't notice you.

Listen to birds and try to imitate their sounds. The better your imitation is, the more interested the birds will be. Pay close attention to what the birds look like, so you can try to find them later in a field guide.

Some of the easiest birds to imitate are the whippoorwill, the bobwhite, and the chickadee. Owls are fun to imitate, too, though it's not always as simple as "who?" or "hoot!" If you hear a deep, loud hoot, you're probably hearing a great horned owl, which lives all over North America. If you hear 8 hoots in a row, you probably are hearing the barred owl. (It's nicknamed the "Eight Hooter.") If you hear a loud noise that sounds like a monkey, but you don't live in the jungle, you're probably hearing another type of call of the barred owl.

Curious as a Bird?

*Learn about the interesting habits and traits of birds.
Then create your own bird book.*

What You'll Need
- reference book about birds
- index cards
- markers
- pen
- stapler

From the tiny hummingbird to the giant ostrich, there are a lot of different kinds of birds in the world. And they all have different habitats. Seagulls and pelicans live along water shores. Penguins live in cold, arctic regions. You can find many strange and colorful types of birds (like the toucan) in rain forests and tropical islands. Even large cities can be home to sparrows, pigeons, doves, and many other varieties of birds. What kind of birds live near you?

Get some books on birds out of the library, study them, and pick out your favorite variety of bird. Afterward, write a minibook on a day in the life of this bird.

Use an index card for each page of your book. Start by drawing a cover on the first index card (put your name as the author). Then write an interesting fact about the bird on each card. Don't forget to leave room for illustrations; include pictures of the bird's shape, nest, and habitat. What does your bird eat? Is it most active during the day or at night? Where does it live? When all of your pages are done, staple them together.

Feathers

If you find a feather you have no doubt that it came from a bird. Feathers have many functions. They keep birds warm, and they keep them dry. Feathers help birds fly. In many species, attractive feathers help the male birds find mates.

Cousin Dino

◆◆◆◆◆◆◆◆

Find modern-day dinosaurs in feathers.

More and more dinosaur scientists (called *paleontologists*) believe birds could be modern dinosaurs. Do you agree? Make a few comparisons of your own to find out. How are birds and dinosaurs different? How are they alike?

What You'll Need
- notebook paper
- pencil

Go outside and look closely at the feet of your local birds. How many claws are on their feet? What are the scales like on the skin of those feet? What kind of tracks do they leave behind as they walk? What do their eyes look like? Where are they placed on their tiny bird heads? By examining modern birds and comparing what you discover to details of extinct dinosaurs, you can decide for yourself!

Examine a Bird Feather

◆◆◆◆◆◆◆◆

Take a closer look at the complex structure of feathers.

What You'll Need
- feathers
- gloves
- bird notebook
- pen
- magnifying glass

Next time you find bird feathers outdoors take some time for a closer look. (Some bird feathers carry disease, so be careful to wear gloves when you handle them.) If you keep a bird notebook, you can add this information to your notes. Most feathers you find will have a hollow quill running down the center. Coming out of both sides of the quill are barbs. Look at them carefully with your magnifying glass. Notice the small hooklike barbules that make the barbs stick together.

Feathers come in 3 basic types: Down feathers have no quill to speak of. The barbs are soft, and the barbules do not stick together. Body (or contour) feathers have downy barbs at the base for insulation, while the upper part forms a flat windproof layer. Flight feathers have no downy parts at all. They are long and stiff and form the shape of the wings.

Draw your findings in your notebook. Using the color and the size of the feather, see if you can figure out what bird it came from. When you are done looking at the feather, put it back where you found it. Laws that protect our nation's birds also protect bird parts. Some feathers can be collected by permit only.

Down and Out

How warm are our feathered friends?

What You'll Need
- down jacket or comforter
- regular jacket or cotton blanket

It's hard to believe feathers keep a bird warm even when rain falls and snow flies. You can find out how it works by wrapping yourself in down. What is down? In simple terms, down is a layer of feathers. On a bird, down is the term for its fluffy little feathers rather than its long, spiny quills. In coats and bedspreads, down is a stuffing of small feathers, whether fluffy or not.

No matter what the definition, the way down works remains the same. Layers of natural feathers hold warmth in. So wrap up warmly in a down jacket or bedspread (ask permission before you use the bedspread) and head out on a frosty winter day. Stand in the cold for a few minutes. Now go inside and change into a regular jacket or wrap up in an ordinary cotton blanket. Spend a few moments in the same cold. Which wrap kept you warmer? Nine times out of ten, down will win.

Nature's Pen

Quill pens were the most popular way to write 200 years ago.

What You'll Need
- large feather
- soap
- water
- scissors
- straight pin
- ink
- newspaper
- paper

Buy a feather at a craft store. It should have a stout quill and be about 10 inches long. Soak the feather in warm soapy water for several minutes. Then rinse the feather and let it dry. Use scissors to trim off the bottom 2 inches of feather from both sides of the quill. Then cut the end of the quill to a point. Use a straight pin to gently clean out the inside of the quill. Be very careful not to crack or break the quill. Finally, ask an adult to cut a small slit in the point of the quill.

To use your quill pen, dip the end in ink. (The hollow quill will hold a little ink.) Blot extra ink on a piece of old newspaper before you write. To write with a quill pen, you need to hold it at an angle. It takes a little practice, but you'll get the hang of it!

Slick Problem

◆◆◆◆◆◆

Why are oil spills bad news for our feathered friends?

Fill a tall glass about ¾ of the way with water. Pour vegetable oil on top of the water to make an oil slick. Stick one feather into the water, and pull it out. You will notice that the oil sticks to the feather.

Compare the feather with oil on it to the feather without oil on it. How has the oil changed the feather? How might the oil interfere with the function of the feathers? One of the functions of feathers is to help ocean birds stay warm. Do you think the feathers function as well when covered with lots of oil?

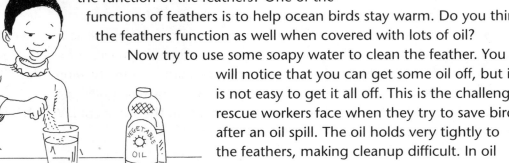

Now try to use some soapy water to clean the feather. You will notice that you can get some oil off, but it is not easy to get it all off. This is the challenge rescue workers face when they try to save birds after an oil spill. The oil holds very tightly to the feathers, making cleanup difficult. In oil spills on the ocean, crude oil is spilled. This is even thicker and stickier than vegetable oil!

Feather Painting

◆◆◆◆◆◆

Feathers are good for the inside of pillows, to tickle your friend's nose, and as great painting tools!

Cover your work surface with newspaper. Pour some paints in a clean foam tray, then pour a bit of ink in a second tray. Now paint a picture on your paper using a different part of each feather: the feather tip, the feather web, and the quill end.

Dip the tip and web in the paint and use them to create soft, sweeping lines. Dip the quill end in the ink to create sharp lines, dots, and points.

Nests

◆─◆─◆─◆─◆─◆

Before birds lay eggs, they build nests to catch and protect the eggs. The mother, and sometimes the father, sits on the eggs to keep them warm. They drive off animals that want to eat the eggs. If they are successful, chicks will emerge from the eggs. The nest then gives the chicks a home while they grow.

 # Build a Bird's Nest

◆─◆─◆─◆─◆─◆

Birds spend lots of time collecting materials to make a cozy nest.

In addition to twigs and leaves, birds like to use bits of string, yarn, lint, and other artificial materials to build and furnish their homes. Take a walk outside and pretend that you are a bird that needs to make a nest. See what building materials you can find. Look for natural materials like leaves and twigs and also for human-made materials.

When you get back home, shape some modeling clay into a bird's nest. Line the inside and outside of the nest with the things you collected until you come up with the perfect bird home. This makes a great piece of art for your home.

> ### What You'll Need
> - natural and artificial materials
> - modeling clay

Experimental Parent

▸▸▸▸▸▸▸

Sit still long enough to learn how it feels to be a bird.

What You'll Need
- large "nest" of straw or leaves
- plastic Easter eggs

If you've ever wondered what it takes to change a clutch of eggs into baby birds, check out the idea we're hatching now. It may look easy to be a mother bird. All they do is sit, right? Wrong. Experts say bird embryos undergo 42 different stages of growth inside the egg. If the mother doesn't turn and care for each egg, the chick might not survive. So why not experiment with warming a nest of your own?

Make a nest out of straw and leaves, and then sit still on a few plastic eggs of your own. Keep all the eggs warm to the touch. Turn them all over at least once or twice an hour. And don't forget, you'll need a friend or pretend bird mate to bring you food and give you potty breaks if you're going to pull this experiment off. Sit for 3 or 4 hours to get an idea of how much it takes to raise a baby bird. You'll understand just how important a mother bird is to her unborn babies.

Egg-sploration

▸▸▸▸▸▸▸

Find out what birds leave behind.

Caution: This project requires adult supervision.

What You'll Need
- stepladder
- work gloves
- soap

When the nesting season in your region is over, why not go on a little "egg-sploration" of your own? Go from tree to tree in an area where birds nest and step up to a whole new world of information. With adult help, use a stepladder to reach abandoned nests. Be sure to wear gloves to protect your hands from bacteria and tiny insect pests.

What do you find inside the nest? Are there tiny eggshell fragments? Whole eggs that didn't successfully hatch? What story do these eggshells tell? How do eggshell colors differ from nest to nest? You never know what fun facts you'll hatch next. When you are finished looking at the nests, leave everything where it was. Be sure to wash your hands with antibacterial soap as soon as you finish this activity.

Be a Bird's Helper

In the springtime, birds are on the lookout for nesting material.
Here's how to give them a helping hand.

You can encourage birds to nest in your area if you provide them with natural nesting materials or artificial materials that birds will accept as well as the natural ones. Cut pieces of string into lengths no longer than 3 inches (or birds can get tangled in it). Short, narrow strips of rag are also useful to birds. Feathers from an old feather pillow are often acceptable as nest lining. If your family discards lawn clippings, save some to dry and give to the birds.

What You'll Need
- string
- scissors
- rag strips
- other nest lining
- berry basket

String, rags, and dried grass can be laid out on the ground or on branches of shrubs for birds to pick up. Hang a used berry basket on a tree limb and fill it with bits of lint or with small feathers.

If you have swallows in your yard, try this trick: In the spring when the swallows first return, go outdoors in an area where you've seen swallows and hold a fluffy white feather in your fingertips as high as you can. The swallows will dive at the feather until one gets brave enough to snatch it from your fingers and take it home to its nest.

Bird-Mart

Make a "home supply" stop for busy birds.

What You'll Need
- large cardboard box
- scissors
- string
- yarn
- dryer lint
- hair from combs and brushes

When nesting time arrives, transform your yard into bird central with this cardboard bird-nest superstore! Cut holes and notches in a large, sturdy cardboard box. Now feed bits of string, yarn, dryer lint, and hair into those holes and notches. Place the box on a high table or on top of a flat roof, then wait and watch. Before you know it, dozens of backyard birds will land on your cardboard shop to find special things for the nests they're building.

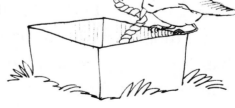

Robin's Egg Treats

Robin Redbreast's eggs don't taste like jellybeans, but these "eggs" do!

What You'll Need
- oven
- measuring cup and spoon
- flaked coconut
- cookie sheets
- 3 bowls
- butter, softened
- sugar
- egg
- lemon extract
- all-purpose flour
- salt
- orange peel
- shortening
- cooling racks
- 1 cup small jellybeans

Caution: This project requires adult supervision.

Preheat oven to 300°F. Spread 1⅓ cups flaked coconut on ungreased cookie sheet. Bake in oven for about 25 minutes or until coconut begins to brown; stir occasionally. Put toasted coconut in bowl.

Increase oven temperature to 350°F. Beat 1 cup butter and ½ cup sugar in a large bowl until fluffy. Add 1 egg and ½ teaspoon lemon extract; beat until smooth. Combine 2 cups flour, ½ teaspoon salt, and ½ teaspoon orange peel in a medium bowl. Add flour mixture to butter mixture; blend.

Separate dough into 36 small balls; roll each ball in toasted coconut until completely covered. Place each dough ball 2 inches apart on greased cookie sheets. Using your thumb, make a dent in the center of each ball.

Bake 12 to 14 minutes or until coconut is golden brown. Remove to wire racks and cool completely. Put jellybean "eggs" in the indentations of cooled cookies. Makes 3 dozen treats.

Bird-Watching

Whether amateur "birders" or professional ornithologists, many people get a thrill from bird-watching. They learn characteristics of birds, such as how they look and the sounds they make. They use books and other people to learn the names of birds. Some birders make checklists to keep track of the birds they have seen.

Watch the Birdie

◇▶▶▶▶▶◀◁

Document which fine feathered friends call your home "home."

Our bird friends help maintain the balance of nature. When you keep a record of just what birds flutter by your window, you begin to understand how that balance works. Why not set a few minutes aside each day to keep track of which birds (and how many) call your house "home sweet home"? Use a few inexpensive bird feeders filled with seed to draw your birds near (this book has some bird feeders you can make on your own). Then sit back and enjoy the show. Make sure to take notes on what you see and when you see it.

1 Bird, 2 Birds, 3 Birds

◇▶▶▶▶▶◀◁

Every year around Christmastime, bird-watchers all over the country get together for a special event. Join the Christmas Bird Count.

You'll learn a lot about birds by spending a day with other people who care about them. The Christmas Bird Count is sponsored by the Audubon Society, an organization of people who are interested in birds. The purpose of the count is to find out how many birds there are and what kinds of birds.

Here's how it works: People form groups, and each group counts birds in a certain area on a certain day. The groups count how many birds there are of each kind. Then, all the groups send their counts to the Audubon Society, which adds everything up to get the big picture. If you'd like to be part of the Christmas Bird Count, call a nature center or bird-watching club in your area for information.

Peep, Peep!

◄►◄►◄►◄►

Could you make yourself understood using peeps and squawks?

As humans, we take our ability to communicate for granted. But what if you suddenly had only chirps and peeps to make your ideas understood? What if our words—hundreds and hundreds of them—were replaced with birdlike tweets and whistles? Take an hour to find out. Try to share one hour with a friend or family member without saying a single word. Chirp when you're hungry. Squawk when you don't like what you've heard. Whistle a happy song when you're content. See if words are the only sounds worth understanding. Then, go outside and try to have a conversation with the birds you see.

How Close?

◄►◄►◄►◄►

Prove you can watch without wounding.

What You'll Need
● ruler

Can birds learn to trust the humans in their world? Why not take a summer to find out? Watch your yard to find out where birds like to gather. First, watch them from your house, talking softly as you look. Then, move outside, but stay close to your house, again talking very softly. Move just 2 feet closer each day, being careful to sit still and make no sudden movements. How close can you get to your feathered friends? If you're patient, you might be surprised.

Where Are You Headed?

◆▶▶▶▶▶▶◀

Here's an easy way to study birds' migration routes.

Migratory birds fly thousands of miles every year. At the library, check out a book about migratory birds. See if your home is on the migration path of any birds. (If it is, watch for them at the times of the year when they migrate.) Then, on a globe or world map, mark the migration paths of some birds. Use rubber cement or other temporary adhesive to attach a piece of yarn to each bird's starting place. Then attach the other end of the yarn to the bird's summer home. Use different colors of yarn for different birds.

What You'll Need
- reference book
- globe or world map
- rubber cement
- different colored yarn

Tweet Repeat

◆▶▶▶▶▶▶◀

Learning a new language is always an adventure, especially when you learn to speak bird.

What You'll Need
- tape recorder
- paper bag
- scissors

Set a tape recorder on "record," and place it near a spot where local birds perch and sing. Slip your recorder inside a paper bag (with a hole cut near the microphone) to protect it from the droppings that sometimes go along with fluttering birds. Let the tape record for at least 15 minutes. Then retrieve your recorder and carefully study the sounds as you play them back from the tape. See if you can mimic the sounds. Practice until it sounds just right. Then sing away when a bird is nearby. Do the tiny creatures react? You'll never know until you try.

Migrating Birds

◆▸◆▸◆▸◆

Follow the spring and fall bird migrations in your area.

If you live in the middle of one of the major flyways, you're in a great place to watch the annual bird migrations. Even if you're not near a flyway, you may still spot birds migrating through your area. Flyways are simply where birds concentrate. Because many migratory birds are attracted to wetlands, locate a marsh, pond, or lake in your area. Find a place near the water where you can watch birds. Use binoculars for a better look. A good bird manual can help. Some of the migratory waterbirds you'll find all over the United States are Canada geese, pintail ducks, mallard ducks, and red-winged blackbirds.

Take notes about the birds you see. You'll probably see a lot more species during the migratory season than at other times. Some birds will stay all year. Others are just passing through. Notice also which birds migrate to your area to stay a season. You may have heard that geese fly south for the winter and north for the summer. But watch what happens in your area. People in certain areas are puzzled when they see geese flying all directions in their area all winter long. They expect the geese to "fly south for the winter," but where geese end up may be as far "south" as they fly. The flocks will remain all winter before returning to their nesting grounds in Canada and Alaska.

Bird Journal

Keep track of the birds you see and learn more about them.

What You'll Need

- notebook
- pen or pencil
- binoculars
- bird guide for your area
- bird-shape stickers or bird pictures (optional)

Most birders keep track of the birds they have seen. You can start your own bird journal and use it every time you go out looking for birds. Get a sturdy, bound notebook, preferably one with a hard cover. An ordinary composition book will work very well. If you like, decorate your notebook with bird stickers or pictures of birds. Reserve the first 2 or 3 pages for your "life list"—a listing of every kind of bird you've seen. You will add to your list each time you go outdoors and spot a bird you haven't seen before.

Now find some good places to watch for birds. Feeding stations, parks, ponds, shores, marshes, meadows, and fences are great places. Take your journal with you each time you go. Find a comfortable spot to sit, and stay quiet as you watch for birds. Take a pair of binoculars with you if you have them. On the top of a fresh page, write down where you are, the time of day, and the date. These are important, because you won't see the same birds everywhere, and you'll see different birds each season. List the names of the birds you see. Sketch or write a description of birds you don't recognize.

Note as many features of the bird as you can so you can look it up later. Record what the birds are doing. Are they feeding, flying, singing, fighting, or displaying? Is there a bird on a nest? Your bird journal entries will teach you a lot about birds. You'll be able to tell which birds migrate through your area and which stay a whole season or all year. You'll get a pretty good idea of which birds are most common, too.

Join and Bird!

The Audubon Society is an organization for people who love to watch birds. Contact your local chapter of the Audubon Society if you're interested in joining a bird-watching club, doing projects that help birds, or taking part in the annual bird census.

Be a Bird Behaviorist

◆◆◆◆◆◆◆

Why do birds do what they do?
Watch the birds and find the answers yourself.

What You'll Need
- notebook and pencil
- binoculars
- bird guide for your area

Because birds are active in the day and aren't too shy, they make terrific subjects for studies of behavior. See how much you can learn from the birds in your area. An easy way to study birds is to set up a feeding station in your yard (see Bird Cafeteria on page 500 for suggestions) that you can see from a window.

Set up a comfortable chair in front of the window and be ready to write down what you see. At first you may only see a confusing jumble of activity, with birds flying this way and that. Some will be at a feeder one moment and on the ground the next. They never stop moving. How can you make sense of what you see?

The best way is to pick something out of the action to observe. You might first observe just one bird. Follow it with your eyes and describe what it does. Then, watch one bird feeder. Describe how the birds act when they are on the feeder. Finally, look for one kind of behavior. Count how many times one bird chases another away from food, for instance. By watching a flock of birds carefully and noting who chases who, you may be able to determine which birds dominate the flock. You can also watch for any peculiar or interesting behavior. For instance, you may notice downy woodpeckers work up a tree trunk as they find insects in the bark. Watch how nuthatches and brown creepers go down the tree headfirst to find insects the woodpeckers miss.

Birds Big and Small

The largest bird alive today is the ostrich. It can reach 9 feet tall and lays 3-pound eggs. The smallest bird is the bee hummingbird, which measures just 2 inches long! It lays 2 eggs at a time, each about the size of a human pinky nail.

Bird Track Tracing

◆◆◆◆◆◆◆

Make an impression—capture the bird tracks.

Have you ever really looked at the delicate tracks of your neighborhood birds? This is your chance to capture and keep a little bird scratch all your own.

Pick an area near a tree often inhabited by birds. Now fill an old cake pan or cookie sheet about halfway with soft, wet mud or very fine sand. Don't fill it too high. It should be wet enough to leave a good impression when you press a dime into the surface and then take the dime away.

Fill an ordinary bird feeder with birdseed, set the seed at the end of the pan, then scram. Come back in a few hours (or

the next day) and see what tracks your feathered friends have made. For extra fun, carefully fill the pan the rest of the way with plaster of paris. Once the plaster dries, you'll have a perfect raised cast of your bird track experiment.

What You'll Need
- old cake pan or cookie sheet
- soft, wet mud or sand
- bird feeder
- birdseed
- plaster of paris
- old bowl and spoon to mix plaster

Stopwatch Takeoff

◆◆◆◆◆◆◆

How long does it take a bird to reach the sky?

What You'll Need
- stopwatch
- paper
- pencil or pen

How long does it take the average bird to go from land to air? That depends on the bird. Do your own personal study. Take your stopwatch outside to your favorite bird sanctuary. The instant you see a bird take off, hit the "start" button. Stop timing when the bird reaches clear sky. Make a note of the time you've logged and the kind of bird that set that pace. Now search for another kind of bird and repeat the process. When you compare notes, you'll be amazed by the individual start-to-finish potential of different birds.

It's Official

There's a lot to learn about your state—including your state bird.

What You'll Need
- field guide to birds

Find out what your official state bird is from the list below. Why do you think that bird was selected? Which bird is the state bird for 7 states? Learn about your state bird from a field guide to birds. Then, whenever you're out hiking, watch for your bird. Can you find any other state birds where you live?

Alabama	Yellowhammer	**Montana**	Western meadowlark
Alaska	Willow ptarmigan	**Nebraska**	Western meadowlark
Arizona	Cactus wren	**Nevada**	Mountain bluebird
Arkansas	Mockingbird	**New Hampshire**	Purple finch
California	California valley quail	**New Jersey**	Eastern goldfinch
Colorado	Lark bunting	**New Mexico**	Roadrunner
Connecticut	American robin	**New York**	Bluebird
Delaware	Blue hen chicken	**North Carolina**	Cardinal
District of Columbia	Wood thrush	**North Dakota**	Western meadowlark
		Ohio	Cardinal
Florida	Mockingbird	**Oklahoma**	Scissor-tailed flycatcher
Georgia	Brown thrasher	**Oregon**	Western meadowlark
Hawaii	Hawaiian goose	**Pennsylvania**	Ruffed grouse
Idaho	Mountain bluebird	**Rhode Island**	Rhode Island red
Illinois	Cardinal	**South Carolina**	Carolina wren
Indiana	Cardinal	**South Dakota**	Chinese ring-necked pheasant
Iowa	Eastern goldfinch		
Kansas	Western meadowlark	**Tennessee**	Mockingbird
Kentucky	Cardinal	**Texas**	Mockingbird
Louisiana	Eastern brown pelican	**Utah**	Seagull
Maine	Chickadee	**Vermont**	Hermit thrush
Maryland	Baltimore oriole	**Virginia**	Cardinal
Massachusetts	Chickadee	**Washington**	Willow goldfinch
Michigan	Robin	**West Virginia**	Cardinal
Minnesota	Common loon	**Wisconsin**	Robin
Mississippi	Mockingbird	**Wyoming**	Western meadowlark
Missouri	Bluebird		

Eat Like a Bird

Think birds don't eat much? Think again.

When people say, "You eat like a bird," they often mean you hardly eat anything at all. But modern bird scientists (called *ornithologists*) have a different perspective. They say that although birds do eat tiny mouthfuls of food, they do so hundreds and hundreds of times each day. They have to eat a lot just to keep their energetic little bodies moving.

So why not try a bird's eating habits on for size? You might not want to feast on invertebrates (bugs and worms), but you can try to eat your food gradually, one tiny bite at a time. See how it affects your energy levels. See how it affects those hunger pains you usually feel 3 times a day. You may never look at birds the same way again.

Backyard Sanctuary

If you like watching birds, you can go out and see them where they live, or you can attract the birds to where you live. Providing birds with food and safe places to live are great ways to attract birds to your yard and learn more about their behavior.

Bird Cafeteria

◆▶◆▶◆▶◆

Set out a feast for the birds and learn what they like best.

Many people put out feeders full of seeds, but you can attract a wider range of birds by offering a selection of foods. Try the following ways of offering foods and see what your birds like best:

- Offer various seeds. You can buy special feeders for fine thistle seed and for larger sunflower seeds. Offer thistle in the summer when goldfinches are around. Sunflower seeds can be out all year.
- Build or buy a table-style feeder on a post to offer peanuts and cut-up fruit (especially cherries).
- Pound a slender nail into a tree and stick half an apple on it, or wedge apple slices between tree branches.
- Cut an orange in half and hang the halves from a branch for orioles.
- Cut a coconut in half. Ask an adult to drill a hole near the edge and hang the coconut from a tree branch. Small, seed-eating birds like to peck at the meat, and larger, more aggressive birds cannot get to it easily.
- On a large flat rock, offer cracked corn to quail and doves.
- Use a flat window feeder to offer cut-up suet from the meat counter. Make sure the window is high enough that dogs, cats, and rats cannot reach. Don't offer suet in the warmer months; it spoils quickly.

What You'll Need

- bird feeders (purchased or homemade)
- thistle seeds
- sunflower seeds
- peanuts
- cut-up fruit
- nail
- hammer
- dull knife
- whole coconut
- drill
- cracked corn
- suet

Bird Haven

◆◆◆◆◆◆

What are some ways you can help your bird friends out?

Imagine that you're going to set up the world's best bird habitat in your back-yard. What would you need? Think of things that people use to attract birds to their yards, and think about the different resources that birds need to survive. Make your bird haven as complete as possible by filling as many of the birds' needs as you can. What kinds of ideas did you come up with for attracting birds? How would the birds use the resources you would provide for them? How would they fulfill these needs if you did not help them? Write down each of your ideas for attracting birds. Next to each one, write down the need that it fulfills. Do you have some of the same needs as the birds? Write down how you fulfill each of the needs that you share with the birds. If you can, use some of the ideas you came up with to make a real bird haven in your yard.

Bake a Bird Cake

◆◆◆◆◆◆

Make your feathered friends happy.

What You'll Need
● measuring cup
● bread crumbs
● unsalted nuts
● raisins
● sugar
● cornmeal
● flour
● birdseed
● peanut butter
● bacon drippings
● string

When we celebrate our favorite friends, we bake them a cake. We can celebrate our feathered friends the same way—by making them a special bird cake and watching them feast for days. Begin with 2 cups of bread crumbs (use mom's old, dry bread crusts—the birds won't mind, and mom will like the fact that they don't go to waste). Mix in a handful of unsalted nuts, 2 handfuls of raisins, 1 cup sugar, ½ cup cornmeal, ½ cup flour, and 1 cup birdseed. Add 8 ounces of peanut butter and some bacon drippings to hold the mix together. Shape the bird snack into "donuts" and freeze. Once they're frozen, carefully hang the bird cakes from your favorite trees and watch the birds chow down.

Milk-Carton Meal

◆◆◆◆◆◆

Put those old milk cartons to good use.

What You'll Need
- empty milk carton
- scissors
- bird cakes
- hole punch
- string

If your yard is a little short on trees with bending branches, hang your bird cakes (see Bake a Bird Cake on page 501) in special milk-carton feeders. Then, instead of shaping the mixture into donuts, fill the bottom of a milk carton with the treat. Punch holes in the carton and run strings from corner to corner, tying them together where they meet at the top. Hang these treats from rain gutters or flagpoles to provide your birds with a safe and delicious treat.

Grow a Bird Feeder

◆◆◆◆◆◆

Sunflowers are natural bird feeders—they grow tall and offer seeds.

What You'll Need
- sunflower seeds
- a garden plot
- tall stakes
- hammer
- string

To grow sunflowers, plant some seeds in a sunny place. Be sure to plant sunflowers in a place where they can be reached with a hose, because they'll need lots of water. You won't believe how fast sunflowers grow and how big and tall they get! When they start to grow tall, have an adult help you hammer a stake in the ground next to each sunflower stalk. Use string to tie the stake to the stalk in several places. Don't forget to water your sunflowers often. In a few months they'll make big yellow flowers. At the center of each flower will be a large cluster of seeds. When the seeds are ready to eat, the birds will know.

Hummingbird Feeder

◆▸▸▸▸▸▸◆

Whip up some special food for these special birds.

Caution: This project requires adult supervision.

Hummingbirds can hover, fly backward, and even fly upside down. They flap their wings up to 78 times per second. All that flapping burns up the calories, so hummingbirds have to eat half their weight in food every day. Of course, some only weigh about $\frac{1}{10}$ of an ounce.

It should come as no surprise that hummingbirds don't eat the same things as other birds. They need high-energy foods, and one of their favorite foods is nectar collected from red flowers. They also love sugar syrup. Here's how to make a hummingbird feeder:

Wash a large, clear plastic soda bottle and remove the label. About $\frac{1}{4}$ of the way from the bottom of the bottle, cut a square hole that is about an inch on each side. Make a crease in the front of the bottle, just above the hole. With an adult's help, boil $\frac{1}{2}$ cup sugar and 2 cups water to make a syrup. Let the syrup cool. Use your finger to cover the hole in the bottle, and pour in the syrup. Put the lid on the bottle. Glue red plastic flowers on the bottle, especially near the hole. Tie a string around the top of the bottle, and use it to hang the feeder.

Ring a Bell

◆▸▸▸▸▸▸◆

Help save your neighborhood birds.

Domestic housecats on the prowl don't mean any harm when they instinctively hunt birds. But they are responsible for the decline of many American songbirds. You can help even the odds. Go to your local craft store and buy the kind of jingle bells you might use during the holiday season. With adult help, tie the bells (on strings) to the lower branches of your songbirds' favorite roost. When cats climb or jump to the lower branches, the birds will have a little extra warning—and time to escape.

Food for Flyers

◆◆◆◆◆◆◆

Try these ideas for simple bird feeders.

Caution: This project requires adult supervision.

Whether you're setting up a backyard wildlife refuge or just want to attract a few birds, you'll enjoy having and maintaining bird feeders in your yard. To make a window feeder, cut a piece of scrap wood (with adult help) as wide as a window. Paint it, then use metal brackets to mount it underneath a window.

Straight peanut butter is too sticky for birds, but you can mix it with equal parts lard or shortening, then stir in cornmeal and sunflower seeds until the mixture is stiff. Stuff the mix into pinecones and hang them up, or spoon into yogurt cups and hang the cups in trees.

To make a fruit feeder, tie long strings to the corners of a half-pint plastic berry basket. Tie the strings together and hang the basket from a tree branch. Put a few cut cherries, grapes, or other diced, brightly colored fruit in the basket. Offer a small amount of fruit at a time and replace it daily. Offer this in the summer when fruit-eating birds are active.

What You'll Need
- scrap wood
- saw
- outdoor paint
- paintbrush
- metal brackets
- peanut butter
- lard or shortening
- cornmeal
- sunflower seeds
- pinecones or yogurt cups
- half-pint berry basket
- string
- scissors
- fruit

Winter Delight

◆◆◆◆◆◆◆

When it gets cold, life is rough for birds. Next time it snows, turn a snow person into a bird's best friend!

What You'll Need
- snow
- bird treats

In winter, when many of the things that birds like to eat are covered with snow, the birds could use your help. Make a snow person, and decorate it with things birds like to eat. That includes birdseed and fruit. Your snow creation is likely to have lots of feathered friends.

You can make several snow people—or even a whole snow family! Use different kinds of food and see if you attract a variety of birds. You may also attract squirrels, rabbits, and other types of backyard wildlife.

'Tis the Season

◆◆◆◆◆◆◆

Decorate a neighborhood tree with these wonderful holiday ornaments for the birds.

What You'll Need
- cookie cutters
- bread
- yarn
- peanut butter
- birdseed

To make holiday tree ornaments that birds will enjoy, use cookie cutters to cut shapes out of bread. Next, poke a piece of yarn through each shape. Spread peanut butter on the shapes, and press seeds into the peanut butter. Hang the shapes from an outdoor tree with the yarn, and watch the birds flock around.

Seed and Feed

◆◆◆◆◆◆◆

Keep your favorite feathered friends from going hungry.

Have you ever noticed exactly where your favorite birds like to gather to eat? Have you ever watched to see what they eat while they're there? You can lend them a hand. Go to your local pet or garden center and buy a bag of birdseed made just for the birds in your yard. Now fill stiff paper plates or recycled pie pans with the seed and string them to lower branches of the trees to help make sure each tweeter gets enough to eat.

What You'll Need
- birdseed
- stiff paper plates or recycled pie pans
- hole punch
- string
- scissors

Duck Bread Distribution

◆◆◆◆◆◆◆

Quack, quack, give something back.

What You'll Need
- old stale bread and cereal products

How often have you watched your folks toss out stale or moldy bread and cereal? Well, stop watching and start retrieving. There are hungry ducks to feed! Take those old edibles to the park or duck pond (or wherever your local mallards hang out) and give the fowl a feast. Be sure to throw the boxes and wrappers away before you leave.

Water Holes

◆◆◆◆◆◆◆

Attract more wildlife to your backyard by offering water all year 'round.

What You'll Need
- hose with nozzle
- water
- pie pan
- fine gravel
- garbage can lid
- small, rigid-sided plastic wading pool
- shovel
- newspaper
- flat river rocks

If you were a bird, could you find enough places in your neighborhood to drink? Do your local water sources dry up or freeze? Make life easier for wildlife with a human-made oasis. First, put a fan-shape nozzle on the end of a hose, and lay the hose in a flower bed or garden that needs watering. Turn the hose on to make a slow, gentle stream. Let the water run across the garden. Birds will be attracted in the evening after a long, thirsty day.

For a pie-pan bird bath, set a large pie pan on level ground. Pour a thin layer of fine gravel into the bottom, and add a rock for birds to sit on and to weigh the pan down. Pour in an inch of water. To make a garbage can–lid bird bath, excavate a shallow hole in the ground, and set the lid in it. Sprinkle gravel in the bottom, add some rocks, and pour in an inch of water. During the winter, have an adult help you keep the water from icing over.

Or for a plastic wading pool pond, have an adult help dig a hole 6 inches wider and 3 inches deeper than the pool. Pour 3 inches of gravel in the bottom for drainage. Put an inch-thick layer of newspapers on the gravel to cushion the pond bottom. Set the wading pool in the hole. Add flat rocks on the bottom of the pool and rocks on one side to make a shallow bathing area. Fill the pool with water. Fill in around the outside of the pool with more gravel. Place rocks, small logs, and plants around the edge to make the pond attractive to wildlife.

Simple Birdhouses

◆▸◆▸◆▸◆▸◆

*Put some of these birdhouses out in the spring
and see what kinds of birds will set up housekeeping!*

Caution: This project requires adult supervision.

Since these houses can't be opened and cleaned easily, they are both one-season houses. You'll need an adult to help you make these birdhouses.

The easiest birdhouse to make is a gourd house. Buy or grow gourds that are at least 4 inches across, with a long neck. Dry out the gourd, cut a 1-inch hole in the round part, and hang it up by the neck. You can also add a perch. Have an adult drill a ¼-inch hole under the larger hole. Then cut a 2-inch length of dowel and insert in the small hole. Glue in place.

What You'll Need
- gourd
- carving knife
- string
- drill
- ¼-inch dowel
- craft glue
- plastic flowerpot
- scissors
- flowerpot base
- decorations

Another easy house begins with a plastic flowerpot. First, run some string through the holes on the bottom. Cut a 1-inch hole in the side of the pot. Turn it over; glue it to a flowerpot base that is larger than the mouth of the flowerpot. Hang it up by the string. If you'd like, you can decorate it with dried flowers, popsicle sticks, or pinecones.

Bird Dos and Don'ts

◆▸◆▸◆▸◆▸◆

Let nature take its course.

When we see a baby bird fall from the nest, it's only natural to want to scoop it up and offer it protection. But when we try to help, we often cause harm. So the next time you see a helpless nestling, take these steps instead.

Try not to pick up the bird unless it is clearly wounded and in danger from another animal. Assuming the bird is not in immediate danger, don't stay too close to the bird or its mother's nest, and don't try to call the bird's mother.

Do move back at least 20 feet from the nesting site, keep quiet, and keep all cats and dogs from the area. Be patient and wait for the mother bird to take care of her hatchling in her own way.

Plant for Your Birdies

◆◆◆◆◆◆

Grow a home for your feathered friends.

Why not plan your garden around the birds you want to attract? Studies show birds prefer these 5 types of plants when searching for the ideal place to nest and live. Evergreens provide cover, winter shelter, and summer nesting sites. Grass (especially if not mowed during nesting season) provides cover for ground-nesting birds. Nectar-producing plants (especially red blossoms) attract hummingbirds and orioles. Fruiting trees and bushes, like cherry trees and grapevines, attract dozens of species of birds for obvious (and tasty) reasons. Be sure to plant trees or bushes that bear fruit every season. Nut and acorn plants, such as oaks, chestnuts, walnuts, and hazelnuts, are good for birds to eat and provide good nesting sites.

Winter Bird Treats

◆◆◆◆◆◆

When the weather gets cold, give winter birds a much needed treat.

Caution: This project requires adult supervision.

To make suet cakes: Put 2 pounds of ground suet in a large pan and add 2 quarts of water. Simmer until all the fat is melted. Strain into a bowl and let it cool, then put in the refrigerator until the fat is hard. Remove the hardened fat and put into a small pan. Melt it over low heat. Add 3 or 4 cups birdseed. Make molds by shaping 2 layers of aluminum foil over the outside of a plastic food container. Pour the suet-birdseed mix into the molds. (Two pounds of suet will make three 4×6-inch cakes.) You can put the cakes on a platform feeder out of reach of squirrels or hang them in a mesh onion sack.

To make bird treats: Mix 2 parts peanut butter with 1 part each shortening, whole-wheat flour, cornmeal, and birdseed. Mix in a large bowl. Roll the mixture into balls and put in a feeder.

What You'll Need
- ground suet (found at meat counters in grocery stores)
- water
- 2 pans
- stove
- 2 bowls
- strainer
- measuring cup
- birdseed
- aluminum foil
- plastic food containers
- mesh onion sack
- peanut butter
- shortening
- whole-wheat flour
- cornmeal

Suet Bell

❖❖❖❖❖❖

All types of birds will love this tasty "dinner bell."

What You'll Need
- birdseed
- bread crumbs
- dried fruit
- suet, lard, or fat drippings
- saucepan
- stove
- yogurt container
- string

Caution: This project requires adult supervision.

First, gather birdseed, bread crumbs, and dried fruit. These ingredients are the "filler" for this project. Next, collect some suet, lard, or drippings from a roast or bacon. (You'll need about ½ pound of suet for every pound of filler.) Ask an adult to melt the suet in a saucepan and mix in the filler. Let the mixture cool a little.

Poke a small hole in the bottom of a yogurt container. Tie a knot in a length of string and pull the string about halfway through the hole. Make sure there are several inches of string inside the container and several inches outside. Have an adult pour the suet and filler mixture into the yogurt container. Leave it there overnight to harden. Carefully remove the yogurt container. Use the string to hang the suet bell in a tree where birds gather.

The Pinecone Café

❖❖❖❖❖❖

A pinecone makes a natural "snack shop" for birds. Here's how to make a pinecone bird feeder.

Tie a string from the top of a pinecone. Then smear lots of peanut butter all over the cone. Next roll the cone in birdseed so the seeds stick in the peanut butter. It may not make your mouth water, but to birds, it's a treat. Hang the pinecone from a branch, and birds will begin stopping by for a snack.

What You'll Need
- large pinecone
- string
- peanut butter
- birdseed

THE ANIMAL KINGDOM

❖◆❖◆❖◆❖

From the lion's roar to the mouse's squeak to the neighborhood dog's bark—animals sure have a way of getting our attention! This chapter has great activities and crafts about all kinds of animals. Learn about your favorite animals, whether they're pets, familiar wild animals, or exotic animals you might have never even heard of! Use your craft skills to help others learn about protecting animals.

It's a Wild Life!

❖◆❖◆❖◆❖

Although bugs and birds are also animals, most people think of things like horses, monkeys, squirrels, and turtles when they think of animals. The animal kingdom is very diverse; it ranges from birds to bats, from camels to corals.

Horsing Around

◆▶◆▶◆▶◆▶

Walk, trot, or gallop your way to equestrian fun.

What You'll Need
● long sticks
● foam chunks
● magic markers

Anyone who's ever watched a horse knows they have at least 3 very distinctive gaits. They walk—the same smooth motion we use when we walk. They trot—a quick step in jerky, one-at-a-time rhythm. And they gallop or canter—a smooth, graceful, long-stepped run. Why not try a game of horse follow-the-leader?

Find a stick that is as tall as your belly button. This will be the body of your horse. Then, take a chunk of foam and decorate it with eyes, a mouth, and a nose. This will be your horse's head. Attach the head to the stick. Hop on that horse (staying on your feet, of course) and ride! See how it feels to ride a stallion (boy horse) or a mare (girl horse).

Get a Raccoon's-Eye View

◆▶◆▶◆▶◆▶

Find out what nature looks like to a raccoon.

Did you know raccoons are related to bears and are only found in North and South America? They are extremely good swimmers—and they even "wash" their food before they eat it!

Go on a hike, but do it the raccoon way: Walk on all fours (or hands and knees), and be very, very quiet. What do you see at this level that you never noticed before? What do you smell? (If you're a good raccoon, you'll be sniffing for anything that smells good to eat.) What do you hear? You probably won't see a raccoon on your hike, since they sleep in trees during the day and are most active at night.

Z Is for Zoo

◆◆◆◆◆◆◆

**An ABC book about animals makes a great gift—
it's like giving someone a trip to the zoo.**

What You'll Need
- notebook
- pen or pencil
- old magazines
- scissors
- glue
- markers
- camera (optional)

An ABC book has one sentence or one page for each letter of the alphabet. A visit to the zoo makes a great topic for an ABC book. The next time you go to the zoo, take a notebook with you. Write down the name of each animal you see. Also write down one interesting fact about each animal. Draw a sketch or bring a camera and take pictures of the animals, too.

When you get back home, make your ABC book. For each letter, think of an animal that starts with that letter. Put its picture on the page. (If you didn't take photos or draw pictures, you can cut pictures out of old magazines.) Then write the animal's name and a fact about the animal. For example, if you saw an aardvark, you might write: The name "aardvark" means "earth pig."

If you come to a letter that you don't have an animal for, think of an object at the zoo that begins with that letter. For "H," you could write about the hot dog you had for lunch! Try to think of an animal or a word for every letter of the alphabet. When you're done, you'll have a book about the zoo, from A to Z!

Animal Defenses

All animals need to protect themselves in the wild. Some are fast and can outrun predators. Others have claws or sharp teeth. Still others have developed unique forms of defense. Turtles have armorlike shells for protection. The porcupine grows sharp quills that ward off an opponent. And the skunk uses a nasty but effective method—it squirts smelly liquid on an enemy!

Walk Like the Animals

◆▸▸▸▸▸▸◆

This is a fun activity to do with a group of friends at a park or beach. Have races where everybody runs like a certain animal.

Decide on a starting and finishing line, and try the following animal races:

Crab race: Racers are on all fours (hands and knees), and must move sideways.

Chimp race: Racers hold their ankles with their hands or drag their knuckles on the ground.

Frog race: Racers squat in frog position and hop.

Can you think of other animals to imitate in your races?

It's an Orangu-phant!

◆▸▸▸▸▸▸◆

Nature has quite an imagination, wouldn't you say? See if you do, too, by inventing an animal.

What You'll Need
- old magazines
- scissors
- glue
- construction paper
- pen

There are some pretty weird-looking animals in nature. Take the platypus, for example. It has a bill and webbed feet like a duck, a furry body and flat tail like a beaver, and it lays eggs like a turtle. Then there's the echidna, an anteater that is covered with prickly spines like a porcupine. Nature has also "invented" lizards with 3 eyes, frogs that glide, and pigs with beards!

See if you can outdo nature. Look through some old magazines to find pictures of animals. Cut out different parts of different animals to invent a new creature. Make a collage of your creature by gluing the different parts together on a piece of construction paper. Once your creation is complete, give it a name and a "biography." Write a story telling how this creature came to be, where it lives, and what it eats. Tell how each of its parts helps the creature survive.

Flash!

Help someone learn about the wild world of animals.

What You'll Need

- 4×6-inch index cards
- pen
- reference books
- old magazines
- scissors
- glue
- markers (optional)

Make some flash cards using 4×6-inch index cards. For each flash card, write a fact or two about an animal on one side of the card. (Read reference books and magazines to learn about animals.) On the other side of the card, put the animal's picture and name. You can cut pictures out of old magazines, or draw them yourself.

You can use your flash cards to help your friends learn about animals. First read them the fact, and then ask them to name the animal. (Example: I live in the water, but I'm not a fish. I'm the world's largest mammal. Who am I? Answer: a blue whale!) Or show them the pictures while covering up the animals' names, and have them guess the names. See if you can stump them, or have them make some cards and see if they can stump you.

All About Animals

One of the best ways to learn about animals is to read all about them.

Go to a pet store, an animal shelter, or the zoo and look at the mammals they have: mice, cats, giraffes. You'll probably find one kind of animal that's your favorite. Ask questions to learn about your favorite animal: What kind of home does it need? What does it eat? How does it play?

What You'll Need

- animal reference books
- paper
- pen

Check out a library book about the animal, read it, and then write a story about all you learned. Remember, the important thing is to have fun getting to know this very special little part of nature.

Moose for a Moment

◆◆◆◆◆◆◆

Imagine walking around all day with a pile of wood on your head that is as much as 6 feet wide and weighs 85 pounds. That's about the size and weight of a moose's antlers!

What You'll Need
- 4-foot long stick
- 2 plastic milk jugs
- string
- construction paper (optional)

Here's how to make and wear your own antlers: Get a stick or dowel that's about 4 feet long. That will be the "rack" part of your antlers. Now, on each side of your "rack," you'll need some "points." You can get the idea by tying an empty plastic milk jug to each side of the stick. Or, make antler points out of construction paper.

When you've made your antlers, hold them on top of your head. Be careful where you turn around. Can you walk through your bedroom door? Remember, if you were really a moose, those antlers would weigh 85 pounds (and you would weigh about a half of a ton), and you'd spend some of your time running at top speed through thick forest. You get the idea: It's not easy being a moose!

Mad About Moose

The moose is one of the largest of North America's wild land animals. It is about as tall as a horse, and a male moose (known as a bull moose) can weigh up to 1,100 pounds! As big as it is, the moose is also a swift animal, able to outrun a horse.

Terrific Turtles

◆◆◆◆◆◆◆

Turtles have been around since the days when dinosaurs walked the earth—millions of years ago. Here's how to make your own turtle "pet rock."

Do you know the difference between a turtle and a tortoise? A turtle refers to all shelled reptiles, but a tortoise is a type of turtle that lives entirely on the land. Turtles come in all sizes. Some can grow as big as 1,200 pounds and live as long as 100 years.

What You'll Need
- rock
- small pebbles
- stone
- craft glue
- paint
- paintbrush
- refrence book (optional)

To create your turtle, begin with a smooth medium-size rock. This will be your turtle's body and shell. Then find 4 similar-size pebbles to use for the feet. Glue the pebbles onto your rock using strong glue, leaving room at one end for the head. Now find a stone slightly larger than the feet to be your turtle's head, and glue it in place. Let the glue dry.

Once the glue dries, it's time to decorate your pet. Paint a face, and then decide what kind of design you want your turtle's shell to have. Many turtles have lovely, colorful designs on their shells. (You can look in a reference book to see some examples.) Or you can come up with your own design. Maybe you want a spiral or checkerboard pattern on your turtle's shell.

Real Live Dragons

Do dragons really exist? Well, yes and no. For years, people living near the small Indonesian island of Komodo told stories of the giant "dragons" that populated the island. Then, in 1912, a group of explorers discovered that the dragons were really large monitor lizards. In fact, the Komodo dragon is the world's largest lizard—it can grow to be more than 11 feet long. It spends its day living in a cave, just like a dragon!

Critters-in-Holes

◁◆▷◆▷◆▷

Critters you can eat: Yummy! You'll love making and eating these sweet, tasty, gooey treats!

What You'll Need

- 48 chewy caramel candies coated in chocolate
- knife
- 48 pieces of candy corn
- vanilla icing
- oven
- shortening
- muffin tins
- 1 package (20 ounces) refrigerated peanut-butter cookie dough
- cooling racks

Caution: This project requires adult supervision.

Have an adult help you cut a slit into the side of one piece of candy. Carefully insert a piece of candy corn into slit. Repeat with remaining caramel candies and candy corn. To create eyes, dot icing on top of each piece of candy.

Preheat oven to 350°F. Grease 12 (1¾-inch) muffin cups.

Remove dough from wrapper according to package directions. Have an adult help you cut dough into 12 equal slices; then, cut each slice into 4 equal sections. Place one section of dough into each muffin cup. Bake 9 minutes.

Remove from oven and immediately press a decorated carmel candy into center of each cookie. Remove to wire racks; cool completely. Repeat until you've baked and decorated all cookies. Makes 4 dozen "critters."

Where's Your Skin?

We take our skin for granted. When we grow bigger, so does our skin. But snakes, on the other hand, actually outgrow their skin. When this happens, the snake needs to shed (or "slough") its skin. It grows a new, larger layer of skin underneath the old one to take its place. Snakes will shed their skin several times in a single year.

Could You Be a Squirrel?

◆◆◆◆◆◆◆

Squirrels bury nuts in the fall and dig them up to eat when food is scarce in winter. Burying the nuts is easy enough. But what about finding them?

Squirrels can be found just about everywhere in the world. There are even real "flying" squirrels that glide from tree to tree. Try your hand at being a squirrel. Hide 20 peanuts in the shell in 20 different places around your house. (Make a list as you hide the nuts, and give it to your parents in case you have trouble finding them all later.) Wait a week, then see if you can find them all. Squirrels use their noses to find their buried treasures, but you'll have to use your memory! If you like, try your luck outside—but don't be surprised if a squirrel finds your secret stash before you do!

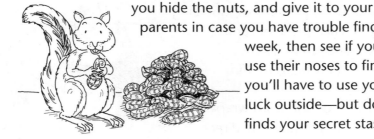

Predator and Prey

◆◆◆◆◆◆◆

How good a predator can you be? Find out by playing this game.

Predators must be good at hiding to sneak up on their prey. If prey animals want to avoid being caught, they must use their senses to detect predators. Many prey species stay in open areas where it's hard for predators to sneak up. To simulate this natural relationship, have one person be the prey animal. With closed eyes, the prey counts to 20 while the predators hide. Every predator must find a separate hiding place from which he or she can see the prey but cannot be seen by the prey. Predators may be close or far away as long as they stay within agreed-upon boundaries.

When the prey finishes counting, he or she may begin looking and may lean in any direction, but cannot leave the starting spot. Predators may change hiding places at any time but must stay where they can see prey at all times. If the prey spots a predator, he or she calls out the name of that person, who is out and must come back to base. When the prey has spotted all predators, choose a new prey.

Hard-Working Animals

◆▶▶▶▶▶◀

Animals help people in so many ways! How many can you think of?

What You'll Need
● paper and pen

This activity is fun to do with a friend!

Name any animal. Then have a friend list the many ways that animal can help people. When your friend is done reciting, see if you can think of any additional ways. Have your friend pick the next animal, so you can recite the list.

For starters, think of what kinds of animals live on farms and ranches. What about companion animals such as seeing-eye dogs? You can make this a game by writing down separate lists, then comparing them. Who can think of the most?

Be a Sculptor

◆▶▶▶▶▶◀

Try your hand at sculpting the animals that live in your neighborhood. Who knows? You may discover a hidden talent.

What You'll Need
● half-gallon milk cartons
● plaster of paris
● scissors
● sculpting tools or dull knife
● pencil

For as long as there have been people and rocks, people have used rocks to make sculptures. For example, the Inuit people of the Arctic carve polar bears and seals from a kind of rock called *soapstone.* Here's how you can create your own masterpiece.

Fill 2 or more half-gallon milk cartons with plaster of paris. Give them plenty of time to dry completely. Then strip off the milk cartons. You'll have blocks of plaster of paris that you can sculpt. Use some simple sculpting tools, which you can get at a hobby or art store, or a dull knife. You may want to draw the shape of your animal on the plaster of paris before you begin sculpting. Begin with a simple animal such as a fish or a seal.

Wildlife Calendar

No need to buy an expensive wildlife calendar when you can have fun creating your own!

What You'll Need
- newspaper
- paints or colored markers
- paintbrushes
- drawing paper
- ruler
- poster board
- scissors
- glue
- hole punch
- yarn or ribbon
- old magazines (optional)

Exploring nature is fun and educational! Make a record of your explorations by creating a calendar.

(If you are using paint, cover your work surface with newspaper first.) With paints or colored markers, make 12 colorful drawings of different wildlife scenes from your neighborhood (for example, squirrels finding acorns, birds eating from feeders, etc.) on 12 separate sheets of paper (make one scene per page). If you don't like to draw or paint, you can cut out colorful magazine pictures of 12 different wildlife scenes.

Measure and cut out 12 sheets of poster board that are twice the length of your pictures (all 12 should be the same size). When you are finished, glue each drawing or picture to the top of a separate sheet of poster board. Then draw a calendar on the bottom of each piece of poster board. Each calendar page should represent a different month. (Copy another calendar around your house so you know how many days there are in each month.) Punch 2 holes in the center top of each piece of poster board, and tie all the pages together with a piece of yarn or ribbon.

Now you have a complete 12-month calendar to commemorate your neighborhood wildlife!

Be an Eager Beaver

◄►◄►◄►◄►◄►

Beavers build their dens with mud and sticks. Build a miniature beaver den from common items.

What You'll Need
- toothpicks or twigs
- modeling clay
- shoe box
- rocks
- leaves
- twigs
- shallow container
- small plastic cup
- scissors

Use your hands to mix the toothpicks or twigs into the clay. (Be careful not to poke yourself!) Shape the clay into a den (like a small cave) with an opening.

To make a beaver habitat, get a large shoe box or other shallow box. (If you use a shoe box, you may want to cut down the sides.) At one end of the box, pile up some more clay, and place the beaver den on it. Place more clay, small rocks, leaves, and twigs over the bottom of the box.

Beavers build tunnels from their dens into nearby ponds. Put a small, shallow container in the bottom of the shoe box as a pond. (A small saucer that goes under a flowerpot makes a good pond.) Use a small plastic cup as your tunnel. Cut the bottom out of the cup. Put the bottom of the cup into the den opening and the top of the cup by the pond. Use clay to attach the cup to the den and to cover the top of the cup so it looks like a tunnel.

This model shows the ingenious home design of beavers. They scurry down to the pond to get water and plants for dinner, then go back home without ever venturing outside where predators might see them.

Now the challenge is yours—what other kinds of animal homes can you make? Do some research in the library, collect your craft supplies, and build!

Chenille-Stem Backbones

◆◆◆◆◆◆◆

Use sculpture to learn that some animals have backbones that run through the center of their bodies, just like humans!

What You'll Need
- chenille stems
- scissors
- pictures of various animals (optional)

Use chenille stems to make skeletons of different animals. Start each skeleton by forming the backbone of the animal. Cut and bend the chenille stems to make other bone parts (legs, heads, tails). Try to make a dog first. Then make other creatures, such as birds, dinosaurs, fish, or reptiles. You might want to try a giraffe or a human. Use pictures of the animals as a guide if that will help you.

Habitat Sort

◆◆◆◆◆◆◆

Living things are affected by both living and nonliving things.

In a habitat, there are living things and nonliving things that may affect the animals that live there. The living things are called *biotic factors.* Plants are biotic factors, as are their leaves, fruits, and nuts. Animals are also biotic factors. *Abiotic factors* are nonliving things that are important to organisms. These are things such as oxygen, temperature, and light.

What You'll Need
- old magazines
- paper
- pencil

Look through old magazines for pictures of animals in their natural habitats. Examine the pictures, then draw 2 columns on a piece of paper. Label one column "Biotic" and the other "Abiotic." List all the living things in your pictures in the Biotic column. List all the nonliving things in the Abiotic column.

Animal Detective

◆▶▶▶▶▶◀◀

Most animals have to worry about being eaten by other animals. So it is quite natural for wild animals to be afraid of you. You may need to learn a few tricks before you are able to spot the presence of animals. You'll also need to be very patient.

 # Trail Tales

◆▶▶▶▶▶◀◀

Find some animal tracks, and try to figure out what the animal was doing.

Observing animal tracks is like reading a detective story. Tracks give us clues about what animals do. Look for animal tracks in freshly fallen snow, on sandy beaches, or in the mud along streams and ponds. Tracks are easier to see if you walk toward the sun, because the shadows make them more distinct.

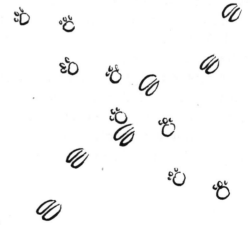

When you find tracks, stop and have a close look. (Push away any leaves and rocks in the way.) Try to determine what animals were there. You'll probably find lots of cat and dog tracks, but you may also see tracks of raccoons, rabbits, muskrats, or large birds. What was the animal doing? Did it come by the water for a drink? Was it traveling across an open field in the snow? If the tracks are deep and far apart, the animal may have been running. Are other tracks nearby? Could one animal have been following the other?

If you see many tracks in one spot, perhaps the animal was nosing around looking for something to eat. Try to follow the tracks as far as you can. If you lose the trail, mark the last track you found and move in circles around it, wider and wider, until you find the next track.

City Wildlife Safari

◆▸◆▸◆▸◆▸◆

There's wildlife even in the busiest parts of the city!

What You'll Need
- notebook
- pencil or pen

When we think of wildlife, we think of bears, cougars, bison, and other large animals. But any animal that normally lives without the care of people can be considered wildlife. This includes birds, insects, fish, and other small animals. You can find wildlife anywhere—even in a city—if you know how and where to look.

Start in a park. Sit under a group of trees and look up in the branches. Watch for birds moving around in the trees. You may also see squirrels in the branches or running around on the ground as they hunt for food. Where there are squirrels, there may also be predators, such as hawks, falcons, or foxes. Look closely at the grass, the leaves of the trees and shrubs, and in the crevices of tree bark. You're likely to find insects, spiders, and other small animals.

After the park, try watching a patch of sidewalk next to a wall or a building. It's "just" concrete, but look closer. Ants may have made a nest in a crack in the concrete. Other insects may use a wall to warm up. Birds come to hunt the insects. You may also see bats hunting insects. Don't be frightened of bats—"nature's mosquito control"—they aren't interested in harming you.

Snake Locomotion

◆━◆━◆━◆

How do snakes move without legs? Find out in this activity.

Snakes are highly evolved reptiles. They move quickly without legs, which gives them some advantage over reptiles that push themselves along with legs while dragging their bellies on the ground. But how is it possible to move without legs? First, get permission to use a snake. You may have a friend who keeps a snake, or you might be able to catch a small garter snake in your backyard. If you aren't experienced in handling snakes, get an adult to help you.

What You'll Need
- snake (a pet or a garter snake from your backyard)
- sandbox or large tray filled with sand
- rake

Rake a sandbox (or a sand tray) level. Use the back of a rake to make the surface smooth. Set the snake at one end of the sand and let it crawl to the other end. Put the snake safely back in its cage, then examine the tracks it left. You'll notice curved indentations in the sand where the snake's body pressed down. The snake uses the curves and coils of its body to press against the ground, moving it forward. Its belly scales, large and rough, give it gripping power like tire treads. Smooth the sand again and see if you can make the snake move at a different speed. See how the tracks change. Are they farther apart? Sometimes snakes move in nearly straight lines. They can use muscle ripples and their belly scales to creep along slowly.

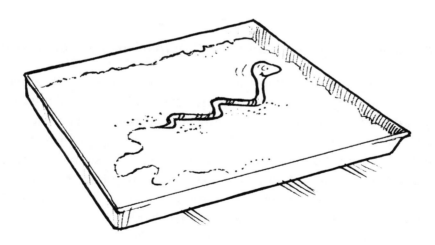

Nightwatching

You may be surprised how many animals live near your house.

What You'll Need
- flashlight
- red cellophane
- rubber bands
- blanket (optional)

Caution: This project requires adult supervision.

Woods, parks, fields, and other places are often full of animals we're not aware of because they come out at night. If you are quiet and still, you can see some of these night creatures.

Go with an adult, and find a safe place in the woods where you can sit and watch. Make sure the spot is quiet and well away from any bright lights. During the daytime, you can remove sticks and rocks, so the spot will be more comfortable. You can also lay a folded blanket out.

Before going out, cover the front of a flashlight with 2 layers of red cellophane. Red light won't affect your night vision, but it is hard for most animals to see. Go outside, and wait a few minutes for your eyes to become adjusted to the dark. Turn on your flashlight, and go to your spot. Allow yourself at least half an hour to sit. Listen carefully for any animal noises. If you hear something, you can slowly move the beam of your flashlight toward it, but try to see it without the aid of the flashlight first.

Mouse Near the House?

Learn to spot signs of small rodent activity in your neighborhood.

Small rodents, such as mice and voles, are shy creatures active mostly at night. You may never know there are any around, but rodents leave behind signs that they've been active. Look around your house and yard, especially at the base of a wall.

Do you see gnawed nuts or cherry pits? Mice chew holes in cherry pits to get at the seed inside. Look also for holes near the base of the wall. These may be mouse holes. Hunt around under pine trees. Can you find pinecones that have been gnawed apart? Squirrels often feed on pinecones and so do mice.

Look in bark dust and other loose mulch for small, raised tunnels near the surface. Voles, often called meadow mice, make these tunnels as they search for plant material. While mice eat mostly seeds, voles eat other kinds of plant material, including flower bulbs. Gardeners don't like vole tunnels in their flower beds.

Who's Out There?

Identify some of the creatures you share your neighborhood with.

If you've ever awakened in the middle of the night and heard strange animal noises coming from "out there," you know that you are not alone. Go to the library, check out a field guide, and learn what animals live in your area. Then take a nature hike (be sure to ask an adult to go with you) and see if you can meet some of your neighbors.

What You'll Need
- reference book or field guide
- notebook
- pen

The best time to do this is either just after it gets light in the morning or at dusk. Most animals are more active at those times than they are during the day. Watch for signs of animals, such as paw prints or animal homes. Keep a journal of your animal sightings.

Try this activity at different times of the year. Do you see different animals during different seasons? When do they gather food or build new homes? When do you see baby animals?

Remember: Never approach or touch a wild animal. Most wild animals are afraid of humans and, if threatened, will try to protect themselves—sometimes by biting. Also, wild animals carry diseases. If you see an animal that seems to be sick or injured, call your city's animal-control department or the police. Don't try to help the animal yourself.

Take an Animal Census

Figure out the animal population of a spot near you.

What You'll Need
- wooden stakes or sticks
- string
- paper
- pen

A census is a count of how many people—or animals—live within an area. In an open field or wooded area, use 4 stakes or sticks to mark off a square that is a meter on each side. Then run string around the 4 sticks to make an actual square. Take a census of all the animals inside the square. Look carefully to make sure everybody gets counted. Look under rocks. (Be polite and put the rocks back when you're done counting.) Look in any bushes or trees. Make a record of your census, telling how many of each kind of insect, spider, and other animal you found living there.

Be a Tracker

*Beat the winter blahs! A great time to learn to read
and follow animal tracks is after a snowfall.*

What You'll Need
- field guide to
  animals that
  shows their tracks

Depending on where you live, you may find the tracks of
dogs, cats, birds, opossums, raccoons, rabbits, squirrels, deer,
coyotes, or other animals. Use a field guide to help you identify tracks. If you live in a neighborhood with lots of dogs,
have fun trying to figure out which dog made which tracks.
Use the size of the tracks as a clue, and also pay attention to
how deep the tracks are. (The deeper the track, the heavier the animal.)

See how far you can follow the tracks. Tracks may lead you to an animal's home. See
if the tracks lead to a source of food. Two sets of tracks may be evidence of a chase.

Plaster Caster

Make a long-lasting collection of animal tracks.

Find a muddy place where animals often visit. Stream banks
and marshes are best since water attracts a wide variety of
animals. You can also make a muddy patch in your backyard
and bait it with a little food.

Once you find a clear track, make a
collar of stiff cardboard to fit around it.
Paper clip the ends of the cardboard
together and push the collar into the
mud around the track. Mix plaster
of paris with water until it is
pourable but not too thin.
Pour about an inch of plaster into the collar. Let it set
before removing. Handle
the cast gently until you can get it home and let it dry
completely. When it is dry, you can paint the track
with acrylic paints if you want.

What You'll Need
- long strip of
  cardboard
- paper clips
- plaster of paris
- water
- mixing container
- spoon
- acrylic paint
  (optional)
- paintbrush
  (optional)

Animal Track Stamps

◆▶◆▶◆▶◆

If you know what to look for, you can read animal tracks like a story.
Make a "rubber" stamp, then invent your own critter tales.

Caution: This project requires adult supervision.

Turn the moleskin to the paper side. With an ink pen, draw the outline of animal tracks. (Use the pictures in a field guide as patterns.) With adult supervision, cut out the shapes with sharp scissors, then peel off the paper backing. Stick the shapes onto a small block of wood. Press your stamp on the stamp pad, and stamp away!

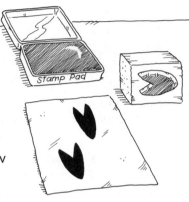

Try making a set of tracks that tell a story. You could show one animal following another, or space tracks farther apart to show an animal running. A cluster of tracks in a small area could show that the animal had found something to eat or something else of interest.

Home Sweet Home

◆▶◆▶◆▶◆

If you look in the right places, you can often see animals in their homes.

Take a hike and see how many animal homes you can find. Look in trees for birds' nests, squirrels' holes, and wasps' nests. Hollows inside trees are squirrels' favorite kind of home, but squirrels sometimes build nests out of leaves high in a tree. You can see these nests in the winter after the leaves fall.

Even if you live in a city or suburb, it's likely that there are opossums and/or raccoons living in your neighborhood. Opossums may "den" in a hollow log or under a bush or house. Raccoons like to live in hollow trees. But when they live near humans, raccoons often like to be very near humans. They often spend their days sleeping hidden in attics or garages or under porches. You'll know you've found a den if you find fur the animal has shed and maybe some tidbits of leftover food. Tell an adult so the animal can be safely removed and taken to a more natural area. Unless an animal has invaded your house, never disturb an animal's home. You could harm the animal, and it could be unhealthy for you.

Frog Raft

◆◆◆◆◆◆◆◆

Ahoy! Who wants to go for a sail on a miniature raft just for frogs?

What You'll Need
- flashlight
- board (18 inches long, 1-inch thick)
- large screw eye
- heavy twine
- candle or small electric lantern
- 2-inch-long nail (if using candle)
- plastic bag (if using lantern)

Caution: This project requires adult supervision.

If you have access to a pond you can visit at night, go frog "hunting." Shine a flashlight out over the pond, and watch for glittering frog eyes. Then launch a frog raft, and see if you can get any passengers.

With help from an adult, insert a screw eye in one end of your board and tie the end of your twine to it. For a light, drive a nail all the way through the board. Stick a candle on the pointed end that comes through the board. If your nights are too breezy for candle flames, omit the nail and candle, and use a small battery-powered lantern instead. It won't be as attractive as a flickering candle flame, but it may still attract frogs. Seal the lantern in a heavy plastic bag, then tie it to the board. Put the raft in the water, and give it a push, then wait quietly for frogs to jump aboard. See how many passengers your raft will attract.

An Orange Frog?

Yes, it's true. While most frogs you see are green or brown, they come in all colors, including red, orange, blue, and black. It's also possible for the common green frog to look orange if that frog has too much yellow pigment in its skin.

Adaptation

◆▷◆▷◆▷◆

Living things must adapt to survive. Conditions in the environment change over days and over centuries, and organisms must find ways to cope with those changes. From cold polar regions to sweltering tropics, from high mountain peaks to the bottom of the sea, living things have adapted to conditions all over the earth.

 # Keeping Warm

◆▷◆▷◆▷◆

How do animals stay warm in the winter? Try this experiment to find out.

What You'll Need
- 4 glass jars of equal size
- water
- 4 thermometers
- leaves
- dry grass
- soil
- graph paper
- pencil
- watch

Mammals have fur and birds have feathers to keep them warm, but even fur and feathers aren't enough protection against stormy winter nights. How can animals keep warm enough to survive?

To find out, fill 4 glass jars with warm water. Record the air temperature, then put a thermometer in each jar and record the water temperature. Now insulate each jar with natural materials. Pile dry leaves around one jar and dry grass around another. Mound soil around a third. Leave one jar uninsulated for comparison.

Record the temperature of the water in each jar every 5 minutes until the jars all reach air temperature. Make a line graph to show how quickly the temperature fell in each jar. Which materials insulate the best? If you were an animal, which material would you make a nest from?

Camouflage

❮◆◆◆◆◆◆❯

Watch wild animals by using their own tricks of disguise.

What You'll Need
- dull-colored clothing
- dark green or tan tarpaulin (or blanket)

If you've ever walked through the woods hoping to see wild animals, you've probably been disappointed. Animals hide when they hear or smell visitors. Learn some animal hiding tricks.

Blending in: Birds see in color, so colorful clothes will give you away. Wear gray, tan, or brown. Mammals don't see color but can tell if your clothing is light or dark compared to the background. Choose clothing that won't contrast with the background.

Changing shape: Wild animals recognize predators and prey by their shape. Many animals have patterned coats, which make it harder for predators to spot them. Drape yourself in a dull-colored tarp or blanket and assume an outline animals won't recognize.

Undercover: Animals hide from predators by using cover, such as bushes, trees, and rocks. Make your own cover: Drape a blanket or tarp over a low branch, tent-style, and sit under it. Be still for at least 20 minutes.

No scents: Wild mammals have an excellent sense of smell. If mammals smell you, they will stay away—even if you hide. When you choose a place to sit, make sure it is upwind of the area you're watching.

Patience: Predators may hide by a water hole for hours waiting for their prey. You must be just as patient. The outdoors isn't a zoo, and animals aren't easy to find. Wild animals follow their own schedules. If you don't see any animals one day, try another day or a different area.

Zoo Favorites

According to the experts at the Denver Zoo, most visitors consider the big cats and elephants their favorite zoo animals.

Fox and Mouse Game

◆◆◆◆◆◆◆

Animals often use their sense of hearing to help them find food and avoid danger. This game will help you and your friends sharpen your ears.

The fox is one of nature's most clever animals. It uses its large ears to help hunt for food. Here's how you can be as cunning as a fox.

Have a group of friends—at least 4—stand in a circle. Pick a person to be the fox. That person will stand in the middle of the circle with his or her eyes closed. Have a mouse (one of the people in the circle) walk in an inner circle around the fox and then return to his or her place in the outer circle. The fox must try to guess who the "mouse" was, using sounds as clues. If the fox guesses correctly, the mouse takes a turn as the fox.

Many animals use their hearing skills to protect themselves in the wild. Rabbits have big ears so they can listen for danger and quickly run away. Can you think of some ways that your ears help you?

Nature's Disguises

◆◆◆◆◆◆

**There's more to the world than meets the eye
when you try some of these experiments with camouflage.**

Nature is an expert at camouflage, a word that means to disguise, or to hide. Here are just a few examples: Polar bears blend in with the ice and snow of their Arctic habitat. If they didn't, they wouldn't be able to sneak up on the prey they need to survive. Ermine and some kinds of weasels have an even more interesting way of camouflaging themselves. In summer, they are brown to blend in with the woods where they live. But ermine and weasels that live in the north turn white in winter, when they are surrounded by snow. This makes it hard for predators, such as coyotes and wolves, to see them. The insects that we call walking sticks look like just that: sticks. They look so much like sticks that you can't tell they're insects unless you see them move.

Take a walk around your neighborhood and see if you can find examples of camouflage. Then, try to imitate nature by camouflaging yourself. How could you dress to camouflage yourself in winter, spring, summer, and fall? Play hide and seek with a friend—see how well you can camouflage yourselves.

What's that Smell?

◆◆◆◆◆◆

Find out how dogs and cats feel when sniffing their way around a park.

What You'll Need
- spray bottle
- water
- strong-smelling flavoring extract (vanilla, mint, lemon)
- measuring spoon

Humans have an amazing ability to distinguish hundreds of different scents, but our sense of smell isn't nearly as well developed as it is in many other mammals. This game will let you "perceive" the world as many animals do—by scent.

Fill a spray bottle with water and add 1 or 2 teaspoons of a strong-scented extract. (Peppermint, lemon, and vanilla work well.) Make a trial spray on a tree to see if the scent is strong enough to detect. Then have the players close their eyes while one person runs ahead through a wooded area with the spray bottle. The person laying the trail should spray trees and other objects along the way. If playing in grassy fields, be careful not to leave obvious foot tracks through the grass. When the trail maker is done, the rest of the players can try to follow the trail.

Polar Bear Warmth

◄◄◄◄►►►►

How do polar bears stay warm in the freezing cold of the Arctic?
Use coffee to find the answer.

What You'll Need
- coffee
- measuring cup
- 2 glass jars
- white cloth
- clear plastic wrap
- food thermometer

Pour a cup of strong black coffee into each of 2 clear glass jars. Let the jars sit until the coffee is room temperature. Cover one jar with a piece of white cloth and the other jar with a piece of clear plastic wrap. Then put both jars in the sun for an hour or more. Use a food thermometer to check the temperature of the coffee in each jar. Which is warmer? Can you explain why?

And now for the polar bear's secret: Polar bears are not really white. If they were, they couldn't stay warm in their Arctic habitat. As you just learned, white reflects sunlight and the heat that comes with it. The hairs in a polar bear's coat are clear. The hollow center of each hair soaks up light from the sun, and the light filters out the sides. That's what makes polar bears look white. Each clear hair carries heat from the sun down to the polar bear's skin. Its skin is black, which means it can soak up heat to keep the bear warm. A polar bear is like the plastic-covered coffee in your experiment: clear on the outside, black on the inside—and plenty warm!

What Hairy Feet You Have!

While you probably knew that polar bears live in cold climates, did you know that their feet have hair on the bottom? Well, they do—that's what keeps the bears from slipping on the ice.

Going Batty

◆◆◆◆◆◆◆

Ever heard the expression "blind as a bat"? Bats do have poor vision, but they have their own special way of "seeing." Find out how by playing bat tag.

Bats get around by using *echolocation*. (Break it into 2 smaller words, *echo* and *location*.) Bats fly around squeaking all the time. Their squeaks "bounce" off objects and echo back to the bat's big ears. Bats use the echo to tell the location of the object. This works so well that they can zero in on (and eat) hundreds of mosquitoes in a single night.

What You'll Need
● blindfold

To play bat tag, you'll need a group of people. You'll also need a big, open area with no trees or other things to run into! Choose someone to be the bat. The others will be insects. Blindfold the bat. The other players spread out. Once the game begins, the bat begins to squeak. The player that is facing the bat should squeak back, like an echo. The bat can move around, but the other players do not move. The bat has to find and tag the other players by listening to their squeaks. When each "insect" is tagged, it stops squeaking. The last "insect" to be tagged is the bat next time.

Clean As a . . . Bat?

Bats have a terrible reputation, and lots of people think they're unclean. But bats wash themselves like cats do, licking their fur very carefully. They comb themselves with their claws, too, and they clean out their ears with a knuckle. So, actually, bats are very clean animals.

How Tadpoles Breathe

With a steady hand and some patience, you can watch tadpoles breathe.

What You'll Need
- tadpole
- clear plastic cup
- water
- eyedropper
- food coloring

Caution: This project requires adult supervision.

Look in shallow ponds for tadpoles. Catch one good-size tadpole, and put it in a clear plastic cup of pond water. When the tadpole is sitting still, fill an eyedropper with food coloring. Slowly and gently lower the tip of the eyedropper into the water until the tip is close to the tadpole's mouth. You may want to practice with a water-filled eyedropper until you can do this without disturbing the tadpole.

Once the eyedropper is in place, slowly squeeze out one drop of food coloring into the water in front of the tadpole. Slowly and carefully remove the eyedropper and closely observe the tadpole. If the animal hasn't moved, colored water will soon stream out from the gills on the sides of the tadpole's head. The tadpole breathes by drawing water through its mouth and passing the oxygen-rich water across gills that contain small blood vessels. The tadpole takes in oxygen from the water and releases carbon dioxide. The water passes out of the gill openings.

Remember to put the tadpole back in the pond when you're finished with the experiment! Frogs are becoming endangered.

Fish Respiration

Fish breathe underwater, which means they take in oxygen through water instead of through air. While a fish swims through the water, its gills absorb the oxygen in the water and pass it through its bloodstream and membranes.

Camouflage Toothpicks

Learn how camouflage can protect some animals.

Add water to each of 3 cups. Add blue food coloring to the first cup, green food coloring to the second cup, and red food coloring to the third. Put 50 wooden toothpicks into each of these solutions and leave them for one day.

Gather a group of volunteers and head out to a green, grassy field with your colored toothpicks. Choose a leader to sprinkle the toothpicks around the field. Depending on the number of people, have the leader give an amount of time to find and pick up the toothpicks, such as 30 seconds. The time allowed should be short enough to make the group feel rushed; you don't want everyone walking over and over the same areas trying to find the toothpicks. Before beginning, tell everyone the rules: To pick up a toothpick they must not kneel or crawl. They need to reach down with one hand and pick up only one toothpick and put that into the other hand. Each time they bend over, they can only pick up one toothpick. Tell them you want to see who can pick up the most toothpicks in the amount of time allotted.

After time has elapsed, have everybody count the colors they have found. Then make a chart that shows the numbers for the entire group. Analyze the data. Were all the captured toothpick colors present in the same amounts?

You probably found that there were less green toothpicks. This is because the green toothpicks were camouflaged against the green lawn. This made it more difficult to find them. In what type of lawn might the yellow toothpicks be hard to find?

Blubber Bags

◆▶◆▶◆▶◆

Find out how seals and whales stay warm, even in very cold water!

What You'll Need
- bucket
- ice cubes
- water
- 2 large plastic bags
- vegetable shortening

Do this experiment with a friend for extra fun. Fill a bucket with ice and water; make sure the water is very cold.

Be sure there are no holes in the plastic bags. Fill one bag about half full with vegetable shortening. Have your friend slip the second bag over his or her hand, like a glove, and slide it into the shortening-filled bag. Your friend should mush the shortening around until it surrounds the hand. Now plunge your bare hand into the bucket of ice water, and hold it there for 20 to 30 seconds. After you take your hand out of the water, your friend should plunge his or her blubber glove into the ice water.

How long could your friend keep his or her gloved hand in the water? Why do you think the gloved hand stayed as warm and comfortable as a seal in the winter?

Now take your turn with the blubber bag, and see for yourself what a difference the "blubber" makes.

Gulping Fish

◆◆◆◆◆◆◆

Water temperature affects a fish's ability to take in oxygen.

What You'll Need

- 2 aquariums
- 4 comet goldfish
- 2 aquarium thermometers
- paper and pen
- water

Fish don't breathe the way you do, but they do get oxygen by gulping in water and pumping it over their gills. The gills are able to take oxygen from the water.

Set up 2 small fish tanks to hold 2 comet goldfish each. (Get advice from your local aquarium store on setting up the tanks.) Once the fish are settled into their new home, observe the temperature of the water by checking the tank thermometer. It should be close to room temperature, between 65° and 70°F. Watch each of the 4 fish, and determine how many times per minute they gulp to take air from the water. Write these figures down.

Gradually add warm water to one tank until, over a period of 20 minutes, you raise the temperature 5°F. Gradually add cool water to the other tank until, over a period of 20 minutes, you lower the temperature 5°F. Do not change the temperature too fast, as this can be harmful to the fish. Record the gulping rates of all 4 fish again.

The fish gulped faster in warm water than in cool water. Warm water contains less oxygen than cool water, so fish in warm water have to work harder to get the oxygen they need from the water.

Conservation

✦✦✦✦✦✦

Many animals are having a tough time surviving, because as human communities spread, they take habitat from animals. You can help the animals by providing additional habitat areas.

 ## A Tragic Lesson

✦✦✦✦✦✦

Oil spills are a terrible tragedy for all of nature. See how they affect animals.

1. Put an ice cube into each of the plastic bags. Squeeze all the air out of the bags, and seal them. Put each of the bags on a separate plate.

2. Soak 2 cotton balls in vegetable oil. Put one of the cotton balls on top of one of the plastic bags. Make sure the cotton ball stays on top of the ice cube. Put the other oil-soaked cotton ball on an empty plate.

3. Put a dry cotton ball on the other plastic bag (on top of the ice cube). Put another dry cotton ball on an empty plate.

> ### What You'll Need
> - 2 ice cubes
> - 2 resealable plastic bags
> - 4 plates
> - 4 cotton balls
> - vegetable oil

4. Let everything sit for 20 minutes. Pick up the 2 dry cotton balls—the one that is on the ice cube and the one that is on the plate. Are they about the same temperature or is one colder? Then pick up the 2 oil-soaked cotton balls—the one that is on the ice cube and the one that is on the plate. Does one feel colder? Pick up the 2 cotton balls that were on the ice cubes again. Does one feel colder? What does this tell you about the connection between oil and keeping warm?

Imagine that those cotton balls are birds, otters, or other animals. When an animal gets soaked with oil, it gets cold, just like the oil-soaked cotton balls. That's because oil destroys the natural insulation that animals have.

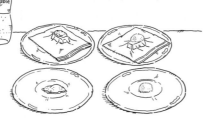

Whenever there's an oil spill, animals die for many reasons. Some are poisoned by the oil. Birds starve to death because they cannot fly to catch food. Some animals die because their food has been killed by the oil. And some animals freeze to death because oil has destroyed their ability to stay warm.

Feed Your Corny Friends

◆◆◆◆◆◆

Make friends with bushy-tailed squirrels, one kernel at a time.

What You'll Need
- dried corn on the cob (from animal feed or gardening stores)
- sturdy string
- stepping stool

It's not good to feed wild animals your favorite foods. Sugary choices like cookies or candy can rot the teeth of wild creatures. And that's bad, because they rely on those teeth for the rest of their lives. For squirrels, nuts are an obvious alternative to candy or cookies. But so is another of our favorite foods—good

old-fashioned corn. Squirrels LOVE corn, and most feed and gardening stores keep dried corn cobs in stock just for those furry friends. So why not try it yourself? Buy a bag of corn, and securely tie it to the lower branches of a tree. Now sit back, and watch these cute rodents feast on the fun. You'll be glad you gave them real eats instead of treats.

Deck the Tree

◆◆◆◆◆◆

Wild animals will appreciate a tree full of treats—especially in the winter.

This activity is fun to do in wintertime, but you can do it any time. Pick a tree in a somewhat secluded spot. In the afternoon, decorate the tree with edible treats for animals. You could use fruit (grapes or pieces of apple, pear, or banana), nuts, bread smeared with peanut butter, vegetables, chunks

What You'll Need
- animal treats
- rake

of cheese, or anything else you think animals would enjoy. After you've finished, rake the ground around the tree until it is smooth.

Come back the next morning to see what treats were eaten and what tracks were left. If you can find an adult who will come with you, you can visit your tree at night and see the animals that go there.

Backyard Wildlife Sanctuary

◆▶◆▶◆▶◆▶

Make a home for wildlife in your backyard!

What You'll Need
- gardening tools (rake, shovel, etc.)
- materials from the suggestions below

Our suburban homes cover a lot of land. You can give some of it back to the animals by turning your backyard into a mini-sanctuary and providing the basics: food, water, and shelter.

If you can, plant native plants that bear the fruit, nuts, seeds, nectar, and pollen that wild animals like to eat. Hazel-nut trees, elderberries, service berries, huckleberries, and wildflowers are terrific.

You can also buy or build bird feeders. Fill the feeders with seeds songbirds prefer, such as sunflower seeds, white millet, and thistle. In the summer, fill hummingbird feeders with nectar made from 1 cup sugar and 4 cups water. In the winter, hang suet feeders.

Water is often scarce. One way to supply water is to set out birdbaths and keep them clean. Put the bowl of a birdbath on the ground for small mammals and ground-feeding birds. Give butterflies a drink, too. Fill a basin with sand, and keep it wet. Place the basin near flowers, where butterflies visit.

Birds and small mammals need safe places to hide, build nests, and stay warm and dry in bad weather. If you can, plant a long hedgerow of native shrubs. Build piles of rocks, brush, or logs for small animals.

For more information on backyard wildlife sanctuaries, call your local Fish and Wildlife Department. They will have brochures and printed material to help you plan a sanctuary for your area.

Your Own Refuge!

Register your own backyard refuge with the National Wildlife Federation. To learn how, write: Backyard Wildlife Habitat Program, National Wildlife Federation, 11100 Wildlife Center Drive, Reston, VA 20190-5362, or visit http://www.nwf.org on the Internet.

"Don't Go!"

Endangered animals are animals that are in danger of becoming extinct. Find out how to help these vanishing creatures.

There are more than 700 species of animals on the endangered list, including the giant panda and the blue whale. Do research to find out some of the other animals that are facing extinction. (Local nature organizations or local zoos are good places to ask.) Then, choose one endangered animal that you especially care about. Learn as much as you can about that animal. Find out where it lives, why it is endangered, and what people are doing to help (and maybe to harm!) it. Most important, find out what you can do to help.

What You'll Need
- reference books
- poster board
- markers

Here's one thing you can do: Make a poster telling others about the animal and how they can help. Try to display your poster in a public place—such as a library or store—where lots of people will see it.

Saving the Animals

An endangered species of animal is one that is in danger of dying out. This danger could be because hunters kill off the animals or it could be because the animal's environment has changed. People can help reverse the situation, though. In 1965, only 6,000 vicunas—a camellike animal that lives in South America—were still alive. People killed vicunas for their wool. By protecting the vicuna from hunting and by giving them an appropriate place to live, there are now about 160,000 vicunas.

Thirsty?

In very hot or very cold weather, wild animals may have trouble finding enough water to drink. Quench their thirst with an animal "drinking fountain."

What You'll Need
- plastic milk jug
- scissors
- tape
- rocks
- large shallow container
- water

In hot weather, the usual sources of water may evaporate or run dry. In cold weather, these same water sources may freeze. Help the animals by putting water out for them.

If the wildlife in your area consists of small animals (such as squirrels, chipmunks, skunks, rabbits, and raccoons), you can make a small water basin out of a plastic milk jug with the top cut off. Put tape around the rim to cover the sharp edge. Make sure the container is shallow enough that these small critters can drink out of it. Put a few rocks in the bottom of the container so the animals don't accidentally knock it over. If predators (such as coyotes or wild cats) live nearby, put the water near trees, so small animals have an escape route if danger appears. If larger animals (such as deer) live in your area, you'll want to use a larger container. A galvanized tub from a hardware store works well.

In summer, refill containers often to offset evaporation. In winter, go out every morning. If ice has formed in the container, break it up and add more water if needed. Remember: Water in small, shallow containers will freeze more quickly than water in large, deep containers. If water is scarce, your "drinking fountains" will attract many animals. At dawn and dusk, stand back at a safe distance and watch them.

Pets

You might have an easy way to explore animal life. Observing your guinea pig, tropical fish, cat, or dog gives you valuable insights into the living world.

Poochy Parade

<><><><><><><>

Proudly parade your puppies!

What You'll Need
- friends with dogs and leashes
- accessories
- portable tape or CD player

Everyone loves a parade. Everyone loves dogs. Why not combine 2 all-American favorites on the next sunny Saturday afternoon? Gather together all your friends with dogs and plot out the event. Whose dogs get along with other dogs? Whose dogs are better on their own? Which dogs are big? Which dogs are extra-small? Pick a theme like "Puppy Love" or "Man's Best Friend," and invent silly, inexpensive doggie accessories—red construction paper hearts gently taped to fur, poster boards hanging from the necks of each puppy's pet person. Then march to one of your favorite doggone songs—"(You Ain't Nothing But a) Hound Dog," "How Much Is that Doggie in the Window?," or maybe even music from *101 Dalmatians*. Be sure someone's parent is on hand to take plenty of pictures. This will be a dog-day afternoon to remember.

Fleas Be Gone!

<><><><><><><>

If you have a cat or a dog, you're probably familiar with fleas. Making an herbal flea collar is a natural way to help keep these pests away from your pet... and you!

If you have a small dog or a cat, you can make a flea collar from a bandanna. Soak the bandanna in a mixture of ¼ cup olive oil and 3 drops of oil of pennyroyal (available at an herb store, natural foods grocery, or pharmacy). Let the bandanna dry, then tie it on your pet. Make sure the bandanna is big enough, and tie it loosely so that it doesn't hurt your pet. After the bandanna is tied, there should be room for you to put 3 of your fingers between your pet's neck and the bandanna. If you have a larger dog, you can make a collar from a strip of cloth that is 6 inches longer than the measurement around your dog's neck.

What You'll Need
- bandanna
- olive oil
- measuring cup
- oil of pennyroyal

Kitty Corner

◆▸▸▸▸▸◀◀◀◀◀◆

Give your outdoor cats a warm place to curl up.

What You'll Need
- old blanket
- scissors
- newspaper "stuffing"
- needle and thread

Many cats prefer spending time outdoors. If you have a kitty friend that lives for wide-open spaces, why not cozy up a corner for those sleepier times? Does your cat have a favorite spot under the rose bush? Does she sleep on the back porch in the sun? Make a mental note of where your cat snoozes.

Now, ask your parents for old newspapers, an old blanket, and a needle and thread. Cut 2 pieces of the blanket into heart shapes about 3 feet across and 3 feet tall. Stitch one side of the heart together at the edges to make a pillow, stuff it with newspapers, then sew up the remaining half at the edges. Then, put your cat's new special pillow in its favorite spot!

Dog Wash

◆▸▸▸▸▸◀◀◀◀◀◆

Polished poochy could mean a pocket full of cash.

Want to try a wet-and-wild moneymaker when the summer months finally hit? Check out the fun and profit possible in washing your neighborhood's pet dogs. Slip into your swim-suit, then let your neighbors know you and a partner will bathe dogs for just $3 a head. Start with the pups in your own backyards.

What You'll Need
- water
- baby shampoo
- plastic bucket
- hose
- old towels

Have one partner gently hold the dog while the other washes. First, wet the dog down, carefully avoiding getting water in its ears or eyes. Pour about 2 tablespoons of generic baby sham-poo into your wet hands and rub them together to make a soap and water paste. Now apply it to the dog's back and chest. Work up a good lather, again, careful of the eyes and ears. Hose all the soap from the dog's body as you rub. Towel excess water off the dog, and collect your cash!

Doggie Diary

Can you talk to the animals? Can they talk back?

What You'll Need
- notebook
- pen

Some experts say our pets have their own distinctive languages, even if we don't know how to interpret what they say. This fun experiment might help you get a clue to doggy dialogue. The next time you have a free day at home with your dog, pay close attention to how he "talks." Does he whimper when he wants to go outside? Write it down. Does he give a loud, short bark when he's hungry? Make a note of it. Now see if you can duplicate the sounds to communicate with your dog.

Sidewalk Pet Portraits

Celebrate neighborhood pets with sidewalk portraits.

What You'll Need
- sidewalk chalk

Does your neighborhood have the world's greatest pets? Why not tell the world? Take out your sidewalk chalk, and let your drawings tell the story. That big spider down the street is scary but sweet—chalk up each of his 8 legs. Great Danes aren't called "great" for nothing. Draw it extra large. Is there a cute new kitty on your block or a pretty canary? Let your drawings tell the story. They're sure to make the neighbors smile.

Salamander Terrarium

◆▶◆▶◆▶◆

Make a cool, comfortable home for a pet salamander.

Salamanders are sold in pet shops. You can find them in woods and ponds, too, but never take one from the wild. Wild animals need to be in their own homes. Before bringing a salamander home, read about it and find out how to care for it.

Rinse aquarium gravel in a sieve before using. Cover the bottom of an aquarium with an inch of gravel. Mound clean gravel up on one side to form a hill about 6 inches high and as wide as half the length of the aquarium. Add enough water to make a pond about 3 inches deep, leaving the top of the mound out of water. (If you use tap water, add a dechlorinator, or let the aquarium sit for 24 hours to allow the chlorine to evaporate.) Cover the top of the mound with forest moss, and dampen it. Put a glass or plastic cover on the aquarium to maintain humidity.

The aquarium is now ready for your guest. Offer it crickets, small worms, or mealworms to eat, or catch insects outdoors to feed it. Try several foods to see what it prefers.

What You'll Need
- salamander
- aquarium
- gravel
- sieve
- moss from woods
- water
- insects as food
- dechlorinator (optional)

A Basket for Bowser

◆▶◆▶◆▶◆

Cats, dogs, and other furry pets will enjoy this fresh grass basket—
any time of year.

Cats love to munch on catnip and other good-smelling herbs.
Dogs—especially dogs who live in city apartments—will enjoy
frolicking with their own little patch of grass. And other pets
such as hamsters, guinea pigs, and—of course—rabbits also
enjoy fresh greens. Find out what kind of "salad" your pet
would enjoy. Then get seeds or seedlings for those plants.
Line the basket with plastic, and poke a few small holes in the
bottom for drainage. Put in a half-and-half mix of vermiculite
and potting soil. Either plant the seedlings, or sprinkle the
seeds on the soil. Water well. If you're starting from seeds, put
plastic wrap over them. Put the basket in a warm sunny spot
indoors. Keep it watered.

> ### What You'll Need
> - herb or grass seeds or seedlings
> - basket without a handle
> - plastic trash bag
> - scissors
> - vermiculite and potting soil
> - plastic wrap

When the plants have grown to fill the basket, give your pets a present! If you keep
the basket in a place where it gets light and keep it watered, the plants will keep growing to replace what your pets eat.

Cat Walking

◆▶◆▶◆▶◆

This purrrfectly wonderful activity will keep you on your toes.

Scientists say cats actually walk on their toes at least 80 percent of the time. Could you
manage that? Practice walking on your toes to your favorite song, counting 1, 2, 3, 4, 5,
6, 7, 8 as you go. When you get to 9 and 10, walk as you normally do. Start your cat
walk again, counting 1 ,2, 3, 4, 5, 6, 7, 8, then walking flat-footed again for steps 9 and
10. How do your legs feel? Want to test a new catlike rhythm? Do the same cat walk to
the beats of your name.

Understanding Your Pet

◆▶▶▶▶▶◀

**If you have pets, listen to them and watch them
to see how they communicate with you and other animals.**

What You'll Need
- notebook
- pen
- markers

Watch your pet's eyes, ears, tails, paws, and fur. And watch their whole bodies. Try to figure out what they "say" by using their bodies. Does your dog or cat ever run back and forth between you and her food bowl? Or between you and the door? ("Lemme outta here!") Does your pet roll over and look at you to let you know she wants a tummy rub?

Animals also use their voices in more ways than you might think. How many different barks does your dog have, and what do they all mean? He probably has one bark for "Someone's at the door!" and another bark for "Hey, you stepped on my paw!" He probably also growls, whines, and makes other sounds. Each sound means he's trying to communicate with you or another animal. It's the same with cats. They may have one meow to say, "Feed me!" and another to say, "Can I come in now?"

Try making a pet dictionary where you record all the different ways your pets communicate and what you think each thing means. You could draw pictures of what your pets look like when they're "saying" different things. The more you pay attention to your pets, the better you'll understand them.

Protective Mothers

Just like a human baby, a newborn animal is small and vulnerable and needs to be protected in the wild. Some animals—called marsupials—keep their young in a small pouch in front of their belly. Female kangaroos and koalas protect their babies this way. A mother crocodile takes a different approach: She carries her young in her mouth to keep them safe from harm!

Fish Keeping

▶▶▶▶▶▶▶

An aquarium is a balanced ecosystem.

What You'll Need
- aquarium
- plants
- fish
- snails

One way to observe an ecosystem with producers, consumers, and decomposers is to set up a balanced aquarium. This requires quite a lot of equipment, some help from your local pet shop, and patience. Consult with an expert at your local pet shop about what you'll need to set up a balanced 10-gallon freshwater aquarium. Once the tank is ready, you can start adding creatures. Include snails to help keep the walls of your tank free from algae. Include a bottom scavenger to help keep the tank clean. Be sure to add fish that can live together, and don't overcrowd your tank. Follow directions for feeding. If you need brine shrimp for food, learn how to raise them yourself. Properly maintained, your aquarium will provide a lot of pleasure, and it will provide a good example of a balanced ecosystem with producers, consumers, and decomposers.

Wet Life

▶▶▶▶▶▶▶

Part of the fascination with SCUBA diving and snorkeling is exploring life in a different world—the world of water. Aquatic organisms, including clams, fish, and whales have many adaptations that help them thrive in their watery habitat.

Marsh Watch

◆◆◆◆◆◆◆

Get close to water wildlife.

What You'll Need
- notebook
- pencil

Wetlands—freshwater marshes, salty estuaries, cold bogs, and woody swamps—are important to wildlife. Wetlands, which provide water, dense cover, and sources of food, are ideal places to watch wildlife. Look around your community for marshes and other wetlands where you can observe animals. Many wetlands are preserved in National Wildlife Refuges, in parks, and on private land. There is bound to be a place with open, shallow water that you can visit.

When you visit a marsh, move slowly and quietly so you don't disturb the wildlife, especially in the spring and early summer when birds are nesting. Find a place near the water's edge where you can sit comfortably. A good observation spot will have some shrubs you can hide behind yet still have a clear view. Be still and silent for at least 15 minutes. It takes that long or longer for the animals nearby to get used to your presence. As the animals come out and become active again, take notes on what you observe. The more often you visit, the more you will see.

Ocean Motion

Creatures in the ocean use many unusual methods to move. Fish swim by moving their bodies from side to side, but whales and dolphins move their tales up and down. Squids and octopuses shoot water out of a nozzle, forcing themselves to move along, and sea slugs creep along the bottom of the sea on a muscle called a foot.

Pond Dipping

◆◆◆◆◆◆◆

Discover the complex world of pond life.

What You'll Need

- stiff wire coat hanger
- heavy wood staples (the kind that are hammered in)
- broomstick
- waterproof tape
- tape measure
- scissors
- cheesecloth or wide-mesh nylon net
- needle and thread
- tall rubber boots
- bucket
- large metal pan (such as an aluminum roasting pan)

Caution: This project requires adult supervision.

One way to explore pond life is to make a dip net and catch living organisms for observation. To make a dip net, bend a stiff wire coat hanger in the shape of a D, leaving the hook in the middle of the straight part of the D. Straighten the hook, and use heavy wood staples to fasten the straightened hook to the end of a broomstick. Fold the wire back over the last staple. Wrap the end in waterproof tape.

Measure the distance around the wire frame. Cut some cheesecloth that width and 18 inches long. Sew the sides together to form a tube. Stitch one end of the tube shut. Sew the open end of the tube to the frame by turning the edge over the frame then stitching the fabric to itself.

To use your dip net, put on rubber boots and wade into a pond (with an adult along). Be careful not to wade in water deeper than your boots. Hold the net in the water with the handle upright and the net resting on the pond bottom. Have a bucket with a little water in it ready in the other hand. Move slowly through the water, and gently move the net up and down. Stop now and then to dump the contents of your net into the bucket. After you've done several nettings, come ashore and dump the bucket into a large pan. Add a little water so your animals can swim while you observe them.

When you are done, return the animals to the pond. Some pond animals (like our native turtles) are endangered because of overcollection.

Underwater Night Life

Some water-dwellers are more active at night than during the day. Here's how to get a close-up look at these creatures of the night.

What You'll Need
- life vest
- strong flashlight
- plastic bags
- tape
- rope
- notebook
- pen

Caution: This project requires adult supervision.

Have an adult go along with you for this project. At night, go down to a dock or a similar place where you can look down into water at least a few feet deep. You could also go out on a pond in a boat. Whether on a dock or a boat, always put on a life vest for safety.

Seal a flashlight into a plastic, zipper-type bag. Roll the bag around the flashlight, then seal it in a second bag. Tape the edges for a watertight seal. Tie a rope to the flashlight, turn it on, and lower it down into the water. Now wait patiently. Soon the light will attract curious creatures. See what kinds of fish and other creatures are active at night. Keep a nature notebook. Draw what you see, and try to identify the animals. Try this in several different areas and compare. See what differences there are between different bodies of water.

Snag Some Shells

Start a collection of treasures and gems from the sea.

A sandy shoreline, especially one protected by an offshore reef, is a great place to collect shells on the morning of a calm

day at low tide, especially after a storm. Strong winds and high waves will have littered the beach with ocean debris. Carry a bucket and some old newspapers for wrapping up your shells.

What You'll Need
- bucket
- old newspapers

When you find a good shell, check it for animals. If it is empty, wrap the shell in newspaper and add it to your bucket.

Eggs Underwater

◆◆◆◆◆◆◆

Have a close look at eggs that pond animals lay.

What You'll Need
- shallow pan
- water
- magnifying glass

In the spring, hunt around the edges of ponds in your area to look for the jellylike eggs of frogs, salamanders, and toads. Salamander eggs lie in stiff masses, often with green algae living inside the jelly. Frog and toad eggs may be laid in strings or soft masses. Pull some loose leaves out of the water; you may find small blobs containing snail eggs on the undersides of submerged leaves. If you have an aquarium with snails, look for their eggs, too.

When you find eggs, put them in a shallow pan with some water and have a look. Use your magnifying glass to observe them. Freshly laid eggs will have little for you to see, but older eggs will have tiny tadpoles inside them. Snail eggs will have tiny white embryonic snails moving slowly inside. Put the eggs back in the water, and mark the spot where you found them.

Return once a week, and check the progress of the eggs. See how long it takes for the tadpoles or baby snails to hatch. Don't take the eggs home in a jar to watch. It's best to leave the eggs in their natural setting, where they will be at the correct temperature and will get plenty of oxygen. The eggs will suffocate in a confined jar.

Water Strider

The water strider is an insect that uses the surface tension of water to its advantage. When it hunts for prey, its widely spaced feet help it run along the water's surface.

Fish Prints

◆◆◆◆◆◆◆

*"Gyotaku"—or fish printing—is a well-respected form of art in Japan.
Make your own beautiful prints using real fish.*

What You'll Need
- fish with large scales
- pan
- brush
- water-based ink or tempera paint
- thin paper (real rice paper is best, but newsprint will work)

You can buy special inks and rice paper for your prints or simply use newsprint and paint. Select a fish with large scales for the best prints. Lay it in a pan, and wipe it clean. Using a brush, cover the fish with a very thin coat of water-based ink or paint. You can make the whole fish one color, or use different colors on the fins, make stripes—whatever you like.

Next, lay the paper on top of the fish. Gently press the paper onto the fish, using your fingers to shape it around the curves of the fish's body. Slowly peel back the paper and look at your print. Try printing again without adding more ink. Sometimes the second print is better. You can make fishy T-shirts and bandannas if you use fabric paint instead of ink or tempera paint.

A Big Fish Story

When you think of a fish, you may think of small ones, such as a pet goldfish. Fish range in size, however, from less than ½ inch long—the dwarf goby—to 40-foot long whale sharks. In 1959, Alfred Dean went fishing off Australia, and he reeled in a white shark that actually weighed 2,664 pounds!

Tidepooling

◆◆◆◆◆◆◆

Learn about the creatures of the rocky tides.

Caution: This project requires adult supervision.

To plan the best time to visit tidepools, get a local tide table from a sporting goods store. Arrive at the tidepools with your adult partner an hour or so before low tide to begin looking as the tide is going out. Sit near the edge of a large pool to observe animals. The longer you look, the more you will see. While actual species will vary at each shoreline, here are some types of animals you're likely to see:

Sea anemones: These simple animals have tentacles around the mouth to trap food. If you gently touch a tentacle, it will feel sticky. This is caused by tiny stingers too small to pierce your skin but able to sting small prey.

Sea stars: Get flat, and watch a sea star in the water moving slowly across the rocks. Can you see the tube feet moving? Sea stars eat mussels, clams, and other shellfish. If you see one with its arms pulled in close and its middle hunched, it's probably eating.

Sea urchins: These close relatives of sea stars look like colorful pincushions. Urchins use their spines for defense as well as to scrape rocks to make round holes to hide in. Can you see long tube feet sticking out between the spines? The urchin uses these to move and to pass food to the mouth on the bottom of the animal.

Crabs: Most tidepool crabs are scavengers. Watch them using their claws to feed. Crabs are usually shy, so be patient and watch for them.

Use your notebook to record what you see and approximately where you see it. You'll notice that some animals live in certain areas of the tidal shore. A guidebook to tidepool animals will help you identify actual species and will help you spot animals found only in your area.

Comb the Beach

◆◆◆◆◆◆◆

Learn why different shoreline organisms live where they do.

What You'll Need
- tide table
- large ball of string
- scissors
- rock
- brightly colored bandannas or scraps of cloth
- notebook
- pencil
- yardstick
- graph paper

Caution: This project requires adult supervision.

Get a tide table from a sporting goods store and look up the next convenient low tide. Arrive at a rocky shoreline an hour before low tide. Find a spot above high tide where you can tie one end of a string to a rock, tree, or a stake. Tie a bandanna to the spot so it's visible. Run the string toward the ocean, stopping as close to the water as you can safely go. Use a rock to hold down the other end of the string.

Starting at the upper end, farthest from the water, write down the most common organisms you see. Work your way slowly down the string. When you see different animals, stop at that spot and mark it with another bandanna. Look back to the first marker and estimate how far down you've dropped in elevation. (Estimate the vertical drop, not how far you've walked.) Continue down the string, adding a bandanna each time you see a different organism.

When you reach the end of the string, wind the string and retrieve the bandannas. As you wind, measure the distance between markers and write that down in your notebook. Get a large piece of graph paper. Let each square represent a vertical foot of shoreline. Use your measurements of vertical distance and the distance between markers to help you draw the shoreline. Then draw in the animals of each zone.

You can use the same mapping techniques to map sandy shores. Rather than using a string, mark a straight line in the sand.

Whale Watching

◆▸◆▸◆▸◆▸◆

With luck, you may be able to spot some of the world's largest animals!

What You'll Need
- binoculars
- warm clothing
- lunch

If you're visiting a rocky coastline on the Atlantic or Pacific oceans, you may be able to watch for migrating whales. Ask local inhabitants about whales in the area. (Rugged, rocky areas of the Pacific coast are good places to watch for rare gray whales in late winter and early spring.) Set out early in the morning on a windless, overcast day to a rocky headland that juts out into deep water. Bring binoculars, extra clothing, and snacks or a picnic lunch.

Watch for the blows of spouting whales. A whale blow looks like a puff of smoke at the water's surface. See if you can identify the whale from its blow. You should also be able to see the whale's dark back.

Use your binoculars to look for tail flukes coming out of the water as the whale dives. (This behavior is called *sounding.*) The whales will surface hundreds of yards or more from where you saw them dive.

If you're near a lagoon where whales gather, you may spot interesting whale behavior. Gray whales will "spyhop," lifting their snouts out of the water to the level of their eyes. If you're lucky, you may see a whale breech—that is, to leap nearly clear of the water and come down with a splash! No one really knows why whales do this. It may be a courtship ritual, a stress-reliever, a way to shake off parasites, or just plain fun!

Flying Fish

◆◆◆◆◆◆◆

Fish seem to fly through the air with this attractive mobile.

Find reference books about fish in your local library. There are many differently colored and shaped fish in the world. Find your favorite in the books, and make a fish mobile that will be sure to catch everyone's attention!

Draw the outline of the fish you have chosen, making sure the outline is about 7 inches long and at least 5 inches high. If you'd really like to go all out, choose 3 different fish and make a large outline shape for each. Trace your initial outline on 5 more sheets of paper—making a total of 6 fish. (If you are making 3 different fish, copy each outline once more—making a total of 2 outlines for each fish.) Use paper clips to hold the 2 fish shapes together, then staple them together at the edges. Staple all around the body except the back of the tail. Make a total of 3 fish this way.

Tear sheets of newspaper into thin strips. Scrunch up the strips, and stuff them into the fish. When each fish is full, staple across the tail to keep the stuffing inside. Paint the fish any way you like. You can paint them so they are realistic, or you can be fanciful with your painting!

Punch a hole in the top of each fish. Cut 3 lengths of string. Tie an end of a piece of string to the top of the fish, and then tie the other end of the string to a coat hanger. Repeat for the other 2 fish. Hang your fish mobile for all to see!

If you don't like fish, why not try a bird, dog, cat, or bear mobile? Your local library has all the books you need to do research on any of these animals!

What You'll Need
- reference books
- 6 sheets of paper
- ruler
- pencil
- scissors
- paper clips
- stapler
- newspaper
- paints
- paintbrush
- hole punch
- string
- coat hanger

Froghopper

◆◆◆◆◆◆◆

Ribbit, ribbit.

We all know dinosaurs became extinct some 65 million years ago. Many scientists believe the frogs of the world could be next to go. These friendly amphibians seem to be facing the same destiny—just like many big cats of the world. Have the frogs and toads in your region started to vanish? Take an afternoon to find out. Head to your local pond or shoreline and watch for hoppers in shallow water!

I Spy

◆◆◆◆◆◆◆

Now you can go snorkeling without even getting your face wet!

So what's there to do when you're standing knee-deep in a lake and you're just not up for a swim? Use a "snorkel mask" to check out what's going on below the water's surface!

First, cut out the bottom of a large ice-cream tub. Cover this hole (and the sides of the container) with a large piece of plastic wrap. Tape the wrap in place. To make sure the plastic wrap stays put, slide a rubber band over it at the top of the container. Do the same at the other end.

Now you're ready for some underwater exploring! Place the plastic-covered end of your mask in some shallow water. Then, look through the open end of the mask and see if you can catch a glimpse of plants and animals in their watery home. Be sure you don't get any water inside the mask, or it'll sink like a stone!

What You'll Need
- plastic 2-liter ice-cream container
- scissors
- plastic wrap
- tape
- rubber bands

THE GREAT OUTDOORS

❖❖❖❖❖❖❖

Hit the trail and discover the wonders of the great outdoors! Whether you head to the mountains, desert, beach, lake, forest, or just your own backyard, you'll find plenty of places to hike or pitch a tent. Learn to camp like a pro, leaving no sign you've been there. Walk in the footsteps of the early explorers. Find out how good food can taste when you cook it outdoors over a fire or a camp stove. And at all times, be a good outdoor citizen. Clean up after yourself, and don't pester or feed the animals. Happy trails!

Leave No Trace

❖❖❖❖❖❖❖

There are three important mottos to remember when you hike in the wilderness: "Leave only footprints. Take only memories (photographs are okay too!). Kill only time." Follow these simple guidelines, and you'll help to protect nature for generations to come.

Shoe In, Shoe Out

◆◆◆◆◆◆◆

Which shoes are best for the environment?

We think hiking boots are best for hitting the dusty trail. But this experiment shows that sneakers could be healthier for the wild and wonderful plants you see along the way. Lay out small cuttings from 6 or 7 of your favorite yard plants (after getting permission from Mom and Dad). Now take normal steps over those plants with your sneaker-covered feet. How do the plant bits look? Did they survive the "hike"?

What You'll Need
- sneakers
- variety of ordinary yard plants
- hiking boots

   Now slip into some hiking boots and repeat the experiment. Are your greens squashed? Hiking boots are much tougher on plant life than ordinary sneakers. So the next time you go for a hike off the beaten trail, do the indigenous plant life a favor and wear your favorite sneaks.

Leave It Alone

◆◆◆◆◆◆◆

Capture the magic of nature without leaving a trace.

What You'll Need
- leaf
- hard surface
- white paper
- crayons (some with the paper peeled away)

As you wander the wonders of nature and the great outdoors, you're bound to see dozens of things you'd love to remember and dozens of images you'd love to take home. But in many natural parks and outdoor centers, it's against the rules to pick a flower or even a single leaf. This project will help you collect memories without hurting a single petal.

   When you see a leaf, gently press it between a hard surface (like a piece of cardboard or a book) and a plain piece of white paper. Now, take a crayon with the paper peeled away and lay it on its side on the surface of the paper. Rub gently across the paper and leaf. Before you know it, you'll have a "copy" of the ridges and textures of that special leaf.

   Flowers don't hold up well to rubbings, but you can take the time to sketch a picture of the blossoms you see. Be sure to make notes about where you saw the flower and what made it special to you.

The Comforts of Home— Outdoors!

◆▷◆▷◆▷◆

How to keep clean out in the wild without harming the environment.

What You'll Need
- shovel
- biodegradable toilet paper (from a camping supplier)
- plastic garbage bags
- paper towels
- pot
- water
- biodegradable soap (from a camping supplier)
- bandanna

Here's how to take care of hygiene in the wildnerness without polluting. To make a one-day latrine, scoop a shallow "cat hole" in the dirt with your heel for solid waste and urine. Bury the waste when you are done. NEVER use waterways as toilets! For overnight camping, dig a latrine (around 10 inches deep) behind some bushes away from camp. Leave dirt and a trowel or shovel by the latrine to cover waste immediately. Keep biodegradable toilet paper in a waterproof container.

To make a garbage disposal, burn fruit peels and plate scrapings in a campfire (if you have one). Put other trash in plastic bags and suspend them from tree limbs. Take them when you leave. Don't bury your garbage, or animals will dig it up later. For dishwashing, wipe the pot out with a paper towel and burn the towel in your campfire (or put it in your garbage bag to throw out). Fill the pot with water and heat it. Add a drop of biodegradable soap. Let the water boil, then remove the pot. Let it cool, then swish the pot clean with a bandanna. Dig a shallow hole outside of camp to dump the soapy water into. Don't dump soapy or dirty water into streams, lakes, or rivers.

Without a Trace

Getting ready to pack up and head home? Be sure to erase all signs of your campsite before you leave! Pick up all trash— including any garbage left behind by campers before you. Leave your campsite cleaner than you found it, and you may inspire others to follow your example. After all, our natural resources are for everyone to share!

Campfire Safety

◆◆◆◆◆◆◆

It is important to keep campfires under control.

What You'll Need
- campfire
- water
- bucket
- shovel

Caution: This project requires adult supervision.

Sitting around a glowing campfire is a fun way to relax after a day of hiking. Unfortunately, many campers don't know how to keep their fires safe. Each year, accidental forest fires burn plants in meadows and forests, kill animals and destroy their habitats, and threaten the lives of people. It is important that when you have a fire, you make it a safe fire. (Never start a fire on your own. Only adults should handle fire.)

First, select a safe spot for your fire. You don't want to put a fire where it could ignite overhead branches or dry grass. If you are at a campground, there may be a fire pit available. If so, be sure to use it. Remove all flammable materials within 5 feet of the circle. Have a shovel ready in case an adult needs to extinguish the fire.

When the fire is burning, an adult should always keep an eye on it to make sure the fire does not spread. You can help by making sure someone in your group is the designated fire watcher.

When your group is done with the fire, extinguish it with water using the "drown and stir" method. An adult pours water on the fire until it looks completely out. Then the ashes are stirred with the shovel and more water is poured on the coals.

Greetings on the Trail

◆▷◆▷◆▷◆▷

Say "hi" in the dirt.

What You'll Need
- stick
- water

In earlier times, explorers marked trees and rocks to help them retrace their steps or communicate with other explorers. In today's campgrounds, carving trees and rocks isn't a very good idea. But you can etch a message in the dirt for the next hiker. Use a sharp stick to carve your comment—your name, a message, a warning about a slippery rock—into the soil. If the dirt is too hard, add a trickle of fresh, clean water (water with no leaves or dirt in it) and then carve your hello. It's one way to reach out to other outdoor lovers without damaging the natural setting you came to see.

Survival Skills

◁▷◁▷◁▷◁▷

One of the exciting things about spending time outdoors is the challenge of leaving the comforts of home. You'll experience new ways of cooking and sleeping. You'll also learn to find your way around in this different environment so you don't get lost.

Know Your Poisons!

◆▶◆▶◆▶◆

Learn to recognize plants that will give you a rash if touched.

What You'll Need

- garden gloves
- drawings or photos of poisonous plants
- poster board or large construction paper
- home medical book
- construction paper
- scissors
- glue

Before you go hiking in the woods, you'd better know which plants have oils that could give you an itchy rash. Help yourself and your fellow hikers by knowing how to recognize the following plants:

Poison ivy has 3 pointed, shiny leaflets; in the summer, poison ivy may have white berries. Found over most of the United States, ivy may cross with poison oak where the 2 plants are found near each other. **Poison oak** is like poison ivy, but the leaves are more rounded and resemble the leaves of a white oak. The plant may be a shrub or a tree-climbing vine and is found mostly on the West Coast, usually in forests and on sunny, dry slopes. It's also found in disturbed places. **Poison sumac** has 7 to 9 pointed leaflets. The leaves are shiny, and it too may have white berries. Poison sumac is found mostly in the eastern United States.

If poisonous plants live in your area, find a specimen in the wild. ALWAYS WEAR GARDEN GLOVES. Photograph or draw it as accurately as you can. Use a home medical guide to learn proper treatment for contact with poisonous plants. Make a poster with this information using cut-out letters from construction paper.

Poison Warning

When you walk the trail, DON'T believe the dangerous myth that you can become immune to poison ivy by eating it. People who have tried it have landed in the hospital! If you come in contact with poison ivy or poison oak, use soap and water to wash the oils off right away.

Camping In

◆◆◆◆◆◆◆◆

Find camping fun in your own backyard!

Camping out miles from home might seem a little scary for beginners.

Camping in can be a great first step. Set up everything you'd normally use for outdoor camping and do your best to pretend you're really in the wild. Cook on the grill (with adult help). No TV, no electricity. (You can use the bathroom facilities inside; that's the only shortcut you'll take.) This is Camping 101, just to get you ready for the real thing.

What You'll Need
- tent
- sleeping bag
- charcoal grill (with adult help)

Orienteering Games

◆◆◆◆◆◆◆◆

Play outdoor games that challenge your map and compass skills.

What You'll Need
- orienteering-style compass with degree markings (such as a Silva compass)
- map of your local area or area of interest
- flags

If you know how to use a map and compass, you're ready for new challenges. These games are great to play with friends, fellow campers, or youth groups. Try the beeline game. Stand on a starting mark. Use a compass to find the exact bearing of a certain landmark within a few minutes' walk. Make sure there are obstacles between the landmarks and the starting point. Measure the distance in paces.

Have all players begin at the same starting point. Give each player or team of players the bearing of one of the landmarks. Tell them to go a certain number of paces in a straight line in their given direction. Don't tell them what landmark to aim for. On your signal, the teams set out. It's up to each team to cope with obstacles, but make sure to be safe and set rules regarding safety and private property. When the teams reach what they think is the destination, they should wave a flag as a signal. Award points to those closest to the landmark.

Give Me Some Direction

Which way is which in the dark?

Do you have a good sense of direction? Here's how to find out. Grab a friend, a blindfold, and a compass. Go to a wide-open space where you can walk in all directions (and fall down if you get dizzy). Have your friend wrap the blindfold around your eyes, then, with you facing north, have him spin you 3 times. Now, he should ask you to walk 2 steps to the north...then south...then east...then west. Make sure he uses a compass to check which way you go.

Solar Cooker

Try using the power of the sun to heat up a hot dog!

This solar cooker uses reflective surfaces and the "greenhouse" principle to generate heat from sunlight. It won't cook raw food but can heat a hot dog. Cut the top flaps off a medium-size cardboard box and turn it on its side. Cut the sides at an angle from the bottom corner up to about the middle of the top. Use the cardboard scraps to make a slanted interior tilting from the top to the back corner. Hold it together with masking tape. Cut a hole in the back of the box to reach through. Cut a door in the back of the slanted interior and hinge it with masking tape. Use masking tape to reinforce weak points in the box.

Line the inside of the box with foil, making a smooth, reflective surface. Cut around the door carefully and use loops of tape to attach the foil to the door. Cover the front of the box with clear, heavy-duty plastic wrap, pull the wrap tight, and tape it in place. Set your cooker in bright, hot sun so that the sun hits the plastic-wrapped front. Put your hot dog on a square of foil inside the cooker. Check after 15 minutes. Turn the box to follow the sun. Try moving the reflective portion to different angles.

How to Get Found

Getting lost in the woods is scary. Make a kit to help you get found fast!

What You'll Need
- aluminum foil
- map
- waterproof carrying bag
- large plastic garbage bag
- mylar emergency blanket
- whistle
- extra sweater or jacket
- unbreakable mirror
- granola bars
- water bottle
- compass

Common sense can keep you from getting lost in the outdoors and get you found even if you do. Before you go, press aluminum foil against the sole of your hiking shoe to make an impression of the tread. Search parties use impressions like these to find a missing person's footprints. Next, study a map of the area you'll be in, and learn the route. Give a copy of the map and your schedule to someone at home.

Then make a "get found" kit to carry in a waterproof bag. Include a large plastic garbage bag with a 10-inch hole in one corner, a mylar emergency blanket, a whistle, an extra sweater or jacket, an unbreakable mirror, granola bars, and extra water. Carry your map and compass in your hand or a convenient pocket. Check the map frequently, stay with your group at all times, and ALWAYS stay on the trail. When camping, don't wander from your site.

If you get lost, stay calm, stay in one place, and let rescuers find you. Establish a base camp. Choose a tree, and stay close to it.

Blow your whistle often, and flash your mirror in all directions to attract attention. If it's cold, put on the extra sweater or jacket. Sit by your tree and pull the trash bag over your head. (Your face should stick out of the hole you've cut.) Wrap the blanket around you for extra warmth and visibility. Blow that whistle. If you are cold, move around, but stay near the tree, which can be a windbreak. If it rains, you can stay dry in the trash bag!

Choose a Compass

◆◆◆◆◆◆◆

Make a compass, and you'll always know in what direction you're headed. You can make either a floating compass or a Chinese hanging compass—or both!

Rub the pointed end of the needle along a side of the magnet, always rubbing in the same direction. Do this about 30 times to magnetize the needle. You can test it by picking up a pin with it. If you will be making both compasses, repeat the process with the other needle.

Floating Compass: Cut a small piece of cork, and push the magnetized needle through it. Fill a plastic cup with water. Carefully place the cork with the magnetized needle into the cup so it floats in the center. The magnetized end will always face north.

Chinese Hanging Compass: Tie an end of a short piece of thread to the center of the magnetized needle, and tie the other end of the thread to a pencil. Place the pencil over the rim of the plastic cup. Again, the magnetized end of the needle will point north.

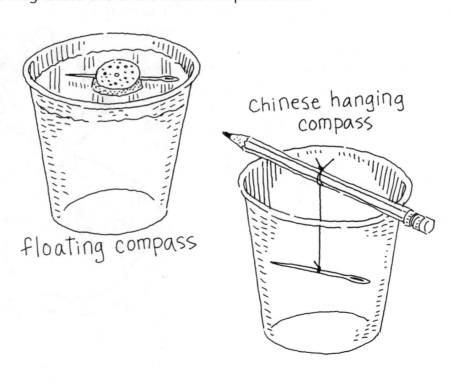

floating compass

chinese hanging compass

How to Use a Compass

Learn to use a map and compass to find your way outdoors.

What You'll Need

- orienteering-style compass with degree markings (such as a Silva compass)
- map of your local area or area of interest

If you learn to use a map and compass, you'll be less likely to get lost in the wilderness. To align the compass, read the directions for the compass and learn which end of the needle points north. Turn the compass until the north arrow on the compass' face is aligned with the north end of the pointer. You are now aligned "north." Observe the letters on the compass: N is north, E is east, S is south, W is west. You'll also find northeast, southeast, southwest, and northwest. Next, look at the numbers. These are degrees, another form of measuring compass direction.

Turn and face any direction. Hold one hand out flat and place the compass on your palm. Point the arrow on the baseplate in the direction you're facing. Turn the dial on the compass until the north-facing arrow is aligned with the pointer. Now read the degree mark that the index line crosses. This is your direction in degrees.

To find your bearing, place the map on the ground and find where you want to start and end. Place the compass so that it matches both points. Turn the dial until "north" points the same direction as the north indicator on the map. The index on the baseplate should now line up with the correct bearing on the dial. Turn the compass in the correct direction.

What You Really Need

What are the camping essentials? According to experts, always bring water, a compass, maps, a daypack, food, extra clothing, matches, a first-aid kit, a flashlight, sunscreen, bathroom paper, a mirror to signal with, and rain gear.

Trail Signs

◆◆◆◆◆◆◆

Early pioneers and explorers marked their way for others to follow.
See if you can do the same thing.

Whenever people have moved through new territory they marked the trail so they would not get lost. American Indians often bent trees to the ground to mark trails. Some of these "trail trees" have now grown to full-size trees. Early explorers and scouts used axe marks on trees. Outdoor youth clubs of today use temporary signs (borrowed from the American Indians) of twigs, grass, and stones.

To play a trail-marking game, have one person lay a cross-country trail through woods or an open field. The person should make trail markers 20 or so paces apart. (Be careful not to harm any live plants when you are making your markers.) Arrow shapes, stacks of rocks, or bundles of grass all say "I went this way." A bend in the grass bundle or a rock beside the pile means "turn this way." Three of anything means "warning." And X means "do not go this way." A circle means "this is the end of the trail." You can use the pictures on this page for ideas, or come up with some of your own. The rest of the players can try to follow the trail and see where the person ended up.

I went this way.

Turn this way.

Don't go this way.

Your Own Fishing Rod

◆▶◆▶◆▶◆

Assemble fishing tackle, and see what you can catch.

What You'll Need

- sturdy stick 4 to 5 feet long
- fishing line
- scissors
- fish hook
- plastic bobber
- bait

You don't need expensive equipment to catch fish. The fish don't care if your tackle is store-bought or homemade. The best type of stick for your fishing rod is strong yet slightly flexible. Bamboo, about ½ inch thick, would be ideal. Find something similar in your own yard or campground.

Let the thick part of the stick be the handle. Tie one end of the fishing line to the handle. Wrap the line in a spiral around the stick until you reach the tip. Tie the line firmly to the tip, but don't cut the line yet. Unroll the line about a foot longer than your stick, and cut it off the roll. You should have a continuous length of fishing line extending from the handle of your stick down to the hook. (That way, if the fishing rod breaks in the middle, you still have the line in your hand.)

Tie a hook to the end of the line. Fasten a bobber to the middle of the line. You'll want to use a ball-shape red and white bobber with a spring-loaded hook that will fasten it anywhere on the line. Now you're ready to fish! Go with an adult who knows how to fish and what to do with the fish when you catch them. For bait, use worms or other material from a sporting goods store.

Fire Building

◆▸▸▸▸◆

Here's how to build a campfire to toast marshmallows over.

Caution: This project requires adult supervision.

Learn to lay and light a fire safely before trying it in the woods. Practice in your fireplace, but NEVER light fires without an adult. When you gather firewood, only pick up what you see on the ground. Don't cut down living trees or break off branches for your fire.

What You'll Need
- shovel
- tinder
- kindling
- larger wood for fuel
- matches
- bucket of water

Start with a fist-size wad of dry tinder (any material catching fire when lit with a match). Wood shavings, dry pine needles, dry moss, pocket lint, and bundled dry grass make good tinder. Then build a small log cabin of pencil-thin kindling around the tinder. Lay some sticks on top of the cabin, but leave space for air flow.

Lay 3 or 4 one-inch diameter sticks of fuel wood on top of the kindling. Light the tinder. When it catches fire, gently blow on it to encourage the flame. Add more fuel wood when the fire is burning. If you're cooking over the fire, wait until there is a good bed of coals. When you're finished, pour water on the fire until the ashes are cool to the touch. Never leave a site or go to sleep without putting the fire out.

A Watering Hole

◆▸▸▸▸◆

In an emergency, you can get fresh water from the soil!

What You'll Need
- shovel
- flowerpot
- clear plastic sheet
- rocks

After getting permission, dig a hole several feet deep or until you hit moisture. Set a flowerpot in the bottom of the hole. Lay a sheet of clear plastic over the hole. Weigh the edges with heavy rocks and seal the hole with dirt. Set a rock in the middle of the sheet, over the pot, so that the plastic leans in. Water will bead on the plastic sheet. Heat from the sun, trapped in the hole, makes water evaporate from the damp soil. The water condenses on the sheet, then drips into the pot.

If you are lost and you can't find damp soil, cut some plant material and drop it in the bottom of the hole. Any moisture in the plants will evaporate, condense on the plastic, and drip into the pot. While you wait, stay in the shade to conserve body moisture. Even if you live far from a desert, try this in your yard. It could be a good science-fair project.

Easy Tent

◆◆◆◆◆◆◆

Who needs expensive stuff?

What You'll Need

- narrow rope or clothesline
- tarp, large sheet of plastic, or old shower curtain
- tent stakes
- 4 small rocks
- heavy twine
- scissors
- foam camping mat or thick blankets

It's fun to camp in the summer. You don't even need an expensive tent if you're just going out for a night in fair weather. This easy shelter will keep off a light rain, but if it begins pouring, you'll want to go in a heavier tent or in the family car!

Stretch a rope between 2 trees, posts, or any other stationary objects. The rope should be about 3 or 4 feet off the ground—lower, if you have a smaller tarp. Drape the tarp over the rope so that it hangs evenly on both sides. If the tarp has metal grommets in the corners, stretch the corners out and hold them down with tent stakes. (If you are using a sheet of plastic or an old shower curtain, wrap each corner over a small rock and tie with twine.) Leave enough twine to tie to a tent stake. If you just poke the stake through the plastic, it will tear.

Make sure the sides of your tent are as tight as you can make them so they won't flap in the wind. If possible, face the tent so the wind strikes the side instead of blowing through. Now, prepare your bed. Put down a foam camping mat to sleep on. (Several layers of thick blankets will work, too.) Air mattresses are cushiony but cold to sleep on. If you use an air mattress, cover it with a foam pad or heavy blankets. The trick to staying warm at night is to have something warm between you and the ground, since the cold ground draws heat away from your body.

Long-Ago Tents

The word "tent" comes from an old Latin word meaning "to stretch." In older times, fabrics were used to shelter people from the elements. Now, our tents are made of much more water-resistant material.

Camp Food

❖❖❖❖❖❖❖

There is something about preparing and eating food outdoors that makes it taste extra delicious. Perhaps it is because fresh air makes you very hungry or perhaps it is the beauty all around as you eat. Whatever the reason, when you look back on your outdoor adventures, some of your fondest memories will be of favorite camp foods.

 ## Camp Desserts

❖❖❖❖❖❖❖

Give your meal a big finish with fun, do-it-yourself desserts!

Banana boats: Peel a banana, then push your thumb in one end until the 3 lengthwise "sections" separate. Remove the "section" near the inside curve or use a spoon to scoop it out. Fill the cavity with tiny marshmallows and chocolate chips. Wrap the banana in foil and place in the coals until the sweets melt (5 to 10 minutes).

S'mores: Break a graham cracker in half and place a 1-inch square of chocolate on it. Toast a marshmallow until it turns golden, then place the marshmallow on the chocolate and set the other cracker square on it. Hold in place and slide the stick out. Squish together and eat!

Baked apple: Cut the core from an apple but leave the bottom intact. Fill the hollow space with brown sugar, cinnamon, and raisins (if you like). Wrap in foil and place in the coals. Let the apple bake about 30 minutes.

Mini-Munchy Cookout

◆◆◆◆◆◆

Sometimes good things come in small packages.

Caution: This project requires adult supervision.

Everyone knows that cooking hot dogs and marshmallows is a campsite tradition. Why not do your roasting in miniature, just for a "little" added fun? Instead of stocking up on standard-size frankfurters, why not pack a bundle of tiny little dogs? Slip these bite-size snacks on a thin stick and heat them up over an open fire. Be careful not to burn yourself, and make sure you have an adult with you to oversee the cookout. After the weenies, you can roast tiny marshmallows!

Let's Have a Cookout!

◆◆◆◆◆◆

Cooking on an outdoor grill is easy and fun.

Caution: This project requires adult supervision.

To make a charcoal fire, place crumpled newspaper (or 2 wax-based fire-starting cubes) in the middle of the barbecue. Pile charcoal briquets loosely over the paper. Leave space between the briquets and the grill. Have an adult help you use a long match or a butane charcoal starter to light the paper. Once the charcoal is burning, put the lid on the grill to hold the heat in while the charcoal burns to coal. (A homemade grill has no lid, so you'll have to wait a bit longer.)

Once you have a good bed of coals, grill something easy, like hot dogs—all they need is to be heated. Set them on the grill and let them cook until they sizzle, turning them once. Once they're hot, put them in a serving dish. Next, shape hamburger meat into patties about a ½ inch thick and place on the grill. Cover and let them cook about 5 minutes. Turn with a long-handled spatula, and finish cooking on the other side.

Dinner on a Stick

◆◆◆◆◆◆◆

All you need is a long, pointy stick to cook up some great food!

Caution: This project requires adult supervision.

Have an adult help you cut pencil-thick cooking sticks about 2½ feet long. Carve one end of the sticks to a point. Slip the food onto the point and push it back so that an inch or so of stick pokes out the other side. Cook the food over a good bed of hot coals (not flames, which will just scorch it). Hold the food horizontally over the coals and turn frequently.

   Hot dogs and sausages: Push the stick through the hot dog or sausage lengthwise, or it may break in half and fall in the fire. Roast over coals, turning constantly, until sizzling. For **kebabs,** cut meat into square cubes. Cut small onions in quarters. Cut potatoes, carrots, or bell peppers into chunks about an inch across. Slip chunks of meat and vegetables onto your stick. Roast over the coals until the meat is done.

What You'll Need

- long, slender hardwood sticks (maple, oak, alder, or ash are good)
- pocket knife (with adult help!)
- ingredients for individual recipes

Food in Foil

◆◆◆◆◆◆◆

Great recipes for the coals of a campfire or on an outdoor grill!

What You'll Need

- outdoor grill (charcoal or gas) or campfire
- heavy-duty aluminum foil
- soup can
- ingredients for individual recipes

Make **chicken and rice** by placing 2 raw chicken breasts on a large piece of foil. Mix 1 can of condensed mushroom soup with ⅔ cup of uncooked instant rice. Seal the foil. Cook over coals for about 20 minutes, turn, then cook 20 minutes longer.

   For grilled **corn on the cob,** husk an ear of corn. Spread with butter, sprinkle with salt and pepper, and wrap tightly in foil. Place on coals and grill for 10 minutes, turning occasionally. To

make **eggs** in foil, shape a square of foil over the end of a soup can to form a cup. Slide the cup from the can and break an egg in it. Set the cup on a grill for 10 minutes or on coals for 3 minutes. Top with grated cheese.

No-Utensil Food

◆▷◆▷◆▷◆▷◆

Let your campfire burn down, then try these no-pan recipes!

What You'll Need
- hot coals
- ingredients for recipes
- string
- scissors
- metal bucket
- salt water

Caution: This project requires adult supervision.

Orange cup breakfast: Halve an orange and scoop out the fruit. Leave the peel intact. Break an egg in one orange cup. Measure mix for one muffin into the other cup and add water. (The batter should half-fill the cup.) Set the cups on hot coals for 10 minutes.

Roasted green corn: Peel the husks back, leaving the cobs attached at the bottom, and remove the silks. Replace the husks to cover the ears and tie in place. Soak the ears for 15 minutes in a clean bucket of salt water. Set the ears upright against a rock near the coals. Turn until all sides are slightly browned. Remove the husks, and eat right away!

Caveman potatoes: With a stick, push aside some coals in the fire. Drop a clean potato in the gap and cover with ashes and coals. Bake 30 minutes. Scrape the coals and roll the potato on to a plate. Allow to cool, then brush off the ashes. Eat by scooping the potato from the jacket.

Make an Outdoor Grill

◆▷◆▷◆▷◆▷◆

Outdoor cooking is even more fun when you make your own grill!

Caution: This project requires adult supervision.

On bare soil, away from flammable materials, make a rectangle in the dirt as long as your grating and 4 inches wider. Use this outline to dig a rectangular, flat-bottom pit 2 inches deep. With help, set the bricks flat on the short sides of the pit. Stack up a second layer of bricks. When making the second layer, overlap the bricks to make a stronger stack. The second layer won't be as long as the first but should be as wide as the grill. Line the pit with at least an inch of sand. This will insulate the ground underneath to prevent fires. When you're ready to cook, remove the grating and pour your charcoal on the sand.

What You'll Need
- grating (from a camping supply store)
- shovel
- bricks or cement blocks
- sand
- charcoal

Food for the Trail

◆▶◆▶◆▶◆

*Next time you go on a long hike,
pack some of these fun foods along with you.*

What You'll Need
● ingredients for individual recipes

Food for hiking should be easy to carry and shouldn't make a mess. Pack your food in moisture-proof containers, such as plastic sandwich boxes, that will keep sandwiches from getting crushed and will contain any spills. Always carry plenty of drinking water. (Don't trust open water sources along the trail.) Try these recipes as a change of pace from the ordinary sandwich-and-fruit lunch:

Hot dogs: Before leaving on a hike, fill a wide-mouth vacuum bottle with hot water. Add a hot dog and seal the bottle. Put a bun in a sandwich bag and condiments in small containers. When you're ready for lunch, your hot dog should be hot.

Instant taco: Pack hot, cooked taco meat in a wide-mouth insulated vacuum bottle. Fill a plastic lunchbox with tortilla chips or a taco shell and sprinkle on grated cheese. If you like, pack chopped tomatoes or lettuce in a separate container. At lunch time, scoop the meat onto the chips, add tomatoes and lettuce, and eat from the chip container.

Walking salad: Cut off the top of an apple. Carefully cut out the core almost to the bottom. Scoop out the pulp of the apple, and mix it with 2 large spoonfuls of cottage cheese, some chopped nuts, and raisins. Stuff the mixture back into the apple shell. Replace the top, and use toothpicks to hold it on. You can eat the salad and most of the container!

Camp Cooking Gadgets

◄►►►►►►

It's fun to make useful "gadgets" for your outdoor kitchen.

Rather than buying things you might only need once, see how inventive you can be with wire and foil. To make a **meat fork,** cut the hook off a stiff wire coat hanger and straighten the wire. Bend the middle of the wire around a thick stick to form a loop. Twist the stick while holding the 2 strands with pliers. Leave about 4 inches of wire untwisted. Separate these to form 2 tines. Remove the stick from the loop in the handle. If the handle sags, wire it to a straight stick.

Ladle: Begin as you did for the meat fork, but leave 6-inch ends. Bend the ends around a tin can or flashlight to form a circle. Wrap the overlapping ends of wire around each other. Shape the bowl of the ladle from foil. Push the bowl through the wire circle. Leave plenty of foil for the overlap, and fold the overlap under the bowl of the ladle.

Biscuit pan: Straighten a wire coat hanger. Fold the wire into a square and twist the ends together. Use any extra wire to form a loop. Using the wire square as a pattern, form a box from 2 layers of foil. Leave several inches for overlap. Place the foil box in the wire square, and fold the overlap down and under the edges of the box. Set cut biscuits in the pan. Sprinkle on a layer of smooth ashes. Set the biscuit pan on the coals. Cover with foil.

What You'll Need

- unpainted coat hangers
- thick stick
- pliers
- tin can or flashlight
- heavy-duty aluminum foil
- wire cutters (with adult help)

Fun and Games

◆◆◆◆◆◆◆

Ever wonder why people sometimes refer to the natural world as the "great outdoors"? Maybe it's because there are so many wonderful things to do and see in nature. Make your time outdoors truly great by having fun with special games as you learn about the world.

 ## On the Right Track

◆◆◆◆◆◆◆

Track down a few facts.

What You'll Need
- notebook
- pencil or pen
- books on animal tracks from the library

We love hiking, but who hikes with us? What animals call that natural territory home? If you keep your eyes carefully trained to the ground, you might find out. Watch for animal tracks as you go. If you find tracks too difficult to spot, look for animal droppings (even animals have to process the food they eat—it's all part of nature).

If there are droppings, tracks won't be far behind. Take out your notebook, and do your best to draw the tracks you find. When you get home, check to find out who might have left them behind. It's fun to know you're never alone.

Finding Bigfoot

"Sasquatch" is real—at least if you use your imagination.

What You'll Need
- garden gloves
- paper
- pencil or pen

Could the mysterious monster "Bigfoot" be more than a myth? Hike through your local wilderness, and search for fun and furry clues—even if you don't quite believe. Keep your eyes peeled for fun clues that could have been left by Bigfoot. Put on some garden gloves and forage around. See a clump of hair? Grab it—it might be a piece of Bigfoot's fur. Spy a tiny piece of bone? Maybe that was Bigfoot's afternoon snack. Is that a cave you see in the distance? Make a note of it. It may be Bigfoot's home. When you get back to camp, write down everything you saw, and make up a campfire story about all the things you've found. You'll have fun trying to scare each other silly!

A Visual "Diary"

You'll remember your next nature trip long after it's over when you create this "natural wonders" wall hanging.

When you go on a nature hike, collect small objects such as twigs, grasses, flowers, nuts, bark, and shells. When you get home, you can weave all the objects together to make an artistic record of your trip.

What You'll Need
- small objects from nature
- 4 sticks or twigs
- jute twine
- wire or small hooks
- craft glue

First, make a frame for your artwork. Tie together 4 twigs or sticks to make a square or rectangle. Next wrap natural jute twine around the frame. Use the twine as a base on which to mount all the other objects. You can weave them through the twine, use small hooks or pieces of wire to hook them on, or glue them on. You could attach the objects to the frame in the order you found them or in an artistic design. Either way, you'll have a unique "diary" of your trip.

Knee-High Hike

❖❖❖❖❖❖❖

Hiking is only human, until you try this trick.

If you want to see hiking from a whole new point of view, why not fall to your knees? Take your next short hike on all fours, as would a puma, chipmunk, or hyena, and see how your perspective is bound to change. Be

sure to wear pants sturdy at the knees and gloves to protect your hands. Then head for the trail. What do you see from this animallike position? What do you smell? How do you feel? Do you begin to get a sense of how vulnerable some creatures of the wild might be? It's a whole new world.

Campsite Bingo

❖❖❖❖❖❖❖

Try this game B-4 you hit the trail.

This is a great way to celebrate the great outdoors—and BINGO is its name-o. It's not traditional bingo. It's a fill-in-the-blank game that has more to do with what you see than what someone says. Take a blank piece of paper and write B-I-N-G-O in big letters all the way across it. Now, grab a partner. (The buddy system is especially important in the wilderness.) Staying close enough to camp to hear each other, search for something that begins with a "B." It can be a bug, a piece of birch, a baseball you packed, or anything else that starts with

"B." Do the same with the rest of the letters in the word "BINGO," using the game pieces on the paper to help you keep track of what you've found. The first team to find all 5 objects wins the game.

Hiking Back in Time

◆◆◆◆◆◆◆

Try "the good old days" on for size.

What You'll Need
- large square of cloth
- walking stick
- beef jerky
- water
- dried fruit

While grownups call hiking "getting back to nature," today's hiking supplies make it a pretty modern activity. So why not take yourself back in time the next time you hit the rugged trail? Pack the way the pioneers might have done. Instead of a fanny pack, grab a square of cloth and tie it around a walking stick. Forget the snack bars and sports drinks. Pack some beef jerky, water, and dried fruit. Think about hiking as a means of transportation, rather than something to do just for fun. You'll come back to the present with a whole new appreciation.

Tic-Tac-Toe

◆◆◆◆◆◆◆

Toss aside that pencil and paper, and play a game of tic-tac-toe with some help from the great outdoors.

X marks the spot! To get started with your game of tic-tac-toe, scratch a game board in the dirt with a stick. Then round up some rocks and pinecones. You and a friend can use them to play tic-tac-toe just like you normally do. Instead of drawing circles and Xs, one of you can use rocks and the other can use pinecones. Just like in a regular game of tic-tac-toe, the first one to get 3 squares in a row wins. If you'd like, you can also play tic-tac-no. It's played just like the game above, except the object of the game is to try NOT to get 3 squares in a row.

What You'll Need
- stick
- rocks
- pinecones

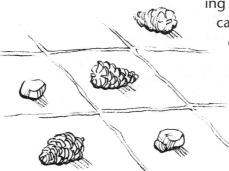

Historical Trails

◆▶▶▶▶▶▶◀

What paths of history are near your hometown?

History will come alive when you walk in the footsteps of famous explorers, pioneers, or early American Indians. Our Historical Trail and Scenic Trail systems began in the 1920s as citizens began piecing together hiking trails on historical routes. It was their vision that led to the National Trail System Act of 1968. All the trails are for foot traffic only, and most of them cross several states.

Check the following list to see which Historical Trails are near you. Make a trail notebook. Keep a record of the trails you've been on. Include some history of the trails in your book, and mark the segments you hike. Our trails are:

Iditarod National Historic Trail (Alaska)
Juan Bautista de Anza National Historic Trail (Mexico, Southwest United States)
Lewis and Clark National Historic Trail (Missouri to Oregon)
Mormon Pioneer National Historic Trail (Illinois to Utah)
Nez Perce National Historic Trail (Idaho, Wyoming, Montana)
Oregon National Historic Trail (Missouri to Oregon)
Overmountain Victory National Historic Trail (Tennessee to North Carolina)
Pony Express National Historic Trail (Missouri to California)
Santa Fe National Historic Trail (Missouri to Santa Fe, New Mexico)
Trail of Tears National Historic Trail (Georgia to Oklahoma)

Sequoias

Some of the world's oldest and largest living trees belong to a family of trees called sequoias (named after Cherokee Indian chief Sequoyah). This family includes redwoods and giant sequoias. In fact, the largest tree in the world—nicknamed "General Sherman"—is a 274-foot giant sequoia. Located in the Sequoia National Park in California, General Sherman is estimated to be between 3,000 and 4,000 years old.

It's in the Bag

Sleeping bags are comfy to sleep in—and great to race in!

What You'll Need
- 2 pieces of rope
- 2 sleeping bags

Are you ready to race? First, lay the 2 pieces of rope on the ground so that they're about 15 to 20 steps apart. Then get a few of your friends together and form 2 equal-numbered teams. Half of each team should stand behind one piece of rope, and the other half should stand behind the other. To get started, have a player from each team get into a sleeping bag. On the count of "3," the players in sleeping bags should hop to the other rope. When they pass that rope, the player gets out of the sleeping bag as fast as possible, and another teammate hops in. The race continues until everyone on the team has had a turn. The team finishing first is the winner. Get hopping!

Flashlight Tag

The fun doesn't have to stop when the sun goes down.

What You'll Need
- flashlights

Before playing, check your playing area for any obstacles that could be dangerous. If you can't remove a hazard, mark it with an extra flashlight. Choose one person to be "it," and give that person a flashlight. All other players run and hide. "It" counts to 20, looks for other players, and "tags" them with a beam of light. Since this kind of tagging can't be felt, players must take "it's" word when they've been tagged. Tagged players go to a jail, such as a large tree.

Players may change hiding places at any time. Part of the fun is that the darkness provides so many hiding places and makes it easier to sneak from one place to another. Be creative when you search for places to hide. Sometimes all you need is a very dark shadow to conceal you.

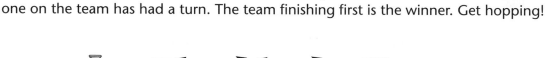

A variation: Give all players flashlights. Players can run around or hide as they choose, but must flash their light every time "it" yells "Lights!" Players can also be required to blink their light every 10 seconds.

Pinecone Pitch

How accurate is your toss?

What You'll Need
- pinecones
- baskets or buckets

Gather as many pinecones as you can in 2 large buckets or baskets. Then take turns emptying the baskets and refilling them from 15 paces. See how accurately you can toss the pinecones. How many did you sink? How many missed? Try from different distances.

Outdoor Alphabet

Go by the letter for outdoor fun.

Searching for an outdoor alphabet can be your ticket to better observational skills as well as a whole lot of hiking fun. As you hike the trail with your parents and friends, call out the letters of the alphabet one by one. If you see an apple, say, "Apple" out loud and move on to the letter "B." If your father sees a bug, you all move on to the letter "C." If your mother sees a canary, you all move on to the letter "D." This is a team game full of team spirit, so cheer each other on. Before you know it, you'll be where you wanted to be—and you will have had lots of fun along the way.

Stack It Up!

How many pinecones can you stack without watching them fall?

What You'll Need
- anything stackable you can find outdoors
- paper
- pen

Start out stacking something easy, like leaves or flat rocks. Then, work your way up to tougher hurdles like tree branches or pebbles. Anything you can stack is fair game. Just for fun, keep records of how many of each item you were able to stack.

Storyteller Scavenger Hunt

◆▶◆▶◆▶◆▶◆

Most of us have gone on a scavenger hunt—a race to find items on a list. But this one has a very creative twist.

What You'll Need
- paper
- pencil
- paper bags for collecting items

Each team (2 or more to a team) must bring back the items on the list (a list like something red, something living, something old, something hard, something soft, something gross). But here's the trick. The winner isn't the one who finds all the items. The winner is the team that finds the items AND comes up with the best story to string them all together.

For example: "Once upon a time, a pioneer girl snagged her red hair ribbon on this old piece of barbed wire, while running from a swarm of pill bugs with runny noses. Why were the pill bugs swarming? To steal her bag of marshmallows, of course. They were tired of sleeping on hard, hard stones." Get the picture? This one is bound to be a laugh magnet.

Tree Tag

◆▶◆▶◆▶◆▶◆

Tag turns over a new "leaf" with this crazy adaptation.

It starts out normally enough. One person is "it" while the others scatter and run. But there are 3 to 5 tree bases, and each runner can only claim sanctuary twice at each tree before they're left with no choice but to run until they're caught.

What You'll Need
- packing tape
- blank paper
- markers
- string

Clearly mark each tree base with a numbered paper and one blank sheet of paper. Attach them with packing tape so you don't hurt the tree and so it can be easily removed when the game is over. Now give each runner a different colored marker tied to a string around their neck. When they get to the base, they must mark the blank sheet with their color-coded "X." Two strikes, and that tree is no longer a free zone. The last player out wins and can either be "it" or pick the next "it." Be sure to remove the paper and tape from the trees when you're done with this game!

Trailblazing

◆◇◆◇◆◇◆

Try this cool variation of hide-and-seek.

What You'll Need
- chalk or sticks for each player

Begin by choosing an "it." Have "it" close his or her eyes (or stand where other players can't be seen) for a specific length of time. The rest of the players run off in the same direction to find hiding places but must mark their paths by chalking arrows on paved areas or placing arrows made of sticks on the ground. Marks should be several yards apart. When the players reach a good hiding place, they leave arrows pointing in 4 different directions. At this point the players scatter and find hiding places within 20 paces of the mark. "It" follows the trail and tries to find all the players.

In a more active version, called "Hares and Hounds," players divide into 2 teams. The "hounds" close their eyes while the "hares" run together in a particular direction, leaving chalk marks or stick arrows along the way. After a 10- or 20-second head start, the hounds chase the hares. The round is over when the hounds spot the hares. The hares must lay trail markers at least every 10 yards.

Leaf, Leaf, Pinecone

◆◇◆◇◆◇◆

A new version of an old circle game.

What You'll Need
- pinecone

This new version of "Duck, Duck, Goose" has a nature-friendly twist. Whoever is "it" must not only touch the heads of the other players, saying, "Leaf, leaf, leaf," but must also drop a big, fresh pinecone in the lap of the victim they choose before running back around the circle without being tagged. The person trying to tag "it" can touch "it" with a hand above the waist or with the pinecone below the waist.

Color Your World

◆▸◆▸◆▸◆▸◆

*This fun matching game will help you find out what colors
Mother Nature likes best.*

What You'll Need
- squares of paper in various bright and dull colors
- scissors
- resealable plastic bag

Collect paper in as many different colors as you can find. Look through cupboards, old colored paper supplies, and any place paper is stored to find old pieces of gray cardboard, faded construction paper, and other dull colors. Collect brighter colors as well, including vivid neon colors. Cut the paper into 2-inch squares. Keep your colored squares in a resealable plastic bag, and bring them along the next time you go hiking or camping.

Give each of the players 5 squares picked at random. Tell them they must find something in nature that matches each of the squares exactly. For instance, a square of green paper may not be the same shade of green as grass. The player must keep looking at leaves, moss, and other plants to find an exact match. See if you can figure out what colors are used most in nature.

You can also let the players pick the colors they want to find. Many people like to pick the neon colors rather than the dull colors, but they soon learn the dull colors are much easier to match, while the neon colors are nearly impossible!

What Is It?

◆▸◆▸◆▸◆▸◆

*You'll have to use all your other senses when you play
this nature version of Blindman's Buff.*

This is a nature game to play with a partner. Have your partner blindfold you and guide you around to touch, smell, and listen to different things in nature. Can you guess what each thing is? Do you notice how things feel, smell, and sound more than you have before? Even familiar places can seem like strange new worlds! Trade places with your partner, letting him or her wear the blindfold while you are the guide.

What You'll Need
- blindfold

Nature Trails

◆◆◆◆◆◆◆

Turn your backyard, local park, or camp into a nature trail.

If you have a favorite natural area, make a trail to point out its interesting features. You can make a permanent trail on private land or a temporary one in a park for a special occasion. Be sure to ask adults for permission.

Make small signs from scrap wood. Paint them, and use paint or permanent markers to write out descriptions of the interesting features or things to do at each station. Nail the signs to stakes. Here are some ideas for stations:

- Give the name of a tree, and list some interesting facts about it.
- Point out a tree that has a bird nest in it. Tell what kind of bird has made the nest.
- State that an animal has made its home near the station. Challenge your readers to find it.
- Have the reader stop and listen for the call of a particular bird that lives near the station.
- Put a station near some sweet-scented flower or other plant.

What You'll Need
- stakes and small thin boards to make signs
- paint or markers
- paintbrush
- nails
- hammer

What's a Whifflepoof?

◆◆◆◆◆◆◆

Try playing this game, used to teach tracking skills, with your friends.

What You'll Need
- small log (about 4 inches in diameter, 18 inches long)
- large nails
- hammer
- screw eye
- rope

To make the Whifflepoof: With the help of a parent or adult, take a small log and drive a few dozen nails into it, leaving about 2 inches of each nail still sticking out, until the log bristles with nails. Take a large screw eye and screw it into one end of the log. Tie a length of rope about 4 feet long to the screw eye.

To play the game: Have one person drag the Whifflepoof through woods or an open field while the other players close their eyes. The person dragging the Whifflepoof should make as long a trail as possible in the area. When the trail is done, the rest of the players attempt to follow it.

Nature's Orchestra

◆▶◆▶◆▶◆

*You and your friends can strike up the band
with these musical instruments made from natural materials.*

What You'll Need
- nature objects
- cans

Remember: Don't harm live plants or disturb animals in their habitats during this project.

With a group of friends, collect rocks, gravel, sand, sticks, shells, and anything else from nature that you can use to make musical instruments. Use your imagination! Put rocks in cans to shake. Use sticks as drumsticks. Maybe you can make a drum from a hollow log or from bark. See if you and your friends can make beautiful music together.

Nature Scavenger Hunt

◆▶◆▶◆▶◆

As you explore nature, be careful not to disturb any plants or animals.

Make a list of things you might find in nature. They should all be things that nature "casts off," such as dropped leaves and seed pods, feathers, small stones, etc. That way, you won't be taking things that nature still needs! Make a copy of the list for each person who wants to join the scavenger hunt. Then set off, alone or in pairs, to find everything on the list. You can even have a race to see who finds the objects first!

What You'll Need
- paper
- pen
- nature objects

Another way to have a nature scavenger hunt is to find things in nature but not touch them or bring them home. When you play this way, you just mark off each thing on your list as you find it.

This activity is a good way to collect the natural objects you'll need for other activities in the book. For example, you could look for pinecones to make pinecone creatures, feathers to make quill pens, interesting leaves for leaf stencils, shells for shell art.

Precious Belongings Pouch

◆◆◆◆◆◆◆

Make this pouch to carry all the precious belongings you'll collect as you go exploring on field trips or nature walks.

What You'll Need
- different colored sheets of felt
- scissors
- ruler
- stapler or glue

Cut a 5×12-inch rectangle out of a piece of felt. Fold up the long end of the strip about ⅔ of the way. Staple or glue the edges together to form a pocket. If you'd like, you can make 2 parallel slits in the back of the pouch so you can thread your belt through the slits. Decorate the pocket by cutting out shapes from the felt (maybe nature shapes, such as leaves, animals, flowers, etc.) and gluing them to the pocket. Now it's time for that nature walk!

Nature B-I-N-G-O!

◆◆◆◆◆◆◆

Try this special kind of bingo that you play in nature.

First, make your bingo cards. Use a ruler to make a grid of 16 squares on a piece of paper. (Draw 3 lines across, and 3 lines up and down.) In each square, write the name or draw the picture of something in nature: a bird, insect, animal, tree, flower, etc. You'll need to make several cards, and make sure

What You'll Need
- ruler
- paper
- pen
- crayons or markers

each card has a different arrangement and at least some different nature objects compared to other cards.

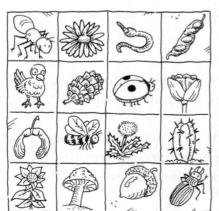

When you're ready to play, get a group of friends and give a bingo card to each person. Go on a nature walk. When a player sees something that is on his or her card, the person marks off that square. The first person to mark all the squares in a row wins. Or, you can play super nature bingo: The first person to mark all the squares on a card wins.

Nature's Bounty

◆◆◆◆◆◆◆

Holidays and birthdays are great times for decorating and gift-giving. Of course, you don't really need a reason to give the gift of nature! And the best gifts are homemade. Try your hand at some of the wonderful crafts in this section. What could smell better than a garland made from real greenery? Or look nicer than homemade wrapping paper? Natural decorations can be ecological, too, if you are careful about collecting your materials.

Holiday Trimmings

◆◆◆◆◆◆◆

Our holidays come to us from hundreds of years ago when life was much simpler. During those times, people used many things from nature in their lives. Making decorations from natural things really spices up the holidays and helps us to remember simpler times.

Birch Bark Valentines

❖❖❖❖❖❖

Make special Valentines out of natural treasures and your own verse.

What You'll Need
- thin birch bark
- natural objects
- ink pen
- scrap of ribbon

The paper birch is an unusual and delicate tree. Its waterproof white bark was used by American Indians to make canoes. It can also be used like paper to make these valentines. Find a paper birch tree with thin strips of bark that have fallen or are already peeling off. Tear off only what you will use. Be careful not to tear off living bark—it could harm the tree!

Next, take a walk in a park, woodland, or other place where you can find early flowers, feathers, or evergreen twigs. With permission, collect a few natural treasures that you think are pretty. Lay your treasures out at home, and let them inspire a valentine poem. Evergreen twigs may make you think of a friendship that is "ever green." Flowers may stand for a blossoming friendship.

When you have composed your poem, write it on a piece of birch bark. Roll the bark around the feathers, flowers, or whatever objects you have used in your verse. Tie the valentine with a ribbon, and surprise someone on Valentine's Day—or any other day for that matter!

Decorated Eggs

❖❖❖❖❖❖

Using onion skins, create a natural dye for a different kind of Easter egg.

Caution: This project requires adult supervision.

Cut the cheesecloth into 6-inch squares. Take an egg in your hand, and place an herb on the egg. Holding the herb in place, wrap a large onion skin around the egg. Place more herbs around the egg, and wrap another onion skin around it. Place the covered egg on a square of cheesecloth. Tightly wrap the cheese-cloth around the egg, and tie it closed with a piece of cotton string. Repeat the process to make more eggs. Have an adult help you boil the eggs in water for 20 to 30 minutes. Take the eggs out of the water, and allow them to cool. Unwrap the eggs, and display them in a gift basket.

What You'll Need
- cheesecloth
- scissors
- ruler
- one dozen eggs
- leafy herbs (such as parsley or coriander)
- assorted onion skins
- cotton string
- pot
- water
- stove
- basket

Homemade Hearts

◆◆◆◆◆◆◆

These cinnamon hearts can be ornaments or valentine greetings.

What You'll Need

- measuring cup
- applesauce
- cinnamon
- white glue
- mixing bowl
- cutting board
- rolling pin
- heart-shaped cookie cutter
- nail
- spatula
- cooling rack
- string or ribbon
- notecard
- pen
- hole punch (optional)

Mix 1 cup applesauce, 1½ cups cinnamon, and ⅓ cup glue in a bowl. Form the mixture into a ball, and chill it in the refrigerator for at least half an hour. (It's okay to leave it in the fridge overnight.)

Next, sprinkle some cinnamon on a cutting board. Roll out the dough until it is about ¼-inch thick. Cut out heart shapes with your cookie cutter. To make the hearts into ornaments or valentines, use a nail to make a hole in each heart. Use a spatula to move the hearts onto a cooling rack. Let them dry for about 2 days.

To make ornaments: Tie a string or ribbon through each heart.

To make valentines: Attach both a string and a valentine greeting. You can write the greeting on a notecard. Use a hole punch to make a hole in the valentine so you can tie it to the heart.

Easter Lilies

◆◆◆◆◆◆◆

Grow these holiday favorites as gifts for your family and friends.

Pour about 4 inches of soil into each of your flowerpots. Put an Easter lily bulb onto the soil, and fill in around it with more potting soil until the bulb is barely covered. Moisten the soil, then put the pot aside in a cool, dark place. After about 2 weeks the stalk will sprout from the bulb. Fill in with more soil. Keep adding soil as the stalk grows until you have filled the pot to within ½ inch of the top.

What You'll Need

- 6-inch wide flowerpots
- potting soil
- Easter lily bulbs
- plant mister

Two months after you have planted the bulbs, bring them into a well-lit room. Mist the leaves daily with a plant mister or spray bottle. In a cool room, the plant will take about 3 months to bloom. In a warm room, it may take 2 months or less.

Nature's Beauty

◆━━◆━━◆━━◆━━◆

Be the apple of someone's eye with this apple centerpiece.

What You'll Need
- polystyrene cone
- scissors
- plate
- apples
- greenery
- toothpicks

Buy a polystyrene cone with a flat top at a craft store. If your cone has a pointed top, cut off the point. Place the cone on a plate. Gather plenty of shiny red apples and some greenery, such as apple leaves or evergreen boughs.

Push a toothpick halfway into each apple. Then attach the apples to the cone by pushing the toothpicks into the cone. Start by making a row of apples around the bottom of the cone, with the apples resting on the plate. Then make another row right on top of that, and work your way to the top. It will work best if you put the bigger apples on the bottom and the smaller ones on top. The last apple should go right on top of the cone.

Use the greenery to fill the spaces between the apples. You should be able to stick the ends of the leaves or boughs right into the cone. Finally, decorate the edges of the plate with greenery, too.

You can also make the centerpiece out of other fruits, such as oranges or lemons.

Going in Circles

◆━━◆━━◆━━◆━━◆

Make your own wreath for Christmas—or any other time of year.

To make the basic wreath, you'll need several vines. You can find grapevines or honeysuckle vines in nature. Collect them in the winter when they are dormant. If the vines are too dry and brittle to bend, soak them in water until they are more flexible.

What You'll Need
- vines
- decorations (leaves, dried flowers)

Bend the vines into a circle. Weave several circles of vine together to make your wreath. Wrap small vines around the wreath to help hold it together.

You can leave your vine wreath plain or decorate it any way you like. For the fall, you could add grape leaves and clusters of grapes to your wreath. (Real grapes won't last very long. You can use artificial grapes or even make your own from clay or paper.) Or decorate your wreath with dried flowers or evergreen and winter berries.

Down-to-Earth Stars

◆◆◆◆◆◆◆

Twig stars make terrific natural holiday tree ornaments.

What You'll Need
- small twigs (several inches long)
- upholstery tacks
- hammer
- yarn
- metallic gold or silver spray paint (optional)
- glitter (optional)

Five-pointed twig star: You'll need 5 twigs, all the same length. Lay them in the shape of a 5-pointed star. Use gold or silver upholstery tacks to attach the twigs at each point. The tacks not only hold the star together, they add a pretty, shining touch. For a really shiny star, spray paint the twigs with metallic gold or silver paint before you tack them together.

Six-pointed twig star: You'll need 3 twigs, all the same length. Cross the 3 twigs in the middle so they make a shape like a 6-pointed star. Wrap the twigs with yarn to hold them together, beginning at the center where all 3 twigs meet. Wrap the yarn around one stick, then the next, then the next. Keep wrapping the yarn (it will make a sort of bull's-eye pattern) until it is close to the ends of the sticks. When you're finished, tie the yarn in the back.

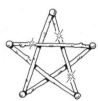

You can use different colors of yarn on the same star to make a colorful design. Or, turn your star into a snowflake by painting the twigs white, wrapping them with white yarn, and adding white or silver glitter.

Spicy Decorations

◆◆◆◆◆◆◆

These spice ornaments not only look good on your holiday tree, they smell good, too.

What You'll Need
- cinnamon sticks
- glue
- ribbon
- decorations
- gold thread

Begin by gluing together a few cinnamon sticks. They should look like a small bundle of chopped wood. After the glue has dried, tie a bright-colored ribbon around the bundle. Then glue on tiny decorations such as other spices (star anise, cardamom pods), holly berries, tiny pinecones, or dried flowers. Let the glue dry. Finally, tie a gold thread around the bundle or just around the ribbon. Use the thread to hang the ornament.

Pinecone Trees

◆◆◆◆◆◆◆

It's easy to turn ordinary pinecones into these unique sparkly decorations!

Caution: This project requires adult supervision.

Gather large pinecones outdoors. Clean off any dirt or leaves. If the cones are closed, ask an adult to dry them in a warm oven until they open.

For beaded "trees": Set the cones upright on newspaper. Pour some white glue in a small dish. Hold a bead with a pair of tweezers, and dip in the glue. Stick the bead on one of the cone bracts. Keep gluing beads on the cone until it is covered. Allow to dry.

For glittery "trees": Pour white glue into one paper plate and glitter into another. Roll the cone in glue first, then glitter. Allow to dry.

Straw Stars

◆◆◆◆◆◆◆

This easy-to-make garland shines naturally in the glow of holiday lights.

First, cut a length of string a few feet longer than you want your garland to be. Next, soak the straw in water for 5 or 10 minutes before using. Cut 6 pieces of straw to the same length, and hold in a bundle. Tie one end of the string tightly to the middle of the straw. The ends of the straw will spring out into a star shape. Cut more straw and make another star 6 inches to a foot down the string from the first one (depending on how big your

stars are). Keep going until your garland is as long as you want it. Tie a loop on either end of the garland, and hang on a wall away from candles or other open flames.

You can make more colorful garlands if you use colored crochet thread, which you can buy by the ball at a craft store. Use red or green for Christmas garlands. Blue also looks nice.

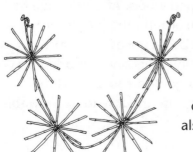

Wrap It Up!

◆◆◆◆◆◆

Create gift wrap using pressed flowers and recycled brown paper bags.

Cut the bottom off of a brown paper bag, and cut it open along the seam. Spread the paper out flat. Wrap your package in the brown paper with the unprinted side out. Now pour a puddle of glue into a glass pan. Add a few drops of water, and mix with a spatula. Add enough water to make the glue slightly runny.

Pick up one of the pressed flowers or leaves with tweezers. Dip it in the thinned glue, then lay it on the side of the package. Place a piece of waxed paper over the flower and rub all over to press the flower onto the paper. Decorate the sides with more flowers and leaves. Allow to dry completely.

What You'll Need
- brown paper bag
- scissors
- tape
- craft glue
- glass pan
- water
- spatula
- pressed flowers and leaves (see page 626)
- tweezers
- waxed paper

Pomander Balls

◆◆◆◆◆◆

These traditional spicy-smelling pomanders make great holiday decorations or gifts.

What You'll Need
- small oranges or apples
- marking pen
- nut pick or toothpick
- whole cloves
- ground spices
- saucer
- ribbon

Select a small, firm apple or orange without bruises. Be sure it is a small one, no more than 3 inches across. (Larger pomanders take a very long time to make and may not dry well.) Use a marking pen to divide the surface up into sections.

Working one section at a time, use a nut pick or toothpick to poke a hole in the skin. Stick the stem of a whole clove into the hole. Go one at a time so you can see how to fit the cloves together. Be patient. Fill one section at a time, allowing gaps between the cloves. The fruit will shrink as it dries, so the gaps will close up.

When the whole fruit is covered, pour ground cinnamon, cloves, nutmeg, or allspice into a saucer and roll the pomander in it. Allow the pomander to dry in a warm place for 2 weeks. Tie ribbons around it and hang in the kitchen or give as a holiday gift.

A Nutty Idea

◆◆◆◆◆◆◆

There are many different sizes and shapes of nuts.
Use a variety to make this lovely nut wreath.

What You'll Need
- wreath base (vine or cardboard)
- shelled nuts
- craft glue
- decorations

Use a vine wreath (see Going in Circles on page 600) or a cardboard ring as a base for a nut wreath. Glue shelled nuts to the wreath. (You can use nuts you find or nuts you buy at the store.) Add other decorations, such as sprigs of evergreen or red bows.

Evergreen Garland

◆◆◆◆◆◆◆

Brighten your home with a fragrant garland made from evergreens.

Gather twigs and branches of fir, juniper, or other evergreens. A walk in the woods after a heavy wind should yield plenty of material lying on the ground. Cut the greenery into 6-inch lengths.

Lay a few twigs alongside a rope at one end with the cut ends of the twigs pointing away from the end of the rope. (Your rope should be the length you wish your garland to be.)

What You'll Need
- evergreen sprigs (trimmings from a Christmas tree or blown-down branches)
- rope
- string or floral wire
- ½-inch wide red ribbon
- 2-inch wide red ribbon
- holiday lights (optional)

Wrap tightly with string or floral wire. Lay a few more twigs on the rope, overlapping the twigs that were tied on. Wrap with more wire. Keep going until the whole rope is covered with greenery.

Next, tie a ½-inch wide red ribbon to one end. Wrap the ribbon in a spiral around the garland and tie off at the other end. Tie large bows of 2-inch wide red ribbon, and attach to both ends of the garland to cover up the rope ends. You can use holiday lights to brighten your garland.

Ice Hangings

◆◆◆◆◆◆◆

When the weather turns cold, you can make these temporary-but-beautiful natural decorations.

What You'll Need
- pie pan
- water
- yarn
- nature objects (flowers, berries, evergreen sprigs)

Fill a pie pan with water and line the edge with yarn, making sure the yarn is submerged in the water. Leave the ends of the yarn loose, so you can hang up your project when it's finished.

Next, arrange your objects in the center of the pan. You can use fresh or dried flowers, greenery, berries, or anything you like. If the temperature outside is below freezing, set your plate outdoors. Or you can place it in the freezer. Wait until the yarn and flowers are frozen completely into the ice before removing.

Once it is frozen, you can remove the ice circle from the pan. (Dip the bottom of the pan in warm water if you need help removing it.) Now hang it up outdoors on a tree, post, or anywhere its beauty can be seen. Watch your creation sparkle in the sun. As long as the temperatures stay below freezing, your ice hanging won't melt away.

Willow Wreaths

◆◆◆◆◆◆◆

Use weeping willow branches or pussy willows to make lovely wreaths.

What You'll Need
- willow branches
- string
- scissors
- ribbon
- decorations

Ask permission from the owner of the willow tree to cut some branches. When the leaves fall from the willow, have the owner help you cut about 15 of the long, slender branches, each twice as long as you want the wreath to measure around.

Bend one branch to make a circle of the right size. Wrap the long end of the branch around itself, spiraling around the circle. Add more branches, and continue the spiral. As best you can, lay each new spiral alongside the old one. Keep going until you have used up all the branches you cut. Tie string around the wreath in 4 places to hold the branches in place. Set the wreath aside to dry for 2 weeks.

When dry, cut off the string and wrap the wreath in ribbon, spacing each turn of the ribbon a few inches apart. End with a large bow. Decorate the wreath with natural decorations such as pinecones, acorns, or dried flowers; or use bright Christmas balls, wooden cutouts, tiny toys, or other ornaments suitable for the season.

Gum Sweet Gum

❖❖❖❖❖❖

*The seed pods of the sweet gum tree are really unusual—
and they can become glittering decorations.*

What You'll Need
- sweet gum pods
- newspaper
- polystyrene wreath base or cone
- toothpicks
- gold or silver spray paint
- ribbon

You can collect the spiky sweet gum tree balls under the trees in the fall. Most sweet gum trees make these balls in abundance! Always check first with the owner of the tree before picking them up. Spread them out on newspaper, and let them dry for several days.

Now pick out a polystyrene base in the shape you want. You can choose a cone-shaped piece for a tree, circles for wreaths, balls, and lots of other shapes. Next, break a toothpick in half, and stick it in one of the holes in the sweet gum ball. Stick the other end into the base. Keep going until the whole base is covered.

Lay your decoration on newspapers in a sheltered place outdoors or in a well-ventilated garage. Ask an adult to spray it with gold or silver spray paint. Put on 3 or 4 coats, allowing the paint to dry between coats. After the last coat, allow the paint to dry completely (at least 24 hours). Add a bow of red or green ribbon. Put one large bow on the wreath or many tiny bows on the cone "trees." Set your decorations out to enjoy or give them as gifts.

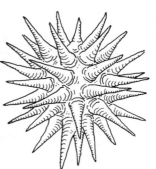

Travel Keepsakes

❖❖❖❖❖❖

Pack your bags, jump in the car, and take off for high adventure! The great outdoors offer great getaways and plenty of opportunities for fun. Pick up some nature souvenirs along the way, and you can cherish your favorite vacation memories long after the drive home!

Beach in a Bottle

◆◆◆◆◆◆◆

Sift a few memories inside a jar.

Ever longed for the ocean with none in sight? This beach in a bottle will help "tide" you over between trips. Find a clean, clear plastic jar with a secure lid (a soap-and-water-washed peanut butter jar works well). The next time you hit the beach, gather up half a jar of clean, garbage-free sand. Now, walk the waterline to see what treasures you can find. Are there shells washed up from the ocean floor? A feather from a seabird? A beautiful piece of drift-wood? A finely polished piece of beach glass? Drop them in the jar along with the sand. Now securely close the jar and take it home. That bottle of beach will remind you of what you love about the shore and why you want to go back soon.

What You'll Need
- clear plastic jar with lid
- sand
- seashells
- feather
- other beach treasures

Sand Clay

◆◆◆◆◆◆◆

Make souvenirs of your beach vacation!

What You'll Need
- old double-boiler
- measuring cup
- sand
- cornstarch
- wooden spoon
- water
- stove
- beach souvenirs
- oven
- baking sheet
- spray varnish

Caution: This project requires adult supervision.

To make sand clay, use a double-boiler that you may scratch up. This mixture is very abrasive! Measure 1 cup fine sand and ½ cup cornstarch in the top pan of the double-boiler. Stir together to mix the sand and starch. With adult help, add ½ cup hot water and stir. Cook over boiling water for 10 minutes or until the mixture is thick and the starch is cooked. Don't let the bottom pan go dry.

After the clay cools, make your sculptures. Decorate them with beach treasures like shells and rocks. With adult assistance, bake your sculptures on a baking sheet at 300°F until dry. Let your sculptures cool at room temperature for a day or so, then have an adult cover them with spray varnish to keep them from flaking.

Shell Wind Chimes

◆▸▸▸▸◆▸◆

Seashells can make beautiful music on breezy days.

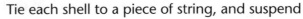

What You'll Need
- seashells (especially clams, mussels, and oysters)
- awl or nut pick
- coat hanger
- string or strong fishing line
- scissors

Caution: This project requires adult supervision.

Shells from animals with 2 shells, such as clams, mussels, oysters, and scallops, make good wind chimes. Pick attractive shells that you don't mind breaking. With an adult's help, take a metal awl or a nut pick and gently work it back and forth in one spot, boring out a small hole for string to run through.

Tie each shell to a piece of string, and suspend it from your coat hanger. Make sure the shells are close enough together to clink. Suspending some shells lower than others makes a nice pattern. Hang your chimes anywhere that the breeze can catch them. You can bring them indoors on very windy days so the shells don't break.

Clamshell Garden

◆▸▸▸▸◆▸◆

You can find clams on the beach—or at a local fish market. Create a miniature garden out of a clamshell.

What You'll Need
- clam half-shell
- small cactus
- craft glue
- sand
- small pebbles (no larger than ⅛-inch in diameter)
- moss
- potting soil
- seeds

To make a cactus garden: Place a tiny variety of cactus inside the clamshell, using a small amount of glue to hold it in place. Fill the shell with a mixture of half sand and half a combination of tiny pebbles and moss. Dampen and place in a sunny spot. Your garden should be watered once a week. Be careful not to overwater it.

To make a seed garden: Sprinkle tiny pebbles along the bottom of the clamshell, followed by a ½ inch of potting soil. Spread moss on top. Dampen and sprinkle on some seeds (grass seeds work well, or you can try alfalfa, clover, mustard seed, radish, or rye). Layer more soil over seeds and moss. Water lightly and keep it in a dark place until the seeds sprout, then move it to a sunny spot.

Forever Fish

◆◆◆◆◆◆◆◆

No one will question your fish stories if you preserve your prize fish forever in plaster.

What You'll Need

- fish
- flat pan
- freezer
- modeling clay
- plaster of paris
- mixing container for plaster
- spoon
- acrylic paints
- paintbrush
- spray acrylic
- hot glue or cement (optional)
- wall plaque (optional)

You may catch a fish so big that you'd love to see it preserved and mounted on the wall so you can show it off to your friends. With some plaster and clay, you can! Clean your fish, and leave the head on. Lay it out flat in a pan. Set it in a freezer overnight and let it freeze. The next day, remove the fish from the freezer. Roll out a slab of modeling clay a little bigger and a little thicker than your fish. Press the fish firmly into the clay. Gently pull it out and see if you like the mold you've made. If there are air bubbles or imperfections, knead the clay, roll it out, and try again.

When you've got a mold you like, put the fish back in the freezer. Mix some plaster in a container until it is about as thick as heavy cream. Pour the plaster slowly into the mold. Try to avoid making air bubbles. Let the plaster dry several hours, then remove it from the mold. Let the plaster dry completely overnight before attempting to remove any clinging bits of modeling clay. Once your plaster fish dries, decorate it with acrylic paints. Use the frozen fish as a color model to ensure that your plaster fish looks as real as possible. After the paint dries, spray it with clear acrylic coating. If you like, use hot glue (with adult help) or contact cement to mount your plaster fish to a wall plaque.

Stay out of the Tide

Remember when you're near a roaring tide to wear sturdy shoes with nonslip soles. Never turn your back on the ocean, because "sneaker" waves can wash away unwary visitors. Always have an adult with you when you're near water.

Art from the Ocean

◆◆◆◆◆◆◆

Seaweed has interesting shapes and textures.
You can preserve them by making seaweed prints.

What You'll Need
- fresh seaweed (available at fish supply stores)
- poster board
- craft glue
- decorations

It's easy to make seaweed prints! Just lay fresh seaweed on a piece of poster board. Arrange it in a nice design, then let the seaweed dry. Seaweed contains a gluelike substance that will cause it to stick to the poster board. When the seaweed is dry, check to make sure it's all stuck to the poster board. If there are loose bits of seaweed, just use a little glue to stick them down. If you like, you can paint your creation, or decorate it with other things you find at a beach—like shells or pebbles.

Seashore Life

The seashore is the part of the world where water and land meet. Fascinating forms of life live there, such as barnacles, winkles, and limpets. Barnacles are small creatures that stick themselves on surrounding rock, waiting for the tide to bring them food. Winkles are like snails; they glide over rocks, scraping food off them with their rough tongue. Limpets are tiny seashore animals that can accurately return to their homes, locating their exact hollow in the correct rock.

Sand Casting

◆▶◆▶◆▶◆

You can make more out of beach sand than castles.
Create unusual sculptures of plaster right on the beach!

What You'll Need
- moist beach sand
- bucket
- nature objects
- paper cup
- plaster of paris
- water
- paint
- paintbrush

To make the mold: Gather a bucket of moist beach sand and carry it to where it won't be disturbed. Now gather some natural objects with interesting shapes, such as seashells. Be careful not to disturb nature areas. Press the objects into the sand, then remove them. The dents in the sand are molds of your object.

To make the sculpture: In a paper cup, mix plaster of paris with water until it is just runny enough to pour. Fill your molds with plaster, and leave them to dry. When they have hardened, remove your sculptures from the sand. You can paint them, or you may wish to leave them in their "natural" state. Always clean up any plaster left on the beach, so that it doesn't damage the habitat.

I See Seashells

◆▶◆▶◆▶◆

Turn an ordinary box into a keepsake container using seashells—
the perfect gift from the sea.

Collect seashells of all different sizes, shapes, and colors. You can also find real or artificial shells at a craft store. Be careful not to collect any shells with the animals still inside them. Then turn your shell collection into a work of art that also houses your favorite items. Glue your shells onto a shoe box in the shape of a picture or any design. You can even spell your name in shells on the top of the box.

What You'll Need
- shells
- craft glue
- shoe box

Homemade Gifts

❖◄►◄►◄►❖

When you take time to make a gift it becomes special. And when you make a gift from the beautiful world of nature it becomes even more special still. Surprise a loved one with a gift from the heart—one that comes both from your hands and from the natural world!

 ## Natural Bookmarks

◄►◄►◄►◄►

Create truly individual bookmarks using the beauty of plants.
These make great gifts for your favorite bookworms.

Lay your pressed plants out on a 2×6½-inch strip of cardboard or colored paper and arrange them until you have a design you like. Remove the plants and dot glue wherever you want to stick the plants. Lay the plants on the glue and allow to dry. If you like, spread some more glue and sprinkle on glitter. Shake the excess glitter off onto a paper. Allow the glue to dry.

Cut a piece of clear self-adhesive paper about 4×6½ inches. Carefully peel off the backing and lay it flat, sticky-side up, on a table. (You may need someone to help you with this.) Turn the cardboard over so the decorated side is down, and lay it in the middle of the self-adhesive paper. Fold the rest of the self-adhesive paper over to cover the back. Trim the ends, leaving a small margin of self-adhesive paper. If you have access to a laminating machine you can laminate your bookmarks instead of using self-adhesive paper

What You'll Need
- pressed plants (see page 626)
- cardboard or colored paper
- ruler
- craft glue
- clear self-adhesive paper
- scissors
- glitter (optional)

Herb Pillow

◆▷◆▷◆▷◆▷

See what "sweet" dreams this pillow of herbs will bring.

Caution: This project requires adult supervision.

Cut 2 squares of fabric to the size you want. Paint a flowery design on one of the squares with fabric paint and let it dry. Put the 2 squares together with the painted side in. With help from an adult, sew the edges of the square with a ¼-inch seam, leaving a 2-inch opening. Turn the pillow right-side out. Now, choose some herbs for your pillow. Tradition holds that chamomile, catnip, and hops bring about peaceful sleep. Have an adult help you dry the herbs so you can fill the pillow. To dry herbs, place them on a cookie sheet. Bake in a 350°F oven for 15 minutes or until herbs are dry enough to crumble.

When you fill the pillow, don't stuff it full; it should be somewhat flat. Sew the opening shut. Tie a ribbon in a bow and sew it to the pillow, or decorate any other way you like with ribbons.

What You'll Need
- fabric scraps
- scissors
- fabric paints
- paintbrush
- needle and thread
- ruler
- herbs
- cookie sheet
- oven
- ribbon (optional)

Be a Nature Artist

◆▷◆▷◆▷◆▷

Try your hand at making botanical drawings.

Botanical means having to do with the science of plants. Botanical drawings are drawings of plants that are both beautiful and scientific. They show all the different parts of the plant, as close to the way they really look as possible. See if you can find some examples of botanical drawings at your library, then create your own.

What You'll Need
- drawing paper or a sketch pad
- colored pencils

You may want to draw your own creations in a spiral-bound sketch pad, and keep adding to your collection. Colored pencils are good to use for botanical drawings, because you can make very exact drawings with them. Start by drawing a simple plant. Label the different parts of the plant (stem, leaves, flower, etc.).

Another way to make botanical drawings is to show a plant at different times of the year. For example, you could make 4 drawings of a tree, showing how it looks in spring, summer, fall, and winter.

Flower Bottles

◆◆◆◆◆◆◆

*These wonderful little bottles make great gifts
for anyone who likes dried flowers.*

What You'll Need
- bottles or wide-mouth jars
- small flowers, seed pods, and seed heads
- scissors
- sand
- plaster of paris
- water
- long tweezers
- cork

Collect bottles, such as salad dressing or vinegar bottles. (Keep in mind, little fingers may work better using wide-mouthed jars. If necessary, use peanut butter or canning jars instead. You can also buy attractive bottles at a craft store.) Clean and dry the bottles, and remove the labels. Now collect and dry small flowers, seed pods, and seed heads. Keep the size of your bottles in mind as you collect your flowers.

Dry your flowers, seed pods, and seed heads (see page 410). Cut the stems to different lengths to form a pleasing arrangement. Mix 2 parts clean sand with 1 part plaster of paris. Add enough water to make a thick liquid. Pour 1 or 2 inches of the mixture into the bottle. Stick the stems inside the bottle into the sand mixture using the tweezers to help you. Allow the sand mixture to dry. Close the bottle with a cork.

You can also make small dried flower scenes by using low, wide jars instead of bottles. Add small figurines or polished rocks and decorate the lid of the jar.

Be a Millionaire

◆◆◆◆◆◆◆

Money is no object with these coins created from natural clay.

Take a small amount of clay and use your palms to flatten and shape it into a coin. Now take a real coin and press it into the clay to make a design. Use different sized coins for larger or smaller clay coins. (You can also use a button or a ring to make an interesting impression.) Let your coins dry for about a week. Then paint them to look like real coins.

To make a medallion or necklace: Before your coin dries, make a hole in the top with a nail. Once it is dry, string silver or gold yarn through the hole. String several together to make a necklace.

What You'll Need
- natural or modeling clay
- coin
- nail
- paint
- paintbrush
- yarn (silver or gold)

Potpourri

*Sweeten your home with flowers and herbs
the same way people have done for centuries.*

Gather sweet-scented garden flowers early in the day after the dew has dried. Pick the petals off larger flowers, pick leaves off herbs, and spread the petals and leaves out to dry on paper towels. Smaller flowers may be dried whole. You can also cut the flower spikes from herbs such as lavender and dry them whole. Experiment to see which flowers keep their scent after drying. You may want to dry petals of colorful but unscented flowers to add color to your potpourri.

Next, blend your herbs and flowers together to make a pleasing scent. You can add spices such as cinnamon, nutmeg, or bay leaves. Try some of the following mixes, or make up your own combinations.

• Lemon verbena or lemon balm, lavender, and violets
• Rose petals, lavender, and bits of orange peel
• Pine needles, rosemary, violets, and bay leaves

Finally, put your mixture (called *potpourri*) into glass containers with lids and decorate with ribbons.

To make sachets: Cut circles of fabric. Place a few spoonfuls of potpourri in the middle of the circle. Draw the fabric in over the potpourri, and tie the bundle with ribbon.

What You'll Need
- scented garden flowers
- paper towels
- spices
- glass containers with lids
- ribbon
- fabric
- scissors

A Spicy Tree

Do you know how cinnamon is made? It comes from the dried bark of a tree. The waste and other parts of the bark are called oil of cinnamon, which is used as a flavoring and has also been used in medicines. Cinnamon was a favorite spice in biblical times, when it was used for perfume and incense.

Herb Vinegar

◆◆◆◆◆◆◆

Anyone who likes to cook will appreciate this special herb vinegar.

What You'll Need
- fresh-cut herbs
- vinegar
- glass bottles with stoppers or screw caps
- masking tape
- pen
- index card
- ribbon

Gather fresh herbs from the garden or buy them from the grocery store. Basil, thyme, sage, marjoram, tarragon, dill, and rosemary all work well. Wash the herbs gently in cool water to remove any traces of dirt. Scrub your bottles out well with soap and water, rinse thoroughly, and put upside down in a dish rack to drain.

Fill the bottles with warm vinegar (cider vinegar, red wine vinegar, white wine vinegar, or balsamic vinegar are best). Add several sprigs of any one herb to each bottle. Cap tightly and label your bottles with masking tape and a pen. Allow the bottles to sit for 2 weeks. Shake them a little every day while they're "brewing." At the end of 2 weeks, you can strain out the herbs and add fresh sprigs if you like, or leave old ones in if they still look nice. For a gift, remove the masking tape label. Decorate an index card to make a pretty label, and tape to the bottle. Add a ribbon if you'd like.

Healing Herbs

◆◆◆◆◆◆◆

Many herbs are known for their relaxing and cleansing properties.

An herbal bath bag is easy to make, and you can use it over and over again. Simply fill your bag with a mixture of dried herbs. (Some examples are listed below.) Then tie the top with a string or ribbon and make a loop at the top big enough to fit over a bathtub faucet. To use your bath bag, hang it from the faucet while hot water is running. (Make sure the bag hangs in the stream of running water.) You can also hang it in the shower. Let it dry completely before storing.

What You'll Need
- cotton or muslin bag (about 4×3 inches)
- dried herbs
- string or ribbon

Herbs that help you relax: Chamomile, Lavender, Marjoram, Mint
Herbs that cleanse and deodorize: Basil, Lovage, Sage, Thyme
Herbs that relieve tired limbs: Bay, Bergamot, Hyssop, Meadowsweet, Rosemary

It's Your Beeswax

◆◆◆◆◆◆◆

Honey bees make beautiful beeswax honeycombs. Make attractive candles that have the color and texture of honeycombs.

Honey bees make wax honeycombs to protect their queen's eggs from nature's elements. The wax is durable, waterproof, and can withstand most temperature changes. The bees also use the honeycombs to store honey or pollen for the cold winter months. It's easy to make beeswax candles. You can

get sheets of beeswax (which are usually made from molded paraffin) and candle wicks at a craft store. A 4×6-inch sheet will make a small candle.

Measure out a length of wick a few inches longer than the width of the wax. Place the wick at one end of the wax. To hold the wick in place, roll the very end of the wax around the wick and press it tightly. Now roll the rest of the sheet of beeswax around the wick. When completely rolled, press the outside edge against the candle to keep it from unrolling.

Beauty in a Bottle

◆◆◆◆◆◆◆

A sand painting in a bottle makes a nice gift. It's also fun to make a collection of them in different-size bottles.

Start with a nice-looking bottle or jar that has a lid. Wide-mouthed jars are easier to work with than ones with narrow tops. Fill it with layers of different-color sand to make a design.

Here are some ideas to try: Alternate thin layers and thick layers. Repeat color patterns. (For example, layer red, orange, yellow. Then repeat the pattern.) Or, tilt the bottle while you add sand. This will make wavy stripes. When the bottle is full, put the lid on. If you don't have colored sand, you can use different textures of sand (coarse and fine) or even sand and pebbles.

Roasted Nuts

Nuts are full of energy-rich oils. That's why they're a favorite food of many forest animals—and us!

◆◆◆◆◆◆

Caution: This project requires adult supervision.

Look for nuts in October and November. What kind of nuts you find depends on where you live. In the east, you'll find hickory, beech nuts, and butternuts. In the west, you may find wild filberts (hazelnuts) or piñon pine. You may also find walnuts and black walnuts planted ornamentally just about anywhere.

What You'll Need
- bag or bucket for gathering
- long stick
- mesh bag
- nutcracker
- cookie sheet
- oven
- salt
- decorative tin

The best time to go nutting is after a wind storm, early in the day before the squirrels have picked up too many. Take a long stick to help you reach nuts still on the branches. Small trees can be gently shaken to loosen nuts. Let the nuts dry in the shell in a sunny place for a week or more. Store them in a hanging mesh bag.

Roasting nuts brings out their flavor. To do this, crack them open with a nutcracker. Spread the meats out on a cookie sheet, and sprinkle with salt. Roast in a 325°F oven for about 10 minutes, stirring several times. Watch them carefully—take them out as soon as they turn brown, or they will burn. Fresh roasted nuts in a decorative tin make a great gift for a "nutty" friend or relative.

Popcorn Frame

◆◆◆◆◆◆

The next time you make popcorn, save some for this fun frame!

What You'll Need
- popped popcorn (air-popped or microwave varieties work best)
- small matte self-standing picture frame
- craft glue
- colored pebbles or marbles

Be sure to let the popcorn cool before starting this project. Don't put butter or salt on it, either. First, glue a layer of popcorn around the edge of the frame. Let the glue dry, then glue some pebbles, marbles, or any other kind of colorful decorations on the frame wherever you want. Let the glue dry again, then fill in any remaining gaps with more popcorn.

Lavender Bundles

◆━◆━◆━◆━◆

Sometimes these are called "lavender wands."
Let their magical sweetness scent your clothes.

What You'll Need
- long stems of lavender
- about 4 feet of ¼-inch wide ribbon for each bundle

This is a very old way of making sachets. Take 15 long spikes of freshly picked lavender. Tie them together right under the flower heads with the ribbon, leaving one end about 10 inches long. Let this end remain inside the bundle. Now bend the stems gently back over the flower heads. Weave the long end of the ribbon carefully in and out of the stems until the flower heads are covered. Wrap the ribbon once or twice around the stems. Draw out the other end of the ribbon, which should now stick out between the stems, and tie the 2 ends together in a bow.

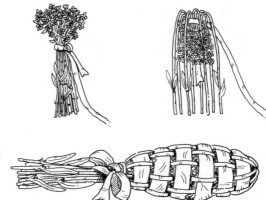

Hang the bundle up to dry thoroughly. When the bundles are ready, slip them into your dresser drawers to make your clothes smell sweet. Plenty of lavender may also help keep moths away, and it smells much nicer than moth balls! Lavender bundles also make nice gifts.

Fun Figures

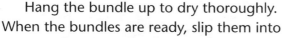

◆━◆━◆━◆━◆

All living things are made of cells. But what if they weren't? What if they were made of pebbles, gourds, or pinecones? Find out how wacky creatures would be if they were made out of different things.

Pebble Sculptures

◆◆◆◆◆◆

All it takes is a little imagination to turn your ordinary pebbles into extraordinary art.

What You'll Need
- pebbles
- thick glue
- acrylic paint or poster paint
- paintbrushes
- decorations

If you have a collection of ordinary rocks that you don't know what to do with, try making sculptures from them. Lay out your rocks and look for interesting features that might suggest faces, animal heads, arms, legs, or bodies. A large, smooth rock might make you think of a beetle. A heart-shaped rock could be part of a pebble valentine. Glue the rocks together with thick, sticky glue. (Hot glue works best, but have an adult help you with the hot glue gun.) Use acrylic paints or poster paints to paint your figures. Decorate your rocks with other natural things you find. An acorn cap makes a good hat. Feathers that you pick up can become tails for your pebble birds. White thistledown or cotton from cottonwoods can make white Santa Claus beards and hair. Give your dog or cat a good brushing and use the hair that comes out as hair for your pebble people. Find a discarded board with a large knothole and put your pebble mice or owls in the hole.

Butterfly Sculpture

To celebrate the New Year, Buddhist monks in Tibet create elaborate yak-butter sculptures to illustrate a different story or fable each year. The sculptures can reach 30 feet high, and they are lit with special butter lamps. Awards are given for the best butter sculptures!

What a Doll!

◆◆◆◆◆◆◆◆

Corn-husk dolls were made by American Indians in what is now the northeastern United States. Here's how you can make one.

What You'll Need
- corn husks
- string
- scissors
- markers
- dried flowers (optional)

Strip the husks from several ears of corn. Let them dry out for a few days. Keep some of the corn silk to use for hair.

First, make the doll's head by rolling up one husk. Put some corn silk on top of the roll. Then put another corn husk over the silk and the rolled-up husk. Use string to tie this piece tightly under the rolled-up husk. This will be the face and neck.

Roll a husk lengthwise to make the arms. Tie the long roll at each end. Put this roll under the neck, and tie it in place. Use several husks to make a skirt. Lay these husks in the front and back of the arms, and tie them in place. Trim the bottom of the skirt so it is even.

To make a blouse: Cut a rectangle out of a husk. Make a cut in one end of the rectangle. The cut should go about halfway through the rectangle. Put the rectangle behind the doll, with the cut end up. The end of the rectangle that is not cut will be the back of the blouse. Fold the cut end of the rectangle over to the front of the doll. This will be the front of the blouse. Cross the 2 flaps over each other and use string to tie the blouse in place.

Finally, draw a face on your corn husk doll. You can put dried flowers in its hand or make a bonnet for its head out of corn husks, too!

In a Nutshell

◆▶◆▶◆▶◆▶

Tiny animal habitats come to life on the half shell.

What You'll Need
- walnut shells (carefully cracked and emptied)
- craft glue
- hobby store grass
- tiny plastic animal and nature objects

These tiny animals in nutty habitats are cute and never need to be fed. Cover the inside of half a walnut shell with glue. Sprinkle a thin layer of hobby store grass (it's like green sawdust) inside the nut. Add a tiny paper bush or watering hole, and then glue a small plastic animal in this cozy, fun place. Once the glue is dry, you'll have the world's teeniest pet zone. Take this pocket-size pal everywhere you go, or you can give it as a gift!

Gourd Puppet

◆▶◆▶◆▶◆▶

Pick out some funny-shaped gourds, make puppets, and put on a show!

You can pick gourds fresh from a garden or find them in markets during the fall or winter.

To Make a Gourd Finger Puppet: Using the long, curved top of the gourd as the nose, paint features for the face. Have an adult help you cut a hole in the bottom of the puppet's "head" and scoop out the contents with a spoon. Allow the gourd to dry, then use your finger as the puppet's neck.

What You'll Need
- small gourd
- paint
- paintbrush
- knife
- spoon
- fabric
- scissors
- needle
- thread

To Make a Gourd Hand Puppet: Turn the gourd upside down and use the long, curved part as the neck. Draw a funny face on the "head." You can dress your puppet with clothes sewn together from fabric scraps.

Pinecone Creatures

◄◆◆◆◆◆►

What kind of wild, imaginary animals can you make out of pinecones?

What You'll Need
- pinecones
- decorations
- craft glue

For each creature, you'll need one large pinecone. You'll also need an assortment of decorations (old buttons, scrap cloth, chenille stems, real or plastic flowers). Use these decorations to turn the pinecone into an imaginary animal. Chenille stems work well for creating legs. When you're done, give your creature a name, and make up a story about it.

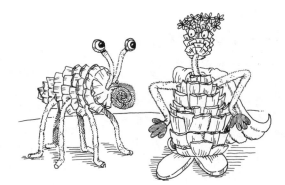

Prickly Pets

◄◆◆◆◆◆►

Those big, prickly burrs from burdock plants can be a pain in the neck— or the foot! Here's how you can change them into cute burr babies.

Burrs can be a big pain in the paw for your 4-footed friends. So, pick them up off the ground and use them for this great craft. Glue several burrs together to make animal shapes. Add tiny twigs for legs, maple wings (they carry the seeds of maple trees) for wings, and other natural decorations to finish them off. You can use tiny dabs of paint to give them eyes. Make a whole zoo of burr babies, and keep them up on a shelf, where they won't bite any toes!

What You'll Need
- dried burrs from burdock plants
- craft glue
- twigs
- maple wings
- paint
- paintbrush

Applehead Dolls

These charming, old-fashioned dolls—made from small apples—look like wise old men and women.

What You'll Need
- small green apples
- peeler
- knife
- wire
- fabric scraps
- scissors

Caution: This project requires adult supervision.

Begin with small, firm apples. Green, unripe apples work the best, so if you know someone with an apple tree you can ask them for some windfallen green apples. Peel the apple, then have an adult help you carve the face with a small knife. Think of how a real face is shaped. The nose and cheeks must stick out, while the eyes are set in, so carve away the front of the apple but leave lumps sticking out for the nose and cheeks. Make exaggerated features, as they will shrink in the drying process. Put the apple in a warm place to dry. This will take a week or more.

When the apple head is dry, bend wire into the shape of a body, with a long neck to stick into the apple head. Dress the doll with clothing cut from fabric scraps.

Garden Crafts

When you take a good look at nature you soon see many patterns—from the arrangement of petals in a flower to the spores on a mushroom. You can use these patterns to create fabulous art!

Paint Box

◆◆◆◆◆◆◆

*Who needs to buy paints and markers when nature
has a free supply of coloring tools for you?*

What You'll Need

- flowers
- leaves
- berries from the lawn or garden
- bark
- soil
- sticks
- rocks
- white paper
- fine sandpaper

The colors you see in flowers, leaves, and berries are from chemicals called *pigments.* Pigments also give color to paints, markers, and crayons. You can use natural pigments to create colorful pictures. Find a variety of flowers, leaves, and berries outdoors. Rub them on the paper to make marks. Experiment to see what kinds of colors you can make, then make a picture with them. Try bark, dirt, sticks, or rocks to see if they will make marks as well.

After you have experimented on white paper and learned to make pictures, try making pictures on fine sandpaper. The colors will come out more strongly, and you will have an attractive picture to frame and put on your wall.

Vine-Covered Vase

◆◆◆◆◆◆◆

*Natural vines add charm to any home. You can use any kind
of jar or bottle to make a simple vase.*

What You'll Need

- jar or bottle
- smooth, flexible vines with leaves removed
- craft glue
- scissors or pruning shears

Put a line of glue around the middle of the jar and press the end of a vine (such as honeysuckle, grape, or clematis) into the glue. Press the vine firmly until it is held in place, then let the glue dry. Once the glue dries, you can wrap the vine tightly around the jar, working up from the middle to the top. Try to wrap the layers as close as possible to one another. If you get to the end of the vine before reaching the top, glue the end in place and start another vine. Once you reach the top of the jar, cut off the end with scissors or shears and glue it in place.

After you've done the top half of the jar, start at the middle again and wrap the bottom half the same way. Let the vase dry for 2 hours before using. You can decorate your vase with leaves, pebbles, or dried flowers.

Make a Plant Press

◄►◄►◄►◄►

A plant press is easy to make and even easier to use.

What You'll Need
- 2 thin boards (about 8×10 inches)
- saw
- corrugated cardboard
- utility knife
- newspaper
- scissors
- paper towels
- nylon webbing straps (1-inch wide)
- 4 D-rings
- needle
- thread
- plants

Caution: This project requires adult supervision.

Have an adult help you cut 2 thin boards to the size you want the press to be, about the size of a paper towel. Then, using the utility knife, cut sheets of sturdy corrugated cardboard the same size as your boards. Cut newspaper sheets twice the size of your paper towels and fold them in half.

To build the press: Lay down a board first, then a cardboard sheet, then 2 paper towels to act as a blotter, and a folded sheet of newspaper. Then add another sheet of cardboard and keep going in the same order. The last things to go on should be one last piece of cardboard, then the other board. Cut 2 straps of nylon long enough to go around the press twice. Slip the end of each strap through 2 D-rings, fold the end over, and sew in place. Ask an adult to melt the other end in a flame to prevent fraying. Wrap a strap once around the press and slip the free end through both D-rings. Turn the strap back, slip it through the bottom D-ring, and pull the strap to tighten.

To press plants: Lay them inside the folded newspapers and spread them out so they don't overlap. Arrange leaves and petals so that they lay flat. Build up your press as described above, using as many cardboard sheets and paper towel blotters as you need. Squeeze the layers together, strap the press tightly, and put it in a warm place for a week or more to dry. Then you can use your pressed plants to make things like bookmarks (see page 612) or stationery (see page 327).

Spore Prints

◆◆◆◆◆◆

Did you know that mushooms can make their own prints?

What You'll Need

- mushroom caps
- white unlined index cards
- black paper
- drinking glass or bowl
- hair spray or acrylic fixative

Find a mushroom in the wild, or get some from the store. (Be careful when handling wild mushrooms—don't eat them!) You will have to find some with the caps open. Look underneath the cap. The gills inside are lined with structures that make and release spores by the millions. Each spore can grow into a new fungus.

Cover half of an index card with black paper. Pop out the stem from the mushroom cap, and place the cap on the card so that half is on the black paper and half on the white. Cover with a glass or bowl and let the cap sit overnight. The next day remove the glass and the mushroom cap. You should see a print of the mushroom spores. Pale spores will show up on the black paper, while darker ones will show on the white. Ask an adult to spray the print with hair spray or acrylic fixative to keep it from smearing.

Weaving Cattails

◆◆◆◆◆◆

Here's one way early American Indians made mats from cattail leaves.

Caution: This project requires adult supervision.

The method used here will make a small sturdy mat, useful for hot dishes, for place mats, or for sitting on outdoors. Cattails can be found growing in many wet areas all over the country (and are also available in craft stores). Just be sure you get permission before you gather them. Cut the leaves from the cattails and spread them out in a sunny place to dry completely. When dry, soak them a few minutes in water. Lay leaves out side by side until you have enough to form a square. Weigh the ends down on one side with bricks. Weave the remaining leaves over and under the leaves you laid out. Then weigh the other ends of the leaves down with bricks, and let the leaves dry.

What You'll Need

- cattails
- scissors
- bricks
- sewing machine
- quilting thread

To finish the edges, have an adult sew them together on a sewing machine using a heavy needle and sturdy quilting thread. If you can't find cattails, try other plants with long leaves, such as daylilies.

A Natural Necklace

◄►◄►◄►◄►

*In Hawaii, people make flower necklaces called **leis**.
You can make a dazzling flower necklace, too.*

What You'll Need
- flowers with long stems

To make a necklace, first you'll need to pick a lot of wild flowers that have long stems, such as daisies. (Be sure to get permission first!) Be careful if you use dandelions, because the same yellow color that rubs off on your hands or chin can get messy.

Here's how to chain them together:

Cross 2 stems at right angles. Loop the vertical stem around the horizontal one so it ends up alongside the horizontal stem. Next lay a third stem at right angles to the 2 horizontal stems. Loop it around both horizontal stems. Keep adding stems this way until your lei is as long as you want it. Tie the last stem to the first flower to make a circle. Aloha!

Looks Delicious!

◄►◄►◄►◄►

You can use real fruit to help you make these lifelike sculptures.

What You'll Need
- fresh fruit
- bowl
- craft glue
- water
- paper towels
- old newspaper
- paintbrush
- knife
- acrylic paints
- acrylic sealer

Start with a variety of fresh fruits such as bananas, apples, oranges, and pears. Pour some white glue into a bowl, and stir in an equal amount of water to dilute it. Tear paper towels into 1-inch strips. You'll need a big pile of paper-towel strips.

Cover your work space with lots of old newspaper. Begin pasting the paper towel strips onto the fruit. Hold a strip over the bowl of glue. Use the paintbrush to push the strip into the glue, wetting it on both sides. Then use the paintbrush to "paint" the strip onto a piece of fruit. Keep adding strips until the fruit is completely covered. Then repeat the whole process until the fruit is covered with 4 layers of strips.

Let the papier-mâché dry completely. Have a grownup use a sharp knife to cut the fruit in half. Then remove the fruit from the papier-mâché shell. Use more papier-mâché to join the halves of your papier-mâché fruit. When it's dry, paint the fruit with acrylic paints.

When the paint is dry, seal the sculptures with at least one coat of acrylic sealer.

Corn-Husk Mats

◆◆◆◆◆◆◆

*These mats are just as useful now as they were
to the pioneers who made them years ago.*

What You'll Need
- corn husks
- darning needle
- quilting thread
- thimble

Dry the corn husks outdoors in a sunny place until completely dry. When you are ready to use them, tear them into strips and soak the strips for an hour in warm water. Tie 6 strips together at one end and braid them together, using 2 strips in each "strand." When you have braided about ⅔ of the way down, add 2 more strips to each strand and keep going. The braid will hold together if your strips overlap one another sufficiently.

When your braid is long enough, tie off the end. Lay it down on a flat surface and begin coiling the braid around one of the end knots. As you coil, stitch the braids together with quilting thread. Use a strong darning needle, and protect your finger with a thimble. Make small mats for coasters or large ones to put under hot dishes on the dinner table.

Flowers Aglow

◆◆◆◆◆◆◆

Use flowers you have pressed to make specialty candles.

Caution: This project requires adult supervision.

Start with a column candle. With help from an adult, melt some paraffin. Paint a thick layer of melted paraffin onto the side of the candle and quickly press a flower into the wet paraffin. The paraffin will work like glue to hold the flower to the candle. Paint another layer of paraffin over the flower, letting it drip between the flower and the candle. This will seal the flower. Put as many flowers on the candle as you like. You can also use feathers to decorate candles in the same way.

What You'll Need
- column candles
- paraffin
- pan
- stove
- paintbrush
- pressed flowers (see page 626)
- tea lights

When the candle has burned enough that there is a 2-inch hole in the center of the column, put a tea light in the hole. Burn the tea light, instead of the column candle.

Dream Weaver

◆▶▶▶▶▶◀

Create unique wall hangings from natural materials.

First you'll need to create your loom. Take a piece of cardboard just a little larger than the size of the weaving you want to make. Cut a row of slits in the top and bottom ends, making each slit ¼ to ½ inch apart. Tie a knot in your string, slip the knot into one of the slits to anchor it, then run the string to the slit on the opposite side. Slip the string behind the cardboard to the next slit on the same side, bring it through, then run it across the board again. Keep going until the whole piece of cardboard is strung, like strings on a guitar.

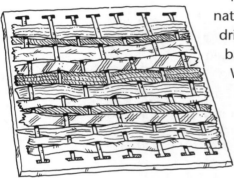

Now collect any kind of natural materials that are long and narrow, such as tall dried grass, strips of dried corn husk or cattail leaves, bark peeled from fallen twigs, or long pine needles. Weave these materials in and out of the strings in any way that pleases you. When your weaving is done, slip the ends of the string off the cardboard. Turn your weaving over, and glue the edges to keep the weaving together.

That's a Lot of Plants!

There are close to 300,000 species of plants that scientists have already named. These plants include mosses that grow close to the ground and huge trees that tower hundreds of feet high. There are plants growing in almost every part of the world today—even in the most difficult climates.

Over the Rainbow

◆━━◆━◆━━◆

You don't need to wait for it to rain to find this rainbow.
Add some color to any plant.

Wash the flowerpot (even if it's new) with dishwashing detergent. Rinse thoroughly and place it in the sun to dry. Apply a 1-inch band of glue around the base of the flowerpot. Wrap violet yarn around the flowerpot, covering the band of glue. Apply another 1-inch band of glue around the flowerpot above the violet yarn. Wrap blue yarn around the pot. Continue gluing and wrapping colored yarn up the flowerpot until it's covered completely. Let the glue set, then put a plant in the flowerpot.

What You'll Need
- clay flowerpot (6 inches in diameter)
- dishwashing liquid
- craft glue
- paintbrush
- yarn (in the following colors: violet, blue, green, yellow, orange, red)
- plant

Grass Prints

◆━━◆━◆━━◆

Grass seed heads make beautiful lacy prints.

What You'll Need
- grasses of various kinds (include seed heads)
- paper
- waxed paper
- water-based paints
- paintbrush
- cloth (optional)

Lay your grasses out on a table and choose those you like the best. Arrange the grasses you like on paper. Try making interesting contrasts between lacy seed heads and thick grass blades. To make your prints, lay the grass on waxed paper. Load a brush with paint and dab the paint on the grass until it is thinly but fully coated on one side.

Lift the painted grass from the waxed paper and lay it, paint side down, on the paper you want to print. Lay another sheet of waxed paper on top and press gently so that the grass makes good contact with the paper. Remove the waxed paper and grass. Watercolor paint works on white paper; tempera looks nice on colored paper. Use fabric paint on cloth to make beautiful grass-printed T-shirts and bandannas!

INDEX

◆◆◆◆◆◆◆